SACRAMENTUM MUNDI

VOLUME TWO: CONTRITION — GRACE AND FREEDOM

SACRAMENTUM MUNDI

An Encyclopedia of Theology

Edited by

Karl Rahner SJ, Münster
and
Juan Alfaro SJ, Rome
Alberto Bellini, Bergamo
Carlo Colombo, Venegono
Henri Crouzel SJ, Toulouse
Jean Daniélou SJ, Paris
Adolf Darlap, Munich
Cornelius Ernst OP, Oxford
José Fondevilla SJ, Barcelona
Piet Fransen, Louvain
Fergus Kerr OP, Oxford
Piet Schoonenberg, Nijmegen
Kevin Smyth, Paris
† Gustave Weigel SJ, Woodstock

© Hermann-Herder-Foundation, Basle–Montreal

Published by Herder and Herder New York · Burns & Oates London · Palm Publishers
Montreal · Herder Freiburg · Éditions Desclée de Brouwer Bruges · Editorial Herder
Barcelona · Edizioni Morcelliana Brescia · Paul Brand Hilversum

SACRAMENTUM MUNDI

AN ENCYCLOPEDIA OF THEOLOGY

VOLUME TWO

CONTRITION
TO
GRACE AND FREEDOM

BURNS & OATES

HERDER AND HERDER NEW YORK
232 Madison Avenue, New York, N. Y. 10016

BURNS & OATES LIMITED
25 Ashley Place, London S. W. 1

1st Edition 1968
2nd Impression 1968
3rd impression 1969
4th Impression 1969

General Editor: Adolf Darlap

First published in West Germany © 1968, Herder KG
Printed in West Germany by Herder
SBN 223 97643 1

ABBREVIATIONS

The following list does not include biblical and other well-known abbreviations.

Whenever an author, not listed below, is cited in an article by name only, followed by page number(s), the reference is to a work listed in the bibliography at the end of the article.

AAS	*Acta Apostolicae Sedis* (1909 ff.)
ACW	J. Quasten and J. C. Plumpe, *Ancient Christian Writers* (1946 ff.)
Billerbeck	(H. L. Strack and) P. Billerbeck, *Kommentar zum Neuen Testament aus Talmud und Midrasch,* I–IV (1922–28; reprint, 1956), V: rabbinical index, ed. by J. Jeremias and K. Adolph (1956)
CBQ	*Catholic Biblical Quarterly* (1939 ff.)
Chalkedon	A. Grillmeier and H. Bacht, eds., *Das Konzil von Chalkedon, Geschichte und Gegenwart,* 3 vols. (1951–54; 2nd enlarged ed., 1962)
CIC	*Codex Iuris Canonici*
CIO	*Codex Iuris Canonici Orientalis* (Unless stated otherwise, the references are to the law relating to persons.)
Collectio Lacensis	*Collectio Lacensis: Acta et Decreta Sacrorum Conciliorum Recentiorum,* ed. by the Jesuits of Maria Laach, 7 vols. (1870–90)
CSEL	*Corpus Scriptorum Ecclesiasticorum Latinorum* (1866 ff.)
D	H. Denzinger, *Enchiridion Symbolorum, Definitionum et Declarationum de Rebus Fidei et Morum* (31st ed., 1957); see also *DS*
DB	F. Vigouroux, ed., *Dictionnaire de la Bible,* 5 vols. (1895–1912)
DBS	L. Pirot, ed., *Dictionnaire de la Bible, Supplément,* continued by A. Robert (1928 ff.)
DS	H. Denzinger and A. Schönmetzer, *Enchiridion Symbolorum, Definitionum et Declarationum de Rebus Fidei et Morum* (33rd ed., 1965); see also *D*
DSAM	M. Viller, ed., *Dictionnaire de Spiritualité ascétique et mystique. Doctrine et Histoire* (1932 ff.)
DTC	A. Vacant and E. Mangenot, eds., *Dictionnaire de théologie catholique,* continued by É. Amann, I–XV, *Table analytique* and *Tables générales,* XVI ff. (1903 ff.)

V

ABBREVIATIONS

Enchiridion Biblicum	*Enchiridion Biblicum. Documenta Ecclesiastica Sacram Scripturam Spectantia* (3rd ed., 1956)
ETL	*Ephemerides Theologicae Lovanienses* (1924 ff.)
GCS	*Die griechischen christlichen Schriftsteller der ersten drei Jahrhunderte* (1897 ff.)
Hennecke-Schneemelcher-Wilson	E. Hennecke, W. Schneemelcher and R. McL. Wilson, eds., *New Testament Apocrypha,* 2 vols. (1963–65)
HERE	J. Hastings, ed., *Encyclopedia of Religion and Ethics,* 12 vols. + index (1908–26; 2nd rev. ed., 1925–40)
JBL	*Journal of Biblical Literature* (1881 ff.)
JTS	*Journal of Theological Studies* (1899 ff.)
LTK	J. Höfer and K. Rahner, eds., *Lexikon für Theologie und Kirche,* 10 vols. + index (2nd rev. ed., 1957–67)
Mansi	J. D. Mansi, *Sacrorum Conciliorum Nova et Amplissima Collectio,* 31 vols. (1757–98); reprint and continuation ed. by L. Petit and J. B. Martin, 60 vols. (1899–1927)
NRT	*Nouvelle Revue Théologique* (1879 ff.)
NTS	*New Testament Studies* (1954 ff.)
PG	J.-P. Migne, ed., *Patrologia Graeca,* 161 vols. (1857 ff.)
PL	J.-P. Migne, ed., *Patrologia Latina,* 217 vols. + 4 index vols. (1844 ff.)
Pritchard	J. B. Pritchard, ed., *Ancient Near Eastern Texts relating to the Old Testament* (1950; 2nd revised and enlarged ed., 1955)
RGG	K. Galling, ed., *Die Religion in Geschichte und Gegenwart,* 6 vols. + index (3rd rev. ed., 1957–65)
RHE	*Revue d'histoire ecclésiastique* (1900 ff.)
RHPR	*Revue d'histoire et de philosophie religieuse* (1921 ff.)
RSPT	*Revue des sciences philosophiques et théologiques* (1907 ff.)
RSR	*Recherches de science religieuse* (1910 ff.)
RSV	Revised Standard Version of the Bible
TS	*Theological Studies* (1940 ff.)
TU	*Texte und Untersuchungen zur Geschichte der altchristlichen Literatur. Archiv für die griechisch-christlichen Schriftsteller der ersten drei Jahrhunderte,* hitherto 62 vols. in 5 series (1882 ff.)
TWNT	G. Kittel, ed., *Theologisches Wörterbuch zum Neuen Testament.* continued by G. Friedrich (1933 ff.); E. T.: *Theological Dictionary of the New Testament* (1964 ff.)
ZAW	*Zeitschrift für die alttestamentliche Wissenschaft* (1881 ff.)
ZKT	*Zeitschrift für Katholische Theologie* (1877 ff.)

C

(continued)

CONTRITION

1. *Concept.* Contrition is an element or aspect in that process of individual salvation which is usually called *metanoia,* conversion (in the sense of change of heart and life), repentance, justification. It can therefore only be correctly understood and judged in that larger context. Since it is a rejection of sin, it presupposes a theologically correct understanding of sin and guilt.

2. *The teaching of the Church.* The Council of Trent describes contrition as "sorrow of heart and detestation for sin committed, with the resolution not to sin again" (*D* 897, 915). The Church's doctrine declares that for anyone who has personally sinned, such contrition has always been necessary as a condition of obtaining forgiveness of the guilt, that it must be linked with trust in the divine mercy, cannot simply consist of a good resolution and beginning of a new life but (in principle) must include the explicit, voluntary rejection of previous life. The same Tridentine doctrine distinguishes between *contritio caritate perfecta* and *contritio imperfecta = attritio,* according to whether the explicit motive of rejection of the sin committed is the genuine theological virtue of love of God or some other moral motive which, while less than the motive of love, is nevertheless a moral one (the intrinsic evil of sin, sin as cause of the loss of salvation, etc.) and is chosen under the influence of God's grace and unambiguously excludes the will to sin (*D* 898). (Mere fear of punishment as a physical evil is therefore not "imperfect contrition", or *attritio;* it would be that "gallows remorse" which Luther rightly rejected, but which he wrongly took to be the Catholic idea of *attritio.*) Perfect contrition (which presupposes at least the implicit will to receive the sacrament of penance) justifies immediately, even before the actual reception of baptism or penance. Imperfect contrition only justifies when linked with reception of the sacrament *(ibid.).* Such voluntary contrition (*D* 915) is not (as the Council understood the Reformers to suppose) an attempt at human self-justification by man's own power, which would indeed make man a sinner. It is a gift of grace by which man entrusts himself to the merciful God (*D* 915, 799, 798). The Church's magisterium forbade (*D* 1146) the partisans of "contrition" and of "attrition" to apply theological notes of censure to one another.

3. *Theological reflection.* a) *Anthropological presuppositions.* Important in the first place for theological understanding of contrition is the general anthropological realization that man as a free spiritual person with a history in time has a cognitive and volitive relation to himself, in regard to his past, present and future and their inextricable interrelations. Consequently man cannot and may not simply leave his past behind him with indifference as something which is no longer real; it still exists as an element of his present, which he himself has brought about in personal freedom, and since he has a relation to himself, he has a relation to his past, and by his present deliberate attitude he gives it its possibly quite different meaning in relation to his future. The degree of explicitness of these interrelationships differs very considerably from individual to indi-

1

vidual, and according to age and situation in life. But it follows from what has been said that man cannot in principle reject forthwith a deliberate attitude towards his past as an element in his relation to himself "now". Consequently, "formal" contrition is meaningful and of itself necessary, but in certain circumstances merely virtual contrition can suffice. By this man turns to God with faith, hope and love, without explicit advertence to his past, for even in this case an implicit attitude to the past is involved in this fundamental decision regarding a human life.

b) *On the phenomenology of contrition.* The repudiation of a past free action which is accomplished by contrition *(dolor et detestatio)* must be very carefully interpreted for it to be intelligible to people today. In the first place it has nothing to do with a psychological, emotional shock (melancholy, depression) which may often, though not necessarily, follow from the bad action for psychological and physiological or social reasons (loss of prestige, fear of social penalties, exhaustion, conflict in the psychic mechanisms involved, etc.). It is more a question of the rejection freely made by the spiritual person of the moral worthlessness of the past action and of the attitude which gave rise to it as its concrete expression. This rejection does not mean flight from and repression of the past, but is the appropriate way for a spiritual subject to face his past, acknowledge it and assume responsibility for it. Nor does this rejection involve any mere fiction or unreal hypothesis ("I wish I had acted differently then"). It has an actual reality as its object: the present disposition of the subject in his fundamental decision and attitude, to the extent that this is partly constituted by the past action. The repudiation does not contest the theoretically and practically undeniable fact that even the evil action in the past was directed to something "good" and has often produced very considerable good (e.g., in human maturity, etc.) which in some cases cannot be left out of account at all in the life of the doer of the action. In this way there arises psychologically an apparently almost insoluble problem, when an event has to be repudiated which, because of its good consequences, can scarcely be left out of account in the person's life. In this case, unconditional turning to the merciful God in love will be a

better method of contrition than analytic reflection on the past.

c) *Contrition as a response.* Contrition derives from God's initiative and must therefore realize that it is a response. It is of course based in essence and in its actual occurrence on the grace of God, like every moral act which is to be of any significance for salvation. It does not therefore bring about God's saving will, which has its definitive historical manifestation in Christ. It is a response of acceptance of that will and is aware that the free acceptance is itself the work of God's saving will. Contrition therefore "causes" justification only by receiving it from God as a pure gift. All the "merit" of contrition, however this is conceived according to different stages of contrition, ultimately derives from a first efficacious grace of God which is preceded by absolutely *no* human merit and work. Whatever is said of such merit (whether thought of as *meritum de condigno* or as *meritum de congruo*), it ultimately simply means, therefore, that God himself effects in our freedom what is "worthy" of him. It is only necessary to avoid the misconception that the activity of our freedom comes less from God than what we undergo passively and automatically.

d) *The formal object of contrition.* The movement of contrite repudiation of one's own past can take various forms because, corresponding to the multiplicity of different aspects of reality willed in their variety by God, there are a multiplicity of moral values which, if affirmed, can form the direct positive intent of contrition and so provide grounds for rejection of what is opposed to them. Yet for all that it must not be overlooked that the multiple world of values which makes it possible for there to be a variety of motives for contrition, forms a unity in which each particular motive points to the whole and is open to it, and that all motives and the response to them are only perfected in God and his love. *Per se* one would even have to distinguish between the intrinsically specifying formal object of an act and the external motive for the positing of the act (though the two can coincide). The formal object of contrition as such, which does not need to be envisaged in a very explicitly conscious way, is always fundamentally the contradiction between sin and the holy God or, positively, God's claim on men because of his holiness. The motives (of a moral kind) which prompt one to posit this act with this formal object can be very multifarious. They can even be "inferior" to the formal object of the act which they "prompt", or can even extend to the formal object of the love of God which in this way becomes the motive of perfect contrition. In what follows, however, we leave out of account this more precise distinction.

e) *Attritionism and contritionism*. On this basis it is possible to understand the attrition-contrition controversy. Attritionism is the doctrine that *attritio* (imperfect contrition, from a motive which is morally good but from the religious point of view inferior to that of unselfish, theological love of God) is sufficient for the sacrament of penance. The term first appeared in the 12th century, and at first meant an inadequate endeavour, insufficient for justification even in the sacrament, to have *contritio* as the repentance which justifies. Later *attritio* was used to mean a genuine repentance prompted by serious moral motives (chiefly fear of divine justice) but not yet based on love. This was opposed by Luther as "gallows remorse" because he identified *timor serviliter servilis* (mere fear of punishment as a purely physical evil) and the *timor simpliciter servilis* (real renunciation of *guilt* out of fear of punishment). Before the Council of Trent, the discussion centred on whether the power of the sacrament itself changed this *attritio* into *contritio* (repentance based on love). Trent recognized *attritio* as a morally good preparation for the sacrament (*D* 898). After Trent, controversy continued on whether *attritio* is sufficient as proximate preparation or disposition for the sacrament or whether in addition an explicit act at least of initial love (which again was variously interpreted) is required (cf. *D* 798). If an at least initial unselfish love of God (*amor benevolentiae* as opposed to *amor concupiscentiae*) is regarded as a proximate disposition necessary even for the sacrament of penance, even if that love is of a kind which is not sufficient for justification without the sacrament, we have contritionism in the form which was current particularly in the 17th and 18th centuries. The controversy between attritionism and contritionism in this form was never decided by the Church (*D* 1146).

On closer examination this controversy is pointless, both in theory and as regards pastoral theology. For where there is no unambiguous renunciation of sin for religious motives, there is no *attritio*. And such renunciation necessarily includes the will to fulfil God's commandments and consequently, before all else, the commandment to love God with one's whole heart. But how would such a will to love God be distinguished practically and in the concrete from love of God? Real attrition and contrition may therefore in the concrete be different in the explicitness with which various motives appear in the foreground of reflective conceptual consciousness, but not in the unanalysed global motivation of the fundamental decision of a human life. The dispute is therefore based on a false reification of the motives on both sides, and on the presupposition that only what is explicitly known as a motive is effectively one. In reality, however, the ultimate fundamental freedom of man cannot remain at all neutral, provisional and indefinite. The God loved in man's fundamental decision is either the true God or an idol of sin. If, therefore, the fatal line is crossed with genuine morality and religion away from sin towards God, there is no danger that God is not yet loved, even if a development *in time* can be assumed to be involved. Furthermore, a distinction would have to be drawn between the proximate disposition for the reception of the sacrament *(sacramentum)* and the proximate disposition for the reception of the grace of the sacrament *(res sacramenti)*. Then the doctrine of attritionism could be applied to the reception of the grace of the sacrament. For it is quite meaningful to assume with Aquinas that the reception of justifying grace (the "infusion of the theological virtue of charity") by an adult can only take place in the act of free acceptance of precisely this gift as such, in other words, in the act of charity. Consequently, in any case the *attritus* becomes *contritus* at least in the sacrament. Where someone has really turned away from sin and towards God, this is a conception which does not present any psychological difficulty, unless the view is held that a motive is only present if it is present in an explicitly conceptual form.

See also *Metanoia, Conversion, Penance.*

BIBLIOGRAPHY. H. Dondaine, *L'Attrition suffisante* (1943); P. Anciaux, *La Théologie du*

Sacrement de Pénitence au XIIe siècle (1948); C. R. Meyer, *The Thomistic Concept of Justifying Contrition* (1949); P. de Letter, "Two Concepts of Attrition and Contrition", *Theological Studies* 11 (1950), pp. 3–33; J. Nuttin, *Psychoanalysis and Personality* (1953); G. J. Spykman, *Attrition and Contrition at the Council of Trent* (1955); P. Anciaux, *Sacrament of Penance* (1962); B. Poschmann, *Penance and the Anointing of the Sick,* Herder History of Dogma (1964).

Karl Rahner

CONVERSION

Sections A and B of this article will deal with the wider notion of conversion as amendment of life; section C with the problem of conversion in the narrower sense, that of a baptized person from a Christian community to the Catholic Church.

A. THEOLOGY

1. *Methodology.* a) The content of the theologically important and indeed central concept of conversion will be presented here from the point of view of dogmatic theology, but that of biblical theology will also be taken into account.

b) It is difficult to distinguish the concept precisely from related theological concepts: faith (as *fides qua*) and consequently hope and love, contrition, metanoia, justification (as an event), redemption. Reference must therefore be made to these terms. In accordance with the corporeal-spiritual, historical and social nature of man, conversion has always, though in very varying degrees, a liturgical and social aspect in all religions, including Christianity (rites of initiation, baptism, penitential liturgy, revivalist meetings, etc.). This can be the embodiment and social side of conversion, but if it is not performed with genuine personal conviction, it constitutes a deformation of conversion and of religion generally. This aspect cannot, however, be dealt with further here.

c) The biblical terms שׁוּב, ἐπι-, ἀπο-στρέφειν, μετάνοια and others are specifically religious terms which denote more than an intellectual change of opinion (as in Greek). They concern the whole human being in his fundamental relation to God, not merely a change of moral judgment and attitude in regard to a particular object (and commandment).

2. *Conversion as fundamental decision.* From the point of view of the formal nature of freedom, conversion is the religiously and morally good fundamental decision in regard to God, a basic choice intended to commit the whole of life to God inasmuch as this takes place with some definite, if only relatively higher, degree of reflection and consequently can be located at a more or less definite point in a lifetime. For the freedom which finds realization in one individual life as a whole is not a mere sum of moral or immoral free actions, simply following one another in time. It involves one act of freedom as fundamental decision. Nevertheless, this fundamental decision is not wholly accessible to analytical reflection. It cannot, therefore, be fixed with certainty by such reflection at a quite definite moment in the course of life. This must always be borne in mind in the theological interpretation of conversion.

3. *Conversion as response to God's call.* From the biblical and dogmatic point of view, man's free turning to God has always to be seen as a response, made possible by God's grace, to a call from God. And he himself in the summons gives what he asks. This call of God is both Jesus Christ himself, as the presence of the Kingdom of God in person, with the demands this involves, and his Spirit which, as God's self-communication, offers freedom and forgiveness to overcome the narrow limits and sinfulness of man. It also comprises the actual situation of the person to whom the call is addressed. This is the precise particular embodiment of the call of Christ and the Spirit.

4. *The content of the call,* which cannot be separated from its utterance, is a summons, imposing an obligation and making obedience to it possible, to receive God, who communicates himself, liberates man from enslaving "idols" (principalities and powers), and makes it possible to have courage to hope for final liberation and freedom in the direct possession of God as our absolute future. The call therefore summons us from mere finitude (since grace is participation in the divine life itself) and from sinfulness, in which man in mistrust and despair makes an idol of himself and of certain dimensions of his own existence in the fundamental decision of his life (since grace is forgiveness). The call is not simply a

command to fulfil particular moral obligations, to "amend one's life".

The content of the call can, of course, also be described the other way round. Where a man is detached from self ("denies himself"), loves his neighbour unselfishly, trustingly accepts his existence in its incomprehensibility and ultimate unmanageableness as incomprehensibly meaningful, without claiming to determine this ultimate meaning himself or to have it under his control; where he succeeds in renouncing the idols of his mortal fear and hunger for life, there the Kingdom of God, God himself (as the ultimate ground of such acts) is accepted and known, even if this occurs quite unreflectingly. In this way the conversion remains implicit and "anonymous" and in certain circumstances Christ is not expressly known (though attained in his "Spirit") as the concrete historical expression of God's definitive self-utterance to man. Ultimately the intention is the same, whether Jesus calls for conversion (*metanoia*) to the *basileia* of God present here and now in himself and confronting the whole man with its radical demands, whether Paul calls us to faith in God who justifies without works through the Cross of Christ, or John admonishes us to pass from the darkness to light in faith in the Son who has appeared in the flesh. All continue the preaching of penance by the prophets of the OT and give it a radical character through the faith that in Jesus Crucified and Risen the call of God, which makes conversion possible, is definitively present and invincibly established, but precisely for that reason imposes the gravest obligation.

5. *The "today" of conversion.* Conversion itself is experienced as the gift of God's grace (as preparation) and as radical, fundamental decision which concerns a human life in its entirety, even when it is realized in a particular concrete decision in everyday life. It is faith as concrete concern about the call, which in each instance uniquely concerns a particular individual, and as the obedient reception of its "content". Conversion is hope as trusting oneself to the unexpected, uncharted way into the open and incalculable future in which God comes (which is predestination). It is a turning from one's past life (freely performed yet experienced as a gift), ending the repression by which the past was detained in sin. It is love for the neighbour, because only in conjunction with this can God really be loved, and without that love no one really knows with genuine personal knowledge who God is. It means standing firm and grasping the unique situation which is only found at this particular moment "today", not soothing oneself with the idea that it will come again, that the chance of salvation is "always" available. It is the sober realization that every conversion is only a beginning and that the rest of daily fidelity, the conversion which can only be carried out in a whole lifetime, has still to come.

6. *Conversion in non-Christian religions* (and even the secular analogies in psycho-therapeutic practice) has to be judged by the same general criteria as are used to interpret theologically non-Christian religions and perhaps even "implicit Christianity".

B. PASTORAL ASPECTS

1. In ordinary Catholic pastoral practice the occurrence of conversion as a central event in the history of an individual's salvation is very often masked. The reasons are easy to see. Baptism, which was *the* event of conversion in the early Church with its baptismal devotion, is in most cases administered to infants. Confirmation also for the most part does not in practice figure as the ritual expression of a conversion. The same applies to our practice of First Communions in early childhood. Furthermore, our pastoral practice treats as the normal case a Christianity lived in a relatively homogeneous Christian society, where the ultimate Christian attitudes and decisions are taken as a matter of course (even if it is questionable whether this is really the case). Practice in the confessional, frequent confession and preaching on morals, which deals chiefly with the particular demands of Christian daily life, also tend to a perpetually repeated rectification and improvement of Christian everyday life on its average level rather than to a fundamental, unique "new birth".

2. Pastoral practice and theology, however, ought not to overlook the phenomenon of conversion as a decisive function of pastoral care of the individual. Not only because freedom in the sense of man's

unique, historical self-realization intended to be final in regard to God, implies a fundamental decision *(option fondamentale)*, but also because a decision of this kind ought to be carried out as consciously and explicitly as possible, since reflection and history are constitutive of man's very essence. From this point of view, conversion is not so much or always a turning away from definite particular sins of the past, as a resolute, radical and radically conscious, personal and in each instance unique adoption of Christian life. And in this, freedom, decision as absolutely final, and grace are really experienced (cf., e.g., Gal 3:5). Furthermore, in a society which in philosophical outlook is extremely heterogeneous and anti-Christian, Christianity in the individual, deprived of support from the milieu, cannot survive in the long run without a conversion of this kind, i.e., personal fundamental choice of faith and Christian life.

3. Pastoral theology and practice should therefore cultivate more the art of spiritual initiation into this kind of personal experience of conversion. Not that a genuine conversion can simply be produced at will by psycho-technical methods. But as clear and conscious as possible an accomplishment of the fundamental Christian decision can be considerably furthered by really wise and skilled spiritual guidance on the part of an individual pastor (as the preambles of faith demand). In an age of atheism which declares it cannot discern any meaning in the question of God even as a question, or discover any religious experience whatsoever, this spiritual initiation into conversion has not primarily a moral decision as its immediate goal, but the bringing about and voluntary acceptance of a fundamental religious experience of the inescapable orientation of man towards the mystery which we call God.

Catholic pastoral practice was and is mistrustful of any deliberate production of conversion phenomena ("methodism", "revivalist campaigns"), and with good reason (regard for "objectivity", fear of pseudo-mysticism, fanaticism, will to preserve the ecclesiastical character and sobriety of Christian everyday life, etc.). Nevertheless, there have also been in existence for a long time in Catholic pastoral practice all kinds of ways of methodically promoting conversion, adapted to the general human and cultural level of Christians, e.g., popular missions, retreats, days of recollection, novitiates, etc. All such pastoral methods directed towards conversion ought, however, to be examined to see whether they are precise enough and correctly adapted to the dispositions of men today which make possible for them a genuine religious experience and conversion. Catholic pastoral practice should realize its own particular dangers and obviate them by a determined effort to provide genuine spiritual guidance towards really personal conversion. The dangers are those of the merely liturgical and sacramental, of legalism, of the practice of comfortable church-going and mere conventionalism, of conforming to the average level in the Church.

4. Since the fundamental decision has perpetually to be maintained or renewed in quite novel situations, the fundamental phases of life constitute so many situations and specific forms of conversion. Puberty, marriage, entry into a profession, beginning of old age, etc. ought to be regarded as situations offering the opportunity for conversion, and pastoral practice ought to know how its spiritual initiation into religious experience and conversion must be specially adapted to fit these situations.

5. From the very nature of freedom, the fundamental decision of which has to be concretely realized and maintained in the multiplicity of particular voluntary choices in daily life, and because of the connection between conversion and the limits of human life, its individual differences and phases of growth, it is understandable that a Christian life may run its course like a slow uninterrupted process of maturation, without very clearly marked breaks (though these are never wholly lacking). On the other hand it may appear as a dramatic event with one or more apparently almost revolutionary conversions which can be dated with considerable precision (as, e.g., with Paul, Augustine, Luther, Ignatius Loyola, Pascal, Kierkegaard, etc.). But even a sudden conversion can be the result of a long but imperceptible development.

C. CONVERSION FROM ANOTHER CHRISTIAN COMMUNITY TO THE CATHOLIC CHURCH

1. Special problems arise on the "conversion" of a Lutheran or Orthodox Christian to the

Catholic Church. What is in question here is not solely (or not even necessarily in all cases) an interior change in the ultimate fundamental attitude concerning the whole of life. It is a change in the ecclesiastical situation of the convert. On the one hand it is conceivable, for example, that in such a case a "saint" may be converted, and then only the external ecclesiastical status would be altered. It is possibly for someone merely to change his denominational membership without special inward change of heart, although this is really needed, and to become a Catholic, even for reasons which have no religious significance at all. The normal case, however, will be one in which conversion to the Catholic Church also involves something in the nature of an inward religious conversion.

2. "It is clear that the preparation and reception of those individuals who desire full ecclesiastical communion is in essence different from ecumenical work; the two, however, are not incompatible, for both derive from God's wonderful design." (Vatican II, Decree on Ecumenism, art. 4.) In practice this conciliar declaration means that the ecumenical work of Catholics as such must take care not to aim at individual conversions to the Catholic Church, for this would bring that work into disrepute and make it impossible. On the other hand, even in the age of ecumenism such individual conversion is legitimate and indeed a duty, the necessary conditions being presupposed. The same applies, therefore, to the endeavours of Catholics and of the Catholic clergy to promote such individual conversions. At all events, however, in case of actual conflict in practice, ecumenical work must take precedence in importance and urgency over individual conversion.

3. The following principles might perhaps be indicated as important in the endeavour to promote individual conversions.

a) If such work is not to degenerate into a false proselytism, the pastoral missionary work at the present day in the countries which are called Christian but are largely de-Christianized ought to be concerned with the re-Christianization of contemporary atheists, of people who belong to no denomination and of the unbaptized, rather than with promoting individual conversions of the kind mentioned. Winning the former to

the Catholic Church then represents simply the final stage of a conversion in the genuine religious sense of the term.

b) In view of the limited pastoral resources in personnel of the Catholic Church, non-Catholic Christians are not in practice suitable "subjects" for the work of conversion, even if this gave promise of success, if they are pursuing a Christian life in the genuine Christian spirit in their own Church and if they would not be much changed or advanced in the central and essential concern of Christianity, which they are of course in a position to live in accordance with their concrete religious possibilities and needs. Consequently, for them a denominational conversion could scarcely mean in practice a conversion in the real sense. It is different with those who denominationally belong to a non-Catholic Church or community but do not practise and religiously speaking are homeless.

c) Anyone who wishes to become a Catholic on genuinely religious grounds may not be turned away but must be afforded most attentive pastoral care.

d) If ecumenical or personal grounds suggest it, the interval of time between recognition of the Catholic Church as the true Church of Jesus Christ and official conversion to it need not be restricted to a very short period.

4. The pastoral care of converts involves more than instruction in Catholic dogmatics and moral theology. As far as may be, it ought to aim, in preparing for the act of entering the Catholic Church, at making this a conversion in the full religious sense of the word. This presupposes a good knowledge of non-Catholic theology and an understanding of ecumenical work. It must endeavour to counter rather than to strengthen a purely negative attitude of protest in the convert against his former ecclesiastical community. It must encourage the convert not to lose any element of his positive Christian heritage by his move, and assist him to cope in faith and patience with the often very imperfect life of the Catholic parish. The pastoral care of converts cannot, therefore, simply be regarded as ended by their conversion.

See also *Metanoia, Freedom, Decision, Ecumenism* I–III.

BIBLIOGRAPHY. E. D. Starbuck, *The Psychology of Religion* (1899); W. James, *The Varieties of Religious Experience* (1902); P. Rousselot, "Les yeux de la foi", *RSR* 1 (1910), pp. 241–59, 444–75; T. Mainage, *La psychologie de la conversion* (2nd ed., 1915); J. Huby, *La conversion* (1919); A. H. Dirksen, *The New Testament Concept of Metanoia* (1932); A. D. Nock, *Conversion. The Old and the New in Religion, from Alexander the Great to Augustine of Hippo* (1933); M.-T.-L. Penido, *La conscience religieuse* (1935); H. Pohlmann, *Die Metanoia als Zentralbegriff der christlichen Frömmigkeit* (1938); J. Behman and E. Würthwein, "μετάνοια", *TWNT*, IV (1942), cols. 972–1004; E. Sjöberg, *Gott und die Sünder im palästinensischen Judentum* (1938); G. Berguer, *Traité de Psychologie de la religion* (1946); M. Nédoncelle, *God's Encounter with Man* (1964); H. U. von Balthasar, *Die Gottesfrage des heutigen Menschen* (1956); W. Gruehn, *Die Frömmigkeit der Gegenwart* (1956); R. Hostie, *Religion and the Psychology of Jung* (1957); W. L. Holladay, *The Root šūbh in the Old Testament* (1958); O.-A. Rabut, *Vérification religieuse. Recherche d'une spiritualité pour le temps de l'incertitude* (1964); K. Rahner, "On Conversions to the Church", *Theological Investigations,* III (1967), pp. 373–84.

Karl Rahner

COUNCIL

I. Theology. II. History: A. Christian Antiquity and Early Middle Ages. B. Late Middle Ages and Modern Period.

I. Theology

1. *Concept.* Councils or Synods are assemblies (σύνοδοι, *concilia*) of representatives of the universal Church or local Churches for mutual consultations and for reaching decisions on Church affairs. A distinction must be drawn between Ecumenical Councils representing the universal Church and the various kinds of particular councils (general, patriarchal, plenary, primatial, imperial and provincial synods).

2. *Historical sketch.* The forms taken even by the Ecumenical Councils have been of diverse kinds. According to existing canon law, no Ecumenical Council can take place unless it be convened by the Pope. The rights of the Pope also include the chairmanship (either in person or through his delegates) of the Council, the fixing of subjects for discussion and the rules of procedure, the location, adjournment and dissolution of a Council, and the confirmation of the decisions reached (*CIC,* can. 222; cf. can. 227). All cardinals, patriarchs, archbishops and bishops, abbots and prelates with an area of jurisdiction of their own, the abbot primate, the superiors of religious congregations and the superiors-general of exempt orders, and also the titular bishops have the right to vote, provided nothing to the contrary had been laid down in the terms of convocation. The theologians and canonists summoned to the Council possess only an advisory vote (can. 223; on representation and premature departure cf. can. 224–5). Council Fathers can also propose questions for treatment at their own initiative, but such proposals are subject to the approval of the president (can. 226). The Ecumenical Council possesses the highest jurisdiction over the universal Church; appeal from the Pope to the Council is excluded; in the event of the death of the Pope the Council is suspended (can. 228–9).

These stipulations codify, in all essential points, the procedure followed at Trent and at the First Vatican Council. Among them there is hardly a point which was not disregarded at one or many or perhaps even at most of the Ecumenical Councils. In particular, it is historically untenable that the "Ecumenical Councils" of the first century were generally convened, presided over and confirmed by the Pope. What all these questions primarily involve are stipulations of canon law, insofar as the constitution bestowed on the Church by the gospel is not embodied in them.

The Petrine office must be effectively represented at an Ecumenical Council, since it is of the essence of the constitution of the Church, of which the Council must be representative. However, this representation was verified in very different ways at the Councils, sometimes merely through subsequent approbation. And it cannot be denied that conflicts have occurred in the past between Church and Pope, or that they may occur in future — as in the possible case of a heretical or schismatical Pope and his "deposition".

Direct representation of the laity at the Councils (and not merely indirect, through the clergy) is not only dogmatically possible, but also desirable from the theological viewpoint of the universal priesthood. The laity's direct knowledge of and responsibility for the world also make it desirable; under some circumstances it is absolutely necessary. On the other hand, a Council directed against the authorities of the Church would conflict with the order of the Church and, in particular, with the nature of the Ecumenical Council, which is intended as a representation of the universal Church, for such representation is not possible without the bishops.

Considerable differences are to be found in every respect between the provincial Councils of the 2nd and 3rd centuries (out of which the Ecumenical Councils developed), the eight ancient Ecumenical Councils of the Byzantine East convened by the Emperor, the papal General Synods of the Latin Middle Ages, the late medieval reform Councils of Christendom, the purely ecclesiastical Tridentine Council of Catholic reform and Counter-Reformation, and the First Vatican Council which was dominated by the Pope.

3. *Theological meaning.* The Church itself is the comprehensive "assembly" (= ἐκκλησία, from καλέω), called together by God himself; it is a "con-cilium" (con-kal-ium, from *concalare,* i.e., to call together; Greek: καλέω) of those who believe. Thus in a deep theological sense the Church itself can be called an "Ecumenical Council of divine convocation". The universal Church, as a fellowship of the faithful, has a conciliar, synodal (collegial) structure throughout; this is true of the local (parish), particular (diocese), provincial and universal Church.

In this perspective the Ecumenical Council in the usual sense (i.e., Ecumenical Council of human convocation) can be described as a comprehensive representation (not merely in the sense of delegation, but as portrayal and as realization) of the Ecumenical Council of divine convocation (of the universal Church), very suitable for consultations and reaching decisions, ordering and shaping the universal Church, but not essential. (The Church is also assembled in a true and very intense manner in liturgical worship, especially at Mass.) The first Christian account of Church Councils expresses this meaning of the Council: "Aguntur praeterea per Graecias illa certis in locis concilia ex universis ecclesiis, per quae et altiora quaeque in commune tractantur, et ipsa repraesentatio totius nominis Christiani magna veneratione celebratur." (Tertullian, *De Paenitentia,* 13, 6–7; *Corpus Christianorum,* II, 1272.)

The idea of representation — whatever form it took — has always been fundamental to an understanding of the Ecumenical Council. The Ecumenical Council is or ought to be an authentic representation of the *ecclesia una* (in concord and moral unanimity of the decisions), *sancta* (the external framework, basic attitude and conciliar decisions should be determined by the gospel), *catholica* (the obligation of individual Churches to recognize the council), *apostolica* (the apostolic spirit, the apostolic witness and — serving these — the apostolic office are decisive for the Council). Insofar as the Holy Spirit operates in the Church according to the promise of Jesus, he also operates in the special event of its representation, in the Ecumenical Council of human convocation. Therefore, the Ecumenical Council can claim a special, binding authority, even if its decrees and definitions are imperfect, fragmentary human words (cf. 1 Cor 13:9–12). Its documents — the doctrinal decrees should be distinguished from the disciplinary ones — only possess the binding character which the Council concerned itself bestows on them. Every Council and every conciliar decree should be understood historically and interpreted in its historical context.

See also *Council* II, *Church, Bishop, Conciliarism, Infallibility.*

BIBLIOGRAPHY. J. L. Murphy, *The General Councils of the Church* (1959); F. Dvornik, *The Ecumenical Councils* (1961); H. J. Margull, ed., *Die ökumenischen Konzile der Christenheit* (1961); P. Meinhold, *Konzile der Kirche in evangelischer Sicht* (1962); H. Küng, *The Structures of the Church* (1965).

Hans Küng

II. History

A distinction is still usual today between assemblies which represent the universal Church by virtue of their composition (Ecumenical Council) or which gather together bishops of a number of ecclesiastical provinces (plenary council) or of a single province (provincial council) and, on the other hand, the diocesan synod. The terms σύνοδος and *concilium* were originally equivalent; there was as yet no hierarchy of different kinds of assembly. Today, 21 assemblies are reckoned as Ecumenical Councils. The authoritative list of these Ecumenical Councils only began to take firm shape in the 16th century. The inclusion of a General Council in this category is settled neither by the application of criteria derived from canon law nor by a synod's view of its own status. The diversity of forms

9

of Church assembly has an independent history just as has the (sometimes retrospective) inclusion of a particular synod in one or other category. Every assembly represents a conscious intention to guide the Church; it follows, therefore, that the history of Councils mirrors changes in the Church's constitution. This factor clearly marks out the middle of the 11th century as undoubtedly the great turning point, for, after the Gregorian reform, the unqualified authority of conciliar decisions was established by papal jurisdiction. The authoritative formulation of the Christian faith and the standardization of Church practice are the constant concerns of conciliar action.

A. CHRISTIAN ANTIQUITY AND EARLY MIDDLE AGES

1. *Pre-Nicene Councils.* No direct line can be traced from the Council of Jerusalem, A.D. 50, to the Church's synodical practice. The initial stages of synodical activity appear only from the middle of the 2nd century onwards. Like the sacred ministries, the synod grew from the meeting of the local congregation for worship. From 175 onwards a growing awareness of the apostolic succession of the episcopate as well as the wider significance of local controversies led to meetings of bishops from several communities. Prior to 325, of course, participation was less on the basis of the imperial provincial system than of the relationship to the mother Church and the geographical distribution of Christian communities. Towards the end of the 2nd century, Italy and Asia Minor had already developed a lively synodal activity; the Church of Gaul did so only sporadically in the 4th century. The first to make the transition from occasional assemblies for specific purposes to regular synods was the African Church in the 3rd century; the last, the Gallo-Frankish Church in the 6th century. Controversy over the date of Easter led at the end of the 2nd century to the first exchange of opinions between groups of synods. Synodal decisions in the 3rd century were communicated to other Churches with a view to securing common policy in the question of the *lapsi* and of Novatianism or to obtaining other Churches' recognition of disciplinary decisions. This rudimentary form of Church universalism nevertheless failed to reconcile differences; African synods in

255 and 256, under Cyprian, dealing with the validity of baptism conferred by heretics, appealed to previous synodal decisions and sided with the Antiochene synod against the Roman view. The authoritarian attitude of Bishop Stephen of Rome did not silence opposition.

While the universal aspect here took the form of an exchange of views between particular groups of councils, with the West taking a leading part, a new form appeared in the Antiochene synods of 252, 264 and 268. In these synods the Western Churches played no part or only a minor one. The Novation question and the heresy of Paul of Samosata, then occupying the attention of the Christian East, led to a meeting of all the Churches from the Black Sea to Egypt. This was a new grouping. The condemnation of Paul of Samosata was the first to be communicated to the entire οἰκουμένη; according to Alexander of Alexandria (320) it was effected by a synod and the sentence of bishops from all places. This same group of councils, embracing almost the entire Christian East, was destined (at the instigation of Constantine) to arrange at Antioch in 324 for the Council of Nicaea, and to provide the majority of the participants. It represented a step on the way to the expression of ecumenicity in the form of a single assembly of bishops. The form taken by this assembly at Antioch later proved to be the prototype of the first Ecumenical Council.

2. *The Ecumenical Councils of antiquity.* The unity of the now Christian Roman Empire following Constantine's victory over Licinius made it possible for the Emperor in the year 325 to summon, open and lead the Council of Nicaea. This was the first of the eight Ecumenical Councils of Christian antiquity, as reckoned by the present-day canon. Representation of all the Churches of both East and West was intended to give visible expression to the unity of the Church as the spiritual basis of a unified empire. In Constantine's view, the security of the empire and the unity of the Church were inseparably linked. This idea was decisive in the completion of the preliminaries. It was strengthened at Nicaea itself by the final agreement about the date of Easter, the reorganization of the Church's districts to correspond to the imperial provincial system and the transformation of regional into provincial councils.

The status of the Emperor in the Council made the assembly of bishops of all the Churches into a kind of imperial council, an imperial institution, and accordingly the Council's decisions were given imperial endorsement and its disciplinary measures were supervised by the civil magistrates.

But adoption by the empire was not itself enough to constitute the ecumenicity of the Councils of antiquity. Not every Council summoned as ecumenical by the Emperor (e.g., Sardica 342/43, Rimini 359, Ephesus 449) proved to be such, for unanimity was not always attainable. Not even the high number of participants was decisive. In 431 it was thought sufficient to invite to an Ecumenical Council at Ephesus only the most important sees, along with a few of their suffragans. Even at Chalcedon — with 500 bishops participating, the largest of the ancient Councils — not all the sees were represented. Above all, the West invariably attended only in the persons of a few representatives. The First Council of Constantinople (381), not intended as ecumenical, united only the Eastern bishops, yet was subsequently recognized as ecumenical by the Council of Chalcedon (451) and by Pope Hormisdas (519). What constituted the ecumenicity of a Council, therefore, was convocation by the Emperor, the eventual agreement of the participating bishops, their awareness that in virtue of their office their assembly represented the Church, and the subsequent acceptance by the whole Church. The conviction that a Council had, as the embodiment of the whole Church and by agreement after free discussion, affirmed the Church's faith and the apostolic tradition, is what established the authority of the Council's decision; it was regarded as an expression of the divine will, unalterable and binding on all Churches.

The structure of conciliar organization did not change in the course of the first seven Ecumenical Councils. The decisions were made by the assembled bishops while the Emperor was responsible for the legal form in which these decisions were expressed. But the balance shifted. The legates of the Bishop of Rome frequently brought with them the view of a Roman synod which already anticipated the matter to be discussed; because the decision reached in Rome represented in essence the view of the Western Church, the papal legates to a General Council acquired incontestable weight. At Ephesus in 431, Cyril of Alexandria and the legates of Pope Celestine worked so closely together that the Fathers of Chalcedon could say in 451 that these two bishops had taken the leadership. Pope Leo I claimed the leadership of the Council at Chalcedon through his legates; all the discussions were dominated by his authority and he determined its decision by his appeal to the succession of Peter. Yet at Chalcedon it was the Emperor Marcian's version of the Creed which was accepted; and the Emperor himself was acclaimed by the Council as the "new Constantine, the new Paul, the new David". Pope Gregory II still admitted Leo III to be Emperor and priest, though he pointed out to this iconoclastic ruler that the title "priest" had only been given to rulers who had summoned Councils with the full accord of the priests in order that the true faith might be defined, whereas Leo had defied the decisions of the Fathers and usurped priestly functions.

The mutual relationship of the two powers was interpreted to mean that the Emperor acted in lawful succession to Constantine as "bishop appointed by God for the external affairs of the Church". The incapacity of the imperial commissioners at the Synod of Ephesus in 449, which turned that stormy assembly into a "Robber Synod", underlined the need for a strong controlling hand. But the apostolicity of the Roman See, which came increasingly to the fore in the 5th century, secured for the Pope an undisputed leadership and authority in doctrinal matters. This tended logically to the recognition of a primacy of jurisdiction. This evolution of full spiritual authority, which as yet went no further than an explicit approval of decisions taken only in the absence of the papal legates, was opposed to the conciliar position of the Byzantine ruler which was incapable of further development, and which was gradually replaced by the Eastern Church's concept of a supreme authority vested in the pentarchy of the five patriarchal sees. Hence, following the confusion over the Patriarch Photius, it remained uncertain whether the Fourth Council of Constantinople (869/70) should, as the Western Church believed, count as the eighth Ecumenical Council or whether the Council of 879/80, also held in Constantinople, should be so regarded, as the Eastern Church desired.

It was in virtue of their doctrinal decisions that the Ecumenical Councils enjoyed clearest precedence over the regional synods. The First Council of Nicaea condemned Arianism and formulated the Creed; the First Council of Constantinople dealt with Arians, semi-Arians, and Sabellians; the Council of Ephesus (431) condemned Nestorianism, that of Chalcedon Monophysitism, and both defined the hypostatic union. The Second Council of Constantinople (553) rejected the Three Chapters of the Nestorians; the next Council in Constantinople (*Trullanum* 680/81) condemned Monothelitism, and the Second Council of Nicaea (787) asserted the legality of the veneration of images. Yet a legally binding hierarchy of Councils had still not established itself. The first four Ecumenical Councils already formed a separate group when Gregory the Great compared them with the four gospels (or Isidore of Seville with the four rivers of Paradise); he accepted the Second Council of Constantinople as ecumenical on the ground that it was in accord with the "four most holy synods". This fourfold group was henceforth regarded as a standard for all other conciliar decisions because it had formulated the fundamental Trinitarian and Christological faith. It was only in the 9th century, however, that Ecumenical Councils were distinguished as such from regional synods, and not finally until the 10th century; in the opinion of theologians they served as a standard for the local synod and were themselves related to the fourfold group, within which the First Council of Nicaea enjoyed special eminence. The pre-eminence of this group is referred to as late as 1080 by Gregory VII, with of course the important qualification that the decisions of these Councils had been recognized by his predecessors.

3. *The General Synods of the German Empire.* The type of synod representative of all the Churches of a Germanic national territory derives from three roots. The Germanic peoples brought with them the idea of a national council, partly from the Christian East and partly from their traditional modes of government; Western Romance territories had only the provincial council or, where partition into provinces was still inoperative, met in regional councils like that of Arles. The Arian kings required councils to be held on the national scale, but held personally aloof. The Visigoth kings only brought their habitual influence to bear after their conversion to Catholicism, while the Merovingians did so as soon as they had consolidated their rule. The first national synods took place more or less at the same time, the Visigoth synod at Agde and the synod at Arles in 506. In 517, the Burgundian synod at Epaon united, for legal reasons, the Church provinces of Lyons and Vienne. The Frankish synod at Orleans in 511 was a definite example of this new type of synod in the Western Church.

The Visigoth synods at Toledo did not all have the character of a national council. Of the eighteen synods held there, long described as national councils, seven have to be excluded as provincial; only the third (589), the fourth (633), the fifth (636), the sixth (638), the seventh (646), the eighth (653), the twelfth (681), the thirteenth (683), the fifteenth (688), the sixteenth (693) and the seventeenth (694) were national councils. After the conversion of Recared, the indigenous Romance population was integrated into the Visigothic state on the grounds of national unity, by way of the episcopate, at the Third Council of Toledo (Toletanum). Chiefly influenced by Isidor of Seville, the Fifth Council of Toledo perfected the national type of council. In questions of faith and in national affairs the general council alone was competent. The Visigothic Church regarded itself as part of the whole Church but the synod claimed the right to examine all doctrinal decisions taken outside the kingdom. There was a second session with the nobles present to treat of national affairs. Like the Byzantine Emperor, the king had the right to summon the synod; by the reading aloud of the *tomus regius* he determined its agenda, and his approval was enough to give its decisions force of civil law. The national council was regarded as representative of Church and State; along with the king, it was the supreme authority in civil and religious matters, laying down and approving laws and supervising their execution. The ecclesiastical and civil affairs of the provinces were regulated in a similar way by the two powers in the provincial councils. When in the years 653–81 the Visigoth monarchy assumed the characteristics of the Byzantine ruler and the Archbishop of Toledo tried to secure patriarchal status, the general council forfeited part of its functions. Instead of exercising normative control over Church and secular power and deciding the legal force of the oath of allegiance which had to be sworn to the chosen king, it became an instrument in the hands of the king for enforcing his will legally.

Provincial and diocesan synods were of little importance in the Frankish kingdom; really important decisions were taken at the national councils, which were largely dependent on the king. The ruler exercised little pressure on the diocesan synods while in the case of provincial synods he claimed only supervisory rights. But from the outset the right to summon the national council and to determine its meeting-place belonged to the king; the choice of the bishops to be invited was also reserved to him; they had to attend in obedience to the royal command and were not allowed to send representatives instead. For these reasons alone, the Frankish national councils had a quasi-civil and parliamentary character. The participants were resident bishops, abbots and clergy. The last mentioned had only advisory functions; from the 9th century onwards the abbots participated in the voting with, in fact, a position equivalent to that of the bishops. Matters discussed were not so much doctrinal as legal and pastoral questions, and more rarely, cases of discipline. The authority of synodal decisions was rooted in the early medieval feeling for law; men wished neither to formulate new doctrines nor to promulgate new law but to re-discover the good old ways. Hence discussion was strongly influenced by authoritative personalities.

In the history of the evolution of national councils a distinction must be made between the Merovingian and Carolingian periods. The Merovingian kings either attended the national council in person or else sent their representatives. They took no part, however, in the formal decisions, claiming only to decide how much civil authority they would lend to Church law. The *canones* thus ratified were binding on the bishops and royal officers. The ecclesiastical council of the Merovingian period became under the Carolingians a court session which externally was like an assembly of the nobility. The king and the council co-operated in making ecclesiastical laws; only when matters affect-ing both the spiritual and temporal spheres were being discussed were secular leaders brought in as among the Visigoths. To this corresponded the existence of ecclesiastical, secular, and mixed capitularies. The sole lawgiver was the king; the bishops acted only by his mandate. In this phase the national council appeared as a section of a national parliament which ordinarily met in two separate groups under the king.

Again, like the national synod of the Visigoths, Charlemagne believed himself able to approve or reject the decisions of foreign councils; he refused to recognize the Council of Nicaea of 787 as ecumenical, and in 794, conscious of his quasi-imperial status at the Frankfurt national council, caused the rejection of Adoptionism in formal agreement with Pope Hadrian I, and even of the veneration of images, in a mistaken interpretation of the text of the Nicene synod. The *Concilium Germanicum* of 743 made regular national councils part of the national constitution. The disintegration of the Frankish kingdom in the 9th century did not alter this regulation; but it could not prevent the atrophy of the council's structure. In the new divisions, the unity of parliament and council was maintained, but only the rulers of the Western kingdom clung to their exclusive right to give decisions force of law; this, however, slipped from their grasp with the rapid disintegration of their power.

The imperial Church of the Saxon-Salic period was in the main governed according to traditional regulations; its synodal decisions, insofar as they were not disciplinary, were therefore of little importance. At this period there was no formal difference from previous synodal law. Synod and Reichstag continued to meet at the same time, though they were not so closely interlocked; the ruler continued to attend as *Vicarius Christi* and "teacher of bishops", and he influenced decisions though legally he only determined their civil validity. It was not the weakening of the Council which determined development, but the integration of the Papacy into the imperial Church by the *Pactum Ottonianum* (962), which joined together the national council and the long standing Roman patriarchal or provincial synod, where in future the important decisions would be made.

B. Late Middle Ages and Modern Period

1. *The papal General Councils of the late Middle Ages.* The temporary union of the old Roman synods with the national council paved the way for the transformation of the former into universal papal General Councils. Under Nicolas I and his successors papal legates constantly attended regional synods and the Pope's immense influence gradually took the form of concrete governmental action even at the conciliar level. The Reform Papacy succeeded to the Emperor at the councils and extended its power of leadership far beyond the limits of the previous period, since now convocation, agenda, and formulation of decisions could be all the more exclusively determined by the Pope; the *Dictatus Papae* of Gregory VII in 1075 declared that no Council might be called universal, even in retrospect, without the Pope's approval. The number of episcopal participants constantly increased, the themes were enlarged to include concerns of the universal Church, and the choice of meeting-place, always conditioned by political considerations, was no longer automatically confined to the city of Rome. The reform Councils of Leo IX at Pavia and Reims (1049), the Roman Synod of 1059 (papal election decree), the Roman Lenten Council of Gregory VII in 1075 (Church Reform) and the Councils of Urban II in Piacenza and Clermont in 1095 (Crusade and Peace of God) were decisive steps leading consistently to the Ecumenical Lateran Councils of 1123 (settlement of the Investiture Controversy), 1139 (schism of Anacletus II), and 1179 (peace with Barbarossa).

It may have been because of the gradual evolution of the Roman provincial synod into a General Council that an ecumenical character was only very tardily attributed to the first meetings of this type of council. The Fourth Lateran Council of the year 1215, which in accord with the wish of Innocent III was by its careful preparations linked again with the great Councils of antiquity, was, along with the Second Council of Lyons (1274) and the Council of Vienne (1311), the only medieval one to be recognized as ecumenical from the very beginning; this Council and the earlier Third Lateran Council dealt with the Catharist heresy. Even the First Council of Lyons (1245), described by Innocent IV

himself as ecumenical, was only later included in the list of such Councils.

The universal authority of these Councils was no longer immanent in their structural origin but was established beforehand, in the view of the canonists, by the papal primacy; material ecumenicity lost in importance. The Popes still wished to know that their decisions had the support of the Council Fathers. At the demand of the assembled bishops and laity, Paschal II in 1112 had to withdraw the treaty of Ponto Mammolo negotiated with the Emperor Henry V; the Lateran Council of 1116 declared the Emperor excommunicated, though the Pope declined to promulgate the ban. The First Lateran Council was summoned to confirm the Concordat of Worms secured by Calixtus II. Lucius III regarded the alteration of a decree issued by one General Council as admissible only by the decision of another. At the Fourth Lateran Council, the Archbishops of Braga and Narbonne opposed any discussion of the primatial status of Toledo on the ground that they had not been called together for that purpose. Even Gregory VII exercised his power to promulgate law at a Council in the traditional way; yet he it was who, in 1075, was the first to declare that the Pope could promulgate laws for the whole Church without a Council, depose or absolve bishops and alter the Church's jurisdictional boundaries. The papal claim gradually made the Pope independent of the Council. In a short period of time Gregory VII promulgated no less than five general laws without a Council. In 1215 Innocent III had the essential work of a Council carried out by a small group of participants gathered together on his own authority. And Gregory X enforced the decisions of the Second Council of Lyons in his own amended form. The provincial councils, whose legitimation depended on the papacy, were in the same period transformed into purely administrative courts.

Change in the composition of the Council corresponded with this development. It was already customary in the Ottonian period for bishops, abbots and lay princes from an area not restricted to the city of Rome to participate. The custom was adopted and, along with a comprehensive agenda, soon extended to all countries of Western Christendom. The First Lateran Council of 1123 was the first to display a *de facto* representation of the Latin Church. The universal diaspora attained systematic representation in 1215. Representatives of the cathedral chapters were added in 1274; at the same time, with the custom of inviting an abbot from each bishopric, the beginnings of a principle of selection emerge which logically pointed towards representation of all orders. The Council of Vienne, under strong pressure by the King of France, Philip the Fair, in the end brought together only a limited number of bishops whose invitation had first to be ratified by the King. As early as the 11th century laymen already had the right to participate in the discussion of matters affecting their interests. Their participation became increasingly a matter of course the more the Council tried to bring together all ranks. Influenced by this development, the Council of Vienne was already a Council of bishops and deputies. From 1215 onwards the College of Cardinals created a special position for itself among these groups; as a small advisory group to the Pope, it often substituted the formula *de consilio fratrum nostrorum* for the older and more comprehensive formula *sacro approbante concilio*.

2. *The Council as representative of all ranks in the Church.* From the Middle Ages onwards, the Church appeared as a predominantly juridical institution, while ecclesiology modelled itself on political society. Radical papalistic canonists regarded the papacy as concentrating the whole Church in its functions, with a fullness of authority subject to no control. The liturgical-sacramental concept of the *corpus mysticum* was obscured in favour of the sociological-realist aspect of the Church and hardened into a *regnum ecclesiasticum, principatus ecclesiasticus, apostolicus, papalis.* Analogously to Christ as the head of his own mystical body, the Pope came to be regarded as the head of the mystical body of the Church. In the Avignon Exile this theory was translated into action in the form of a centralizing absolutism. Then the election of a Pope and anti-Pope in 1378, the background to which made any settlement of the dispute impossible, at once brought to light the limits of papal efficiency and permitted a second, hitherto little observed, range of ideas to come to the fore. This new conception, though it also started from the corporative idea, instead of concentrating the community in its apex to the exclusion of the legitimate claims of its members, regarded the apex as a delegation of the authority of the total community, from time to time renewed by an election which involved the endorsement of each act of government. This range of ideas which began to appear in the 13th century in tentative and sporadic fashion, began to harden after 1378 into a theory which is given the general title of Conciliarism.

Only in the early 15th century was agreement reached that the Council was the basis for the restoration of the Church's unity, though in this context the basis of the Council needed a different structure from its late medieval one. At the Council of Pisa (1409) cardinals of both obediences declared the two Popes to be heretical by reason of their personal inflexibility in questions of Church unity, and therefore deposed. They elected a new Pope; and the Church was now split into three obediences. The Council of Pisa regarded itself as a General Council, but its decisions were rendered obsolete by the Council of Constance, 1414–18 (itself only subsequently recognized as ecumenical), when it decided to annul all three papal titles and in 1417 elected a new Pope of uncontested legality, Martin V. The Councils of Pisa and Constance were also attended by delegates from the universities and almost all the princes. Pisa was dominated by the cardinals; in Constance the Emperor appeared as *advocatus ecclesiae,* in effect for the last time. But the awareness of representing all members of the Church and so of authorizing its own decisions was first fully expressed at the Council of Constance. The division of the Council into nations, a move directed against control of the Council by the Curia, and already foreshadowed at Vienne, was now applied even to the voting procedure with all participants having equal voice.

The *Haec Sancta* decree of the Council of Constance is still disputed today because, provoked by the flight of John XXIII, it subordinated the papacy to the will of the Church represented in a Council, and, in the later decree *Frequens,* obliged it to pursue a programme of reform dictated by the Council. Regarded by many while it was still being drafted simply as a way out of a particular emergency, it was later held by Conciliarists as sanctioning their theory of the Church which regarded the Pope as, in principle, subordinate to a universal Council. This question was constantly debated throughout the entire 15th century. In pursuance of the programme of regular Reform Councils, laid down at Constance. Eugene IV in 1431 summoned a General Council to Basle, but a general weariness of Councils soon caused it to disband. Appealing to the decree *Haec Sancta,* a section of the Council continued to meet and gradually established itself as a supreme legal and administrative court of the Church; attended by hardly any bishops and increasingly by professors and procurators, this assembly set about taking over the long term direction of the Church in the style of a modern parliament. But by their election of the anti-Pope Felix V in 1439, the Basle Conciliarists discredited themselves. When Eugene was negotiating with the Greeks about Church union in 1437 at his Council at Ferrara (transferred to Florence in 1439) — this Council is reckoned today along with Basle as the seventeenth Ecumenical Council — most of the Christian powers remained neutral, partly from uncertainty, partly because of a latent Conciliarist attitude. Only when the French king abandoned his neutrality in 1449 and Felix accordingly resigned, did the Council, which had been transferred from Basle to Lausanne in 1443, break up without any decision.

The Conciliarist theory was still not completely overthrown, for in the thought of the time Council and Church reform continued to be closely connected. The papacy saw in this connection of ideas a constant threat to its supremacy, the more so because the Council was actually misused in this way as a political weapon. Louis XII of France actually arranged a *conciliabulum* directed against Julius II which met at Pisa in 1511 and renewed the decrees of the Council of Constance. The Fifth Lateran Council (1512–17), which consciously ranked itself with the papal General Councils, had no difficulty in suppressing this attempt to revive Conciliarism.

3. *The Ecumenical Councils of the modern period.* With certain modifications, the nineteenth Ecumenical Council, at Trent, maintained the structure of the papal General Councils of the Middle Ages and fixed the pattern of succeeding Councils. Called for by the German Protestants, who were still thinking in terms of the type of Council so recently rejected, the Council of Trent by its very success led to a strengthening of papal authority. The idea of a representation of the whole Church was rejected; with its relatively small number of participants and its permanent majority of Italian bishops, the ecumenicity of the Council depended once again on the papal convocation, the support of the participants and the papal confirmation of its decisions. Invitations were sent only to bishops, generals of orders and representatives of monastic congregations, all of whom voted as individuals, and to the secular powers, whose delegates, however, had no voting right; the direction of the Council was entrusted from now on to papal legates.

The course of the Council of Trent falls into two main periods: the so-called Imperial Epoch (1545–52) was directed to dealing with the Lutheran Reformation in an enforced co-operation with an absent Emperor; at the request of the French king, the second epoch (1562/63) was devoted rather to Calvinism. Summoned in 1536 by Paul III under pressure from Charles V, and adjourned without opening, after the naming of Mantua and Vicenza as meeting-places, it was only after the Peace of Crépy that the Council was able to meet, in Trent. In 1547–51, because of typhus, it was transferred to Bologna and was suspended until 1562 because of the rebellion of the German princes. If we take into account the immediate consequences of the Council, for example the acceptance of its decisions in various countries, a process which lasted in part into the 17th century, it begins to take on the dimensions of an epoch even in terms of duration. In significance it rivals the First Council of Nicaea.

Hoping for union with the forces of reform which had already broken away, the Council from the outset tackled simultaneously the two main tasks of affirming traditional doctrine and of bringing about a comprehensive reform of the Church. Since the majority of the Council Fathers lacked a clear concept of the Church, the Council did not succeed in producing an exhaustive and systematic presentation of doctrine but was content with particular measures of reform and doctrinal clarification, with a view to closing the gaps which had arisen in the existing system under the impact of Protestant thought. But the few German Protestants who were present for a short time (1551–52), and then the Peace of Augsburg (1555), made it clear that differences were irreconcilable. The word "Catholic" came to be used more and more, instead of "Christian", now that Christendom was divided.

In retrospect the Council of Trent proved to be the starting point for a renewed Church within a changed environment. Men came to terms both institutionally and spiritually with the division of Christendom. Against this background, the implementation of the Council's decisions was not a process of adaptation to the previous Church tradition; tradition was integrated into the *corpus* of the decrees, which now was regarded as adequate, complete and final, in contrast to the view of many of the Council Fathers. Pius IV established a Congregation for the authoritative interpretation of the decrees; Pius V published an official edition to guide their execution, and Gregory XIII entrusted the supervision of the implementation of the decrees to the nuncios. Respect for the Council's decisions, thus raised to a unique status, shaped the so-called Tridentine system, down into the 17th century; this system in turn determined the new characteristics of Church administration. The vertical hierarchical aspect was superimposed upon the character of the Church as a fellowship; it displaced the collegial function of the cardinals and of the episcopate, this being taken over by curial Congregations and by the supervisory functions of the nuncios. This was one of the main reasons why the Church had to wait more than 300 years for the next General Council.

The First Vatican Council (1869/70) was convoked to put an end to the spiritual confusion of the 19th century, which affected even Christians, by clarifying the Catholic faith and the Catholic view of the Church. The *Syllabus* had been the first step. The only constitutions to be promulgated were the *Dei Filius,* dealing with the relation between faith and knowledge, and *Pastor Aeternus,* dealing with the extent of papal jurisdiction and doctrinal infallibility. The Council ended prematurely with the occupation of the Papal States by Piedmontese troops as a result of the Franco-Prussian War; decrees in preparation on the Church and pastoral questions never reached the voting stage. The definition of the Pope's primacy and infallibility, intended as part of a comprehensive definition of the Church, thus remained a torso. The primacy question presented the greater difficulty in view of the inherent

rights of the diocesan bishops. But widespread alarm was aroused by "infallibility" even before the Council opened. Yet this definition did not have the unhappy consequences which had been feared. While excluding existing Gallican ideas, it also set limits to extreme ultramontane views; in substance it did not go beyond the traditional doctrinal teaching of the 13th and 16th centuries. The declaration of the universal jurisdiction of the Pope, on the other hand, was fraught with far greater consequences in the intensification of curial centralization.

In its formal structure the Second Vatican Council (1962–65) differed neither from the First Vatican Council nor from the Council of Trent. Summoned by John XXIII, directed by a special commission, its decisions solemnly ratified by the personal presence of the Pope at the close of each session, it, too, assembled bishops, superiors-general of exempt orders, and prelates with their own special sphere of jurisdiction, all having an individual vote. But unlike the First Vatican Council which was in large measure an assembly of the bishops of the entire world, the composition of the Second Vatican Council was no longer exclusively European in character. Another difference at the last Council was the presence once more of lay people, invited as observers (not as *oratores* of the Christian powers as at Trent). And this time the non-Catholic Christian Churches and alliances accepted the invitation to send observers.

The careful preparation (a further contrast with the Council of Trent) together with the collaboration between the preparatory commission and the appropriate central authorities of the Curia gave rise to an impression that the Fathers of the Second Vatican Council were to be allowed simply to give formal approval to previously prepared schemata. But a sense of collegial responsibility and independent initiative already established itself in the episcopate in the first plenary session, and this soon led to the formation of new groupings linking up with the system of episcopal conferences already in existence for over a century in some places such as Belgium and Germany and extending it, rather than the quite insignificant provincial synods, on the horizontal plane, with its own authority and a limited power of legislation. The representation of the non-Catholic Churches ensured that the themes

17

were always discussed in the context of the hope for future reunion. Decisive was the declaration of John XXIII that the task of the Council was not to repeat traditional theology nor to condemn errors but rather to examine abiding doctrine and to interpret it in contemporary terms. The division of a Council's tasks into dogma and discipline which had existed since the earliest Councils was thus overcome by a deeper fundamental pastoral concern, and the defensive post-Tridentine attitude was abandoned. The consequences of this approach cannot yet be foreseen.

See also *Reform* II C, *Avignon Exile*, *Conciliarism*, *Bishop* IV.

BIBLIOGRAPHY. J. D. Mansi, *Sacrorum conciliorum nova et amplissima collectio,* 31 vols. (1757–98), new edition, completed and ed. by L. Petit and J.-B. Martin in 60 vols. (1899–1927); *Monumenta Germaniae Historica inde ab anno Christi 500 usque ad annum 1500,* series *Concilia* and *Constitutiones* (1826 ff.); C. J. Hefele and J. Hergenröther, *Conciliengeschichte,* 9 vols. (1855–1900); J. Haller, *Concilium Basiliense,* 8 vols. (1896–1936); C. H. Turner, *Ecclesiae occidentalis monumenta iuris antiquissima,* I–II, 3 (1899–1930); C. J. von Hefele and J. Hergenröther, *Histoire des conciles d'après les documents originaux,* trans. by H. Leclercq, 9 vols. (1907 ff.); N. Valois, *La crise religieuse du XVe siècle. Le pape et le concile, 1418–50,* 2 vols. (1909); E. Schwartz, ed., *Acta conciliorum oecumenicorum,* 25 vols. (1910–40); C. Butler, *The Vatican Council,* 2 vols. (1930); H. Barion, *Das fränkisch-deutsche Synodalrecht des Frühmittelalters* (1931); C. de Clercq, *La législation religieuse franque de Clovis à Charlemagne* (1936); V. Martin, *Les origines du Gallicanisme,* 2 vols. (1939); S. Kuttner, "Conciliar law in the Making", *Miscellanea Pio Paschini,* II (1949); G. Schreiber, ed., *Das Weltkonzil von Trient, sein Werden und Wirken,* 2 vols. (1951); C. de Clercq, "La legislation religieuse franque depuis l'avènement de Louis le Pieux jusq'aux fausses décrétales", *Revue de droit canonique* 4 (1954); 5 (1955); 6 (1956); B. Thierney, *Foundations of Conciliar Theory* (1955); W. Ullmann, *The Growth of the Papal Government in the Middle Ages* (1955); H. Jedin, *The History of the Council of Trent,* 2 vols. (1957–61); J. Gill, *The Council of Florence* (1959); H. Jedin, *Ecumenical Councils of the Catholic Church. An Historical Outline* (1960); F. Dvornik, *The Ecumenical Councils* (1961); G. Dumeige, ed., *Histoire des Conciles œcuméniques,* 12 vols. (1962 ff.); *Conciliorum Oecumenicorum decreta,* ed. by Centro di Documentazione and Istituto per le Scienze religiose (2nd ed., 1963); H. Jedin, *Strukturprobleme der Ökumenischen Konzilien* (1963); J. Vives, *Concilios visigóticos e hispanoromanos* (1963); M. Wilke, *The Problem of Sovereignty in the Later Middle Ages* (1963); R. Aubert, *Vatican I* (1964).

Odilio Engels

COVENANT

1. *Before the biblical revelation.* The pagans of the ancient East know nothing of a covenant which binds the divinity to man. But they know that there are relations between man and his god. Not only is the divinity witness and guarantor of pacts between men, it also intervenes in the life of man; it hears prayers and supplications; it can heal and give long years of life; it has certain wishes, not always clear, and is irritated with those who transgress them and they fall thereby into misery. It has its favourites and its elect, often predestined long beforehand, and it grants them power and descendants. It adopts them, because men, like gods, can be its children. It sustains their life, guides them by revealing itself in dreams or otherwise, saves them from danger and preserves them from illness. The religious paganism of Babylon, Egypt, and Syria culminates in an ill-defined kinship where the god, brother, mother, or father, penetrates human life but does not really raise it to his own level. As the Gilgamesh epic tells us, "When the gods created mankind they gave it death for its portion but kept immortality for themselves." Yet the hero of the epic, the son of a goddess, was two-thirds divine. For paganism the union of God and man does not go beyond sharing in dominion over the earth and the divinized forces of nature.

2. *The patriarchs.* While the gods of pagan kings and believers disappear from history one after the other, the God of Abraham remains a living God. And from being the God of one man, he becomes the God of a clan, a nation, a Church. But in the beginning, the patriarchs' manner of honouring their God differs little from the way in which their contemporaries honour theirs. He makes them repeated promises (Gen 12:1; 13:15; 15:1, etc.) and at the same time gives them his directives (Gen 26:2; 46:3, etc.). The true God binds himself closely to Abraham, just as according to the belief of the times the *ilu* (god) Gilgamesh made himself the associate *(tappu)* of Enkidu, a man, and received offerings of association from him. In the same way, at Ugarit in the 13th century B.C. the god Ansukka receives such offerings from a certain Takhulu. But the treaties of "alliance" concluded by Abraham (Gen 21:27, 32) and Isaac (Gen 26:28), and

so on down to David (2 Sam 5:3), are rather treaties between men with the divinity as witness, treaties of vassallage of which we have numerous examples outside the Bible.

3. *Moses and the covenant.* The covenant between God and his people of which Moses is to be the intermediary goes beyond the association between God and the patriarchs, though the biblical redactor again uses the word *bᵉrīt,* as he did when speaking of Abraham in Gen 15:18. The Mosaic covenant is preserved for us in two conflated traditions, one of which puts it at Sinai (Exod 19:1, 2, 18; 34:2), the other at Horeb (Exod 17:6; 33:6; cf. Exod 3:12b). The resulting narrative is complex. Without entering into detail, we note that the Covenant of Sinai is presented above all as a sacred meal in the presence of God (Exod 24:1f., 9f.), and that it is sanctioned by a decree of the Lord (Exod 34:10–28) in which, like the kings of the time, he regulates the worship, the sacrifices, and the annual feasts at which the people comes into his presence, "to the house of Yahweh" (v. 26).

In the other narrative, the covenant is presented rather as a contrast based on the Decalogue (Exod 20:1–17). Moses repeats these "words" to the people and they pledge themselves solemnly to carry them out, after a rite performed in front of twelve *stelae* representing the twelve tribes, in which the blood of victims is poured on the altar and sprinkled on the people. It seems probable that this rite was renewed at the sanctuary of Gilgal where twelve *stelae* were set up (Jos 4:20). In both traditions it is Moses who writes down the order of God which is the condition for the blessing given to his people. The covenant with Israel is not simply an alliance based on the bonds of blood, as between kindred; it is a conditional alliance in which the people is bound to respect the demands made upon it in the moral and religious order.

4. *From Joshua to David.* Joshua is the heir of Moses and it is this Ephraimite who makes Israel master of the mountains this side of Jordan. His activity culminates at Shechem in the temple of the "God of the covenant *(bᵉrīt)*". A solemn covenant is made in which his followers, as well as other peoples for whom fidelity will be more difficult (Jos 24:19, 25), pledge themselves to the Lord who must be served. A great stone is set up as a witness (Jos 24:26) near the oak of the sanctuary (cf. Jg 9:6). This is the stone, apparently, on which Joshua inscribed the text called the "curses of Shechem" ("stones", plural: Jos 8:32), in accordance with the prescription of Moses in Deut 27:4 ff. Henceforth the promises made to the patriarchs, the "words" of Horeb-Sinai and the blessings of the twelve tribes (Deut 23, which is to be attached to Gilgal), are accompanied by curses. Shechem is the meeting-place of the so-called "amphictyony" of the tribes of Israel, where they renew their covenant every year and where each tribe provides for the upkeep of the central shrine for one month.

The life of Israel during the period of the Judges is marked by infidelities, chastisement, appeals to the Lord, and the re-grouping of the people around the warrior God enthroned on the ark of the covenant who delivers his people. The danger was even greater in the time of Samuel when the transition was made, not without opposition, from the amphictyony to the monarchy, from the judge to the anointed king. The danger came from the Philistines. The function of the monarch in the ancient East was to protect the people and give it prosperity in the name of the national god. First Saul and then David were chosen as *nāgīd,* shepherds of the people of God. But the institution of kingship was only indirectly dependent on the covenant. Later texts speak above all of the covenant made by God with David (Ps 89:4).

5. *The covenant under the monarchy.* For the theology of the covenant, the establishment of the monarchy is of central importance. David instals the ark of the covenant in his palace, and it will then be placed in the most sacred part of the national temple built by his son. A difficult verse (2 Sam 23:5) in which the "house of David" is mentioned already affirms that God "has made with me an everlasting covenant". The monarchy introduces a note of perpetuity, or rather stability, into the covenant, and the permanence is manifested by the dynastic national sanctuary which attracts the festive pilgrimages of the nation. It is true that the northern tribes, Israel, abandon the dynasty after the death of Solomon. But the ark of the covenant, along with the tables of the law, make it

always possible for the faithful to find the true God, as Isaiah says (Is 8:14–18). The ark of the covenant is confided to a priesthood (2 Sam 8:17) which under Solomon is restricted to Zadok and his sons (1 Kg 2:35). It is perhaps to this priestly group that we owe the preservation of the national traditions which are found in the synthesis which critics call the Yahwist document (J) of the Pentateuch. As in 1 Sam 7, it insists more on the promises and the blessings than on the covenant, but the demands of God are indicated in the law for the Pasch (Exod 13) and in the code of Exod 34:17–27.

6. *The prophets.* It fell to the prophets, at the decline of the monarchy, to develop all the latent virtualities of the Mosaic covenant. But a crisis began which was to lead to the revelation of a "new covenant" after the rupture of the old. They are not mutually exclusive, because the same God is author of both. Nevertheless, a profound change ensues in the structure of the Israel of God.

The crisis makes itself felt first of all in the northern kingdom, which was more exposed to the disturbing influences of the international trends of the day. The continuity of the dynasties was constantly interrupted, and as early as the Aramaean wars of the 9th century the prophets appear, like Elijah and Elisha, as the religious guides of the people, taking the place of an incompetent monarchy. They appeal to the traditions of the past. Elijah makes a pilgrimage to Horeb, and a new synthesis of the national traditions is probably made, inspired by the prophetic outlook — the Elohist document (E) of pentateuchal criticism. It goes back beyond the monarchy and the conquest to base itself on the Mosaic tradition of which the levitical clergy is the depositary, especially the clergy of Dan, who are the descendants of Moses, and perhaps the clergy of Bethel. But the latter, descendants of Aaron through Phinehas (Jg 20:26–28), were more contaminated.

The covenant is an unequal contract, conceived on the lines of a treaty of vassalage, where the people binds itself by oath to carry out the stipulations of Yahweh its God. This solemn undertaking was preceded by a history in which God, the sovereign protector, the "shield of Abraham" (Gen 15:1), protected the patriarchs and their descendants against all the powers with whom the Israelites were tempted to enter into alliances.

But the Yahweh of Horeb alone is God, and it is he who gives the people its good things (Hos 2), and not the Baals to whom Israel "prostitutes" itself like a wife unfaithful to her husband. Israel has been unfaithful from the beginning (Hos 11) but the covenant allows of repentance and penance (Exod 33:5–6), just as Jacob's family purified itself before going to Bethel, by "putting away the foreign gods" (Gen 35:2–5).

The ancient curses of Shechem are transformed into a punishment, which Yahweh finds hard to inflict, as is revealed in the heart-rending cries of Hosea and Isaiah (ch. 1). He "roars from Zion" (Amos 1:2), irritated by its injustices and transgressions. As the true king of Israel, the God of Micah upbraids the princes of the house of Jacob who ought to have "known justice" but prove to be enemies of goodness and lovers of evil (Mic 3:1). Yahweh is so much the Lord of Israel that according to Ezekiel he went so far as to give statutes that were not good and ordinances by which they could not have life (20:25), having them kill their first-born and allowing wicked foreign customs to come in. Instead of letting the people perish by its sins, God is so faithful to the covenant that he takes responsibility for their misery and makes of it a chastisement to lead the people to repentance and penance.

But the evil is so profound, Jerusalem is a city so deeply "rusted", that the rust can no longer be removed (Ezek 24:6), and the prophets say clearly that the covenant has been broken off. Amos had already seen Yahweh standing upon the altar and destroying the sanctuary (Amos 9:1). Instead of this cultic image, Hosea speaks of the divorce between Yahweh and Israel. The Israelites can accuse their mother, "for she is not my wife and I am not her husband", says Yahweh (Hos 2:2 [4]). Micah sees the mountain of the temple transformed into a wooded height (Mic 3:12). Jeremiah is the most explicit. Taking up once more the image of divorce used in Hosea, he recalls the law of Deut 24:1–4 to affirm that a new marriage should be impossible (Jer 3:1): the nation has changed gods (Jer 2:11). "The house of Israel and the house of Judah have broken my covenant which I made with their fathers." (Jer 11:10.)

At the beginning of his ministry Jeremiah still thinks that there is room for repentance and return to God (Jer 3:6–18; 18:8), but later it seems to him more and more impossible (Jer 13:33), as God withdraws from him the right to intercede (Jer 14:11). A *new covenant* will be needed (Jer 31:31–34). Ezekiel takes the same attitude (Ezek 16:59–63). The covenant has been broken (v. 59), but God will remember it (*zaqar*, very important for the theology of the "memorial" of the covenant) and "raise up" *(heqim)* an eternal covenant (v. 60) in which Sodom and Samaria will share, "but not on account of the covenant with you" (v. 62).

Finally, for Deutero-Isaiah as for Jeremiah (Jer 30:17), Israel is a forsaken wife (Is 54:1, 6), but God redeems her; his love is unshakeable and from now on he has "a covenant of peace (*shalom,* fullness)" for his bride which is likewise unshakeable (Is 54:10). This eternal covenant is founded on God's "steadfast love for David" (Is 54:3) in which the nations will share (v. 4), the only condition being that men turn towards Yahweh the God of Israel (v. 7) and abandon their evil ways.

7. *Towards the new covenant.* The prophets have thus orientated the theology of the covenant towards new horizons and a new foundation. It is less a pact than a gracious act of God. It is based rather on God's promise than on Israel's dedication. Though it maintains the just demands laid down in the Decalogue of Moses, it will be founded on the favour accorded to David. For Ezekiel the good shepherd will be no ordinary king but a new David "raised up" by God, to "make a covenant of peace" (Ezek 34:23–25).

Deuteronomy, which is so close to Jeremiah, had already voiced this new way of thinking. The covenant undoubtedly remains a pact in the nature of a treaty of alliance, with stipulations, undertakings, blessings, and curses. But above all it is a free act of God (Deut 7:7ff.), founded on the promises made to the patriarchs. Its implementation supposes love above all Deut 6:4ff), the memory of God's great deeds (Deut 6:12), and fidelity. The king is a brother who draws inspiration continually from the law (17:14–20), and Moses is rather a prophet than a law-giver (18:15). As for Jeremiah, fidelity is essentially a personal question for each man before God (24:16), rather than a collective loyalty to the covenant on the part of the nation. Hence circumcision of the heart is demanded rather than that of the flesh (Deut 10:16). But the object of this covenant is a life with God among brothers, in which strangers too will share, even the Egyptians (23:9).

The "priestly" texts of the Pentateuch deepen and enlarge this notion of the covenant under the influence of Ezekiel. The texts no longer speak of "concluding" a covenant, but of "giving" or "establishing" it, and "covenants" appear in the plural (Gen 6:18; 9:11; 17:7, 19; Exod 6:4). St. Paul reminds his readers that the OT contained covenants (Rom 9:4). Each of them comprises a gift, a demand, and a sign. God "establishes" the covenant of Noah for all humanity. God continues to sustain life in spite of cosmic catastrophes, but only for those who do not shed blood; and the sign is a cosmic one: the rainbow in stormy weather. The second covenant is the covenant with Abraham, an eternal covenant under which God grants progeny. It calls for integrity *(tamim)* of conduct before God, and its sign is bodily circumcision (Gen 17:1ff.). The third covenant is that of Moses on Sinai (Exod 19:5 — this is however disputed, cf. Lev 26:45), given in memory of the covenant with the patriarchs (Exod 6:4ff.). It makes of Israel a kingdom of priests and a holy nation by reason of the calling of Aaron and the institution of the priesthood and the sanctuary. By the covenant of Noah the covenant was broadened to take in all nations; by that of Aaron, the covenant was given a greater depth of holiness and consecration: it is the covenant of salt (Num 18:19) and therefore incorruptible. Since it is a gift and a unilateral action on the part of God, though it still requires a personal response from the individual who lives under it, it could well be translated by διαθήκη in the Alexandrine version.

This divine διαθήκη, which is a testamentary disposition of one's goods in favour of an heir, or the deposition of the written document in a shrine, appears in the book of Daniel as the holy covenant which many are to forsake under persecution (Dan 11; cf. 9:4). In Ecclus the word is used to translate not only *berit* but *hoq* (law, decree), a word which covers the whole will of God for man, especially the date of his death (Ecclus 14:12, 17; 16:22), though it still means also the eternal covenant, the law of life (17:11, 12), the divine commandments (41:19; 46:20; 45:5). Aaron is the beneficiary of the eternal covenant (45:15) of peace (v. 17), while David receives a royal covenant (*ḥoq mamleket,* 47:11) from God. Ecclus also speaks of covenants in the plural, but there is only one "book of the covenant", the law promulgated by Moses (Ecclus 24:23). This law is identified with Wisdom, which shared in the creative action of the Most High and took root in the people where the divine glory dwells (Ecclus 24:11). It is a liturgical Wisdom, which officiates in the holy tabernacle (v. 10) and is the giver of food and life (v. 19), being the earthly paradise restored which is watered by the life-giving stream of Ezek 47, which also flowed from the temple.

8. *The covenant of the New Testament.* The NT speaks comparatively rarely of διαθήκη, 35 times in all, of which 17 are in the Letter to the Hebrews. In the writings of Qumran the term is very frequent, and the "new testament" is mentioned not only in the *Damascus Document* but almost certainly in the commentary *(pesher)* on Habakkuk. *The Rule of the Congregation (1 QSa)* of the "men of the covenant" includes regulations for meals, to which only those who have undergone two years of probation are admitted (*Rule of the Community [1 QS],* 6, 20–21) and from which one can be excluded for certain faults.

The word covenant does not appear at all in the Johannine literature, except in one quotation from the OT in the Apocalypse. It is the Letter to the Hebrews, with its interest in liturgy, which speaks of it most frequently. Jesus of Nazareth is the mediator of the new covenant (Heb 9:15) and he is the surety (ἔγγυος 7:22) of a covenant better than the former one made with the fathers. "By the blood of the eternal covenant" the Lord Jesus has become the great shepherd of the sheep (13:20). By his death which has redeemed the transgressions of the first covenant, he has given the promised eternal inheritance to those who are called (9:15–16): the allusion to the death of the testator in v. 17 is unmistakable. By his own blood, not by the blood of goats, he enters with our humanity into the eternal sanctuary not made with hands (9:11f.) and purifies our conscience from dead works so that we may worship the living God. This covenant had been promised by God, and the letter quotes Jer 31:31 (8:8), while at the same time it recalls the blood of the covenant of Sinai (9:20). To sanctify the people by his own blood, Jesus suffered "outside the gate" (13:12), and the faithful must go forth from the camp (v. 13) to offer the sacrifice of praise (v. 15), because they have an altar (θυσιαστήριον) "from which those who serve the tent have no right to eat" (v. 10).

The Pauline letters likewise contrast the two testaments or covenants (Gal 4:24). The true διαθήκη is the firm arrangement in which God's promises were embodied (Eph 2:12) and which the gift of the law could not annul (Gal 3:15, 17). It is nonetheless a "new covenant" of which Paul and the apostles are the ministers (2 Cor 3:6). Christ has lifted the veil which hid the face of Moses and which prevented the "old covenant's" being understood (2 Cor 3:14). This was only a covenant of circumcision (Acts 7:8).

Having read the Letter to the Hebrews we are not surprised to find that the great instrument of the establishment of the new covenant was the Lord's Supper: "This cup is the new covenant in my blood. Do this as my memorial." (1 Cor 11:25) This translation, proposed by J. Jeremias, is the one which is most in keeping with the ritual texts of the OT which we have seen above. The Lucan narrative of the Last Supper, like that of Paul, likewise mentions the "memorial" (Lk 22:19) and the "new covenant". Matthew (26:28) and Mark (24:24) also speak of the "blood of the covenant" in a formula which like that of Paul and Luke recalls the sacrifice of Exod 24:8, but what is said to be "new" is the wine, the fruit of the vine, drunk by Christ with the apostles in the kingdom of God which has been established. As in John (Jn 6:54f.), the "eucharistic" meal (Mk 12:22 and par.) is the meal where Christ "raises up" his followers to eternal life in the last days or the last times (Heb 1:2), once the kingdom has been established by his death in the shedding of his blood, and by his resurrection. The sign of Daniel is given from this moment on (ἀπ' ἄρτι, Mt 26:64; ἀπὸ τοῦ νῦν , Lk 22:70), and the transition from the old to the new covenant has taken place before "this generation" (Mk 13:30; Mt 24:34; Lk 21:32) has passed away.

See also *Biblical Historiography, Old Testament Theology.*

BIBLIOGRAPHY. J. Jeremias, *The Eucharistic Words of Jesus* (1955); G. E. Mendenhall, *Law and*

Covenant in Israel and the Ancient Near East (1955); E. F. Siegmann, "The Blood of the Covenant", *The American Ecclesiastical Review* 136 (1957), pp. 167–74; G. Widengren, "King and Covenant", *Journal of Semitic Studies* 2 (1957), pp. 1–32; K. Baltzer, *Das Bundesformular* (1960); H. Wildberger, *Jahwes Eigentumsvolk* (1960); W. Eichrodt, *Theology of the Old Testament,* 2 vols. (1961–67); G. von Rad, *Old Testament Theology,* 2 vols. (1962–66); J. Coppens, "La Nouvelle Alliance de Jer. 31:31–34", *CBQ* 25 (1963), pp. 12–21; A. Jaubert, *La notion d'alliance dans le judaïsme aux abords de l'ère chrétienne* (1963); L. Krinetzki, *Der Bund Gottes mit den Menschen nach dem Alten und Neuen Testament* (1963); D. McCarthy, *Treaties and Covenant* (1963); R. Schmid, *Das Bundesopfer in Israel* (1964); R. E. Clements, *Prophecy and Covenant* (1965); E. Gerstenberger, "Covenant and Commandment", *JBL* 84 (1965), pp. 38–51.

Henri Cazelles

CREATION

I. Theology: A. Meaning of the Term. B. The Old Testament. C. The New Testament. D. History of the Dogma. E. Systematic View. F. Conclusion. II. Genesis: A. Title. B. Methods of Interpretation. C. Structure and Contents. III. Protology. IV. Beginning and End.

I. Theology

A. MEANING OF THE TERM

The term "creation" expresses the way in which the world and everything pertaining to the world have their origin, ground and final goal in God. It can mean, actively, the creative action of God, and passively, the totality of the world.

The concept was expressed in various languages by terms taken from various realms. The Greek Bible preferred κτίζειν which originally meant "to make habitable" and then "to found" (a colony, a city). The corresponding Latin word is *condere,* but the Latin Church preferred *creare,* the strict meaning of which was "to beget". This is the word which was taken over by the Romance languages and then in English, while the Germanic languages used *Schöpfung,* probably akin to the English "shape". None of these words were derived from a pre-Christian religious usage. Hebrew, however, had a word which was reserved for the divine action. Along with more general terms for making or forming, the word בָּרָא (Ezek, etc.) was used from prophetic times on, to designate God's action on the world, on

Israel and in the establishment of eschatological salvation. This consistent usage is characteristic of the biblical doctrine of creation.

B. THE OLD TESTAMENT

1. The Semitic peoples honoured the gods of nature, and myths embodying natural processes were the basis of their speaking of the gods. "The loneliness of Israel in the company of the religions of the world" (von Rad, II, p. 352) stems from the fact that it learned to know God not from nature but from history (Vriezen, p. 199). Israel first knew God as the saviour of the nation; belief in creation grew out of the experience of God's saving deeds (Vriezen, pp. 153f.; Renckens, p. 54).

Belief in creation did not form part of the original kernel of the religion of Israel. The older confession of faith includes the saving actions of God in history but not his creating the world (Deut 26:5–10). Some few ancient texts may reflect belief in creation but it only becomes an explicit theme in the late monarchical period (von Rad, I, pp. 149f.; Vriezen, pp. 195f.). Belief in creation was an extension of faith in Yahweh as the God of the covenant, of history and of the promises.

The process was probably as follows. The God of Israel gradually revealed himself as Lord of all mankind, and hence the story of the patriarchs was prefaced by the genealogies and the story of paradise, which gave a link between Abraham and all men. Then Yahweh also appeared as Lord of the forces of nature, using them as weapons in the liberation of Israel (Vriezen, p. 34). Faith in the God of the covenant begins to take in the whole world. This is the mental climate in which the affirmations and hymns about creation arose (cf. especially Deutero-Is, Jer, Ps). The doctrine of creation serves to confirm God's loyalty to his covenant (Jer 31:35–37) or to illustrate God's sovereign power in the history of salvation (Jer 27:5). God throws all the mighty forces of the world into his work of salvation. Hence creation and deliverance are hymned and praised in one breath as the marvellous works of God (Is 42:5f.; 45:24–28; Ps 74:13–17; 89:10 to 15, etc.). Creation, like the deliverance from Egypt, testifies to the power, the goodness and the fidelity of God.

2. Belief in creation was then given its classical form in the first chapter of Genesis (1:1–2:4a), which serves as an all-embracing prologue to the history of salvation. Creation is not regarded as a timeless revelation which takes place in the orderly course of nature (von Rad, I, pp. 152f.) but a historical and salvific work of God which launches history. It is now generally recognized that Gen 1 does not intend to provide a description of the coming to be of the world. Once this is understood, the doctrine of the passage may be more clearly seen:

a) *The whole world owes its being entirely to the free, sovereign action of God.* God speaks, and creates by his word. This theme, which occurs here and there in other religions, is strongly stressed in Gen 1, and recurs constantly throughout Scripture. The world, like Israel, subsists by virtue of God's word in his covenant. It is not a divine emanation, the natural result of a necessary process of theogony (von Rad, I, p. 156). It exists in so far as God addresses it.

b) *The world is "good".* The ancient cosmogonies have, as a rule, a markedly dualistic character. Our world, with its mingling of good and evil, comes from an encounter, a conflict, between a good principle of order and light, and an independent principle of disorder and evil. Even Gen 1 uses images taken from such notions, but de-mythized. All things implicitly obey the effortless command of God; they simply correspond to the divine will (Gunkel, p. 103). And since from the start Israel knows God as its loving Lord, it is fundamentally impossible for its faith to see the world as a hostile power. Hence the OT view of the world has a tranquillity, a warmth and clarity which we seek in vain outside the Bible (Vriezen, pp. 197f.). But faith in creation is no ground for naive optimism. Like the covenant, the creative word can become judgment (*ibid.*, pp. 206f.).

c) *The world exists for the sake of man.* Man is the real object of God's love, as the making of the covenant showed at once. He is the true partner in the covenant of creation, the viceregent of God and his image. In obedience to God he is to subject the world to himself (von Rad, I, p. 160). Man must not bow to the mysterious forces of nature. He must, on the contrary, make them serve him. With this, the world loses fundamentally all divine status, though it can be recognized as a sign and a word given to man by God (von Rad, II, pp. 350–2).

Creation itself is regarded as a sort of covenant given to man by God (Vriezen, pp. 153f.). The very existence of the world is to some degree a salvific work (von Rad, I, p. 152), since it is the theatre of the power and fidelity of God, who entered upon a covenant with Israel and the human race (e.g., Jer 33:20–25; Ps 89; 119:89–91; cf. 1 Pet 4:19).

Efforts have constantly been made to discover *creatio ex nihilo* (as it is formulated in 2 Macc 7:28) in Gen 1. The question is an anachronism, because it supposes that creation is envisaged from the *terminus a quo*, whereas the ancient creation texts are concerned only with the *terminus ad quem*. But the world is explained as containing nothing that does not depend on God's action; all goes back to him.

3. There is a further analogy between creation and covenant inasmuch as creation is also considered as a force dominating history. In the Bible, the world is not a stable cosmic order which was set up by creation once and for all. It is "much less a being than a happening" (von Rad, I, pp. 165, 429f.). Creation is, therefore, a promise ordained to a fulfilment (Vriezen, p. 358). It is entirely caught up in the relationship between God and man, of which eventful history salvation is the goal. Hence the one word ברא can indicate the original creation, God's actions in history and his final salvific intervention. In Deutero-Is above all creation and redemption appear almost as one and the same act of God's dramatic initiative (von Rad, I, p. 151). God's creative action is not simply a thing of the past, it takes place here and now and is yet to come.

Though Gen 1 makes creation the beginning of all things, belief in creation is not reduced to a mere protology. Creation is an act of the present instant, and remains true to itself till the hour of eschatological salvation. The association of creation, conception and resurrection in 2 Macc 7:22–29 is characteristic (cf. Rom 4:17). Creation is not a sort of neutral setting for the drama of salvation. It is part of the *magnalia dei* and a salvific act, since it founds and sustains the whole history of salvation.

This is a truth of which primitive Christianity and the ancient liturgy were still aware.

Thanksgiving for creation was given a fixed place in the solemn prayers of the Eucharist (Congar, pp. 189–94).

4. *Wisdom.* Along with this history-centred view which was inspired by the very kernel of faith in Yahweh, a more cosmological attitude also developed, probably under the influence of Egyptian and Hellenistic "wisdom" (von Rad, I, pp. 442 f., 463). The world becomes a spectacle (Job 36:25 f.), and the object of human research (Wis 7:17–20). It evokes astonishment and humility (e.g., Job 28; 38–39) and hymns of praise (Ps 8; 19; 24; 33; 93; 96; 104; 148; Ecclus 42; Dan 3:52 ff.; Pss 24 and 104 may be pre-exilic, Vriezen, p. 195). Here creation holds the centre of the stage and becomes the absolute foundation of faith (von Rad, I, pp. 153, 463). It almost becomes proof of the existence of God (Wis 13:1–9).

Here creation and salvation are not linked by means of history but through wisdom. Wisdom, which is considered almost as a subsistent entity (Prov 8:22–31; Ecclus 1:1–10; 24:1–34; Wis 7:22–8:1; 9:9–18) is the first work of creation, the instrument which God used to make heaven and earth. In the book of Wisdom, it is described as the master craftsman (Wis 7:21; 8:6). As the divine plan for the world, it is "poured out" upon creation (Ecclus 1:9) so that the world is irradiated by a glory which points back to God (von Rad, I, pp. 460–2). To know and follow this wisdom is salvation, since it is God's will for man and is identified with the law (Ecclus 24:1–34; Bar 4:1; von Rad, I, p. 458). To follow after wisdom is to partake of life, since God's creative will is directed to life (Wis 1:13 f.; 2:23).

This opens up the way for an important development, because creation is inscribed throughout the whole realm of profane nature. But it is not without its dangers. As long as the cosmological contemplation still concentrated its faith on the living and loving God of the Fathers, it constituted an enrichment. But where faith in creation loses sight of the history of salvation, the image of the creator can pale into that of a neutral, almost indeterminate being (Vriezen, p. 359).

C. The New Testament

1. The *synoptic preaching* provides very few allusions to the doctrine of creation. The present salvation is in the foreground, and creation is only evoked as a background on a few occasions (Lk 11:50; Mk 13:19; Mt 25:34; apropos of marriage, Mt 19:4–8; Mk 10:6–9).

But in the *prayer* of the community creation is chanted as one of the *magnalia Dei* (Acts 4:24; cf. Rev 4:11; 10:6; 14:7). Liturgical influence is also suggested by the formula which speaks of all things coming from God and moving towards him (1 Cor 8:6; cf. Rom 11:36; Eph 4:6; Heb 2:10), though here the orientation to God is predicated particularly of the community, which is the new creation.

In the preaching addressed to pagans, however, creation has its place (Acts 14:15–17; 17:24–28; Bultmann, pp. 69 f.). It should be noted, however, how strongly the immediate significance of creation is stressed, as a force pervading history (Scheffczyk, p. 15).

2. The New Testament is very conscious of the *power of evil*. In Paul and John the word cosmos can even indicate a reality hostile to God. It is true, of course, that this dualism is a moral one, and not strictly ontological. But it runs counter to the permanent and fundamental optimism of faith in creation, and greatly weakens the existential import of this faith as the inspiration of a joyous Yes to the world (Bultmann, pp. 492 ff.). The fulfilment of creation in Christ displays most vividly the inadequacy and brittleness of the old creation.

3. The *Christocentric character of creation* can only be discussed here insofar as it forms a new element in the doctrine of creation. It is at once apparent when Christ is designated as the new Adam, when the existence of the faithful and the Church is considered as a new creation, and when baptism is seen as a re-birth in which the events of the Exodus and of creation are renewed. Christ is the man who is God's image (2 Cor 4:4; Col 1:15), in whom the ancient word of creation has been fully verified. There is an allusion to the role of Christ in creation when the words "through Jesus Christ" are added to the "from God" of 1 Cor 8:6. But Christ was first recognized as Lord of salvation, and only then as Lord of creation; the development is the same as in the OT (Ratzinger, col. 462; Scheffczyk, p. 19).

Col 1:15–17, Heb 1:2 ff., 10–12, and Jn

1:1–18 then proceed in their different ways to identify creative wisdom and the word of the creator with the man Jesus Christ. These texts were the foundation of the doctrine of the pre-existence and the two natures of Christ. It should be noted, however, that they are also affirmations about the historical figure of the man Jesus Christ. The tendency to eliminate history, which is found in the description of the creative role of Wisdom, is now radically avoided. In the man Jesus Christ, God's creative word is fully uttered, and his plan of creation definitively accomplished in his saving acts. Jesus is truly the creature willed by God in creation.

Here the ultimate truth of the ancient theological proposition, that man is the goal of creation, is displayed to the full. Here it can also be seen that creation is obedience, partnership in a covenant. This mystery also affirms the unthinkable proximity of the creature to the creator: the Son who is in the bosom of the Father is a man. Creation is orientated to this intimacy.

Creation is history, because it makes man and his whole world reponsible to the creative will of God and thus involves all creation in the drama of refusal and forgiveness (Rom 8:19–21). All things are from God, and look for his Lordship, when he will be all in all (1 Cor 15:28).

D. History of the Dogma

The dogma of creation had no very chequered history. Faith in creation had its place in the liturgy. The oldest creeds confess the *Pater omnipotens,* with *omnipotens* designating not abstract omnipotence but God's sovereign rule, and *Pater* probably expressing his role as first cause and creator (Kelly, pp. 134–9).

From the 4th century on, this confession is enlarged by the words *factorem caeli et terrae* etc. But *creatio ex nihilo* was emphasized as early as the middle of the 2nd century, as in the confession of faith in Hermas (*Mand.,* 1, 1; *Vis.,* 1:6), which is often cited. It was done polemically against Gnostic dualism, and in apologetics to counter the philosophical view that matter was eternal. In the anti-Arian struggle, creation from nothing was often contrasted with the generation of the Son by the Father in unity of being.

The opposition to dualism and to the eternal matter of Greek philosophy soon made cosmology and protology the chief interests in the Church's doctrine of creation, an attitude which has persisted down to recent times. The view of Irenaeus, centred on the history of salvation, found little echo. The documents of the Church are directed against the dualism or the Priscillianists (*DS* 191, 199, 285 f.) or of the Catharists (*ibid.,* 800) or against the pantheistic tendencies of 19th-century idealism (*ibid.,* 3001 f.; 3021–5). This polemic against philosophical error gave rise to a one-sided philosophical view on the part of the Church (Congar, pp. 203 f.).

The reflections of Augustine, however, on the nature of time were important. They maintained on principle the unity of creation and conservation and thus avoided a purely protological concept. The contribution of Scholasticism was a strong emphasis on causality, which was corrected and enriched among the great Scholastics by the notion of participation. But the influence of such principles on current preaching remained restricted, so that to a great extent a purely protological approach prevailed, with emphasis on efficient causality.

This was a very naive type of faith in creation and proved unequal to the challenge of science. For theology, creation as the action of God became further and further removed from the chain of natural causes, and was restricted to the beginning of the world which was being placed further and further back, or restricted to a few exceptional cases in the history of evolution. A reaction set in only in recent years (Teilhard de Chardin).

E. Systematic View

Since creation implies a comprehensive action of God on the world and a total relationship of the world to God, it transcends all categories of thought. It is easier to say what it is not than what it is. It is easy to criticize standard definitions, but to indicate lines of thought which give a positive approach to its meaning is a task which is never mastered fully. Let us therefore first examine what it is not.

1. Creation is not an answer to the question of the origin of the world and of evolution, as posed by science. Science talks of causes

in intra-mundane categories, and to reduce creation to such categories would be to misinterpret it and ignore its character as a divine act (Beaucamp, pp. 71-75). Creation can never be met or grasped in terms of experience (Sertillanges, *Dieu ou rien?*, I, p. 96).

2. The doctrine of creation is not a proof of the existence of God nor a theodicy. It is based on a knowledge of the living God which is communicated only by the history of salvation. It is true that one can argue from the contingence of the world to its origin from absolute being, but it is questionable whether this origin can be recognized as creation (Vatican I, *DS* 3026; on which see Scheffczyk, pp. 150f.). Theodicy is actually made more difficult by the doctrine of creation, since it makes the question of evil still more acute.

3. Certain metaphysical systems, like pantheism, emanationism and dualism cannot be reconciled with the doctrine of creation. But this does not make it the equivalent of a metaphysics. If it were, it would lose its link with faith in the redemption and thereby its essential character. The last word of creation is uttered in the God-man; but that the creator was so interested and involved in his creation will probably never be deduced by metaphysics.

We are now in a position to turn to the positive aspects.

1. The following general presuppositions are to be made:

Personal categories are the most suitable to express creation. It is the action of the personal God and the person is the most characteristic of his creations, so that "the full dimensions of the creature can only be seen in the personal creature" (Volk, p. 516). Hence the concept of authorship or responsibility is better than that of causality (cf. Hengstenberg).

Creation embraces the whole reality of the world; not just its beginning but its whole existence, including its consummation; and not just its static being, but its dynamism and activity.

2. In the standard description, the formula *productio rei* is defective, because it con-centrates attention exclusively on the beginning and is impersonal in character. *Ex nihilo* is easily misunderstood, as if a "nothingness" preceded it. *Secundum totam substantiam* could suggest that only the static substance, but not the activity and perfectioning, was the result of creation.

3. Creation means that everything without exception is God's action and God's beneficent action towards man.

a) God is the author of all. He is this as the personal Saviour-God who has revealed himself as pure love and initiative. This means that creation is a spontaneous act which can have no other source or cause but the initiative of love. The definition of Vatican I concerning God's freedom means positively (*DS* 3002, 3025) that all reality originates in the pure initiative of God's love. This love does not presuppose its object, but brings about its lovableness (Guelluy, p. 55, after Augustine).

b) The object of creation is everything, without exception, in all its dimensions.

"Without exception": this is the positive meaning of *ex nihilo*. The whole of reality comes from God's action and is comprised by it.

"In all dimensions": in the unity of beginning, development and fulfilment, including not only the material creation but man, and man not only as nature and a datum imposed on man himself, but as person and freedom, who realizes himself and freely affirms, fetches in and perfects himself and his world around him. In contrast to frequently held opinions, it is probably necessary to emphasize that man is created precisely in his free act.

The creative act of God does not eliminate the action proper to the creature, it brings it about. "God empowers the creature to found itself on itself" (Hengstenberg, p. 108). Though the doctrine of creation was always aware of this (cf. the *concursus*), it was always exposed to the danger of slipping into a sort of deism, according to which God created the power to act, while the activity itself stemmed only from the creature. Such a misunderstanding becomes all the more pernicious when science has shown the world as a closed system of natural energy which constructs itself in a natural process. For it would then appear that the creative activity of God was being excluded more and more by the intrinsic activity of the world, and that the creature was in competition with the creator (cf. Vatican II, *Gaudium et Spes*, art. 34). The resistance of the faithful to the theory of evolution stems to a great extent from this misunderstanding of creation.

It must be clearly understood that God creates a "world coming into being" (Schoonenberg), which is bringing itself about and is precisely a creature by doing so. This means, however, that the creative act of God is not to be considered as an extrinsic condition of or a supplement to the intrinsic activity of the creature, but as its inmost core. Even in my activity God is more intimate to me than my inmost self. The creator is not "a cause within the category of causes besides others in the world but the living and transcendent ground of the world's own movement" (K. Rahner, "Bemerkungen zum Begriff der Offenbarung", *Interpretation der Welt* [1965], p. 715).

c) Creation is God's beneficent action towards man. "To believe in creation is to see Someone behind all things ... to see the world as a gift" (Guelluy, p. 55).

The "motive" of God's creative act is described by Vatican I in the words, "ad manifestandam perfectionem suam per bona, quae creaturis impertitur" (*DS* 3002), of which the official explanation was, "ut bonitatem suam creaturis impertiret (*Collectio Lacensis*, VII, pp. 85 f., 110). Creation is pure generosity, the act of loving and giving.

Hence the goal of creation is man, as person and as community. Only man can receive love as love. Everything exists in relation to man, who in the course of history gathers the cosmos to himself, takes in himself gradually in his freedom and so responds to the creative word with all the strength of his own being and of the world.

The fullness of human existence is identical with the glory of God. The more man realizes himself, and the world in himself, the brighter the glory of the creator radiates from him. And insofar as man, as such a perfected freedom, himself thanks God, he gives glory to God. "Gloria Dei vivens homo; vita autem hominis visio Dei." (Irenaeus, *Adv. Haer.*, IV, 20, 7; *PG*, VII, col. 1037.) Thus Jesus the Lord is the goal of all creation, the final Yes of God to his work and the full Yes of man to God (cf. 2 Cor 1:20).

F. Conclusion

Creation is to be considered as the free act of God whereby he gives the world and man entirely to man, as a gift of his goodness and as a task to be carried on to a fulfilment in which man responds to this word of his creator with the fullness of his own being and of his world. Creation means that man is revealed as one addressed by God in such a way that the whole of reality comes to him as a word of God, summoning and inviting him to an equally total response.

See also *Causality, Deism, Dualism, Evolution, God, God-World Relationship, Materialism, Natural Theology, Salvation* III A, *World.*

BIBLIOGRAPHY. See the various works on the *Theology of the Old Testament* by W. Eichrodt; E. Jacob; O. Procksch; J. van Imschoot; G. von Rad; T. Vriezen. — W. Foerster, "κτίζω", *TWNT*, III, cols. 1000–35; P. Donelly, "The End of Creation", *TS* 2 (1941), pp. 53–83; 4 (1943), pp. 3–33; A.-D. Sertillanges, *L'idée de création et ses retentissements en philosophie* (1945); J. van der Ploeg, "Le sens du verbe hébreu bara", *Muséon* 59 (1946), pp. 143–57; P. Humbert, "Emploi et portée du verbe bara (créer) dans l'AT", *Theologische Zeitschrift* 3 (1947), pp. 401–22; J. Kelly, *Early Christian Creeds* (1950); E. Brunner, *The Christian Doctrine of Creation and Redemption*, Dogmatics 2, 1952; J. Brinktrine, *Die Lehre von der Schöpfung* (1955); H. Volk, *Schöpfung und Entwicklung* (1955) in K. Barth, *The Doctrine of Creation*, Dogmatics 3, in 4 vols. (1958–61); E. Beaucamp, *La Bible et le sens religieux de l'univers* (1959); M. Flick and Z. Alszeghy, *Il Creatore. L'inizio della salvezza* (1959); H. Hengstenberg, *La naissance du monde*, Collection Sources Orientales 1 (1959); C. Trésmontant, *La métaphysique du Christianisme* (1961); G. Wright, O. Michel and G. Gloege, "Schöpfung", *RGG*, V, cols. 1473–90; K. Heim, *The World: Its Creation and Consummation* (1962); M. Schmaus, *Katholische Dogmatik*, II/1 (6th ed., 1962); R. Guelluy, *La création* (1963), biblio.; L. Scheffczyk, *Schöpfung und Vorsehung* (1963), biblio. (E. T. in preparation); J. Ratzinger, "Schöpfung", *LTK*, IX, cols. 460–66; K. Rahner, "Schöpfungslehre", *ibid.*, cols. 470–74; Y. Congar, *Le Thème de Dieu-Créateur dans la tradition chrétienne* (1964), pp. 189–222; H. Gunkel, *Genesis* (6th ed., 1964); H. Renckens, *Israel's Concept of the Beginning. The Theology of Genesis 1–3* (1964); P. Schoonenberg, *God's World in the Making* (1965); K. Rahner, *Hominisation*, Quaestiones Disputatae 13 (1965); P. Smulders, *Het visioen van Teilhard de Chardin* (5th ed., 1966).

Pieter Smulders

II. Genesis

A. Title

The first book of the Torah or Pentateuch is generally known by the name "Genesis", which is taken from the Septuagint. The contents may be described as "the beginnings". Theologically, the Book of Joshua is a continuation of the Pentateuch, since it describes the fulfilment of promises made in Genesis, and hence it would be better to speak of a Hexateuch rather than a Pentateuch.

B. Methods of Interpretation

The method of literary criticism was initiated for the Pentateuch over two hundred years ago, by B. Witter and J. Astruc, in an effort to explain the origins of the books, which had hitherto been mostly ascribed to Moses. The documentary theory associated with the name of J. Wellhausen may be said to have brought this line of research to a sort of conclusion. In this view, the Pentateuch is composed on the basis of four sources, J (the Yahwist, 9th century), E (the Elohist, 8th century), D (the Deuteronomists, 7th century) and P (the Priestly Code, 5th century). A further analysis was attempted on the basis of form-criticism, developed chiefly by H. Gunkel and H. Gressmann, who sought to trace the pre-literary genesis of the documents. They succeeded in demonstrating that they were not the creation of individual authors but rather the depositaries of ancient traditions which had been later combined by various schools. This method is now taken a step further by research into the history of traditions, which investigates the growth of the various traditions, as they were handed on in different circles, from their early to their final forms. Finally, the history of redaction tries to determine the principles and themes by which compilers and redactors were inspired at the various stages of the growth of tradition and when it was given its final form. These refined methods are used in combination to throw light on the highly complex process through which the Pentateuch was evolved (see, for instance, the systematic schema in Ernst Sellin and Georg Fohrer, *Einleitung in das Alte Testament* [1965], p. 30).

C. Structure and Contents

The fifty chapters of Genesis are usually divided into two sections: the history of origins (chs. 1–11); and the history of the patriarchs (chs. 12–50). Though the division is more marked than any which occurs in other OT books, the sections are united by the figure of Abraham.

1. *The history of origins.* Many efforts were formerly made to discover in the history of the origins elements of the most ancient traditions of mankind, or to treat them as a phenomenon with parallels in ancient oriental literature and hence as an effort to explain the origin of the world and man in terms of myths. The view now increasingly favoured is that Gen 1–11, and especially 1–3, were from the start aetiological prophecy, orientated to the past. The redactors, confining themselves almost exclusively to J and P, undertook the tracing of the activity of God back to the beginning, to provide theological information about the origin of the universe and to make the universally significant decisions of the first men a preface to the beginning of historical revelation with Abraham. This enabled them to explain the historical experiences of their people at the hands of God and the interpretation of these experiences as given by God. In this perspective, the primitive history ceases to be a statement about the origin and nature of things put forward for its own sake, and is seen to have a functional significance for the revelation which followed in historical times. The following main themes may be noted:

a) The creation by God is affirmed in both strata: P, 1:1–2, 4a; J, 2:4b–25. Gen 2 and 3 form a literary unity. The double narrative, in which J is completed and enlarged by P, stresses the fundamental importance of God's creative act, a theological truth which remains of the utmost importance for the understanding of man and the world in the present day. The procedures also give us to understand that it is impossible to gain a complete grasp of God's action from any one approach. For any sort of comprehensive view, many aspects must be envisaged. The first narrative develops in a majestic monotone the theological proposition, "For God has created everything", and shows how his work of dividing and organizing brought all creatures into existence, in a sort of pyramid, from chaos to mankind. The narrative uses the word בָּרָא, which is reserved for the creative action proper to God. It expresses a type of production for which there is no analogy, and which comes about by the "Word" of God, which thereby becomes the bridge spanning the gulf between God and the creature coming into being. The development of the doctrine of creation moves towards the NT by means of a deeper scrutiny of the "word of God" (cf. Jn 1; Col 1:14–17, Heb 1:2). The three-fold בָּרָא in the description of the creation of man (v. 27) indicates that the creative energy of God is most fully deployed here. Man is said to be created according to the image of God, to distinguish him from other creatures which were made "according to their kind" (vv. 11 f., 24 f.). He has therefore a share in the divine sovereignty (cf. Ps 8:5 ff.; 145:12) which enables him to perform his task of ruling the world (v. 28).

In a warmer, more picturesque fashion, the second narrative places man as the first creature at the centre of a circle upon which God constructs the world which is orientated to man. He is made partly of earth and partly of a divine life-force, the two being linked in an essential unity. This unity is to be regarded as the pre-philosophical basis of biblical anthropology. The narrative is so arranged as to stress, along with the origin of creation, God's permanent care for man. The region he lives in is provided with trees and plants, his loneliness is ended by the creation of the woman. The imagery shows that the woman is similar to the man, and because of like nature, of like dignity. In view of his actual experience of the urge of the sexes for one another, the author then projects this strong orientation of man and woman towards marriage back to the good beginnings of creation, before the fall.

b) Paradise and original sin. It is now conceded that Paradise is not to be understood as a historical or geographical entity. In order to avoid the difficulties involved in trying to harmonize it with the findings of the relevant sciences, it is probably correct to understand Paradise chiefly as a profoundly harmonious human existence, a state of complete equilibrium in the *integritas* of the first men. How long this special state lasted is a matter for debate, possibly only for a moment of his existence. The supreme

happiness of this special situation was man's friendship with God (3:8), which was also a magnificent promise and a glimpse of the fulfilment towards which the course of history runs, the *eschaton* of Is 25:6–8.

Man's most excellent gift is the freedom intrinsic to his person which makes it possible for him to decide for or against God on the basis of the commandment, 2:17. For with freedom comes temptation and the possibility of a wrong decision. The serpent, the embodiment of the evil principle, attributes envious designs to God and promises the woman neutral country from which she can pass judgment on God and his command. Thus the urge to be incomprehensible is awakened in man, and the fascinating desire to be master of secrets beyond the human horizon, so as to reach ultimately a region where he will be free of God. Thus the essence of original sin is that man wills to be independent of God in a monstrous arrogance and content himself with creatures. This total absorption in the world produces not man's glorification but shame and disappointment. Gen 3:14–19 describes man's present situation on earth: the right order is disturbed in man's relationship to God, to his fellowmen and to the infra-human creature. But man accepts (3:20 f.) his new situation, no longer in immediate proximity to God, and God extends to him his care and protection in a new way. The new situation is radiant with the promise of the final victory over the Adversary (3:15).

c) In spite of the succinctness and obscurity of Gen 4, it is clear from the crime of Cain that original sin does not remain an isolated deed of pre-history. In the very next generation the decision is taken once more against God, in the personal sin of fratricide. The way of man on earth is thereby designated as one of sin and guilt; at the same time, he is denied the possibility of blaming his forefathers. The path of sin leads him further and further away from God (4:11). Gen 4 has still another function in the structure of the history of origins. It forms the necessary link with the statements of 6:5 ff., according to which man's wickedness has transgressed all tolerable bounds, so that God determines to destroy it.

d) Even granted the possibility that popular traditions from ancient pre-history may be contained in Gen 6 f. (cf. the non-biblical legends of a deluge, e.g., in the epic of Gilgamesh), modern exegesis is quite clear that the judgment of God depicted in the deluge is not to be taken as a precise historical description. The authors of Gen 6f. rather used the legends of their environment to show the full significance of the calamitous history of the first men and to depict the flood as a judgment brought upon themselves by men. God's "repentance" (6:6) gives one to understand that the whole purpose of man's being is frustrated by sin and that he has no further right to exist in the eyes of God. It exemplifies the perpetual threat of destruction which hangs over man in God's judgment on sin. But what was the occasion of well-merited punishment in 6:5 ff. is the reason for mercy and compassion according to 8:21. The prologue and epilogue of the story show that man is the object of a struggle which is starting between justice and mercy, in which the love of God constantly intervenes on the side of man and ultimately triumphs. After the flood the time of God's patient endurance begins (Rom 3:25).

e) The covenant with Noah (9:8–17) is one of its foundations in the history of salvation. This bond between God and man after the deluge creates a new state of peace and is given visible form in the rainbow. It is the covenant of the order of creation and a divinely-guaranteed renewal of the creative act. All creatures are relieved of their basic anxiety for their lives. Hence the blessing pronounced on creation in 1:28 is renewed in 9:1. The covenant is also the foundation and beginning of the new salvation which is promised, and is open to all men who are ready to observe the ethical order intrinsic to creation and to strive for a personal relationship to the creator God.

f) The many nations and the chosen one (10f.). In Gen 10, P, probably drawing on an ancient map, depicts the multiplicity of the nations, as willed by God, since they are all traced back to the one ancestor, Noah. Thus they remain a vast unity, linked to God by a covenant. But their unity seems to J ambivalent. The tower of Babel reveals the danger of a union to which men are impelled by arrogance as they concentrate their forces against God. God wills rather that the nations of which he has made one family in the covenant with Noah should preserve their independence. This new Fall then becomes

the stepping-stone to a new way to salvation. Contrary to man's hostile plan, inspired by arrogance, of forcing unity upon the peoples, God himself will assure the true fellowship of all nations by linking them to Abraham, who has been specially chosen for this purpose (11:16–32). The history of the origins ends in the story of God's triumphant salvific will, which is revealed in Abraham as an inexhaustible blessing for all men of all ages.

2. *The story of the patriarchs.* With Gen 12 we reach a stage for which the ancient East supplies historical sources and which is also to be taken as historical to some extent in the Bible. On the historiography of the Bible in general it may be said that it is "pragmatic, purposeful", hence that it does not intend to use its sources critically and reflect the past in faithful detail in a sequence of cause and effect. Its intention is to use a historical substratum of a more or less extensive range to emphasize God's special intervention on behalf of certain men and also the divinely inspired interpretation of his action. Hence it is concerned with giving the history of salvation. In the first part of this section, the main theological theme, which also links together the individual figures which appear, is the great blessing bestowed by God on Abraham. It was in view of this blessing, according to J, that Abraham was chosen by God and the new way of salvation which leads to Christ was opened (12:1–3; 18:18f.; 22:18; 26:4; 28:14).

The ancient scepticism which saw in Gen 12–50 a frieze of legends or sagas, or tried to present the patriarchs as gods reduced to men, is giving way to the notion that they are really historical figures, even though the Bible gives only meagre details about them (cf. W. F. Albright, J. Bright, R. de Vaux). In the light of archaeological discoveries, which have now multiplied, they may be dated between the 20th and the 16th century B.C.

a) The most significant figure by far is Abraham. In many respects he may be regarded as the ideal for man's attitude when confronted with God's work of salvation. God summons this semi-nomad whom he has chosen, to leave behind him his homeland and his past and go into the land of Palestine. Thus the situation of pilgrimage hand in hand with God becomes a determining (existential) structure of God-centred man, who is henceforward the object of a special promise from God. From now on the course of the history of salvation is determined by promise and fulfilment, not as religious categories which can be defined and depicted by man in advance, but as basic structures of the salvific action of God, as is shown in the repeated promise of the land and of a son and heir, and finally in the birth of Isaac. Abraham's response to God's intervention is an act of faith, of which the content is a renunciation of all earthly assurance and a self-dedication to God which the patriarch has constantly to effect (15:6). Faith in this sense forms the basis for the justification of the believer, that is, for the rightness of a life which has been set in order by God. Abraham's life of faith is so exemplary that he is honoured in Rom 4:16 by the title of "the father of us all" in faith. As at other stages of the divine activity, here too the new relationship is given the status of a covenant. It is, in fact, in the form of covenant that God realizes his plan of salvation throughout the whole history of salvation. A two-fold tradition expounds the most important theological aspects of this covenant (Gen 15 [J] and 17:1–14 [P]). It enables the elect of God to have a theophany (18) and makes him the familiar friend of God (18:17ff.). But the demands of God on one who is united to him in faith are very great. The aging man is called on to wait patiently, when hope of a son seems to have become futile, humanly speaking (16). When he is at last a happy father, he is given the unheard-of command to sacrifice his beloved son and thereby the one vehicle of the promise and the whole future (22). What is really envisaged is the steadfastness of a faith which refuses nothing to God, though there is also another point in the story, the condemnation by God of human sacrifice.

b) The figure of Isaac is much less vividly drawn (24–27). His function is to maintain the covenant with God and to transmit the blessing.

c) With Jacob, however, the human element in the bearer of the blessing becomes strikingly manifest. The interplay of divine election, human sin (the fraudulent acquisition of the birthright and the blessing, 25:29–34; 27) and the punishment for sin is typical of the co-operation of God's plan and human freedom. Since Jacob does not make a breach in the foundations of the election

and works in faith for the things of God, even though by unjust means, God holds fast to his choice. But the patriarch suffers heavy punishment for his fault, in the hostility of his brother, in being banished from his paternal home, in being cheated by his father-in-law and in the pain inflicted on him by his children. Purified, he returns with a new name and a new blessing to the land of his fathers (32:22–32). But here too new disasters befall him, till he is forced by famine to seek refuge in Egypt.

d) At the centre of the last part (37–50), which differs notably in its formal structure from the previous chapters, we find the figure of Joseph, who rises to astonishing heights of success at the court of Pharaoh. However, according to 49:8–12, the further realization of the plan of salvation is not to come through the favourite son of Jacob who dominates the immediate present, but through Judah. His transgression with Thamar, which is not palliated (38) makes him the ancestor of David (Ruth) and hence of the Messiah (Mt 1). In contrast to the continuous gradual realization of the plan of salvation which has been stressed previously, the sapiential and didactic element focuses the attention in the story of Joseph. He represents the embodiment of Israelite humanism. His figure is built up chiefly of elements of Egyptian literature. Joseph shows the possibilities which life with God opens up in this world while he is also displayed as a sign for the world which points unmistakably to God. His life and his place in Egypt are also inserted into the theme of the divine guidance of the chosen people. Joseph is an indispensable link with the events of the exodus (see Exod).

To sum up: according to Genesis, God's revelation does not take the form of the communication of knowledge and secrets. It is essentially manifested in the various ways in which God guides his chosen friends. Their response is the permanent sense of being on the march towards God. They have to practise this all their lives, either by "walking with God" like Enoch (5:22) and Noah (6:9), or "walking before God" (17:1) like Abraham and his house.

See also *Old Testament Books* I, *Form-Criticism, Creation* I, *Man* I, *Original Sin, Covenant, Biblical Historiography*.

BIBLIOGRAPHY. Commentaries: H. Gunkel (6th ed., 1964); O. Procksch (3rd ed., 1934); P. Heinisch (1930); J. Skinner (2nd ed., 1930); B. Jacob (1934); C. Simpson (1952); L. Pirot and A. Clamer (1953); R. de Vaux (1953); F. Michaeli (1960); G. von Rad (6th ed., 1961); U. Cassuto, vols. I–II (1961–64); J. de Fraine (1963); E. Speiser (1964); H. Junker (4th ed., 1965); C. Simpson, *The Early Traditions of Israel* (1948); A. Dublarle, *Le péché originel dans l'Écriture* (1958); R. de Vaux, *Bible et Orient* (1967); J. de Fraine, *La Bible et l'Origine de l'homme* (1961); W. F. Albright, *The Biblical Period from Abraham to Ezra* (1963); H. Gross, "Hauptthemen der Urgeschichte", *Lebendiges Zeugnis* I (1964), pp. 63–78; H. Renckens, *Israel's Concept of the Beginning. The Theology of Gen 1–3* (1964); W. H. Schmidt, *Die Schöpfungsgeschichte der Priesterschrift* (1964); J. Bright, *A. History of Israel* (1960); J. Vergote, *Joseph en Égypte* (1959).

Heinrich Gross

III. Protology

1. *The concept.* Protology is a term formed on the analogy of eschatology to designate the dogmatic doctrine on the creation of the world and man, paradise and the fall, hence the doctrine of the origins. In the ordinary text-books of dogmatic theology the subject is generally treated under "De Deo Creante", "De Deo Elevante", "De Peccato Originali". These seemingly disparate themes form a real unity. For protology describes in terms of dogma one half of the permanent proprieties and existentials of each individual human being, that is, the permanent and unavoidable pre-conditions, established by God or by man himself (in his origins), for the exercise of man's free decision for or against God. The other "half" of his situations is described in the dogmatic treatise on soteriology. The two together make up theological anthropology, since the total "essence" of man is only really disclosed in the history of his fall and salvation which takes it beyond an implicit preliminary self-understanding. There is a more than material connection between the themes of protology, because the beginning is a permanent determination of man, and hence like eschatology can only be grasped in a retrospective aetiology in the light of each changing historical situation. And hence the progress of the history of salvation is the progress of protology in the progressive development of its starting-point.

Since it is only in Jesus Christ and his Pneuma that man knows explicitly and through official revelation that he can be, and has been throughout his history, the subject of an absolute self-communication of God (which can be surpassed only by the beatific vision), it is only since Jesus Christ that a full protology is possible and hence also intelligible in its formal nature. This also explains, for instance, why a doctrine of the "first things" including the supernatural elevation of man and original sin was only possible in the NT. The general doctrine of creation (on the beginning of the world) can undoubtedly be taken as an element of protology, because it is not ultimately an account of what once happened without reference to man, but the doctrine of the immediate, but nonetheless ancient creatureliness of the world as the environment of man — a world which itself only attains its true being in the Spirit.

2. *Present-day problems.* a) There is need of a clearer demonstration of the *a priori* and *de facto* inner unity of protology. This would affect the treatment of the actual components and complete its themes, which are not fully envisaged in the dogmatic treatises which now correspond to protology. Once we ask what are the universal and permanent proprieties of man which are theologically accessible and existentially relevant, we are provided with a set of themes which are only partially treated in the manuals of scholastic theology. The matter of protology would then include, for instance, the historicity of man, the unity of mankind and its history (which is more than mere biological monogenism) and the sexual nature of man (which should not be left to moral theology). Even the theology of Gen 1–11 contains more matter than is treated explicitly in the theology of the schools.

b) Formal or transcendental theological protology, which presupposes such matters as the doctrine of creation and the original state of man, needs to be more explicitly developed. The general horizon within which the questions of material protology are put must be interrogated as to its constitution and its proper history. In such formal protology light would be thrown on the correspondence between protology and eschatology as well as their real difference, which is not simply obvious (as is supposed in theories of "return to paradise", and the like).

c) The permanent, justifiable, dialectical but not contradictory opposition to a profane protology "evolving from below" must be demonstrated. Such protology, including natural history, evolution and hominization, age of the world and of mankind, characteristics of primitive man, etc., is not and cannot be protology strictly speaking. It would have to be shown that the protology sketched in the light of Christian eschatology, as already given in Jesus Christ, is concerned with a beginning which is "withdrawn" from our grasp, and which therefore cannot on principle be attained in secular sciences of the origin of the world and man, while still not contradicting them. The adoption of the doctrine of creation into dogmatic anthropology does not exclude but rather provides for a correct understanding of an evolutionist cosmology and some understanding at least of man as situated within such an evolution of the world, of which the goal is man.

See also *Creation* IV, *Last Things, Person* II, *Man, States of Man, Original Sin, Salvation* III B, IV B, *Existence* III B, *Revelation* I, *Monogenism, Evolution, Sex* I.

BIBLIOGRAPHY. G. Delling, *Das Zeitverständnis des NT* (1940); O. Cullmann, *Christus und die Zeit* (2nd ed., 1948), E. T.: *Christ und Time* (1951); H. U. von Balthasar, *Theologie der Geschichte* (2nd ed., 1950); J. Pieper, *Über das Ende der Zeit* (1950), E. T.: *The End of Time* (1954); P. Levert, *L'idée de Commencement* (1961); J. Mouroux, *Le Mystère du temps* (1962), E. T.: *The Mystery of Time* (1964); H. U. von Balthasar, *Das Ganze im Fragment* (1963); B. Welte, *Heilsverständnis* (1966); *Mysterium Salutis*, II: *Die Heilsgeschichte vor Christus* (1967); and literature on *Creation* I, IV, and *Eschatology*.

Adolf Darlap

IV. Beginning and End

1. Beginning and end — in the concrete form of birth and death — are basic elements in human and hence religious experience. As a being with a history, man seeking to master consciously his destiny inevitably asks after his beginning and his end, since he recognizes that the action now possible to him and demanded of him is limited by previously existing conditions and is orientated to a supreme end — the goal of human existence. But a formal ontological analysis shows that the beginning is not an individual first moment in a series of many comparable moments, but the opening of a possibility of a totality which matures from its beginning to its end (as towards its goal). Hence the notion of beginning goes beyond that of a formal external time, being intrinsic to the totality which it opens up and being the start of a duration determined at every moment within the whole by its beginning. The beginning provides the totality with its essence and the consequent conditions of its realization. Thus the beginning appears as the sum total, as it were, of the concrete pre-conditions of the historical being of man.

Since, however, man as a personal being shares the history of the one humanity, and at least the essentials of the history of human origins are part of the inescapable pre-conditions of each individual life, each man's beginning includes not only the givenness and launching of his own history but the beginning of humanity in general.

The relationship to his beginning, as the acceptance of himself, is one of the basic acts of man. But the beginning is not only the givenness of the abstract essence which is present in the self-realization of man. It is also a concrete factualness ("facticity") which is the mere start of a future self-realization and potentially greater than any given moment of its self-realization. Hence the concrete beginning is necessarily shrouded in hiddenness, the obscurity of the origin. The potential beginning cannot contain the explicit truth of the historically present. To this extent, the beginning is extrinsic to and withdrawn from man, since it is present and intrinsic to him only as the unmasterable pre-condition of the existence experienced as his own positing and act. Like the end, the beginning is for man an insuperable limit.

a) It is only possible to speak of a beginning where what is opened up is a totality and open — where the beginning itself, even as the unattainable limit, can be transcended by the free, posited existence. Hence "authentic" beginning can only be personal. Only the authentic beginning, as absolutely without antecedents which belong to itself, as in no way explicable as the end of another movement, can be the basis of "intrinsic temporality", where the individual moments are not equivalent parts of a homogeneous duration but qualitatively different in their temporality.

b) Since the beginning opens out on the end, and the beginning is only fully itself in the end, there is an intrinsic connection between protology and eschatology (here understood as formal elements of an existentialist anthropology). Man's sense of himself as at once finite and infinite brings home to him the hiddenness both of his beginning and his end. The mystery penetrating and transcending both is phenomenologically the same. The presence of the end in ever greater measure in man's self-acceptance and self-realization is also a like presence of the beginning.

c) Man necessarily fails to grasp the beginning as the beginning, if thrown back on himself alone. His self-understanding takes the form of myth, or the profane nihilism of an empty, formal scheme of time. Hence an adequate protology and exact knowledge of the concrete beginning is only possible in the light of revelation, as long as the fulfilment is not there. Hence protology must be theological, deriving either from the word of revelation concerning the concrete *eschata,* or from the hidden entry of the end into the present which is expressed in words.

2. For the concrete understanding of the beginning as determined by revelation, reference must be made to the subjects treated under *Creation* I, *Evolution* II, *Original Sin, Man* and *Person.*

Here we shall confine ourselves to the scriptural doctrine of the "Beginning" (omitting the creation of the world). The primary point to be considered is the following. Where God intervenes directly in history to give an essentially new determination to the situation of man in the history of salvation, there is in this sense an authentic beginning (a new beginning, a new creation), since the possibilities of the existing beginning are directly modified in their origin, as deriving from God. Hence Christ is the true beginning of salvation, above all because in the radically new beginning of the resurrection he has shown himself the mediator of salvation for all ages (Col 1:15, 18; 1 Cor 15:20, 23; Rev 3:14; 21:6; 22:13b). Hence all the divine pre-conditions of man's action, all man's reactions to the divinely-appointed beginning from which all proceeds, are characterized in Scripture as "in the beginning" or "from the beginning": the Logos (Jn 1:1; 1 Jn 2:13); the salvific will of God which has always regulated history (Eph 1:4; 3:9 ff.; 2 Thess 2:13); the devil (Jn 8:44; 1 Jn 3:8); the calling (Jn 15:27); the first preaching of the gospel (Heb 2:3; 5:12; 6:1; 1 Jn 2:7; 3:11; 2 Jn 5f.); the sending of the Spirit at Pentecost (Acts 11:15); the start of Christian existence (Heb 3:14). But occurrences which are contrary to the original plan contained in the beginning are characterized as "not from the beginning" (Mt 19:9).

3. In addition, there are the formal structures which determine the concrete beginning as a totality.

a) The original givenness of the beginning. By this we understand the constitution of the personal spiritual being as such, insofar as it can only be posited by a directly creative act of God, so that it is in concrete immediacy to God as the unconditioned free cause not subject to time, perfect of itself and hence not seeking its own perfection in its action. It follows that this original givenness is one of the intrinsic existentials of man. This immediate dependence on God necessarily implies that the beginning can never be mastered. The beginning is directly instituted by God and hence is outside man's control insofar as his action is always subsequent and derivative with regard to the beginning and can never really exhaust it. But since this primordial beginning is truly posited as the beginning of a process of becoming which is not just change from one state to another of equivalent actuality, but tends to true fulfilment, the beginning is truly a potentiality and hence exists as the hidden beginning which is only adequately disclosed to the being in question in its history.

b) The beginning as an imperative. Since the spiritual being is capable of the *reditio completa in se* by virtue of its transcendence towards being as such, the hiddenness of the beginning does not mean that it is left further and further behind as the spiritual being enduringly develops. The beginning is that towards which the spiritual being moves, to become what it is, in the process of historical self-realization through which the beginning is more and more clearly disclosed. On account of the primordial givenness of the beginning, the potentialities of a given being are only given as such in him, and hence are imposed on him by God as obligatory and unavoidable tasks which he must discharge in knowledge and decision. Hence in spite of the supreme originality of the beginning man can deny it (cf. Job 3) or use its hiddenness to ignore or misinterpret it. Or again, he can accept it as the divine disposition more and more fully as it is revealed to him in the course of his history and thereby attain the precise fulfilment assigned to him. Hence the beginning matters for the end, as the end for the beginning.

c) The beginning as origin of the maturely valid. The authentic and primordially posited beginning gives rise to a truly temporal sequence, but by virtue of its being itself directly posited by God is not a moment of a time really antecedent to it. Hence the goal of the movement which it launches is not the end as termination but as fulfilment of this temporal sequence, where the harvest of the time run is preserved as valid and definitive. Hence what corresponds to the authentic (intrinsic) givenness of the beginning is not the end as a terminal stage within continuing time, but the fulfilment which absorbs a time which may be thought of as continuing. The beginning is truly a potentiality. Of itself it enters the time in which alone its fulfilment can be brought to maturity. It thus exposes itself to the incalculable sway of God over these open possibilities in time, and the end, though the safeguarding, fulfilment and revelation of the beginning, is not just the implementation of the law of the beginning by which man was launched. The beginning rather lives by virtue of the movement towards the fulfilment whose achievement is accomplished by God. For he alone is both beginning and end at once, and hence as transcendent unity both separates and combines beginning and end in the finite, and communicates himself in grace to the finite being as this transcendent unity of beginning and end.

4. The end is the whither of the beginning as its goal. And then it is the fully-formed existence of that which was posited with the beginning as that which had to mature in order to be; or it is the limit which defines the totality of the existence. This end may be realized in various ways which are analogous to one another, according to various potentialities in question.

a) Whether the material world has an authentic end which may be discerned by inspection of it, that is, whether it is orien-

tated to a permanent goal of perfection which will absorb its temporality on a higher plane beyond which any essentially new phase is inconceivable, or whether it merely continues to go through new phases of what is fundamentally the same thing, is a question which we need not try to decide. So too it remains an open question, philosophically and theologically, whether simple inspection of the world can show that it had a beginning. (It is unthinkable that the material world should tend to nothingness; its possibility of non-being by virtue of its createdness remains a purely transcendental threat.) But the question is not ultimately important, because there is no such thing as a material world *qua* purely material, which could be interrogated in the concrete as to its intrinsic destiny. Theologically we are compelled to affirm that there is a history of nature, and hence an end and object of nature simply because it has been posited by God as the pre-condition and setting of the history of the spiritual creature which ends up in the free self-communication of God to the spiritual creature (as the history of salvation). Hence at least the *de facto* end of the history of nature will preserve all the natural elements which can enter into the fulfilment of the created spirit.

b) The end of the biological as such is the re-establishment of the beginning. As a spatio-temporal element demarcated within nature as a whole, the biological rests on the purely material and physical which it integrates into itself. It is exposed to being a mere undifferentiated moment of the "history" of all nature. Hence each individual biological element can have an end which is terminal. But this does not exclude the fact that the end of the biological as such is the regaining of the beginning, its self-propagation. At this level one can begin to see to some extent that the end is not the cessation of what hitherto was and now is simply no more, but the taking over and the attainment of potentialities which were given with the beginning merely by virtue of its transcendent cause and are achieved in time as an inheritance.

c) The end of the spiritual personal being, in keeping with his ontological nature, that is, one which knows itself and takes conscious possession of itself, in keeping with its beginning, is the freely activated acceptance of the authentic beginning. The proper concept of end in theology is the end which is achieved in the history of freedom before God and orientated to God. This end is neither the negation of being nor an ultimately arbitrary caesura in a time which had indeed a beginning but now runs on indefinitely. It is a real fulfilment of time which ends temporality because it ends up in the absolute validity of freedom, the definitiveness of decision. Maturing freedom is always achieved in the decision between possibilities opening on the future, and hence in view of the totality of free possibilities, that is, in view of and by virtue of the end. The various types of end distinguished above in relation to the ontological degrees of beings are so many possible modes (though obviously not equally true) in which man can understand the end. Since man is irresistibly drawn towards his end — though the mode of approach may be falsified by efforts to resist the insistent end — and since his present existence is engaged on a sketch-plan of his future, even if timorously, the end is present as what is to come, displaying itself as a task, a summons and an imperative. Thus the end permeates and determines every instant of existence and constitutes its uniqueness. Insofar as this still outstanding but present end is the end of a finite being, it is never absolutely within its power but is determinant in its veiled and sovereign impact. But insofar as the being in question opens out towards its end and appropriates it as truly its own, the end is at the same time something produced by it. The incalculable (diastatic) unity of impinging end from without and maturing end from within is the mystery which always enshrouds the clearness of the present.

5. Since men are essentially historical beings, their self-understanding and notion of salvation in each individual actual existence must involve an aetiological retrospect of a truly temporal past and the prospect and sketch-plan of a truly temporal future, embracing the life of each and of all mankind. Hence this basic reference cannot be whittled down to the atomized actualism of a demythologization or a simply existential interpretation. And the historical "descendence" (in tradition) may not be truncated in favour of a one-sided "transcendence" towards the future, in the Marxist utopian fashion, just as the imperative of the future may not be suppressed by the conservative effort to restore an unchanged past.

6. Man must learn from the future and from his end, which are part components of his present, how to understand his actual existence. But where existence is directed to a supernatural goal, and hence determined by revelation strictly so called, this revelation — which speaks of man's present constitution in the order of salvation — must also speak of his future as still outstanding and as having arrived, while it speaks of his end. Hence this utterance must be couched in terms of a realized (actualist) eschatology and of a genuine "later on", a tension of now and later, and be embodied at once as the now and the end in an actual event which is temporal — and can therefore only express the now by the future and the genuine future only by the present. This is the hermeneutical principle which must be applied to all eschatological assertions. Where they are not "realized", they are understood one-sidedly, and when the realization blocks the perspective of the temporal future, the realization is false.

See also: *Order* IV, *Essence, History* I, *Time, Creation* I, *Eschatology, Myth, Demythologization* I, II, *Nihilism, Evolution, Existence* III, *Death, Salvation* III, *Original Sin.*

BIBLIOGRAPHY. M. Heidegger, *Sein und Zeit* (1927 ff.), E. T., *Being and Time* (1962); G. Delling, "ἀρχή", *TWNT*, I, cols. 476–83; A. Delp, *Der Mensch und die Geschichte* (1943); K. Jaspers, *Vom Ursprung und Ziel der Geschichte* (1949); K. Barth, *Church Dogmatics*, III/2; K. Rahner, *Theological Investigations*, IV (1966), pp. 323–46; A. Darlap, "Fundamentale Theologie der Heilsgeschichte", *Mysterium Salutis* I (1965), pp. 3–153; and literature on *Creation* I.

Adolf Darlap

CREEDS

The Church has traditionally used creeds or symbols in its liturgy. Here we shall study the origin and structure of these formulas to show their theological importance and meaning.

1. *The earliest creeds.* The word symbol *(symbolum)* appeared first of all in the Latin Church (in particular in Africa: Tertullian and Cyprian). The East at first used expressions

such as πίστις, μάθημα, ἔκθεσις, πίστεως (exposition of faith); the word *symbolon* appeared in the middle of the 4th century (Council of Laodicea, can. 7). The writers who explain the term *symbolum* understand it as a "sign of recognition", a "formula of initiation": the symbol is the formula whereby Christians are initiated into the mystery of the faith and the sign by which it can be recognized that they profess the true faith. Other interpretations (Augustine, *Sermo,* 213, 1) see in the symbol a summary of the true faith (see below).

Different formulas of confession of faith are already to be found in the NT. The simplest and perhaps also the most primitive are the professions of faith in Jesus Christ, the Son of God and Lord (1 Cor 12:3: κύριος Ἰησοῦς; Rom 10:9; Heb 4:14; 1 Jn 4:15; cf. Acts 8:37, Western text). This profession is often accompanied by the mention of certain facts from the history of Christ and these are always the same: his virginal birth, his crucifixion under Pontius Pilate, his resurrection (already in 1 Cor 15:3–5; Ignatius of Antioch, *Eph.,* 18:2; *Smyrn.,* I; *Trall.* 9:1; *Magn.,* II).

On the other hand we know of formulas of faith with two members, addressed to God the Father and to Jesus Christ (1 Cor 8:6; 2 Tim 4:1), and also ternary formulas (2 Cor 13:13 and again *Clem.,* 58, 2; *Ign. Magn.,* 13, 1. 2, etc.), which recall the commandment given by Jesus to baptize "in the name of the Father and of the Son and of the Holy Spirit" (Mt 28:19), a formula no doubt already stylized through liturgical use.

Much later on in Justin, Irenaeus and Tertullian we find more developed formulas which set forth the content of the true faith within the framework of a trinitarian formula, into which is inserted the confession of Christ, connected either with the mention of the Holy Spirit (Justin, *1 Apol.,* 61; Irenaeus, *Haer.,* 1, 10, 1, etc.) or with that of the Son (Tert., *Virg. vel.,* 1). Here we are dealing with much more developed theological texts. But in the 2nd century we know of shorter formulas already fixed through liturgical use.

For example, in the apocrypha *Epistula Apostolorum* (Asia Minor, 160–70):

"I believe in the Father master of the universe,

and in Jesus Christ our Saviour,

and in the Holy Spirit the Paraclete, and in the holy Church and in the remission of sins."

Or the liturgical formula of the papyrus of Der-Balizeh, which could represent an Egyptian ritual of the 2nd century(?):

"I believe in God the Father almighty,

and in his only Son Our Lord Jesus Christ,

and in the Holy Spirit and in the resurrection of the flesh in the holy Catholic Church."

The Creed of the 2nd century is then the echo of the primitive confessions of faith which go back to the apostolic kerygma and to the revelation of Jesus Christ himself. It is from these that all the later symbols in the East as well as in the West derive.

2. *The Roman Symbol or the Apostles' Creed.* At the beginning of the 3rd century the Roman symbol appears already fixed in the form that with a few additions was to be definitive. The *Apostolic Tradition* of Hippolytus, which could in fact represent the Roman usage at the beginning of the 3rd century, describes the rite of baptism and quotes the triple interrogation addressed to the candidate:

"Do you believe in God the Father almighty?

Do you believe in Jesus Christ, the Son of God, who was born through the Holy Spirit and the Virgin Mary, died and was buried, rose living from the dead the third day, ascended into heaven and is seated at the right hand of the Father (and) will come to judge the living and the dead?

Do you believe in the Holy Spirit, in the holy Church and in the resurrection of the flesh?"

Here we must make two important observations:

a) The creed was not first of all a rule of faith (see below), but a profession of baptismal faith. St. Cyprian (*Ep.,* 69, 7) speaks of "baptizing with the symbol" *(symbolo baptizare),* and relates the formula of the symbol *(symboli legem)* to the baptismal interrogation. The symbol is the profession of faith that the catechumen makes at the moment of his baptism. In the 4th century the baptismal catechesis was organized on the plan of the symbol (Cyril of Jerusalem, Theodore of Mopsuestia). St. Ambrose and St. Augustine commented on the symbol to the catechumens at the time of the solemn *traditio symboli.*

b) This triple interrogation informs us about the structure and the meaning of the symbol; the symbol or creed is a formula with three members, and a profession of faith in the Trinity (*symbolum Trinitatis,* Firmilian of Caesarea, Cyprian, *Ep.,* 75, 11), to which was associated a profession of faith in Christ whose life, death and resurrection was our salvation. Tertullian had already remarked that the baptismal confession was a development of "what the Lord determined in the gospel" (*De corona,* 3).

The text of the Roman symbol of the 4th century has been preserved in Greek in a letter of Marcellus of Ancyra to Pope Julius I (*c.* 340, in Epiphanius, *Haer.,* 72, 3, 1). The original language appears to have been Greek, which justifies our dating it back to the middle of the 3rd century:

"I believe in God (the Father) almighty,

and in Jesus Christ, his only Son our Lord, who was born of the Holy Spirit and the Virgin Mary, who was crucified under Pontius Pilate and was buried; the third day he rose from the dead, ascended into heaven, is seated at the right hand of the Father from whence he will come to judge the living and the dead,

and in the Holy Spirit, the holy Church, the remission of sins, the resurrection of the flesh, the life eternal."

Thus there existed at Rome from the 3rd century a symbol formula *(R)* which, although a little less developed, is identical to the received text *(T)* which appears in its present form in St. Caesarius of Arles (d. 542). The shorter formula *(R)* is the starting-point for all the Western creeds which are otherwise known to us (Gaul, Spain, Africa, Brittany). The longer formula *(T)* was not composed at Rome; no doubt it originated in Gaul and was perhaps enriched by Eastern contributions. It eventually spread throughout the whole of the West and even returned to Rome (in the Carolingian era), where it had been supplanted in the baptismal liturgy by the so-called Nicene-Constantinopolitan Creed.

So we must reject the legend which had already appeared in the 4th century (St. Ambrose, Rufinus), and which could date back to Syria in the 3rd century, according to which the creed was drawn up by the apostles themselves (the attribution of each of the twelve articles to one each of the twelve apostles appeared in Gaul in the 6th century);

but the teaching of the creed itself, whose connections with the NT we have shown, goes back, without any doubt, to the apostolic preaching.

3. *The Eastern creeds.* Apart from the profession of faith of St. Gregory Thaumaturgus, Bishop of Neocaesarea in Pontus (d. *c.* 270), which does not appear to be a liturgical (baptismal) formula, we have evidence of the Eastern form of the creed only from the 4th century and then in its more developed forms. But all that we have said above justifies our affirming that it also goes back to the confessions of trinitarian and Christological faith. Under the forms in which we possess them (the creeds of Jerusalem, Caesarea, Antioch, Cyprus and Mopsuestia) the Eastern creeds show more diversity than the Western symbols, no doubt as a result of reaction against heresies. When the Church wanted to define its faith at Nicaea against the heresy of Arius, it did so in the framework of a baptismal creed (that of Caesarea or Jerusalem) with the addition of technical formulas (ὁμοούσιος). And this was to be the case with all the other formulas which were successively worked out in the course of the trinitarian controversies of the 4th century. "The ancient *credos* were *credos* for catechumens, the new *credos* were *credos* for bishops." (C. H. Turner.)

The origin of the Creed of "Constantinople" remains in dispute. It is possible that Epiphanius who quoted this symbol in 374 (Ancor. 118, 9–13) was its author and that the Council of 381 took it over. The text was read at the Council of Chalcedon as the creed of the Council of Constantinople and this attribution has become traditional. But in any case there is no question of a development from the formula of Nicaea and the expression the "Symbol of Nicaeo-Constantinople" is inexact.

This creed supplanted the other baptismal symbols of the East (and even for some time that of Rome). It was introduced into the eucharistic liturgy in Syria in the 5th century (by Peter the Fuller), the custom then spread to the West, first of all to Spain, then to the imperial court, and finally in 1014 to Rome at the request of Henry II.

4. *The Athanasian Creed.* The symbol *Quicumque,* called the "Athanasian Creed", is not a baptismal symbol but first a profession of

faith in the Trinity and then in Christ (Chalcedon Christology). It has nothing to do with St. Athanasius and is of Western origin. Many names have been proposed as its author (St. Ambrose, Vincent of Lerins, Fulgentius of Ruspe, St. Caesarius of Arles, etc.), but no certain conclusion has been reached. It seems to have been drawn up in Southern Gaul in the 5th or 6th centuries. It spread through the West during the Carolingian period. From the 9th century onwards it was recited on Sundays at Prime, but since 1955 this is no longer the case, except on the feast of the Trinity.

5. *The creed and the rule of faith.* The creed is the summary of the pre-baptismal catechesis (which explains, for example, why we find no reference to the Eucharist in it, this being reserved for the "initiated") — a catechesis which echoes the apostolic preaching. In this respect it can pass as a witness to the apostolic tradition and enjoys a pre-eminent authority. But it does not express the whole content of the doctrine of faith: in ancient Christian literature we know of more developed confessions of faith which summarize and expound the faith that the Church received from the apostles and their disciples (thus Irenaeus, *Adv. Haer.,* I, 10, etc.; Tertullian, *Praescr.,* 13, *Virg. vel.,* I; Origen, *De Princ.,* I, *Praef.,* 4). These confessions for the most part retain the trinitarian structure and are not unrelated to the profession of baptismal faith. Irenaeus speaks of the rule of faith received in baptism, I, 9, 4. But they are not to be identified with the baptismal symbol and it would be futile to try to reconstruct the "symbol" of Justin or Irenaeus from them, as has been attempted. They are theological expositions which do not represent the ritual formula of the profession of baptismal faith.

These writers speak in this connection of the "rule of faith", *regula veritatis.* Essentially these expressions signify that it is the truth of faith itself which is the rule (Irenaeus, II, 28, 1). But soon these formulas of faith began to be considered as normative. Thus the creed which at the beginning was not identical with the rule of faith became the "rule of faith". It seems that this took place at Nicaea which formulated its faith in the framework of a baptismal creed: the "faith of Nicaea", the expression of "the faith professed by the Fathers according to the Scriptures", is the touchstone of orthodoxy. At the Councils of Nicaea and Chalcedon the "symbol" of Nicaea and that of "Constantinople" are the norms which are referred to so as to judge the orthodoxy of a teacher and to express the Catholic faith against a heretic. The baptismal creed had become the rule of faith. If it is the responsibility of the magisterium to formulate the creed and to complete it on a point about which there has been dispute (e. g. ὁμοούσιος), the creed is also the rule to which the magisterium must refer as the expression of the apostolic tradition. In later centuries we again come across formulas of faith, either official ones (the Council of Toledo, 400 or 447) or private ones *(Fides Damasi, Clemens Trinitas, Quicumque)* which are expressed in the framework of the creed. The *Professio fidei Tridentina* of Pius IV (1564) again takes up the Nicene Creed.

BIBLIOGRAPHY. *D* 1–40, *DS* 1–76; P. Schaff, *The Creeds of Christendom, with a History and Critical Notes,* 3 vols. (1877); J. Lebreton, *Histoire du Dogme de la Trinité,* II (1928), pp. 141–73; D. van der Eynde, *Les normes de l'enseignement chrétien* (1933); C. H. Dodd, *The Apostolic Preaching and its Developments* (1936); P. Nautin, *Je crois à l'Esprit-Saint dans la Sainte Église pour la résurrection de la chair* (1947); I. Ortiz de Urbina, *El Símbolo niceno* (1947); B. Capelle, *An Early Euchologium* (1949); O. Cullmann, *The Earliest Christian Confessions* (1949); J. de Ghellinck, *Patristique et Moyen âge,* I, 2: *Les recherches sur les origines du symbole des Apôtres* (1949); J. Crehan, *Early Baptism and Creeds* (1950); J. N. D. Kelly, *Early Christian Creeds* (1950); J. Quasten, *Patrology,* I (1950), pp. 23–29, III (1961), pp. 32–33; B. Altaner, *Patrology* (1960), pp. 47–50, 319–21; C. Eichenseer, *Das Symbolum Apostolicum beim heiligen Augustinus* (1960); A. Hahn and A. von Harnack, *Bibliothek der Symbole* (4th ed., 1962); F. W. Danker, *Creeds in the Bible* (1966).

Pierre-Thomas Camelot

CRUSADES

1. *Name and nature of the movement.* Since the 18th century the term "Crusades" (medieval Latin *cruciata,* 13th century) has been applied to all the armed pilgrimages and military expeditions, sponsored by the medieval Church, that were undertaken against unbelievers and heretics by the *crucesignati* — people who had taken vows and wore a cloth cross sewn on their garments.

The idea of the crusade, a special form of the idea of the just and holy war, looms large in the history of Western piety and thought, casting its shadow beyond the age of the Crusades proper, over the voyages of discovery and the Turkish wars down into quite modern times. It found its first embodiment between 1095 and 1291, in the expeditions made to the East to restore Christian sovereignty over the Holy Places. Early or isolated forms of Crusades were the Byzantine wars against the Arabs and the Spanish Reconquista (from the 8th century on), and the expeditions in the West against the heathen, heretics, or schismatics — Slavs, Albigenses, Hussites, and so on. But the Eastern Crusades are the most striking historical embodiment of a central characteristic of medieval Christendom — the belief that the City of God could be built within time. They gave concrete shape to the basic forms of life in the ordered medieval world, Christianity and feudalism, as expanding universalist forces and yet forces making for hierarchical order.

Complex motives mingled in them which can only be understood against the background of general conditions in the West between the 11th and 13th centuries, so that any uniform approach to the nature and objects of the individual Crusades would fall wide of the mark. They can be seen as many things: a new phase of the barbarian invasions and colonial occupation; a consequence of economic and social change; a trial of strength, or even mere adventure, on the part of knighthood, now rising to the position of a governing class; a spontaneous outburst of pent-up religious ideas; the expression of the consciousness of Western Christendom as a community; an early form of imperialism, particularly in the case of France; the first European mass-movement; an expression of the papal will to power; or even a special form of missionary zeal to dominate the world.

From the point of view of universal history, the Crusades are part of the global struggle between East and West for control of the borderlands of Western Europe against Asia — a struggle that began in antiquity between the world of Graeco-Roman culture and Persia, and despite changes of cast still goes on today. The Crusades in the strict sense, though not always animated by the same motives in hierarchy and people, can be distinguished from other wars of a religious flavour, by the juridical basis Pope Urban II gave them at the Council of Clermont in 1095. The second canon of this Council, and the celebrated papal address delivered there, set up the Crusade as a definite institution under canon law. All who marched on Jerusalem (later to other places as well) not for worldly glory or money but *sola devotione* to free God's Church, were granted the remission of all punishment due to sin *(omnis poenitentia peccatorum)*: the first proclamation of a plenary indulgence. Frivolous violation of the crusader's oath brought down excommunication. A series of privileges, sanctioned by papal bulls since the Second Crusade, gave legal protection to the crusader and the family and possessions he had left at home.

Urban II looked on the Crusade as renewing the Peace of God on a universal basis. The extraordinary response which greeted the appeal from Clermont is to be accounted for by the fact that the canon attached secular privileges, and the promise of further religious and material benefits, to the gaining of the indulgence. Contemporary biblical exegesis, identifying that age and its Christian people with the OT people of God and their function in the history of salvation before the coming of Antichrist, declared the Crusade to be the work of God ("Deus le veult!"), the "Gesta Dei per Francos", for as the Lord says, "Ab Oriente adducam semen tuum et ab Occidente congregabo" (Ps 43), "Erit sepulcrum eius gloriosum" (Is 11). From the Second Crusade onwards the sermon on the Crusade, with its new interpretation of certain biblical texts by papal legates, formed part of the juridical basis of that institution.

2. *Antecedents.* The rise of the crusading movement and the course it took become intelligible if one examines its antecedents. We shall only indicate a few of them here. Since the NT forbids killing and enjoins peace, and on the other hand teaches the duty of obedience to authority, the attitude of Christianity towards war is an ancient and crucial problem; and constant confrontation with the State, and the conflict of the Christian state with pagans and heretics, led the Church to work out a Christian ethics of war. The pioneering patristic idea of the *bellum iustum Deo auctore* for keeping the peace (St. Augustine) but also as a missionary duty (St. Gregory the Great) was fused with Germanic maxims of martial glory, loyalty, and the right of resistance. At the time of the

investiture conflict the idea that God willed a *sanctum praelium* against the enemies of the Church gained in strength, although the traditional rule that clerics must not bear arms continued in force.

Much was done to Christianize the feudal nobles and the knights by the Cluniac reform, with its demand that the Church's sphere of competence be extended into lay society. It likewise stood squarely behind the 10th and 11th century movement for the Peace of God, resistance to the Arabs in Spain, and the growing popularity of pilgrimage. Monastic reform, broadening into a general reform of the Church, strengthened hierocratic tendencies in a regenerate papacy conscious of its primatial duties as the supreme authority set over all the Christian world; and the idea of the Crusades fitted in in the most natural way.

Pilgrimages to the Holy Land were a tradition that reached back to the days when the Emperor Constantine built his basilica over the Holy Sepulchre, where legend asserted the true Cross was preserved that had been found by his mother St. Helena. In the year 630, victorious over the Persians who had penetrated to Jerusalem, the Emperor Heraclius brought it back to Golgotha: in a literal sense the first Crusade. But by 640 Syria and Palestine had succumbed to a new attack from Asia; under Mohammed's successors the breath-taking Arab expansion had made Islam the mighty rival of the Christian world. Christianity and Islam sometimes faced each other in arms. On three fronts the Arab onslaught was halted: in the Near East, in Spain, and in Sicily (718 before Constantinople; 732 at Tours and Poitiers, reconquest of Toledo 1085; 11th-century Norman wars in Southern Italy against Arabs and Byzantines). But for long the world was ruled from the citadels of the two powers: Rome and Cordoba in the West, Constantinople and Damascus (Baghdad from 750) in the East.

Apart from more or less religious border-fighting — "pre-Crusades" — the two cultures lived side by side in reasonable tranquility. Christians continued to make pilgrimages to Santiago de Compostela and Palestine, the latter ruled by the Egyptian Fatimites from 969. A Western sense of responsibility for the Holy Land and for the Christians of the East was kept alive by the Frankish protectorate over the Holy Places

which Charles the Great had negotiated with Baghdad, by pilgrimages, and by the reports which travellers brought back. A brief persecution of Christians and the destruction of the Holy Sepulchre by an unbalanced Fatimite ruler (1009, 1020) called forth a first encyclical on the Crusade by Pope Sergius IV, which failed to arouse enthusiasm, and then transformed the pilgrimages to Palestine into mass-expeditions (like that of 1064–65, led by the Archbishop of Mainz and the Bishop of Bamberg, in which between seven and twelve thousand people took part).

Relations between Byzantium and the West were a further important element in the Crusades. The estrangement between the Old Rome of the Latin-German West and the Greek New Rome, which had been growing since Carolingian times, and rivalry between the two empires and ecclesiastical systems for the prestige of Roman tradition led to the schism of 1054. Thus the seal was set on the division of the ancient Christian world. Small wonder, then, if a radical change in the Eastern political situation from the mid-11th century brought about a political *rapprochement* between the Rome of the East and the West, but left the problem of ecclesiastical reunion to poison future relations.

The Mohammedan threat in a new form, that of the Seljuk Turks from the steppes of Asia, ended the Arabian caliphate of Baghdad in 1055, subjected Byzantine territory to new pressure, and set up the sultanate of Roum (Iconium). Christendom was profoundly shocked by the fall of Jerusalem in 1070, and the appeals of the Eastern Emperor for aid moved the West to intervene. First there was the abortive papal project for a Crusade in 1074, and then the summons to a Crusade in 1095 whose motto was: armed support in exchange for Church reunion. Byzantium and the Emperor Alexius I expected mercenaries to help recover Asia Minor and Syria, but not a flood of "Frankish" armies whose leaders would turn out to be rivals of their State and Church. To Byzantines the Latin states of the East became a cancer in the body of Greek Romania. The divergent aims of West and East and the experiences of the Normans' anti-Byzantine policy sowed the seeds of future trouble. The conviction of the *perfidia Graecorum* grew.

3. *Course of the Crusades.* Authors do not always agree in their enumeration of the

seven to nine major Crusades to the East. The many lesser expeditions were seldom of more than local importance.

a) *The First Crusade,* 1095–1101, an enterprise of knights and people in which no king took part, occupies a special position because of the religious enthusiasm it awakened, the success it achieved, and the space historians have devoted to it. When the chaotic "Peasants' Crusade" under the hermit and "vagus" Peter of Amiens had been wiped out, the main expedition followed, organized by the papal legate Adhemar of Le Puy and French and Norman princes (Godfrey of Bouillon, Raymond of Toulouse, Bohemund of Otranto, and others). Advancing by land and sea it captured Jerusalem and set up the Latin princedoms of Edessa, Antioch, and later Tripoli, in loose feudal dependence on the Kingdom of Jerusalem. This creation of a wholly unique set of supernational States "Outremer", with a population composed of various Western strains, Greeks, and Armenians and its own Latin patriarchate subject to Rome, theoretically the possession of all Christendom but in fact political rivals of Byzantium, was the work of individual crusading princes — the colonial flower of Western feudalism.

Besides the chroniclers (especially Fulcher of Chartres and William of Tyre), we have the Assizes from the late 12th century onwards to give us an insight into the constitutional structure of the feudal monarchy of Jerusalem. Henceforth the Crusader States, an exotic microcosm of the Western macrocosm, were involved in the destinies of the East just as they were in those of their originally Western dynasties (such as the houses of Toulouse, Lusignan, and Ibelin). It was for their defence that the subsequent Crusades were undertaken. For their needs, too, the orders of spiritual knighthood were founded in the 11th century (Knights of St. John, Knights Templar, Teutonic Knights) to provide pilgrims with hostels and armed protection: typical embodiments, in institutional form, of the religious and military crusading ideal. St. Bernard of Clairvaux laid down their programme in 1128 in his letter to the Templars, *De laude novae militiae.*

b) *The Second Crusade,* occasioned by the fall of Edessa in 1144, was the high-watermark of the crusading movement. Prepared by the compelling religious genius of St. Bernard of Clairvaux, it was soon regarded as a "universal enterprise" of Christians against the unbelievers of the world because it combined a Turkish war with the Spanish Reconquista and German colonization of the Slavonic East (Crusade against the Wends, 1147). Its only success was the capture of Lisbon; the expedition to the East, a project of the Kings of France and Germany (Louis VII and Conrad III), became bogged down in political planning and proved a complete disaster that heralded withdrawal from the Levant. Disillusion and doubt whether Crusades were really God's will gave birth to a critical attitude which henceforth counteracted the theory of the holy war.

c) With the *Third Crusade,* 1189–92, a reaction to the fall of Jerusalem in 1187, the world debate between Christianity and Islam was raised to a high political plane in the sight of all. The West, Byzantium, and Islam faced each other in the person of brilliant rulers; on the one hand the Emperor Frederick Barbarossa, Philip Augustus King of France and Richard Lionheart King of England; on the other the amiable and gifted follower of Mohammed, Saladin, who led the reunited Moslems of Egypt and Syria into an offensive *jihad* in the grand manner; and then Barbarossa's imperial counterpart, Manuel I Comnenos, who revived the idea of Byzantium's universal dominion. And yet, thanks to friction between Church and Empire, England and France, the Crusade ended in a number of disastrous individual actions. Once Barbarossa was drowned in the Saleph the Christian forces disintegrated. A treaty arranged a *modus vivendi* between Christians and Moslems in the Holy Land, where an armistice was henceforth periodically renewed. Outremer, having lost its heart, now survived only in Cyprus, conquered by Richard Lionheart, which remained the last outpost (becoming Turkish only in 1571), and recaptured Acre, capital till 1291 of the mutilated Kingdom of Jerusalem. The epilogue, Richard's imprisonment by the Babenbergs and Staufens and his ransoming, revealed that the Crusade was being used for selfish political ends by the rival powers within Europe.

d) *The German Crusade,* 1195–98, was an expression of the Hohenstaufen imperial idea in its death-throes. To the mind of Henry VI, heir to the imperial policy of the Staufens and the Mediterranean policy of the Normans, the Crusade was to be a step towards a universal, hereditary Empire by establishing feudal control over Cyprus and Lesser Armenia.

On the failure of this second attempt to bring the Empire into Eastern politics, a rift grew between the idea and the reality of the crusading movement. Innocent III, mightiest successor of the reforming Popes, tried to bring the movement into the service of the hierarchy, re-organizing it with the aim of recovering all the former Christian territories in Palestine, restoring papal supremacy over them and over the schismatic Eastern Church as well. But all the Crusades now attempted became caricatures of the *bellum iustum*.

e) Typical was the *Fourth Crusade, 1202–4.* Instead of recovering the Holy Land it captured Constantinople, because the proud maritime Republic of Venice, whose trading privileges Byzantium had trespassed upon, under its Doge Enrico Dandalo, an aged scoundrel, had cleverly exploited a disputed succession to the Greek throne and wrested the Crusade to its own purposes, rising on the ruins of plundered imperial Constantinople to become mistress of Mediterranean commerce on the threshold of Asia. What the West gained thereby was the doubtful benefit of a weak Latin Empire of Constantinople — stillborn, for in 1261 it once more fell into the hands of Byzantium, which had survived in Asia Minor as the Empire of Trebizond — and a multitude of costly relics which were offered to the disappointed pilgrim as partial compensation for the relics of Jerusalem. In the end all the hopes that the papacy cherished for a reunion of the Churches came to nothing. High-sounding appeals for a new Crusade — masterpieces of persuasive rhetoric — popularized in France by the legate Jacques de Vitry met with a macabre response in the *Children's Crusade* of 1212. Thousands of children aged up to twelve gathered about fanatical shepherd boys in Southern France and the Rhineland and started for the Promised Land, because of the biblical promise, "Their's is the kingdom of heaven". They perished miserably in the ships of merchants who had embarked them. On the other hand rulers kept their heads, as we see from Philip II's *Stabilimentum crucisignatorum,* which set forth the privileges of crusaders in order to ensure that these should not interfere with the rights of the State (to legislate, try criminals, and collect taxes).

f) No ruler took an active part in the *Fifth Crusade,* 1217–21. It meant the loss of Damietta, the metropolis on the Nile, which had been captured shortly before, for since the Third Crusade Egypt had been regarded as the key to Jerusalem. The Church put the failure down to the delaying tactics of the Hohenstaufen Emperor Frederick II, who had taken the vow in 1215. Thus the Crusades once more became an issue in German imperial politics. When conflict dramatically broke out anew between papacy and empire, the Church demanded that the *negotium terrae sanctae* become a *negotium imperii,* and acceptance of that demand can be said in a sense to have been a *reductio ad absurdum* of the ecclesiastical idea of the Crusades. For the second occupation of Jerusalem (1229), during the Sixth Crusade, took place peacefully, by treaty between the Sultan and the excommunicated Emperor. As consort to Isabella, heiress of Acre and Jerusalem, Frederick II crowned himself King of Jerusalem without any ecclesiastical ceremony in the Basilica of the Holy Sepulchre and issued a proclamation of peace to the Christian world, while the Pope laid the Holy Places under interdict — a strange and ephemeral fulfilment of the dreams of Christendom, with the papal idea of the Crusades in open conflict with this beginning of the *raison d'état.* Outremer was bled white by the struggle between Guelph and Ghibelline carried over to the East. In 1244 Jerusalem was lost forever. The last Hohenstaufens were left only the empty title of King of Jerusalem.

g) Still marked by desperate religious valour, the tragic *final phase of the Crusades* was once more the work of France, this time of the remarkable king St. Louis IX. His first expedition, 1249–50, again met with disaster before Damietta. The second, 1270, was halted at Tunis by the king's death, which meant defeat for both the crusading and the secular policy of the house of Anjou, heir to the Sicilian monarchy of the Normans and the Hohenstaufen. In 1265 the last footholds of the Latin Christians in Syria, weakened by anarchy and faction, fell to the Egyptian Mamelukes, who had just defeated Ghengis Khan's Golden Horde. With the fall of Acre in 1291 the doom of Christian rule in the Holy Land was sealed. The fall of Constantinople, 1453, then began the age of the Turkish wars.

4. *Assessment.* In the light of their actual history the Crusades seem a tragic episode of bloodshed in the name of God, motivated by intolerance and political ambition, a sacrifice of human life out of all proportion to the ends that were sought. Modern research seeks to weigh the benefits of the Crusades against the harm they did — benefits like the widening of Europe's geographical horizon, increased trade because the Arab blockade of the Mediterranean was broken (chiefly advantageous for the maritime Italian cities), advances in the technique of warfare, a livelier exchange of art and culture, and so on.

But a purely objective weighing-up of advantages and disadvantages will hardly do the age justice. Taking a wider view, we shall perceive that the Crusades did not merely express the ecclesiastical and political universalism of the Middle Ages, were not only a decisive stage in terms of the time in the global process of assimilation and separation between West and East. Beyond all that they were a turning-point in religion and spirituality. While the crusading idea became secularized, disillusion and criticism produced the realization that a spiritual pilgrimage to Jerusalem could be made without joining an armed expedition to the East. For, said the critics, it would be fatuous to hurry off in search of the true Cross if the Crucified himself is neglected at home — to put out a neighbour's fire if one's own home is burning down. Too rough-and-ready a treatment of the letter of Scripture brought about a certain return of exegesis to allegory. But of more practical import for the future was the seed of tolerance, sown, for example, by St. Francis of Assisi before Damietta in 1219, when he risked his life in an attempt to convert the Sultan instead of fighting him. Then from the later Middle Ages on the peaceful Franciscan and Dominican missions went side by side with the older method of making war on unbelief.

See also *War, Reconquista, Invasions (Barbarian), Investiture Controversy, Occident, Islam, Reform* II B, *Pilgrimage, Tolerance.*

BIBLIOGRAPHY. *Recueil des historiens des croisades,* ed. by Académie des Inscriptions et Belles-Lettres (1841–1906); D. C. Munro, *The Crusades and Other Historical Essays* (1928); R. Grousset, *Histoire des croisades et du royaume franc de Jérusalem,* 3 vols. (1934–36); G. A. Campbell, *The Crusades* (1935); A. S. Atiya, *The Crusades in the Later Middle Ages* (1938); M. Villey, *La croisade. Essai sur la formation d'une théorie juridique* (1942); P. Rousset, *Les origines et les caractères de la première croisade* (1945); S. Runciman, *A History of the Crusades,* 3 vols. (1951–53); J. Richard, *Le royaume latine de Jérusalem* (1953); P. Alphandéry, *La chrétienté et l'idée de croisade* (1954); K. M. Setton, ed., *A History of the Crusades,* 2 vols. (1955–62); A. Waas, *Geschichte der Kreuzzüge,* 2 vols. (1956); F. Gabrielli, *Storici arabi delle crociate* (1957); A. C. Krey, *The First Crusade. The Accounts of Eye-Witnesses and Participants* (1958); H. E. Mayer, *Bibliographie zur Geschichte der Kreuzzüge* (1960); A. S. Atiya, *The Crusade. Historiography and Bibliography* (1962); id., *Crusade, Commerce and Culture* (1962); J. A. Brundage, *The Crusades. A Documentary Survey* (1962); R. Hill, ed., *Gesta Francorum et aliorum Hierosolimitanorum,* Latin and English (1962); H. Treece, *The Crusades* (1963).

Laetitia Boehm

CULTURE

1. *Meaning of culture.* The word culture, from the Latin *colere,* to cultivate, in the sense here discussed means a certain kind of environment as changed and shaped by man, and also the human activity that leads to the cultural pattern. The notion of culture may be differentiated from the notion of civilization, the latter meaning the cultural sphere formed by technology in the service of the external necessities of life and practical utilitarian achievements. In this sense, civilization, in contrast to the originally creative culture, is taken to mean a social order primarily determined by a utilitarian approach. This view is not shared by the Romanic nations who regard civilization as the core of all culture; to them civilization is the sum-total of different types of social phenomena. This whole has various aspects, religious, moral, aesthetic, scientific, or academic, and is present in all groups of human society. This is why one speaks of the various historical or geographical civilizations or cultures, treating the terms as synonymous, the former stressing the subjective and the latter the objective aspect.

As culture does not exist in the form of a perfect world, individual or society, but only in relatively limited forms, one can speak of cultures as conditioned by or happening in history. Man's culturally creative attitude distinguishes him from the animal which is firmly held by its environment and lives within a strictly limited sphere of action, based on instinct, never able to go beyond these limits. Unlike the animal, man is unsure of his instincts but, because of his mental gifts, he is able to reach beyond his natural surroundings although he too remains conditioned by the finite world. This transcendence, the metaphysical possibility of basically limitless human thought and desire, culminates in man's freedom, the hidden driving force of all cultural creativity. His concern for his physical welfare, a place to live, good social relations and making a worthy environment for himself, drives man, over and above purely utilitarian considerations, to impress upon his world his striving for the infinite, his unrest which torments him and at the same time brings him joy and which is due to the insufficiency of his finite experiences, so that his world reflects this striving and unrest. Culture can therefore be seen in the works of man and in his creative activity as a reflection of his striving after higher things.

2. *Aspects of culture.* Culture has a so-called objective aspect in the sense of a successful achievement produced by man, which remains for him and his fellow-men as something which has been given form and meaning. But as culture in the objective sense can only have life in relation to man, the subjective and objective aspects cannot be separated either in the creative act or in the way the work is regarded afterwards. Both are part of a living culture: one cannot experience subjective culture without the historical presence of cultural values or objective products of this culture. Neither objective culture as the sum of cultural values nor subjective culture as the cultural attitude of individuals and groups can rest or exist in itself. They are part of the mainstream of historical tradition which depends for its life on the success or otherwise of this interaction of objective and subjective culture. Morals and customs are also contributory factors in culture; their rise or decline can be measured by the level of the culture concerned, although the reciprocity of objective and subjective culture must also be taken into account, for there can be signs of moral decay within very high objective cultures which are, however, no longer realized subjectively.

The growth and progress of culture is limited by the dependence of human life on historical conditions. The infinite aims of human endeavour are embodied within a historical situation with limited cultural possibilities. Every generation selects what it wants out of its cultural inheritance. This is usually done polemically, i.e., as a rule anything that was regarded as of value by the previous generation will be discarded by the new generation because it is faced by new, as yet unmastered, possibilities, and it can only find enough energy for further development if it excludes or forgets what has gone before. This kind of development explains why revolutions and renaissances occur over the centuries and why culture does not progress in a straight line.

Culture is essentially a social phenomenon, although it can only be realized in the individual through an encounter with other minds. Naturally such an encounter presupposes an objective cultural environment and a certain level of personal culture, as present in the most diverse traditions, e.g., a richly developed language which is in itself an objective cultural medium. This historical process of cultural encounter comes about through the initiative of individuals who form élites and create a mental climate which will always fire individuals with new enthusiasm and within which nations can find their spiritual home. Such an élite can only fulfil their aspirations if allowed scope by their fellow-men and they must have scope if their culture is to endure.

There is a close, if strained, connection between culture and power, for political leaders have always tried to impose unity on nations by the use of power and even force. All wars have been more or less cultural crusades against "barbarism". But the very attempt to impose culture by brute force stands in inner contradiction to the nature of culture because, however much good will and mental effort there may be, culture cannot be "forced". Culture needs freedom of the mind, and it is a basic duty of the state to ensure it; only then can the urge of the spirit become achievement of the spirit. If culture is taken to be the expression of a people's mental and spiritual life, it will be seen that culture only reflects the relation between the objective existence of certain cultural products and the state of the educational level of the people. If the two do not correspond, a culture is liable to decay or die, while conversely maintenance or growth of a cultural level depends on a rise in the educational standard of a people. The individual encounters this process in the form of traditions which induce him to consider his attitude towards his cultural heritage. Depending on the degree of interest he takes in this heritage, he will be able to understand and explain the history of his forbears. There is a reciprocal relationship between culture and history, the knowledge of one's own past.

What is known as objective culture, as expressed in various historical traditions, generally crystallizes in institutions. These form, as it were, the river-bed which the living river of culture has made for itself over the centuries. But just as the bed only has a purpose together with the living river, culture as an institution only makes sense together with unhampered creativity. Culture is not only a product of intellect and will, it is also influenced by impulses of quite a different kind, such as play. Play is not confined to children, but remains, as a liberal art, the soul of all conscious creativity, academic or scientific, and even more in art, philosophy and religion. If usefulness is the only criterion, as seems too often the case in our modern rationalized way of life, the will to play will have insufficient scope, thus excluding the creative element which is an essential part of culture.

This is the same as saying that culture can only exist where there is *leisure*. Leisure, as distinct from free time, means in this context an act of that inner freedom which man must cherish and safeguard within himself, if he is not to be a slave to matters of immediate material usefulness but remain open to the things that lie above immediate utility and practical success. Such leisure is the fruit of mental composure, the spiritual centre of freedom, which will remain dormant and ineffective whenever man allows himself to be driven by things of immediate importance and does not find time for recollection.

The effort to ensure conditions in which culture may flourish cannot just be a matter for the individual, especially today when he is involved in a productive process which may perhaps leave him free time externally, but enables him less and less to make creative use of this free time.

Just as leisure has an essential connection with culture, so religious worship, the reli-gious expression of society, is also a basic ingredient of all cultural development. The remarkable thing about the spiritual connection between cultus and culture is that man's creative powers of expression, which manifest his creatureliness before the Creator, are far more than merely rational forces. Here we see how fertile in symbols are human creativity and co-operation, not only in the sphere of religion and art but also in that of customs. The source of these sensible expressions is man's freedom which is the counterpart of God's creative freedom.

Thus there can be no doubt that religion, in which man submits to God, is one of the chief sources of culture. The assertion that religion and culture are incompatible rests on a misunderstanding of both religion and culture. Man, through his religious attitude, makes room above all for God in his life and thus endeavours to maintain freedom; at the same time he opens the way to a spiritual formation of his world and thus makes possible a free encounter of cultural worlds, individuals and peoples. Of course religion does unmask a certain view of culture which holds that man's proper attitude towards culture should be to "consume" as many cultural goods as possible, a view encouraged by modern science which can put before man a limitless number of such "goods". It is not the amount of culturally valuable objects that is relevant for actual life, however high these values might be, but what man makes of them for himself and his fellow-men.

3. *Unity and diversity of culture*. The necessity for a meeting of cultures in the interest of peace between nations is often asserted. Not infrequently this intention, good in itself, conceals the illusion, or even the claim to power, that seeks to unite mankind within a world culture, or even to force man into it. Such aspirations are based on the erroneous idea that culture can be made or organized, for it is the politician's temptation to want to make men fit into a plan. But unity and peace among nations, from the cultural point of view, presupposes a diversity of the cultural world. Unity and freedom will be assured if each people tries to respect and understand the difference in others. This necessity for reverence for the creative richness and uniqueness of the minds and spirit of the various peoples and individuals

also applies to cultural propaganda. One must not confuse action against lack of culture with cultural work proper, nor is the organization that does cultural work synonymous with the work itself. However good the organization may be, it will not succeed in maintaining or furthering culture, if it is not animated by reverence for a genuine personal freedom which is the primary source of the creative life of culture.

Something must be said in this connection about the relationship between culture and science; there are two aspects to be considered. Insofar as science offers man greater scope for freedom and a peaceful social life, it is itself a cultural factor, no different from all the other human activities which can be moulded by culture. But science, through establishing better communications, can also be used for spreading culture, which often fosters the illusion that a quicker and more perfect spread of cultural matter is doing culture a great service. This is, however, a very dangerous mistake, because such a rapid spread can in fact destroy culture. Only if something is done at the same time to make men ready to receive real cultural values, will science be a help by disseminating culture. But if this prerequisite is absent, the flooding of whole sections of the population with cultural works will do more harm than good, for science is quite unable to create the right atmosphere. The mysterious process of growing maturity and readiness for culture always takes place within the very narrow framework of human encounter. If this creative framework is restricted or destroyed, as always happens under totalitarian systems, the source of all cultural creativity and receptiveness is blocked.

4. *Cultural crises and their causes*. Such crises happen quite frequently as peoples or generations succeed each other and fail to establish contact, because there has been a radical change in conditions owing to some political or social upheaval; the old ideas about the world or mankind are questioned, the future is regarded as all-important, and men turn passionately to new ideas. The same happens after violence and hostilities between peoples of different cultures: there follows a struggle for a synthesis between the old and the new, or else the higher culture displaces the lower, although the culture of the victor is not always the winner. Contact between religion and culture is also rarely established without crises.

Cultural history which deals with the development and the crises of the various cultures, examines the laws of growth and change in the various types of society and has been taking the social changes increasingly into account. As freedom is the source of all culture, it follows that culture can only flourish where there is a certain degree of political and economic freedom. Originally the only bearers of culture were free citizens, while slaves were practically excluded. History has shown again and again how oppressed and unfree peoples or classes fought for equal rights in revolutions and then entered cultural history themselves, and how they overthrew political or economic systems which, they were convinced, barred their way to freedom and therefore culture. It has become a commonplace in our industrial and democratic age that all culture should be open to all and that all have equal political and economic rights as a matter of principle. But this egalitarian world is unable to recognize and evaluate the different degrees of achievement and, even less, of spiritual development which should reflect the difference of degree of inner freedom, the source of all culture. The inevitable fact of inequality of achievement and mind is expressed by an order of freedom which must be maintained, safeguarded and encouraged by the political and economic order. This inner order of freedom is the very soul of culture. Whenever this order is upset there will be a cultural crisis.

Culture is a whole that cannot be ascertained and certainly not analysed in the same way as some concrete object. Just as one can tell that there is a soul or life in an organism because this highly complicated structure is functioning harmoniously as a whole, the loss of any part within the very complex whole organism of the history of mankind has always been a danger to culture.

The development of culture in history sometimes takes place organically, while at other times it erupts in revolution, depending on the type of encounter between groups or peoples. There are a great many stages, some near the primitive cultural level, some nearer the highly advanced level. There has never been such a thing as a purely natural state of man. Man's very first tools show that, even at this early stage, man's urge to create went beyond the purely utilitarian. Theories which overlook this basic fact lose themselves in one-sided speculation and abandon the solid ground of reality.

See also *Church and World, World, Transcendence, Society* I, *History, Power, Tradition, Education* I, *Leisure, Play, Religion, Liturgy* I, *Art* I, *Science* I, *Communications Media*.

BIBLIOGRAPHY. O. Spengler, *Decline of the West*, 2 vols. (1926–28); H. Bergson, *The Two Sources of Morality and Religion* (1935); J. Huizinga, *In the Shadow of Tomorrow. A Diagnosis of the Spiritual Distemper of Our Time* (1936); M. Blondel, *Lutte pour la civilisation et philosophie de la paix* (1939); P. Hazard, *European Mind, 1680–1715* (1939); P. A. Sorokin, *The Crisis of Our Age. The Social and Cultural Outlook* (1941); J. Burckhardt, *Reflections on History* (1943); C. Dawson, *Religion and Culture* (1948); T. S. Eliot, *Notes Towards the Definition of Culture* (1948); J. Ortega y Gasset, *Dehumanization of Art and Other Writings on Art and Culture* (1948); A. J. Toynbee, *Civilization on Trial* (1948); J. Huizinga, *Homo Ludens. A Study of the Play-Element in Culture* (1949); A. Rüstow, *Ortsbestimmung der Gegenwart. Eine universal-geschichtliche Kulturkritik*, 3 vols. (1950–57); A. Weber, *Prinzipien der Geschichts- und Kultursoziologie* (1951); *Interrelation of Cultures. Their contribution to International Understanding*, ed. by UNESCO (1953); H. Freyer, *Theorie des gegenwärtigen Zeitalters* (1955); A. Portmann, *Biologie und Geist* (1956); H. Fischer, *Theorie der Kultur. Das kulturelle Kraftfeld* (1965).

Robert Scherer

CURIA

I. Historical Evolution. II. Reform and Present Structure.

I. Historical Evolution

The Acts and Letters of the apostles show us that from the very outset they used fellow-workers in carrying out the mission Christ had entrusted to them. At Jerusalem, the apostles considered the advice of the presbyters and settled jointly with them the controversy that had been raised by the Judaizers (Acts 15:6–23). Previously they had already appointed seven men to see to the needs of the poor (Acts 6:1–6); and it was quite normal for them to use amanuenses or secretaries: Peter used Silvanus (1 Pet 5:12) and Paul Tertius (Rom 16:22). In short, from the very beginning the apostles had three kinds of helpers: some in Church government, others in the preparation of

documents, and others again in the administration of temporal goods, foreshadowing in a simple way what bishops' curias were to be like with the passage of time.

During the early centuries the fellow-workers of the Pope were hardly different from those each bishop had in his own diocese. In the 4th century we find three permanent organs about the Pope, corresponding to the three original kinds of helpers: the presbyters, the notaries with their "scrinium", and the deacons. But henceforward those rudimentary organs begin to evolve and specialize, with the more frequent appeals of particular Churches to the Vicar of Christ and his spontaneous interventions on behalf of the universal Church. But the Pope's helpers were not called the Roman Curia until the 11th century, and the term has only in very recent times been confined to the ministries which help him govern the universal Church (St. Pius X, 1908). Those who help the Pope to govern the diocese of Rome are the Cardinal Vicar and his diocesan curia, the Vicariate of Rome.

1. *From the presbyterate to the Sacred Congregations.* a) From the 4th century onwards the presbyterate *(presbyterium),* as advisers and judges, were the Roman Pontiff's chief assistants. At first they comprised all the presbyters and deacons of Rome; later they were only the leading, or cardinal, deacons and presbyters; and from the 8th century there were also the cardinal bishops, the bishops of the suburbicarian dioceses.

Nevertheless the Popes until the 12th century convoked Roman councils to deal with important business. After that time the Roman councils were replaced by the *Consistory*. The word is of Byzantine origin and means the college of the three ranks of cardinals (which already resembled the present Sacred College) in its capacity as the Pope's permanent advisers and fellow-judges.

b) From the 13th century onwards the judicial functions of the Consistory were entrusted to a new body, the "Auditorium", which eventually developed into the Apostolic Tribunals of the "Sacred Roman Rota" and the "Apostolic Signature". But the Consistory kept its full powers to advise the Pope and govern with him until the 16th century, when the various Congregations of cardinals arose, each appointed to help the

Pope with a particular aspect of Church government.

c) The first Congregation was set up by Paul III in 1542 to guard the integrity of the faith (it was called the Holy Inquisition, then the Congregation of the Holy Office, and today is the Congregation for the Doctrine of the Faith); the second by Paul IV in 1564 to carry out the decrees of the Council of Trent (the "Congregation of the Council"); and the third by Sixtus V in 1586 for matters concerning religious (later it was called the Congregation for Bishops and Regulars, and from 1909, the Congregation for Religious). Then the same energetic Pope Sixtus created fifteen Congregations, five for the government of the Papal States and ten for the government of the Church universal.

Of the latter Congregations two continued to function till recently: the Consistorial Congregation and the Congregation of Rites, from which the Congregation of Ceremonies soon branched off. As already indicated, the new system of Congregations deprived the old Consistory of its functions, reducing it practically to an ornament. Some thirty Congregations arose, disappeared, fused, or underwent transformations during the 17th, 18th and 19th centuries, only two of these surviving the reform of Pius X: the Congregation for the Propagation of the Faith (Gregory XV, 1622) and the Congregation for Extraordinary Affairs (Pius VII, 1814).

2. *From the Notaries to the Chancellory and other Offices.* a) *The Apostolic Chancellory.* The 4th century Notaries with their Scrinium gradually changed from a mere office for drawing up, dispatching and storing papal documents, into an administrative organ of great importance called the Apostolic Chancellory (13th century). It was headed by the "Primicerius" of the Notaries, called Chancellor and later Vice-Chancellor, the Pope's right-hand man, especially in business that was dealt with outside the Consistory. But the Apostolic Chancellory had its heyday at Avignon because appointment to bishoprics and abbacies was now normally reserved to the Popes. John XXII (1316–1344), who had been Chancellor at the French court, reconstructed the Apostolic Chancellory, setting up seven different bodies of officials to expedite bulls and rescripts: examiners, *minutantes, glossatores,* and so on. By the end of the 15th century, however, the Vice-Chancellor's powerful influence in Church government had waned. The Apostolic Chancellory was reduced to its original proportions — an office of notaries who merely drew up papal bulls.

b) *The Apostolic Datary.* To a considerable extent the rapid decline of the Apostolic Chancellory resulted from the establishment of the papal Datary. The decisive importance of the date for the validity of a papal bull meant that the duties of the Datary were extended. At first he merely dated documents; then he had to witness the signing of them; then he laid the relevant petitions before the Pope in the first place. Soon he had to have assistants, and finally became the head of a new office called the Apostolic Datary (16th century, it would seem). The Datary became a still weightier affair when certain benefices and dispensations were at its disposal. Then in the 17th century the number of reserved benefices dwindled, and competition from new curial bodies contributed to the decline of the Datary, until by the 19th century almost its only business was the granting of dispensations from the impediments to marriage.

c) The *Secretariat of State.* Meanwhile the Secretariat of State had grown in importance. It dates back to the days of Clement IV (1266–1268), who entrusted certain Notaries of the Apostolic Chancellory with the confidential and especially the diplomatic correspondence of the Holy See. These Notaries were called Secretaries, and under Martin V (1417–1431) became the office of the Privy Seal. Innocent VIII made it the Apostolic Secretariat (1487), one of whose members, the *Secretarius domesticus,* was to be the Pope's trusted adviser and his right-hand man in the world of politics, especially once Leo X (1513–1521) had created the Apostolic Nuncios. When the Cardinal Nephews began to control the domestic and foreign policy of the Pontifical State, the *Secretarius domesticus* drifted into the background and was eclipsed under Paul III (1534–1549) by the new *Secretarius intimus* of the Pope, who was usually the Cardinal Nephew's adviser and therefore began to be called the Secretary of State, possibly during the pontificate of Clement VIII (1592–1605). Three factors contributed to giving that dignitary's office, the Apostolic Secretariat, its present shape: the practice begun by Innocent X (1644–1655) of choosing the Secretary of

State from among the cardinals, the dissolution of the college of secretaries, and the suppression of nepotism (by Innocent XI, 1678, and Innocent XII, 1692). Thus the amplest powers were automatically gathered into the hands of the Cardinal Secretary of State — powers further enhanced by the privilege that prelate had of direct access to the Pope, who used him and his Secretariat not only to direct the policy of the Pontifical States but also to make known his will to the other "departments" of the Roman Curia. When reorganizing the government of his dominions, Pius IX made the Secretariat, that many new secretariats were set Ministers and head of the ministry for external affairs.

d) *Other Secretariats*. So multifarious were the documents originally handled by the Privy Council and then the Apostolic Secretariat, that many new secretariats were set up, each with its special task. The first of these was the Secretariat for Briefs, which came into being in the pontificate of Alexander VI (1492–1503) to deal with ordinary briefs *(brevia minuta),* so called to distinguish them from briefs of a diplomatic nature. When Innocent XI abolished the Apostolic Secretaries in 1678, he set up an independent office parallel to the Secretariat of State — the Secretariat for Briefs to Princes temporal and ecclesiastical. To its lot fell the original tasks of the Privy Council, and others such as the drawing up of the Latin allocutions which the Pope addressed to the Consistory. In the 18th century the Secretariat for Latin Letters branched off from the Secretariat of State; it was directly under the Pope's orders. Finally, the Secretariat for Memoranda arose at some date which it is difficult to ascertain.

3. *From the deacons to the Apostolic Camera*. After the Edict of Milan the hitherto scanty material possessions of the Roman Church, which the deacons administered, began to multiply. There were gifts from the Emperors and the faithful (4th century), taxes from lands or monasteries placed under papal protection (9th century), feudal dues, "Peter's Pence" (11th century), and the various fees connected with benefices, which rapidly multiplied until they reached their maximum in the 14th and 15th centuries. As these possessions grew, so did the organs charged with administering them; the *Vestiarium,*

the *Palatium* (8th century), and finally the *Apostolic Camera* (11th century), under the Chamberlain, or Camerlengo, who was later chosen from among the cardinals. Naturally enough, the great days of the Apostolic Camera coincided with those of the Chancellory — the pontificates of John XXII and Benedict XII. It comprised a network of "Collectores", rent or tax collectors, which covered all Europe, and a body of officials — administrators, lawyers, and judges — resident at the papal court.

Historical circumstances in the 16th and 17th centuries which dried up most of the Apostolic Camera's sources of income, also changed its structure. Only its personnel at Rome remained, reduced in numbers and with new duties. In the 17th century the Vice-Chamberlain was Governor of Rome, and under Pius IX the Cardinal Chamberlain was Minister of Commerce, Agriculture, Industry, Mines, Arts and Science.

4. *Reform under St. Pius X*. At the end of the 19th century the Roman Curia was a maze of Congregations, Tribunals, Secretariats, and Offices, whose functions were not precisely demarcated Executive power overlapped with the judicial, ecclesiastical affairs with the relics of the government of the Papal States. With a foresight like that of Sixtus V, St. Pius X reorganized the Roman Curia in 1908, eliminating the superfluous, innovating where necessary, and trying to define the field in which each ministry was to operate. His task was simplified by the loss of the Papal States, which made possible a reform along purely spiritual lines — in contrast to the Avignon reform (which in any case affected only the Chancellory and the Apostolic Camera) or even that of Sixtus V. The Code of Canon Law (which came into force in 1918) embodied the reform of Pius X, with some slight adjustments by Pope Benedict XV. It sets forth what has been substantially the recent structure of the Roman Curia: three sets of bodies: (i) The *Roman Congregations,* eleven in number; to the eight that we have mentioned must be added the Congregation of the Sacraments, set up by St. Pius X (who first called it the Congregation of Matrimony), the Congregation for Seminaries and Universities, which was created by Benedict XV (1915) but traces its ancestry to Sixtus V's Congregation *pro Universitate Studii Romani* (1588), and

finally the Congregation for the Eastern Church, founded by Pius IX within the Congregation for the Propagation of the Faith and made independent by Benedict XV (1917). (ii) Three Apostolic Tribunals (cf. can. 258–9). (iii) Six Offices: the Apostolic Chancellory, the Apostolic Datary, the Apostolic Camera, the Secretariat of State, the Secretariat of Briefs to Princes, and the Secretariat for Latin Letters. We should note that St. Pius X merged the Secretariat for Ordinary Briefs in the Secretariat of State and abolished the Secretariat for Memoranda.

For the reforms of Paul VI and the present structure of the Curia, see part II of this article.

See also *Pope, Cardinal, Avignon Exile.*

BIBLIOGRAPHY. B. Ojetti, *De Romana Curia* (1910); J. B. Ferreres, *La Curia Romana según la novísima disciplina decretada por Pio X* (1911); V. Martin, *Les Cardinaux et la Curie* (1931); id., *Les Congrégations Romaines* (1931); N. Del Re, *La Curia Romana* (2nd ed., 1952); C. Pichon, *Le Vatican* (1960); P. C. van Lierde, *Dietro il Portone di Bronzo* (1961).

Ignazio Gordon

II. Reform and Present Structure

The demand for "decentralization" in the Church, which was heard during the preparations for Vatican II, became more and more strongly linked as time went on with the demand for reform of the Curia. In an allocution to the members of the Curia (21 September 1963, *AAS* 55 [1963], pp. 793–800), Paul VI responded by announcing his intention of reforming the Curia. He invited the Council to discuss the question, and the main results of the discussions were then embodied in the decree on the bishops *(Christus Dominus).* The Council asked for reform of the Roman Curia "of which the Roman Pontiff makes use in the exercise of his supreme, full and immediate authority over the universal Church". The Curia should be "adapted to the needs of the times, of the various regions and the different rites, especially in regard to its numbers, titles, spheres of jurisdiction, procedures and co-ordination of functions" (art. 9). The decree also called for the internationalization of the staff, so that the central officials and organs of the Catholic Church should have a truly world-wide character. Above all, some bishops, especially diocesan bishops,

should be appointed as officials. Laymen were also to be more widely consulted (art. 10).

In a further allocution to the Council (18 November 1965, *AAS* 57 [1965]) Paul VI again spoke of reform, and soon after initiated a gradual change, with the new name and orientation of the Holy Office (7 December 1965), the implementation of the Council's decree on the missions, which brought changes into the Congregation *De Propaganda Fide* (6 August 1966) and the abolition of papal reservations with regard to minor benefices, which left the Apostolic Datary without any functions (*AAS* 58 [1966], pp. 673–701; 947–90).

These first steps heralded the definitive reform of the Curia, which was promulgated by Paul VI in the Apostolic Constitution *Regimini Ecclesiae Universae* of 15 August 1967 (with effect from 1 January 1968). The Constitution sets forth in a preamble the reasons for reform — mainly the changed conditions of modern times, and the *vota* of the Fathers of Vatican II — and outlines the main principles on which the reform is based. Then follow some general norms, and in a third section, the various "departments" are described in particular.

1. *Main principles.* The three major departments of the Curia are retained (with certain changes): the Congregations, the Tribunals and the Offices, to which certain Secretariats have been added, along with a Council for the Laity and a Department of Statistics. A number of diocesan bishops are to be members of the Congregations. Co-ordination between the Congregations is to be assured by the common discussion of matters which fall under several jurisdictions, and by regular meetings, convoked by the Cardinal Secretary of State, of the heads of the various departments. For the greater good of the universal Church, the members of the Curia are to be drawn from all over the world. Prefects, members and consultors are in future to be appointed only for five years, though their term of office may be prolonged by the Pope. Cardinal Prefects cease to function at the death of the Pope, except the Cardinal Vicar-General of the Roman diocese, the *Camerarius* (Chamberlain) and the *Paenitentiarius Major,* who must, however, submit matters ordinarily dealt with by the Pope to the College of Cardinals.

Laymen are to be called in as advisors. As regards the judiciary, the powers of the Rota are extended to all cases involving the nullity of matrimony; the powers of the Apostolic Signatura are extended to all matters of ecclesiastical administration. The Apostolic Chancellory becomes the sole department concerned with drawing up Apostolic Letters. A new ministry is set up for the finances of the Holy See and the Vatican City.

2. *General norms.* The Roman Curia consists of Congregations, Tribunals, Offices and Secretariats. All Congregations have the same juridical status. In case of conflict, the decision rests with the Apostolic Signatura. The Congregations are composed of cardinals nominated by the Pope. For matters of major interest, plenary sittings of the Congregations must include diocesan bishops named as members by the Pope. Special rules obtain for the Congregation for Religious in this matter, and for the Congregation of Propaganda (see below). Each Congregation is headed by a Cardinal Prefect, who is helped by a secretary and sub-secretary appointed by the Pope. Prefects and secretaries are appointed for five years but may be confirmed in office, and need to be so confirmed within three months of the election of a new Pope. The various officials cannot claim the right to promotion by virtue of their appointment. The Pope also appoints consultors, likewise for five years. Each department must transmit its statistics to the central office. Judicial matters are to be submitted to the competent tribunals. As regards the bishops, apart from their place in the plenary sessions of the Congregations as mentioned above, the Constitution orders that the wishes of episcopal councils and similar bodies are to be kept in mind. They are to be notified, if possible, of decrees which are of special interest to their dioceses, before such decrees are promulgated. Bishops are to receive quinquennial questionnaires, so that a general survey of the needs of the Church may be provided. Other languages than Latin may be used.

As regards *negotia mixta,* in which several jurisdictions are involved, the Congregations in question must consult together, under the Cardinal Prefect of the Congregation to which the matter was first submitted. In minor matters, Cardinal Prefects or secre-

taries consult together. As circumstances demand, the Prefects of the Congregations for Bishops, Clergy, Religious and Catholic Education meet at certain times. Further co-ordination is to be assured by the Cardinal Secretary of State, who convokes the heads of all departments (a sort of "cabinet meeting").

3. *The departments in detail.* The *Secretariat of State* (Papal Secretariat) is headed by the Cardinal Secretary of State, who is helped by a Substitute and an Assessor. The Secretary of State is the "Prime Minister" of the Pope, both for the universal Church and the Roman Curia. *Sede vacante,* the Substitute retains control of the office, being responsible to the College of Cardinals. The Papal Secretariat now includes the offices for Latin Letters, for minor briefs, for certain affairs of the diocese of Rome and for the collection of news. Along with the Council for Public Affairs, it takes special interest in the Council for Communications Media, and supervises the Department of Statistics. The Governor of Vatican City is responsible to the Secretary of State.

Council for Public Affairs of the Church. The "Consilium Sacrum pro Publicis Negotiis" is the new name for the former "Congregatio pro Negotiis Ecclesiasticis Extraordinariis". Its Prefect is the Secretary of State, who has here a special secretary and sub-secretary. Unlike the Secretariat of State, which can deal with all civil and religious matters, the Council is restricted to dealings with civil governments and diplomatic relationships.

The Congregation for the Doctrine of the Faith. The "Sacra Congregatio pro Doctrina Fidei" (formerly the "Holy Office") is charged with safeguarding faith and morals. Its officials include a *Promotor Iustitiae.* It examines new doctrines, promotes learned congresses on such matters and consults with the bishops of the regions concerned. Authors are not to be condemned unheard. Its jurisdiction embraces matrimonial matters involving the *privilegium fidei* and the dignity of the sacrament of penance. It keeps in touch with the Biblical Commission. As for the other departments, detailed rules will be published for its internal regulations.

The Congregation for the Eastern Churches. This is the former "Congregatio pro Ecclesia Orientali". The Eastern Patriarchs and the Prefect of the Secretariat for Christian Unity are *ex officio* members, and its consultors include the secretary of the latter organ. There is a section for each oriental rite. Its competence extends to matters in which Orientals are involved with "Latins". It has all the faculties which the other Congregations have for the Latin rite, though it transmits to the proper tribunals matters which concern them, while the rights of the Apostolic Penitentiary remain untouched. Latin missionaries come under its jurisdiction *qua* missionaries. On matters concerning Islam, it co-operates with the Secretariat for Non-Christians.

The Congregation for Bishops ("pro Episcopis"). This is the former "Congregatio Consistorialis". *Ex officio* members include the Prefects of the Council for Public Affairs, of the Congregations for the Doctrine of the Faith, for the Clergy and for Catholic Education, with the corresponding secretaries as consultors. It deals with the erection of new dioceses, in consultation with episcopal conferences, with the nomination of prelates (consulting the Council for Public Affairs where the civil government is interested), with episcopal administration and retirement, the holding of local synods and episcopal conferences (for which it supplies norms) and general directives for pastoral work. Attached to it are councils for the apostolate of emigrants, seamen, aviators, and nomads. The Prefect invites the heads of the Congregations for the Clergy and for Religious (and for Catholic Education where necessary) to consult on matters of interest to all clergy.

The Congregation for the Discipline of the Sacraments ("de disciplina Sacramentorum") leaves doctrine, rites, law-suits and matrimonial cases of nullity to the proper tribunals, but deals with such matters as dispensations from the eucharistic fast, questions of non-consummation of matrimony, the validity and obligations of major orders.

The Congregation of Rites ("Rituum") has two sections, one for (Latin) liturgy and other devotions, the other for processes of beatification and canonization. The reform of the liturgy is to be pursued by the special Council for the implementation of Vatican II's Constitution on the Sacred Liturgy, whose conclusions are to be submitted to a plenary session of section I of the Congregation of Rites. The *Promotor Fidei* and other judicial and medical experts continue as before. A bureau of hagiographical research (set up in 1930) remains at the disposition of both sections.

The Congregation for the Clergy ("pro Clericis"). This is the former "Congregatio Concilii" (i.e., of Trent, see above). It has three sections, one mainly concerned with priestly life and ministry, the second with preaching and catechetics, the third with the administration of temporal goods. The usual provisions are made for co-ordination with other Congregations (and episcopal conferences).

The Congregation for Religious and for Secular Institutes. The "Congregatio pro Religiosis et Institutibus saecularibus" corresponds to the older Congregation for Religious, but now with two sections. It deals with religious life and discipline (not, e.g., with education) and is to set up councils or conferences of major superiors.

The Congregation for Catholic Education ("pro Institutione catholica") is the new name for the Congregation for Seminaries and Universities. It embraces lay and clerical education, with one section for seminaries (diocesan and religious), another for universities and higher studies and a third for Catholic schools in general.

The Congregation for the Missions (or for the Propagation of the Faith), the former "De propaganda Fide", has the title of "Congregatio pro Gentium Evangelizatione", to which the ancient title "De propaganda Fide" is added as an alternative. Its *ex officio* members include the Presidents of the Secretariats for Christian Unity, for Non-Christians and for Non-believers. In major matters, plenary sessions include missionary bishops named as members by the Pope, possibly with deliberative voice. One of the tasks of the Congregation is to provide news of the missions. It also supervises missionary institutes in the home countries as regards rules and administration, in keeping with the rules laid down by the Congregations for Religious and for Education. Financial accounts are to be laid before the papal ministry of finance.

The Secretariat for Christian Unity ("ad christianorum unitatem fovendam") includes as *ex officio* members the Prefects of the Congregations for the Oriental Churches and for the Missions, with corresponding consultors. To its normal duties is added the task of implementing the conciliar Decrees on Ecumenism. It also deals with matters which affect Jews from the religious aspect.

The Secretariat for Non-Christians ("pro non christianis") fosters dialogue with all those who at least "have a religious sense". It has an office attached for dealings with Moslems.

The Secretariat for Non-Believers ("pro non credentibus") studies atheism and explores the possibility of dialogue.

The Council for the Laity ("Consilium de Laicis") and the Commission "Justice and Peace", according to the norms already laid down in the motu proprio *Catholicam Christi Ecclesiam* of 6 January 1967, pursue the tasks outlined in the Pastoral Constitution of Vatican II on the Church in the Modern World.

The judiciary comprises three tribunals. The *Supreme Court* is the "Supremum Tribunal Signaturae Apostolicae", to which for instance appeal may be made from decisions of the various departments of the Curia, or in cases of conflict of jurisdiction.

The Rota ("Sacra Romana Rota") remains the tribunal for dealing with cases of matrimonial nullity.

The Sacred Penitentiary ("Sacra Paenitentiaria Apostolica") deals with matters of the internal forum, including non-sacramental matters such as indulgences.

The "Offices", which with the Papal Secretariat and Council for Public Affairs, the Congregations, the Secretariats and the Tribunals is the fifth main division of the Curia, are five in number. The Apostolic Chancellory ("Cancellaria Apostolica") draws up all apostolic constitutions, briefs, bulls, etc. Thus there disappear: the Apostolic Datary, the Chancellory of Briefs, the Secretariats of Briefs to Princes and for Latin Letters. The Ministry of Finance ("Praefectura rerum oeconomicarum S. Sedis") is a commission of cardinals, aided by experts, including an Auditor General *(Ratiocinator Generalis)* which supervises Church expenditure and presents an annual budget and balance-sheets. The *Camera Apostolica,* under the Cardinal Chamberlain, administers the goods of the Holy See, *sede vacante*. The *Administratio Patrimonii Apostolicae Sedis,* for which taxes are levied by the Ministry of Finance, looks after papal property in particular. The *Praefectura Palatii Apostolici* is a fusion of the Majordomo, the Office of the *Maestro di Camera* and the "Congregatio Ceremonialis".

It is concerned with State visits of and to the Pope, papal audiences and travels, etc. The only new office (along with the Finance Ministry) is that of Statistics *(Ecclesiae Rationarium or Officium Statisticum),* which collects and co-ordinates statistics from the parish level upwards throughout the Church.

Thus in the reform of the Curia, the main *vota* of Vatican II — internationalization, the presence of diocesan bishops, consultation of laymen — have been implemented. A further step, if not exactly towards "decentralization", at least away from "permanent civil service" rigidity, is the termination of office, at least in principle, every five years, or at the death of the Pope. The speeding-up of procedures is promised, and though there is still a certain amount of overlapping between the various Congregations — as is inevitable, since, for instance, religious orders interest Propaganda, Bishops, Clergy and Education in various ways and degrees — and some division of functions which is traditional rather than obvious — such as the distribution of marriage cases between the Congregation for the Faith, for the Sacraments and the Rota — sufficient provision has been made for consultation and co-ordination. "Decentralization", which means primarily that the exercise of the papal primacy through the Curia should take place with due regard for the college of bishops, is chiefly assured by the presence of diocesan bishops at plenary sessions of the Congregations, and by the consideration to be given to the wishes of episcopal conferences — of which the Synod of Bishops will, no doubt, be a competent and impressive mouthpiece.

See also *Avignon Exile, Bishop* III, *Cardinal, Censorship, Church* III, *Ecclesiastical Law* III, *Ecclesiastical Tribunals.*

BIBLIOGRAPHY. J. H. Bangen, *Die Römische Kurie* (1854); M.-D. Bouix, *Tractatus de Curia Romana* (1859); F. M. Cappello, *De Curia Romana iuxta reformationem a Pio X sapientissime inductam,* 2 vols. (1911–13); A. Monin, *De Curia Romana* (1912); E. Hugues de Ragnau, *The Vatican. The Centre of the Government of the Catholic World* (1913); M. Martin, *The Roman Curia As It Now Exists. An Account of its Departments* (1913); B. Ojetti, *De Curia Romana* (1916); G. Trezzi, *La posizione giuridica della Santa Sede nel diritto internazionale* (1929); V. Martin, *Les cardinaux et la curie* (1930); P. Torquebiau, "Curie romaine", *Dictionnaire du Droit Canonique,* IV, cols. 971–1000; E. L. Heston, *The Holy See at Work* (1950).

Kevin Smyth

D

DEACON

The diaconate is the lowest degree of the consecrated hierarchy in the Church's visible structure; the term means doing a particular service. It is an office that figures in the earliest pages of Church history, and the fact that the NT uses the Greek word διάκονος in a strict sense to designate this ecclesiastical office shows us that service is its special characteristic. Everywhere in the NT the word διάκονος means a servant or an official minister.

It is possible to discern the character of the diaconal office in the Acts of the Apostles, the letters of St. Paul, and the earliest monuments of Christian tradition. Though Acts 6:1–6 does not use the actual word διάκονοι, it shows deacons being appointed, by the laying on of hands (χειροτονία), to administer the goods of the Hellenistic community on a permanent basis. These "seven men" are found preaching the word of God and conferring baptism in Acts 6:10; 8:5; 8:35, etc. In St. Justin's liturgy deacons dispense the Eucharist to those attending the sacrifice and also to those who are absent (*Apol.,* I, 65). St. Paul speaks of them as forming a hierarchical rank in the Church (Phil 1:1) and requires that they possess such personal qualities as will assure them real authority in their service of the faith, thanks to their blameless manner of life (1 Tim 3:8–12). Tradition confirms this triple office of the deacon: liturgical, doctrinal and charitable.

On the other hand tradition constantly insists that deacons are helpers of the bishops in the service of the Church. St. Ignatius of Antioch calls them "his counsellors" (*Philadelphia,* 4; *Smyrn.,* 12, 2); he declares that they are "entrusted with the ministry of Jesus Christ" (*Ephesus,* 6, 1) and that they "are not ministers of food and drink but servants of the Church of God" (*Trall.,* 2, 3); accordingly they must be reverenced "as God's commandment" (*Smyrn.,* 8, 1). St. Polycarp calls them "ministers of God and Christ and not of men" (*Philippians,* 5, 2). St. Cyprian says that deacons were instituted by the apostles, "as ministers of their episcopate and of the Church" (*Ep.,* 3), whence they are entrusted with "the *diaconia* of sacred administration" (*Ep.,* 52). The *Traditio Apostolica* states that "they are not ordained for the priesthood but for the service of the bishop, to do such things as he may command" (n. 9). And the *Didascalia Apostolorum* says that deacons must be the ears, the mouth, the heart and the soul of the bishop (1, II, 26, 3–7); accordingly they must resemble him, though in a "more active" manner, so as to "accomplish the truth, filled with the example of Christ" (1, III, 13, 1–6). Today the Roman Pontifical says that deacons are chosen "for the service of the Church of God", that their task is "to serve the altar, to baptize, and to preach", and that consequently they shall be called "fellow-workers and fellow-ministers of the body and blood of the Lord".

Bearing in mind that the Eucharist is the central mystery of the Church and that all ecclesiastical ministry proceeds from the altar, we may say that the hierarchical rank of the diaconate, according to the constant tenor of tradition, stands halfway between the general priesthood of the faithful and the special priesthood of bishops and priests. Accordingly the diaconate is "the order instituted by the apostles in the name of God and Christ, whose fully accredited representatives they were, in order to actuate and direct the task of the priestly people, which is to offer itself unreservedly to God" (Colson).

This explains why tradition considered the hierarchy of bishops, priests and deacons, with their different offices and powers, as at once in their leadership of the eucharistic community, and hence always maintained the sacramental character of the diaconate. It demanded the same exclusive dedication from all the sacred ministers. And it was in this perspective that the law of the Latin Church imposed celibacy on bishops, priests and deacons from the 4th century on.

At the present time there are considerable differences in discipline between the Eastern and the Latin Churches: the former has preserved the diaconate as a permanent and separate rank, both among the parish clergy and in the monasteries, whereas the latter only allows the bishop to confer the order on those who propose to go on to the priesthood (*CIC,* can. 973) and requires all clerics in major orders to observe celibacy (can. 132).

The Second Vatican Council provided an opportunity to discuss the revival of the diaconate as a permanent status. This matter had in fact been raised four centuries earlier at the Council of Trent, where the Fathers discussed the restoration of all the orders below the priesthood. In fact, in a schema which adapted the functions of the various orders to the needs of the day (but which was not debated), the Council suggested that in future "ministries shall be carried out only by persons ordained for each". This was to be done "so that the functions of the sacred orders may be restored, according to the practice of the ancient Church", and "so that heretics may not dismiss them as superfluous" (session XXIII, can. 17 de ref.). Despite its limited purpose, however, the Tridentine decree remained a dead letter. It had no influence on further developments.

Recent proposals to restore the diaconate have given rise to a good deal of theological reflection. It is pointed out, for example,

that ordination to the diaconate gives the candidate certain duties, but no essential powers beyond those conferred by baptism. Moreover, scarcely one diaconal function can be mentioned which the Church may not also confer extrasacramentally. The same may be said of the grace bestowed by ordination to the diaconate: since the functions of that order may be conferred outside the sacrament, we must admit that the Holy Spirit also gives the appropriate supernatural aid outside the sacrament. And in fact laymen carry out liturgical functions recently introduced in connection with the renewal of the liturgy — reading, commenting, leading the congregation in prayer, etc. — and exercise the apostolate or the ministry of the word, without any need of the ordination which is proper to the clerical state.

But the functions assigned by tradition to the diaconate show that it is an office with many functions which remains within the basic unity of the ministry performed on behalf of the priestly people. Hence the real question is not the opportuneness of its revival, but that of developing and determining its mediatory function between special and general priesthood. Now to that end one must be prepared to consider having many different forms of the one permanent diaconate, according to which function or ministry happens to predominate, all invested with a certain dignity and all necessary to the Church's pastoral work. No sounder theological argument, in fact, for restoring the diaconate as a permanent rank in the Latin Church can be found than the general law of grace in the sacramental order, according to which the rite must bestow the grace it signifies.

Doctrinal reflection does not stop at this point. Thorny questions arise when one tries to determine how diaconal functions are related to the activities of laymen in the Church. Nor is it much easier to demarcate the ministry of the deacon from that of the priest.

The Second Vatican Council reaffirms, in its Dogmatic Constitution on the Church, the essential features of the diaconate in accordance with tradition. Deacons, the lowest rank in the hierarchy, become such by the laying on of hands and are fortified by sacramental grace; they are not ordained to be priests but to serve the people in union with the bishop and his priests, through the liturgy, the word of God, and works of charity.

So far as discipline is concerned the Council has advanced a step beyond the present rules of canon law (cf. can. 741; 845, § 2; 1147, § 4; and 1274, § 2) by considerably increasing the liturgical functions proper to the deacon in the Latin Church; but whether they shall be exercised is left to the discretion of authority. Some of these powers are important: for example, the right to keep the Eucharist, to assist at and bless marriages, to preside over the worship and prayer of the faithful, to administer sacramentals, and to conduct funeral rites.

The Council has solemnly announced that in principle the diaconate may be restored as a separate and permanent rank in the hierarchy of the Latin Church. How this is done will depend on the decision of each episcopal conference when sanctioned by the Sovereign Pontiff. But that principle has been proclaimed for entirely practical reasons: the conciliar text "takes into account the fact that given the present discipline in the Latin Church there are many areas where few are available to discharge these functions, so necessary to the life of the Church". On the other hand, whereas the law of celibacy continues to bind young men aspiring to the diaconate, a notable exception is made: with the consent of the Roman Pontiff, it is now permissible to ordain "men of mature years even if they be married".

The paths have been smoothed for the diaconate in the Latin Church since the Second Vatican Council. The change in the self-understanding of the Church signalled by the Council will bring with it a changed notion of Church offices and functions. The task now is to combine the long-standing tradition with the *aggiornamento,* and much time and courage will be needed before the diaconate will be ripe for its new juridical definitions.

BIBLIOGRAPHY. J. W. Deidle, *Der Diakonat in der Katholischen Kirche, dessen hieratische Würde und geschichtliche Entwicklung* (1884); H. W. Beyer, "διάκονος", *TWNT,* II (1935), pp. 81–93, E. T.: *Theological Dictionary of the New Testament,* II (1965); B. Reiche, *Diakonie, Festfreude und Zelos* (1951); K. E. Kirk, ed., *The Apostolic Ministry* (1947); H. Krimm, *Das Diakonat in der frühkatholischen Kirche* (1953); W. Schamoni, *Married Men as Ordained Deacons* (1955); M. Simon, *St. Stephen and the Hellenists in the Primitive Church* (1958); P. Winninger, *Vers un renouveau du diaconat* (1959); J. Colson, *La fonction diaconate aux origines de l'Église* (1960); A. Kerkvoorde, *Où en est le problème du diaconat?* (1961); K. Rahner and H. Vorgrimler, eds., *Diaconia in Christo. Über die Erneuerung des Diakonates* (1962); N. Jubany, *El diaconado y el celibato eclesiástico* (1964).

Narciso Jubany

DEATH

1. *Introduction.* It cannot be said that the theology of death usually receives in scholastic theology the attention which the theme deserves. People think they know from everyday experience what death is, and quickly turn to the question of what comes after death, as though the theology of death only began there. Yet death necessarily also contains within itself all the mysteries of man. As the Constitution *Gaudium et Spes* of Vatican II notes, it is the point where man in the most radical way becomes a question for himself, a question which God himself must answer. Furthermore, Christianity is the religion which regards the death of a certain man as the most fundamental event of the history of salvation and of world history. Finally, death is not something which happens to a man alongside much else. Death is the event in which the very man himself becomes his definitive self. It is therefore certainly and eminently a topic for theology.

Death is an occurrence which concerns a man as a whole. Now man is a unity of nature and person, i.e., a being who, on the one hand, even prior to personal free decision is constituted in existence in a certain way which has its determinate laws and consequently necessary development, and, on the other hand, disposes of himself freely, so that he is finally what he freely wills to consider himself to be. Death is therefore at once a natural and a personal occurrence. If biology does not really know why all life, and in particular man, dies, then the reason for death which is given by faith — the moral catastrophe of mankind (Rom 5) — is the only reason propounded for the undeniable universality of death among men. And this theological reason also furnishes the certainty that even throughout the future the inevitability of death will be one of the necessary forces dominating human reality, and that death can never be abolished.

2. *Magisterium and Scripture.* Before attempting a definition of death, it will be well to mention the pronouncements of the magiste-

rium expressly concerning death. Death is a consequence of original sin (*D* 101, 109 a, 175, *DS* 413, *D* 788 f.). This does not of course mean that if there were no original or personal sin man would have continued in perpetuity his biological life in time, or that before "Adam" there was no death in the animal kingdom. Even without sin man would have ended his biological, historical life in space and time, and would have entered into his definitive condition before God by means of a free act engaging his whole life. Death as we know it now, as part of man's constitution subject to concupiscence, in darkness, weakness and obscurity regarding its actual nature (see below 3), is a consequence of sin. This does not mean that we can necessarily be successful in distinguishing between death as personal fulfilment of life and death as a manifestation of sin. Consequently all men in original sin are subject to the law of death (*D* 789). Even those who according to 1 Cor 15:51 will be found alive at Christ's second coming, must attain eternal life by a radical "change" which in substance is the same as death. With death man's individual history finally ends (cf. Lk 16:26; Jn 9:4; 2 Cor 5:10; Gal 6:10). The doctrine of apocatastasis has always been rejected by the Church (*D* 211; cf. *D* 778, 530, 693). At Vatican I a definition was projected regarding the impossibility of justification after death (*Coll. Lac.,* VII, 567). In this way any doctrine of transmigration of souls is rejected as incompatible with the conception of the uniqueness and decisive dignity of human history and the nature of freedom as definitive decision.

3. *Definition of death.* a) Christian tradition gives a provisional description of death in the phrase "separation of body and soul". This implies that the spiritual principle of life in man, his "soul", assumes in death a different relation to what we are accustomed to call the "body". But it does not say much more than this. Consequently the phrase is not a definition of death adequate to metaphysical or theological requirements. For it is absolutely silent about the characteristic feature of death, that it is a human event concerning man as a whole and as a spiritual person, an event which concerns his very essence: his definitive free, personal self-realization. This must certainly not be

conceived as occurring "with" or "after" death, but as an intrinsic factor of death itself. Whilst plants and animals "perish", only man "dies" in the proper sense.

The above-mentioned description of death is also inadequate because the concept of separation remains obscure and leaves room for some very important distinctions. For since the soul is united to the body, it clearly must also have some relationship to that whole of which the body is a part, that is, to the totality which constitutes the unity of the material universe. This material unity of the world is neither a merely conceptual sum of individual things nor the mere unity of an external interaction of individual things on one another. As the soul by its substantial union with the body as its essential form also has a relationship to this radical unity of the universe, the separation of body and soul in death does not mean the absolute cessation of this relation to the world so that the soul (as people like to think in a neo-Platonic way) becomes absolutely a-cosmic, and otherworldly. It is much truer to say that the termination of its relation to the body, by which it maintains and forms the latter's structure and delimits it from the whole of the world, means a deeper and more comprehensive openness in which this comprehensive relation to the universe is more fully realized. In death the human soul enters into a much closer and more intimate relationship to that ground of the unity of the universe which is hard to conceive yet is very real, and in which all things in the world communicate through their mutual influence upon each other. And this is possible precisely because the soul is no longer bound to an individual bodily structure.

This conception also follows from the scholastic doctrine that the substantial act of the soul as *forma corporis* (*D* 481) is not really distinct from it, and therefore could only absolutely cease if the soul itself were to cease to exist, and were not immortal, as philosophy shows and the Church's dogma affirms. A substantial relation to matter of this kind, identical with the soul itself and not one of its "accidents", can change but cannot simply cease. It must also be taken into consideration that even before death the spiritual soul through its embodiment is already in principle open to the whole world and is therefore never a closed monad without windows but is always in communication with the whole of the world. Such a comprehensive relation to the world means that the soul, by surrendering its limited bodily structure in death, becomes open towards the universe and a co-determining factor of the universe precisely in the latter's character as the ground of the personal life of other incarnate spiritual beings. Indications of this are, for example, certain parapsychological phenomena, the Church's doctrine of purgatory, of the intercession of the saints, etc. Purgatory, for instance, would mean that the soul, even after surrendering its bodily structure and through that surrender, experiences in its freely posited self-determination more clearly and acutely its own harmony or disharmony with the objectively right order of the world and, conversely, itself contributes to determining the latter.

b) Another definition of death states that death is neither the end of man's existence nor a mere transition from one form of reality to another having something essentially in common with it, namely, indefinite temporal sequence; death is the beginning of eternity, if indeed and so far as we may use the term "beginning" at all in regard to this eternity. The totality of created reality, the world, grows in and through incarnate spiritual persons, and the world is in a certain sense their body. Their death slowly brings the universe to its own final stage. Yet this immanent maturing of the world towards its consummation, like that of the individual human being, is at the same time, in a mysterious dialectical unity, a rupture, an ending from without, by an unpredictable intervention of God through his coming in judgment, of which "no one knows the day or the hour" (Mk 13:31). Man's death is, therefore, an occurrence passively undergone, which man as a person faces powerlessly as coming from outside. But it is also and essentially personal self-fulfilment, "one's own death", an act which a man interiorly performs; death itself (rightly understood) is the act, not simply an attitude the human being adopts towards death but which remains extrinsic to it.

Death, therefore, as the end of the man as a spiritual person, is an active consummation from within brought about by the person himself, a maturing self-realization which embodies the result of what a man has made of himself during life, the achievement of total personal self-possession, a real effectuation of self, the fullness of freely produced personal reality. At the same time the death of man in his unity but as the end of his biological life is simultaneously, and in a way which affects the whole man, an irruption from without, a destruction, so that a man's own death from within through the act of the person is at the same time an event of the most radical spoliation of man, highest activity and greatest passivity in one. And in view of man's substantial unity it is not possible simply to divide these two sides of the one death between soul and body, for this would dissolve the very essence of human death.

c) Because of this ambiguous duality, death is essentially obscure, i.e., it is not possible, humanly speaking, to say with certainty in the concrete case whether the full term of life reached in death is not in fact the emptiness and futility of the individual in question as a person, which till then was concealed, or whether the apparent emptiness in death is only the outward aspect of a true plenitude, the liberation of the person's true essence. Because of this obscurity, death can be the punishment and expression of sin, the culmination of sin, mortal sin in the proper sense, or the culmination of the whole act of a man's life in which he surrenders himself in faith to the incomprehensible mystery of God, which has its most radical manifestation in man's dispossession by death. In this definition of death there is no question of asserting that this essence is realized precisely at the chronological instant of medical "extinction". Death in this view is an event which is ultimately identical with the one history of man's freedom in its totality, which creates man's definitive condition, inasmuch as this event is completed "at" (rather than "by") the end, which is marked by extinction in the medical sense.

4. *Christ's death*. Since Jesus Christ became man of the fallen race of Adam and assumed "the flesh of sin" (Rom 8:3), he entered human life in a situation in which it reaches its fulfilment only by passing through death in its ambiguous, obscure form. Consequently he took death upon himself inasmuch as in the existing order of things it is an expression and manifestation of the fallen state of creation in both angels and man. He did not simply offer a certain satisfaction for sin.

He enacted and suffered death itself, which is the expression, manifestation and revelation of sin in the world. He did this in absolute liberty as the act and the revelation of that divine grace which divinized the life of his humanity and by reason of his divine person of necessity belonged to him. In that way, however, death became something absolutely different from what it would be in a human being who did not possess in his own right the life of grace and perfect freedom secure from any weakness of concupiscence. It is precisely by its darkness that the death of Christ becomes the expression and embodiment of his loving obedience, the free transference of his entire created existence to God. What was the manifestation of sin becomes, without its darkness being lifted, the manifestation of an assent to the will of the Father which is the negation of sin. By Christ's death his spiritual reality, which he possessed from the beginning and actuated in a life which was brought to consummation by his death, becomes open to the whole world and is inserted into this whole world in its ground as a permanent determination of a real ontological kind. (Cf. on this feature of human death in its realization by Christ, the biblical affirmation regarding Christ's descent into hell.)

The world as a whole and as the scene of personal human actions has, therefore, become different from what it would have been if Christ had not died. Possibilities of a real ontological nature have been opened up for the personal action of all other men which would not have existed without the death of our Lord. By that death his human reality and the grace which was definitively ratified by the real concrete human freedom precisely of his death, became a determining feature of the whole cosmos. To the innermost reality of the world there belongs what we call Jesus Christ in his life and death, what was poured out over the cosmos at the moment when the vessel of his body was shattered in death, and Christ actually became even in his humanity, what he had always been by his dignity, the heart of the universe, the innermost centre of all created reality.

5. *Dying*. Knowledge, even if mostly an implicit knowledge, of the inevitability of death, though not of its when and where, intrinsically determines the whole of life. In this knowledge death is always already present in human life and only by this does life assume its full gravity, through the necessity of its activities, the uniqueness of its opportunities and the irrevocability of its decisions. Just as personal failure before the absolute claim experienced in conscience is the most poignant, so death is the most tangible expression of man's finitude. But precisely in the explicitly conscious presentiment of death in natural mortal anguish it is apparent that life itself points limitlessly beyond death. For in mortal anguish death does not appear (as in the mere fear of death) only as a possibly painful single event at the end of life, but rather as an event of such a kind that in face of it man is freed from his attachment to all that is individual and he is confronted with the truth, namely, that in death the fundamental decision which a man has made in regard to God, the world and himself, and which dominates his whole life, receives its definitive character (Jn 9:4; Lk 16:26; 2 Cor 5:10; D 457, 464, 493a, 530f., 693). Man hopes that at the same time it means fulfilment, yet he remains uncertain whether this is achieved. The will of man maturing from within to the totality and finality of his attitude to life is always alienated by the dispersion of bodily existence and is robbed of its power of disposing of all in a coherent whole. He therefore cannot bring to open, unambiguous certainty the totality of a definitively composed personal life which he strives for. Consequently the act of human life remains essentially impenetrable in face of death, threatened from without, and in death finally comes to its sharpest contradiction, the simultaneity of highest will and extreme weakness, a lot which is actively achieved and passively suffered, plenitude and emptiness.

This fundamentally obscure and ambiguous situation of death is the consequence of original sin which affects all men and becomes in them a natural expression of the fall of man in Adam from his grace-given immortality (cf. Rom 5:12; D 101, 175, 793), the clear fulfilment of an earthly existence transfigured by communion with God. According to whether a man wills autonomously to understand and master this death, due to original sin and beyond his clear power of control, which he accomplishes as a personal action throughout his life, or whether he holds himself open in death with unconditional readiness in faith for the incomprehensible God, his death will become either a personal repetition and confirmation of the sinful emancipation of the first human being and so the culmination of sin, definitive mortal sin, or it will be the personal repetition and appropriation of Christ's obedient death (Phil 2:8) by which Christ inserted his divine life into the world itself. In this way it becomes the culmination of man's salutary activity. Conformation to the death of Christ, anticipated throughout life in faith and sacraments, is now personally accomplished and becomes a final blessed "dying in the Lord" (Rev 14:13), in which the experience of the end becomes the dawn of perfect fulfilment.

See also Being II, *Asceticism, Martyrdom, Resurrection* II, *Apocatastasis, Transmigration of Souls, Last Things, Concupiscence, Immortality, Body, Soul, Purgatory, Hell* II.

BIBLIOGRAPHY. J. A. Fischer, *Studien zum Todesgedanken in der Alten Kirche* (1954); H. Volk, *Der Tod in der Sicht des christlichen Glaubens* (1958); E. Wasmuth, *Vom Sinn des Todes* (1959); P. Althaus, *Die letzten Dinge* (8th ed., 1961); M. Heidegger, *Being and Time* (1962); J. M. Demske, *Sein, Mensch und Tod. Das Todesproblem bei M. Heidegger* (1963); R. Troisfontaines, *I Do Not Die* (1963); L. Boros, *The Moment of Truth. Mysterium Mortis* (1965); K. Rahner, *On the Theology of Death,* Quaestiones Disputatae 2 (2nd ed., 1965).

Karl Rahner

DECISION

1. *Introduction.* Freedom is the self-determination which stems from the transcendental openness of the spirit for the absolute and unconditional. Hence it appears essentially as freedom from outside coercion and thus as freedom or indifference with regard to possibilities that are open to it. It is *liberum arbitrium,* the power of *choosing.* This does not mean that the possibilities of choice are always of equal value. In the most important choice to be made by finite freedom, the choice between good and evil, one particular course is commanded and another forbidden, which, though it remains possible, means that freedom fails of its goal and is diminished.

Apart from utterly indifferent matters, every choice (and all the more so, the more important the decision) is characterized by the impossibility of a total rational assessment of the pros and cons of the actual possibilities. This is also true of moral choice, since finite reflection does not find the good merely good, and evil presents itself with positive aspects. The ultimate reason is that the rational investigation is not just an independent prior condition of the act of choice but an integral moment of it (or of a choice also prior to it). Further, we must choose to make this choice (and not merely choose its object), though this may be done unconsciously, the decision to make the choice being prescribed by custom, convention, etc. This "basic choice" is, no doubt, known in the self-transparency of the spirit, but it cannot be objectified consciously again. The effort would lead to a regress *ad infinitum.* Hence choice is not an irrational procedure, but it surpasses, or, as it may be, provides the first basis for rational reflection (on self).

In this sense, every choice has the character of a decision. This essential element is particularly noticeable where it is clear that one cannot evade a certain choice (as one might perhaps wish to, having had experience of its unaccountability) — except by a new choice, that of refusal to choose. It is clearest of all where the inevitability is also a matter of time, that is, when there is a deadline for decision. "Decision, though freedom is its presupposition, is forced upon us." (H. Lübbe.)

2. *History of the problem.* The Greek theory was that man should be a "spectator" — though this attitude must be seen as a reaction, like tragedy and the mystery religions, against the oppressive and universal cosmic law of ἀνάγκη or τύχη. Jewish-Christian thought, inspired by religious experience, introduced the concept of decision to the Western mind. Here man is seen as essentially a being faced with decision. Cf., for instance, "See, I have set before you this day life and good, death and evil. If you obey the commandments of the Lord your God, ... by loving the Lord ..." etc. (Deut 30:15f.) "Today, when you hear his voice, do not harden your hearts ... as long as it is called 'today' ..." (Heb 3:7–15.)

An hour is set for decision, because the call of God's grace can be missed, being unrepeatable. And the necessity of decision dominates the whole of human life in the general sense that it is limited by death. This does not mean that life is merely a testing-ground or time of trial for something totally different, as if the world was only a stage on which we played a part. Life itself becomes in the decision the definitive thing, man's eternity; salvation and loss do not lie on the periphery, but are the very makings of what he is and has become. This truth is transmitted above all in Augustinian and Franciscan schools of thought and in the theology of the Reformation, till it finds in the 19th century its most effective spokesman in S. Kierkegaard (along with Newman and later Blondel). Through Kierkegaard it came to dominate existentialism.

3. *Description.* A description of decision must place it at the centre of the person, by which knowledge is also to some extent determined, though this does not necessarily imply an irrational voluntarism, because the ontological self-determination of the basic act of finite freedom is to be distinguished from subsequent reflection in terms of categories. (And vice versa, where this reflection is pushed to the point of an adequate "scientific" explanation of decision, we have reached the level of ideology.) At the same time, decision demands reflection — since it is only by articulating and thinking out his transcendental self-realization in human categories that man can really bring it about — though such reflection cannot eliminate the element of decision. For this decision is not just concerned with the general norms under which the case for decision is to be subsumed, as "prudence" demands. It must use "the logic of existential knowledge" (K. Rahner) to achieve a "discernment of spirits" (St. Ignatius Loyola) which will go beyond (not contrary to, as situation ethics suggests) the general norms to make the call of "the hour" audible as such. But such knowledge, for all the certainty it gives, provides no safe-deposit of security to which we hold the key. It is, on the contrary, an element of this unavoidable decision itself.

Above all, this reflection provides no security about the "spirit" of the decision itself, about its ultimately determinative motivation. This is due to the very nature of freedom itself, as also to the fact that the individual's decision is also determined to some extent by those of his environment. It is further complicated by original sin, which places each man in a ruinous situation (not simply eliminated by the redemption), unable to tell absolutely how far he merely accepts the situation resignedly as the inevitable co-determinant of his decision, or how far he willingly enters into it and ratifies it.

Thus the play of reflection and decision, of self-assurance and act, points on to the relationship between the individual decisions and that basic decision *(option fondamentale)* which is made at the core of the person and is responsible for his essential way of self-determination — by which he makes himself what he is. It is this which produces the individual decisions, but in such a way that it is only explicated and realized in them, and the individual decisions may just as well be described as practising for and leading to the basic one. This incompleteness which marks temporal being and becoming allows us to note the merely relative value of previous decisions, to go beyond them and even to abandon and reverse them. Nonetheless, freedom is bent on making an absolute and unconditional decision. The basic decision does not hover, as it were, in a timeless region above the individual decisions, though it cannot be definitely identified with any of them — say, with the last decision up to now, or even with the definitely final decision.

But there are crucial, "decisive" moments, and the final, irrevocable situation of man is therefore of supreme importance. At death, the nature of decision is most vividly manifest. (Here death need not coincide with what is medically the end; being man's "last word" about himself, essentially a human act, it may have already been pronounced beforehand.) Death is indivisibly action and passivity, above all a call to renunciation, like every decision. It issues from the whole experience of life, of which it bears the stamp, but by affirming or revoking the past, gives life its definitive character. And here once more there is no totally conscious lucidity in the demarcation, either for the dying man or for the looker-on. The darkness and brightness in which inward knowledge of the self is wrapped allow of no final analysis. Here the temptation which besets every decisive situation stands out at its clearest: despair, flight (including the escape into "theorizing"), defiance and disintegration — as does the due answer: resoluteness, generosity, self-surrender and hope in the God of life, who guarantees the definitive wholeness of salvation.

If, then, death is where decision shows up

most clearly, death is also and above all the place for the central basic act of man, the religious act, and what has been said of death can be applied at once to the act of faith, which involves an irremediable tension between the *rationabile obsequium* (the *praeambula fidei*) and the *sacrificium intellectus,* and in both of these, between the "act" of man and the grace which evokes and sustains them. This is what is studied in the *analysis fidei.*

See also *History* I, *Existence* II, III, *Situation* II, *Concupiscence, Death, Religious Act, Faith* IV.

BIBLIOGRAPHY. J. Fuchs, *Situation und Ethik* (1952); C. von Krockow, *Die Entscheidung. Eine Untersuchung über Ernst Jünger, Carl Schmitt, Martin Heidegger* (1958); K. Rahner, *The Dynamic Element in the Church,* Quaestiones Disputatae 12 (1964); H. Lübbe, "Zur Theorie der Entscheidung", *Colloquium Philosophicum* (1965), pp. 118–40.

Jörg Splett

DEISM

Deism designates a defective form of thought with regard to the relationship between God and the world. It reduces God's function as ground of the world's existence to his giving it its first impulse. According to the classical comparison of God with a clock-maker, which is found as early as Nicolaus of Oresmes (d. 1382), God wound up the clock of the world once and for all at the start, so that it can run on and produce world history without his creative conservation and his concurrent influence to bring about the activity of the creature. Any free action of God's grace in man's history (by the word of revelation, by miracles to signal revelation, etc.) is therefore radically excluded.

This deistic conception of God corresponds to a basic development of the modern mentality. Science has provided a natural explanation for many phenomena which were once attributed to a miraculous intervention of God; there is no need to trouble God any longer to act as stop-gap wherever natural causes fail — for the moment — to explain things, as Newton, for instance, still did with regard to deviations in the orbits of the planets. To this extent the deistic solution is justified. It leaves too many things out of account, however; and it is not radical enough. The idea of a first cause

on the periphery of the world should really have been abandoned when the Copernican system replaced the Ptolemaic. The new theory of the universe, however, is obscured by misunderstandings down to the present day, and has not been well enough exploited for it to have penetrated the general consciousness (cf. J. A. T. Robinson, *Honest to God,* 1963). Kant subjected the deistic view of the production of the world to a devastating criticism (*Critique of Pure Reason,* B 480 ff. = 4th antinomy).

This criticism of a merely horizontal view of causality does not, however, affect that of classical metaphysics, which considers that the "vertical" creative and conservational action of the "first" cause is needed, not merely for the initial origin of a series of causes, but for the continued existence of each of its intrinsically contingent elements. The transcendence of God in this view is not that he is localized outside the world: it is ontologically supra-mundane while being at the same time most intimately and indissolubly immanent to everything produced by this type of causality. God is not a power in the background, but the inmost ground of being — as the abyss of mystery. This concept gives due weight to what Heidegger calls the "ontological difference" (between being and beings) which deism neglected, or, from another point of view, to the analogy between unconditioned being and conditioned beings and their modes of activity.

Basically, the philosophical refutation of deism is already given in the essential nature of real meta-physical knowledge (as, for instance, in knowledge of the contingent *as such*), since this leads with compelling force over to the essentially different order ("higher" or "deeper", as one wills) of God's transcendent and immanent relationship of maker to the world. Deism is given the lie most powerfully and effectively by the God of Israel and the God of Jesus Christ, since his free acts of saving grace give effect and testimony to his transcendent immanence in the world and its history.

See also *History, Salvation* III, *Absolute and Contingent, Analogy of Being, Transcendence.*

BIBLIOGRAPHY. A. S. Farrar, *A Critical History of Free Thought* (1862); L. Stephen, *History of English Thought in the Eighteenth Century,* I (1876); W. Dilthey, *Gesammelte Schriften,* II (1914; 7th ed., 1964), pp. 90 ff., 246 ff.; E. Troeltsch, *Gesammelte*

Werke, IV (1925), pp. 429 ff., 845 ff.; R. Pettazzoni, *The Allknowing God* (1956); W. Philipp, *Das Werden der Aufklärung in theologiegeschichtlicher Sicht* (1957); G. van der Leeuw, *Religion in Essence and Manifestation. A Study in Phenomenology,* 2 vols. (2nd ed., 1964).

Walter Kern

DEMYTHOLOGIZATION

I. General. II. Existential Interpretation.

I. General

1. *The problem.* Bultmann was not the first to affirm the existence of myths in the NT. It was he, however, who centred the theological and exegetical problem on the question of the necessity of a demythologization. And it is because of what he sought to do that the problem of demythologization occupies many theologians and exegetes at the present time.

The idea of the necessity of demythologization is already found several times in Bultmann's early works. It was in 1941, however, that he gave it systematic exposition under the title *New Testament and Mythology.* This lecture-manifesto was to have considerable repercussions. The discussions that it provoked are not yet over. The problem of demythologization still remains extremely topical.

Bultmann's fundamental idea was that of the abyss which separates the world in which the NT was conceived and expressed, from our own. The world-view to which the NT is tributary is mythical, whereas the one to which we refer explicitly or implicitly is scientific. According to Bultmann we are to regard as mythical the mode of representation in which what is not of this world, the divine, appears as though it were of this world, as human, the beyond as something here below; a mode of representation according to which, for example, God's transcendence is thought of as spatial remoteness, and in virtue of which ritual worship is viewed as an action transmitting by material means forces which are not material. Modern thought, on the contrary, inevitably conditioned by science, is characterized by the principle of immanence, according to which the reason for phenomena cannot be sought except in the phenomena themselves, without any possibility of a gap in their succession.

It appears evident to Bultmann that the NT world-view was a mythical picture. He describes that universe as a three-tiered structure (heaven, earth, hell) whose parts communicate with each other, man's earth being the scene of supra- or infra-terrestrial influences rather than shaped by the decisions and work of those who live on it. It is a mythical history of the world that presents it as now in the power of Satan, sin and death, rushing towards its imminent end in a universal catastrophe, after passing through extraordinary "tribulations" which will only be ended by the coming of the celestial Judge bringing salvation or condemnation. According to Bultmann there corresponded to this mythical world-picture a mythical representation of the saving event "which forms the proper content of the New Testament message": the sending down to earth of the pre-existent Son of God who effects by his death the expiation of sins, rises from the dead, is raised to heaven at the right hand of God . . .; and this saving work is rendered present to men in an equally mythical manner in the sacraments.

Demythologization must, therefore, Bultmann maintains, be radical. It cannot consist merely in eliminating certain elements and retaining others, but must reach to the very heart of the NT message. That, in fact, is where it is most urgently imperative, since it is the very kernel of the NT to which we must penetrate in order to draw sustenance from it.

Moreover, the necessity of demythologization does not derive for Bultmann solely from the need of adapting the NT message to the modern mind. "It is rather a matter", he writes, "of enquiring whether the message is purely and simply mythical or whether the very attempt to understand it and its specific intention, does not lead to the elimination of myth." The NT in fact aims at doing something quite different from transmitting to us a mythical picture of the world which it shares with other documents of its period. It does not aim at communicating a world-view but a living word of salvation, a word, therefore, which must be really heard in order effectively to transform human existence.

Thus the idea of demythologization represents for Bultmann only the negative aspect of an enterprise which is intended to be essentially positive and strives for maximum fidelity to the NT itself. This positive aspect finds its chief expression in his programme of existential interpretation. Is it possible, however, to accept a problem of demythologization stated in these terms? This question must now be examined.

2. *Unacceptable aspects of Bultmann's idea of demythologization.* For several reasons we cannot accept the problems of demythologization as Bultmann formulates it. In the first place it is based on distorting over-simplifications. There are over-simplifications in the way in which allegedly mythical data of the NT are expounded. In the book that Karl Barth devoted to him, Barth inquires what interest there can be in listing in a "caricatural" way, as Bultmann does, all those elements, in reality of very different kinds, which he simply lumps together in the category of myth. Does the NT doctrine of the sacraments, for example, belong to the same kind of thought and raise the same problems as the three-tiered picture of the world? And is it so astonishing to find transcendence expressed by reference to space? Do we, who can no longer re-enter the mythical universe, succeed in removing all traces of spatiality from our thought? Does not our picture of the world become strangely mythical again when we speak of the "sublimity" or "loftiness" of a thought or a life or a testimony?

Consequently the radical opposition which Bultmann establishes, or claims to observe, between the world-view of the first Christian generations and our own, is quite evidently due to an over-simplification with pernicious consequences. It was in the same sort of way that Lévy-Bruhl and his school believed they could establish a fundamental difference between what they called the "pre-logical" mentality of primitive peoples and the logical mentality of civilized societies. At all events it seems difficult to admit a real discontinuity between the mode of thought and way of seeing things of the apostolic generations and our own mode of thought and of looking at the world today. The technology of two thousand years ago was certainly very different from the kind that dominates our lives in the 20th century. Nevertheless the first tools foreshadowed our technology. The fishermen of Tiberias and the temple tradesmen had more than a merely mythical relation to the world. Conversely the relations which link modern men to that same world are not solely of a scientific and technical kind. It is sufficient to recall the world of art or poetry. Depth psychology also shows the enduring function of myths, and ethnologists are continually coming to a better realization of their deep significance. From this point of view Bultmann displays a narrow rationalism which is largely out of date today.

He does indeed speak of the symbolic power of myths. Their meaning, he points out, is not so much to give a "picture of the world" as to express "the way man understands himself within his world". But he attributes to mythical representations only a very general meaning. And consequently the NT data which he regards as "mythical" hold no other meaning for him than to indicate the "importance" of the subject of which the text speaks: the Christian event. The break noted between the world of the NT and ours is paralleled by an equally deep disjunction between the (non-mythical) sense of the biblical data and the (mythical) mode of expression in which those data are presented.

But would it not be legitimate to ask whether the principle of these various divisions is not to be found in the denominational position of the man who formulated the project of demythologization? Was the abyss which Bultmann thinks he observes between the world of the NT and our own not created in the first place by a movement which itself consisted in breaking with the historical reality of the Church and the continuity of its tradition? And is it not that "abstraction" from the world and history which we meet once again in the hiatus asserted to exist between the concrete images and their meaning, between alleged myths and a kerygma which ends up by having no content?

The weakness in Bultmann's manner of stating the problem of demythologization ultimately derives from the fact that he does not extend his criticism to the initial situation from which his inquiry starts and on the basis of which he draws his conclusions. No doubt he rejects any idea of making modern man the measure of all things. Yet it is certainly on the basis of modern man, or more exactly of his rationalist illusions, that he defines and criticizes the allegedly mythical world of thought inhabited by the men of the NT. He has not in fact profited by the criticism of "modernity" which Nietzsche in particular undertook and which a whole current of contemporary philosophy continues to carry further. From this point of view, Bultmann has not profited from the teaching of Heidegger, on whom in other respects he so deliberately draws. For Heidegger it is characteristic of modern times to see the "world" in terms of its own epoch. It would therefore involve from the very start a radical misunderstanding of myth to speak of a "mythical picture" of the world. At the very least it would mean contemplating the myth from outside and, in fact, turning the very narrow point of view of modern man into the absolute norm.

3. *Demythologization and Catholic theology.* Catholic exegesis is in principle immunized against this danger by the duty it acknowledges of fitting into the movement of a tradition extending from apostolic times to the present day. That is why it will never entirely recognize its own problem in Bultmann's demythologization problem. But that does not mean that the question is of no concern to Catholic exegesis.

Although the problem of demythologization is in part linked to the denominational position of the man who has drawn a whole programme from it, certain aspects of the problem cannot fail to concern Catholic theology too. The latter can share Bultmann's preoccupation to the extent that this consists simply in seeking out and expressing as adequately as possible and in the most effective way the data of faith contained in Scripture. From this point of view one could say that all theology embodies what is authentic in Bultmann's project.

The term demythologization is not appropriate, however, to describe this enterprise. It may well suggest that the NT presents us with myths in the proper sense, whereas the NT formally rejects them (cf. 1 Tim 1:4; 4:7; 2 Tim 4:4 . . .) and claims to bear witness to a real history. This essential link with history, maintained not only by NT but also by OT revelation, explains why it has been possible to describe that revelation as a veritable process of demythologization (so, for example, G. von Rad, *Old Testament Theology*). What at most can be found in the biblical writings are terms and images, originally connected with myths, but which are employed as part of a whole context where quite evidently they bear an entirely new meaning. Consequently, to equate the hermeneutical problem with a problem of demythologization would reduce it to a relatively superficial undertaking. The search for and elucidation of the meaning of Scripture, ceaselessly pursued for generations, represent a very much profounder and more exacting task.

Does this mean that the problem raised by Bultmann corresponds to no special difficulty and that the modern times to which he refers have brought no new obstacle to our understanding of the Bible in faith, not only in regard to the OT but also to the NT? It would certainly be vain to claim that the critical sense has not considerably developed in the last two thousand years or that the relation of men of the 20th century to the Bible is still spontaneously the same as that of the Fathers of the Church or of medieval theologians. The modernist crisis at the beginning of the present century, for example, shows that a certain tension can develop between the traditional affirmations of faith and the task that is proper to criticism. At the present time, too, attention has been drawn to the difficulties which are met with in harmonizing perfectly developments in dogma and exegetical research. That means that an often difficult effort is needed to harmonize our modern critical demands with an understanding of the faith which will be identical with that of the apostolic and indeed of all Christian generations.

See also *World Picture, Science* III, *Existence* II, III, *Kerygma, Modernism, Dogma* II.

BIBLIOGRAPHY. R. Bultmann, *Glauben und Verstehen*, 4 vols. (1933–65); K. Barth, *R. Bultmann. Ein Versuch, ihn zu verstehen* (1952); F. Gogarten, *Entmythologisierung und Kirche* (3rd ed., 1953); H. W. Bartsch, ed., *Kerygma und Myth*, 2 vols. (1953–62); E. Fuchs, *Das Programm der Entmythologisierung* (1954); R. Marlé, *Bultmann et l'interprétation du Nouveau Testament* (1956); L. Malevez, *The Christian Message and Myth. The Theology of Rudolf Bultmann* (1958); E. Castelli, ed., *Il problema della demitizzazione* (1961); R. Brown, "After Bultmann, What? An Introduction to the Post-Bultmannians", *CBQ* 26 (1964), pp. 1–30; J. Cahill, "R. Bultmann and Post-Bultmann Tendencies", *CBQ* 26 (1964), pp. 153–78; W. Schmithals, *Die Theologie R. Bultmanns* (1965).

René Marlé

II. Existential Interpretation

1. *Nature.* The idea of existential interpretation corresponds to the positive aspect of Bultmann's hermeneutical project, just as demythologization expresses its negative side. "Myth", he explains, "does not call for a cosmological interpretation, but an anthropological or rather an existential one . . . In the mythology of the New Testament, it is not the objective content of the representations in itself that must be studied, but the understanding of human existence which these representations express." To extract this "understanding of human existence" implied in all that the biblical texts present to us, and to show what vital significance for man's life the different statements of Scripture can, and in fact are intended to, have, are the aims of existential interpretation.

2. *Its necessity.* It must not be thought that the project of existential interpretation only springs from interest in man and from a regard for intelligibility leading to the elimination of everything which exceeds man's measure. The principle of existential interpretation does not belong to one of those types of rationalism which are unwilling to recognize any reality except what the human understanding can grasp. In fact that principle, prior to expressing a human need, finds its justification and in a certain way its necessity, in God himself. Reference to human existence is, in fact a condition of an authentic religious language. One cannot speak seriously of God without speaking of the relationship to him, for there is no standpoint at which one would be external to God, ultimately. God is "the reality which determines our existence . . . Hence, if one wishes to speak of God one must obviously speak of oneself". (*Glauben und Verstehen*, vol. I, pp. 28f.)

3. *A committed and responsible interpretation.* "To speak of oneself" does not, however, mean to talk of one's experiences or inner states, as if we regarded these as direct manifestations of God's action in us. It is not a matter of speaking "about" our existence, but of speaking "out of" it, with it as starting-point. There is this strange truth about our existence, which also applies to that of God: we can speak about neither of them in strictly proper terms, and neither is at our disposal. "Two features alone" of this thought-defying existence "are clear; firstly, that we have the care and responsibility of it: *tua res agitur;* secondly, that it is devoid of all security and we cannot provide it with any, for in order to do so we should have to stand outside it, we should have to be God." In other words, the reference to existence in no way aims at linking us to the familiar universe of our experience or ideas, but very much rather to project us into the heart of the most ineluctable and hopeless of situations and hence to challenge us. It is the condition of all authentic religious language, because there is no authentic religious language which is not concerned with the decision of faith.

4. *Method.* Though it is impossible to speak "about" existence, the latter is not to be assimilated to something irrational which understanding cannot grasp at all. On the contrary, existence is never without an "understanding of existence", just as our ideas and utterances express in a very general way a certain concrete existential attitude or manner of approach. It is in this relation between existence and understanding, which makes them in some respects co-extensive, that the legitimacy of existential interpretation can be founded. But that relation may be more or less immediate and more or less evident. That is why it is necessary to employ a practical method aimed at bringing fully to light the significance for existence of NT assertions which concern it only indirectly and which may even at first sight appear quite alien to it.

Existence, in fact, may be expressed directly in certain very simple words: I love you, I hate you, I forgive you . . . More often it finds expression by seeming to speak of what is other than itself. The aim of existential interpretation is then to show how it is existence which is really speaking and, by showing this, to display the true goal of existence.

To achieve this, this interpretation uses a particular technique drawn from a particular philosophy which, under the name of "existential analysis", lays bare the general structures of human existence and so supplies "the concepts thanks to which it is possible adequately to speak of human existence".

Existential interpretation aims at remaining on this formal plane, indicating the general significance for existence that the text to be interpreted may possess, but leaving to man's freedom the practical recognition of the validity of that significance. It remains on the plane of structures, and that is why it is called existential in the universal sense (existenzial), aiming solely at opening out the possibility of an authentic and personal decision, which will then be called existential in the concrete sense (existenziell).

5. *Criticism.* It is theologically legitimate to seek for a principle of existential interpretation which will retain faith in its original dimension, that of a summons to man. Only such a reduction of faith can appeal to each man in his authentic situation in each age. The words of Scripture are "Spirit and life", and hence it can be useful to use certain methods of analysis and indeed a language elaborated by philosophy.

The limits, and therefore the dangers, of existential interpretation are determined by the idea of existence which is taken as the starting-point. Obviously it is only acceptable if the existence in question, and the understanding we can achieve of it, can be radically called in question and be opened up to new horizons. K. Barth reproached Bultmann for wanting to confine biblical revelation within a carapace of existentialist philosophy. Without attempting to go into the grave question of the relations of philosophy and theology, of man's quest for God and the answer which revelation provides, we must be content to note that the existence to which Bultmann refers (since he is the chief advocate of existential interpretation), is of a very formal type, in which the body, work, "natural" relations with the world and with one's fellow-men play practically no part. Within the framework of that existence several features or fundamental components of revelation are not given their full importance: in particular everything concerned with the objective chronological facts of history, or the intimate, disinterested and potentially contemplative knowledge of the mystery of God. An existential interpretation undoubtedly makes God's claim and promises stand out clearly, and this helps us to understand how God's action on us in Christ is *propter nos et propter nostram salutem.* But such an interpretation also provides an articulate though always analogous statement about God's revelation and his work of salvation.

It is not possible to say *a priori* what might be achieved by an exegesis and a theology inspired by the endeavour to make contact with existence, yet freed from the limitations imposed on Bultmann by the philosophy and anthropology which explicitly or implicitly he takes as his frame of reference.

See also *Myth, Existence, Religious Act, Language.*

BIBLIOGRAPHY. E. Dinkler, "Existentialist Interpretation of the New Testament", *The Journal of Religion* 32 (1952), pp. 87–92; H. W. Bartsch, ed., *Kerygma and Myth,* 2 vols. (1953–62); R. Marlé *Bultmann et l'interprétation du Nouveau Testament* (1956), ch. 3; L. Malevez, *The Christian Message and Myth. The Theology of Rudolf Bultmann* (1958), ch. 2; H. Ott, *Denken und Sein. Der Weg M. Heideggers und der Weg der Theologie* (1959); M. Heidegger, *Being and Time* (1962); E. Fuchs, *Hermeneutik* (3rd ed., 1963); G. Hasenhüttl, *Der Glaubensvollzug* (1963); J. M. Robinson and J. B. Cobb, eds., *The Later Heidegger and Theology,* New Frontiers in Theology 1 (1963); O. Rodenberg, *Um die Wahrheit der heiligen Schrift* (3rd ed., 1963); J. M. Robinson and J. B. Cobb, eds., *New Hermeneutic,* New Frontiers in Theology 2 (1964); K. Frör, *Biblische Hermeneutik* (2nd ed., 1964); C. von Til, "The Later Heidegger and Theology", *The Westminster Theological Journal* 26 (1964), pp. 121–61; H. G. Gadamer, *Wahrheit und Methode* (2nd ed., 1965).

René Marlé

DESPAIR

1. Despair as a *sin* consists in the relinquishing of present or possible hope. It is, therefore, the voluntary rejection of a consciously recognized dependence of man upon his fellowmen and upon God, as well as of the corresponding duty of seeking perfection and salvation in harmony with them. The motives for despair can be various; it may be, for example, moral sloth (accidie, acedia) which shrinks from the effort of following Christ and which prefers earthly blessings to union with men or God; or it may be a lack of confidence which fears the responsibility of links with others or refuses to surrender to the known will of God. Fear of God may hold acts of despair in check, but only the virtue of hope can truly overcome despair itself.

2. To be able to despair in the *moral sense,* a man must have recognized his duty of

placing his hope in God and his neighbour, and he must at the same time be in the position to reject that love which is asked of him if it should appear as of no value to him for any reason. This means that a man is by nature bound to God and his neighbours, and that he may also freely reject this bond by treating it as of less than absolute value.

Hence, sinful despair is only possible in those who at least are capable of the personal relationships which enable them to perceive and to accept the love of another. This presupposes a sufficient experience of love bestowed on them. Only those are capable of despair in the full sense, however, who have not only withheld their own response, but also consciously choose to do so. For in spite of the recognition of their own nothingness, they arrogantly choose to live for themselves alone and arbitrarily refuse to place their hope in love.

3. Such an attitude is glorified in contemporary literature and in various forms of nihilism which, after rejecting the faith, has despaired of reason also. Indeed, one may speak of a renaissance of despair. This can be expressed in euthanasia, suicide, pseudo-heroics in the face of death, as well as in the flight towards hedonism. From the religious viewpoint, every attempt to attain justification through works is seen as an expression of disguised despair. For this reason it is accepted that the task of the law within the divine plan is either to drive us to despair or to bring us to the point of placing our hope entirely in Christ. Despair, like those limitations of our freedom which spring from sin in general, cannot be adequately grasped in psychological terms. Every sin is in its root a form of despair, which consists of a rebellion against our recognized duty of being dependent in our self-fulfilment. It is a rejection which can be made good again only by means of repentance and forgiveness. Ultimately every resistance to offered grace is an act of despair. It is for this reason that scholastic theology always related despair to the sin against the Holy Spirit.

4. Accordingly, one cannot speak of despair in the moral sense when proffered love cannot be recognized as such, or when one does not possess sufficient will-power to respond to it and to open himself trustingly to others and to God. This incapacity is often pathological, and in such a case one must seek to enlist the aid of psychiatry and psychotherapy. There are doubtless many forms of melancholy and scruples which are due to mental illness, as well as other disturbances caused by delusions and fantasies or other emotional stresses which induce feelings of despair and block either partially or completely the capacity to form relationships and which may eventually lead to suicide. In contra-distinction to this there is another type of despair which is based upon a metaphysical incapacity resulting from the under-development of the perceptive capacity and freedom, so that the naturally negative response to hardship cannot be neutralized. For this reason one cannot call the hopeless attitude of "moral outlaws" despair in the moral sense; it results from a man's inability to see in God and other men anything else but enemies who wish him evil. A man can be driven to such a state if he is unworthily treated and never has the chance of experiencing the joy of another's love, or if he is unable to recognize the blessing and providence of God in the incomprehensible and bitter experiences of his fate.

See also *Hope, Human Act, Nihilism, Death, Law, Grace.*

BIBLIOGRAPHY. J. Pieper, *Über die Hoffnung* (1935); S. Kierkegaard, *The Sickness Unto Death* (1941); A.-M. Carré, *Espérance et désespoir* (1954); J.-P. Sartre, *Being and Nothingness* (1957); B. Häring, *The Law of Christ*, 2 vols. (1961–66), see Index; G. Marcel, *Problematic Man* (1967).

Waldemar Molinski

DEVIL

I. Demons. II. The Devil.

I. Demons

1. *Hermeneutical problems.* The particular way in which angels and demons figure in Old and New Testament revelation, and the indisputable use that is made there of modes of representation drawn from outside revelation, even though in Scripture these belong to the mode of expression, not to the content asserted, make it important to be cautious about the traditional method of harmonizing and systematizing the scattered indications of Scripture. This method worked

indiscriminately, without taking into account from text to text the different relations between content and mode of representation (e.g., the sublunary realm of the devils [Eph 22:2; 6:12]; the apparently direct aetiological ascription of very natural events such as illnesses to diabolical causes). Such a procedure takes no account of the lack of clear distinction between content and mode of expression in Scripture, nor of the fact that it is probably only possible to speak of any dogmatically defined doctrines about evil spirits because the Fourth Lateran Council (*D* 428; cf. *D* 237, 427) applies to angels and devils, which it assumes to exist, the doctrine that everything apart from the one God is radically created. The intention was to emphasize the universal validity of this principle, so that there is no absolute primal evil, only finite evil due solely to the free decision of creatures. It was, however, assumed that prior to the free decision of the individual and of human beings generally, the world already has an element of what is evil and hostile to God. And it must be admitted that these definitions imply the existence of personal non-human beings, and that this is also guaranteed by the ordinary magisterium and tradition (cf. *D* 2318). Consequently, further statements can be made about these realities with the help of general Christian principles. But only those few statements can be made which really follow from this initial position and which are really implied by the data indicated.

It must always be borne in mind that it is in fact ultimately a question of unmasking the apparently numinous evil in the very appearance it has arrogated to itself (cf. also Jn 12:31). This kind of evil is still found, for example, in only apparently demythologized form in German Romanticism and the later M. Scheler, and in the kind of confused popular Christian piety which in fact makes personal diabolical evil into an equal partner with God in dialogue and action. That can apply to created good in nature and grace but not to evil.

It must also be remembered that the theological starting-point of demonology excludes any description of the essence and activity of these diabolical powers. They have their own specific nature and influence precisely where the realities which can be experienced within this present world have a depth and power which, although created, are beyond man's command. Consequently it is neither possible nor permitted to distinguish them from the earthly realities. If the substantial and personal character of these powers is disputed, it can no longer seriously be maintained at the same time that "from the world which is God's good creation, an inherently groundless resistance to God breaks out against God's action — and this is inexplicable either in anthropological or sociological terms" (G. Gloege in *RGG,* vol. II, col. 3). For there would be no real agents involved. However, such personal beings may certainly be thought of not as spirits (like goblins) "in" the world, but precisely as the (regional) "principalities and powers" of the world and its history, in the form of refusal of God, temptation of men and perversion of the world.

2. *Scripture.* a) *Old Testament.* The fundamental human experience of evil found expression in the ancient East in a complicated demonology which also influenced the early stages of the OT. But the more firmly rooted the belief in Yahweh's absolute dominion over all things visible and invisible, the more any cult of demons was stigmatized as idolatry, an abomination before Yahweh (Deut 18:9–13). There are "evil spirits" sent by God (Is 34:14) and others like the demons of the steppes such as Azazel to whom the scapegoat was despatched on the day of expiation (Lev 16:10). The calling up of spirits from the dead is mentioned in 1 Sam 28:13; cf. v. 9. They cause ritual impurity, like contact with corpses, and hence are forbidden figures, Lev 19:31; 20:6, 27; Deut 18:11. The terminology of the Septuagint shows that it carried out a consistent process of identifying demons and pagan gods. It uses δαιμόνιον as a noun, and thus introduces the notion of the Greek δαίμων, a being with divine power, mostly baneful in nature, which can be conjured up by magic. It also speaks of such beings as μάταια, "nothings". With the growing influence of possibly Persian demonology in the time of the Exile (most evident in the book of Tobit, "Asmodeus"), in later Judaism the demons are ranked under Satan as fallen angels (*Jubilees,* 10:8, 11). Various mythical accounts tell of the "fall" of the demons (battle of the stars cf. Is 14:12). Against them under Michael fight the ἄγγελοι, the

powers which mediate between God and man (Deut 10:13).

b) *New Testament.* This conception of evil spirits persists in the NT, where the devils appear principally as cause of illness and possession (Mt 17:15, 18). Illness (physical: Mk 9:14–29; mental: Mk 9:20ff.) is a sign of the hopeless condition of the bodily world. But moral faults and eternal damnation are not attributed to the work of demons, nor all types of bodily illness. Hence the demons, and their conquest by Jesus, display only the damage to or the re-establishment of concrete human existence. There is no trace of spiritualism. The healing of men is a σημεῖον of the dawn of the kingship of God. Since this kingship is indissolubly linked with the person of Jesus, the devils subject to Satan (Mk 3:20ff.) struggle against Jesus. But the power of the devil and of his subordinate spirits, which is chiefly displayed in the NT in the realm of possession, is already broken, since the kingship of God has already begun with Jesus' coming and work. The Church took over like Jesus the ideas of apocalyptic Judaism concerning demons. Jesus possesses the "pure" Spirit and hence makes war on the demons, the "impure" spirits. The claim of Jesus to drive out demons in the power of the "holy" πνεῦμα is one of the main pre-Easter Christological principles and a decisive presupposition for the title of "Son of God". That the devils in the NT appear primarily in the anthropological, and only derivatively in the cosmic domain, explains the attempt to interpret the devils as the abyss of what ought not to be in man, and which is not identical with himself. Jesus' combat with the evil spirits is continued by his disciples (Mt 7:22; Mk 9:38f.; Mk 6:6, 7, 13 par.; Lk 10:17–20; Mk 16:17) and the primitive Church (Acts 8:7; 19:11–17). But the Church's combat with diabolical disorder also implies total rejection of magic, superstition (Acts 13:8ff.; 19:18f.) and soothsaying (Acts 16:16). Recognition of the spirits leading astray into error and illusion (1 Cor 12:1ff.) is only possible in the power of the Holy Spirit (1 Cor 12:10). The primitive Church looked forward to the final defeat of Satan and his demons at the coming of the glorified Kyrios (Rev 20:1f.; 7–10).

3. *Dogmatic theology.* a) In view of the created and non-human character of these various spiritual, personal principalities and powers, all that is affirmed of the natural essence of the angels must be ascribed to them too.

b) In accordance with the teaching of faith regarding their existence, we must maintain with equal certainty the plurality of such non-human demoniacal powers. The antagonistic divisions of evil in the world even within itself (despite Mt 12:26) may be regarded as a sign of this in actual experience.

c) They are to be thought of as having in their personal, purely spiritual nature (i.e., not of the same kind as earthly space-time), an essential, natural and therefore personal relation to the world, to nature and so to the history of salvation and perdition (cf. Mt 4:1ff.; 2 Cor 12:7; Lk 22:31; 1 Thess 3:5; Jn 8:44; 1 Pet 5:8; Jas 4:7; Eph 6:11, 16; *D* 428, 793, 806, 894, 907, 909). They carry this relation into effect naturally and personally by realizing an indestructible order of essences in guilty opposition.

d) We may accept, as against Hugh of St. Victor, Peter Lombard, Alexander of Hales and St. Bonaventure, the view commonly held today that the devils had an objective finality directed to supernatural fulfilment, just like the good angels, but renounced it (cf. also *D* 1001, 1003f.).

e) From the general principle stated above, it follows that they culpably shut themselves off from a perfect fulfilment by God, and did so definitively (cf. Jn 8:4; Jude 6; 2 Pet 2:4; 1 Jn 3:8; Mt 25:41; Rev 20:9; *D* 211, 237, 427ff.). This decision must in accordance with c) and d) have some relation to the universal supernatural finality of the world in Christ. The victory of Christ over sin as such is therefore the end of the power of the evil spirits (Lk 10:18; Mt 12:28; cf. also *D* 1261, 1933).

See also *Angel* I, *Possession, Superstition.*

BIBLIOGRAPHY. R. C. Thompson, *The Devils and Evil Spirits of Babylonia* (1903/4); M. Dibelius, *Die Geisterwelt im Glauben des Paulus* (1909); P. Perdrizet, *Negotium perambulans in tenebris. Études de démonologie gréco-orientale* (1922); M. Summers, *The History of Witchcraft and Demonology* (1926); W. R. Smith, *Lectures on the Religion of the Semites* (3rd ed., 1927), pp. 119–39, 441–6, 538–41; P. Billerbeck, *Kommentar zum Neuen Testament aus Talmud und Midrasch,* vol. IV (1928; repr. 1956), pp. 501–35; W. Foerster, "δαίμων", *TWNT,* II (1935); pp. 1–21, E. T.: *Theological Dictionary of the*

New Testament, II (1965); L. Thorndike, *A History of Magic and Experimental Science,* 6 vols. (1947–51); *Satan,* Études Carmélitaines (1948); E. Langton, *Essentials of Demonology. A Study of Jewish and Christian Doctrine* (1949); S. Eitrem, *Some Notes on the Demonology in the New Testament,* Symbolae Osloenses, suppl. 12 (1950); M. T. Unger, *Biblical Demonology* (1952); G. B. Caird, *Principalities and Powers* (1956); R. H. Robbins, *The Encyclopaedia of Witchcraft and Demonology* (1959); T. Ling, *The Significance of Satan. New Testament Demonology and Its Contemporary Relevance* (1961); H. Schlier, *Principalities and Powers in the New Testament,* Quaestiones Disputatae 3 (1961); L. Cristiani, *Evidence of Satan in the Modern World* (1962);

Adolf Darlap

II. The Devil

1. *Methodological considerations.* a) By "the devil" we are to understand, in a sense to be defined, the "highest" of the evil spirits. It is clear that the background for a theologically correct idea of the devil will have to presuppose and include all that has been said in the article on *Angel.* Explicit reference must be made to it.

b) Firstly, the devil (leaving out of account for the moment the question of his exact relation to the other demons) is not to be regarded as a mere mythological personification of evil in the world; the existence of the devil cannot be denied. Secondly, the devil, like the other evil spirits, cannot be regarded, as in absolute dualism, as an independent counterpart to God. He is a finite creature whose evil remains comprised within the scope of the power, freedom and goodness of the holy God. We must therefore apply to the devil whatever theology has to say about evil, sin, its permission by God in a positive divine intention, about the negative character of evil, the impossibility of an evil substance, about concrete, finite good as the goal even of evil freedom etc. Thirdly, the teaching of Scripture and revelation about the devil (as about evil spirits in general) appears rather to be a natural presupposition of human experience which is incorporated, critically corrected, into the doctrine of the victory of the grace of God in Christ and of the liberation of man from all "principalities and powers".

c) Once it is clear that the doctrine of angels, demons and the devil is the conscious conceptual interpretation of natural experience of a variety of supernatural princi-palities and powers (and not derived directly from the word of revelation properly so called), the findings of comparative religion become intelligible. Such a doctrine can be, and is, widespread. Interpreted and criticized, it penetrates revealed religion slowly from outside. It does not necessarily at first distinguish clearly between good and bad principalities and powers. It may overestimate such powers in a polytheistic way or again it may reduce the great powers of polytheism to the mere rank of angels or demons under the one God. Reflection on a certain hierarchical order among these princi-palities and powers may be more or less advanced, and such hierarchical arrangement can underestimate the natural heterogeneity of the spiritual personal world prior to man and the inner contradiction of the "realm" of evil, or it may in the concrete identify the evil spirits with the one devil, or employ the term devil as a summary formula for the evil principalities and powers. Remarks of this kind apply to some extent to the Old and New Testaments.

d) All this shows that the doctrine of the devil has really a very simple content which has nothing to do with mythology in the proper sense. The calamitous situation which man recognizes as his own, presupposed by the message of redemption and at the same time overcome by God's grace, is not one that is constituted solely by human freedom. A created freedom contributes to its consti-tution, one which is supra-human and antecedent to the history of human freedom. The opposition to God which appears as prior to man in man's calamitous situation, is itself manifold. "Evil" even in itself is disunited, and in that way constitutes man's situation. But this intrinsic disunity of evil itself which is at once one of the factors of its power and of its powerlessness, is not such that it could destroy the unity of the world, of its history (even in evil) or the "unity" of the calamitous situation in its opposition to God. Evil is still something like one kingdom, one rule. That is what is meant when we speak of a highest among the evil spirits, the devil. And this shows that we can only speak in a very vague sense of "pattern" in the disunity of evil in the world and consequently of a chief among the evil spirits. This is so, if for no other reason (though it is not the only one) than that the hierarchy among the good angels is very difficult to determine, because of course each of those angels is a radically unique being.

2. *Scripture.* a) The Septuagint translated the Hebrew *sātān* (adversary) by διάβολος. This word then passed into the various European languages. The names διάβολος and Satan at first bear various very wide meanings, then become narrower and coalesce in the demonology of later Judaism. The devil is then the prince of the angels who with his adherents fell away from God and was thrust out of heaven.

b) The NT assumes the general Jewish teaching about evil spirits and the devil. New designations of the devil are: the evil one (Mt 13:19, etc.), the enemy (cf. Lk 10:19), the ruler of this world (Jn 12:31, etc.), the god of this aeon (2 Cor 4:4), murderer from the beginning and father of lies (Jn 8:44). A new feature is the opposition between Christ and the devil. The devil's enmity with God reaches its historical culmination in Jesus' passion (Lk 22:3, 31; Jn 13:27; 1 Cor 2:8) but also its final defeat (1 Cor 2:8; Jn 12:31; Acts 12:7ff.), just as the exorcisms of devils were the prelude to the victorious coming of God's reign in the person of Jesus. This opposition continues in the history of the Church until the devil is finally cast into hell (Rev 20:8, 10).

3. *Dogmatic theology.* a) Most of what has been said by the magisterium about the devil is to be found in connection with doctrinal pronouncements about evil spirits and has the same content (their creation as good, their own sin and eternal reprobation: *D* 427ff., 211; *DS* 286, 325); a certain power over sinful man and his death is ascribed to the devil (*D* 428, 788, 793, 894) and his power is taken from him by Christ's redemption (*DS* 291, *D* 711f., 894). But the Church's doctrine guards against exaggeration of the influence of the devil's temptations on the sins of man (*D* 383, *DS* 2192, *D* 1261–73, 1923). The devil (*diabolus*) is often tacitly assumed to be a sort of chief of the evil spirits. Vatican II is very reserved about statements concerning the devil, but they are not avoided altogether. We are freed by the Son of God from the devil's domination (Constitution on the Sacred Liturgy, art. 6; Decree on the Church's Missionary Activity, art. 3 and 9). "The evil one" led men astray into sin but his power was broken by Christ's death and resurrection (Pastoral Constitution on the Church in the Modern World, art. 13; cf. art. 2).

b) Speculative theology will take into consideration that the multitude of principalities and powers, by the very fact of their creation as part of the unity of the world, cannot be without a certain hierarchical order and gradation (cf. Mk 3:24). This order is not destroyed even by their guilt, because there cannot be an absolutely powerful sin which totally destroys specific nature and unity. This provides the basis for the idea of a leader of the evil spirits (Mk 3:22), called the devil, as the representative of all the principalities and powers. But it is not possible to attempt to individualize the devil as distinct from the rest of the evil spirits (cf., e.g., *D* 242 and 243). Particularly in regard to the devil as head of the demons, Christian piety must avoid the picture of Antichrist as a counterpart to God in history on an equal footing with him. The devil is a creature who must retain a created essence which is good and which he must employ according to its nature even to be capable of evil ("natura eius opificium Dei est": *DS* 286, *D* 237f., 242, 457).

4. *Kerygmatic treatment of the devil.* a) There is no reason to put the doctrine of the devil in the forefront of the hierarchy of truths when preaching the faith today, as was to some extent done in earlier times (e.g., by Luther). Not because there is no enduring statement of faith concerning the devil, but because what it means for the actual practice of Christian life can be said, as far as its decisive content is concerned, even without explicit teaching about the devil. And at the very least, because access to this doctrine is relatively difficult for people today. Nor is the devil mentioned in the great creeds. Consequently we must very definitely avoid drawing on the traditional arsenal of popular pictures of the devil (distinct classes of demons with special functions, proper names for some devils, etc.). Probably the exorcisms at baptism, etc., will have to be more soberly expressed in the new liturgy. In defending genuine dogmatic teaching about the devil, appeal to spiritualistic phenomena or to phenomena of possession are generally ineffective, for both meet with scepticism from

men accustomed to the scrupulous empiricism of the natural sciences.

b) When an explanation and defence of the Church's teaching about the devil is required, e.g., in expounding the NT, liturgical texts, etc., people today must first have their attention drawn to the sinister suprahuman power of evil in history. This has its ground in the doctrine of the "principalities and powers", and this prevents its being glossed over and reduced to triviality. It need not be overlooked or contested that in such an argument it is not, and need not be, possible to draw a perfectly clear distinction between what is purely conceptual projection based on the experience of evil in history, and what is actually specifically affirmed about these substantial, created and personal principalities and powers, provided that such an intrinsic content of the affirmation is not denied in principle. It can also be helpful for the understanding of this teaching to point out that such principalities and powers, in accordance with their nature, which remains good, always retain a constant positive function (actus naturalis) for the world. It is not possible to object to this doctrine by asking why God does not remove the waste-products of the personal history of spirit completely from his creation. The free and eschatological refusal to open the natural activity of their essence into the mystery of God's free self-communication in grace does not destroy that natural activity as a permanently valid factor in the world.

See also Angel I, Dualism, Antichrist, Evil, Possession (Diabolical), Spiritualism.

BIBLIOGRAPHY. J. Bremond, Le Diable, existe-t-il? Que fait-il? (1924); M. Garçon, Le Diable. Étude historique, critique et médicale (1926); M. Rudwin, The Devil in Legend and Literature (1931); B. Rigaux, L'Antichrist (1932); G. de Libera, Satana (1934); W. Foerster and G. von Rad, " διάβολος", TWNT, II (1935), pp. 69–80, E. T.: Theological Dictionary of the New Testament, II (1965); H. Colleye, Histoire du diable (1946); Satan, Études Carmélitaines 27 (1948); R. Dubal, La psychoanalyse du diable (1953); B. Caird, Principalities and Powers (1956); R. H. Robbins, The Encyclopaedia of Witchcraft and Demonology (1959); E. Reisner, Le démon et son image (1961); H. Schlier, Principalities and Powers in the New Testament, Quaestiones Disputatae 3 (1961); A. Winkelhofer, Traktat über den Teufel (2nd ed., 1962); C. Journet, The Meaning of Evil (1963).

Karl Rahner

DIALECTICAL THEOLOGY

Dialectical theology is the name given to a movement of thought which appeared within Protestant theology after the First World War and which at that time held the place in theologico-philosophical debates which the problems of demythologization and existential interpretation have occupied since the Second World War. Its chief protagonists were K. Barth, E. Thurneysen, E. Brunner, F. Gogarten and R. Bultmann.

1. The beginnings of dialectical theology. The common viewpoint of these theologians was presented to the public in the course of the same year. Between 1921 and 1922 Gogarten published The Religious Decision, Brunner, Experience, Knowledge and Faith, Thurneysen, Dostoievsky, and Barth, the second edition of his commentary on the Letter to the Romans, which Bultmann received favourably. During the autumn of 1922, Barth, Gogarten and Thurneysen founded the journal Zwischen den Zeiten, with G. Merz as editor. This was intended to be the organ for their work together, and Brunner and Bultmann soon began to contribute articles to it. It was in the same year that an observer gave to the newly-founded circle the name of "dialectical theology".

But unity was soon seen to be unstable. Dialectical theology was the first form of a theology of the word of God which was to appear in many different guises. What characterized the movement at the start was the reaction of its first supporters against the traditional liberal theology. Disturbed by the needs of the pastoral ministry and by the spiritual crisis caused by the war, they sought a new basis in the writings of Blumhardt, Kutter, Kierkegaard, Overbeck, Dostoievsky, etc. They held that traditional Protestant theology, centred as it was on religion and piety and studying their manifestations in human psychology and history, was really only speaking about man, whilst all the time it believed that it was speaking about God. They went on to affirm the transcendence of God in relation to all human knowledge and every human work, including religion; the sovereignty of the divine revelation in Jesus Christ, the authority of the Bible. They affirmed that sinful man, even when he believes, always stands before God with empty hands. And so they came back once more to the thought of the Reformers without returning to ancient Protestant orthodoxy.

The second edition of Barth's commentary on the Letter to the Romans is generally considered as the most vigorous and radical expression of "dialectical theology". So we must look at it first and then go on to define the rest in relation to it.

2. *Barth's dialectic*. Dialectic is produced by negation. In Barth's *Epistle to the Romans* this appears under the name of *critical negation*. It means the negation or denial that God himself pronounces upon man in the death and resurrection of Christ. And so it appears that there is a relationship with God only to the extent that God dialectically suppresses man. It is through judging us that God gives us grace; it is in the "no" of his anger that we hear the "yes" of his mercy. All human existence, religion included, stands in subjection to the divine "no". The true God, who can never be regarded as an object, is the origin of the *krisis* of every "objective" thing, the judge, the negation of this world.

This critical negation creates *distance*. A "line of death" separates God from man and time from eternity: what Kierkegaard called an infinite qualitative difference. God cannot be discovered either in experience or in any historical entity. In Jesus Christ he is revealed precisely as the "Wholly Other", as the unknown God. The Calvinist notion of the *majestas Dei* here informs what Barth takes from R. Otto or from the religious philosophy of neo-Kantian inspiration. Even in the most exalted communion between God and man, God remains God and man nothing but dust and ashes. Their encounter takes place only in the miracle and paradox of faith.

But the cross of Christ throws a bridge over the distance between God and man, by the very act of setting it up. "Critical negation" has a *dialectical* character; which means that it includes in itself an assertion and its reversal, which tend to ultimate unity. As the *unknown* God, God is *known* in Jesus. "Insofar as he is the non-being of things, he is their true being." "Judgment is not annihilation; by it all things are established." This characteristic appears to the full in the dialectic between Adam and Christ, which constitutes both our justification and our resurrection. "The dualism of Adam and Christ, between the old and the new, is not metaphysical but dialectic. The dualism exists only insofar as it dissolves itself. It is a dualism of movement . . . (For) the *krisis* of death and resurrection, the *krisis* of faith, is the change of the divine 'no' to the divine 'yes'. There is no subsequent reverse movement."

Yet this turning or transition does not take place in human psychology and human history. It is the *actus purus* of an incomprehensible event in God. Just as the resurrection of Jesus is not a historical event alongside the other events of his life and death, so the new life that it introduces into my being is not an event alongside the other events of my own existence. The new man that I am is not what I am. "It is only by faith that I am what I am (not!)." "We can only believe and may believe that we believe." This faith is essentially hope, an awaiting for an eternal future. Insofar as it is man's act, it is pure "empty space", just like the life of Jesus itself. The non-historical character of the relationship between God and man (i.e., the notion that it is not worked out within the bounds of human history) is most clearly expressed in this celebrated declaration: "In the resurrection the new world of the Holy Spirit touches the old world of the flesh, but touches it as a tangent touches a circle, that is, without touching it. And precisely because it does not touch it, it touches it as a frontier, as a *new* world." The history of salvation unfolds on the frontier of time and eternity, in "the eternal moment".

As human endeavours, religion and the Church stand in the shadow of sin and death; for us the ethical problem is a mortal sickness. Religion, the Church and moral action are of value only as sign, witness, parable and reference, "an allusion to the revelation itself which is always far beyond all historical reality".

The situation of theology is the same. The theologian must speak about God; but as a man he cannot do so. All his talking will be only "witness rendered to the truth of God". To that end, he must follow by preference the dialectical way, which contains and unites within itself both the dogmatic and critical ways, by keeping his gaze fixed on their common presupposition, the living and ineffable truth which stands at the centre and which gives their meaning to both affirmation and negation. This centre, namely the fact that God has become man, can be neither apprehended nor contemplated and so cannot be directly expressed. All that remains is to relate the statement and the negation *to one another,* to illuminate the "yes" by the "no" and the "no" by the "yes", without ever stopping for more than a moment at the "yes" or on the "no". The dialectician must not forget that his speaking rests on "the presupposition of this original living truth, which is to be found there at the centre".

In 1927 in his preliminary sketch of *Church Dogmatics* Barth again explains, and in practically the same sense, that dogmatic thought is dialectic thought, i.e., a thought expressed in contradictories, moving endlessly from affirmation to negation, with no conclusive statement. But he purposely replaces the theme of critical negation by a definite assertion of the faithfulness of God. No longer does he say that God is the Wholly Other, nor that faith is empty space. He tries to introduce revelation into history. The *Church Dogmatics* was to emphasize this feature even more. It also gives great prominence to the "yes" that God says in Jesus Christ and no longer puts forward the idea that theology must be dialectics.

3. *The dialectic of Gogarten, Bultmann and Brunner.* The thought of Gogarten, Bultmann and perhaps to a lesser degree that of Brunner from about 1921 to 1924 was remarkably close to Barth in the role given to negation. "The idea of God", said Gogarten, "signifies the absolute *krisis* of everything human, and that means of all and every religion." Bultmann wrote: "God signifies the complete suppression of man, his repudiation, his being called into question and his judgment." And Brunner: "It is only in the *krisis* where man comes to an end, that grace can intervene as grace." All of them held that revelation and faith transcend historical knowledge and religious experience, that God is revealed in Jesus Christ as the Wholly Other, that he pronounces an essential "no" which accompanies an original and final "yes", that justified man remains a sinner and can only believe in the divine pardon. For them, however, the radical opposition of time and eternity does not separate two worlds, as with Barth. It divides the world which is our world. Dialectic or *krisis* is not as in the *Epistle to*

the Romans, the *actus purus* of an incomprehensible event in God. The moment in which it takes place is not an eternal moment beyond all time, but the unique and specific moment when the Word of God made flesh encounters the human decision of faith. But it must be said that this difference is hardly perceptible; especially as Barth affirms that divine revelation is the reply to the question of human existence.

But after 1926, when the others made room for the decision of faith by integrating into their theology, as a necessary presupposition, the understanding that man has of himself, it was quite clear that they conceived dialectical theology in a way quite different from Barth.

For Gogarten, the reason for which all speaking about God is dialectical is that we have no knowledge of God that is not at the same time and first of all knowledge of ourselves. It is not our relation to God, but our existence which is dialectical. The duality of the creator and the creature does away with the possibility of dialectic relationship, because it prohibits all unity and all relative exchange between the two terminal elements. There is only a dialectic of the creature, a dialectic within history, insofar as my present decision takes away and takes up my perishable past and thus confers upon it an imperishable character. Gogarten then explains that the constitutive element of history is faith in creation, the content of this faith being the encounter with the individual *thou* and the response to the call of one's neighbour. His later work sought to base relations between the individual and society on the *I-thou* relationship and here his analysis leans heavily upon the work of F. Ebner and M. Buber.

Bultmann likewise declared that theology cannot speak of God without at the same time speaking of man, and that consequently in its statements it presupposes a particular conception of man. This "pre-comprehension" he takes over from Heidegger after 1928: man's being is "historical", that is, its lot is at every moment at stake in the actual situations of life and moves through decisions in which man chooses himself as his *own possibility.* The expression "dialectical theology" actually means insight into the historical nature of man and of human speech in relation to God. The proposition: "God is merciful to me", is dialectical, not in the

77

sense that it must be completed and made more precise by the correlative mention of God's anger with the sinner (which is also accurate), but insofar as it is historical, insofar as it expresses the irruption of the grace of God.

For Brunner, the knowledge of man through himself, to which the unbeliever can come, and which as such is taken up into theological anthropology, constitutes the point of insertion of revelation in human reason. Wholly a sinner, but without ceasing to be the image of God, in the formal sense, man is a contradiction. That is why the divine summons is both an attack upon and the fulfilment of man. That is also why theology must be dialectical. The word "dialectical" can be paraphrased as: "reflecting contradiction". Because the word of God encounters man in contradiction, it stands itself "in contradiction"; its message is of the God who is man, wisdom which is foolishness, freedom which is the service of God, etc. And so it is most properly expressed through paradox.

4. *The parting of the ways.* Thus in spite of their differences, Brunner, Bultmann and Gogarten all agree that the dialectical character of theology is based on human existence, and not on the event of revelation which is the denial or rejection of it. Barth accuses them of accepting a second sovereign court of appeal besides the word of God (*Zwischen den Zeiten,* 11 [1933], pp. 297–314). He continued to maintain that human existence can only be contemplated in the light of the word of God. He deliberately excludes everything in his earlier writings which might suggest that theology was based on a philosophical analysis of existence (see his *Church Dogmatics,* vols. I/1 and VII). He no longer holds that divine revelation is the answer to the question of human existence.

When Gogarten joined the "German Christians" in 1933, Barth announced that he was to cease collaborating with *Zwischen den Zeiten,* and the editor stopped publication. The following year Barth emphatically rejected the "natural theology" which Brunner was developing. From then on each member of the group went his own way. And the vital influence behind their thought is no longer principally that "critical negation" which had first united them. Barth continued to develop his positive interests in his *Church Dogmatics* which has now reached the doctrine of the atonement (vol. IV/3, second part). Bultmann's theological programme of demythologizing and existential interpretation is pursued by Bultmann himself, E. Fuchs, G. Ebeling and others.

See also *Analogy of Being, Analogy of Faith, Demythologization, Existence* III.

BIBLIOGRAPHY. E. Brunner, *Erlebnis, Erkenntnis und Glaube* (1921); F. Gogarten, *Die religiöse Entscheidung* (1921); E. Brunner, *Die Mystik und das Wort. Der Gegensatz zwischen moderner Religionsauffassung und christlichem Glauben dargestellt an der Theologie Schleiermachers* (1924); K. Barth, *Word of God and Man* (1928); E. Brunner, *Theology of Crisis* (1930); id., *The Word and the World* (1931); R. Bultmann, *Glauben und Verstehen,* 4 vols. (1933–65); K. Barth, *Epistle to the Romans,* trans. from the 6th ed. by E. C. Hoskyns (1933); E. Brunner, *The Mediator* (1934); id., *God and Man. Four Essays on the Nature of Personality* (1936); E. Brunner and K. Barth, *Natural Theology, Comprising "Nature and Grace" by Emil Brunner and the Reply "No!" by Karl Barth* (1946); C. von Till, *The New Modernism. An Appraisal of the Theology of Barth and Brunner* (1946); H. U. von Balthasar, *Karl Barth, Darstellung und Deutung seiner Theologie* (1951; 2nd ed., 1962); H. Bouillard, *Karl Barth,* 3 vols. (1957); K. Barth, *Theology and Church* (1962); J. Moltmann, ed., *Anfänge der dialektischen Theologie,* I: *K. Barth, H. Barth, E. Brunner* (1962), II: *R. Bultmann, F. Gogarten, E. Thurneysen* (1963); T. F. Torrance, *Karl Barth. An Introduction to His Early Theology, 1910–1931* (1962); K. Barth, *Dogmatics in Outline* (new ed., 1961); H. Hartwell, *The Theology of K. Barth. An Introduction* (1964); B. A. Willems, *Karl Barth. Eine Einführung in sein Denken* (1964); H. Küng, *Justification* (1967).

Henri Bouillard

DIALECTICS

The origin of the term "dialectic" (διαλέγεσθαι, "to discuss", i.e., the for and against, thoroughly, by means of dialogue) points to the sphere of reasoning (λόγος, Spirit), but can have many shades of meaning. We here examine (1) the early history of the term, (2) its main usage, as seen in Hegel, (3) the correctives to be applied to Hegel, with the resulting perspective of (4) a dialectic of freedom and (5) its theological significance.

1. *Early history of the term.* The history of the philosophical concept begins with Heraclitus's question: "How is that which differs

from itself at agreement? Harmony is the tension of opposites, as in the bow and the lyre" (Fragment 51). This unity in tension is the basic law of the spirit, which it displays in all the polarity of worldly reality: day and night, life and death, war and peace, good and evil. The paradoxes of Zeno invoke against the phenomenon of movement the absolute logical contrast of being and non-being, as does Parmenides. This is the proto-type of a dialectic of pure negation. In the opposite direction, the Sophists exploit the trivial contradictions of immediate experi-ence against the universal validity of ethical norms. The spiritual and universal is de-fended by Socrates in the Platonic dialogues, where he uses the "dialectic" method of refuting mere opinions which are too readily accepted. In Plato (*Republic,* VI, 511), "dia-lectic" is the faculty of attaining the forms in themselves, through the opposites in which they are mediated. The later dialogues define the intrinsic connections of such basic concepts as being and nothingness, the one and the many, the self and the other. Aristotle uses "dialectic" for the argument from probabilities. But he also uses it for the probing and explicitating process of investi-gating opposites (1004b, 25; 1078b, 25 ff.), and in his notion of act and potency laid down the basis of a "dialectic of reality" which corresponds to the movement of the empir-ical world itself. For the Stoics, dialectic was part of logic, and meant the art of putting arguments and refuting objections. The neo-Platonists regarded it as the contemplation of the process of becoming in the world.

In the later tradition (scholasticism, mysti-cism, Nicholaus of Cusa), the dialectical thought-forms of (neo-) Platonism and Aris-totelianism continued to be stressed, rather than the meaning of the term in logic. Dialectical thought was given new dimen-sions in the Christian faith in the incarnation and Trinity. In Kant, the word took on once more a pejorative sense. Dialectic is the logic of the (inevitable) phenomenal, by which reason is carried away if it leaves the solid ground of experience and is thus trapped in the antinomies of reason. In Fichte, and above all in the systematic analysis of Hegel, dialectic is *the* logic of being, the inward Logos which pervades all reality.

2. *Hegel.* In the *Enzyklopädie,* nos. 79–82, Hegel describes the dialectical movement of

thought according to the following three moments: a) the abstract or intellectual moment which distinguishes clearly-defined concepts; b) the negative rational moment in which these concepts pass over into their opposites; c) the positive rational moment which comprises "the unity of the deter-minations in their opposition" (*ibid.,* 82). He does not speak of thesis, antithesis and synthesis, but of the universal and immediate "in itself" which becomes "for itself", exteriorizes, expounds, particularizes itself in its elements as it posits its contrary. This mediation leads to that which is "in and for itself" which comprises in one the self and the other as the fully formed individuality and the new "mediated immediacy". The dialectical movement takes up the initial position into the (preliminary) end position, where it is preserved on a new plane though taken away. The antithetical force of the negation, when applied to itself leads to synthesis with the original. (The simple negation shows the progressive and revolu-tionary trend of dialectic, while the double negation displays its conservative and reac-tionary character.) The effect is the process itself. "The truth is the whole."

Dialectic is the way in which the Spirit comes to consciousness of itself, extrapolat-ing itself by positing its opposite to find itself. Its self-externalization as the world is its entrance into its own depth and fullness — an "immanent outgoing". The process by which the Spirit explicitates itself is the law of becoming and being in the universe, from immediate, general being as the starting-point of the logical movement, to the absolute Spirit which knows itself in all, as the completion of the whole system. It takes in the various degrees of material nature, organic life, human spirit, law, State, history, art and religion, including the mysteries of the Christian faith: all is "taken up" in the concrete universality of the all-embracing Spirit. The dynamism which launches and sustains all is the discrepancy between the final goal and the emergent realities, whose very inadequacy forces them to strain on-wards till the Spirit has worked itself out in and through all and so become utterly itself in the all of knowing, the "circle of circles" of its dialectical spirals.

3. *Criticism of Hegel.* The Marxist criticism of the Hegelian dialectic took the form of

demanding its complete reversal, from top (the Spirit-idea) to bottom (material production): the determinant element is matter. The dialectical cycle which tends towards the universal self-identity of the Spirit by its reconciliation with the existent must be broken by a constant revolutionary negation based on the irreconcilable non-identity of the material (cf. T. W. Adorno, *Negative Dialektik* [1966]). Kierkegaard, in his *Philosophical Fragments,* protested against the Hegelian dialectic as a "Gnostic" bracketing of God and the world, and opposed to it the uniqueness of the free person, the moments of decision, the scandal of the historically unaccountable, the leap of faith. "Dialectical theology" insisted on the sharpest possible contradiction between God and the world; any mediation would be the work of Antichrist. The "dialogical" approach worked out since 1920 by such authors as F. Ebner and M. Buber tries to open up systematic *a priori* thinking for the relationships of interpersonal experience.

4. *The dialectic of freedom.* The dialectic of Hegel leaves no loop-holes for attack from outside; and it is not easy to distinguish between dialectic as a valid method and an erroneous system. But the Hegelian dialectic of knowledge can be adopted — transposed and re-cast — into an open dialectic of freedom (which we can do no more than indicate here). What is, in fact, the necessary presupposition of the dialectical movement? It is not matter — which is in any case only the penultimate stage as an opposite — but the reality of the free will, the real opposite of the Spirit's knowing. This in fact is what was recognized by Hegel when he placed the *decision* to arrive at true knowledge at the outset. The freedom of the subjectivity is the condition of possibility of true objectivity. Since freedom determines the self-consciousness of the Spirit as it comes to know, it is never fully absorbed by it. Its immediacy is not lost in the process of mediation, of which it is the permanent and all-pervading foundation. This makes it impossible to reduce the "other" to a mere moment in the self-apprehension of the subject, as the totality of the Spirit embraces both. It is the specific law and function of the will to achieve "in" the object the identity of the Spirit as subject and object. Hence the ultimate must necessarily be the affirmation of the other qua other.

In contrast to the necessary essences and all-embracing unity of a purely cognitive system, we have the finite which is permanently valid in its diversity and multiplicity, the individual which is permanently significant, a historicity which is free and not summed up already, the hope of the new and the hopeful act in creative fellowship. In the space thrown open by a dialectic of freedom, the constructive elements in Hegel's thought retain their real force: the intensity of experience, the relentless effort to close in on the concrete, the resolution of over-rigid schemes of thought, the reconciliation of ostensible opposites, the manifestation of the spiritual structure of all beings — compare the scholastic transcendental, "omne ens est intelligibile" — and the meaningful contradiction of the contradictoriness of things. The free reality of the human spirit which dialectic supposes experiences itself, in its truth-obscuring fragility, as posited by a primordial freedom. It is welcomed and wooed to its own selfhood.

5. *Theological significance.* We may now consider the theological significance of an open dialectic. The structural law is provided by the metaphysics of creation: "The closer a being is to God ... the greater is its natural tendency to self-realization" (Thomas Aquinas, *De veritate,* 22, 4). The degree in which true selfhood is realized is the co-efficient of the constitutive transcendental relation to God, who gives and sustains being creatively, and it is also the co-efficient of free mastery of self. Dependence and freedom are here not in inverse proportion, but are dialectical equivalents of each other. The creative freedom of God makes men free. The supreme liberating inauguration of human being in its essential fulfilment takes place in the personal union of the Logos-God with human nature in Jesus Christ. Its effective expression is also in the fellowship, the *one* earthly and eternal community of the "Christus totus caput et membra" (Augustine) in the Spirit of the unity of the Father and Son — called grace *(ad intra)* and Church *(ad extra)*. Here too, in the expansion beyond space and time of the fundamental union of God and man in Christ, "grace presupposes nature" — in the literal ontological sense of "positing it beforehand" — "and fulfils it". In the creative, incarnational, grace-giving and Church-founding event of the union,

which makes man freer and freer, we can
see manifested and active the "immanent"
Trinity of Father, Son and Spirit, which is
the primordial instance of personal relation
and mutual constitution in the spirit, and
hence of dialectic.

At the same time, the original event of
Christ, with the liberating installation of man
in the Spirit-fellowship of the *Christus totus,*
provides the universe for all the further
dialectical traits, which now, with a certain
inevitability, make up Christian faith and life:
the relationships of presupposition as between faith and knowledge (and on a higher,
more systematic degree of reflection, between
philosophy and theology); history and revelation; human *religio* and the gospel of the
apostles of Jesus; letter and spirit; sacramental gesture and word; love of God and
love of the neighbour. All of which is given
unfathomable depth by the relation of
opposition between human sin and divine
redemption (cf. Rom 5:20f.), in the cross of
Jesus Christ: the utterly real and not merely
"speculative" Good Friday.

See also *Spirit, Act and Potency, Marxism* II.

BIBLIOGRAPHY. J. McTaggart, *Studies in
the Hegelian Dialectic* (1896; repr. 1964); E. Hein-
tel, *Hegel und die analogia entis* (1958); H. Ogiermann, *Materialistische Dialektik* (1958); H. Dahm,
Die Dialektik im Wandel der Sowjetphilosophie
(1963); T. W. Adorno, *Drei Studien zu Hegel*
(2nd ed., 1966); K. Kosík, *Die Dialektik des
Konkreten* (1967).

Walter Kern

DIOCESE

A diocese is a territorial corporation established by the competent ecclesiastical authority. It is part of the people of God having
at its head its own shepherd, and in its own
district represents the Church.

A. HISTORY OF THE WORD

Deriving from διοικεῖν, meaning "to keep
house", "to administer", the word διοίκησις
signified an administrative district and in
Roman law became a technical term for
political organizational units of varying
sizes: city districts, portions of a province,
and after the division of the empire into

12 districts under Diocletian (297), the larger
unit comprising several provinces. The usage
whereby diocese refers to the greater unity
and province to the smaller, follows the
legal language of the Eastern Churches. According to a usage dependent upon the civil
division of areas of jurisdiction which was
already in use by the time of the First
Ecumenical Synod of Nicaea (can. 6) and
which was fully confirmed by the Synod of
Chalcedon (431), the diocese indicates a large
area of jurisdiction composed of several
ecclesiastical provinces (called ἐπαρχίαι at
that time) with an exarch (later a patriarch)
at its head. The simple unit of episcopal
jurisdiction was called παροικία up to the
12th century and was later referred to (as it
still is) as an *eparchy;* diocese was never used
in the East with this meaning.

The development of usage was completely
different in the West; there diocese never
referred to the larger districts of Church
organization. The ordinary episcopal district
was also here called *parochia* or *paroecia* and
comprised at first the urban community, then
after the second half of the 4th century the
city and rural areas of an episcopal see.
Diocese was first used in this sense by Innocent I (*Ep.,* 40, in *PL,* XX, 606f.), though
it was as yet not a fixed term and meant
either the community of a bishop's city, the
rural area or the entire diocese, or at times
even a Church province. Parish and diocese
were used in the same sense for a long time.
It was only in the 13th century that diocese
was used technically to indicate the community over which the bishop ruled.

B. NATURE AND FORM OF THE DIOCESE

The diocese is a part of the people of God at
whose head stands the bishop; he represents
for the flock entrusted to him the invisible
Lord and, together with his priests, so joins
the faithful in unity with Christ that in this
unit of the Church "the one, holy, catholic,
and apostolic Church of Christ is truly active
and present" (Vatican II, Decree on the
Bishops' Pastoral Office, art. 11). The division into episcopal Churches is an essential
element of Church order, as the bishop is the
line of succession to the apostles and as such
is entrusted with a divine mission and the
authority which is necessary for the exercise
of his episcopal tasks (*ibid.,* art. 8). The
diocese is consequently no mere administra-

tive district of the Church, but represents the whole Church in its own area, being united through its bishop to the Pope and the college of bishops. It is an essential part which reflects the whole.

Just as the image of the bishop has been determined from primitive times (Ignatius, *Ad Magnesios,* 6; 7; *Ad Smyrnenses,* 8; 9) by his relationship to a given flock, so too the juridical status of the diocese is determined by the juridical nature of the episcopal office, which is of divine right but which must always be determined in concrete particulars by the Church. The recognition of the fact that the bishops are not vicars of the Pope but of Christ, will not alter the situation, for the episcopal office based on succession to the apostles was from the beginning a hierarchically-ordered office which extended from the leadership of a given local Church to the various types of higher episcopal authorities (metropolitans, exarchs, patriarchs) and to the supreme pastoral office of the Pope. Thus the episcopal office has this particular characteristic, that jurisdiction over a given local Church bestowed by ecclesiastical tradition or by a special legal act can be at the same time the basis of a more extensive episcopal charge. The bishop of a diocese is thus integrated into a hierarchical organization which necessitates a demarcation of jurisdiction for each office. As a typical basic ecclesiastical office, the episcopal office serves the organization of the people of God and thereby the orderly realization of the saving mission of the Church. Hence the divinely-instituted office requires to be given concrete form in time and space, and this occurs in the establishment of a diocese which in the early Church was done by the exercise of the office, from which the legal boundaries followed, and in later times by a formal act of the competent authority. The establishment of a diocese necessarily involves the establishment of an episcopal office; a community is created which is given a head through the mediation of the office. In this sense the diocese and the episcopal office conjoined to it are of ecclesiastical law and can, as ecclesiastical organizational structures, be changed or abolished.

The establishment of dioceses essentially follows territorial divisions, i.e., Christians living in a certain district are formed into a community under a bishop ("territorial corporation"). By this means each Christian has his own pastor (the "territorial principle"). Dioceses are generally named after the city of the bishop's residence, i.e., his see. By way of exception, there are sometimes *personal dioceses,* especially when the marriages of Catholics of another rite seem to need their own prelate; in such cases, however, the jurisdictional boundaries within the rite concerned follow territorial boundaries, so that here too the diocese is territorial. Communities on purely personal foundations can enjoy extensive exemption from the jurisdiction of the local ordinary, but are not called dioceses. The competent authority for the establishment, alteration and suppression of dioceses in the Latin Church is the Pope (*CIC,* can. 215, § 1) and in the Eastern Churches normally the patriarch with the consent of the patriarchal synod, or the major archbishop (*CIO,* can. 159; cf. can. 248, 327, § 1, 328).

With regard to the size of dioceses there are no fixed specifications. Every attempt to derive such specifications from the nature of the diocese and the episcopal office have been in vain, because here the concrete ecclesiastical situation plays a decisive role. The Church has always oriented itself upon the city in its erection of a diocese, "ne episcopi nomen et auctoritas vilipendatur" (Synod of Sardica, can. 6). This will probably be future practice also, though in view of the change in sociological structures care must be taken to estimate the actual importance which a city has with reference to the larger territorial divisions. Vatican II discussed the delimitation of dioceses and recommended a re-organization in the near future, with a view to dividing or merging dioceses according to need, changing boundaries, or moving episcopal sees to more appropriate localities (Decree on the Bishops' Pastoral Office, art. 22). In an attempt to preserve the organic unity of each diocese, general guidelines were issued which foresee, among other things, a) that each diocese should form a territorial unity; b) that the size of the territory and the number of its inhabitants should be such that the bishop is able to carry out all his duties in a proper manner, while it should be large enough to provide sufficient scope for the activities of the bishop and his clergy; c) that there be offices, institutions, and organizations proper for all the functions of the local Church, and the means for supporting these should be available or at least foreseen in the immediate future.

A more important and practicable requirement would seem to be the establishment of a reasonable relationship between the number of clerics involved in diocesan administration and the number of priests occupied in pastoral care. If the modest requirements of the *CIC* are followed with regard to the establishment of a diocese, the number of those required for its administration will be twenty or thirty, while the number of priests in pastoral work will be about ten to twenty times as great. Such a ratio would ensure that the diocese was an efficient and capable organization and that it would fulfil its tasks in the framework of the entire Church. The diocesan organization of large cities, especially those that number several million inhabitants, present special difficulties; these are in need of a new type of inner organization *(ibid.)*. The organizational unity must be maintained, while appropriate distribution of labour ensures that the bishop's duties towards his people are carried out in a meaningful way.

Forms of organization sometimes substituting for the ordinary diocesan form are abbeys and prelatures *nullius (abbatia vel praelatura nullius)*; the apostolic administrature; in the mission countries the prefecture apostolic and in the case of rapidly developing missions which outgrow the prefecture, the vicariate apostolic. In modern times the trend has been to establish dioceses in missionary districts as soon as possible.

C. Appointment of Bishops

1. *History*. In early Christian times the bishop was chosen by clergy and laity with the supervisory assistance of the neighbouring bishops. The Council of Nicaea (can. 4) gave the metropolitan the right of approval and consecration; at the election at least three bishops must be present, who take part in the election as well as in the examination and the confirmation of the candidate. The presence of three bishops is retained today in the rite of consecration. With the rise of absolutism, the occupancy of episcopal sees became a matter of state politics. The emperors often intervened in the election and appointment of bishops. The right of election, which was firmly defended by Leo the Great, seemed in the laws of Justinian to have become a mere

right to propose names in the East; the clerics and prominent laymen were to propose to the metropolitan persons they thought suited for the dignity. The seventh general council (Nicaea, 787) gave bishops (in can. 3) the right of nomination and declared appointment by civil rulers to be invalid. The practice in the East was that the bishops of the province presented three candidates, the most worthy of whom was then to be consecrated by the metropolitan.

In the West this procedure was changed under the influence of Germanic customs which gave a decisive voice in the matter to the monarch. The right of election was replaced to a great extent by royal nomination. For Charlemagne this was an expression of the power given to him by God. The political power of the episcopacy consequently grew and its bestowal became mostly a matter of royal investiture. The notion of special rights over the Church affected in particular the dioceses of southern France. In general the distinction between the spiritual office and lay investiture became so obscured that the bestowal of both by the king was also represented in the signs of the office (the crozier, and since Henry II, the ring). The reform movement demanded that the right of bestowing offices be given back to the Church, especially the right of a free episcopal election by clergy and people (Leo IX at the Synod of Rheims, 1049). The investiture dispute ended in the restoration of the right of free episcopal election. The growing power of the cathedral chapter eventually resulted in excluding the lower clergy and the laity from such elections. The right of election was changed from a mere agreement to an actual choice. Towards the end of the 12th century the electoral rights of the cathedral chapter were generally recognized and were given force of universal law by Innocent III. With this development, which was favoured by the Popes, the right of approbation and of consecration finally rested with the Apostolic See.

The influence of the Bishop of Rome did not at first exceed his rights as metropolitan and patriarch; only the early custom whereby communion with Rome was sought by means of *epistolae synodicae* actually resembled a form of approbation. Since the 9th century the Popes were accustomed to intervene in the appointment to episcopal sees in the case of deposition or transfer. Disputes concerning elections came increasingly under the verdict of Rome. At the same time papal influence in episcopal consecration was growing. Gregory VII at the Lenten Synod of 1080 was able to assert that the power of approbation in the case of episcopal elections was held by the Apostolic See or by the metropolitan (can. 6). This right was also often used to exert influence on the election itself. By means of papal reservations, applied at first only occasionally, then to certain sees and finally universally by Urban V (1363), the powers of the chapter were first undermined, and then juridically suppressed, when the papal chancellory adopted universal reservation into its rules.

The disputes about the Council of Basle, which had rejected all general reservations not contained in the *CIC,* led to the recognition of the electoral rights of the cathedral chapter in the Concordat of Vienna (1448), though with considerable limitations. After initial opposition, episcopal election became the rule in the German Empire. But elsewhere, partly in the wake of the disputes centring on the Council of Basle, the right of nomination was conferred on the king by papal privilege, as an extension of the papal right of investiture, e.g., in France (Concordat of 1516), in the crown-lands of the emperor, and elsewhere. The Spanish crown possessed in its European and South American lands the right of presentation and nomination which derived from its right of patronage, or from papal grant. Princes who failed to secure the right of nomination influenced appointments by intervening in elections. Thus in feudal bishoprics they gained the right of specifying the candidates whom they did not favour, and thus could exclude *personae minus gratae* from the election.

With the decline of the Catholic royal houses the right of nomination fell mostly into disuse; the way was already partly prepared before the *CIC* for the institution of papal appointment. In mission areas the papal rights were never disputed, and were scarcely touched by concordats and customary laws. There developed here a practice of drawing up lists of candidates whereby the Apostolic See was informed by the bishops of a country, partly also by the cathedral chapter, concerning persons suited for the episcopal office either in general or with regard to a particular see. The historical roots of this procedure lay in the Irish custom of

domestic nomination which was basically a canonical right of election emptied of its legal force. In the U.S.A. this practice is maintained in the form given it in the 19th century.

2. *Prevailing law*. a) In the Latin Church the Pope appoints bishops freely (*CIC,* can. 329), wherever he is not bound by law to accept the choice put forward by those who have right of election, nomination or presentation. The bestowal of the episcopal office is exclusively the Pope's in every case (can. 332, § 1); he exercises his right in the case of a previous election by approval of the candidate and in the case of nomination or presentation by canonical installation. The electoral rights of the cathedral chapter are still retained in the Swiss bishoprics of Basle, Chur, and St. Gall, in the German bishoprics (outside Bavaria), with the limitation of a choice from three candidates to be proposed by the Pope, and in Salzburg. In Alsace-Lorraine the right of nomination has been retained (by the concordat of 1801). Reminiscent of the old right of patronage, the limited right of choosing from the papal panel of three candidates is granted to Spain (1941); Portugal possesses a merely formal right of presentation for its East-Indian bishoprics (1928). The practice of presenting lists of candidates, which originated in mission countries, is in force almost everywhere, normally in such a way that the bishops of a certain area periodically (every one, two or three years) propose the names of suitable candidates for the episcopacy, though for certain sees lists are proposed either by the cathedral chapter concerned or by the bishops of the area or by both. The panel of candidates serves solely to supply information to the Holy See; only in Bavaria does it have a legally binding character.

Through the concordats concluded after the Second World War, the influence of the State on episcopal appointments is generally limited to putting forward general political considerations. This means that no legal obstacles hinder the freedom of the Holy See. Enquiries about political misgivings are also made, as in France, where there is no concordat to enforce the process. Vatican II expressed the desire that in the future the State be denied the right to propose candidates for diocesan sees, and desired that those

States which still enjoy such rights and privileges should relinquish them of their own accord (Decree on the Bishops' Pastoral Office, art. 20).

b) In the Eastern Churches the laws governing episcopal appointments are substantially those of Christian antiquity. The new canon law for the Eastern Churches takes this tradition into account and provides that the Pope should freely appoint the bishops or approve the properly elected candidates (*CIC*, can. 392, § 2). Generally, however, an election is held by the synod of all the residential and titular bishops of the patriarchate, the preparations and the actual management of which are in the hands of the patriarch (can. 251 ff.). To expedite matters, canon 254 provides that the choice is made from a panel drawn up by the electoral synod and approved by the Holy See, while consecration and enthronement may follow at once. No formal confirmation by the Pope is necessary, because it is already implicitly given; the Holy See must merely be informed of the election having taken place. If an electoral synod is impossible, the patriarch arranges an election by letter, with the permission of the Holy See, whereby two bishops must assist the patriarch as examiners (can. 255).

D. The Legal Position of the Diocesan Bishop

1. *Episcopal jurisdiction.* The authority of the diocesan bishop, like that of every other bishop, is essentially based on his episcopal consecration (Vatican II, Constitution on the Church, art. 21); it is defined in greater detail and becomes actual authority through the conferring of a diocese. The old dispute whether a diocesan bishop has his pastoral power from God or from the Pope has been decided by Vatican II; the heads of local Churches are not vicars of the Pope but vicars and envoys of Christ; their ecclesiastical authority is exercized in the name of Christ (*ibid.*, art. 27). This assertion of the Council is found in the teaching on the pastoral office which it distinguishes from the teaching and priestly offices; it applies likewise, however, in the spheres of the teaching and priestly offices as it is the one sacred authority of the bishop which is active in all three offices. In the Decree

on the Bishops' Pastoral Office it is further asserted that "as successors of the apostles, bishops automatically enjoy in the diocese entrusted to them all the ordinary, proper, and immediate authority required for the exercise of their pastoral office. But this authority never in any instance infringes upon the power which the Roman Pontiff has, by virtue of his office, of reserving cases to himself or to some other authority." (Art. 8.) With this declaration the original rights of the episcopate are fully restored.

A far-reaching clarification of this question, was already given in practice in the motu proprio *Pastorale munus* of 30 November 1963. Here the diocesan bishops were granted an imposing array of new powers, which also belong *de jure* to apostolic vicars and prefects, permanently appointed apostolic administrators as well as abbots and prelates *nullius,* and which can also be delegated to coadjutors, auxiliary bishops and vicars-general. The previous system of granting faculties to bishops (by way of concession) which since Trent was covered by the legal term *tamquam Sedis Apostolicae delegatus,* has been replaced by a system of papal reservations. With respect to former law this means a radical change in the relationship between the Pope and the diocesan bishop; the presumption is now in favour of the latter, that he has all the powers necessary for the due exercise of his office. But this is not a revolutionary change, since canon law had preserved many of the original rights of the bishop, such as that of conferring all benefices in his diocese (can. 1432, § 1).

The rights of the bishop are here presumed, in contrast to papal reservation. How these basic decisions of the Council will be implemented technically is still to be seen. A list might be made of the matters and cases which would be reserved to the Pope or another authority (patriarch, episcopal conference). Though such a method might correspond to the conciliar requirements, it does not appear to be well suited for defining adequately the authority of the diocesan bishops. Even under the new system of the relationships between Pope and bishop it remains true that the diocesan bishop is bound to rule his diocese "ad normam sacrorum canonum" (*CIC,* can. 335, § 1).

The diocesan bishop stands in a hierarchically-ordered structure which contains besides bishops and their head (college of bishops and Pope) intermediate offices in the form of the higher episcopate (patriarch, metropolitan) and collegial organs (synods, episcopal conferences); the office of the diocesan bishop therefore requires a positive definition of its rights and duties to which the explicit reservations in favour of the Pope or other authorities can well be joined. In this connection it should be noted that the problem of the precise definition of authority is quite different in the legislative sphere where it is imperative to give universally binding norms for the entire Church or for separate groups of Churches, and in the judicial and administrative spheres which are concerned with the implementation of norms, or with making regulations for situations not envisaged by such norms. In art. 8b of the Decree on the Bishops' Pastoral Office the individual diocesan bishops are given faculties to dispense those over whom they exercise lawful authority from a general law of the Church in particular cases, where they consider such dispensations useful for the spiritual good of their subjects — unless special reservations have been made by the supreme authority of the Church. Though the basic declaration on the authority of the diocesan bishop in art. 8a still awaits implementation, which can hardly come in fully mature form before the reform of canon law, the faculties envisaged by art. 8b have already been implemented for the Latin Church by the motu proprio *De Episcoporum Muneribus* of 15 June 1966. This is a provisional regulation, valid as from 15 August 1966 and due to expire with the promulgation of the new code.

The motu proprio recalls that the norms of canon law and later regulations are still in force, provided that they have not been revoked — unless they have been clearly abrogated in whole or in part by the Council, or replaced by a new organization of the matter involved. Only can. 81 is changed in part by art. 8b of the decree, insofar as faculty to dispense has been conferred on the bishops independent of special circumstances and merely envisaging in a general way the spiritual welfare of the faithful. The motu proprio extends these faculties to the prelates juridically of equal status with diocesan bishops, that is, to vicars and prefects apostolic (can. 294, § 1), permanent apostolic administrators (can. 315, § 1), abbots and prelates *nullius* (can. 323, § 1); and rightly so,

since authority serves the spiritual good of the faithful. The authority may be exercised with regard to all the faithful who are subject to the local ordinary because of their domicile or other juridical titles (no. VII) but not over religious in their quality of religious, and not at all over members of exempt clerical orders, so that the unity of religious discipline may not be disturbed (no. IX, 4). This is a departure from previous practice, which allowed religious the possibility of benefiting by general dispensations, and restricts the efforts which have been made to bring religious more fully under the bishop even in his *jurisdictio gratiosa*. The faculties apply only to dispensations in the strict sense (can. 80), but not to the granting of permissions (a notion very difficult to distinguish from that of dispensation); nor do they apply to the granting of faculties, indults or absolution. The general Church laws for which the faculty of dispensation is granted do not include *leges constitutivae* (constitutional laws) or the rules for judicial procedure, since these do not directly affect the spiritual welfare of the faithful.

This restriction, which is justifiable in itself, is not free from contradictory elements and does not throw sufficient light on the matter, since the distinction between *leges constitutivae* (a concept unknown to canon law) and laws which express a command or prohibition is left vague. The reason for granting a dispensation, according to can. 84, must have to do with the spiritual welfare of the faithful, if the dispensation is to be legal; otherwise, it is illicit and invalid. Without prejudice to the faculties specially granted to papal legates and higher prelates, the Pope reserves to himself a total of twenty cases of dispensation (no. IX). These are mostly cases in which hitherto the Pope has never granted a dispensation, or only rarely and because of particularly grave reasons. But they include some cases where the reservation hardly seems justifiable, as for instance a dispensation from the course of philosophy or theology, both as regards the time and the main subjects involved (no. IX, 7), or dispensation from the eucharistic fast (no. IX, 20). The reservations are concerned with the obligations of the clerical state, including the celibacy of priests and deacons (no. IX, 1–3), the duty of denunciation enunciated by can. 904 (no. IX, 5), the requisites for the reception and exercise of holy orders (no. IX, 6–10), for the celebration of matrimony (impediments and obligation of the form) and *sanatio in radice* (no. IX, 11–18). Absolution from a censure is not a dispensation in the technical sense, but the remission of a penalty, like absolution from a penance. The reservation of absolution from a censure laid down by general law, when imposed or recognized as existing by the Holy See (no. IX, 19), points clearly to the fact that we still await the necessary reconsideration of the absolution of reserved penalties, which is so necessary for the spiritual welfare of the faithful. Pastoral prudence suggests that only those censures should be reserved to the Holy See which are already reserved *specialissimo modo* in the present canon law.

The pastoral authority of the diocesan bishop is divided into three functions. a) The bishop is legislator, i.e., he can impose general precepts on his diocese within the framework of universal or particular Church law. Episcopal legislation is normally promulgated in the diocesan periodical, and comes into force as soon as promulgated, unless otherwise indicated. The diocesan synod has no legislative powers (*CIC*, can. 362). b) The bishop is judge in his diocese (can. 1572), though he must appoint an official and a synodal judge for the exercise of the ordinary judicial functions. In matters concerning him or his curia he cannot act as judge, nor should he do so in penal matters and more important disputes (can. 1578). Decisions regarding diocesan administration are made by him, in his ecclesiastical court. c) The bishop is the administrator of his diocese, though he is bound in certain cases to seek the advice of the cathedral chapter. For detailed discussion of the organization of the administration see below E and F.

2. *Episcopal duties.* The diocesan bishop is charged with the proper exercise of the salvific mission of the Church in its doctrinal, priestly and governing office (see Vatican II, Constitution on the Church, art. 24–27, and Decree on the Bishops' Pastoral Office, arts. 12–21).
a) *Magisterium.* As a representative of the Church's magisterium, the diocesan bishop is responsible for the preservation and proclamation of the word of God in his diocese (can. 1326). He must guard the purity of doctrine in the spoken or the written word (can. 336, § 2; 343, § 1; 1384, 1395), though he has no independent authority to settle disputed questions. He is bound to preach the word of God himself and to employ others in this ministry (can. 1327); he gives the canonical mission of teaching and preaching (can. 1328, 1338); he is responsible for the instruction of the faithful in Christian doctrine (can. 1336); he establishes and inspects seminaries and schools (can. 1352, 1372).

b) *Sacerdotium.* The bishop is the high-priest of his diocese; he is bound to offer holy Mass for his diocesans on Sundays and holidays, including those which have been suppressed (can. 339). The mention of his name in the celebration of the Eucharist is a sign of communion with the bishop who is responsible for the administration of the sacraments and all other sacred ministries in the diocese. The conferring of holy orders is reserved to the bishop (can. 955), as are the consecration of the holy oils (can. 734, § 1), and of churches (can. 1147, § 1), and in the Latin Church the normal administration of confirmation (can. 783, 785).

c) *Regimen.* The bishop is responsible for the organization of the diocese: the establishment of the diocesan curia and the appointment and change of all officials, the establishment, alteration, or termination of minor offices (can. 394, § 2; 1414, § 2; 1423 ff.), especially those of parish priests and curates, the organization of parishes into deaneries and the appointment of minor ecclesiastical officials (can. 152, 1432, § 1); papal reservations (can. 1434, 1435) are to be revoked (Vatican II, Decree on the Bishops' Pastoral Office, art. 31). The bishop administers diocesan property and has the right to impose taxes (can. 1355 f.; 1429, 1496, 1504 ff.). He has the duty of supporting those ordained for his diocese (can. 981, § 2) and of distributing justly diocesan revenues. He fixes stole fees and Mass stipends (can. 831, 1234). Except in cases of exemption, he supervises clergy, laymen, religious houses, associations, institutions (churches, chapels, schools, hospitals, cemeteries), and especially the management of church property. In the case of abuses he can intervene authoritatively. He is obliged to make visitations of his diocese (can. 343–6) and to submit reports to the Holy See, in person, at intervals (*visitatio liminum*).

E. The Diocesan Curia

The diocesan curia is the staff of officials employed in the government of the diocese. It has no corporative organization and does not possess the character of a juridical person. Officials within the diocesan curia are: the vicar-general who is in charge of general administration; the *officialis* (Chancellor) and the synodal judges, the promotor of justice, the defender of the (marriage) bond, the synodal examiner, the parish consultors, the chancellor, and the notaries. The cathedral chapter does not belong to the diocesan curia, but has a voice in certain administrative matters.

The most important official in the diocesan curia is the vicar-general. He is the representative *(alter ego)* of the bishop in matters of general administration, in discretionary and in obligatory matters. The bishop can either limit the authority of the vicar-general as fixed by law, or he can also in special circumstances provided for by law broaden his powers by special mandate (can. 368, § 1). The vicar-general is bound to follow the directives of the bishop, in contrast to the Chancellor, and may not exercise his authority contrary to the mind of the bishop (can. 369). The office of the vicar-general has proved itself to be of great value in the larger dioceses. Normally only one vicar-general is to be appointed for each diocese to safeguard the unity of administrative practice. However, if differences of rites or the growth of the diocese require it, several may be appointed; in the former case their authority is confined to certain persons, in the latter it can apply to certain matters or (what is generally more practicable) certain districts, so that each vicar-general is responsible for one part of the diocese (can. 366, § 3). This last possibility is, however, disputed.

In order to give auxiliary bishops a position corresponding to their episcopal dignity, Vatican II created the episcopal vicar *(vicarius episcopalis)* who by virtue of his office exercises in a designated district of the diocese or in a special task or over the faithful of a different rite the authority which canon law assigns to the vicar-general (Decree on the Bishops' Pastoral Office, art. 27). This position is in itself unnecessary, as the office of the vicar-general is so flexible that it could be made to include such tasks.

Nevertheless, it must be recognized that this new legal figure, though it was instituted for the sake of the auxiliary bishops, is independent of the episcopal dignity and can also be conferred upon simple priests. What is new in this legislation is that the bishop must make his auxiliary bishop or bishops vicars-general or at least episcopal vicars, with corresponding authority, in the exercise of which they are not responsible to the vicar-general, whether the latter is a bishop or not, but to the diocesan bishop alone. Also, the auxiliary is to retain this office in the case that the episcopal see is vacated (*ibid.,* art. 26). Further, *sede vacante,* the office of vicar capitular should be entrusted to the auxiliary; but the cathedral chapter retains the freedom to appoint a non-bishop to the office of vicar capitular. A coadjutor bishop, who in future must have right of succession, must be appointed by the diocesan bishop to the office of vicar-general; in special cases greater powers can be given to him by the competent authorities *(ibid.).*

There is no lack of salutary warnings by the Council that the unity of diocesan administration must be assured and that between the diocesan bishop and his coadjutor or auxiliary fraternal love should prevail. Proposals for some type of collegial diocesan government (under the formula "una sub et cum Episcopo diocesano" were eventually discouraged by the Council. The diocesan bishop remains the shepherd of his flock, but with the appointment of coadjutors and auxiliaries he must accept the fact that in the co-ordination of diocesan administration he can no longer rely solely on the vicar-general.

F. Collegial Bodies

1. *Permanent collegial bodies.* Apart from the cathedral chapter (*CIC,* can. 391–422), or council, where there is no chapter, the code envisages a council of administration for Church property (can. 423–8), which is to consist of the bishop and two or more other members, who should be experienced in civil law (can. 1520); there is nothing to prevent laymen being members of this board. The bishop must consult this board in all important matters. The board has only a consultative role but in certain cases foreseen by law (e.g., can. 1532, § 3; cf. 1653, § 1) or provided for by foundations, it has also a deliberative voice. Vatican II desired that in

every diocese a pastoral council should be instituted, composed of priests, religious, and laymen under the presidency of the diocesan bishop. The task of the council is to consider matters pertaining to pastoral care and to suggest practical measures (Decree on the Bishops' Pastoral Office, art. 27). A special concern of Vatican II was the revival of the presbyterate (Constitution on the Church, art. 28); the diocesan bishop is to meet his priests for discussion of pastoral problems, individually and as a group, if possible at regular intervals.

As a practical measure in this direction, Vatican II (Decree on the Ministry and Life of Priests, art. 7) envisages the obligatory erection of a council of priests which will be representative of the presbyterate. The council is to be given a statutory status corresponding to modern needs. The task assigned to the council of priests, that of effectively supporting by their counsel the episcopal administration, corresponds essentially to that of the pastoral council, and is hard to distinguish from it, unless the latter confines itself to defining the problems while the former envisages practical measures. In practice the two will have to work together. A special task of the council of priests will be to consider the welfare of the presbyterate itself, which needs a new organization to assure contact with the bishop and between the priests themselves. And this will be the most effective contribution of the council of priests to the pastoral efforts of the bishop.

2. *The diocesan synod.* This representative assembly of the diocesan clergy meets at least every ten years. It is convoked and presided over by the bishop. Its duty is to advise the bishop, who is the sole legislator in the diocese (can. 362). Through their representatives, the clergy thus have a statutory opportunity of putting forward suggestions and proposals on urgent questions of diocesan government, especially with regard to forms of pastoral care and problems of the priestly life. It has a right to decide on the nomination of synodal judges, examiners and counsellors (can. 385, 1574), who are proposed by the bishop and confirmed by the collegiate vote of the synod.

See also *Ecclesiastical Regions, Ecclesiastical Office* I, *Ecclesiastical Tribunals, Bishop* III.

BIBLIOGRAPHY. S. D'Angelo, *La curia diocesana,* 2 vols. (1922); P. Hofmeister, *Bischof und Domkapitel nach altem und neuem Recht* (1931); K. Mörsdorf, *Das neue Besetzungsrecht der bischöflichen Stühle mit besonderer Berücksichtigung des Listenverfahrens* (1933); G. E. Lynch, *Coadjutors and Auxiliaries of Bishops* (1947); L. Mathias, *The Diocesan Curia* (1947); K. Rahner and J. Ratzinger, *The Episcopate and the Primacy,* Quaestiones Disputatae 4 (1962).

Klaus Mörsdorf

DISCERNMENT OF SPIRITS

1. *Introduction.* God's self-communication which is the source of Christian life in the Church through Christ, is also a revelation of himself: a movement, a call, and speech perceptible to men. To the outward hearing of the gospel corresponds in the hearer an inner perception of the hidden word of God (Mt 11:25). The divine glory radiates in the hearts of those who hear the good news of Christ (2 Cor 4:4–6). They enter into an experiential fellowship with God (1 Jn 2:3ff.). He "draws" his own, and they are taught by him (Jn 6:44f.). God has given them a special capacity to perceive his action, a special "sense" (1 Jn 5:20). Without this God could not be understood (Mk 4:12). The magisterium of the Church also affirms that "God touches the heart of men through the illumination of his Holy Spirit" (*D* 797), he "rouses" and "calls" (*D* 814). The Holy Spirit "admonishes" and "invites", and without his "speaking and rousing there is neither a beginning made along the way of virtue, nor progress, nor attainment of everlasting salvation" (Leo XIII, *Divinum Illud*). But Satan is also active within men, disguised as an angel of light (2 Cor 11:14). This is the reason for the admonition, "beloved, do not believe every spirit, but test the spirits to see if they are from God" (1 Jn 4:1). This is the capacity for the discernment of spirits, which St. Paul includes under "charisms" (1 Cor 12:10), not as though it were a prerogative seldom to be exercised, but because it presupposes spiritual maturity for the full exercise of the gift and its manifestation as a grace. It has its origin in love: "that your love may abound ever more and more, with knowledge and all discernment" (Phil 1:9–10). Love possesses an instinct which finds spontaneously the appropriate attitude: "love is patient and

kind; love is not jealous or boastful; it is not arrogant or rude" (1 Cor 13:4ff.).

2. *Theological considerations.* Seen from the viewpoint of systematic theology, the ultimate norm for the discernment of spirits is the non-objectivated consciousness of God, accessible to all Christians, which is contained in the exercise of the theological virtues. When communicating himself in grace to men, God brings about in them the acceptance of this communication and the response to it. This is above all the movement of faith-hope-charity. In them (according to a *sententia quasi communis*) God is present to the consciousness, in a non-objectivated way, as the formal object of these virtues, as the light which illumines the objects of these virtues in their act, though it is a light which is never itself "seen" (in the sense of an ontologism). It is only experienced together with the objects of these virtues in the course of their exercise. Such a consciousness of God can thus never be the object of introspection. Nor can it be a guarantee of the state of grace. Nevertheless, such an experience, since it involves an experience of God, is already an initial directive from the will of God, providing a real norm for the discernment of spirits, though one that is only a concomitant experience in a non-objectivated way. The religious and moral impulses in the inner life of man ("natural" or supernatural) which are in harmony with such a light, are "from the good Spirit", i.e., they ultimately correspond to the concrete will of God in a given case (even when they are directly conditioned by "natural" elements). Every impulse, "natural" or preternatural, which clouds this light is "from the evil spirit", i.e., is against the will of God in such a case.

This "instinctive" norm is at the disposition of the justified during lawful work and recreation as well as prayer. For the theological virtues in whose acts this norm is contained are also exercised in such activities, since work and recreation also spring from the centre of the person which is characterized by supernatural forces, especially by love. But this means that love and all it entails come implicitly into play during such work and recreation, even when the Christian does not think expressly of God. Here too love (as *caritas implicite actuata*) brings with it implicitly its fullness of life. Hence too it contains the non-objectivated consciousness of God, with the light, force, joy and peace which this consciousness radiates. Work and recreation are permeated by it, and hence by the "instinctive", non-objectivated norm for the discernment of spirits.

The effect of the theological virtues is a transformation of the "natural desire" of man for God and of the knowledge and the love which is active in this openness. Hence, the consciousness of God is all the more perceptible, the more a man actually partakes of the experience of this transcendence in the fulfilment of the *natural* orientation toward God. This occurs in the discovery of the transcendence of the spirit, whereby the spirit is experienced as something more than a part of this world and this time; it occurs when one lives from one's personal and spiritual centre, which is the free and responsible source of all one's activity and of one's judgments in ethical questions, in aesthetic experiences, etc.

Any further insight and any further criteria for the discernment of spirits can only result from a deepening of that elementary and non-objectivated consciousness of God which accompanies all Christian activity. This further illumination varies, according to the different degrees in which God freely communicates himself. There are periods of "consolation" and of "desolation". There are times of "illumination" and "inspiration"; and there are other times when the light, joy, warmth and power of the presence of God shrink almost to vanishing-point, where only the basic will remains. Hence the rule of spiritual tradition in such a case, that one should adhere to the decisions taken in time of consolation.

God who reveals himself in the heart of men through Christ, also reveals himself outwardly in the words and deeds of Christ and in the Church. But both of these self-communications are the *one* saving activity of God. Thus the response of men to this action of God must be a unified one; a listening to God that integrates both the voice of God from without and from within. Ultimately, the inner, non-objectivated consciousness of God takes on its Christian character only by being constantly integrated with the faith of the Church.

The true presence and activity of God necessarily manifest themselves in their "fruits": these are the credible evidence of that presence, and hence the further necessary criteria for the discernment of spirits. "The fruit of the Spirit is love, joy, peace, patience, kindness, goodness, faithfulness, gentleness, and self-control" (Gal 5:22, 23); "for the fruit of light is found in all that is good and all that is right and true. And try to learn what is pleasing to the Lord; take no part in the unfruitful works of darkness" (Eph 5:9–10). No one who lives in the Spirit denies Christ (1 Cor 12:3). As God also reveals himself in the visible Church, Scripture can say: "let what you have heard from the beginning abide in you . . ., then you will abide in the Son and in the Father" (1 Jn 2:24); and likewise: "whoever knows God listens to us, and he who is not of God does not listen to us. This is how we distinguish the spirit of truth from the spirit of error" (1 Jn 4:6).

The living contact between both forms of the activity of God led more and more, in ecclesiastical tradition, to a set of "rules for the discernment of spirits". They are useful especially for important and difficult decisions, but should also be part of the habitual Christian wisdom in the search for the will of God in other concrete actions. They remain, nevertheless, only general rules which are only of use in conjunction with the individual guidance given by the basic non-objectivated experience of God.

See also *Charity* I, *Revelation* II.

BIBLIOGRAPHY. R. Guardini, *Das Gute, das Gewissen und die Sammlung* (1931); J. de Guibert, "Discernement des esprits", *Dictionnaire de Spiritualité*, III, cols. 1222–91; K. Rahner, *The Dynamic Element in the Church,* Quaestiones Disputatae 12 (1964); id., *Betrachtungen zum ignazianischen Exerzitienbuch* (1965).

Karl Vladimir Truhlar

DISPENSATION

1. "Dispensation" is derived from the Latin *pendere,* because the "dispensator", in the days before coinage was introduced, had to weigh the bronze used for making payments, as we are told by Varro (*De lingua latina,* V, 183): "ab eodem aere pendendo dispensator", and Festus (*De verborum significatione,* s.v. "dispensator"): "Dispensatores dicti qui aes pensantes expendebant, non adnumerabant." *Dispensatio* then came to mean the administration of a patrimony or the public treasury, and also, like the Greek οἰχονομία, the prudent distribution of goods, even spiritual goods as 1 Cor 4:1 has it: "dispensatores mysteriorum Dei". But to distribute goods fairly and prudently was necessarily to consider cases where it seemed appropriate to make an exception to the general rule. Hence a dispensation could be defined as an exemption from a law, or the abrogation of a law in special cases, granted by the wielder of authority.

2. The granting of dispensations is undoubtedly a characteristic institution of the Church; indeed it is usual for canonists to indicate this fact when they define a dispensation; thus Rufinus (12th century), for example, "Canonici rigoris casualis derogatio" (cf. H. Singer, *Die Summa decretorum des Magister Rufinus* [1902], p. 234), and Wernz (*Ius decretalium,* I [1905], p. 138) "Relaxatio legis ecclesiasticae in casibus particularibus a competente superiore ecclesiastico ex causa cognita et sufficiente facta". For the Church must see that justice and equity prevail as far as possible; and since it exists in order to distribute spiritual goods, any departure from the objective norms in its government is far more serious than in civil government, since it is with these goods that the members of the Church must find salvation. In the State the need for adjustment is less urgent, since the goods it bestows belong to the natural order and as such can more readily be dispensed with; here wise legislation, providing suitable remedies and taking account of the variety of persons and situations involved, will generally satisfy the demands of equity. But the power of dispensation in the Church is not confined to the author of the law but also rests, derivatively, in subordinate authorities for use in urgent cases or special circumstances (*CIC,* can. 81–83), so that dispensations are duly available.

The legislator is not absolutely bound to grant a dispensation, because if he were, there would be no difference between being dispensed and being excused from obeying the law; and the dispensation must achieve some sort of higher purpose that would not be served, were the dispensation not granted — which means that failing sufficient reason for it, a dispensation would be at best illicit, as the Council of Trent indicates (sess. 25, cap. 18 de ref.): "Sicuti publice expedit legis vinculum quandoque relaxare ut plenius, evenientibus casibus, et necessitatibus (at least remotely), pro communi utilitate satisfiat."

3. The code of canon law provides for dispensations in connection with a) administration of the sacraments and granting of indulgences; b) freeing people from vows and oaths, and dissolving marriages that are valid but have not been consummated; c) freeing people from penalties; d) relaxation of the law, according to can. 80. In the case of a), dispensation still has the general sense of the distribution of goods. As to b), many authors (since Suarez) accept that there is no dispensation in the strict sense, but that a juridical act done in accordance with the law is annulled. In this way, they hold, the natural law (which is here involved) remains immutable. For our own part this view presents no less difficulty than the other; for it appears to us that to annul an act (such as a vow or a marriage) is simply to dispense from the law which provides that the act shall not be annulled. We should say, rather, that in such cases, given a reasonable cause, the law, both derivatively and as regards the authorities, becomes conditional and one from which the Church can dispense. Such a view preserves a clear distinction between dispensing from vows and quashing them. When vows are quashed, authority does indeed annul the act of a person whose will was subject to the authority at the time of the act, that is, who was not in a position to take his decision quite independently of the authority; and therefore the vows are quashed by a jurisdiction that is ordinary, not delegated. Finally, in the case of c) we seem to have a true dispensation, since a person is freed from a penalty sanctioned or imposed by law.

4. At least in principle it is important to distinguish between exemption (from a law) and *epikeia*. Whereas the person dispensed is placed beyond the reach of the law by an executive act on the part of the legislator or someone who exercises his authority (it should be noted that executive and legislative power in the Church are in the same hands), the person excused from the law is placed beyond its reach by the nature of things, by the serious difficulty he would have in obeying it which outweighs the good that would result from his obedience. The individual's judgment that he is in such a situation is called *epikeia*.

See also *Law, Equity, Vow*.

BIBLIOGRAPHY. M. A. Stiegler, *Dispensation, Dispensationswesen und Dispensationsrecht im Kirchenrecht* (1901); W. J. Sparrow Simpson, *Dispensations* (1933); A. Douville, *De la dispense* (1935); A. van Hove, *De privilegiis et dispensationibus* (1939); G. F. Reilly, The General Norms of Dispensation (1939); J. Lederer, *Der Dispensationsbegriff des kanonischen Rechtes* (1957).

Olis Robleda

DISPOSITION

1. A being which is changing, which acquires new determinations, states and attributes, requires certain conditions either intrinsically in itself or in its external circumstances, if it is to be able to receive the new determinations, etc. These conditions are called a disposition for the new determination, to which the disposition stands in the relation of potency to act (in the widest sense of the term). This relation may be found in all orders of reality, so that there are physical, juridical and moral dispositions. The relationship of condition, between disposition and "act", may derive from the nature of the two realities, e.g., mathematical knowledge as condition of the solution of a problem of calculation. Or it may be the result of legal enactment, e.g., a certain age for episcopal consecration. The disposition may "demand" the "act" (e.g., economic production requires remuneration) or not (e.g., canonical age is required for ordination but gives no right to it). A disposition may always be present or may be produced specially. To bring it about may be a duty or may be left to a person's discretion. In certain circumstances it may be brought about by the act for which it is to be the disposition, or by another cause. The lack of a disposition or the impossibility of producing it may entail the absence of the act or the impossibility of achieving it. It must not be overlooked, however, that God as omnipotent cause standing outside the system of finite, temporal things, can always produce a disposition if he absolutely wills the act for which the disposition is meant to prepare. For example, God can produce the repentance which is the disposition for forgiveness of personal sin. Consequently, the doctrine of the necessity of a disposition for

a particular grace (justification) does not involve any diminution of the sovereignty and power of the grace of God.

2. The doctrine of disposition has an important field of application in the Catholic theology of grace and justification. If a human being who is fully capable of using his reason and freedom is to obtain justification (sanctifying grace), certain free acts intrinsically ordained to salvation (*actus salutares,* acts of faith, hope and contrition) are absolutely necessary (*D* 797 ff., 814, 817, 819, 898), by the very nature of the case — the freedom of the person and justification itself. The first antecedent grace which in the very first instance makes possible such salutary and disposing acts (supernaturally elevating grace) and which in fact effects these acts in their very freedom (efficacious grace), is independent of any moral disposition on the part of man. God can bestow it even on the sinner who has no merit to show for it. There is no "natural moral merit" as disposition for saving grace as Pelagianism held (*D* 811, 813). The first salutary movement of man towards God, which is then a disposition for man's further advance in salvation, occurs without any disposition morally effected by man as its condition. It occurs by the free initiative of God's grace, in which God gives grace on account of his universal salvific will. Consequently, the whole process of salvation remains until its perfect fulfilment (and despite all merits) based on this initial disposition which God alone has produced by his grace without prior religious or moral conditions on the part of man. Where, however, such a salutary act is freely posited through God's grace, its "degree" (i.e., its actual personal and potential depth and resoluteness) is a disposition for further salutary activity and as such the "measure" of the grace (e.g., grace of justification) bestowed for this further salutary activity (*D* 799).

3. The concept of disposition is also used in the field of sacramental theology. An adult must prepare himself for the reception of a sacrament and for the grace of the sacrament, for despite their character of *opus operatum* the sacraments are not causes which operate magically (*D* 799, 849, 819, 898). In other words, the adult must not have merely the intention of receiving the sacrament, but for the fruitful reception of the sacraments he also requires a certain disposition, faith, hope and at least an inchoative love (as in contrition). This disposition which is ultimately dependent on the efficacious, freely bestowed grace of God, but which is freely brought about, is the measure, but not the cause, of the grace given by the sacrament as instrumental cause (*D* 799). Yet it must be noted that the sacrament itself as a religious event and by the grace offered in it, can deepen this disposition or even produce it where it does not exist, so that in this way the grace offered in the sacrament finds in the disposition the measure of its acceptance.

It is an urgent task of sacramental theology and of preaching on the sacraments to bring out even more clearly the unity of the objective action of God in man by grace in the sacrament and the subjective salutary action of man occurring in grace (which is precisely the "disposition"). We must not be content casuistically to determine the minimum disposition for the various sacraments and so encourage the prejudice that the sacrament does the rest, or does so if received with the maximum frequency (Eucharist, sacrament of penance). It is meaningless to increase the frequency with which a sacrament is received if there is no growth in the personal moral participation by the individual in the accomplishment of the sacrament, i.e., in his disposition. In the case of sacraments which can be validly received without being fruitful (sacraments which confer a sacramental character: *D* 852; and matrimony: *D* 2238), the disposition can be supplied or personally deepened after the reception of the sacrament and so the effect of the sacrament can be obtained or deepened. It is important to realize this, particularly on account of the practice of infant baptism. Pastoral endeavour ought to promote the rekindling of sacramental grace on a higher level (baptism, priestly ordination: 1 Tim 4:14; 2 Tim 1:6; matrimony) by deepening the personal attitude to a sacrament already received but lasting in its effects. This may be done by preaching, devotion, meditation (renewal of baptismal vows, e.g., at the Easter Vigil, retreats for married couples, the celebration of sacerdotal jubilees, etc.). This is no make-believe but true growth in sacramental grace.

See also *Existence* III, *Contrition, Habitus, Grace, Justification, Merit.*

93

BIBLIOGRAPHY. K. Rahner, *Hörer des Wortes. Zur Grundlegung einer Religionsphilosophie* (1940; 2nd ed., 1963); H. Bouillard, *Conversion et grâce chez Saint Thomas d'Aquin* (1944); R.-C. Dhont, *Le problème de la préparation à la grâce. Débuts de l'École Franciscaine* (1946); D. Iturioz, *La definición del Concilio de Trento sobre la causalidad de los Sacramentos* (1951); R. Aubert, *Le problème de l'acte de foi* (3rd ed., 1958); J. Mouroux, *I believe* (1959); H. de Lubac, *Discovery of God* (1960); H. Bouillard, *Blondel et le Christianisme* (1961); B. Häring, *The Law of Christ*, 2 vols. (1961–66), see Index; J. Alfaro, *Fides, Spes, Caritas* (2nd ed., 1963); K. Rahner, *The Church and the Sacraments,* Quaestiones Disputatae 9 (1963); H. de Lubac, *Le mystère du Surnaturel* (1965); H. Bouillard, *The Logic of the Faith* (1967); H. Küng, *Justification* (1967).

Karl Rahner

DOCETISM

Docetism is an effort to interpret the incarnation and life of Jesus in the framework of dualism. It holds that Christ had only an apparent body (δοκέω, seem or appear) and therefore denies various dogmas bearing on the Incarnation. At the birth of Christianity, the dualism of Gnosis was widespread in the Graeco-Roman world. The clash with Christianity gave rise to a series of heresies that claimed to offer a rational explanation of the mystery of Christ. It was a basic assumption of all these heresies that matter was inherently evil. Therefore God, being pure spirit, could not be united to it. As applied to Christ, the doctrine takes various forms: some flatly deny any true humanity in Christ, some admit his incarnation but not his sufferings on the cross, while others ascribe to him a special body not subject to human miseries.

1. *History and doctrines.* a) *Apostolic times.* Certain passages in the gospels (Mk 6:45 ff.; Mt 15:22 ff.; Jo 20:24 ff.) seemed to favour early Docetist views. After the departure of the Lord and then the death of his last witnesses, the tendency towards Docetism gained strength. Some have thought that Colossians and the Pastoral Letters contain anti-Docetist allusions. This is not quite accurate: St. Paul is concerned there with Judaizing tendencies. But St. John may well have Docetism in mind: 1 Jn 4:2 and 2 Jn 7 should be compared with 1 Jn 1 ff., where the bodily reality of the Lord is stressed. Modern exegetes believe that St. John is

attacking various groups of heretics; they all combine a Christological error with moral errors and seem to be converts from paganism who later abandoned the faith.

b) *St. Ignatius of Antioch* plainly combats Docetism. He vigorously reminds his readers that Jesus is the descendant of David and the son of Mary; that *in very truth* (this is said fifteen times) he was born and ate and drank; was persecuted and crucified; died, and then rose from the dead. None of this was mere appearances (δοκεῖν) as the heretics assert. Our salvation is anchored in that Christ who is as real as the chains in which Ignatius was brought to his martyrdom in Rome.

c) *St. Irenaeus* wrote against Valentinus and his followers, who maintained that Jesus passed through Mary as water does through a channel; at the baptism in the Jordan he was united with the pneumatic Christ but at the Passion the two separated again. Ptolemaeus preached substantially the same doctrine. The distinction between a passible Jesus and an impassible Christ was maintained by the Judaizer Cerinthus and the Ophites, among others. Strictly speaking, it is no part of Docetism. Basilides is more of a Docetist in explaining the problem by a gross deceit: Simon of Cyrene took Christ's place on the cross, while Christ ascended into heaven.

d) *Tertullian* in his treatise *De Carne Christi* defends the reality of the Lord's human nature and refutes certain doctrines of Valentinus and Marcion. The latter, a disciple of the Gnostic Cerdon, held that Christ was not born of Mary but appeared in Capernaum as a grown man.

e) *Clement of Alexandria* mentions some Encratites and their leader Julius Cassian, an out-and-out Docetist. Clement himself, like Origen, occasionally makes statements that have a Docetist flavour.

f) *Hippolytus of Rome* is one of our chief sources of information about Docetism, which he calls a heresy. He describes and refutes it in his *Philosophoumena.*

g) *St. Augustine,* especially in *Contra Faustum,* attacks the Gnostic and Docetist doctrines perpetuated in Manichaeism.

h) *Later Docetism.* These errors were revived by the Catharists and Albigenses. Influenced by the rationalist Enlightenment, B. Baur denied that Christ was in any sense a historical person. He saw Christianity as the product of the Greek genius.

2. *Pastoral significance*. Docetism, officially condemned by the Church at Chalcedon and hence disposed of as a theological problem, had first caused grave damage in the moral order, as among the Encratites, especially as it called in question two of the fundamental doctrines of Christianity, the Incarnation and the Redemption. It also affected the motherhood of Mary, the credibility of the Church and the nature of the sacraments. Christian preaching was constantly menaced by the danger of emphasizing so strongly the transcendence of God that the mystery of the Incarnation no longer seemed compatible with it.

In keeping with the Christology of Chalcedon, Christian spirituality naturally and historically took on two main forms: that of the following of Christ and that of the divinization of man. The former emphasizes in particular the historical Christ, placing the true and full humanity of Christ in the foreground. The spirituality which takes as its ideal the divinization of man must remember that there is no direct approach to God except through the Logos "in the flesh". Any denial or diminution of the significance of the humanity of Christ for salvation is basically coloured by Docetism.

See also *Gnosis, Gnosticism, Incarnation, Jesus Christ* IV, *Catharists, Enlightenment*.

BIBLIOGRAPHY. C. Maurer, *Ignatius von Antiochien und das Johannesevangelium* (1949), pp. 45–58; A. Houssiau, *La Christologie de St. Irénée* (1955), pp. 151 ff., 188 ff., 236 ff.; C. Moeller, *Mentalité moderne et Évangélisation* (1955); R. Cantalamessa, "Méliton de Sardes. Une Christologie antignostique du IIe siècle", *RSR* 37 (1963), pp. 1–26; J. Liébaert, *L'incarnation*, I: *Des origines au Concile de Chalcédoine* (1965), ch. i; K. Rahner, "The Eternal Significance of the Humanity of Jesus for Our Relationship with God", *Theological Investigations*, III (1967), pp. 35–46; R. Schnackenburg, *The Letters of John* (in preparation), passim.

Enrique Fabri

DOGMA

I. Theological Meaning of Dogma

A. DOGMA IN CHRISTIANITY

1. For an understanding of dogma and its necessity in terms of a philosophical anthropology, it is to be noted that there is a transcendental necessity for man as mind and spirit (and consequently for every human society) to affirm certain truths absolutely. And this in principle has to be done through their conceptual formulation (though in certain circumstances this may be of a merely pre-scientific kind), at least in logic, formal ontology and ethics. This necessity can only be contested and denied self-destructively. Consequently man's existence is essentially a "dogmatic" one. It can be shown that since man must act he must to some extent necessarily affirm some contingent facts as unconditionally valid. In view of this, historical revelation and the acceptance of propositions to be affirmed absolutely cannot be repugnant to man's nature. The absolute character of the claim and obligation of dogma is addressed precisely to man's freedom; dogma expresses a truth which can be rightly heard and attained only in the free decision of faith (*D* 798, 1791, 1814). And freedom as knowledge in action achieves its own true nature only in absolute commitment. Dogma and freedom are, therefore, actually complementary terms. Precisely because the Church proclaims dogma (and not in spite of doing so), it must appeal to and respect this freedom (*D* 1875; *CIC,* can. 752, § 1; Vatican II: Declaration on Religious Freedom).

2. The actual nature of dogma is not, however, deduced solely from the abstract idea of divine communication of truth and its obligatory character, but from revelation in the concrete. For a) revelation is the saving event, in which God communicates himself to the free, spiritual person and does so in such a way that the immediate recipient of the communication is the community, the Church, which is constituted precisely by this. And b) this self-communication by God has reached its definitive, eschatological stage. For by God's definitive and unsurpassable saving action in the incarnate Word, revelation is concluded (because it now directly opens out on the vision of God), and God's definitive word is present (even if

embodied only in the enigma of human speech). Consequently, dogma now exists in the full sense of the absolute and supreme claim by which ultimate salvation and perdition is decided. Hence dogma is not merely a statement "about" something, but one in which, because it is an "exhibitive" word with a "sacramental" nature, what it states actually occurs and is posited by its existence: God's self-communication in grace which is also the grace of its absolute acceptance (faith). In the proclamation and the hearing of dogma in faith, therefore, what is affirmed is itself present.

3. Dogma has an ecclesial, social character. For the revelation which is the ground of dogma is addressed and entrusted to the Church, and is so in the unity of its three elements, as word, as event and as the revealed and communicated reality of God himself. The Church is both hearer and preacher of God's revelation. The latter does not cease to be God's word because it is spoken by the Church. Consequently, dogma is not only the unifying pattern of a common act of hearing but also the unifying pattern of God's word being addressed to all. And since this word remains the ever-new event of God's gracious self-communication in the history of the Church, and therefore always has to be spoken afresh, there has to be dogmatic adaptation and development of dogma (and not merely of theology) and history of dogma. Since in the proclamation of dogma the one, identical and definitive revelation of God in Christ takes place which has taken place once and for all (ἐφάπαξ), dogma is the *form* of the abiding validity of the tradition of the deposit of faith in the Church which itself remains always the same. Dogma helps to constitute the unity of faith and makes it visible. Consequently, when it is determined and proclaimed, there always occurs not only a manifestation of the reality to which it refers, but also a terminological determination of common linguistic usage. The definition of a dogma often consists just as much in fixing the common mode of expression as in distinguishing between true and false propositions.

4. To the extent that dogma is God's absolute self-communication in the form of human truth to the Church and through the Church, it is integrated into the religious act.

For this act has a complex but unified structure, deriving from the very essence of man, comprising and actualizing all his powers in its circumincession; it therefore itself is "life". Dogma as believed is in itself "life" and, provided it is rightly affirmed and personally assimilated, stands in no need of any subsequent defence in respect of its value for life. In itself it is a source and standard of authentic piety.

5. Since God's word is announced in human terms, dogma is in vital contact with the whole mental life of man. It employs in principle not only the common terms of every day but, like Scripture itself, can use the terminology of human learning and science if the needs of a particular intellectual situation require it. Usually in doing so it critically modifies them and to some extent brings them nearer to everyday usage. Such a use does not, however, sanction a scientific or philosophical system itself. Everyday language and that of science and learning are not after all essentially different. Conversely, knowledge of dogma provides a spur to building up a Christian philosophy, such as may be used in apologetics.

B. NATURE OF DOGMA

Dogma in the sense in which the term is used nowadays in the Church and in theology (a usage which only became definite and universal in the 18th century) is a proposition which is the object of *fides divina et catholica,* in other words, one which the Church explicitly propounds as revealed by God (*D* 1792; *CIC,* can. 1323, §§ 1, 2), in such a way that its denial is condemned by the Church as heresy and anathematized (*CIC,* can. 1325, § 2; 2314, § 1). It may be so propounded either by the ordinary and universal magisterium or by a papal or conciliar definition. The decisive characteristics of dogma (divine origin, truth, the obligation to believe it, immutability, incarnational structure as a genuine union of divine and human unmixed and undivided, etc.) are therefore dealt with under more general headings such as revelation, faith, theology, the ecclesiastical magisterium. The declaration that a proposition expresses a dogma is also the highest theological qualification.

Two elements are therefore required formally to constitute a dogma. a) A proposition must be set forth by the Church explicitly and definitively as a revealed truth (formal element). This does not necessarily require an express definition. b) This proposition must belong to divine, public and official Christian revelation (in contrast to private revelation). Consequently, it must be contained in the word of God addressed to us in Scripture and/or tradition (material element).

The declaration of Vatican I on the object of *fides divina et catholica* (*D* 1792) makes this the unambiguous and generally accepted definition of dogma. A few questions regarding more detailed interpretation remain open, however, and are controverted in theology. These are chiefly the following.

a) The question how exactly dogma taught by the ordinary magisterium can be distinguished from the rest of its teaching which is not, or not yet, presented explicitly and with absolute finality engaging the whole authority of the Church's magisterium, as revealed by God. On this matter the admonition of *CIC,* can. 1323, § 3, must be noted, but at the same time it must be remembered that in the concrete the practice of Christian faith can never relate solely to actual formal dogmas. The latter are only possessed in a personal way appropriate to the nature of the Church if they are assimilated in connection with other knowledge, convictions and attitudes. Consequently, the importance of drawing an exact distinction between the two must not be exaggerated, and in fact is not possible with absolute precision (cf. *D* 1684, 1722, 1880, 2007 f., 2113, 2313).

b) The question how we are to think of dogma as being contained in divine revelation. It is indubitable that much is taught by the Church today as dogma (and therefore as contained in revelation) which was not always taught as such or even consciously recognized as such. Consequently, the essential condition of forming part of revelation can doubtless be satisfied by one truth being contained in another truth. The question is, therefore, what "implication" (on the first use of this term in the language of the magisterium cf. *D* 2314) is necessary and sufficient for it to be possible to regard a proposition derived from primary revelation as still constituting a communication from God attested by God himself, and believed on this ground because of his authority (formal, or merely virtual implication; virtual implication which requires for its explication a material premiss not derived from revelation, or explication purely within considerations themselves revealed; a kind of implication different from that of formal logic; subjective or purely objective implication). No unanimity of view has been reached by theologians in these questions. Post-Tridentine theology was for the most part inclined to regard as potential dogma only those propositions which can be explicated from the original deposit of faith by a rigorously formal logical procedure without the use of "natural" premisses. At the present time, however, in view of the actual facts of the development of dogma there seems to be an increase in the number of theologians who also identify as potential dogma propositions which explicitly formulate what was "virtually" implicit. These theologians endeavour in various ways to explain, by various interpretations of this virtuality, why propositions of this kind can also be considered as communicated by God himself and as directly guaranteed by him.

c) The question whether dogma and defined proposition are identical or not, i.e., whether in addition to dogma there can be other defined truths of the Church, guaranteed with absolute authority by the Church, and if so, which (dogmatic facts; truths of a purely "ecclesiastical faith", which is not an act of faith in the word of God as such but which is directly based simply on the [divinely appointed] authority of the Church as such [Catholic truths]).

C. DIVISION OF DOGMAS

1. *According to content and scope.* General (fundamental truths of Christianity) and special (particular) dogmas (fundamental articles, articles of faith, *regula fidei*). Although of course the formally equal value of all dogmas as guaranteed by God and definitively held by the Church must be emphasized, a division of this kind is justified. For according to the reality signified, dogmas have objectively different importance for salvation (cf. Vatican II, Decree on Ecumenism, art. 11). For this reason canon law, for example, does not qualify every heretical denial of a dogma as total apostasy from Christianity (can. 1325, § 2). The strictest measure regarding fundamental dogmas is applied when a distinction is drawn between dogmas necessary or not necessary for salva-

tion. This is determined by whether they must be believed explicitly for salvation to be possible — either because they are a necessary means or prescribed as necessary (*necessitas medii — necessitas praecepti*) — or whether a *fides implicita* in them is sufficient. Since God's revelation, the teaching authority of the Church and divine faith refer to "theoretical" and to "practical" affirmations, these various types of proposition can all be dogmas.

2. *According to their relation to reason.* Dogmas pure and simple (only knowable through revelation: mysteries in the strictest sense), and mixed dogmas (the contents of which can also be known by natural reason). Even on the supposition that truths which really are wholly accessible and intelligible to reason can also be believed by a person who knows them, mixed dogmas still differ from the truths of reason materially identical with them. For when they are attained and believed on the basis of the whole of revelation and saving faith, they present their content under a supernatural formal object, in a context and with the aspect of pure dogmas quite inaccessible to the apparently identical affirmation of reason. On the other hand, such dogmas are an expression of the fact that God's revelation really concerns the actual world of man himself. They show that articles of faith are not *a priori* propositions relating to some particular function of man, but involve the whole reality of man.

3. *According to the way they are propounded by the Church:* formal and (simply) material dogmas, according to whether the formal element in dogma (cf. B 1 a) is already present or not.

D. MODERNIST CONCEPTION OF DOGMA

Negatively, the concept of dogma in Modernism was characterized by a) the rejection of an authentically supernatural reality and consequently of a mystery which can only be known through a personal self-disclosure on the part of God. "Dogma" expresses man's experience of himself in his religious indigence and only in that way something of the "divine". Another feature was b) the rejection of the genuine possibility of intellectual statement of the reality to which dogma refers, a statement which would belong to the constitution of religious experience itself. For Modernism, the conceptual, intellectual proposition which constitutes dogma is not merely "inadequate" to the reality signified, nor is it an "analogical" statement, which orientates and directs man into mystery utterly beyond his scope. For Modernism, dogma is secondary and derivative as compared with religious experience, which can possess the reality signified, in total independence of conceptual expression in dogma. Viewed positively, dogma, according to Modernism, is a derivative expression of religious experience, unavoidably necessary for the religious community, but always subject to revision or even to change into its contrary, and religious experience itself is given an immanentist interpretation (cf. *D* 2020 ff., 2026, 2031, 2059, 2079 ff., 2309–12).

See also *Fundamental Theology, Theology, Revelation, Freedom, Conscience, History* I, *Tradition, Religious Act, Religious Experience, Modernism, Protestantism* IV.

BIBLIOGRAPHY. A. Harnack, *Lehrbuch der Dogmengeschichte,* I (4th ed., 1909), pp. 3–22, E. T.: *History of Dogma* (reprint 1958); L. de Grandmaison, *Le dogme chrétien. Sa nature, ses formules, son développement* (1928); R. Bultmann, *Glauben und Verstehen,* 4 vols. (1933–65); E. Dublanchy, "Dogme", *DTC,* IV (1939), cols. 1574–1650; K. Barth, *Church Dogmatics,* I: *The Doctrine of the Word of God,* part 1 (1949), para. 7; H. de Lubac, *Catholicism. A Study of Dogma in Relation to the Corporate Destiny of Mankind* (1950); A. Hartmann, *Bindung und Freiheit des katholischen Denkens* (1952); H. W. Bartsch, ed., *Kerygma and Myth,* 2 vols. (1953–62); J. Koopmann, *Das altkirchliche Dogma in der Reformation* (1953); F. Buri, *Dogmatik als Selbstverständnis des christlichen Glaubens,* I (1957); H. Diem, *Dogmatics* (1960); Y. Congar, *La foi et la théologie* (1962); G. Ebeling, *Nature of Faith* (1962); G. Ebeling, *Word and Faith* (1963); W. Elert, *Structure of Lutheranism* (1963); E. Fuchs, *Hermeneutik* (3rd ed., 1963); W. Joest and W. Pannenberg, eds., *Dogma und Denkstrukturen* (1963); J. M. Robinson and J. B. Cobb, eds., *The Later Heidegger and Theology* (1963); C. Journet, *What is Dogma?* (1964); J. M. Robinson and J. B. Cobb, eds., *New Hermeneutic* (1964); W. Kasper, *Dogma unter dem Wort Gottes* (1965); H. Ott, *Theology and Preaching* (1965).
Karl Rahner

II. Development of Dogma

A. REVELATION AND DOGMA

1. "In many and various ways God spoke of old to our fathers by the prophets; but in these last days he has spoken to us by a Son."

(Heb 1:1f.) These words indicate the progressive character of God's revelation which culminated in Christ. In him the final and definitive stage of that history has been enacted: in Christ God has spoken his final and unsurpassable word to men. What went before Christ (the OT law) was a preparation, a training for the revelation that is embodied in him, for the faith we must have in him (Gal 3:23ff.). "For all the prophets and the law prophesied until John" (Mt 11:13); but Jesus is the fullness of revelation; he says of himself, "All things have been delivered to me by my Father, and no one knows the Son except the Father, and no one knows the Father except the Son and anyone to whom the Son chooses to reveal him." (Mt 11:27.) Jesus revealed to the apostles all that he had "heard from the Father" (Jn 15:15). But this text, which must be interpreted in the light of other texts, only means that Jesus has revealed all that is necessary to salvation. After the Ascension, therefore, the supreme work of the Holy Spirit is to recall Christ's words to the apostles' minds (Jn 14:25). Now Christ was revelation in his own being, not merely by his preaching but also by his life, death and resurrection, because all this manifests the mystery of God's salvation to us. Man's response to God speaking is faith, the acceptance of a message (or testimony) from God (Jo 3:11f., 32–36). A purely human interpretation of the life, death and resurrection of Jesus would be only human speculation, not the word of God, and as such, unacceptable to faith. But the apostles are authentic and privileged witnesses and interpreters of Jesus' own revelation. Thus St. Paul says of his gospel (the interpretation of the Lord's life, death and resurrection): "I did not receive it from man, nor was I taught it, but it came through a revelation of Jesus Christ." (Gal 1:12; cf. 1:16f.) Probably Jn 16:12–15 refers to such inspired interpretation of Jesus' spoken message. Such interpretative additions are limited by their object, since they are always confined to the mystery of Christ, the new messianic order of salvation; cf. Lk 18:30. They complete the preaching of Jesus (i.e., give it its fullness by teaching "all the truth", those many things which according to Jn 16:12 Jesus still had to say), which is why Jesus declares that the Spirit "will take what is mine".

2. This process of authentic interpretation of the message of Jesus, through inspired meditation on the saving acts of the Lord, and hence not restricted to human insight but aided by revelation, is restricted in time to the age of the apostles and of the primitive apostolic Church. In any case we must sharply distinguish between the foundation period of the Church (apostolic age) and its subsequent history. This the Church has done by condemning the proposition: "Revelation, constituting the object of Catholic faith, was not completed with the apostles" (*D* 2021; cf. also 783, which presupposes this doctrine by linking "the purity of the gospel", which the Church must preserve, with that foundation period). No doubt it was with the same idea in mind that the apostles themselves looked on their message as a deposit that must be faithfully preserved (1 Tim 6:20; 2 Tim 1:13f.), without any alteration or addition (Gal 1:8f., where St. Paul repudiates "any gospel contrary to [παρ' ὅ, outside] that which we preached to you"). This deposit is a "paradosis" (2 Thess 2:15; 3:6): transmitted by the apostles, who received it from the Lord (cf. 1 Cor 11:23), it must be handed down from age to age because the gospel must be preached until the end of time (Mt 28:20). The first sub-apostolic generation is well aware of the dividing line. The Apostolic Fathers consider themselves different from the apostles (for example, the *First Letter of St. Clement,* 42; St. Ignatius of Antioch, *Letter to the Romans,* 4, 3) and base what they say on apostolic doctrine (*1 Clem,* 42, 1f.), a deposit received from the apostles (St. Polycarp, *Letter to the Philippians,* 7, 2) to which nothing may be added and from which nothing may be taken away (*Didache,* 4, 13; *Barnabas,* 19, 11). The sub-apostolic Church holds that its first duty is to preserve the deposit of revelation.

As an absolute guarantee of that mission, the Church and its supreme shepherd the Pope have been promised "the Holy Spirit, not so that by revelation they might make known new doctrine, but so that by the assistance of the Spirit they might preserve inviolate and faithfully expound the revelation handed down by the apostles, that is, the deposit of faith" (*D* 1836, with reference to the successors of St. Peter; but they are endowed with the same infallibility as the Church and for the same purpose; cf. *D* 1839). Notwithstanding the faithful preservation of the deposit, certain truths contained in it may on occasion recede into the background. Perhaps, indeed, such a thing is inevitable. Considering the wealth of content in Christianity and the limitations of man who is called on to live that religion, it is never possible for all Christian truths to occupy the foreground of interest and attention at the same time. But neither can the Church ever repudiate or lose a revealed truth, or allow the central truths of the gospel to become obscured (*D* 1501; cf. also 1445).

B. Problem of Development of Dogma

1. On the other hand the Church's duty is not simply to preserve the deposit of revelation but also to interpret it, authoritatively setting forth its content (*D* 1800, 1836). It must preach its message in every age and to every nation, which obviously involves more than the mere repetition of set words. The constant effort which the Church must make to convey its message in intelligible terms leads to a growing understanding of that message. Furthermore, since the gospel is chiefly concerned not with obvious truths but with mysteries that do not carry conviction of themselves, a Christian who accepts the gospel by faith, relying on the authority of God who attests it, is induced as it were automatically to make an effort to grasp the objective content of his religion (cf. St. Thomas, *De Veritate,* q. 14, a. 1, 6). Now this effort is the deepest sense of theology as the understanding of faith and the noblest function it has, though understanding is limited by the mystery of God. Further, as St. Thomas says (II, II, q. 2, a. 3, ad 2), when we make this effort, the grace by which we make an act of faith (the light of faith) gives us a connatural knowledge of the thing that is believed. This connaturality in the act of faith is always a new kind of adhesion to the object of faith (*De Veritate,* q. 14, a. 8, c.); but it may also, by a sort of instinct, give one a better understanding of that object. This process goes on both in individual Christians and in the Church as the holy people of God, as a supernatural *sensus fidei.* In the latter, it is the infallibility, since this efficacious grace means that "the faithful as a whole, who have received the anointing of the Spirit (cf. 1 Jn 2:22, 27) . . . cannot err in faith" (Vatican II, Constitution on the Church, art. 12). It is by this operation of grace that

Christ brings about in his mystical body "the growth that is from God" (Col 2:19), "until we all attain to the unity of the faith and of the knowledge of the Son of God, to mature manhood, to the measure of the stature of the fullness of Christ . . ., from whom the whole body, joined and knit together by every joint with which it is supplied, when each part is working properly, makes bodily growth and upbuilds itself in love" (Eph 4:13 and 16).

2. This growth in our understanding of the gospel becomes dogmatic development in the strict sense when the fuller insight that has been reached is infallibly proclaimed by the Church's magisterium to be a truth contained in the deposit of revelation, that is, a dogma (cf. *D* 1792). The solemn promulgation is the climax of the process, which now enters the express understanding of the official Church. The historical fact of development is undeniable, however it is to be explained, since certain dogmas cannot be found as truths of faith before a given moment in history (the truth concerned may have been known before but the Church did not teach that it was revealed), or the truth as such was not yet known at least in its present form.

3. If revelation is a deposit that has been complete since the end of the apostolic age, then the new dogmas must have been objectively contained in the deposit from the start. For only what has been really "said" by God (in his revelation and in the interpretative words accompanying the history of salvation — which is always more than can be communicated as propositions through the medium of Church preaching) can be the object of faith. Whether this includes conclusions deduced from the data of revelation with the help of non-revealed premises, is a matter of controversy. And the mode in which a later dogma is objectively implicit in the original revelation, and subjectively explicated has not yet been adequately explained theologically. Hence there is no uniform Catholic view of how the climax of a development is contained from the start in the deposit of faith, that is, of what are the objective limits of the development of dogma. It may be said in general, however, that a clear distinction must be made between the development of dogma and the apostolic task of making the

truths of faith one's own in a process of intellectual elaboration. Now that no new public revelation could be looked for, such a process would seem to be a human creation, not a message from above which the Christian could believe as God's word. The goal of dogmatic development must be a truth which can be the object of divinely-revealed faith, and it would seem that the only possible object of divine faith is what God has actually said, taken in the same extension as is the human word (an extension sometimes wider than the implicit content that is discoverable by purely logical analysis), and not what can be deduced from God's word. It will not do to argue that God knows what deductions can be drawn from his word: that fact does not make such deductions a part of his word. When God is pleased to use human words, what he says must be understood according to the rules governing human language.

On the other hand, the Church's definition of a dogma is purely declaratory: the truth defined must be God's word beforehand, and nothing the Church may do can make it so. At any rate it is important to stress the fact that while the term of the development of dogma must be objectively contained in the deposit and must remain demonstrably of a piece with it, still, as the word of God, the new dogma may well evolve otherwise than by logical analysis of the gospel. By virtue of the connatural knowledge of faith, certain goals of dogmatic development may be attained by a procedure insufficient to generate logical certainty and using only arguments of congruity. Once the dogma has evolved, the task theology has of showing its homogeneity with the deposit will sometimes be a difficult and delicate one. The theologian is not always helped in his search by any guidance from the magisterium, which on occasion simply defines that a truth is revealed without giving any indication of where it is revealed.

4. Now in saying that the growth of dogma is rooted in understanding of the deposit, we have suggested the forces behind that growth (cf. Vatican II, Constitution on Divine Revelation, art. 8). The Church's infallible magisterium takes the final step, bringing the process to a close and sanctioning it, presenting a truth to Catholics as a dogma to be believed (cf. *ibid.;* also *D*

1792). It is within the framework of this concern to answer the questions men ask that the role of heresy in the development of a number of dogmas needs to be considered.

Theological reflection is a second factor in development. It has undoubtedly a vital function in the Church and stems from the psychological need of clarifying the truths of faith. Theological reflection, insofar as it is the *intellectus fidei,* and not mere deduction in the Aristotelian sense of a (theological) science, is obviously a factor of the development of dogma in the strict sense. Only such efforts to understand the faith can give rise to "truth of faith" which were included in the original deposit. Such reflection is stimulated by the same factors as work on the magisterium, though very often the work of understanding better proceeds to a certain extent independently of outside forces, when the very obscurity of an element in the deposit invites reflection.

A third factor is the consciousness of faith or the instinct of faith *(sensus fidei)* in the faithful as a whole, founded on the grace-given connaturality of this sense with the objects of faith (Vatican II, Constitution on the Church, art. 12). The living faith which guarantees knowledge by connaturality works above all in the realm of Christian spirituality and life. This explains the preponderant role of the *sensus fidei* in the development of the Marian dogmas, according to many theologians (Dillenschneider). Meanwhile, the distinction between the Church teaching and the Church learning was generally understood to signify that the latter was a passive partner. But there is no such thing as passivity under the action of grace. A proper understanding of the role of the faithful in the development of dogma throws light on a profound saying of Paulinus of Nola: "Let us seek the word of God in all things. Let us hang on the lips of the faithful, since the Holy Spirit inspires them all." (*Ep.,* 23, 36.)

5. This list of factors which influence the development of doctrine in one way or another shows that the history of dogma and the lines along which development proceeds are fully contingent. Had historical conditions been different, other themes would have emerged. But the contingency of the lines of development does not mean that the results arrived at are contingent. All that comes

DOGMA

under an infallible declaration of the Church, which is the last stage of the development of dogma, is absolutely irreformable (*D* 1800, 2145). Nonetheless, this infallible answer to a previous question can open up avenues to new questions. The ensuing answers will form new stages in dogmatic progress which will gradually explicitate further what is already acquired. The immutability of definitions does not impede further development (*D* 1800). This also shows that though dogma is necessarily expressed in a given language making use of the concepts of a given culture, the multiplicity of potentialities means contingency of growth but not deficiency in the results. Infallibility excludes the use of inappropriate terms (and has always done so). If, therefore, certain terms have not only been used by general councils but explicitly ratified by them, we are not free to depart from such terms (*D* 2311).

See also *Bible* I B, *Apostolic Church, Apostolic Fathers, Heresy* I, *Spirituality, Dogma* III.

BIBLIOGRAPHY. J. H. Newman, *An Essay on the Development of Christian Doctrine* (1878); A. Gardeil, *Le donné révélé et la théologie* (1910); M. Tuyaerts, *L'évolution du dogme* (1919); F. Marin-Sola, *L'Évolution homogène du dogme catholique*, 2 vols. (2nd ed., 1924); L. de Grandmaison, *Le dogme chrétien. Sa nature, ses formules, son développement* (1928); P. Lynch, "The Newman-Perrone Papers on Development", *Gregorianum* 16 (1935), pp. 402–47; W. Ong, "Newman's Essay on Development in Its Intellectual Milieu", *Theological Studies* 7 (1946), pp. 3–45; H. de Lubac, "Le problème du développement du dogme", *RSR* 35 (1948), pp. 130–60; C. Dillenschneider, *Le sens de la foi et le progrès dogmatique du mystère marial* (1954); C. Journet, *Esquisse du développement du dogme marial* (1954); F. Flückinger, *Der Ursprung des christlichen Dogmas. Eine Auseinandersetzung mit A. Schweitzer und M. Werner* (1955); O. Chadwick, *From Bossuet to Newman. The Idea of Doctrinal Development* (1957); C. Pozo, *Contribución a la historia del problema del progreso dogmático* (1957); J. H. Walgrave, *Newman et le développement du dogme* (1957); M. Werner, *The Formation of Christian Dogma* (1957); M. G. McGrath, *The Vatican Council's Teaching on the Evolution of Dogma* (1959); C. Pozo, *La teoría del progreso dogmático en los teólogos de la escuela de Salamanca* (1959); H. Rondet, *Les dogmes changent-ils?* (1960); K. Rahner, "The Development of Dogma", *Theological Investigations,* I (1961), pp. 39–77; H. Hammans, *Die neueren katholischen Erklärungen der Dogmenentwicklung* (1965); K. Rahner, "Considerations on the Development of Dogma", *Theological Investigations,* IV (1966), pp. 3–35; G. Biemer, *Newman on Tradition* (1967).

Candido Pozo

III. History of Dogma

A. As a Theological Discipline

History of dogma as a theological discipline and an integral part of dogmatic theology itself, is the methodical, systematic investigation and exposition of the history of the various individual dogmas and of the whole Christian understanding of faith, studying the mutual relations of its various constituents and its relation to the themes and epochs of the history of ideas. In contrast to the history of revelation, the history of dogma begins with the close of revelation in Jesus Christ and of the apostolic preaching. Yet even in Scripture it discovers its subject-matter in paradigm, because in Scripture itself "theology" is already found (even though it is theology guaranteed by inspiration), which may be distinguished from the original revelation-event. Consequently there is already development of dogma there.

Since dogma does not consist only of explicit definitions of the extraordinary magisterium, the distinction, possible in principle, between the history of dogma and the history of theology cannot always be clearly effected. As a result, the history of theology is mostly written as part of the history of dogma. At the basis of the history of dogma lies the fact of the development of dogma and at the basis of this the intrinsically temporal, historical character of man, and therefore of his knowledge of truth. For dogma is God's truth heard, believed and formulated in human, historically conditioned terms by man in this world. Moreover, dogma is a living function of the Church, which in an essentially historical and socially articulated process has to accept, make explicit and proclaim the truth bestowed and guaranteed by God himself, in ways appropriate to the ever-changing intellectual perspective of the world around it. The method of the history of dogma is a *theologically* historical one. It is not merely a part of the general history of civilization and religion, but a theological discipline, and therefore regulated by faith. At the same time, however, it is genuine critical history using the method proper to such history. The unity of the two methods is possible because it is already present in the inquirer and in the subject-matter of the history of dogma: genuine *history* under *grace*. The history of dogma inquires into the meaning and scope of dogmatic propositions (and therefore cannot wholly be separated from dogmatic theology), but does so in order to determine and understand the history of these propositions; it is therefore not dogmatics pure and simple. It also comprises the greater part of the history of heresies, because the meaning of dogmatic definitions is often clearest when they are confronted with their contradictories.

History of dogma establishes the meaning and scope of the various dogmatic propositions, compares them with one another, traces the development of the formulas employed, discloses the forces at work in their development (objective, personal, cultural, social, etc.), endeavours to grasp the dynamic trend of that development towards the future and so to prepare future dogmatic theology. It does not seek only what remains the same in the same faith under its changing forms (the apologetical aspect of the history of dogma), but also the differences and sequence of these changing forms themselves. It does so, not only because it is only in this way that the meaning and justification of the later statement of the faith (perhaps formulated in an actual definition) is made clear, but also because only in this way is the fullness of the Church's awareness of its faith manifested. For the history of dogma does not advance only in linear fashion from the less explicit and less determinate towards a more explicit formulation incapable of any further improvement. In principle the history of the understanding of the faith is always incomplete and open towards the future. The past ("tradition") always remains as source and critical measure of what comes later and is never fully replaced by later formulation in such a way as to be rendered superfluous for dogmatic theology itself. It follows that genuine history of dogma can only be pursued in living contact with a dogmatic theology which exposes itself to questions set by the actual preaching of the gospel today and tomorrow.

B. As Subject-Matter of Historical Research

1. *Preliminary hermeneutical considerations.* It is impossible of course to recount in detail here the history of all the statements of faith in dogmatic theology. Even a brief survey, if it is not to confine itself to the purely external facts of a few of the most important dogmas, depends on whether some fundamental features and structures of this history can be indicated. This in turn depends on whether despite the incalculable freedom of this history on the part of God and of man, it is possible to find an objective guiding principle for its formal division into epochs which would make it possible to analyse it in a theologically appropriate manner. On account of the close relation between Church history (assuming that this is understood and analysed in a truly theological way) and history of dogma (as a decisive factor in the former), it is to be expected from the start that the structural principle sought must be identical with, or a specification of, the principle of a theologically interpreted Church history. This refers us to what was said about this structural principle of Church history in the article on Christianity, which must be considered again here in regard to the specific features of the history of dogma. It becomes clear that for the purpose of the analysis, methodical arrangement and characterization of the history of dogma, it is possible to make use of the encounter and dialogue between the understanding of the faith formed within the Church and the world situation which confronts and makes demands upon that understanding. This does not mean that the determination of the structure of the history of dogma is given over to a random element alien in character to the nature of dogma and its history. For on the one hand the history of dogma itself develops as a history of the faith which is aware that it is called responsibly to answer for its hope (cf. 1 Pet 3:15) and the promise accepted therein. And on the other hand a theological interpretation of the "secular" intellectual situation and its history would show that this itself is disposed by God in relation to the growing attainment of full self-awareness in the understanding of the faith. And since its coming, Christianity has contributed to determine that situation even in the apparently secular domain. Consequently Christianity encounters itself in that situation, often in something Christian which the Church has not yet explicitly realized. The actual history of dogma took place, therefore, not in the style of a purely logical continuity of statement and explana-

tion, but in the perpetual interaction of sacred and secular history, history of faith and of thought, which cannot wholly be displayed in theoretical form. Of course, to a history of dogma composed on this basis, further subsidiary divisions would have to be added for its more precise articulation: in regard to organization (what institutions actively promote the historical growth of dogma and theology?), history of style (interaction of history of dogma and literary history), individual history (the uniquely great thinkers of original creative power), social history (theology in its dependence on a particular social and economic situation), Church history (interaction of history of theology and other aspects of Church history), etc. All these in turn are mutually interdependent. It is impossible here, however, to go into such patterns of arrangement and division.

2. On the basis of these hermeneutical considerations the following can be said about the phases and course of the history of dogma.

a) Just as Christianity only reached its full development as the universal religion of all nations when it found tangible historical realization among all nations and civilizations through the intermediary of the unity they had historically achieved in a "world civilization", so too the Church's dogma. It too only attains its own full development when as a message of salvation in the course of history, it encounters, in a dialogue involving both partners, the whole mind of the world in the epoch of world civilization, and by this dialogue contributes to determine the further course of history and shares in it, in a manner which cannot be foreseen today. In this perspective, the history of dogma has two great epochs, that of the process of the attainment of this full development and that of global dialogue with the entire unified (which does not mean peacefully reconciled) mind of humanity. The first fundamental period is only now slowly coming to an end, the second only just beginning (cf. Vatican II, Decree on the Church's Missionary Activity). From this point of view, the whole previous history of dogma was "local", the dialogue of faith with Judaism in the time of Christ, Hellenism in Roman antiquity and the Occident later. All this contributed to make the Church a competent partner in the dialogue which divine revelation was to continue with the world as a whole. The great task of earlier times was to show, in the actual process of dogmatic development which the Lord of history and not men's deliberate thinking engineered, that the message of Christianity is not tied to any particular stage or region of man's self-understanding. This meant that the understanding of the faith had to be detached from the mental horizons of Judaism and Hellenism, to become, as it ought to be, a dialogue with the "world".

In the latter process, the Church has to take cognizance, in an ever-increasing measure, of three truths. The first is that it is permanently confronted with a permanently distinct secular partner, which demands a growing acceptance of the "worldliness" of the world, of its relative autonomy, of its basic inability to be fully "consecrated", of the powerful forward drive of its dynamism, the resulting distance between Christianity and any given, stable order of social and political economy, etc. The second truth is that the Church really has a message for the life and history of this partner. This means a growing knowledge in faith of Christian anthropology with its bearings on the secular sphere, where it insists on the free personal subjectivity of man, greater theological insight into the nature and foundations of natural law, into the need for the "humanization" of man individually, into the possibilities and ethical bounds of man's self-manipulation, the rejection of an esoteric indifference to a sinful world to be abandoned to its corruption, etc. The third truth is that the Church must uphold against the world all that is most truly its own and not of the world. This is the story of the defence and interpretation of its supernatural message about God and his gracious self-communication against efforts to reduce it to a human ideology, the story of the "discernment of the Christian spirit", of a theology of the endless task of detachment from the world, which justifies the action of the Church. These are the three truths which had to become more and more clear and explicit — in many concrete forms, no doubt, which cannot be fully embodied in a system — in the former period. It is on this basis that the faith of the Church can now take up in earnest the dialogue which is now beginning with a unified and independent world.

b) To some extent, therefore, this first great period of the history of dogma (and of theology) permits of further analysis. Measured by the usual themes and divisions of the traditional history of dogma, this analysis may apparently not be very sharply defined and profound, but it should be remembered that the importance for personal salvation of later formulations of dogma as compared with earlier, and therefore of the history of dogma in this respect, should certainly not be exaggerated. In this case, too, what is more important is the enduring element in the Church. Consequently, the structural analysis can only really be based on the notion of the encounter with successive epochs in the history of civilization. This principle, however, rightly makes some of the changes and advances in the history of dogma appear less significant than they seem in a history of dogma written on purely positivist lines. The first great period of the history of dogma can perhaps be divided theologically into phases as follows, to give a general sense of the movement of ideas which took place in it.

(i) The history of dogma in the *primitive Church,* which for the most part took place in Scripture itself. Here the early Church's new sense of faith was expressed spontaneously and directly with the means available in the world of the OT (and only marginally with those of Hellenism). Precisely by doing so, it went beyond the mental perspectives of that world. What was radically new (the universality of the gospel of the absolute mediator of salvation in death and resurrection) was envisaged on the basis of the divinely ordained OT (theology of the fulfilment of Scripture), and so had to preserve continuity with (Rom 9–11; opposition to Marcion), and distinction from, its pre-history (the Pauline theology of freedom from the Law; polemics against the Jews; theology of separation of the Church from the Synagogue, cf. Letter of Barnabas).

(ii) The theology of the first contacts with *Hellenistic civilization.* In the 2nd and 3rd centuries the universalism of the message of the Christian faith, disengaged from the particularity of its origins, met for the first time a mental perspective of a certain universality — a philosophy and (to a certain extent) a world-empire. For the boundaries

of the Church coincided in practice with those of the Roman empire. On the other hand, within those frontiers there was a "pluralism" of East and West etc., which later took on in fact tragic dimensions: schism, cessation of dialogue between Eastern and Western theology. This first encounter, still under the cross of persecution, produced, as was to be expected, a first general response which, as a comprehensive outline (details of which therefore were to be worked out later), was to serve as a permanent model. The response to secular universalism (Hellenistic Gnosticism as the catchment of Eastern and Western conceptions of man, a "system" with religious application) inevitably developed in two directions and phases. On the one hand there was the defensive self-affirmation of revelation from above against its absorption in human Gnosis; the conquest of Gnosticism by the theology of saving *history* together with the first theology of tradition and the formation of the Canon (Irenaeus). On the other hand there was in a positive sense the first attempt at a systematization of the Christian faith with Hellenistic instruments, with all the dangers this involved, as Origenism shows. The negative and positive dialogue with the real world led to the beginnings of a theology of martyrdom and asceticism (virginity: Methodius), and also, in opposition to an esoteric conception of the Church in Montanism and Novatianism, a theology of a soberly realistic but affirmative relation to a truly redeemable world (where "canon law" had a place).

(iii) The third period extends *from the turning-point under Constantine to the beginning of "modern times",* comprising, that is, the theology of the "imperial Church" of antiquity and that of the medieval West. This is ultimately a single period because despite the change in ethnic substratum the same mental perspectives dominated (Platonism and Aristotelianism as a cosmocentric philosophy). Both in Roman and medieval times Christianity was involved in the same task, that of assimilating a civilization already to some extent formed by Christianity, even in its distinctive rational, secular and dynamic character and which was (because of this providential fact) to be the active agent of the creation of the intellectual unity of the world in the second great period.

Significance for the theology of the imperial Church. This meant a theology of the radical

105

distinction between God and world in opposition to the latent panentheism of Arianism, the elaboration of an orthodox theology of the Trinity in which the Logos and Pneuma, the principles of the economy of redemption, are not derivatives of the true God but are the absolute God himself. The Trinity continues to be seen as "economic" and for just that reason, as immanent. In this way there was also preserved, both as a matter of course and in opposition to Manichaeism, at least the outlines of a theology of a good created world established in its own reality by God. The temporal, historical character of man, of salvation and of faith itself was firmly maintained in principle against an (ultimately Gnostic) closed system of the world, by maintaining the doctrine of the "resurrection of the flesh" and rejecting that of apocatastasis. Protology and eschatology, however, scarcely advanced theologically beyond the statements of Scripture.

There was a theology of the radical acceptance of this world distinct from God, through the elaboration of orthodox Christology balanced between separation (Nestorianism) and confusion (Monophysitism, Monotheletism). In Christology the Christian conception of the general relation between God and the world finds expression during this period: the closest proximity of the world to God is also its most complete liberation to be itself.

Other matters remain unsettled or an open question for the West, or else are only found discussed in a rudimentary way; the true relation between Church and world (the State) is still (despite Gelasius) to a large extent obscured by an imperial theology of the sacred state (in Byzantium), and this was only really shaken for the first time in the investiture controversy. Augustine developed for the first time a universal theology of history, but in such a way that the danger of an identification of "Christian" State and God's Kingdom (represented by the Church but not identical with it) was not yet banished; in Augustine (in particular by his doctrine of free grace for the individual in his personal life of salvation which is not simply an aspect of the cosmic and "incarnational" process of divinization), the first outline of an existence-centred orientation is found. But this is linked with a questionable pessimism as regards salvation after original sin. In his opposition to Donatism he upholds an institutional conception of the Church, but his appeal to the secular arm against Donatism linked Church and State in a questionable way that was to have grave consequences.

Significance for medieval theology in the West. In the same fundamental perspective "progress" in the history of dogma can broadly be characterized as follows.

At first there was a fairly complete systematization of Christian dogma with the help of an Aristotelianism of Platonic and Augustinian stamp (cf. the theological *Summas*). This meant an approach to dogma in a cosmocentric and not in a "transcendental" or personal, existential, anthropocentric or really historical perspective. But it also meant, at least in principle, the emancipation of a secular philosophy relatively independent of faith and theology. By way of the doctrines of the independence of secondary causes (Aquinas) and of the supernatural character of grace, it led for the first time to a recognition of the independence of the secular world and at the same time represented a unity of world and Christianity, though one conditioned by the age.

There was a clearer distinction between the Church and the world. An initial theological analysis of the social constitution of the Church showed its independence of the State (even a "Christian" State). The relation between collegiality and primacy was not yet worked out, as Conciliarism shows. There was still a tendency to incorporate the secular order directly and completely into that of salvation and its mediation by the Church. Hence the notion of the *corpus christianorum* and the *sacrum imperium*.

(iv) The theology of the *transition from a culturally and intellectually restricted milieu into the situation of the world Church*. Wherever this era of transition to modern times is considered to have begun, as early as Aquinas or in the later Middle Ages, at the Reformation, the Enlightenment or the French Revolution, at all events its end has come, broadly speaking. This is reflected even in the Church. Vatican II's dialogue was with the world as a whole, with non-Christian religions and with "atheism", in "religious freedom". That era of transition constituted the period of immediate preparation (more or less well exploited) of the Church and especially of its theology for the present "pluralistic" world which is being rationalized and humanized by technology. That preparation involved the ecclesial and theological mastering of the pluralist situation within Christianity itself by elaborating distinctive doctrines in the face of the Reformation (in controversial theology), and by entering into positive discussion with non-Catholic Christians (in "ecumenical theology"). The "emancipation" of the world continued, as progress was made in the doctrine of natural law, in the theory of society *(ius gentium)* and a distinctively Catholic but flexible social doctrine. There was optimism about salvation, in contrast to Jansenism, and the rudiments of a positive theology of non-Christian religions. The Church recognized its distinction from other social structures of secular society and its autonomy and capacity for independent action (Vatican I and II). The Church proclaimed more clearly the essentials of Christianity against the theology of the Enlightenment and Modernism. It disengaged itself from a particular mental perspective determined in advance by the conditions of a particular epoch and place by the admission of historical criticism into exegesis and theology and the advent of the history of dogma and of biblical criticism. There was a growing familiarity with a limited pluralism of philosophical systems through recognition of an Eastern theology and through growing acceptance of the anthropocentric transcendental philosophy of modern times and of a philosophy of the temporal, historical nature of man, as possible instruments of orthodox theology. There developed a theology of freedom and of personal conscience in a pluralist civil society. The conflict between natural science (theory of evolution) and theology was gradually eliminated. Post-Tridentine Scholasticism of the Baroque period was itself a phenomenon of transition. As in the Middle Ages, the attempt was made with considerable success to construct a vast system which would integrate into itself the whole secular view of the world. At the same time, however, theological understanding slowly began to respond to the new situation that was approaching. Examples of this were the first attempts at historical theology, the independent pursuit of philosophy, the development of international law, of the psychology of faith, of freedom under grace.

C. Relevance to Pastoral Activity

1. The pastor today must have some knowledge of the history of dogma. Only in this way can he announce the Word of God with the inner flexibility which is necessary today precisely in order to preserve true orthodoxy. If he is to have the courage to open out new perspectives and to change relative emphases, he must know how rich in variety of perspectives and emphases the history of the Church's preaching and theology has been. He must have learnt from the history of dogma that serious questions and profound difficulties regarding faith can often only be dealt with slowly. In this way he will be ready in his own situation to practise patience and hope in faith. Through his studies in the history of dogma he should have learnt to go beyond monotonous repetition of dry catechism statements and to draw on the wealth of tradition as a whole.

2. The pastor should realize that he plays his part in the advance of the history of dogma. Preaching the faith is not merely repetition of a simplified theology, but an anticipation of theology. Its living vigour, its problems and solutions carry the history of dogma onwards. And it is precisely that dynamic movement towards the future of preaching which ought to give life and energy to the pastor and which gives the question of the past the gravity and significance without which the history of dogma would degenerate into mere erudition.

See also *Theology* I, II, *Church History, Christianity* I, *Dualism, Hellenism and Christianity, Occident, Man* II, *Person* II B.

BIBLIOGRAPHY. A. Harnack, *Lehrbuch der Dogmengeschichte*, 3 vols. (1886–90; 4th rev. ed., 1909–10), E. T.: *History of Dogma*, 7 vols., trans. by N. Buchanan; K. Werner, *Geschichte der Katholischen Theologie. Seit dem Trienter Konzil bis zur Gegenwart* (2nd ed., 1889); F. Loofs, *Leitfaden zum Studium der Dogmengeschichte*, 2 vols. (1889; 5th ed., 1951–53); R. Seeberg, *Lehrbuch der Dogmengeschichte*, 4 vols. (1895–98), E. T.: *Textbook of the History of Doctrines*; L. J. Tixeront, *Histoire des dogmes dans l'antiquité chrétienne*, 3 vols. (1905–12), E. T.: *History of Dogmas*, 3 vols. (1910–16); M. Jugie, *Theologia dogmatica Christianorum orientalium ac ecclesia catholica dissidentium*, 4 vols. (1926–35); G. Ebeling, *Kirchengeschichte als Geschichte der Auslegung der Heiligen Schrift* (1947); E. Hocedez, *Histoire de la Théologie au XIXᵉ siècle*, 3 vols. (1948–52); W. Koehler, *Dogmen-*

geschichte als Geschichte des christlichen Selbstbewusstseins, 2 vols. (3rd ed., 1951); M. Schmaus, Beharrung und Fortschritt im Christentum (1951); A. M. Landgraf, Dogmengeschichte der Frühscholastik, 4 vols. (1952–56); H. U. von Balthasar, A Theology of History (1964).

Karl Rahner

IV. Dogmatics

1. *General description.* Dogmatics is the science of the Church's dogma, i.e., systematic reflection undertaken on methodological principles appropriate to dogma and aiming at as comprehensive a grasp of it as possible. This involves reflection on everything necessary or helpful, in method or content, for the understanding of dogma. As in every branch of knowledge, reflection on its own history is an integral part of dogmatics. Its first and proper object is Christian revelation (from the formal point of view: fundamental and formal theology; from the material point of view: "special" dogmatic theology). This also includes those dogmas which concern the Christian accomplishment of man's salvation in nature and grace and which therefore have a directly moral significance.

Since dogmatics is a part and indeed the central part of Catholic theology, it is a science of *faith,* i.e., it is pursued by the believer in the light of faith. For all its scientific reflection, therefore, it is a "committed" knowledge of the saving self-manifestation of the triune God in Christ and in the Church as his Body. And because revelation and dogma primarily exist as the faith of the Church, dogmatic theology from the start is an ecclesiastical science. It is of course always pursued by individuals, but its starting point is always the Church's kerygma, as heard, believed and announced by all the faithful and the Church's ministry. And it returns to the Church's understanding of its faith as source of an understanding of the faith which develops and is perpetually renewed. Kerygma (and its derivative, dogma) is of course always a summons calling for men's actual submission to the mystery of God. But it has a content, for it is the proclamation of the historical saving deeds of God (and of the ultimate, "eternal" structures implied in them: dogma as concerned with "essences"). Dogmatic theology, therefore, also has a historical and "metaphysical" content. In many respects it remains a historically-conditioned discipline (depending on historical presuppositions of

the prevailing world-view etc.). Yet the historical situation which is properly its own is that of the definitiveness of historical revelation in Christ. This does not diminish the divinely-created and grace-endowed reality of the world or nullify analogical statements about it ("affirmative" theology); but through this revelation, direct and permanent access to the enduring, "silent", adorable mystery of God in himself is available, really, and not merely ideologically or in mystical contemplation ("negative" theology as an intrinsic constituent of truly Christian theology, and one which must permeate the whole). Through this historical "eschatological" situation which is proper to it, dogmatic theology always transcends the historical limitations which in other respects affect it.

2. *Distinction from other theological disciplines.* a) *From moral theology.* By the themes which constitute its content, moral theology remains intrinsically a part of dogmatic theology. For God's self-communication in grace and faith is a theme of dogmatic theology precisely because this self-communication of God himself (as the very substance of revelation as such) is the principle of man's action in regard to salvation. Now moral theology rightly understood concerns precisely this kind of human activity. It is only on practical grounds, therefore, that (since the Baroque period of Scholasticism) it has — quite rightly — been established as a separate discipline. This was done in particular because in this section of dogmatic theology many auxiliary sciences have to be called upon which do not concern the other sections of dogmatic theology. But even with the present-day division of these branches of study for technical reasons, dogmatic theology does not relinquish themes of "moral theology" (*De peccato; De gratia; De virtutibus infusis,* etc.), and in Vatican II's Decree on Priestly Formation, moral theology is strictly charged not to neglect its authentic dogmatic origin and purpose.

b) *From exegesis and biblical theology.* Scripture is, of course, always the *norma non normata* of all theology, because it permanently opens out for us genuine access to God's definitive self-disclosure in Jesus Christ. But biblical theology as such (and the exegesis which it presupposes) cannot itself be dogmatic theology or take its place. This is so even if it is assumed that biblical theology, being an ecclesiastical science, must be carried on within the Church's understanding of its faith and not merely as part of the scientific study of religion. Precisely because it is to be a critical (and therefore distinct) standard and a perpetually fresh source of dogmatic theology (*D* 2314), biblical theology must not seek to take over the task of demonstrating and critically testing the legitimacy of its own exegesis in the history of the Church's teaching, throughout the history of the development of the Church's dogma. Nor should it attempt to effect the "actualization" of the message of Scripture in order to renew the kerygma of the Church in the encounter of the Church's understanding of the faith with whatever is the predominant secular conception of man. This quite apart from the question of the relation in which non-scriptural tradition, in the "material" sense, stands to the content of Scripture (cf. on this the cautious formulas of Vatican II in the Constitution on Divine Revelation, according to which at least the extent of the Canon and the inspired character of the absolute norm of faith *cannot* be derived from Scripture alone, so that Scripture itself requires a "dogmatic" foundation supplied by the understanding of the faith by the Church and its tradition). Precisely these tasks which cannot be fulfilled by a biblical theology as such are those of dogmatic theology. This distinction between the two in no way settles of course the loftier question (which is omitted here) whether at least biblical theology (as opposed to purely textual exegesis) is nevertheless not actually, in a profounder and more exact theological methodology, an essential constituent of dogmatic theology itself. The latter after all has to listen to Scripture itself (the *themata biblica:* Vatican II, Decree on Priestly Formation, art. 16) and not merely supply *dicta probantia* from Scripture for its own theses.

c) *From fundamental theology.* From its nature as the demonstration of the credibility of the actual occurrence, i.e., existence, of Christian revelation, fundamental theology is certainly distinct from dogmatic theology, which is systematic reflection on the content of faith. Yet two things must not be overlooked. Fundamental theology is a theology of Christian *faith,* not metaphysics and philosophy of religion. Furthermore, at the present day in particular, a purely abstract,

formal demonstration of the credibility of the existence of revelation would seem to be insufficient. Nowadays each of the various mysteries of faith requires an initiation into its credibility and the possibility of its actual concrete assimilation by the individual. Only such initiation in its totality, therefore, would represent an adequate demonstration of the credibility of revelation. Whether such a task should be carried out to a large extent by special dogmatic theology alone (dogmatic theology cannot renounce the task entirely) or whether fundamental theology itself is to assume the task, is a secondary question, of a more technical and pedagogical kind, which cannot be settled here. In the latter case fundamental theology would certainly be considerably extended, and in a certain way would have to keep before it the whole of dogmatics and interpret its fundamental affirmations in relation to the "credibility" (concrete assimilability) and so perhaps discover the true nature of that *cursus introductorius* which the Vatican II plan of studies calls for without precisely determining in what, from the methodological point of view, it consists.

d) *From other theological disciplines.* All other historical and regulative theological sciences can be summed up and distinguished from dogmatic theology by the fact that though theological disciplines, they relate to history and the (desirable) action of the Church insofar as this is not determined solely by its enduring nature, i.e., by dogmatic ecclesiology. These sciences include, therefore, Church history with the history of liturgy, history of law, history of ecclesiastical literature (patrology and the history of theological literature, history of theology); practical theology (i.e., canon law, pastoral theology with catechetics, liturgical studies, homiletics). These disciplines study the Church as it appears in the human contingencies of history and in the action flowing from the authority for free decision granted to the Church together with the norms of such action: the Church as the (divinely effected) response of men to God's word.

3. *Methodology of dogmatic theology.* An important instruction is given in the Decree of Vatican II on Priestly Formation (art. 16). Dogmatic theology must be *positive* theology, i.e., it must begin with the "biblical themes" and the history of the continued proclama-

tion of the biblical message of salvation by the Church in preaching, authoritative doctrinal pronouncements, history of dogma and history of theology. But then it also has to be "speculative" and systematic, i.e., it has to serve a really personal assimilation of the truth as heard historically. That, however, demands a confrontation of the revealed truth heard with the totality of the hearer's (transcendental and historically-conditioned) conception of himself and of the world. Of course the two phases of theological work in dogmatics, the historical and the speculative, cannot simply follow one another chronologically, for they mutually condition and involve one another. It is noteworthy that the decree of Vatican II is clearly departing from the too exclusively analytic dogmatics of later Scholasticism and neo-Scholasticism, in which the "positive sources" were consulted too onesidedly simply in support of certain traditionally prescribed theses. Historical revelation should obviously be listened to receptively and serenely, even for what is not already current in the explicit consciousness of theology. Living dogmatic theology is also always a "philosophical" work, for any particular conception of man and the world is expressed principally in the prevailing philosophy of the age, while dogmatic theology speaks in human terms (just as revelation itself does). Now these human terms require perpetually to be called in question anew, both in the light of revelation itself and of human experience (transcendental and historical).

This does not mean that dogmatic theology presupposes a complete philosophical conception of man which has come into existence absolutely independently. On the contrary, obedient hearing of revelation alters the historical situation of philosophy and therefore philosophy itself. In fact it is quite conceivable that dogmatic theology in the future may integrate philosophy into itself even more fully, because it is the more comprehensive and more radically concrete and vital study, and nothing really philosophical can remain entirely a matter of indifference to it. Only theology itself can consider the method of its listening, because this is determined by its own proper object (the historically personal self-manifestation of the absolute God to the free consent of faith and love, not to mere *theoria*). Hence from the critical point of view of theology itself its object comprises metaphysics (as statement of the hearer's self-comprehension) and also hermeneutics, for dogmatic theology is also fundamental and formal theology, though it cannot be reduced to hermeneutics. Theory of historicity and historical experience on the one hand and history and its concrete experience on the other are never purely and simply identical. And salvation consists in encounter with historical reality itself, not merely in the acceptance of formal historicity.

4. *Inner structure of (special) dogmatic theology.* The fundamental difficulty of an intrinsically appropriate arrangement (articulation) of dogmatic theology lies in the fact that its object is at once "essential" and "existential". The revelation of God which finds expression in it is not primarily a doctrinal communication of truths in propositional form comprehensible in themselves independently of the moment of time of their communication. That moment is not merely extrinsic to them. Revelation and its history is at one and the same time salvation and history of salvation. "Revelation" as God's *action* among men, which, it is true, has an intrinsically constitutive gnoseological factor, can therefore only be received in historical experience which remains alive and is correctly heard as anamnesis and as "prognosis" (hopeful statement about the future as the accomplishment of what is experienced). Consequently, dogmatic theology must be an account of sacred history. It must be a historical science not only in the handling of its "sources" but also in regard to its object. It can therefore never simply be concerned with "theological conclusions", simply taking its highest "premises" for granted. At the same time, however, dogmatic theology is necessarily a study of essences and to that extent systematic: the history recounted has a unity and a coherent structure which have to be taken into consideration, and which need to be examined in a general, formal and fundamental theology. The basis of that history is always the permanently identical reality which has a history and which has to be grasped theologically: God's one turning in grace to the world. In it the immutable essence of God appears. And that history has entered the eschatological phase in which the historically contingent and the essential, in their historically conditioned and changing mutual

relationship, have converged definitively and indissolubly (and only as a consequence of this is it possible really to distinguish them). That history has therefore reached the phase in which the Church pursues theology according to its content and also its form.

On the basis of the unity and difference of the historically existential and essential aspects of all dogmatic theology, it is understandable that there cannot be a compulsory and universally received structure and consequent articulation of the various dogmatic tractates. It is only possible to explain the chief kinds of emphasis of possible dogmatic theologies. At one extreme there is a dogmatics which is almost purely and simply an account of redemptive history. At the other there are those which are either almost purely systems of theological conclusions, assuming the history with its content as a prior datum, or else consider practically nothing but the formal structures of that history and their incorporation in a formal theology of the enduring structures of the history of redemption and revelation or in a hermeneutics of the manner of their incorporation. A "pure" type of dogmatic theology would contradict the inner plurality of its object and claim presumptuously to grasp adequately the unity of this object.

See also *Dogma* I–III, *Revelation, Kerygma, Magisterium, Moral Theology* I.

BIBLIOGRAPHY. MANUALS: F. Diekamp, *Theologiae Dogmaticae Manuale*, 4 vols. (1932–34); E. Brunner, *Dogmatics,* 3 vols. (1949–62); J. Brinktrine, *Katholische Dogmatik. Einleitung in die Dogmatik* (1951); J. Pohle and J. Gummersbach, *Lehrbuch der Dogmatik,* 3 vols. (1952–65); L. Ott, *Fundamentals of Catholic Dogma* (1955); K. Barth, *Church Dogmatics,* ed. by G. W. Bromiley and T. F. Torrance, 5 vols. (1956 ff.); P. Althaus, *Die Christliche Wahrheit. Lehrbuch der Dogmatik* (5th ed., 1959); M. J. Scheeben, *Handbuch der Katholischen Dogmatik,* 6 vols. (3rd ed., 1959–61); M. Schmaus, *Katholische Dogmatik,* 5 vols. (1960–64); *Le Mystère chrétien. Théologie Dogmatique,* I ff. (1961 ff.); O. Weber, *Grundlagen der Dogmatik,* 2 vols. (3rd ed., 1962–64); J. Feiner and M. Löhrer, eds., *Mysterium Salutis. Grundriss einer heilsgeschichtlichen Dogmatik,* 5 vols. (1965 ff.). OTHER LITERATURE: O. Ritschl, *Dogmengeschichte des Protestantismus,* 4 vols. (1908–27); M. Grabmann, *Geschichte der scholastischen Methode,* 2 vols. (1909–11; repr. 1956); M.-R. Gagnebert, "La nature de la théologie spéculative", *Revue Thomiste* 44 (1938), pp. 3–17, 213–55, 645–74; J.-F. Bonnefoy, *La nature de la théologie selon St. Thomas* (1939); J. Friedericks, *Die Theologie als spekulative und praktische Wissenschaft nach Bonaventura und Thomas von Aquin* (1940); M.-D. Chenu, *La théologie comme science au XIIIe siècle* (1943); M. Grabmann, *Die theologische Erkenntnis- und Einleitungslehre des hl. Thomas von Aquin* (1948); F. Buri, *Dogmatik als Selbstverständnis des christlichen Glaubens* (1956); M.-D. Chenu, *La théologie est-elle une science?* (1957); C. Dumont, "La réflexion sur la méthode théologique", *NRT* 83 (1961), pp. 1034–50; 84 (1962), pp. 17–35; K. Rahner, "The Prospects for Dogmatic Theology", *Theological Investigations,* I (1961), pp. 1–18; id., "A Scheme for a Treatise of Dogmatic Theology", *ibid.,* pp. 19–37; M. Kähler, *Geschichte der protestantischen Dogmatik im 19. Jahrhundert* (1962); P. Fransen, "Three Ways of Dogmatic Thought", *Heythrop Journal* 4 (1963), pp. 3–24; J. Blenkinsopp, "Biblical and Dogmatic Theology", *CBQ* 26 (1964), pp. 70–85; C. H. Ratschow, *Lutherische Dogmatik zwischen Reformation und Aufklärung,* I (1964); H. Ott, *Theology and Preaching* (1965); K. Rahner, "Exegesis and Dogmatic Theology", *Theological Investigations,* V (1966), pp. 67–93.

Karl Rahner

DOGMATISM

The dogmatic procedure, which is the exposition of certain structures of thought *(dogmata)* without investigation of their intrinsic justification, is of itself legitimate. It is only when it is used in a field where it is not applicable that it becomes dogmatism and has a derogatory sense.

1. This occurs when the procedure is used in philosophy, whose essential function is to investigate its objects with regard to the ultimate grounds of their being and can only make responsible assertions on these terms. Its terms of reference do not include dogmatic assertions. Dogmatism was originally taken in too wide a sense, when it was used (in *Diogenes Laertius,* IX, 74) to characterize any positive exposition of doctrinal propositions in opposition to the scepticism of the later Hellenistic period. The term dogmatism has also been used in neo-Scholastic philosophy, since J. L. Balmes, to describe the apparently indispensable procedure by which the "fundamental truths" are pre-supposed (the existence of the "I", the principle of contradiction, etc.). But this is to overlook the fact that such basic acquisitions are not amenable to proof, being their own justification (or being justified by the indication of their pre-rational grounds). For Kant (Critique of Pure Reason, B XXXV) every metaphysic which neglects the critique of the

faculty of knowledge itself is dogmatism. Philosophical thought since Kant is open to the charge and the danger of dogmatism, insofar as it fails to deepen and complete the ancient and medieval pre-occupation with the object by the transcendental method orientated to the subject. Present-day linguistic analysis and Heidegger's philosophy of being have also posed the problems of the historicity of thought and speech with regard to the fundamental matters which all non-dogmatic philosophy has to investigate today. Tradition and authority have indeed a profound significance for philosophy but this function is limited to that of sign-post and impulse for the investigation of the matter itself.

2. In theology, however, the dogmatic procedure is not only legitimate. It is of fundamental importance. Dogmatic theology derives from the divine revelation embodied in Scripture the dogmas of faith which are not of themselves perspicuous to human reason. But even these would degenerate into merely dogmatist assertions if they were put forward with a mere reference to later authoritative doctrinal formulae and no effort was made to demonstrate as clearly as possible that such formulae are based on the original source of faith. Fundamental theology also tries to meet the indisputable demands of scientific criticism (as does apologetics), by affirming the "extrinsic" reasons of credibility for the fact of revelation — though not appealing to the "intrinsic" justification of the truths of faith themselves.

3. In the various sciences, and especially in the teaching of the natural sciences, the student has to accept much of what he learns on the authority of his teachers, which is of course confirmed by other experts. Here too a type of instruction which insisted too much on the personal authority of the teacher could be called dogmatism. Above all, a scientist would be guilty of a pernicious dogmatism in his methods, if he applied uncritically the demands and limits of his own field of science to that of others. The acquisition of non-scientific knowledge follows basically the same lines as the corresponding sciences, but the necessity of a critical, non-dogmatic justification of the knowledge in question can never be greater than the degree of maturity attained by the learner.

See also *Transcendental Philosophy, Being, Existence* II, *History* I, *Dogma* I, IV, *Fundamental Theology, Apologetics, Knowledge.*

BIBLIOGRAPHY. E. Rothacker, *Die dogmatische Denkform in den Geisteswissenschaften;* H.-G. Gadamer, *Wahrheit und Methode* (2nd ed., 1965), pp. 256–69, 307–15, 487 f.; K. Rogmann, *Dogmatismus und Autoritarismus* (1966).

Walter Kern

DUALISM

A. Notion

In general, dualism, in contrast to monism, is used to describe the view which reduces reality to two equally primordial and mutually opposed principles. The various forms of dualism are determined by the ontological natures of these principles and by the manner of their opposition. Since the total reality can neither be simply two realities which have nothing at all to do with each other, and it cannot be simply one reality, the question of how the historical forms of dualism are to be understood involves the basic question of the origin of, or the ultimate relationships and distinctions between, all reality. A readiness to condemn out of hand the historical forms of dualism could lead one to miss the real problem, just as much as if one refused to investigate the nature of the unity of reality. Dualism cannot be avoided by taking refuge in the (false) alternative of simple unity, but only by clarifying the relationship between duality and unity.

Purely speculative theorizing on the problem cannot provide a solution. The actual duality-in-unity of existence cannot be realized and resolved except in the duality-in-unity of the dialogue which is lived out in the love between the "I" and "You". But since man has renounced this love by original sin, and hence has falsified his relationship to himself as well as to God, existence, both in the individual and in society, must always be experienced as to some extent dualistic. This existential dualism, affecting man to his very core because it is a dualism of personal relationships and of the will, is the most radical of all forms of dualism. Man can ultimately prescind from all other forms of theoretical or practical dualism, but not from the dualism of man himself in his deliberate self-contradiction as sinner. This contradiction in man's will which he is impotent to obviate strikes home all the more violently because it is also projected on to God, and so is re-affirmed as a quasi-metaphysical dualism — as a contradiction between what is and what ought to be.

In face of this distress which plagues all human existence throughout its history, all facile speculative attempts at reconciliation remain unconvincing. Hence for instance, throughout the history of religions various types of dualism sought to express themselves directly in more or less mythical forms. But this effort to provide man with symbols of salvation for the understanding of his destiny remained unintelligible to abstract conceptual thought. The direct interpretation of life offered by such religions has a justifiable tendency to choose contradictory images, of which the intrinsic mutual relevance generally has to be divined. But the experience of existence given in Christian faith also knows the pain of being torn by conflicting imperatives. This contradiction, since it cannot be attributed to God's antagonism, is felt all the more sharply as a flaw in all experience within this world. And so far from being always resolved at once by faith, it rather becomes more acute. Indeed, it is only in the initial experience of salvation that it can be fully revealed. This existentially dualistic situation, tragic because combining salvation and doom, cannot be resolved by any theoretical reflections. The believer can only hold out under it, in a hope inspired by the initial experience of salvation, till the unimaginable mode of salvation is realized definitively in actual truth. Nonetheless, it is always the Jewish-Christian religion which counteracts the hardening of the various forms of existential dualism into the finality of metaphysical determinism, to which the contradiction in the will so readily resigns itself.

B. The Morphology and Theory of Dualism

1. *History of philosophy.* Western philosophy begins with the question of the *one* "material element" which persists throughout all change and is the principle of all things. Abandoning the mythical explanation of reality, this quest for the elements or the one basic element — the ἀρχή — of the cosmos erects into a "principle" the unity experienced in the multiplicity of reality and so induces a mentality which henceforth urges the thinker to look for the ultimate grounds of reality. Since it is never a search for one isolated ultimate principle, but for the unity-in-duality of this principle with its own reality which it has itself produced, the history of the quest for the origin of all reality is also the history of various types of monism and dualism which combat or complement each other.

Though the first exponents of natural philosophy among the Greeks tried to reduce the cosmos to one primordial element — Thales, for instance, to water, Anaximenes to air and Anaximander to "the unbounded" (ἄπειρον) — the question of the connection of all reality in the one ἀρχή suggested in each case was not explicitly raised. But Heraclitus and Parmenides posed more clearly the problem of the ultimate opposites and their compatibility (immutability and movement, imperishability and finiteness, truth and appearance). Inspired by the traditional (Eleatic) understanding of being, and also by the thinking of Socrates, a fundamental metaphysical dualism crystallized in the philosophy of Plato, with the opposition of the "forms", the authentic eternal being, and the appearances of this being, which make up nature as it comes to be and passes away. This duality between eidetic, authentic being and the non-being (μὴ ὄν) of transitory appearances cannot be an absolute dualism in the mind of Plato, since the form of all forms, the good, is ultimately the source of all beings. For Aristotle, the form exists essentially only as the form of concrete substance, combining with the "matter" informed by it to make up the concrete sensible thing. But though it is true that Aristotle's hylemorphism constitutes a fundamental advance on Plato, it is scarcely possible to bring together in a unified relationship the basic elements of his philosophy — matter and form, act and potency, immortal νοῦς ποιητικός and mortal νοῦς παθητικός, unmoved mover and moving world, supralunar and sublunar cosmos.

When Greek philosophy was adopted by Christianity, the Fathers and the scholastics opposed all forms of radical or metaphysical dualism, in the light of their faith in the one God and creator — Augustine, for instance, basing himself on Plato and the distinction between sensible and suprasensible being, as more sharply delineated by Plotinus; Thomas Aquinas interpreting the νοῦς of Aristotle as transcendence orientated to the God beyond the world, who is the origin and principle of all reality. On the whole, Greek philosophy, in spite of its initial quest of the one ἀρχή, displays a tendency towards a dualistic conception, while the following age of patristic and scholastic thinking was inspired by faith in the oneness of God — reinforced in the Middle Ages by the notion of the hierarchy of being — and strove to eliminate all metaphysical dualism. But here too the *prima principia* were not systematically thought out in view of their intrinsic and mutual relationships; such systematizing only flourished in modern times.

Nicholas of Cusa was mainly preoccupied by the problem of the union of the ultimate opposites, not merely in his speculative thought, but as a dominant element of his whole life. The themes of the *coincidentia oppositorum* which he developed were later to engage the attention of German idealism, under the headings of "identity" and "difference". Modern pre-Kantian philosophy is characterized by the more radical way in which it poses the problem of the ultimate opposites, which it approaches in the light of the Cartesian dualism of *res cogitans* and *res extensa* and the "pre-established harmony" of Leibniz.

Kant brought the whole of his speculative effort to bear on the problem thus posed, endeavouring to grapple with dualisms which his own empiricism and rationalism made even more pointed, and seeking either to reduce them to a synthesis in the unity of a critical philosophy or to reject them entirely. Nonetheless, it may be said that Kant is still haunted by a dualism which affects the two sources of knowledge, sense perception and intellect, and appears in the distinction between the thing in itself and its sensible phenomenon, between moral duty and inclination and between practical and theoretical reason in general.

Fichte attacked the problems left by Kant with an energy and a drive for systematization of unique intensity. He reduced all reality to three principles, each intelligible in the light of the others, all being modes of manifestation of the one primordial origin, which, however, is not itself a principle and is only known as a limit or in the positing of a limit. Fichte's thought was always dominated by the question of the ultimate difference between, or the two-fold unity comprising, the Absolute (God) and absolute appearance (creation). The basic theme in Hegel and Schelling is also "identity and difference".

While Fichte left open the questions posed by the contradictions of history, which he held could not be solved by speculative theory, Hegel, though taking these contradictions equally seriously, tries to see them as ultimately resolved in the absolute "idea" or God, as the "identity of all identity and non-identity". Under the influence of German idealism, especially that of the Kantian type, Schopenhauer attributes the cleavage throughout nature to the blindness of will, and since for him the world is only will and representation, his main interest is to rid himself from the will itself which is the source of all contradiction. This he tries to do through art, *ascesis* and inward mortification, understood in Buddhistic terms.

The trend of positivist and materialist philosophy since Hegel was to pay little attention to systematic principles of thought. Dualistic themes like matter and consciousness, body and soul, reason and instinct, the contrast between sciences of the mind and of nature were treated on a rather naive level. Nietzsche's declaration of war on Christian morality and indeed on all Christian and idealistic thought stemmed from his conviction that these doctrines of salvation really promoted dissociation, and was carried on with a passionate longing for the undivided life which by creating its own transcendence ultimately makes itself its own God and can thus abandon all dualistic types of self-expression. Heidegger's approach was to show that the miserable state of man was due to the erection of the subject-object dualism into an absolute, and that this dualism itself sprang from the predominance of conceptual thought. With the effort to surmount this by means of essential thinking, that is, thought directed to the relation between subject and object as such, and to the whence of this relationship, "being", understood as a transcendent communication, Heidegger finally tries seriously to abandon all thinking in terms of systems, to try to say simply how the event of existence comes about as the there-ness of being.

2. *History of religions*. In the cosmological dualism of the cosmos-centred thought of China, the whole life of the universe is

set in motion and sustained by Yin and Yang, the opposition of the male and female. The religion of Zarathustra, in the form, that is, of Iranian Mazdaism, understands the history of the world as the struggle between the equal and opposite forces of good and evil. In the Samkhyra philosophy of India, which must be regarded as a soteriological dualism, salvation comes through the separation of soul and body. In Plato's anthropological dualism the body also appears as the prison of the soul (*Gorgias,* 493a). Gnosis also seeks liberation from the body to enable man to ascend to the heavenly world of light.

In the apocalyptic of late Judaism an eschatological dualism gradually develops, which regards the history of the world as an aeon of misfortune, death and sin, at the mercy of wicked demons till the other aeon dawns which is full of goodness and blessing: "The Most High has not made one aeon but two" (*4 Esdr,* 7, 50). The conflict between chthonian and uranian gods, represented, for instance, in Greece by the struggle between Zeus and the Titans, among the Germans between the earthly Vanas and the heavenly Aesir, can be termed a numinous dualism, which is intensified when the godhead itself has two visages, as in many Indian religions — for instance, Varuna and Indra. These religious dualisms rarely see themselves as such, since they do not reach the stage of conscious and articulate reflections. They are a way of reacting directly to destiny, in an effort to use such images to attain self-understanding and mastery of life.

3. *Biblical theology.* Faith in the one Lord who is creator and lord of creation's history rules out of course on principle any absolute form of dualism in the OT. Nonetheless, it leaves room for Israel to display its strength of mind in its refusal to attempt facile reconciliations of the unfathomable contrast between sin and forgiveness, misery and salvation. This uncompromising realism persists into the NT, where the new experience of salvation is still expressed antithetically, especially by Paul and John. The dialectical movement of Paul's thought, faced with the enormous task of at once combining and separating Judaism and Christianity, can find expression only in the form of antithesis: the law and the promises, works and faith, flesh and spirit or the old and

new man, the inner and the outer man. The Gospel of John is dominated by the experience of the opposition between light and darkness, grace and law, life and death, truth and the lie, spirit and flesh.

4. *Dogmatic theology.* It was first necessary to refute Marcion, who appealed to Paul to set up a contrast between the God of might of the OT and the God of mercy in the NT, proposing therefore a dualism between the Old and New Testaments. At the same time Gnostic and Manichean dualism, appealing to the Gospel of John, had to be rejected. When the great dogmatic themes of God and the world, grace and freedom, faith and knowledge came to be enunciated, the forms of expression chosen were those of a modified or restricted dualism which maintained the oppositions and refused to adopt the short-sighted solutions of monism. Hence the rejection of pantheism, predestination and (absolute) Pelagianism as well as of fideism and rationalism. The basic (soteriological) problem, the surmounting of the existential dualism of the "mystery of iniquity" by the "mystery of salvation", is left open for an eschatological solution. Nonetheless, it is the task of present-day theology to attempt an explicit reconciliation of the dualism between Church and world, word and sacrament, office and charism and so on. In general, dogmatic theology must reflect more purposefully on itself and its history, for its self-understanding and justification, since only a dogmatic theology of this self-searching type can perform the heavy task of studying theology as a consistent whole and thus avoid the dualism which threatens to separate dogmatic theology from exegesis.

See also *Monism, Reality, Original Sin, Salvation, Hope, Pre-Socratics* (and other philosophical articles), *Gnosis, New Testament Theology* II, III, *Predestination, Pelagianism, Fideism, Apocatastasis.*

BIBLIOGRAPHY. S. Pétrement, *Le dualisme dans l'histoire de la philosophie et des religions* (1946); id., *Les dualismes chez Platon, les gnostiques et les manichéens* (1947); A.-D. Sertillanges, *Le problème du mal,* I (1948); G. Mensching, *Gut und Böse im Glauben der Völker* (1951); G. Quispel, *Gnosis als Weltreligion* (1951); H. J. Schoeps, *Urgemeinde, Judentum, Gnosis* (1956); H. Jonas, *Gnosis und spätantiker Geist,* 2 vols. (I, 3rd ed., 1964; II, 2nd ed., 1958); id., *The Gnostic Religion* (1958).

Eberhard Simons

E

EARLY CHURCH

The early period is of particular importance in Church history, as is seen not only from the long debate on the subject but above all from the intrinsic structures of the early Church, which grew out of its unique situation and problems. It is also a historical unity, clearly distinct from the following Constantinian period.

A. THE DEMARCATION

The early Church covers the period from about A.D. 30 till its recognition as a religion of the empire under Constantine the Great (306–37). Though the Church only became "established" in course of time, basically under Theodosius I (380), the decisive change came at the beginning of the 4th century, with the change in the State's attitude to religion, as evinced by the Edict of Toleration under Galerius (311) or the Peace of Milan, between Constantine and Licinius (313). It would be wrong, however, to over-emphasize the new externals of the Church at the expense of historical continuity. Still, this turning-point shows how closely the Church is linked with world history, even for the demarcation of its chronological stages.

The three hundred years of the early Church can be divided according to internal factors.

1. The apostolic and sub-apostolic age is basic for the whole history of the Church. When this, the "primitive Church", is regarded as the age of the giving of revelation, it is primarily the concern of NT history. But without prejudice to the unique importance of the ἀποστολικοὶ χρόνοι (Eusebius, *Hist. eccles.*, III, 31, 6), when revelation was committed to writing, the notion of primitive Church may well be extended to take in the following period, up to Irenaeus of Lyons (*c.* 180), when the mind of the Church was formed as regards the extent of the apostolic testimony to Christ — the period of the formation of the canon. This extension of the notion is also justified by the fact that it was in these years that the "église naissante" (P. Batiffol) developed its characteristic structures — the personal and oral transmission of tradition and the formation of creeds in the struggle against heresy. Though the origin and development of such forms pose many problems, on the whole the period is characterized by its determination to take on ecclesiastical form.

2. In the following period, *c.* 180–313, these structures already determine essentially the image of the Church, which claims a universal mission in the Roman empire. It has rightly been termed the period of the Great Church, in view of its numerical growth, its constitutional development and its intense theological activity. The 3rd century prepared the ground for the development which ensued in the following ages. In spite of intense persecutions on the part of the State, the Church presents itself to a crisis-racked empire as a ferment of unification. It makes Greek and Hellenistic culture its own in a resolute and flexible process of adaptation. The history of the Great Church is that of a growing openness to the world of the empire,

where a unity of Church and State is achieved once more when the religious policy of Constantine begins to aim at an imperial Church. Thus the history of the Church from the death of Jesus to its recognition by the State displays a consistent trend, which allows us, and even forces us, to see it as a well-marked whole.

B. PHASES OF DEVELOPMENT

The aptness of the divisions outlined above still leaves room for problems with regard to the individual phases. On the whole, schematic verdicts take the finer points of research into account. But there is often disagreement on details, due in part to the special (dogmatic) implications of this period.

1. *The primitive Church*. This period is naturally the most debated, since the characteristic structures of the Church were determined by its origin. NT research is decisive in our verdict on the genesis of the Church, which based itself from the start on faith in Jesus of Nazareth as Christ and Lord. Conscious of fulfilling Jesus' will (the acts whereby he founded a Church), the believing community came together and proclaimed him, from Pentecost on, as the promised Messiah. But this faith, the response to the word of the hidden Messiah and the exalted Lord, did not merely launch the Church, it remained constitutive of the people of God all through its history.

a) The first concrete manifestation of the ἐκκλησία is the primitive community of Jerusalem, its faith and theology nourished by the traditions of Israel but also influenced by special trends among the Jews. Parallels are drawn in particular between the Qumran community and the primitive Church, though the independence of the latter, in the central fact of faith in Christ, remains unquestionable. But Jewish Christianity went on to develop in various ways by no means free from tension. And its theology and Church order were still strong influences in the early Church after the catastrophes which befell Jerusalem in A.D. 70 and 135. Following in the footsteps of Jewish missionaries, Judaeo-Christians spread the gospel outside Palestine, especially eastwards. This activity, which soon gave rise to heterodox trends, was reflected for centuries in the Christian writings "adversus Judaeos".

b) We must not underestimate Jewish Christianity, but the turning-point in Church history was the mission to the gentile Hellenistic world, initiated by Peter (Acts 10:48) and carried on vigorously by Paul. The emancipation from the Law asserted in this type of preaching was ratified at the Council of the Apostles (49 or 50), which meant an official break with Judaism. Freed from the restrictions of the Law, the Church threw itself open to Hellenistic culture with its far-reaching effects on language (Bible, liturgy), thought-forms (theology, dogma) and sociological structure (the State). The subsequent interchange left its mark on the Church both in its imposing universality and in the limitations thus placed upon it. The new orientation did not affect the legitimacy of the Jewish-Christian branch, but it led in practice to the general acceptance of the structure of gentile Christianity — a process conditioned by historical factors and for that very reason of supreme interest.

c) The missionary urge of the primitive Church was obviously not inhibited by apocalyptic expectations of an imminent parousia. The structure of the communities also assures us that believers were prepared for an "intermediate period" from the start and hence could absorb the delay of the parousia without too much shock. New problems were posed thereby, but their importance also came from their being symptoms of Christian existence in history. This perspective explains the increasing emphasis on pastoral and paraenetical elements, which is apparent as early as the pastoral letters and makes itself strongly felt in the Apostolic Fathers. Obviously, there was a certain relaxation of Christian effort which led to the Christian message of salvation being presented as a code of morals. And ecclesiastical regulations did not simply result from disappointment about the parousia, but from the desire to fortify the Church during the "intermediate period" (Acts 20:18–35). As early as apostolic times, the constitutional organization of the Church set in, on the basis of the office of the apostles, which went back to the institution of Christ. Existing models suggested themselves, especially the organization of Judaism under "elders", which was adopted by the primitive Church. Out of this collegiate structure the monarchical episcopate crystallized. It soon became the dominant office in the

117

Church, as the precedence of the charisms gradually disappeared.

Under pressure of circumstances, even greater emphasis was laid on Church office in post-apostolic times. In the struggle with the advance of heresy, the revelation received from the apostles was linked more strongly with the bearers of office. In particular, the timeless myths of Gnosticism in all its forms were opposed by a history-centred tradition and the succession of the ancient episcopal sees, especially of Rome (Irenaeus). Thus, to preserve the purity of the gospel, the primitive Church adopted a constitution in which local and universal Church formed a closely-knit but thoroughly pluralistic unity, a κοινωνία which the celebration of the Eucharist fostered and voiced.

To designate this process as "Proto-Catholicism" (Frühkatholizismus) is to assume a norm for primitive Christianity which can scarcely be justified historically, but must be arrived at by an interpretation aiming at the heart of the gospel. The transition from a purely biblical and charismatic Christianity to the institutional Church of history is already reflected in, for instance, Acts. That the initial stages of "Proto-Catholicism" are already evident in the NT supports the (Catholic) conviction that the early Church was essentially identical with the Church of the beginning.

d) The theology of the primitive Church is characterized by the effort to formulate the faith in terms of NT vocabulary, using suitable thought-forms of Hebrew or Hellenistic origin. The needs of preaching, liturgy and apologetics gave the process a doctrinal orientation. Judaism had to be shown that Jesus of Nazareth was the fulfilment of OT testimonia; the heathen world demanded a new approach, quite apart from the discussion of polytheism, which is clearly depicted in the works of the early apologists. The adoption of Hellenistic categories was not without danger, but was on the whole a missionary necessity. It was the only way in which the Christian message could find an echo in the world of paganism.

e) The Christian Churches and hence the primitive Church suffered from being a minority, and had to be content with a subordinate role, in numbers and social status, among the many religions of the Roman empire. Nonetheless, the constant intercourse between the local Churches shows that they had the sense of an all-embracing unity. Though holding itself aloof from the world, the primitive Church was ready to come to terms with the State, recognizing precisely its earthly authority (Rom 13). Persecution in this period was rather the result of a ground-swell, manifested in local upheavals in the nature of pogroms. The loyal addresses of the apologists to the emperors heralded the fundamental conflict between Church and State.

2. *The Great Church of early Christianity.* The epoch of the Great Church began about the end of the 2nd century. In spite of oppressive measures Christianity became firmly established numerically and structurally and so paved the way for the Church of the empire.

a) The growing importance of Christianity is best shown by the systematic character of the persecutions. Previously sporadic, they are now organized by the State on a broad scale to further its policy of the restoration of paganism. Under Decius (249–51) and Diocletian (285–305) they reached their height. There were heroic examples of fortitude, but also constant displays of mediocrity, which forced bishops like Cyprian to pose once more the ancient problem of Christian sin, in this case apostasy, when the persecution had passed.

b) The general response to the Christian message justifies the appellation of Great Church in this period. According to prudent estimates, at the beginning of the 4th century Christians numbered some seven million in a total population of fifty million in the Roman empire, that is, about fifteen per cent, very unequally distributed. The geographical expansion can be traced very definitely. In the West, the missions penetrated Gaul, Spain and the marginal zones of Germany and Britain, and Christianity was equally widespread in the East (Edessa). But here racial characteristics and the fluidity of the imperial *limes* were already engendering special forms of Church life. In spite of the considerable growth of the Great Church, throughout all classes of the population, the majority were still pagan under Constantine, even in their reactions to the crises through which they were passing.

c) Pastoral measures had to be taken in the Church to cater for the influx of Christians in great numbers. The institution of the catechumenate ensured the formation of believers and provided the religious and spiritual instruction which was so imperative in face of the pagan world. The sacramental rites and in particular the celebration of the Eucharist were adapted to meet the new situation; thus, for instance, the spirituality of the times was profoundly marked by the theology of baptism, as also by that of martyrdom. Within the Church order, there developed a multiplicity of ministries under the bishop, to assure a well-regulated pastoral care. The territorial divisions mostly followed the existing organization of the empire. At the same time, bishoprics began to be organized into higher (patriarchal) unities, whose hierarchical heads demonstrated the limits of the Roman claim within the college of bishops. Theological reflection on the primacy, which began in this age (Cyprian), is characterized by a clear consciousness of the rights of the bishops.

d) The development of theology in this period was of major importance in the history of the Church. In spite of much resistance, the original conflict between the cross and Greek culture *(paideia)* was smoothed out; desire for well-defined concepts and debate with or polemics against Hellenism (especially neo-Platonism) made it necessary to reflect more and more on revelation. At Alexandria, Clement (d. before 215) and Origen (d. 254) sought to re-interpret and systematize the faith, using well-known principles of interpretation (typology, allegory) and philosophical categories to present revelation for the first time in a scientific form. Origen also made serious efforts to produce a critical text of Scripture as the basis of his studies (the hexapla). It must be admitted, however, that exegesis was at times inadequate to its task, as may be seen from its reserves as regards the message of the cross, which was presented in a theology of symbols which was undoubtedly profound but nonetheless made the character of scandal less apparent. It was, no doubt, a concession to the mentality of the times.

The major themes of the future were already intoned by the theologians of the Great Church. Following Irenaeus of Lyons (d. about 202), the Alexandrians emphasized the continuity of the redemption in Christ with the whole history of salvation, and hence necessarily made Christ central in their thought. As the Oikonomia (dispensa-tion, redemption) became the object of theological reflection, the question at once arose as to the agents of this one salvific action. The problems posed by Monarchianism, with its effort to reconcile the godhead of Christ and monotheism, gave rise to subtle speculation (Logos Christology, subordinationism) which opened the way to Arianism. Another point worth noting here is the tension between biblical language and the philosophical concepts which were put forward as the sole means of advance in theological thought. Against the Gnostic doctrine of self-redemption the Church found itself compelled to stress salvation by grace. Here too the Fathers strove to preserve the links in the history of salvation (the fall of man, the mission of the Spirit) while guiding future theological language by careful distinction (e.g., between *imago* and *similitudo, natura* and *gratia*). Delicacy of expression and profundity of symbolism characterize their efforts to describe the mystery of the Church; the individual Christian was clearly seen as a member of the Church (e. g., in the discipline of penance).

e) The keen sense of belonging to the Church did not, however, prevent Christians from recognizing how much they differed. This diversity was soon to express itself linguistically as well as in the organizational independence of the chief Churches. The redistribution of the Roman empire into a tetrarchy under Diocletian was a deliberate effort to tip the balance in favour of the East, and the effect of this administrative measure on the Church was to set independent developments on foot which were based on differences of temperament and culture. Diversity within the Church found its most marked expression in the variety of liturgies which evolved in each main regional Church. But the essential unity did not suffer from such diversification.

Thus situation and task clearly distinguish the Great Church from the primitive Church, on whose traditions it is wholly based, though developing themes of its own, as is proved notably by the rise of a Christian art.

C. THE SIGNIFICANCE OF THE EARLY CHRISTIAN CHURCH

The early Church was always held in high esteem, because it was supposed to embody

Christianity in its purest form. It was undoubtedly a high point in Church history, though its normative character has been exaggerated and oversimplified, especially in more critical views, which were influenced by the theory of a steady "deterioration". Jerome was lauding this era for its martyrs, contrasting the depravation of the Church in his own day (*Vita Malchi*, 1). The revivalist movements of the Middle Ages likewise conjured up the ideal of the *ecclesia primitiva*, against which they measured their own Church. For the Reformation also the early Church was the norm, insofar as it was precisely in this period that the truth of the gospel maintained its uncompromising claims. As classicism turned once more to antiquity, the early Church gained a new measure of esteem, as the canon of "noble simplicity and tranquil grandeur" was applied to it. Even in modern Church history the postulate of the pure and unadulterated Church of the beginning is still put forward, especially in the discussion of the "turning-point" under Constantine.

In this schematic view, the early Church is undoubtedly idealized, in a way which cannot survive historical analysis, highly as the age may be esteemed. The view is influenced by the notion of natural evolution, and looks for a renewal of the Church in a return to the "youthful freshness" of its early days. Though such notions do not correspond to facts or to the nature of the historical process, we must still ask whether the early Church has a normative character and what these norms may be.

In principle, it must be affirmed that the Church, even as a supernatural entity, is essentially involved in history and hence must undergo evolution: it has a beginning which determines in a certain way the whole future. Since the acts of Jesus as founder of the Church aim at the permanence of the believing community in history, the "Twelve", as immediate witnesses of the word and transmitters of the office, have a central function. Hence too "the sub-apostolic period of proximity to the sources remains dogmatically relevant and historically definable, singular and valuable in a way that can neither be repeated nor surpassed" (K. Rahner). The unique status of the apostolic age is guaranteed by the canon of inspired Scripture; and the age of the primitive Church, the time of the formation of the canon, preserves the full gospel, marking the boundaries against apocryphal writings and heterodoxy.

Along with this fundamental and essential value, the early Church has a special role even from the point of view of history. Even taking into account the obvious defects, we must affirm that the first centuries represent a high point. The active responsibility for the gospel and life according to the gospel in a hostile environment remain exemplary. Hence when due consideration is paid to each historical "hour" *(kairos)*, the development of Christianity may be judged in the light of the early Church.

See also *Church History, Qumran, Apostolic Church, Canon of Scripture, Judaeo-Christianity, Hellenism and Christianity, Alexandrian School of Theology, Apostolic Fathers, Martyrdom, Ecclesiastical Office, Charisms.*

BIBLIOGRAPHY. A. Harnack, *The Expansion of Christianity in the First Three Centuries,* 2 vols. (1904/5); P. Batiffol, *L'Église naissante et le catholicisme* (6th ed., 1927); A. Ehrhard, *Urkirche und Frühkatholizismus* (1935); H. J. Schoeps, *Theologie und Geschichte des Judenchristentums* (1949); J. Daniélou, *The Theology of Jewish Christianity* (1958); W. Marxsen, *Der "Frühkatholizismus" im Neuen Testament* (1958); H. von Campenhausen, *Kirchliches Amt und geistliche Vollmacht in den ersten drei Jahrhunderten* (2nd ed., 1963), E. T.: *Ecclesiastical Authority and Spiritual Power in the Church of the First Three Centuries (1967);* J. Daniélou and H. Marrou, *The First Six Hundred Years,* in: *The Christian Centuries,* I (1964); K. Baus, *From the Apostolic Community to Constantine,* Handbook of Church History, ed. by H. Jedin and J. Dolan, vol. I (1965).

Peter Stockmeier

EASTERN CHURCHES

A. Notion. B. Unity and Diversity. C. Schisms and Reunions. D. Rites and Churches. E. The Orthodox. F. Byzantine and Slav Theology. G. Doctrinal Bonds and Conflicts between East and West. H. Some Points of Doctrine. I. The Catholic Church and the Eastern Churches.

A. Notion

In the term Eastern Churches, the geographical reference derives from the world-view of antiquity, and means the Eastern part of the Roman empire. Like the sun, the gospel comes from the East, from Palestine. "You shall be my witnesses in Jerusalem, and in all Judaea and Samaria, and to the end of the earth." (Acts 1:8.) The first Churches were founded in Jerusalem and from there Churches were founded in Samaria, Antioch, Cyprus, Asia Minor, Greece, Crete, Syria, Persia, Egypt, Armenia, Ethiopia, Georgia, India and later in the Slavonic lands. Of great importance for the division into East and West was the division of the Roman empire after the death of Emperor Theodosius I (395). The boundary ran between Italy and Greece. Accordingly, we understand by the Eastern Churches those Churches which originated in the Eastern empire and those which were dependent on them. Within this Eastern Church a hierarchical structure was soon formed, within the empire in the form of patriarchates and outside of it (in Persia, Armenia and Georgia) in the form of catholicates. As the seat of the Emperor, Constantinople tried to assert its primacy among the Eastern patriarchates (Alexandria, Antioch, and later Jerusalem) since the 4th century.

B. Unity and Diversity

Christ sent the apostles to teach, baptize and make disciples of all peoples (Mt 28:19-21). This threefold commission is the basis of the essential unity of the gospel in both East and West: in doctrine, in sacrifice and sacraments, and in the essential structure of the Church as founded upon Peter and the apostles and transmitted through their successors. It is also the basis of diversity a) in the way in which the truths of faith were presented (the Synoptics, John, Paul; the Greek, Latin, and Syriac Fathers), b) in the many Eastern and Western liturgies, in sacrifice, sacrament and blessings, and c) in the legal and administrative structure. Such variety, naturally arising from the differences of peoples and cultures, could only become a hindrance to unity after separation from the universal Church and its magisterium. Differences in doctrine only harm unity when they depart from revealed truth or deny a dogma.

Differences are also legitimate in rites whether rites are understood as the customs used in the celebration of the Eucharist, the administration of the sacraments, fasting, etc., or in a broader (juridical) sense as the customs, laws, and discipline of a local Church, includig rites in the narrower

sense (cf. *CIC,* can. 98). Since various Eastern Churches (Catholic and non-Catholic) use the same liturgical rite, while representatives of the same people belong to different rites, a distinction must be made between the various Eastern liturgical rites and the various Eastern Churches or communities.

C. Schisms and Reunions

Of decisive importance for the Eastern Churches were the three great divisions brought about by Nestorianism, Monophysitism and the controversies between Old and New Rome, i.e., between Rome and Byzantium (Constantinople). Hence the turning-points were the ecumenical councils of Ephesus (431) and Chalcedon (451) and the year 1054, to which the definitive break between East and West is usually dated. To the history of the divisions there corresponds the history of the attempts at reunion by Rome and unions that were actually effected through the centuries. The union with the Maronites (1181) was a lasting one. The reunions brought about by the Councils of Lyons (1274) and Florence (1438/39-45) with the Greeks and other Orientals did not last. The major reunions of recent times are those of Brest-Litovsk (1595) with the Ruthenians (Ukrainians and White Russians) and of Alba-Julia (1697) with the Rumanian Siebenbürgers. There have been smaller groups of Uniat Albanians since the latter half of the 15th century in Southern Italy, of Uniat Serbians in Creatia since the end of the 16th century, and later also Uniat groups among the Bulgarians and the Greeks. Greater success in the Near East attended the efforts of the Latin religious orders under the protection of the Western powers, especially France. Approximately every fourth Christian there is Catholic. But even here there was a series of divisions and reunions. The unions with the Chaldeans, Syrians, Melchites, Armenians and Copts are important. In India, the Portuguese brought about a measure of union with the Christians of Malabar (Diamper, 1599). Since 1930 many other Malabar Christians have accepted the union (the Malankarese).

D. Rites and Churches

There are five Eastern rites: the Alexandrian (among Copts and Ethiopians), the Antiochene (among West Syrians, Maronites and Malankarese), the Chaldean (among the Syro-Chaldeans and Malabarites), the Armenian, and the Byzantine which has the most numerous branches (among the Greeks, Melchites, Bulgarians, Russians and Serbians, Ruthenians, Ukrainians, Russian Old Believers, Rumanians, Georgians, Albanians, Hungarians, Japanese, Chinese, Africans in Uganda, in Italy in the monastery of Grottaferrata near Rome, and among the Italo-Albanians). The Eastern rites are distinguished by venerable antiquity, the pomp and splendour of their ceremonies and their deep piety.

The term "Eastern Church" is often used, but it is inexact. In fact, the local Eastern Churches or Eastern communities do not form a unity. They comprise five more or less united groups: the Nestorians, the Monophysites, the Orthodox, the Catholic Uniats and the Protestants. Of the once very numerous group of Nestorians who in the Middle Ages penetrated as far as India, China and Mongolia, there are now only about 70,000, mainly in Irak, and 5,000 in India. The Monophysites are considerably stronger (some fourteen million all told), opponents of the definitions of Chalcedon and for this reason more recently called the "non-Chalcedonian Orthodox". They include the Copts and Ethiopians, the West Syrians (mainly in India) and Armenians. The strongest of all the Eastern groups is the Orthodox. They include the ancient patriarchates of Constantinople, Alexandria, Antioch and Jerusalem (all together about two million). Numerically the strongest Orthodox Churches, however, are those in Greece (8 million) and in the Communist countries (as far as one is able to tell): in Russia, Rumania, Yugoslavia, and Bulgaria (all together perhaps 80 million). The number of émigré Russian Orthodox in the four different communities of the Moscow patriarchate, the Paris hierarchy, and two hierarchies in the U.S.A. may be around one million. In general, each Eastern rite includes a Catholic group. The Maronites, Italo-Albanians, Slovaks and Malabar Christians are all Catholic, while the Georgians, Esthonians, Latvians, Finns, Japanese and Chinese have no Catholic counterparts. There are also Eastern Christians in various countries who have gone over to Protestantism (the Mar Thoma Christians in India; the Nestori-

ans who went over to Presbyterianism in the U.S.A.; the Ukrainians who became Congregationalists in Canada). There are Protestant missions in the Near East.

There are numerous patriarchates in the Churches separated from Rome; besides those already mentioned, the Coptic and the Ethiopian (since 1959), those of the Monophysites of Antioch (Jacobites; the Jacobites of India have a catholicate) and of the Nestorians; there are two catholicates and two patriarchates of the Armenians; one catholicate of the Orthodox Georgians; the patriarchates among the Orthodox in Russia, Serbia, Rumania and Bulgaria are more recent. The Orthodox Church of Greece is autocephalous (with the Archbishop of Athens at the head), as are those of Cyprus, Albania, Poland and Czechoslovakia. For the Catholics of the Eastern Churches there are six patriarchates (the Coptic, Syrian, Maronite, Melchite, Armenian, and Chaldean) and one *Archiepiscopus maior* with patriarchal rights among the Ukrainians. There are metropolitans for the Catholic Ethiopian Church (1), the Malankarese (1) and the Malabar Christians (2), the Catholic Rumanians (1) and the Ukrainians (3). The remaining Catholics of the Eastern Church are directly under the Apostolic See (with the exception of the two groups in Yugoslavia and Hungary which are subject to a Latin bishop).

E. THE ORTHODOX

The Churches of the Byzantine rite are given many different names: the "Orthodox Church of the East", the "Orthodox Church", or simply the "Eastern Church". It is also known as the "Church of the Seven Ecumenical Councils", or, after its main representatives, the "Byzantine-Slavonic" or the "Greek-Slavonic Church". This great Church of the East, which today is spread over the whole world, represents, like the Monophysite, no strict unity, but is made up of a number of separate national Churches grouped according to patriarchates and later as autocephalous Churches, i.e., local or national Churches each of which has its own head and is autonomous. Some of the autonomous Orthodox Churches are very much at variance with each other (for example, the Russian émigré Church first at Karlowitz, later at Munich and New York, in its relation to the

Moscow patriarchate; and the Russian Old Believers in their relation to the chief Russian Church).

F. BYZANTINE AND SLAV THEOLOGY

The inner development of doctrine is historically closely connected with the external divisions of the Eastern Churches. The history of Eastern piety, asceticism, and mysticism is very instructive. After the patristic age, which is usually considered as closing with John Damascene (d. *c.* 749), that is to say, after the time of the Trinitarian and Christological controversies (especially those of Arianism, Nestorianism, Monophysitism and Monotheletism), and after the time of the first seven ecumenical councils (from the first to the second Council of Nicaea, 325–787), the conversion of the Slavs began in the 9th century. In the same century the temporary schism under the Patriarch Photius heralded the separation between Christians of East and West which has obtained since the middle of the 11th century. Further, the history of the Christian East cannot be understood without reference to the Arab, Mongol, and Turkish domination and the Crusades undertaken against Islam. In the middle of this period occurred the unfortunate conquest of Byzantium by the Crusaders (1204) and the setting up of the Latin Empire there (1204–61). The conquest of Constantinople by the Turks (1453), which put an end to the Orthodox Byzantine Empire, affected even more deeply the history of Orthodoxy. It was only in the 19th century that the Balkan countries ceased to be under Turkish rule. As the separation of the Orthodox East from Rome had marked effects on doctrine, one can date the beginning of Orthodox theological history as about the middle of the 11th century.

The history of Byzantine theology, however, as a continuation of Greek patristic theology, began much earlier. Its main periods may be characterized as follows: the period of the iconoclast disputes, 730–850; the period from Photius to Cerularius, 850–1050, i.e., the beginning of the controversy on the procession of the Holy Spirit; the period from Cerularius to the Latin Empire in Byzantium, 1050–1200; the period between the conquest of Constantinople by the Crusaders and the Hesychasm of Gregory Palamas, 1200–1330; the period from Pa-

lamas to the conquest of Constantinople by the Turks, 1330–1453. The centre of Orthodoxy then shifted from Constantinople to Kiev and then to Moscow and St. Petersburg. Greece and the Balkan countries are still recovering from the time of Turkish domination.

The history of Slavonic Orthodox theology may be divided into the following periods: from its beginning in Bulgaria (9th–10th century) and the Kingdom of Kiev (10th–11th century) to the rejection of the Union of Florence; the period after the Reformation; the great period of the Kiev School (end of the 17th and beginning of the 18th century); the beginning of the great Russian Schism, that of the Raskolnians (at approximately the same time); the replacement of the patriarchates by the Holy Synod under Peter the Great (1721); from the anti-Protestant Reform in Russia (1836) until the Communist Revolution of 1917, or from the origin of Slavophile theology to 1917; and lastly, the recent period since the revolution of 1917 which saw the reinstitution of the patriarchates for the Russian Church through the Pan-Russian Council of 1917/18, but which also brought oppression and persecution. Many theologians fled and founded centres of Orthodox theology in other countries, the most notable of which are the Orthodox theological Institute of St. Sergius in Paris and the Orthodox Seminary of St. Vladimir in New York.

Byzantine theology felt the influence of philosophy from the beginning, especially that of Plato, Aristotle and Plotinus, though different schools, as in the West, can hardly be distinguished. The influence of Western Scholasticism can be traced only from the 14th century on. Catholic influence predominated in the post-Tridentine Orthodox theology, even within the Kiev school; but Protestant influence was strong in the school of Theophanes Prokopovič who assisted Peter the Great in his reform of the Church. Since the reform carried out by the chief procurator of the Holy Russian Synod, Protasov, in the year 1836, Catholic influence has predominated in the official Russian theology, but Protestant influence in the theology of Alexius Chomjakov. Byzantine theology reached its last heights in Gregory Palamas, whose synthetic power showed itself not so much in the teaching on the nature and energies of God as in Mariology. The last important Byzantine and also Palamite theologian was George Scholarius, whose aim was to synthesize Byzantine and Scholastic theology.

In the 16th and 17th centuries the Orthodox sought to protect themselves from the influence of Protestant ideas by making use of teaching borrowed from Catholicism and the Scholastics. This is clear (i) from the three answers of the Patriarch of Constantinople, Jeremias II, to the Protestant theologians of Tübingen (1576; 1579; 1581); (ii) from the condemnation by Patriarch Cyril Contarenus of the confession of faith of the Patriarch of Constantinople, Cyril Lucar (d. 1638), which had been influenced by Calvinism, and (iii) especially from the fact that the Synod of Jassy (1642) confirmed the confession of faith of Peter Mogila, and the Synod of Jerusalem that of the Patriarch of Jerusalem, Dositheus. The *Confessio* of Dositheus has recently been regarded as the apex of a doctrinal *rapprochement* between Orthodoxy and Catholicism. The well-known Orthodox theologian Gabriel Severus (1541 to 1616) also based himself in his disputes upon Catholic teaching. In the theological school of Kiev since the end of the 17th century, even the scholastic method penetrated. In this school, founded in 1631 by Peter Mogila (1596–1646), philosophy was introduced as a discipline in 1685 and theology in 1690; in 1701 it became a theological academy. While in the first centuries following the conversion of the Slavs in Bulgaria, Serbia, and in the Kiew and later in the Moskovite Kingdoms, theological writings, such as there were, showed Greek influence — in Moscovia still apparent under Maximos the Greek (Maksim Grek, d. 1556) who is called the "first illuminator of the Russians" — the Kiev Academy later became so important in its own right that it attracted not only Ruthenians, i.e., Ukrainians and White Russians, but also Moscovites, Greeks, Rumanians, Bulgarians and Serbs. There the authority of Aquinas was unchallenged. His *Summa* was mostly known through the commentaries of the Jesuits Gregory of Valencia, Suárez, Hurtado, Arriaga, and De Lugo.

Theologians also frequently appealed to other Catholic authors, especially Bellarmine, on whom the famous work of Stephan Javorsky against Protestantism, *Kamen Very* (*Cornerstone of the Faith*) depends. Javorsky (1658–1722) had studied in Kiev and with the Jesuits, and in 1700 was named Patriarchal Administrator by Peter the Great. The publication of his main work met with great difficulties. His teaching on justification, merit and good works, the form of the Eucharist, purgatory and the canon of Scripture was that of Catholic theology. The Kiev school taught the same doctrines, with the inclusion of the Immaculate Conception of Mary, but it did so in terms of the Byzantine-Slavonic tradition and liturgy rather than by appealing to Catholic theology.

Opposition to the *Cornerstone* of Javorsky was led by Theophan Prokopovič (1681–1736), the counsellor of Peter the Great who after the death of the Emperor became Archbishop of Novgorod. He introduced a theology with Protestant leanings into the Moscow Kingdom. Born in Kiev, Prokopovič became a Catholic in his youth, joined the Order of St. Basil, and studied in Rome. Upon his return, however, he again espoused the faith of his parents, taught at the Kiev Academy and was appointed rector. In 1716 he was called to Petersburg by Peter the Great. His writings influenced Russian handbooks of dogmatics from *c.* 1759, and he is considered the founder of systematic theology in Russia. He was the first there to separate dogmatic from moral theology, while also attempting to synthesize the various treatises of theology. His dogmatic teaching was completed only later by Samuel Mislavsky (1782); Prokopovič himself only wrote a tractate on the gratuitous justification of the sinner by Christ, which was strongly influenced by Luther. Even earlier than Prokopovič, however, Lutheran elements had penetrated the writings of some of the Greek theologians (e. g., the Catechism of Zacharias Gerganos and the confession of faith of Metrophanes Kritopulos). But in the Byzantine sphere nothing is seen of the Protestantism which showed itself in the writing of Prokopovič, as regards Scripture as the sole rule of faith, the canon of the OT, ecclesiology, and justification. The last representative of the theology of Prokopovič was the famous Metropolitan of Moscow, Philaret Drozdov (1782–1867), as can be seen from the first editions of his catechism.

A change came in the year 1836 with Count Protasov, who had been educated for 15 years in Jesuit schools and was somewhat partial towards the Latins. It was through him that the confessions of faith of Peter Mogila and Dositheus as well as the work of Stephan Javorsky again became influential. He promoted the study of the Fathers and introduced patrology into the theological curriculum. A number of textbooks of dogmatic theology were produced in Russian, which were in use until the Revolution of 1917 and are still read today by the students of theology in the Russian Patriarchate. Philaret was forced to revise his catechism, much against his will. The third edition appeared in 1839 and was frequently reprinted since then. Protosov sought to have his reform measures carried out by imperial decrees, but in this he was not entirely successful.

Along the lines of Prokopovič's theology, there now arose the increasingly influential school of Slavophile philosophy and theology. It was influenced by the German idealism (especially of Schelling and Hegel) which it sought to combat, but was also inspired by the ancient oriental patristic and ascetical tradition. Its first philosophical leader was Ivan Kirejevsky (1806–56), while its theological head was his friend Alexis S. Khomyakov (1804–60). Vladimir Soloviev, the most important Russian philosopher and lay-theologian (1853–1900), also began as a Slavophile, but then came to differ from them more and more on central theological issues. In 1896 he privately accepted the Catholic creed. Khomyakov, who influenced most Russian Orthodox theologians greatly in the sphere of ecclesiology, was a moving force in the new independent Russian theology. He was followed by several representatives of the official theology (including E. Akvilonov and P. Svetlov) but especially by the better-known of the Russian theologians abroad (L. Karsavin — who, however, died as a Catholic — V. Zenkovsky, S. Bulgakov, G. Florovsky, and the internationally known philosopher N. Berdyaev). Karsavin, Bulgakov, and Berdyaev were also under the influence of Soloviev who was at the origin of Russian Sophia theology. The main representatives of the latter were P. Florensky and S. Bulgakov, and the movement also attracted L. Karsavin, S. and E. Trubeckoy and V. Ivanov.

Much may be learned of modern trends from the acts of the First Congress for Orthodox Theology (Athens, November to December 1936); the controversy between Moscow and Constantinople over the primacy within Orthodoxy; the efforts of the Orthodox to attain inner and outward unity (as on the occasion of the Pan-Orthodox conferences in Rhodes, 1961, 1963 and 1964, and Belgrade, 1966); the attempts to clarify the relations of the Orthodox Churches to the ecumenical movement and to the World Council of Churches, to Vatican II and to the Catholic Church.

G. Doctrinal Bonds and Conflicts between East and West

The history of the Eastern Churches and their relations to the Catholic Church is closely connected with the dogmatic and liturgical disputes which led to the separation or which arose in the centuries following it. It must first be stressed that between Catholic and Orthodox teaching — and also, more or less, that of the other Eastern Churches — there are large areas of agreement. This is also true of the liturgy and the sacraments, as well as the spiritual life. All Eastern theologians — with few exceptions — look for revealed truth not only in sacred Scripture, but also oral tradition. Most of them oppose the principle of "Scripture alone" and adhere to the principle of "Scripture in the Church". They consider Scripture and tradition to be linked to each other and to form a unity. There are differences of opinion as to the extent of oral tradition: some limit it to the explanation of Scripture, while others rather stress a tradition independent of Scripture. All Eastern theologians hold the books of Scripture to be inspired. The Orthodox agree with Catholic tradition in their canon of the books of the NT; but in the canon of the OT, with regard to the so-called deuterocanonical books, the Russians, Rumanians and Serbians have differed to some extent since the 17th century while the Greeks have wavered. The Greeks consider the Septuagint as the only authentic translation of the OT.

The sources of tradition for the Orthodox are above all the ancient professions of faith: in the first place the Nicene-Constantinopolitan Creed, and then the so-called Athanasian Creed in its Greek translation. To these are added the decisions of the first seven ecumenical councils (sometimes an eighth is added: the Synod of 879–80 under Photius), together with the decrees of the Trullan

Synod complementing the two Councils of Constantinople (553 and 680–81). Basic also to Orthodox teaching are the writings of the Fathers, of whom Athanasius, the three Cappadocians, Chrysostomus, the Pseudo-Areopagite, and Maximus the Confessor are given places of honor. Less often, John Damascene is quoted, and of the Latin Fathers only the Popes Leo I and Gregory I — the reason being ignorance of the Latin tongue, as for the Latins it was a lack of Greek. It was only in the Byzantium of the 14th century and then later in the Kiev school that the Latin Fathers were quoted with more frequency. In the post-Reformation period, the touchstone of orthodoxy were the "Confessions of Faith", whose authority remained very great for about two centuries. In the following period these came under criticism, especially the Confessions of Mogila and Dositheus, for their too great dependence upon Catholic teaching.

There are, no doubt, differences of mentality between the Orthodox East and the Catholic West; but there is also much in common. These differences should neither be exaggerated, nor glossed over where they affect the faith. Photius's primary objection against the Latins was the teaching on the *filioque*. It is impossible to prove, as V. Lossky maintains, that all the differences between East and West in the spiritual life go back to the doctrine of the procession of the Holy Spirit, i.e., from the Father alone, or from Father and Son. In general, there is agreement in both East and West that the main source of dissension lies in the recognition or denial of the Roman primacy. Besides the *filioque* and its addition to the creed, Photius names as points of controversy (in his letter to the Archbishops of the East in 867, in his *Mystagogy of the Holy Spirit* and elsewhere) the primacy of the Bishop of Rome, the Latin custom of fasting on Saturday, the use of milk, cheese, etc., in the first week of Lent, priestly celibacy, and the exclusive power of bishops to dispense the sacrament of confirmation. In the 11th century, at the time of the final separation, this list of Latin errors was notably enlarged. Michael Cerularius enumerates twenty-two such errors, especially the use of unleavened bread at the celebration of the Eucharist. Many of these complaints do not concern the faith at all, but only discipline (e.g., the shaving of the beard, marriage of priests,

wearing of rings by the Latin bishops, etc.), as Archbishop Theophylactus of Bulgaria then pointed out.

From the 12th to the 15th century the number of complaints against the Latins rose to over sixty. Then came the controversy about the fire of purgatory and the form of the Eucharist. The Council of Florence (*D* 691–4) settled five controversial questions: (i) the Holy Spirit proceeds "from the Father and the Son" and likewise "from the Father through the Son"; (ii) the addition of the *filioque* to the creed is justified; (iii) the Eucharist may be celebrated with either leavened or unleavened bread according to the custom of East or West; (iv) between heaven and hell there are purifying punishments for the souls of penitent sinners; (v) the Roman Bishop, as the successor to Peter, possesses a universal primacy in the Church. Maximus the Greek (d. 1556) recognized only three "great heresies" of the Latins: the *filioque,* unleavened bread and the fire of purgatory.

Of the greatest importance today in the dialogue between Catholics and Orthodox, as well as the other Eastern Churches separated from Rome, are the following: the primacy and infallibility of the Pope and in connection with this, the hierarchical structure of the Church; the *filioque* and its addition to the creed; the unknowability of the essence of God; the juridical conception of redemption; the eucharistic epiclesis as the form of consecration; the Immaculate Conception of the Mother of God and her Assumption into heaven; the last things. Yet it must be stressed that while on each of these points the great majority of the Orthodox depart from Catholic teaching, there have always been, among Eastern theologians, very great differences of opinion, for or against Catholic teaching. Since the separation the number of doctrinal differences has grown. In the beginning the differences were concerned with individual dogmatic and liturgical questions, but since the separation from the Catholic Church and the denial of its magisterium as a binding norm of faith, the differences have become more profound and have had effects later in fundamental theology and even in philosophy. Revealed truth has further unfolded itself inside as well as outside the Catholic Church and it was interpreted in different, often opposing ways.

H. SOME POINTS OF DOCTRINE

One task of the present-day ecumenism is to distinguish merely ritual or non-essential differences from the essential ones and to limit controversy to the essential. Even at the time of Photius and Cerularius, and indeed before the completion of the schism, the real underlying reason for the separation was the differing types of hierarchical structure. Hence, we must first discuss the Eastern conception of Church structure, and then, more briefly, the problem of the knowledge of God, modern Sophia theology, Christology and soteriology, the Mother of God and her privileges, and finally the sacraments and the last things. This will throw light on what is the characteristic in the Orthodox approach to theology, especially in modern times, and the way theology, patristics, and liturgical piety are united.

1. *The Church.* Like the local Church (bishop, priests, and people), the universal Church has been hierarchically organized from antiquity. The local Churches were not merely juxtaposed. They were organically united and interwoven. There was fellowship and inter-connection, and even mutual dependence, just as one part of an organism is dependent on the others. The individual local Churches were dependent upon the assembly or the council of the regional Church and ultimately upon the universal Church whose head, according to Catholic teaching, is the successor of Peter. In the first centuries the government of the universal Church by the Bishop of Rome was restricted to a minimum, as the Church only gradually developed fully its hierarchical organization, and communication in the modern sense was not possible. Much was necessarily left to the local and regional Churches to decide. This situation gave rise in the very first centuries to the patriarchates, which were to be so important for the Christian East, and which stood, as it were, between the primacy and the episcopacy. The precedence of old Rome as the see of the successor of Peter was acknowledged in the Byzantine East before the temporary and then the final separation, although of course some were ready to question the primacy, first in practice and then on theoretical grounds. This was done, at least virtually, by the drawing up of can. 3 of Constantinople and can. 28 of Chalcedon. That the hierarchy instituted by Christ possesses the supreme authority in the Church, has till modern times never been doubted in the Christian East.

Before and after the separation there were two theories especially which were put forward with regard to the supreme authority in the Church: that of the pentarchy and that of the ecumenical councils. To these there must be added in modern times the theory of the *Sobornost* and eucharistic ecclesiology. Between all these theories there is a historical and theological connection. The theory of the pentarchy attributes the highest jurisdiction to the Patriarchs of Rome, Constantinople, Alexandria, Antioch, and Jerusalem. Three forms of this theory may be distinguished. The first was put forward by the defenders of the cult of images, especially by Theodore of Studiou (759–826) and Patriarch Nicephorus of Constantinople (d. 829). Theodore speaks of the "five-pinnacled body of the Church"; he asserts that the true councils are those accepted by all five patriarchs. The power given to Peter (Mt 16:19) belongs in the concrete to the successors of the apostles and the five patriarchs. On the other hand, he recognizes the Roman primacy. According to Nicephorus, the patriarchs together with the Bishop of Rome represent the whole Church in its ordinary jurisdiction.

A second form of the pentarchy was formulated in opposition to the primacy of Rome and was systematically developed by the Byzantine canonist Theodor Balsmon towards the end of the 12th century. He traces the origin of the Eastern patriarchates to the apostles or to the second ecumenical council, but of the Roman patriarchate to the Emperor Constantine. He thinks that the patriarchs are the visible head of the Church representing the invisible Christ; they have power over all the Churches, just as the five senses serve to govern the body; all the patriarchs have equal power. Another form of the pentarchy excludes Old Rome as apostate. Such a "tetrarchy", i.e., a diminished pentarchy, was put forward by Maximus the Greek. As the theory of the pentarchy is based upon the patriarchates which were not directly instituted by divine right, it includes a relative element. Hence the number of the patriarchs among Orthodox and Uniats has grown in the course of the centuries; among the Orthodox especially in modern times, because of their principle that every country or people can and should have their own independent Church government. The last-mentioned form of the pentarchy went hand in hand with the development of polemics against the Roman primacy: it is not of divine institution but is based only upon ecclesiastical law; the episcopal office of Peter was passed on to his successor but not his primacy; the Pope has fallen into heresy; Christ is the one invisible head of the Church; the primacy is based on the False Decretals (of "Isidore"); Rome has turned the primacy of love into a primacy of jurisdiction.

2. *Authority in the Church.* The supreme authority of the patriarchs, which developed from custom, was given juridical force by the ecumenical councils. The patriarchs and bishops, however, make their decisions about the concerns of the entire Church only at ecumenical assemblies. The ecumenical council remained the organ of supreme authority for the Eastern theologians, even when they denied the universal primacy of the Pope. There were, however, seven ecumenical councils up to the separation of the Churches in the 11th century, which were recognized both in the East and in the West. (In the Catholic West the eighth is considered to be the Council which condemned Photius in 869–70; while in the East the eighth is sometimes considered to be the Photian Council of 879–80.) The Eastern theologians termed the Orthodox Church "the Church of the seven ecumenical councils". In more recent times, however, the Archpriest Sergius Bulgakov objected strongly to the opinion that in the living Church of Christ there could only be seven ecumenical councils, as new problems continually arise and demand a common solution. For Orthodox theology this is the greatest problem: how is the lack of an ecumenical council in the East for more than a thousand years to be explained or justified? Efforts have hence been made in the past years, by means of preparatory pan-Orthodox conventions, to prepare for a new ecumenical council. In the Catholic Church, the series of ecumenical councils was continued from antiquity, through the general councils of the Middle Ages up to Vatican II.

For Orthodox theology, the reunion councils have a special importance among the Catholic ecumenical councils: that of Lyons (1274) and that of Ferrara-Florence (1438/9 to 1445), especially the latter. For at these councils, under the leadership of the Byzantine Emperor and the Patriarch of Constantinople, the whole Orthodox world was represented. It was, according to the traditional Eastern as well as Western concept, properly convoked and ecumenical. The union, however, lasted only a short time and was then completely abandoned again. Orthodox theologians attempt to justify this delayed rejection of the council by putting Florence on a level with the "Robber Synod" of 449, asserting that the bishops who accepted the union with Rome were apostates, whereas the entire people under divine inspiration unanimously rejected the false union.

There are indications of a similar explanation as early as the history of the Council of Florence written by Silvester Syropulos, but it was first clearly formulated by the Russian lay-theologian Khomyakov, whose explanation has grown in popularity among the Orthodox. Khomyakov thought he could substantiate his opinion by the letter of the Eastern patriarchs of 1848 with its negative answer to Pope Pius IX who had invited them to union with Rome. According to Khomyakov, the conciliar decrees must be either accepted or rejected by the whole Church community, for there had been heretical councils in which Emperor, bishops, patriarchs and Pope had accepted false teaching. Infallible faith could not depend upon a hierarchical order but is preserved by the people of the Church as a whole. The gift of faith must be clearly distinguished from the tasks of the hierarchy (i.e., sacramental and disciplinary authority). Infallibility in the Church does not rest on individuals, but on the entire Church united in love and holiness. To divorce true faith and true knowledge from the mutual love of all the faithful would be the error of rationalism, with which he reproaches the Christian West. The Church is unity, freedom, and love. Khomyakov sees Catholicism as unity without freedom and Protestantism as freedom without unity, whereas Orthodoxy is the synthesis of unity and freedom in love (one is reminded of the Hegelian thesis-antithesis-synthesis).

The followers of Khomyakov give this conception of the Church the Russian name of "sobornost", as Khomyakov took the word "Catholic" in the creed (in Slavonic "sobornyj", from the root "sobirati", i.e., gather) not in the extensive, but in the intensive sense: it is not the physical diffusion of the Church, but the free and perfect unity and unanimity of all the faithful. Even earlier than Khomyakov, Russian theology knew of a doctrine similar to that of the Gallican Richer and the Synod of Pistoia, according to which the bearer of infallibility is the entirety of all the faithful, while the bishops in council act as their delegates. The theology of Khomyakov was under ecclesiastical censure in Tsarist Russia until the beginning of the present century. E. Akvilonov (1894) tried to introduce Khomyakov's ecclesiology into official ecclesiology, and was followed by well-known Russian theologians, priests (P. Svetlov, P. Florensky, S. Bulgakov, G. Florovsky, V. Zenkovsky, G. Grabbe) as well as laymen (N. Berdyaev, L. Karsavin — who, however, died a Catholic — and N. Arseniev). These are mostly Russian *émigrés*. To these must be added the well-known Bulgarian theologian, the Archpriest S. Zankov. Among the Greeks the ideas of Khomyakov are still largely unknown. Still, in recent times Balanos, Bratsiotis and especially Alivisatos have favoured them, while Greek theologians such as Dyovuniotis and Trempelas have been critical.

The original neo-Russian ecclesiology is largely influenced by Khomyakov and Soloviev, as is especially clear in the understanding of the Church which one finds in N. Berdyaev and S. Bulgakov. For both, the Church is the mystical body of Christ, a divine-human organism ("Bogočelovĕčestvo"), the transfigured divine world. Soloviev sharply criticized Khomyakov's conception of the Church: it represented the Church in its idealized image of unanimity, which did not correspond to fact among the disunited Orthodox Churches. Moreover, the Russian Church since 1917 was divided into a plurality of hierarchies. In view, no doubt, of these difficulties, the Archpriest N. Afanasiev, professor at the Orthodox Theological Institute of St. Sergius in Paris, recently attempted to place the Orthodox ecclesiology on a new foundation, or rather, to return again to the original conception of the primitive Church. He distinguishes between *universal* and *eucharistic* ecclesiology.

In universal ecclesiology, the Church is considered as an organism whose parts are the local Churches. The fullness of Church life is to be found only in the entire Church; the local Churches are only subordinate parts of the whole. Such a conception is foreign to the writings of the NT, especially those of Paul, and to the early Church. Yet this false conception took the place of the original ecclesiology since the 3rd century, in the East as well as in the West, in the West especially in the form of the Roman primacy. The jurisdiction of the Roman pontiff over the whole Church would reduce the dioceses to the status of parishes.

According to Afanasiev, the principles of eucharistic ecclesiology, on the contrary, are based on 1 Cor 10:16–17 and 12:27, where Paul speaks of the body of Christ and his members, of those who share one eucharistic bread and who, though many, form one body. The source and the fullness of Church life is to be found in the eucharistic assembly of the local Church. Ignatius the martyr describes how the bishop together with the priests and people celebrates the Eucharist; and each local Church is for him the Catholic Church, autonomous and on an equal level with the other local Churches to which it has a living relationship and whose teaching and decrees it freely accepts. No doubt Rome exercised a primacy even in Christian antiquity, but it was not a juridical primacy; it was one of prestige, service and love. There is no real subordination of one local Church to another. The primitive Church had no juridical structure. Power, jurisdiction, law — these are categories borrowed from the Roman Empire and from the civil State. Here we note that Afanasiev, who tries to exclude every form of law from the Church, was originally a professor of canon law. The truth lies surely in between: true ecclesiology must be eucharistic as well as universal, and in the Church there is both love and law.

3. *The nature of God.* In the Eastern theological tradition the absolute transcendence of God is stressed: God dwells in inaccessible light (1 Tim 6:16). The Fathers of the 4th century inculcated this doctrine in the struggle against Eunomius. On the other hand, the Eastern ascetical tradition taught that God can be experienced in a mystically immanent way. Gregory Palamas, Archbishop of Thessalonica (1296–1359), attempted to harmonize these conflicting doctrines: one must distinguish in God between

the absolutely unknowable essence and the knowable perceptible attributes, the energies or the activity of God. Among the divine energies, which are eternal and uncreated, grace and the "light of Tabor" which was seen by the three chosen disciples and by the mystically gifted ascetics, have a special place. There is a real distinction in God between his nature and his energies, between his nature and the three divine persons. The energies are not immanent but the outward revelations or processions of the divine nature. About the middle of the 14th century this teaching was first condemned in Byzantium, but in 1351 accepted at a council and prescribed and remained dominant in the Greco-Russian Church for nearly two centuries. Then it fell into oblivion. In recent years the Russian theologians above all, especially Florovsky and Meyendorff, have tried to prove that the Palamite teaching was the genuine Eastern tradition. The year 1959 was celebrated in Thessalonica as the Palamas-Jubilee. The first volume of a new edition of his works has already appeared.

4. *Sophia.* The new Russian Wisdom-teaching, Sophiology or Sophia theology, was developed from the teaching of Soloviev especially by Florensky and Bulgakov. It is as it were the link between theology and *oikonomia* and it ponders the foundation of the world, its beauty and its splendour in God. It enquires especially how man, the microcosm, how humanity in its totality, and above all how the human nature of the God-man is founded in God; how the incarnation of God and the divinization or transfiguration of the world is possible. In the Sophia theology, Plato's theory of ideas lives on. To substantiate the theory the wisdom texts of the Old and New Testaments are used, among others, as well as the writings of the Fathers, the Eastern liturgy and iconography. Soloviev, Florensky, and Bulgakov see in the winged angel of the Sophia-icon of Novgorod not a representation of Christ, but one single great being, the ideal humanity. Accordingly, divine wisdom appears not as the person of Christ (cf. 1 Cor 1:24), to whom the Hagia Sophia in Constantinople is dedicated, but as the one divine nature of all three persons considered primarily in the person of the Word and the Spirit, insofar as the creation is founded in the nature of God and is his

image. At the same time, however, wisdom is depicted as the ideal creation itself, either as its prototype or as the transfigured, divinized creation. Wisdom then appears to be identical with God and distinct from him; as one with the creation and yet distinct from it, or intermediate between God and creation. For this reason the followers of the Sophia theology are accused of introducing, like the Gnostics of old, an intermediate being, indeed a fourth hypostasis in God, or of confusing the world with God in a pantheistic way. In the ensuing controversy, the teaching of Bulgakov was condemned as erroneous by the Moscow and Karlowitz hierarchy. Nonetheless, the Sophia theology conveys a great universal insight which contains much truth.

5. *Christology.* In recent times the Orthodox theologians have attempted to develop further the dogma of Chalcedon, especially Bulgakov with his Sophia theology, Soloviev with his concept of the God-man and Vladimir Lossky with his patristic studies. The problem of the divine self-consciousness of Christ was also discussed in connection with Protestant theology of the 19th century, even before the controversy about the "I" of the God-man in Catholic theology. New Russian theology returns again and again to the motif of the self-emptying of Christ, with new attempts to explain Phil 2:5–11. As Bulgakov identifies person, consciousness, and "I" in Christ, he attributes only one consciousness to the God-man and teaches, like Apollinaris of Laodicea in antiquity, that the Logos, the Word, took the place of the human soul in Christ.

6. *Soteriology.* Russian Orthodox soteriology developed in an independent direction about the beginning of the 20th century, primarily under the influence of Metropolitan Philaret of Moscow, Khomyakov and Dostoievsky. Representatives of this new soteriology are Světlov, later Patriarch Sergius of Moscow (d. 1944), Metropolitan Antonius (1917/18, candidate for patriarch; d. 1936), Tarejev, Nesmelov, and S. Bulgakov. Concepts of Catholic theology such as the satisfaction or merit of Christ sound suspect to these theologians and remind them of Roman or medieval penal law, or of debits and credits or bank transactions. The struggle against the juridical elements of such con-

cepts led some of these theologians to deny the objective aspect of redemption through Christ, the result of the life, suffering, death and resurrection of Christ as already at hand before its application to the redeemed, and to allow only the subjectively conscious aspects of redemption, such as the merciful love of Christ, his compassion for sinners, his example and the acceptance of his influence by repentant sinners. Tarejev stresses the redeeming value of the temptations of Christ; Nesmelov the soteriological meaning of his resurrection. Like Philaret, Svetlov and Bulgakov attempt to reconcile love and justice. Philaret propounds the mystery of redemption on three levels; in the eternal loving plan of the triune God, in the historical life and death of the Redeemer, and in the history of the Church for each Christian.

7. *Mary.* Since the patristic age there has always been theological speculation concerning Mary in the East, especially in homilies on the feasts of the Lord and the feasts of the Nativity of Mary, her Presentation in the Temple, the Annunciation, and the Assumption. The authors of theological textbooks treat of her in Christology. Only recently have monographs on Mary appeared: among the Russians, e.g., S. Bulgakov, *The Burning Bush* (1927), and among the Greeks, J. O. Kalogerou, *Mary the Ever Virgin Mother of God According to Orthodox Belief* (1957). At the centre of Orthodox Mariology stands the virginal motherhood of Mary; stress is laid on the sublimity and holiness of Mary, her share in the redemption, her place as mediatrix. This Mariology flourished strongly among Byzantine theologians in the 14th century, as it did again in our days among the Russian Sophia theologians, especially Florensky and Bulgakov. The Byzantine theologians see Mary together with her Son in the centre of the cosmos, as the recapitulation and goal of world-history (cf. Eph 1:10). For the Sophia theologians Mary is the embodiment of the Wisdom, the heart of the Church and the centre of creation. Most Orthodox theologians today deny the Immaculate Conception of Mary. Many consider the Assumption of the Mother of God into heaven only as a pious opinion and not a revealed truth.

8. *The sacraments.* In the sacramental theology the separation of East and West has meant divergent development in more than one respect. Among the controversial subjects were the sacramental character, the validity of sacraments dispensed outside of the one Church (especially baptism if not by triple immersion), the repetition of confirmation, the penance or satisfaction in the sacrament of penance, the indissolubility of sacramental marriage. The largest place, however, was taken by the controversies concerning the Eucharist: leavened or unleavened bread; the necessity of the epiclesis for the consecration of the elements; communion of children under the age of reason; and communion under both species. The only really dogmatic question concerns the necessity of the epiclesis. An explicit Orthodox sacramental theology only arose in the post-Reformation period, leaning heavily on Trent. Efforts to discard Catholic (as well as Protestant) influences and to reflect on the genuine Eastern tradition brought many differences to light and gave rise to new controversies, especially on the question of sacraments in general: the nature of grace, its action in the sacraments; the repetition or non-repetition of certain sacraments; the author and the number of the sacraments; their validity and efficacy outside of the Church. The Orthodox in great part reject a too juridical conception of the sacraments.

9. *The last things.* The ordinary doctrine of the Orthodox (as of Catholics) is: after death there can no longer be any atonement or merit; the general resurrection is yet to come; at the last judgment the good will be definitely separated from the evil; rewards will differ according to merit; the renewal of the world will follow the judgment; prayer for the dead is justified. Other than this there is no fixed teaching among the Orthodox on this subject. The controversy on the fire of purgatory, ever since 1231/32 and especially at the Council of Ferrara-Florence, centred on whether the sufferings of purgatory are caused by fire and whether the lot of the deceased will be decided before the last day. Some Orthodox theologians deny that there are any torments in purgatory and assert that God forgives the souls of the deceased in view of the prayers of the Church. The Council of Florence defined the existence but not the fire of purgatory. In the following period, many Greeks and Slavs held fast to the teaching on an intermediate state, while

131

others vigorously repudiated it. The teaching of the credal books is not consistent, so that many authors still waver.

The doctrine of the intermediate state is also testified to by the Byzantine liturgy. Besides this, the conviction is widespread among Orthodox theologians that it is only at the last judgment that the good and the evil will receive full reward or punishment in body and soul, as was taught already by Photius in the 9th and Theophylactus in the 11th and 12th centuries, and by Mark of Ephesus at the Council of Florence. Other Byzantine theologians, however, taught an immediate recompense for the souls of the good who have been purified, and for the unrepentant wicked, as was later defined at Florence.

After the council the doctrine of the delay of the recompense spread more among the Greeks, while the Slavs, especially the representatives of the Kiev school, held the Catholic position. Orthodox as well as Catholics agree that the resurrection of the body brings with it a fuller bliss for the good and a greater torment for the wicked. In the catechism of Philaret of Moscow, the good are granted only the vision of Christ immediately after death, the vision of God after the last judgment. Hence many recent Slav theologians differ with regard to the final recompense immediately after death. Some are convinced, on the basis of a homily of John Damascene which found its way into the Byzantine liturgy, that with death the lot of the unrepentant sinner is not irreparably decided. This belief was nourished by the rite of a last anointing of the dead, originating in the 13th century, which included prayers that the soul of the deceased might be freed from hell. While the Greeks found the doctrine of purgatory suspect because it seemed to reflect the error of Origin on the apocatastasis, various Russian authors, such as N. Berdyaev and S. Bulgakov, uphold the teaching of Origin and deny the eternity of an objective hell.

I. THE CATHOLIC CHURCH AND THE EASTERN CHURCHES

The Catholic Church has always considered itself to be the one Church of Christ and hence has continually worked for reunion after each schism, the Holy See being partic-

ularly active. This is evident from the long history of the attempts at union and their partial success. But the attitude of the Catholic Church towards the Christian East has not always been the same; it has changed in keeping with the times. There have been alternating periods of great understanding and also deep estrangement. Undoubtedly, sympathy and concern for the separated Eastern Churches received a decided impulse from Pope John XXIII, and from the Council convoked by him, a feature of which was the new ecumenical movement in the Catholic Church. Yet this did not happen all of a sudden, but was prepared by a series of papal letters and measures undertaken by Pius IX, Leo XIII, Benedict XV, and especially Pius XI. A movement interested in the Eastern Churches has long existed in Germany, France, and elsewhere. Pius XI made the Benedictine monastery of Amay-sur-Meuse in Belgium, later Chevetogne, a centre of the movement. Benedict XV founded the Pontifical Oriental Institute in Rome, which was then greatly helped by Pius XI, whose encyclical *Rerum Orientalium* of 8 September 1928 recommended study of the Eastern Churches and especially their theology. Scholarly and informative periodicals have been published for years by the Benedictines, Augustinians, Assumptionists, Dominicans, Jesuits, and other orders to further the knowledge of the Christian East.

Vatican II not only promulgated a special Decree on the Eastern Catholic Churches, but also included in this decree (art. 24–29) and in the Decree on Ecumenism (in Part I of the third chapter: art. 13–18) a special reference to the Eastern Churches separated from Rome. These decrees express great esteem for the institutions, liturgy, and traditions of the Eastern Churches. The first decree speaks of the local Eastern Churches, of the preservation of their spiritual heritage, of the venerable institution of the patriarchate (all Catholic Eastern patriarchs are equal in dignity; their rights and privileges are stressed); it speaks also of the sacramental discipline, the celebration of feasts, of contact and inter-communion with the separated Eastern Churches (the practice with regard to *communicatio in sacris* is modified; cf. the Decree on Ecumenism, art. 8). In the second decree the elements which unite East and West are stressed.

See also *Occident, Nestorianism, Monophysitism, Monotheletism, Cappadocian Fathers, Apocatastasis.*

BIBLIOGRAPHY. M. Jugie, *Theologia dogmatica Christianorum orientalium ab ecclesia catholica dissidentium,* 5 vols. (1926–35); S. Bulgakov, *The Orthodox Church* (1935); F. Heiler, *Urkirche und Ostkirche* (1937); M. Gordillo, *Compendium Theologiae Orientalis* (3rd ed., 1950); B. Schultze and Johannes Chrysostomus, *Die Glaubenswelt der Orthodoxen Kirche* (1961); N. Zernov, *Eastern Christendom* (1961); J. Meyendorff, *The Orthodox Church* (1962); E. Benz, *Eastern Orthodox Church. Its Thought and Life* (1963); *The Orthodox Ethos. Essays in Honour of the Centenary of the Greek Orthodox Archdiocese of North and South America* (1964); *A Pan-Orthodox Symposium* (1964).

Bernhard Schultze

ECCLESIASTICAL AUTHORITY

Ecclesiastical authority *(potestas sacra)* is the authority which the Church has been given by Jesus Christ to be exercised in his name in carrying out the mission entrusted to it.

1. *Basis in the nature of the Church.* In the language of Vatican II *potestas sacra* means the power which Jesus Christ has given the Church to exercise in his name, in the discharge of ministries he has established in his Church in such a way that they have to be carried out by special authorities (Constitution on the Church, art. 18). The ministry here referred to is the basis of the hierarchical structure of the new people of God which is essential to the Church. This structure is an element of the sacramental significance of the Church. As a visible community founded in Christ and for Christ the Church is the sign of salvation which the Lord has set up for all men, "as it were a sacrament in Christ, that is, a symbol and instrument of the closest union with God as well as of the unity of all mankind" *(ibid.,* art. 1). The Church is sign of salvation in that the divine element proper to it shines through and becomes tangible in the human element, especially by the fact that the Lord, the invisible head of the Church, is visibly represented in the Church by men. Thus, as the Council teaches *(ibid.,* art. 8), the Church presents a close analogy to the mystery of the incarnation of the Son of God, for "as the divine Word uses the human nature which it has assumed as a living instrument of salvation indissolubly united to itself, so in a very similar way the Spirit of Christ uses the social organization of the Church, which it animates, to build up his body" (cf. Eph 4:16).

All members of the people of God, clergy and laymen alike, have the same dignity as Christians and share in the threefold task of the Church — the teaching, priesthood, and pastoral office. The only difference is in the manner of the collaboration, and that difference follows from the different ways there are of being a person in the Church. So it is not for those invested with ecclesiastical authority to take the whole saving mission of the Church upon themselves; rather "they must be shepherds to the faithful, scrutinizing each one's accomplishments and charisms so that all may work together in harmony, each in his own way, at the common task" (Vatican II: Constitution on the Church, art. 30). So "the whole body, joined and knit together by every joint with which it is supplied, when each part is working properly, makes bodily growth and upbuilds itself in love" (Eph 4:16). The part the pastors of the Church have to play is one of pure service (διακονία). It is a matter of loving self-sacrifice for the disciples, such as is depicted in the parable of the Good Shepherd (Jn 10:1–28). Authority in the Church must be this kind of service and solicitude for the good of the people, not lording it over them (cf. Mt 20:24–28).

A person possesses ecclesiastical authority not simply because he is conscious of having received a personal charism from God, even one recognized by the people of God, but solely because he has been called to power in tangible, juridical form. Thus the hierarchical structure of the Church means that it cannot have a charismatic structure. At the same time the charisms are an essential part of the Church. They are gifts of the Holy Spirit who is at work in all the members of God's people; they are part of the Church's daily life, and in times of stress are also given in the form of special gifts. The Holy Spirit "gives to each according to his will" (1 Cor 12:11). As the Council teaches (Constitution on the Church, art. 12), it is for those who preside over the Church (cf. 1 Cor 14:37f.) to judge whether the gifts are genuine and how they can be fittingly used; and those authorities are particularly admonished not to extinguish the Spirit but to examine everything and keep what is good (cf. 1 Thess 5:12, 19–21).

2. *Two powers or three?* The Council's doctrine on ecclesiastical authority underwent a considerable evolution. The 1963 schema (22 April), which was discussed in the assembly hall, taught the doctrine that there is a threefold authority *(triplex sacra potestas):* authority to teach *(potestas docendi),* sanctify *(potestas sanctificandi),* and govern *(potestas regendi).* That of 1964 (3 July), which was voted on, abandoned the doctrine of the threefold power and in place of *potestas* used the word *munus.* Article 28 of the latter schema spoke of the "potestas sacra tum ordinis tum iurisdictionis, quae ex missione Christi in Episcopis resident"; but this version too was abandoned in the final text. We can gather from the textual alterations what difficulties the Council experienced in connection with the doctrine on ecclesiastical authority.

The distinction between the power of order and the power of jurisdiction, which has been made since the 12th century, led in the Latin Church to a real division of the one ecclesiastical power and a corresponding division of the hierarchy into a *hierarchia ordinis* and a *hierarchia iurisdictionis.* What this distinction means becomes quite clear when we consider that it was not episcopal consecration but the bestowal of episcopal office which made a bishop; indeed a good many "bishops" were not even deacons in sacred orders. In the Roman Catechism (pars II, cap. 7, q. 6) we are told: "Ordinis potestas ad verum Christi Domini Corpus in sacrosancta Eucharistia refertur. Iurisdictionis vero potestas tota in Christi corpore mystico versatur." This formula, which attempts to sum up the teaching of classical Scholasticism, was increasingly taken to mean that the power of order has to do with administering the means of divine grace and the power of jurisdiction solely with the outward government of the Church. In this view the power of order becomes a sacramental power, because it relates to the administration of the sacraments, and the pastoral power a juridical one, since it governs the people of God by juridical means. Now contrasting sacrament and law in this unfortunate way quite obscured the original sense of the distinction, made it

impossible to discern the Church's nature as a whole, and above all opened a gulf in men's minds between the Church as a religious society and the Church as a juridical society. To take a typical example, it was now a riddle why *iurisdictio in poenitentem* should be required as well as priestly orders for valid absolution in confession *(CIC, can.* 872). At least when distinguishing between the powers of order and jurisdiction men did remember that the one power derives from ordination or consecration and the other — except for the Pope's supreme authority — from canonical mission (can. 109); but even in the *CIC* justice was not done to the distinction (cf. can. 145, 210, for example).

The idea of a threefold power is of recent origin. It goes back to the doctrine of the three offices of Christ and the Church (magisterium, priesthood, government), which must not be understood as offices in the juridical sense but as duties and ministries. The doctrine of the triplex *munus* is neither biblical nor patristic in origin but derives from Martin Bucer and John Calvin. Lutheran theologians adopted it only in the middle of the 17th century, having originally recognized only two offices *(sacerdos — rex).* To Catholic tradition the doctrine of the threefold office is alien. First in Eusebius, when he is explaining the name Χριστός, and more often later, even in the Roman Catechism, we find the observation that priests, kings, and prophets were anointed in the OT. It was only the theologians of the Enlightenment who borrowed the notion of the threefold office from Protestant theology in the late 18th or early 19th century. Much use was made of it by Vatican II. The doctrine of the *triplex munus* notably helps us towards a systematic idea of Christ's work and its continuation in the Church; but it must be observed that there are also other helps to that end — medieval theologians recognized as many as ten offices — and that the three offices, as the conciliar documents make quite plain, cannot be sharply distinguished. Lutheran theologians nowadays consider the doctrine no more than a "rule of thumb". It was the German canonists Ferdinand Walter and Georg Phillips, in the earlier 19th century, who connected the doctrine of the three offices with the doctrine on ecclesiastical power. They assign each office a power of its own, so that the powers remain unconnected side by side. Now this cuts away the whole network of relations that subsist between the two poles, order and jurisdiction, because of the distinction between order and canonical mission; it destroys too the bonds which link the powers of order and jurisdiction with the three offices of the Church and must do so unless we are to sacrifice the unity of ecclesiastical power. Apparently that is why the Council abandoned the threefold division which figured in the schema of 1963.

Because the threefold division of ecclesiastical power was related to the three offices, it became the practice to define the three powers by their tasks — *potestas docendi, potestas sanctificandi,* and *potestas regendi* — which, without quite obliterating it, more and more obscured the distinction drawn on another basis between *potestas ordinis* and *potestas iurisdictionis.* Insofar as the old distinction between *potestas ordinis* and *potestas iurisdictionis* survived, it was felt necessary to assign the magisterium *(potestas docendi)* to one or the other; and so it fell to the power of jurisdiction. Canonists in particular — who generally speaking continued to distinguish between the power of order and the power of jurisdiction — related the former *(potestas ordinis = potestas sanctificandi)* to the priestly office and the latter *(potestas iurisdictionis = potestas regendi et docendi)* to the office of teaching and government. Several pronouncements of the Council reflect this school of thought, especially the statement that the bishops as a body succeed the college of apostles in the office of teaching and government ("in magisterio et regimine pastorali", Vatican II: Constitution on the Church, art. 22; cf. also Vatican II: *De Ep.,* art. 3, where the words "ad magisterium et regimen pastorale quod attinet" were added in the final version of the text). At the same time it can hardly be denied that the college of bishops succeeds the college of apostles in the priestly office as well. The Council seems to say as much in declaring that "by divine institution the bishops take the place of the apostles as pastors of the Church" (Constitution on the Church, art. 20); for the *Ecclesiae pastores* discharge all three offices of the Church. If the priestly office did not fall within the competence of the episcopal college, how could it be correct to say that that college possesses full *(plena)* and supreme power in the Church *(ibid.,*

art. 22)? The only question is which concrete tasks can be discharged by a college and which only by a physical person.

3. *Unity in duality.* By calling *sacra potestas* all ecclesiastical authority with which the pastors of the Church are invested, the Council teaches that that authority is one; and at the same time, as we shall see in more detail (under point 4), declares that the same ecclesiastical authority works through two channels—holy orders and canonical mission. But the Council does not definitively lay down what sort of unity ecclesiastical power possesses. That is a matter for scholars to examine, and in fact they have recently begun a systematic historical study of the canonical doctrine on ecclesiastical power.

a) *History of the distinction between the powers of order and jurisdiction.* If we are to understand why the distinction was originally made, we must recollect that the power of order and the power of jurisdiction rest to the same extent on the Lord's mission. Christ is invested with the fullness of both powers, but as a power that is absolutely one. He authorizes the apostles to do various things — to proclaim the good news, celebrate the Eucharist, forgive sins or retain them — in general to bind and to loose. But it is fruitless to examine the differences among these powers in search of the future distinction between the powers of order and jurisdiction; and in any case what is important about the distinction does not derive from any objective differences between the powers. A need to distinguish between order and jurisdiction arose when the Lord's mission passed to men. The Lord gave the apostolic mission by word alone, without a sensible sign; at least we have no record of any symbolic act. But as soon as the apostles appoint successors in their mission and helpers in their ministry, we encounter a sign: the laying on of hands. The laying on of hands efficaciously imparts God's Spirit to a man and clothes him with apostolic authority. Once ecclesiastical office was organized on a local basis, a man was ordained for the service of a particular church. Ordination was also bestowal of office.

Throughout the first millenium this principle of "incardination" held its ground, as it still does in the Eastern Churches today. But when ordained men came to grief this interweaving of order and office presented a serious constitutional problem. From the very first it was accepted that an ordained man who fell away from the faith or seriously offended against Church order was no longer fit to rule the people of God. He was removed from office. The difficult question then arose whether the personal failings of such a person extinguished every single power he received at ordination; in particular, whether an ordained man degraded from office, or outside the Church, could still administer the sacraments. High views of the Church's holiness fostered a puritanism, at Alexandria and Carthage, which held that serious sin incapacitated a man for any spiritual function. This puritanism degenerated into fanaticism in Montanism.

With the hierarchical Church of the bishops, based on sacraments and law, Tertullian contrasts a Church of the spirit — for him, the true and essential one. The bishops' Church is successor to the apostles only in outward discipline; the Church of the spirit, gathered together and governed directly by God's Spirit, has the fullness of the divine mission. As the Lord says that "where two or three are gathered together in my name, there am I in the midst of them" (Mt 18:20), so the spiritual Church is constituted when three people meet in the Holy Spirit. The Spirit "gathers together that Church which consists of three" (*De pud.*, 21). "Where the ecclesiastical *Ordo* does not gather, you offer sacrifice, you baptize, you are your own priest; for wherever there are three, there is the Church, even if the three are laymen" (*De exhort. cast.*, 7). Here the need for ordination is bluntly denied; the capacity for spiritual functions depends on possession of the Spirit. Tertullian's dualistic notion of the Church — partially reflected in his distinction between two baptisms, a sacrament of water and a sacrament of faith — ultimately rests on a Christological dualism. The principle which dominates Tertullian's mind — no spiritual capacity without personal holiness — made a lasting impression on St. Cyprian. But in his case instead of splitting the Church it narrowed down the circle of those who possess the Spirit. The principle of unity in the Church, for Cyprian, is the hierarchical Church of the bishops, built upon Peter. Only where the lawful bishop is, is the Spirit found, and only subordination to the bishop gives one assurance of salvation. Thus he bases pos-

session of the Spirit on legitimate ordination, but at the same time on the personal holiness of the man ordained: serious sin deprives a minister of the Spirit and of spiritual power alike.

During the controversy about the baptism of heretics it emerged as apostolic doctrine that baptism administered by heretics is valid. The Donatist schism, which occurred over the question whether ordination conferred outside the Church is valid, led to no definitive dogmatic explanation. St. Augustine pointed the way to the solution with his doctrine of the sacramental character, but as re-ordination was still practised in the early Middle Ages we can see that the victory of the Augustinian theology of the sacraments over Cyprian's spiritualist, and also juridical concept of the Church was very long delayed. Much light was thrown on the problem by the controversies over the validity of absolute ordination — ordination without assignment to a particular church. The Council of Chalcedon (451) sanctioned the ban on absolute ordination by providing that those so ordained possess an ineffective laying on of hands (ἄκυρον = *vacuam, irritam*), and to the disgrace of the consecrating prelate cannot officiate anywhere (can. 6). It is not doing this canon justice to suggest, in the light of later knowledge, that the Council does not question the validity of absolute ordination but only forbids the use of the power received. On the contrary, the fact that the Council pronounces absolute ordination ineffectual is eloquent proof that the concept of ordination was still embryonic at that time.

Spirit and office had been so closely interwoven since the earliest days of Christianity that it was quite impossible for a statement on ordination to apply to one element but not the other. Precisely because men could not disentangle spirit from office and could not see how they differed and how each bore on the other, a fierce struggle over the foundations of the Church's constitution went on down into the 12th century. Absolute ordination was really not a problem of speculative theology but one of apostolic tradition. Once it was realized — as had long been assumed in practice, first in isolated cases and then generally — that ordination can be valid apart from simultaneous incardination, the distinction between the powers of order and jurisdiction was fixed. Thanks to the tedious wrangling men now saw that the one power could not be lost, because it was bestowed by holy orders, and that the other could be lost, because it was bestowed by canonical mission.

b) *Difference and inter-relation.* Just as each power has its proper nature, each also has its proper function, luminously set forth in the parable of the vine (Jn 15:1–11). There the Lord speaks of two forces at work in the Church: the vine, from which life flows into the branches, and the vinedresser, who cuts away barren branches and purges fruitful ones so that they may bear more fruit. Both are divine forces, both at work in the Church but in different ways — one generating and one ordering. We have the same functional difference in the powers of order and jurisdiction. The power of order is the principle of life. It is given forever and is always efficacious; but being liable to abuse in human hands, it needs to be ordered and directed in the right channels. The power of jurisdiction is the ordering principle. It is able to act as such because it is formally different from the power of order and especially because it is separable from its possessor, and therefore can effectively deal with threats to the Church's life arising from personal factors. Other characteristics are akin to this one. The power of order is so bound up with the person who is ordained that it can be efficaciously used anywhere in the Church, for example, in saying Mass; it is communitarian by nature. On the other hand, the efficacy of the power of jurisdiction — apart from the supreme power of the Pope and the episcopal college — is limited, either as to territory or as to persons, and thus demarcates the local communities which are necessary for the orderly government of the people of God. True, the power of order also contributes to this end, for it produces the ministers who must rule the people of God and celebrate the liturgy (cf. can. 948). But it is not holy orders alone, it is only bestowal of the power of jurisdiction that creates the relationship of subject and superior, binding the shepherd to his flock and to the other shepherds and providing a basis for the proper exercise of the ecclesiastical powers conferred both by holy orders and by canonical mission.

The difference of function between the two powers also reveals their deep reciprocal connection, so that we may speak of a oneness in duality. First of all, the degrees within the hierarchy of order closely correspond to the degrees within the hierarchy of office. The system of relative ordination fully respects this unity, ordaining and conferring office by the same act. In the system of absolute ordination the unity of the two powers is ensured because a given office can only be bestowed on those who are in the appropriate orders. For example, only a priest can be given a parish. In the Latin Church at the moment orders and offices are still separate at the appointment of a bishop; but the bishop-elect only becomes a real bishop at his consecration, and he is always consecrated to a particular see, just as in the system of relative ordination. The manner in which both powers are exercised testifies no less plainly to their intimate connection, which in some cases goes so far that we must speak of a single reality. This is certainly true of the sacrament of penance. Here the two powers are so closely combined that priestly orders and jurisdiction jointly effect sacramental absolution (can. 872).

The polarity of the relationship between the powers of order and jurisdiction may be compared with the foci of an ellipse, supposing these to be movable. Each of the two powers has its own connections with the three offices, because both the power bestowed by holy orders and that bestowed by canonical mission operate, each in its own way, in the priesthood, magisterium, and government that compose the Church's work.

Thus holy orders and jurisdiction are two complementary elements of the one ecclesiastical power which Jesus Christ entrusted to his Church.

4. *Episcopal authority.* The combination of order and jurisdiction is closest in the bishop, to whom both types of hierarchy are proper. He is at the summit of the *hierarchia ordinis,* and in the *hierarchia iurisdictionis* he will be found at any one of the levels that reach from the supreme jurisdiction of the Pope, through the higher episcopal ranks, down to the office of diocesan bishop. Through all these hierarchical gradations episcopal consecration forms the ontological basis of the bishop's ministry and also of his authority, in such a way that we must assume the existence of an inner kernel unaffected by

the difference between the powers of order and jurisdiction. I consider this kernel to be his personal episcopal character and above all the inalienable power which a bishop always has to confer valid holy orders (though it be not automatically licit for him to do so), which ensures that despite human weakness ecclesiastical authority will always live on in the Church. Catholic tradition thinks of the bishop as the shepherd of a flock. And so a bishop is always consecrated to a particular see, an act which also confers on him the episcopal office, according to the ancient concept preserved in the Eastern Churches (*CIO*, can. 396, § 2, n. 1). The Latin Church still observes the custom in its liturgy, at least. But consecration and the conferring of office, whether done separately or in the one act, are essentially different processes and not interchangeable. In particular we must remember that the canonical mission distinct from orders cannot be given *"through* lawful customs which the supreme, universal authority of the Church has not abolished" or *"through* laws which the said authority has made or recognizes" (cf. Vatican II: Constitution on the Church, art. 24); of its nature, it must come from the competent authority, *according to* law or custom, by nomination, confirmation of election or the like.

Because the Council did not treat the problems connected with episcopal consecration and canonical mission in the same context, difficulties of interpretation arose which the *Nota praevia explicativa* largely resolved. The Council teaches that episcopal consecration bestows the fullness of the sacrament of order (*ibid.*, art. 21). As to the effects of episcopal consecration we read: "Besides the ministry of sanctification *(munus sanctificandi)*, episcopal consecration confers the ministries of teaching and government *(munera docendi et regendi)*, which by their nature can only be exercised in hierarchical communion with the head and members of the episcopal college." Here the Council follows the view outlined above (under point 2) that the power of order relates to the priestly office and the power of jurisdiction to the office of teaching and ruling.

However, we must not therefore conclude that the sacred power — which the Council depicts as a unity — is not embodied in all three offices. But what is the meaning of a sacramental transmission of offices, if they cannot (of their nature) be exercised unless another element intervenes, namely hierarchical communion with the head and members of the college? On this point the *Nota praevia* says (art. 2): "Consecration gives one an ontological participation in the sacred offices, as is clear from tradition, including liturgical tradition. The word offices *(munera)* is advisedly used instead of powers *(potestates)*, which might be taken to mean a power ready for use *(de potestate ad actum expedita)*. Now so that a power ready for use may be available there is need of a canonical or juridical determination by hierarchical authority. This determination of power may consist in the bestowal of an office or the assignment of subjects, and is made according to norms approved by supreme authority. An additional norm of this sort is required by the nature of the case because these are offices which must be exercised by a number of ministers who co-operate as a hierarchy according to the will of Christ." This is nothing new, and the *Nota praevia* can rightly appeal to what the Constitution says about canonical mission when describing the episcopal office. By collating the separate statements which the Constitution makes about order and office the *Nota* sheds light on the statement about the effects of episcopal consecration. Episcopal orders and episcopal office are connected because the powers deriving from order and office complement each other, joining together to form an episcopal power ready for use. The *Nota praevia* gives us to understand that this does not solve all questions concerning the relation between office and order, and explicitly leaves it to the theologians to analyse the problems involved in the licit and valid exercise of power.

The relation between order and office is often envisaged thus: episcopal consecration bestows full episcopal power, but that power is "in bond" and cannot be used until it has been released by bestowal of an office. In this view the only business of episcopal office is to unchain power and if necessary chain it up again: office has a purely formal function, no real content. The *Nota praevia* explains why the power conferred by holy orders needs completion by pointing out that the episcopal ministries have to be carried out by several persons and therefore require a precise juridical determination — and the assignment of a flock, that is, the bestowal of episcopal office, is mentioned. Now this in itself is recognition that office has more than a merely "liberating" function. But it is necessary to point out — and this seems to be the essential point — that episcopal consecration must always have the same effects and that therefore the many gradations in the episcopal ministries cannot derive from order: they must derive from office. Pope, patriarch, metropolitan, and diocesan bishop are all in the same episcopal orders; but with regard to office they occupy different hierarchical ranks, all designed to ensure orderly government and to safeguard the unity of the people of God. Now the Church's constitution is such that the Pope's supreme jurisdiction and every higher episcopal office — like that of patriarch or metropolitan — relates to a particular see: that Pope, patriarch, and metropolitan are at the same time pastors of a particular diocese, like any other local ordinary. This peculiarity in the Church's constitution, which has no parallel in the temporal sphere, follows from the fact that the local Church is not simply part of a whole but in its domain represents the whole Church. It manifests the collegiate structure of the Church's constitution and the inner bond between episcopal order and episcopal office.

W. Bertrams has made a remarkable attempt to interpret the structure of ecclesiastical power by distinguishing between *structura interna* and *externa*. He holds that the sacrament of order bestows the fullness of episcopal power, or rather constitutes it substantially and ontologically. He accepts the division of this one episcopal power into order and jurisdiction, and relates these as usual to the three "offices", in such a way that the power of order relates to the *munus sanctificandi* alone and the power of jurisdiction to the *munus docendi et regendi* alone. The ontological groundwork is not sufficient unto itself; it has an intrinsic tendency to take on outward form. If this happens we have reached the first stage of *structura externa*. And the power of order can in fact achieve such a full outward form. It has, Bertrams supposes, no direct effects in the Church as an external society. The case is otherwise with the power of jurisdiction, which has direct effects in the Church as a juridical external society. So a further element, a new stage of *structura externa,* is now

required: *recognitio, incorporatio* or *communio,* which is provided by *missio canonica*. This consists in defining a concrete ministry or concrete task, or assigning a pastor to a definite flock. *Missio canonica* unchains, liberates the fullness of episcopal power which the sacrament has substantially bestowed. But it is not something accidental in relation to the (pastoral) power of jurisdiction. Since the *structura externa* — bodiliness — is an essential element of human society and therefore also of the Church, the power of jurisdiction cannot be constituted *ex toto* until *missio canonica* supervenes.

We cannot feel altogether satisfied with the strict assignment of the power of order to the *munus sanctificandi* and the power of jurisdiction to the *munus docendi et regendi;* all teaching and government in the Church are also related to the power of order; and so too sanctification is related to the power of jurisdiction. If one agrees with Bertrams, the distinction between the powers still threatens to become a divorce which at least borders on a rigid distinction between the sacramental order and the social and juridical order. To suppose that the power of jurisdiction is substantially conferred by ordination but still requires an essential element from outside, only postpones the problem of the relation between order and office. But it does mean that consecration is intrinsically orientated to being joined to a concrete office by means of *missio canonica*.

See also *Church* III, *Bishop* IV, *Clergy, Laity, Ecclesiastical Office, Hierarchy.*

BIBLIOGRAPHY. R. Sohm, *Das altkatholische Kirchenrecht und das Dekret Gratians* (1918); J. Fuchs, *Magisterium, Ministerium, Regimen. Vom Ursprung einer ekklesiologischen Trilogie* (1941); M. Kaiser, *Die Einheit der Kirchengrundlegung nach dem Zeugnis des NT und der Apostolischen Väter* (1956); R. A. Strigl, *Grundfragen der Kirchlichen Ämterorganisation* (1960); K. Nasilowski, *De distinctione potestatis in ordine in primaeva canonistarum doctrina* (1962); W. Bertrams, *De relatione inter Episcopatum et Primatum* (1963); B. Fries, *Forum in der Rechtssprache* (1963); J. McKenzie, *Authority in the Church* (1966).

Klaus Mörsdorf

ECCLESIASTICAL FINANCES

Church finances include all arrangements and activities of the Church for providing the financial means necessary for carrying out its mission.

1. *General.* a) *Basis in divine law.* The Church, following the will of its divine founder, works in the world as a visible community. That is not possible without financial means. Therefore she claims the God-given right to acquire, own and administer earthly goods, in complete freedom and independently of any other power (*CIC,* can. 1495, § 1). (i) The beginnings of Church finances are to be seen already in the NT. Jesus and his apostles receive offerings which are administered in common and which serve to meet the expenses incurred by the group (Lk 8:3; Jn 12:6). St. Paul reminds the Corinthians of the Lord's command that "those who preach the gospel should live by the gospel" (1 Cor 9:14). The communities in Asia Minor organize a collection for the "poor among the saints in Jerusalem" (Rom 15:26; 1 Cor 16:1 ff.; cf. too Mt 10:10; Lk 10:7; Acts 2:45; 4:34 ff.; 11:29). (ii) Church financing has not merely been impeded in many ways by public authorities but it has also been attacked within the Church itself. Viewing the spiritual nature of the Church in a rigid and unbalanced way, people put forward the view (doubtless in many cases out of a genuine anxiety about the seductive power of money) that the use of earthly possessions is not reconcilable with the spirit of the gospel. Such people overlook the fact that Christ's chief concern in warning about the danger of riches was the freedom of the heart for God. Now this freedom is to be judged not by possessions as such but by the use to which they are put. (iii) Divine law sets clear limits to Church finances, which have not always been observed with the necessary fidelity. The Church can be responsible for possessions and the use of money only to the extent demanded by its mission of salvation. It must be extremely careful in its dealings with these very earthly things and always be on its guard to ensure that money will serve the spirit and that the spirit may not be sacrificed to material interests.

b) *Decentralization.* The Catholic Church has no centrally directed system of finances. There exist many accounts or financial arrangements very varied in size and significance. (i) The independent finances of the Holy See and of the dioceses and parishes correspond to the territorial divisions. The financing of parishes is connected with that of dioceses more or less closely and with a greater or lesser degree of independence according to the circumstances of each country. In addition to this there are the religious institutes whose independent finances provide not only for their own needs but supply also considerable means for the foreign missions, for Church schools and for works of charity. Finally there are many foundations and associations with their own financial means which largely provide the economic basis for specific institutions founded for apostolic or charitable purposes. (ii) The decentralization that began to take place more rapidly in the 18th century of the hitherto more highly centralized diocesan finances, has been determined more by economic considerations than by ecclesiastical requirements and need not affect the unity of Church action; it can enable the Church to adapt more easily in its various sectors to the conditions of the various countries. Modern rationalization of financing tends to bring about a greater concentration of small, otherwise non-viable financial units.

2. *Financial needs.* a) *Personal needs.* Following the command of the Lord, those who serve the altar and preach the gospel should also live by the gospel (cf. 1 Cor 9:13 f.). This places on the Church the responsibility for the support of its clergy and its lay employees. (i) According to the traditional system of benefices every cleric should be given a benefice, the revenue from which should provide him with a living befitting his state of life. But the ancient benefices are for the most part so impoverished that they can no longer fulfil their function and the erection of new ones with sufficient foundation is scarcely possible; areas with a newly organized Church community have either no livings at all or none with a sufficient foundation. Accordingly new sources of income must be everywhere found to provide a salary befitting their state in life for the clergy, whether they are still active or retired. This has not yet been everywhere satisfactorily achieved. (ii) Since the Church today so emphatically upholds social justice, it will have to be very conscientious itself in paying a just wage to the lay people who are engaged in very great numbers in full-time work in its service.

b) *Material needs.* (i) Buildings. At the present time the Church's need for buildings has greatly increased. This is occasioned partly by the considerable growth in population (urbanization, housing schemes), but also by the greater desire for more adequate church furnishing and equipment. New churches, presbyteries and parish centres must be built, old buildings repaired and adapted to modern needs. Provision must also be made for centres of administration, seminaries, retreat houses, etc. (ii) Needs of administration. In line with more recent developments there is a constant and increasing need at the higher levels of Church organization for administrative requisites (office equipment, telephones, circulars). (iii) Liturgical needs. The dignified administration of liturgical services is not possible without material means (vestments, heating, lighting). In comparison with the central significance of the liturgy for the life of the Church, the expenses it involves are small and have remained relatively stable.

c) *Need for alms.* Christ on one occasion, after having preached to the people, exclaimed: "I have compassion on the multitude . . . If I send them away fasting to their home, they will faint in the way." (Mk 8:2f.) The Church follows in the footsteps of its Master when it busies itself in loving care for the bodily needs of men. For the sake of the credibility of its preaching it cannot be content with a simple exhortation to help, but must itself be active in giving help. This service of charity must not in an industrial society be restricted to personal alms to the needs but must also provide or support welfare institutions (orphanages, rest homes, homes for the aged, etc.).

d) *Need for schools.* The Church must give instruction in the faith for eternal life; it has the rights of a mother in respect of its children to whom it has given supernatural life in baptism. It thereby receives from the gospel the mission and right to interest itself in providing schools. This it can do in many countries only by maintaining its own school system; in other countries it is able to open Church schools in conjunction with the State school system. Even though many States provide help for the upkeep of such schools in a more or less satisfactory manner, there remains nevertheless a burden for those responsible for Church financing which can

only be borne through great self-sacrifice on the part of the faithful.

3. *Provision of means.* a) *Income from Church collections.* Voluntary offerings of the faithful are the oldest and most characteristic way of providing for needs. They were made originally as *oblata* at the Holy Sacrifice. Nowadays considerable sums accrue from offerings, mostly of smaller sums but given with a certain regularity. They are indispensable, especially in politically restricted areas, for the needs of the missions and the diaspora, for the works of charity and for special schemes of help *(Misereor, Adveniat).* As signs of a realization of responsibility, readiness for sacrifice and charity, these offerings correspond in a special way to the nature of the Church. From the financial point of view they present a difficulty inasmuch as the income from them is difficult to assess in advance and tends to fluctuate.

b) *Private sources of income.* The Church claims the right to make use of all the ordinary means of acquiring income to the same extent and with the same freedom as all other subjects of ownership rights. In ecclesiastical practice the possibilities of earning income in this way are in fact restricted. (i) Up to the time of the secularization of Church property and the devaluation of money and revenue from land and capital, ownership played an important part. The land still held by the Church is chiefly in the form of scattered farms; apart from monasteries and welfare institutions, it is for the most part not worked directly by the Church but rented to small farmers. The revenues from capital ownership are greatly diminished through successive devaluations and are of no great financial significance. Of more significance probably are the revenues from direct economic activity, especially in monasteries (hospices, publishing centres, bookshops, etc.). (ii) That Church agencies own and run business enterprises cannot be criticized in principle. Yet it is essential to see to it that they are conducted with care from the business point of view and along lines of honourable competition and that socially the interests of all who are involved are respected. It should not be forgotten that all economic activity of the Church is exposed in a particular way to the eye of the public and that a failure in this matter does grievous injury to the credibility of the Church's message.

c) *Official Church income.* The Church claims the right, independently of State authority, to demand offerings from its faithful when the necessary means cannot be provided otherwise. In the course of history it has built up a complex system of collections for local, diocesan and papal needs, the administration of which has been a severe burden on its activity. Nowadays there are three important forms of official levy: (i) Fees. The Roman and diocesan curiae charge fees for the various kinds of voluntary services (distinctions, dispensations, the formalities of appointments) and for law cases. For parish priests the stole fees are important; they are felt more and more to be a hindrance to pastoral work. (ii) Dues. In many countries the faithful are obliged, as they would be in an association, to pay dues, regulated in amount and collected by the Church itself. (iii) Church taxes. These are payments made by the faithful in accordance with a State means test ("means tax") and collected, sometimes by State officials, on a percentage basis arranged in agreement with the Church. This method of providing revenue distributes the burdens evenly and provides substantial and predictable means not otherwise easily available to the Church. Yet there is a disquieting aspect to this: what ultimately belongs to God should not be mechanically collected by civil servants but should be consciously given as an offering.

d) *State grants.* State salaries had their origin at the time of the secularization and the transition from the right of presentation. They are nearly always in favour of diocesan institutions and are often made the subject of agreement and secured in a Concordat. As well, many States provide special subventions, as for Church schools. Finally, there are also indirect aids by exemption of the owners of Church property from paying State taxes.

4. *Needs and tasks.* The Lord has ordained that, just as he did himself, so too his Church should share in the limitations of all flesh. One of these limitations is the impossibility of fulfilling the Church's apostolic mission without money. No matter how essential an element in the life of the Church it is, the question must be continually asked: how does the Church stand in this matter in the view of its founder and what consequences must be drawn from the answer for its existence here and now? (i) The Church must, in loyalty to the self-emptying and poverty of its Head, seek to regulate its finances so that in it the mystery of poverty remains visible to men. (ii) To the social accountability called for in the economic life of today must correspond a spiritual accounting in the financial life of the Church, i.e., the responsible official must earnestly examine his conscience as to how far the religious mission of the Church is being furthered by his use of money. (iii) Christian charity demands a financial equalization to avoid imposing greater sacrifices for a smaller result on the faithful in poorer dioceses than in those that are better off. (iv) Money for Church purposes is almost entirely provided by the laity. It is right and understandable that they should share in discussion and decision on the uses to which such money is to be put. (v) The Church should give more publicity to its financial arrangements. This would be the best antidote to suspicion and unfounded speculation on the matter of Church finances.

See also *Charity* III.

BIBLIOGRAPHY. M. Pistocchi, *De bonis Ecclesiae temporalibus* (1932); G. Sabatini, *Del patrimonio ecclesiastico* (1934); T. Bouscaren, *Canon Law Digest,* 4 vols. with supplements (1934–61); G. Forchielli, *Il diritto patrimoniale della Chiesa* (1935); J. Wenner, *Kirchliches Vermögensrecht* (3rd ed., 1940); C. Berutti, *Institutiones Iuris Canonici,* IV (1940), pp. 461–549; L. Mier, *Sistemas de dotación de la Iglesia católica* (1949); M. Conte a Coronata, *Institutiones Iuris Canonici,* II (4th ed., 1951), pp. 447–516; G. Vromant, *De bonis Ecclesiae temporalibus* (3rd ed., 1953); A. Ottaviani and I. Damazia, *Institutiones iuris publici ecclesiastici,* I (4th ed., 1958), pp. 325–46; F. Capello, *Summa Iuris Canonici,* II (5th ed., 1962), pp. 547–94; T. Bouscaren and A. Ellis, *Canon Law, a Text and Commentary* (rev. ed., 1963); W. Wilken, *Unser Geld und die Kirche* (3rd ed., 1964).

Josef Lederer

ECCLESIASTICAL LAW

I. Concept and System: A. Definition and Division. B. The Foundations of Law. C. Special Nature and Task of Church Law. D. Binding Power and Limits of Law. E. Sources. F. The Science of Canon Law. G. Revision of Canon Law.

I. Concept and System

A. Definition and Division

1. *Definition.* Ecclesiastical law, or canon law, is the entirety of the norms of the law laid down by God and by the Church, which regulate the constitution and life of the Church of Jesus Christ united under the Pope as its one visible head. The laws of the State which regulate Church affairs, which apply where the Church is "established" in the State, are civil and not ecclesiastical law. Law which arises from agreement between Church and State, especially through concordats, is both ecclesiastical and civil law.

2. *Division.* Ecclesiastical law is distinguished according to its origin either as divine or as human law. Divine law is either positive divine law as expressed in revelation, or natural law based on the order of creation. Human law (purely ecclesiastical law) is either the result of legislation or of custom.

Divine law is unchangeable. But the following considerations should not be overlooked in this regard. For a certain institution to qualify as an expression of divine law it is not necessary that it be found explicitly as such in the pages of sacred Scripture; it is enough if it is unanimously considered by the ecclesiastical magisterium to belong to the inalienable nature of the Church and has some sort of basis in sacred Scripture. No greater demands can be made upon legal institutions in this regard than are made with respect to dogmatic assertions. Also, it is necessary to be mindful of the intrinsic law of development in the Church. Like the development which characterizes organic life, the course of Church history has been marked by the stirrings of new tendencies and new developments under the guidance of the Holy Spirit which have given rise to offices and institutions which in their fully developed form are considerably different from those of primitive Christianity and the early Church. As the instrument of God, the Church has an essential share in the creation of these institutions. With regard to those juridical forms which the Church considers to be essential to its being, the process is an irreversible one.

The purely ecclesiastical portions of Church law are changeable. Human law always has one relation, and often a two-fold one, to divine law, insofar as the juridical authority legitimately functions in virtue of divine law, and insofar as formal ecclesiastical law largely codifies what is materially divine law.

B. The Foundations of Law

The justification for the existence of law in the Church is in the very nature of the redemptive work of God. The bringer of revelation is the God-man Jesus Christ; redemption is achieved in the historical actions centred on his person. Historicity cannot be divorced from society, and society cannot exist without law. The redemptive work of God and the means he chose for its realization contain the presuppositions and the basis for a juridical order.

1. *Preaching.* Revelation is the saving activity of God in Jesus Christ. The answer to revelation and to the offer of salvation which it contains is faith, which is essentially also obedience (Rom 1:5). Insofar as the content of revelation is intelligible, it represents a doctrine which is imposed by God upon all men. The teaching of Jesus must be retained unfalsified and conscientiously observed (Mt 28:20; Jn 17:6–8). The Christian message is the proclamation not only of the words of Jesus, but also of his life, his works and his suffering. Redemption is unthinkable without the underlying historical events of the death, burial and resurrection of Jesus. Saving faith encompasses all these actions (Rom 10:9). To substantiate the factual nature of the resurrection of Jesus, Paul offers the proof of witnesses (1 Cor 15:5–8). These historical events are an essential part of the gospel; to abandon them is to destroy Christianity (1 Cor 15:2). Since God willed to effect the salvation of mankind through the unique and unrepeatable history of Jesus Christ, his will includes the obligation of proclaiming historical facts; these facts are the norm of the contents and of the form of the preaching. The relation of preaching to these concrete historical

facts and the duty of handing on this tradition unchanged are of a juridical nature.

The juridical character of the Church's preaching is also based on the fact that it is done in the name of Christ and by his mandate. In order to be able to proclaim the resurrection of Jesus, it is not enough to be an eye-witness of his apparitions; it is also necessary to be commissioned by the risen Christ and to be empowered by the Holy Spirit (Acts 10:42; 1:8). To become a witness of Christ one must possess both an inner charismatic element, the power of the Spirit, and an outward juridical element, the authorized mission.

2. *Confession of faith.* The preaching of the salvation bestowed through Christ must correspond in content and form to the message of the witnesses of the events themselves, namely that of the apostles. The Christian communities persevere "in the teaching of the apostles" (Acts 2:42). For the preaching of the decisive events of salvation the missionaries used fixed concepts and expressions (Acts 4:10; 8:12; 9:20). Paul showed himself to be in conscious agreement with the preaching of the entire Church, not only in the general sense of what he preached but also in the very expressions and formulas he used (1 Cor 15:11, 14). Thus, preaching necessarily involves a fixed confession of faith.

Similarly, the sacramental activity of the Church cannot dispense with its efficacious performative and significant words and with fixed formulations of the faith. The Christian is dedicated to Jesus Christ in baptism; the meaning of the baptismal event makes the profession of faith in Jesus Christ and the acknowledgment of acceptance by Jesus Christ indispensable. The neophyte must acknowledge that Jesus is the Lord (Rom 10:9; Eph 4:5) and the minister baptizes in the name of the Lord Jesus (Acts 8:16; 19:5; 1 Cor 1:13). With these the necessary formulas of the baptismal creeds come about. This is also true of the trinitarian creeds (cf. Tertullian, *De Spectaculis,* 4; *Constitutiones Apostolicae,* VII, 41), and baptismal formulas (Mt 28:19; *Didache,* 7, 1–3; Justin, *Apologia,* 1, 61, 3; Tertullian, *Adversus Praxean,* 26; *Constitutiones Apostolicae,* VII, 43). Christian community worship, like the worship of the Jewish people, always embodied remembrance and praise of the great deeds of God in history. The unique, historical, and fixed character of this proof of the providence and faithfulness of God requires an established formulation. Formulas of faith, therefore, have had a place in the worship of the Christian community from the very beginning (1 Cor 12:3; cf. 2 Cor 1:20) both in the liturgy (1 Cor 16:22) and in the preaching of the word (Tit 1:9; 1 Thess 4:14ff.; 1 Cor 15:1ff.; Heb 1:1ff.; 1 Jn 1:1ff.; Acts 1:4ff.; *2 Clem,* 1, 1). They are the normative basis of both liturgy and preaching. The ordinand is required to make a profession of faith (1 Tim 6:12) and is bound to adhere to this profession (2 Tim 2:2). Thus from the beginning, there was a dogmatic tradition in the primitive Church. The formulations of the faith used by the apostles and their followers have an authoritative character; they comprise the norms of Christian teaching, and to them the following generations of Christians are bound.

3. *Tradition.* Primitive Christianity was conscious of being chosen and saved through the historically unique activity of God in Jesus Christ. It belongs to the very foundation of the Church's existence to hold fast in faith to this event and to attest and hand on the confession of faith in it. Paul bids the Corinthians to preserve the tradition which he passed on to them (1 Cor 11:2, 16). If God has covenanted himself to mankind in a binding way, mankind has the duty of accepting, attesting and transmitting faithfully the truth thus received. Each generation must hand on unchanged to the next that which it has received from the previous one (1 Cor 11:23; 15:3; 2 Tim 2:2). When the witnesses of the event of Christ transmit their experiences and their faith, they found the tradition. The obligation to hold to that which is handed on and the duty to transmit it further loyally, are, in the ecclesiastical community, of a juridical nature. Inasmuch as the recipients are bound to hand on that which they have received, they are subject to a juridical bond.

The tradition-principle is related to the hierarchical principle of Church order by the concept of succession. The direct lineage of a tradition is the guarantee of its correctness, of the soundness of teaching (2 Tim 1:13f.). The handing on of the truth is the presupposition of the authority of the teachers. Their authority is based on the fact that the teachers form a link in the chain of tradition, and that the transmittor is closer to the origin of the traditional doctrine than the recipient. The necessity of forming a link in the chain of witnesses or teachers, is of a juridical nature. The methods of active tradition and the criteria of objective tradition are likewise juridically determined.

4. *Dogma.* Those to whom the divine revelation or the doctrinal tradition of the Church is entrusted must preserve it (1 Tim 6:20); and that active preservation expresses itself in doctrinal declarations and definitions.

The revelation of a truth by God and the founding of an institutional Church implies at once, according to God's intention, the declaration of this truth officially, authentically and in a binding way by the Church. The Church has the task of formulating the faith in clear concepts, insofar as it can be comprised in true propositions, and of binding its members to the profession of such formulations. At the same time it has the right and the duty to give binding interpretations of the official declaration of the faith, to determine when teaching departs from this, and to decide finally and imperatively disputed questions. Both the authoritative declaration of the truths of faith and the authoritative decision on doctrinal questions have normative value and are of a juridical nature.

The most important expression of the ecclesiastical magisterium is the infallible definition, which is the explicit and irreformable declaration of a proposition as revealed truth. Dogma is a truth of revelation in the form of an ecclesiastical law, a law of faith. To the obligation of accepting divine revelation, there is added the obligation by virtue of ecclesiastical law.

5. *Worship.* Jesus commissioned and empowered the apostles to baptize, to celebrate the Eucharist and to forgive sins in the sacrament of penance. Only those who are commissioned and empowered can validly (or lawfully) perform these liturgical actions. In the execution of their commission and in the exercise of their authority the ministers are bound to the will of Christ; they can and must only perform these actions in the manner which the Lord has determined. When they duly carry out the commands of Christ, God works infallibly with them and through them. The imparting of grace is

linked to a fixed order determined by divine law.

This bond is especially clear in the celebration of the Eucharist. At the Last Supper, Jesus charged the apostles to continue to celebrate the meal in the future, after his death and return to the Father; he bade them do it in that form which he himself had used (Lk 22:19; 1 Cor 11:24f.). Jesus instituted the essence and the form of the celebration. Only when the disciples do what Jesus himself did, is the memorial of Jesus and his sacrificial death proclaimed, i.e., only then is the death of Jesus made present in its saving power. The Christian communities recognized that they were bound by the command to celebrate the Lord's Supper and to celebrate it in the manner instituted by Jesus himself. Only if the celebration of the Eucharist is carried out by authorized members of the Church, with the elements and words which the Lord himself used, is the command of Jesus fulfilled and the full content of the celebration guaranteed. But where the reality and the validity of a liturgical event is bound to delegated faculties and the observance of certain norms, law comes into force.

The duty to observe the command of Jesus and to hold to the form which he himself used are juridical elements, from which as the Church became clearer about the meaning of Jesus' command and of the eucharistic celebration, other norms followed, especially the injunction of worthiness. Paul saw clearly that the nature of the commemoration of the death of the Lord implied necessary consequences for behaviour of the community and of the individual. The Eucharist stands in closest relation to the last meal of Jesus. When the community eats "this bread" and drinks of the cup, it "proclaims the death of the Lord" (1 Cor 11:26), it celebrates the memory of the death of Jesus. At the same time, the Eucharist brings us into communion with the glorified Christ. "The cup of blessing which we bless, is it not a participation in the blood of Christ? The bread which we break, is it not a participation in the body of Christ?" (1 Cor 10:16.) From the knowledge that the community joins itself to the living Lord in the celebration of the Eucharist and particularly in the partaking of the food and drink, there follows the demand for worthiness on the part of the participants. Whoever takes part in the sacred meal "unworthily" makes himself "guilty of profaning the body and blood of the Lord" (1 Cor 11:27) because he does not distinguish the body of the Lord from ordinary food. Starting from the requirement of worthiness in the participants, the Church made explicit the individual elements of the requisite conditions and made them obligatory.

In a similar way the other sacraments also clearly show their intrinsic relationship to law. In the sacrament of baptism the pouring of water and the invocation of the name of Jesus brings the candidate into the fellowship of Christ's disciples (Mt 28:19; 1 Cor 12:13; Eph 5:26; Tit 3:5). The process as such is necessary for the attainment of salvation through union with Christ. Without this Christian initiation which is accomplished in baptism, the reception of the other sacraments is not possible; baptism is the prerequisite by divine right. For the efficacy of baptism, both elements of the process, contact with water and the pronouncing of the words, are indispensable. Their determination and association are elements of an institution of divine right.

In the sacrament of Orders the gift of grace is mediated by the outward juridical act of the imposition of hands (1 Tim 4:14; 2 Tim 1:6). The power thus bestowed distinguishes clerics from laymen; it either confers the office or disposes a subject for the reception of such and is thereby the basis of the juridical organizational structure of the Church.

6. *Office.* It belongs to the nature of Christianity that the divine both appears and veils itself in human form. In Christ, God has really and actively entered into history, though veiled in the form of Jesus of Nazareth, who as a child lay in a manger (Lk 2:12, 16) and was known as the son of Joseph (Lk 3:23), and as a man died hanging upon a cross (Mk 15:24f., 37). The manner in which the divine and the human are thus conjoined so that the human serves the divine, though it at the same time conceals it, runs through the whole of the redemptive work of God. It also characterizes the organization and the activity of the Church. The Church is the organ and the instrument of the kingdom of God. It is of divine origin and contains divine treasures; it is vivified and sustained by divine power. But it is also a society of men and is subject to the historical

and sociological conditions of such society, which include authority and order. The special nature of authority and order in the Church is that they are determined in their essential features by the founder of the Church himself. Jesus handed on to the apostles the mission which the Father had given to him (Mk 3:13–19); the disciples preach in his name and by his mandate (Lk 10:16). Because sent by Jesus, they can give a message which demands response, and take binding decisions.

In certain regards Jesus delegated the power which he had received from the Father to the apostles (Jn 13:20; 20:21). This delegation took place in their vocation and mission by Jesus (Mk 3:14 par.; Mt 28:19; Acts 9:27; Gal 1:15f.). A mandate given by a historical act is of a formal and therefore a juridical nature; a formal action in the past is the basis of the apostolic status and gives it a juridical character.

Jesus established in the Church a power of binding and of loosing (Mt 18:18). He thereby conferred upon the Church the power to impose obligations and to absolve from obligations, i.e., in the first place to make and abrogate laws. The exercise of the power of binding and loosing is assured of divine ratification.

The two essential elements of the constitution of the Church, the primacy and the episcopacy, go back to Jesus. From the manner of their institution or bestowal, we can conclude to their nature. The formally juridical nature of the conferring of Christ's authority is very clear in the special case of Peter. The pastoral mandate announced by Christ (Mt 16:18f.) was given to the head of the apostles before witnesses and was repeated three times (Jo 21:15–18). This public commission by Jesus is the warrant of that mission; authority rests upon a formal act of conferring. The use of a juridical formula indicates that it is the conferring of an office. An office is a stable set of rights and duties which is conferred upon someone by the competent authority and gives to the official actions of that person an objectively binding power; it is an institution which is essential and proper to law.

The Church therefore recognized from the start the existence of ecclesiastical offices. The apostles knew that they had certain powers and duties. They proclaimed the word of God and called for obedience to it

(Gal 4:14; 1 Thess 2:13; 2 Cor 5:20); they celebrated the liturgy and performed baptisms (Acts 2:41; 1 Cor 1:14), the Eucharist (Acts 20:7–11), the imposition of hands (Acts 6:6; 8:15–17; 1 Tim 4:14; 5:22; 2 Tim 1:16); they founded and ruled Churches (Acts 8:14f.; 15:2; Rom 15:15; 1 Cor 11:34; 2 Cor 10:13–16; 13:10; 2 Thess 3:4) and they exercised disciplinary and judicial functions in the Church (1 Cor 5:3–5; 1 Tim 1:20). Because of their mission, the apostles could claim the obedience of the community (Rom 15:18; 1 Cor 14:37; 2 Cor 10:18; 13:13).

These offices in the Church did not cease with the death of the apostles; they handed on their ordinary power to proclaim the word, to dispense the sacraments and to rule the Church, to other men chosen as their representatives and successors (1 Tim 4:14; 2 Tim 1:6). Those whom the apostles appointed were considered to be appointed by the Holy Spirit (Acts 20:28). The apostles acted, therefore, by the mandate of God and with his approbation. The directives which they issued for the handing on of their transferable powers have the character of divine law. "The line already drawn in *1 Clem*, 42, 4 — God-Christ-apostle-bishop — is thus not a shift in the direction of the juridical, but reflects the data of the NT." (H. Bacht, *LTK*, I, col. 738.) Thus, the hierarchical structure and the juridical nature of the Catholic Church are shown to be of divine law. To speak of the Church as juridical simply means that the Church "is bound in its outward form to a historical, and basically closed revelation and that in the essential characteristics of this outward form, as contained in Church law, it cannot be changed" (H. Barion, "Katholische Kirche", *RGG*, III, col. 1505). As our knowledge of divine law is bound up with the development of dogma as a part of revelation, growth and progress is possible in the recognition of the elements of Church organization which are of divine right, and consequently in the elaboration of the basic order of the Church.

C. Special Nature and Task of Church Law

Church law is law in an analogous sense, i.e., it is both similar and dissimilar to civil law. It is similar in that it agrees fundamentally with civil law in its nature and goal; but it is dissimilar in that it is the order of a supernatural community instituted by God.

1. *Special nature.* Church law is a spiritual law: its basic elements were determined by Christ himself. Ecclesiastical legislators are directly or indirectly authorized by revelation. Matters regulated by canon law stand in more or less close relationship to the life of grace in the mystical body of Christ.

a) *Mediation of salvation.* Church law, by its attempt to harmonize the interests of individuals and of the community, seeks to bring about peace, justice, certainty, and freedom in the Church. By preserving order, it does its part in making the Church a suitable instrument of the mysterious divine activity within it. Thus, the ultimate purpose of this order is to lead the individual to his eternal goal. Because Church law is not separable from the Church and because the visible and hierarchically ordered Church is necessary for salvation, canon law has a function in the mediation of that grace. This is true both for divine and for human law, though in different degrees and in different ways. It remains true that salvation is a free grace of God, even though the observance of law is indispensable in the attainment of salvation.

b) *Inward and outward spheres.* One characteristic feature of Church law which is of special significance is its distinction between the inward and the outward spheres *(forum externum* and *internum).* As with all forms of juridical order, Church law begins with the external. But it does not remain with the externals: it strives to give insight and awaken a free personal response. Outward and inward concerns should normally correspond. What is of decisive importance in the last analysis, however, is the inward attitude. Thus, in the case of conflict, the inward intention has precedence over the declared will. An example of such a case is the marriage consent (can. 1081, § 1; 1086). Of course the inward intention can only be relevant in law, if it can somehow be demonstrated. This is true, for example, of the *poenitentiae signa* in the question of the granting of Church burial (can. 1240, § 1) and of the repentance required for the lifting of excommunication (can. 2242, § 3). The evidence of the activity of grace in the inward sphere can mitigate in an individual case the necessary universality of the law and can take account of individual persons and circumstances. In the inward sacramental sphere, in the sacrament of penance, Church law penetrates to depths beyond the reach of civil law.

c) *Aequitas canonica.* Canonical equity consists of a higher justice, which, in its concern for the spiritual good of the whole or of an individual, may in certain cases mitigate the strictness of the law (as is most often the case) or (rarely) intensify it. The subordination of law to equity is an attempt to allow moral values to predominate over the letter of the law, and thus to realize the ideal of justice in the juridical sphere. Canon law distinguishes between *aequitas scripta* and *non scripta,* according to whether the law itself prescribes a procedure according to equity, or whether an action guided by equity is only possible by virtue of general legal principles. Equity obliges and justifies one in taking cognizance of the local, temporal, and personal circumstances of a given case. It is a dynamic principle of Church law.

d) *Particular legislation.* The *CIC* is fundamentally adapted to particular legislation, i.e., laws that are made for a certain locality or a personally defined legal group. Differences in particular laws, insofar as they are based on a necessary and legitimate adaption of principles to special circumstances and relationships, are fully justified. The Church can and must express its Catholic nature also in its legal order. It should be observed, nevertheless, that countries and continents, and therefore also the different types of communities within the Church, are coming more and more into contact as a result of improved means of communication. For this reason, the justification for particular legislation, at least of that which represents a modification of general laws, must be constantly reviewed by the competent ecclesiastical legislators. The faithful all too easily take offence at the differences in the ecclesiastical law in neighbouring countries, when they cannot see that the differences are due to varying situations or to political situations.

e) *Continuity.* Church law is the order of a spiritual community with a history of almost two thousand years. The goal remains the same, though the means may vary, within relatively narrow bounds, however, as the essential means of salvation are intrinsic to the Church. Because of this, even purely ecclesiastical law reveals a marked continuity. Furthermore, to educate the members of the Church to respect for the law and to avoid uncertainties, a certain permanence of jurid-

ical institutions is indispensable. Changes and especially inconsistencies following rapidly upon each other in the same legal sphere undermine confidence in the lawgiver and also the obedience of the subjects. Likewise, individualistic anticipations of an awaited or desired change disrupt the unity of observance. Those entrusted with the implementation of Church law easily lose sight of the entire state of legislation. The result may be defective or unworkable changes in law. Changes in law thus demand great circumspection and profound historical studies. This conservative trait of canon law, which is also an intrinsic trait of law in general, does not imply an easy-going dependence upon tradition or a blindness to necessary changes; it implies rather the preservation of the valid, the rejection of unjustifiable experiments, the quest for permanent norms, an effort to preserve continuity and creativeness while maintaining sound tradition.

2. *Tasks.* a) *The preservation of order.* The activity of the Holy Spirit in the Church does not exclude the need for law in the maintenance of right order; it is the basis of that need. Those who are appointed as shepherds of the Church by the Holy Spirit (Acts 20:28) are under the guidance of that Spirit when they make and implement laws, a guidance which in certain acts of doctrinal legislation can even preserve from error and equip with infallibility. God himself, according to revelation, sustains the human endeavour to maintain good order. In reference to the gift of prophecy, Paul writes, ". . . God is not the God of confusion but of peace" (1 Cor 14:33).

The Church laws apply to the faithful, to those who have become bearers of the Spirit through baptism and confirmation (Rom 8:9). The Spirit of God, who dwells within them, enables them to recognize the precepts and prohibitions of the law as the way of the Spirit and fulfil the demands of the law from inner conviction. Observance of the law is the fruit of redemption and of the gift of the Holy Spirit. Nevertheless, the Spirit also bestows the gift of the proper use of freedom under the law. The law of the Church does not enslave the faithful but helps them to become more and more Christian in daily life. It is a part of that imperative of the realization of salvation which in Christianity is inseparably bound to the indicative of the presence of salvation (O. Kuss).

b) *Protective function.* Church law has an essentially protective function: it has in the first place the task of guarding the purity of doctrine by fidelity to tradition. A typical expression of this function is that all teaching in the name of the Church has as its unvarying prerequisite the *missio canonica*. The task of protecting the purity of teaching is carried out also by other prescriptions of doctrinal legislation, such as the rules governing censorship and the making of professions of faith. The servants of the Church must present in their teaching not opinions but truths of faith.

The most fully worked out part of the *CIC* and the most important in pastoral work is the section on marriage laws. Its basic purpose is to preserve the sacredness of marriage and its indissolubility. The ideal is the marriage between partners of the same faith who are blessed with children.

Church law must also have a developed penal law, providing for ecclesiastical penalties and courts. Sanctions express the will to live and the desire for justice. A community which leaves unpunished those who offend against its own ideals gives the appearance of having but a low estimation of the good things it offers; it invites violation of its laws and imperils its own existence. In its system of penalties the Church shows its fidelity to the truths of revelation and the seriousness of its mission in the world. Insofar as the holiness of the Church is the moral task of its members, it is also served by the Church's penal legislation. Justice demands that the public law-breaker be recognized as such and that compensation be made for his misdeeds in the form of a restriction of his rights. One who discredits the community to which he belongs, deserves that the community in some way withdraw itself from him. Just as observance of the law is deserving of praise, so too its violation is deserving of censure. In view of the different possible violations and the degrees of responsibility involved, a gradated penal system is required to deal with them justly. Starting from the traditional penalty of excommunication, the Church has developed an organized system of penalties. The Church does not forget, however, that its mission sets a limit to punishments, and that it cannot presume to anticipate the eschatological judgment of God.

D. BINDING POWER AND LIMITS OF LAW

1. *Binding power.* The human law promulgated by the holders of ecclesiastical office of divine institution, or by their delegates, claims obedience for two reasons. In the first place their power to command derives directly or indirectly from Jesus; they stand, in a sense, in the place of God. In the second place, the common good of the Church requires the rule of law in ecclesiastical life, even in matters that appear to be of secondary importance. Just law opposes caprice and ensures due uniformity of action. How far uniformity should extend is a matter of opinion; but not its basic necessity.

Purely ecclesiastical law restricts as a rule its demands upon the faithful to a minimum. It is to mistake the meaning and the goal of the law to think that he who fulfills that law has done enough, that he has thus "fulfilled all justice". The demands of God can in individual cases reach further than the laws of the Church. The law determines what is under normal conditions indispensable for the common good and for the salvation of the individual; it fixes the lower limit. It cannot and will not set a limit upwards. It is left to the enlightened Christian conscience of the individual to determine what God requires from him here and now over and above the codified law.

Between law and love there is no real opposition; the rule of law is rather the expression of the maternal love of the Church. The most elementary and minimal effort of love must be to create order and justice, stability and freedom. This is precisely what the law seeks to realize. Love must therefore normally first fulfil the law and give to each one his due before it seeks to do something more. Conflicts between the common and the individual good are inevitable. The ensuing hardships must either be borne for the sake of the common good or may be removed or lessened by dispensation and privilege, two legal processes which exemplify the principle of the equity at law. By dispensation we mean here the removal of the obligatory character of a law in a concrete case; by privilege the institution of an exceptional rule in favour of individual need. Both measures, however, are to be used with discretion and restraint, for every deviation from the rule tends to lessen the validity of the norm, not in itself but in the eyes of those subject to the law.

Ecclesiastical law does not deprive the faithful of responsibility for their actions, but rather heightens it. It is true that the course of our personal actions is irrevocably determined by divine law, and similarly in the sphere of purely ecclesiastical legislation one is normally to presume that the law is to be followed both in its particulars and according to its letter. Nevertheless, the Christian must always take account of the circumstances of his actions; he must remember that the law represents only a minimum demand which he must complete in a spirit which accepts law not as an alien power but as an expression of his personal will. The observance of the law will not be seen as his own achievement but as the fruit of the Spirit. For Paul the new creation in Christ (2 Cor 5:17; cf. Eph 2:10, 15; 4:24; Col 3:10) is the "canon", i.e., the guideline, the rule for the behaviour of the Christian (Gal 6:15f.). Responsibility may cause the Christian to go beyond the law and do more than it commands. But it may also permit, suggest or even require that the law be disregarded. Justification for such freedom with regard to purely ecclesiastical law is: grave fear, necessity, and grave disadvantages as recognized by law (can. 2205, § 2). Another justification would be the elimination of the end envisaged by the law (cf. can. 21).

A decision against the law demands great discretion and high moral seriousness. *Epikeia* (equity, "sweet reasonableness") is a moral virtue; it measures the grounds for excusation against the weight of the law, i.e., its importance for the community and the individual. One's own relationship to the law, and especially the duty of avoiding scandal, must also be considered. The legislator denies the validity of the excuses given above when disregard of the law would lead to contempt of the faith or of Church authority or to harm to souls (can. 2205, § 3). The way of true Christian obedience lies between the extremes of a false legalism and libertinism. The Christian must guard himself from the two-fold error of believing either that he himself can attain salvation by his observance of the law or that the observance of the law is indifferent to salvation.

2. *Limits.* The law of the Church is necessary for the realization of salvation; it is the necessary condition for its mediation. Nevertheless, it is not itself the saving event or the reality of salvation. Rather, canon law is inwardly and essentially directed to a meta-canonical sphere: it has its significance and its necessity for salvation not in itself but in its transcendence towards the meta-canonical sphere (G. Söhngen).

In the framework of ecclesiastical life, canon law has a comprehensive task insofar as juridical order is always necessary; but of itself it is incapable of making an essential contribution to the life of the Church. Law does not create life but protects and maintains a life which is already present. Great expectations attached to changes in the law are usually disappointed. Too much cannot be asked of the law. On the other hand, spiritually gifted personalities have also made use of law to prepare the way for their ideas. The great reform movements in Church history have always had repercussions upon Church law. The reformers were aware that ideas need a juridical embodiment if they are to endure and be efficacious. Spiritual renewal intends, and indeed must intend, to shape the practice of ecclesiastical life and hence also ecclesiastical law. Thus, such movements as the Carolingian, Gregorian, and Tridentine Reforms have also proved to be sources of new legislative activity. They gave to the collection and systematization of canon law powerful and enduring impulses. Renewal in the Church and highpoints of juridical development generally go hand in hand. Not a few of the most eminent Popes were also capable canonists.

E. SOURCES

1. *Up to the CIC.* The most important source for the law in force up to Pentecost 1918 is the *Corpus Iuris Canonici*. It is composed of the *Decretum* of Gratian, the Decretals of Gregory IX *(Liber Extra)*, of Boniface VIII *(Liber Sextus)*, of Clement V *(Clementinae Constitutiones)* and the two collections of *Extravagantes (Extravagantes Ioannis XXII, Extravagantes Communes)*. The *Corpus Iuris Canonici* is not a code but rather a group of various collections and law books. It embraces a period of about 400 years.

The development of ecclesiastical law did not stop with the completion of the *Corpus*. The Council of Trent and the legislation of the Popes of modern times, such as Benedict XIV and Pius IX, produced much new material which was scattered in diverse sources frequently difficult of access. General need was felt for a codification, i.e., a unified, authentic summary of the current common law.

2. *The CIC*. The main source of the present law is the *Codex Iuris Canonici*. Pope Pius X began the work of codification; the new code was promulgated on 27 May 1917 and came into force on 19 May 1918. The *CIC* first appeared as Pars II of vol. 9 (1917) of the *Acta Apostolicae Sedis*. Editions of the *CIC* were published with and without references to sources. Appended to the text are various important documents. The index published with it was the work of Pietro Gasparri; Gasparri and I. Serédi published in the years 1923–39 the *Codicis Iuris Canonici Fontes*, in nine volumes. The authentic interpretations of the *Pontificia Commissio ad Codicis canones authentice interpretandos* have been collected by I. Bruno up to 1950 (1935, 1950).

The *CIC* is intended as a law book for that part of the Church which uses Latin as the language of its official worship, though it also has limited application to the communities of the Eastern rite. For the latter a separate book of law is being compiled. In spite of its many borrowings from the law of the Latin Church, justice is being done to the special characteristics of the Oriental rites.

3. *Subsequent development*. Since the *CIC* came into force, law has been steadily developing and in many respects, due to the legislative activity of the Popes and the Roman Congregations, it has gone beyond the *CIC*. One could mention here the extensive legal activity of Pius XII which broke new ground in several areas. Of special significance is the constitution concerning the election of the Pope, *Vacantis Apostolicae Sedis*, of 8 December 1945. Similarly John XXIII issued new prescriptions, e.g., concerning the administration of suburbicarian sees, the episcopal dignity, the right of option for cardinals, and supplements to the constitution on papal elections.

John XXIII announced a revision of the *CIC* on 25 January 1959, and appointed a commission for that purpose. The revision has many tasks to cope with. To bring the code abreast of the development of the last 50 years will demand many additions and changes. A greater systematization and unification of legal language is necessary; the declarations, trends and goals of Vatican II must be translated into law, as far as is possible and necessary. The Council itself laid down a sort of programme for legislation, outlining its principles, especially in its Constitution and Decrees on the Liturgy, Instruments of Social Communication, the Church, Eastern Catholic Churches, Ecumenism, Bishops' Pastoral Office, Religious Life, Priestly Formation, and the Apostolate of the Laity. Under the impulse issuing from Vatican II, Paul VI promulgated new laws, such as those concerning the powers of the bishops, and the institution of a synod of bishops. Partly in imitation of the conciliar decrees or in their implementation, Congregations of the Roman Curia have been active in legislating. The Congregation for the Doctrine of the Faith issued instructions on cremation and mixed marriages, and the SC Rit. instructions on the implementation of the Constitution on the Liturgy. Similarly particular law has been considerably increased in consequence of Vatican II and the legislation which followed it.

New treaties have been concluded between the Church and various States, such as the concordat with Spain, with the Dominican Republic and with Venezuela, the *modus vivendi* with Tunisia, and the treaty with Austria.

F. The Science of Canon Law

1. *Definition*. The science of canon law is the systematic study and presentation of the law of the Church in itself and in its historical development.

2. *Method*. Canonists employ three methods: a) the historical method which traces the development of law in connection with the entire inward and outward development of the Church; b) the dogmatic method whose task it is to show which juridical norms are binding law, to explain them and their application; c) the philosophical method which attempts to explain the relation of the individual laws to all the rest and to the legal principles themselves, and also to show the agreement between the laws and the nature and goal of the Church, thus building up a system of canon law. It is also the task of the canonist to exercise responsible criticism with regard to the laws based upon human institution, by pointing out mistaken developments and encouraging reform.

The mixture of the juristic method of formal text-interpretation in canon law with the method of logical deduction from general principles and from the theological sources of Scripture and tradition in moral theology, gaining ground ever since the 16th century, has for a long time given way to the analytical movement back to the sources.

3. *History.* Church law is as old as the Church, yet for the first eleven centuries it received no special systematic treatment; it was taught in the schools as a part of theology. The earliest method which we find in canonistic literature is almost exclusively that of a simple collection of legislative documents. In Italy in the 11th century there was a renewed interest in antiquity and especially in Roman law. The schools of jurisprudence in Bologna ushered in a period of high development of Roman law under the influence of the scholastic method which was then gaining ground.

Inspired by this example and hoping to remedy the many contradictions in Church law which had resulted from the uncritical collection of old and new, general and particular, spiritual and temporal law, the Camaldolese monk Gratian, teacher of theology in the monastery of St. Felix and Nabor in Bologna, made a new collection of church law, the *Concordia discordantium canonum,* later called the *Decretum Gratiani,* probably between 1100 and 1120. His work is really a textbook in which the commentary is woven into the text itself. Gratian had the gift of arranging existing material clearly; he was able to elaborate the guiding principles of the canons, to bring out contradictions and to find, in the spirit of canon law, the right solution for actual or apparent antinomies. He was the first to teach canon law as an independent discipline. This was the beginning of the science of canon law which was soon to be zealously studied at the new universities.

Canonistic science schooled itself in the work of composing glosses, commentaries, and summaries of the law books promulgated by the Popes, all of which were gathered together along with private collections into the *Corpus Iuris Canonici.* It was, however, also — thanks to important figures such as Popes Alexander III, Innocent III, and Innocent IV who themselves went through that schooling — in a certain sense the co-creator of canon law itself. The technically perfected and flexible *Ius Canonicum* was enforced as the common law of the whole Church, having world-wide significance next to the *Ius Civile* and forming with it up to modern times the *Ius Utrumque.*

In the period of the classical canonists, the period of the Glossators (between Gratian and Johannes Andreae, d. 1348), the system of canon law was so soundly developed that it remained determinative in the following centuries and even for present-day law. The two main divisions of study concerned the *Decretum* of Gratian, and the collections of Decretals.

In the period of the post-classical canonists, the epoch of the post-Glossators (*c.* 1350–1550), the traditional teaching was further handed on; the literature was predominantly practical.

In the period of the neo-classical canonists (*c.* 1550 to the 19th century), alongside the older and more exegetical method, a new systematic method was employed which maintained the traditional study of the original sources, but which arranged that material in a single comprehensive work. The authors of the great commentaries of this period are still today identified to some extent with the *auctores probati.*

In the 19th century there was a variety of systematic presentations of canon law, some of which are especially deserving of attention. The history of canon law made great progress.

Ever since the *CIC* came into force the systems based on the Decretals and the *Decretum* of Gratian have been definitively superseded. The method of interpretation of *CIC* was for the first time officially determined by two instructions from the Sacred Congregation of Studies dealing with teaching and examinations in view of academic degrees. The text of the *CIC* is to be studied according to the analytical exegetical method; independent synthetic presentation is excluded. The Constitution *Deus Scientiarum Dominus* of 24 May 1931, requires the application of the historical and philosophical method as well as the exegetical one for an appropriate understanding of canon law. Commentaries generally keep within the limits of practical exegesis. Not a few of them, however, try to penetrate deeper into the basic principles of law and to grasp the inner relation between the norms.

The promulgation of the *CIC* gave a great impetus to the study of canon law. The number of text-books has risen notably; a variety of monographs on the history of church law and on dogmatic aspects of law have appeared; new periodicals devoted to canon law have been launched. In France a dictionary of canon law is almost complete.

The history of canon law has received special attention. The jubilee of Gratian in 1952 gave a lively impulse to historical research. In France a new history of the Law and the institutions of the Western Church is in process of publication. In Washington in 1955, the canonist S. Kuttner founded the Institute of Research and Study of Medieval Canon Law, for the purpose of collecting and examining all the material relating to canon law in the Middle Ages. The immediate goal of this work is a survey of the present state of studies in this field and the critical edition of the works of the "Decretists" and "Decretalists", as well as a new edition of the *Decretum Gratiani* on the basis of broader source-material and modern literary criticism.

4. *Place of Church law in science.* Canonistic science, in keeping with its subject matter, stands between theology and jurisprudence. It is closely linked to theology because it derives its principles from various theological disciplines and presupposes them, e.g., dogmatics — the very basis of canonical science is the Church in its dogmatic conception and in its dogmatic juridical order; and secondly, as *theologia practica,* it completes the system of theological science. From jurisprudence canonistic science took over its formal method. And there was a far-reaching reciprocal influence between the matter of civil and canon law and between ecclesiastical and civil jurisprudence. In a word: "canonistic science is a theological discipline using the method of jurisprudence" (K. Mörsdorf).

5. *Auxiliary disciplines.* Among the auxiliary disciplines which canonistic science needs for the expounding and explanation of its principles we must distinguish between those of theology and jurisprudence. Theological auxiliaries are exegesis, which points out the elements of divine law; dogmatics, which with its dogmas is the foundation of ecclesiastical law; moral theology, which expounds the moral law as basis of ecclesiastical law; pastoral theology, which indicates how ecclesiastical law can best be implemented for the salvation of souls; and Church history and the history of liturgy, which include the description of the development of canonical institutions. The auxiliary disciplines of jurisprudence are: the study of natural law, which provides the basic concepts; Jewish law, insofar as the OT was in many respects the model for ecclesiastical institutions; Roman law, insofar as the Church often modelled itself on it, erected civil into ecclesiastical law (*leges canonizatae*) and used Roman law as a subsidiary; Germanic law, because canon law adopted various Germanic principles and institutions; constitutional and administrative law, where the Church has an established relationship to the State, and its law — as in Germany — is recognized as an element of public law; international law, insofar as State and Church meet in concordats, etc.; and finally economics, since the principles elaborated hold good to a great extent for the administration of ecclesiastical property.

G. REVISION OF CANON LAW

The Synod of Bishops which met for the first time on 29 September 1967, in Rome, laid down the following principles for the revision of canon law, and once approved of by the Pope, they will be normative for the work of the commission in question. The special nature of ecclesiastical law as the means of ordering a spiritual society is to be taken into account. The external forum is to be both kept apart from and co-ordinated with the internal. The pastoral intention is to be primary. The principle of subsidiarity is to be maintained. Personal rights are to be assured. Penal laws need to be simplified. The new law governing judicial procedures must aim at speeding up the processes of law. The division of the *CIC* is to be more strictly systematic. The spirit of love, moderation and equity is to predominate throughout. No decision has yet been taken about the three possible structures of the new code of law: a) a single codex for the whole Church, b) separate codes for the Western and Eastern Churches, or c) a basic law for the whole Church, to be completed by codes for the various Churches.

See also *Law, Authority, Order, Church, Ecclesiastical Office.*

BIBLIOGRAPHY. F. Maassen, *Geschichte der Quellen und der Literatur des kanonischen Rechts im Abendland* (1870); J. F. Schulte, *Geschichte der Quellen und der Literatur des kanonischen Rechts von Gratian bis auf die Gegenwart,* 3 vols. (1875–80); E. Friedberg, ed., *Corpus Juris Canonici,* 2 vols. (1879–81; repr. 1955); A. Salante, *Fontes Juris Canonici selectae* (1906); F. X. Wernz, *Ius decretalium,* 6 vols. (1908–15); G. le Bras, *Legacy of the Middle Ages* (1926); A van Hove, *Prolegomena* (1945); J. Leclercq, *Le fondement du droit et de la société* (3rd ed., 1947); N. Jung, *Le droit public de l'Église dans ses relations avec les États* (1948); A. Hagen, *Prinzipien des katholischen Kirchenrechts* (1949); G. Michiels, *Normae generales Iuris Canonici, Commentarius Libri I CIC,* 2 vols. (1949); S. Mayer, *Neueste Kirchenrechts-Sammlung,* 4 vols. (1953–62); G. Michiels, *Normae generales Iuris Canonici* (1954); W. Ullmann, *The Growth of Papal Government in the Middle Ages* (1955); J. Gaudemet, *L'Église dans l'Empire Romain* (1956); P. Bouchet, *Canon Law* (1958); R. F. Begin, *Natural Law and Positive Law* (1959); R. Bidagor, *Lo spirito del diritto canonico* (1959); G. May, *La potestad de la Iglesia. Análisis de su aspecto jurídico* (1960); R. Metz, *What is Canon Law?* (1960); Y. Congar and B.-D. Dupuy, eds., *L'Épiscopat et l'Église universelle* (1962); P. Fedele, *Lo spirito del diritto canonico* (1962).

Georg May

II. History of Ecclesiastical Law

The more one is concerned today to gain a personal understanding of the various aspects of the faith and of Christian life within the divinely-willed institutional framework of the Church, the less one may consider the history of canon law as a subject remote from reality and of interest only to a few specialists. A knowledge of the history of law is necessary for a fuller understanding of present-day law and jurisprudence, since these are the result of an organic development, often centuries long and influenced by the most varied exigencies of the life of communities and of society. And possibly no other branch of history reflects so directly and hence so faithfully the realities at work and the prevailing social needs. Finally, the history of canon law is in a very special way the expression of the organized social life of the Church, that is, of the life of the visible Church, which is so closely linked to the truths of faith and which indeed enters the faith itself. In this way, the history of canon law is a necessary source of knowledge of Church history in general and also of particular aspects of that history, e.g., internal and external organization, discipline, public wor-

ship, disputes, divisions, periods of decadence and movements of reform, etc. Their many legal aspects demand a knowledge of law and its history. So too the relations of the Church with the surrounding world, in the spheres of political institutions, social life, international affairs, history of religions, science in the most general sense, art, charitable works and even economics, etc., mean that a deeper knowledge of such spheres, and sometimes even the initial understanding, comes only through the history of canon law. One need only glance at the collections of ecclesiastical laws throughout the centuries to convince oneself of the wide influence of ecclesiastical law. Starting from these suppositions, we shall attempt to trace the main lines of the history of canon law and give a general view of its significance.

The history of canon law is divided into three fields of study, which, because of the difference in their objects and partly also because of the difference in their methods of treatment, can be considered separately. There is the history of the sources or the collections of laws, the history of canonistic science, and the history of the various legal institutions. Each of these will be subdivided into periods without reference to the others, for this corresponds better to the particular nature of each, though the periods sometimes coincide for two or three of the branches.

A. HISTORY OF THE SOURCES

The two main sources are the *Corpus Iuris Canonici* and the *Codex Iuris Canonici.* In the centuries preceding the former collection, compilations were inspired by the practical need of having the authoritative norms available, but even more so by other needs, among which two in particular were compelling. One was the need for a healthy uniformity in face of the centrifugal tendencies of particular law, which had been detrimental to Church unity; the other was the effort to reform Church life where it had been endangered or decadent. The multiplicity and variety and even the contradictions in the content and the form of these collections were then themselves a hindrance to the knowledge and application of the authentic norms, and compelled canonists to seek to harmonize and unify both the collections and the norms themselves. Such a service was rendered by the Camaldolese monk Gratian in his work *Concordia Discordantium Canonum* (*c.* 1142) which was to become the basis and the first part of the *Corpus Iuris Canonici*. The other parts of the *Corpus* which were the combinations of the central papal legislation (Decretals) and general theological knowledge, are the collections of Gregory IX (*Liber Extra,* 1234), of Boniface VIII (*Liber Sextus,* 1298), of John XXII (*Clementines,* 1317), and two collections of *Extravagantes,* later added to these. This *Corpus* contains the essential norms of canon law up to the *CIC*. Further compilations were limited to more or less correct critical editions of conciliar norms, papal decretals, rulings of the organs of papal government, as well as other special legislation. Such activity, however, never again resulted in a single collection. These latter compilations also included of course outdated, altered and contradictory rulings. In order to deal with this new multiplicity and the resultant difficulty of recognizing which laws were currently in force, and to eliminate the consequent uncertainties, the central authorities undertook, after various private attempts, to "codify" the valid law of the whole Church, i.e., to re-classify it and to publish it in a new form corresponding to modern codes of law. This was done at Pentecost 1917. The reform of the *CIC* ordered by John XXIII deals less with the form of the legislation than with its content. This is to be brought abreast of new conditions, and must now be guided by the disciplinary decrees and the general directives of Vatican II.

B. THE SCIENCE OF CANON LAW

This treats not only of the systematic study of the ecclesiastical laws in their principles and concrete forms, with enumeration, explanation, and application; but it also deals with the methods of the science of law, the literary genres of research and presentation, the life and work of the various canonists, the organization of studies and teaching institutes, the various doctrinal trends, and relationships to other disciplines. In the first thousand years of the Church there was no canonistic science in the proper sense. It was Gratian, who by treating the existing valid canonical texts in the light of jurisprudence, and as an independent subject, laid

the foundations of canonistic science strictly speaking. The resulting school of the Decretists, and that of the Decretalists who studied papal legislation, represent the first great stages of the development of the science. They produced the classical canon law and are rightly called the classical canonists. In their approximately 200-year long activity (1150–1350), based on international centres — especially Bologna, Paris, the Rhineland, and the Anglo-Norman territories — they produced, at least in essential features, a complete and methodically structured system, the Decretal law (so called because of the sources which mainly employed the Decretals). This is still the basis of Church law. Then followed a period of imitative work by the Post-Glossators, or Conciliarists, lasting for almost 200 years, which only produced summaries of existing law and applied it to new cases. The period following the Council of Trent and its disciplinary reforms is called the neo-classical or golden age. It produced the great commentaries, characterized in part by new and independent methods of presentation. Every competent canonist must know them and make use of them, according to the rules of interpretation given by can. 6. There were also summaries *(Institutiones),* introductions, monographs and historical works. The latter, together with the works imitating the format of civil law on the "public and private" law of the Church and presentations of the laws governing State Churches, owe their origin either to movements towards national and State Churches which were antagonistic to the Church, to the Enlightenment and the philosophical systems linked to it, and also to the internal disputes such as Episcopalism and the apologetical efforts which it provoked. While the substance of canonistic teaching suffered in many ways from all these influences, the science as a whole gained through a deepening of its historical and philosophical elements and through the progress of the theory of civil law both in regard to content and to form. The nadir of canonistic science was in the 19th century, in which the confusion and multiplicity of systems obscured above all the presentation, already made extraordinarily difficult by the state of the sources and the difficulty of access to them. This period ended with the edition of a unified codex. This did not, however, lead to a rejuvenation of canonistic

155

studies, as they remained more or less confined to purely practical exegesis. One can expect a new impetus from the reform of canon law which is already under way, and which will affect the very substance of the laws.

C. History of the Legal Institutions

This third section treats of the development of the ecclesiastical norms themselves. It treats of the development of individual legal institutions and groups of regulations formed around a general subject matter in the fields of constitutional law, legislation, judicature, exercise of authority, disciplinary measures, the administration of Church affairs in the broadest sense of this canonical expression, i.e., including the sacraments, liturgical matters, teaching, etc.

Authors are not agreed upon the division of this section into periods. According to the present state of research, however, it appears that the most practical schematization is that proposed by U. Stutz, which though variously interpreted by other authors, is generally retained in its essential chronological divisions. Thus we distinguish a) the development of law in the Church of the first three centuries; b) the period from the 4th to the 7th and 8th centuries which was marked by a definite influence from Roman law; c) the period from the 7th and 8th centuries to the 12th, characterized by Germanic influence; d) the following period marked by scientific study and systematization of ecclesiastical law by the "classical" scholastics, and the legislation of the Popes (12th to the 14th century); e) the period dominated by reform legislation, especially that of the Council of Trent and of the papal organs which implemented and continued these reforms (15th to the 18th century); f) finally the period of legislation necessitated by the rise of various anti-ecclesiastical and anti-religious movements extending from the 18th century to the present. g) We may add that a new and important period has just begun with the decrees of Vatican II and the reform of the codex now proceeding.

The presentation of this inner development of Church law presents great difficulties: the extent of the material, the variety of legal institutions, and the changes which have ensued through harmonization, abrogation, exclusion, or new legislation, would demand too much space to give even a summary historical account of development. An even greater difficulty presents itself because of the fact that large areas have not been explored at all. Hence certainty is impossible, till scientific monographs are available on the main institutions. Though we shall nevertheless attempt a sketch of the history here, it will only be a characterization of each period according to its main lines, and with due reserves.

1. *The early Church.* In this period we can observe the emergence of the basic forms of Church constitution and its deliberate organization as "public law": in its hierarchy, the monarchial episcopacy, the division without loss of conscious unity into dioceses and provinces. The elements of divine right emerged more clearly, along with those of apostolic origin, and there was a constant growth in positive law elaborated by ecclesiastical authorities. Custom was gradually transformed into law, and private institutions emerged. As the influence of civil legislation was slight, owing to the hostility of the State toward the Christian religion, the Church developed its own juridical concepts in the light of its own essential structures. But it also freely adopted such elements of civil law as seemed suitable to its purposes.

2. *The influence of Roman law.* The freedom which the Church attained in the 4th century and its power of assimilation made it possible for the Church to develop its juridical forms freely in every direction and to put them effectively into practice. Roman law, so fully developed in many ways, could be used as a model. Indeed, the Church was in some measure forced to adopt elements of that law, especially in the East. This influence had such an effect upon ecclesiastical juridical development that the period can truly be characterized as Roman in its stamp and orientation, though it was always properly ecclesiastical law in the sense that all forms of obligation were consciously based on the authority of the Church. The marriage laws illustrate this convincingly.

This period also witnessed the development, to a great extent based on Roman models, of the territorial organization and administration of the Church, judicial procedure and penal law, personal and real law, and also the monarchical form of authority. The latter was due partly to the demands of divine law, and partly to the influence of Roman law which in this case corresponded with primordial ecclesiastical structures; the monarchical structure constantly gained ground against surviving democratic elements. The whole of Church government became more markedly centralized: the sole ordinary authority in the diocese was the bishop, in the province the metropolitan, in the patriarchate the patriarch, in the entire Church the Roman Pontiff. Stress was laid on the public character of the whole of Church life, which thus received a strongly community-centred character. The effect was deeply felt, for example, in worship, in administration, and in the reception of the sacraments (the penitential discipline is an especially good example of this). The life of prayer was also "social". All this placed a special emphasis on authority as such and the abstract notion of ecclesiastical office as a function. The entire legislation for property, clearly determined as it is by public ends, is also largely influenced by this legal conception.

3. *The influence of the Germanic legal structure.* Even after the dissolution of the Roman Empire, which had so providentially served the initial spread of the Church, the Church continued to live according to Roman law among the new Germanic kingdoms. Only with the 7th and 8th centuries did Germanic law begin to influence the ecclesiastical sphere. This was due to the mass conversions of the Germanic peoples and their chiefs, the close bond between the secular and ecclesiastical powers, the fact that ecclesiastical rulers were also secular princes, the close relationship of Pope and Emperor, and finally the long period of papal decline and the poor state of scholarship in the Church. Another notable influence was that emanating from the missionary activity of the insular Churches (Ireland, England, and parts of Northern France).

Under these influences canon law assimilated quite varied and sometimes quite foreign elements which radically altered the legal structure of the Church in many respects. It has been asserted — and in many ways rightly — that the law of the Church became unduly "real", insofar as the feudal laws and the laws of benefices, which not only dominated the whole law of property but also the laws concerning ecclesiastical offices and the personal laws connected with them, were strongly concerned with material goods. This concern overshadowed the essentially spiritual nature of ecclesiastical offices. The relation between *principale* and *accessorium,* between end and means was reversed, the whole of Church life was too much subjected to temporal concerns; it became worldly and materialistic; the subject was made to serve the object. Secular princes and the laity exercised an excessive and decisive influence in Church matters, in their own temporal interests. Finally, the clergy itself was "secularized". The legal structure of the Church in this period seemed, therefore, because of these extraneous elements, to be less properly ecclesiastical; older elements were transformed into their contraries, or at any rate largely overlaid with new ones.

The diocesan organization was broken up by the chorepiscopate, the archdeaconate, the archpresbyterate, the deanery, and by a system of benefices outside episcopal control. Episcopal authority was fragmentated or divided, or limited by autonomous authorities, e.g., chapters, exempt territories, or immunities. What authority remained was strongly coloured by Germanic custom. In place of the monarchical centralization of authority, Church government underwent a decentralization which was due not only to the multiplicity of clerical administrators just mentioned, but also to their independence by virtue of the real law of property. Thus there were a large number of ordinary administrative offices besides the episcopate. The metropolitan structure also decayed and could neither arrest nor assimilate this development in the dioceses.

In such a climate the community character of Church life fell more and more a victim to subjective and individualistic attitudes, while public law so pronounced in the previous period, increasingly gave way to concepts and practices of private law. The Germanic concept of the sovereignty of the people, and the interest in private associations gave rise to various democratic elements, e.g., the chapters, the confraternities, pious associations, orders, etc. Personal law determined the juridical relationships of the various groups: courtiers, vassals, ministers and cities had their own laws, all of which of course furthered even more the particularism which had affected ecclesiastical law. Germanic elements also penetrated judicial procedure, e.g., the extensive use of oaths, the ordeal, certain forms of testimony, publicity of procedure; in penal law ecclesiastical excommunication entailed a civil ban. Penances could be replaced by monetary gifts or performed by substitutes, etc. Besides the completely changed form of property laws, this period also saw the introduction of stipends on the occasion of spiritual functions and ministries, e.g., stole fees and other taxes, the *regale,* etc. Naturally there was a similar development in the administration of the sacraments (private penance, marriage impediments, etc.), participation in the public worship, and the life of piety. Personal law was also affected by the same sort of real law which governed the holding of office, though on the other hand it was also enriched by the new forms of ecclesiastical legislation for chapters, confraternities, religious orders, etc.

Though a richness and variety of new juridical elements and institutions were brought into the Church, it is also clear that Church life and discipline suffered. Many things were not taken over organically; some of them in fact could not really be assimilated at all as they were too foreign to the Church's spirit, structure, and tradition. The situation could only be dealt with by the supreme authority in the Church, the universal papal jurisdiction, which, when it had recuperated its strength undertook the work of reconstruction which has since become known as the Gregorian Reform. This reform, as seen from the viewpoint of the history of canon law, had deeper and broader roots as well as much more extensive significance for the whole of Church life than is generally supposed. It eliminated — unfortunately often by violent means which did much harm to the Church — the absolutely incompatible elements, and assimilated definitively all that was in any way tolerable.

4. *Development from the 12th to the 14th century.* The inner organic fusion of all these elements into a unified and coherent system in which the private institutions could be made to correspond with the general body of legislation and in which all the individual elements would be clarified, unified, and permanently organized according to their nature, forms, and function — all this comprised the scholarly labour which the universal legislative activity of the Popes at first supported, and then actively led. This systematic elaboration of canon law in its entirety came about from the 12th to the 14th century. This "Decretal law" was scientifically studied, purged of essential obscurities and inconsistencies and moulded into universal law, in spite of the diversities of its origin. Its binding force was specified as universal, particular, exceptional or privileged. Its interpretation and development were given solid bases by the distinction between unalterable (natural, or positive divine) and other law, and by the clear definition of legislative organs. Since the universal authority of the Pope was effective in practice and accepted doctrinally, this universal ecclesiastical law was also papal law.

The direct and indirect influence of papal law can be seen from another factor which figured in the creation and modification of law, growing in strength from the 13th century on. This was the statutory law of the new religious orders, especially the mendicant ones. Their democratic but centralized organization and their apostolic activity reflected the general juridical order, because they followed consistent directives and led faculties from the Pope. Their direct pastoral ministry transformed the passive and local exemption of monks and convents into external activity and so destroyed the remnants of diocesan centralization still surviving in the parishes. This process was furthered by the permanent association of laymen with religious through the institution of "Third Orders", confraternities and other pious sodalities under the control of the orders. Through the centralized and unified government of the orders, their papal faculties, and their juridical status, the crumbling diocesan and territorial centralization was restored on a higher level — that of the universal and centralized papal authority, which could appeal to a primacy of divine institution. Thus the way was prepared for reform, which, in spite of setbacks to the central government of the Church (decline of the papacy in the Avignon period, the Western Schism, the Conciliarist theory), could only be carried out by this authority.

5. *Reform legislation: the Council of Trent.* Reform of ecclesiastical law had become

necessary not only because of the break-up of the political and social order of the Middle Ages and the totally new situations which had then to be catered for, but also because of grave disturbances and upheavals within the Church. These were set on foot by heresies of a more practical than speculative nature, and when they became movements which detached Christians from the universal Church, had permanent effects on its whole future history. At the same time, no doubt the Church gained other adherents in the New World, but there an intense missionary effort was to meet new problems.

The reforming efforts of the old Church finally found an effective expression in the Council of Trent. Besides the solution of dogmatic questions on matters of faith, it was to determine the principles of the reform and the new order of Church life. The local authority of the bishops was, with the help of the universal authority of the Pope, effectively restored; new directives placed the selection, formation, and discipline of the secular and religious clergy on a sounder and more modern basis; the functions of the clergy were adapted to the needs of the times. This was done in every sphere of organization: the administration of the sacraments, religious instruction, government, and the administration of property. Abuses with regard to benefices, still possible and hence temporarily rife under Decretal law, were attacked at the roots, so that the priority of the office and the subordinate role of ecclesiastical property were in fact recognized and preserved. The unwieldly formalism of legal procedure was simplified (smaller panels of judges, summary proceedings, trials or rulings *ex informata conscientia*) and by the elimination of the delays caused by the possibility of appeals. The bishop gave judgment as legate of the Pope, and could no longer be simply passed over in administrative procedures. These principles were implemented and further developed after the conclusion of the Council by the permanent officials of the papal government, which guaranteed the necessary internal and external uniformity. The main agents were the Congregation of the Council (so named after the Council) which functioned till the reform of the Curia in 1967. It is now the *Congregatio pro Clericis*.

The missionary activity of the Church opened a new and extensive area for the development of Church law. The discovery of new peoples in need of evangelization and the need to re-convert the separated Christians demanded a new approach. The work was first carried on by the new religious orders, in a non-co-ordinated way, with or without assistance from secular rulers. But it was then taken in hand by the Holy See itself and given directives through the newly-founded Congregation for the Propagation of the Faith. In the Spanish and Portuguese conquests, the royal right of patronage meant that the older juridical order was often applied, especially in the Americas. But in all other countries directly under its jurisdiction Propaganda elaborated a special missionary legislation which took local conditions, stages of development and national peculiarities into account. Thus was created the legal system of Propaganda which differed in many respects from that of the Decretals and its developments. As the missionary activity was organized on a uniform basis, and its hierarchical heads excercised their functions in the name of the Holy See, the norms, as the Church desired, were central, uniform and flexible, directed to immediate pastoral needs. They were not linked, much less subordinated, to the laws governing property. The existence of the central authority meant that new problems could be envisaged in the light of harmonious development and new needs. This new legislation necessarily reacted on Decretal Law and its post-Tridentine development, since the same supreme central authority directed both, but above all because missionary territories, when ready for it, were incorporated into the ordinary ecclesiastical jurisdiction, and could not, of course, renounce their existing law. Thus, missionary law gradually penetrated Decretal Law at many points.

6. *The Enlightenment (18th century) and the following period.* The new teachings of the Enlightenment, rationalism, liberalism, legal naturalism and positivism, the exaggerated forms of political absolutism, as well as the subsequent democratic trend of state leadership and of public life — all this marked deeply the thought and the life of the time and could not but have a profound effect upon ecclesiastical life. The concrete manifestations of these new attitudes were the State Church, even in countries which remained Catholic

(under Gallicanism and Josephinism); a growing estrangement between Church and State, and finally their separation; conflicts within the Church such as those provoked by the modern movements of Episcopalism and Febronianism, together with the trend towards the formation of national Churches. Inroads, sometimes grave, of temporal rulers into the ecclesiastical sphere, individualism and reactionary democratic elements, were very detrimental to Church discipline, and especially to ecclesiastical authority and its practical recognition. But they were also the occasion of considerably greater freedom, e.g., in the administration of the sacraments, as well as of further development of the laws for religious, penal law, etc. New zeal prompted the defence of the rights of the Church, of the faith, and of the genuine spiritual life of the faithful. The Church sought to cope with the new situation by an active bilateral concordat-legislation, by further intensification of pastoral care by both higher and lower clergy and by an even stricter spiritualization of the ecclesiastical law of property as well as of penal law.

In the course of these endeavours many of the more strict and formal prescriptions of the law were replaced by more flexible ones better adapted and adaptable to the new situations. However, this revision of internal and external relationships in such a necessary process of defence and reconstruction had the effect of further strengthening centralization. In the same way the newly-founded religious communities moved towards an even more pronouncedly monarchical, hierarchical and centralized organization, with special emphasis on the apostolic activities of pastoral care, schools, care of the sick and other works of Christian charity, and also on missionary activity. This naturally brought with it a corresponding harmonization of the laws affecting religious, which in turn reacted on general ecclesiastical law. In this period of development, the Church, which had once allowed itself to be influenced, positively or negatively, by the almost universal Roman law, could not but be influenced by modern State law, which was being progressively codified since the 18th century. All in all, it may be said that the spiritualization of the whole Church law, pursued since the Tridentine period, was decidedly advanced in this period.

7. *Vatican II.* This Council, pastoral in its whole outlook, initiated an entirely new period for the history of canon law. Though it produced no new formal innovations in law, it nevertheless specified in its constitutions, decrees and declarations, the principles and directives which are to determine the reform of the Codex already in progress as well as the substance of ecclesiastical law. We need only refer to the constitutional aspects of the constitution on the Church, on the synod of bishops, and especially on the episcopal conferences; the important decrees on the office of bishops, the life and work of the priest, the deaconate as an independent office, religious, the place and the apostolate of the laity, the education and formation of priests, missionary activity, relations to other rites, separated Christian brethren and non-Christian religions; religious freedom, public worship, the sacraments and their administration, the means of forming public opinion in the Church. The elimination of the benefice system from ecclesiastical laws on property and offices, the decisions on the attitude of the Church to the problems of modern society and culture — these in particular will have lasting effects. Here it is especially clear that the history of canon law is important for the proper assessment of the present juridical order.

See also *Church History, Ecclesiastical Law* I, III, *Gallicanism, Episcopalism, Reform, Curia.*

BIBLIOGRAPHY. P. Fournier and G. le Bras, *Histoire des collections canoniques en occident depuis les fausses décrétales jusqu'au Décret de Gratien,* 2 vols. (1931/32); I. Zeiger, *Historia Iuris Canonici, II: Historia Institutorum Canonicorum* (1940); A. M. Stickler, *Historia Iuris Canonici Latini,* I: *Historia fontium* (1950); B. Kurtscheid, *Historia Iuris Canonici. Historia Institutorum,* I: *Ab Ecclesiae fundatione usque ad Gratianum* (2nd ed., 1951); G. le Bras, ed., *Histoire du droit et des institutions de l'Église en Occident,* 1: *Prolégomènes* (1955); H. E. Feine, *Kirchliche Rechtsgeschichte,* I: *Die katholische Kirche* (3rd ed., 1955); G. le Bras, *Institutions ecclésiastiques de la Chrétienté médiévale,* in: *Histoire de l'Église,* ed. by A. Fliche and V. Martin. vol. XII (1959 ff.); W. Plöchl, *Geschichte des Kirchenrechts,* 4 vols. (1959–66); C. Duggan, *Twelfth-Century Decretal Collections and Their Importance in English History* (1963); J. Gaudemet, *Droit canonique. Introduction bibliographique à l'Histoire du Droit et à l'Ethnologie juridique* (1963); *Études d'histoire du droit canonique dédiées à Gabriel le Bras,* 2 vols. (1965).

Alfons M. Stickler

III. Code of Canon Law

A. HISTORY

At the time of Vatican I there was a general recognition of the need for a summary and revision of canon law. Legislation was dispersed in many different collections and this gave rise to uncertainty about the status of current law. The most important source was still considered to be the *Corpus Iuris Canonici;* but this included norms long superseded, changed, outdated, or doubtful. The reform begun by Trent was decisively influenced by papal legislation and by the Congregation of the Council which brought to maturity the reforms of Trent. The rulings and jurisprudence of the Roman Curia, the *vigens Ecclesiae disciplina,* became more and more the norm of ecclesiastical life, and the text-books and commentaries of the *probati auctores* took the place of the missing code.

In his concern for pastoral problems, Pius X undertook the difficult work of codification. In his motu proprio of 19 March 1904, *Arduum Sane Munus,* he announced his plan and indicated the basic lines of its implementation. Obsolete laws were to be abrogated and a code modern in content and form was to be drawn up. The composition of the commission which was entrusted with the work of codification changed often in the course of the years, but its head remained the same: Pietro Gasparri, first secretary of the special commission of Cardinals, and then after his elevation to the cardinalate the *relator* of the commission. The bishops and the Catholic universities were asked to co-operate, and as the draft of the first part was finished it was laid before the bishops for criticism and comment. Certain areas which were in special need of reform were treated before the rest in the years 1908 to 1910 (reform of the curia, matrimonial law, removal of parish priests). These reforms showed that the codification was in progress, though as yet in strict secrecy. It had progressed so far that neither the death of Pius X nor the outbreak of the First World War could seriously hinder its completion. Benedict XV, in a private Consistory of 4 December 1916, announced the completion of the Codex; on Pentecost, 27 May 1917, the *Codex Iuris Canonici (CIC)* was promulgated by the bull *Providentissima Mater Ecclesia,* though the solemn act of promul-gation took place only on the vigil of Sts. Peter and Paul. The Codex came into force on Pentecost, 19 May 1918. It originally appeared as *Pars II* of vol. 9 of the *Acta Apostolicae Sedis* (1917). Subsequent editions were issued with and without a supplement indicating the sources in the older law. Cardinal Gasparri composed the preface and analytical index.

The *CIC* is the lawbook only of the Latin Church, though it also has limited applicability to the Eastern Churches. The Latin Church and the Eastern Churches, as parts of the one Church, are in constant relationship to each other, and if the *CIC* intended to regulate the order of the Latin Church in the most complete manner possible, it had also to include the relation of the Latins to the Orientals and vice versa. These questions of inter-communion were regulated according to the principle of the equality of all rites.

The success of the Holy See in its codification of the law of the Latin Church prompted it to undertake the much more difficult task of codifying the law of the Eastern Churches. The work was begun by Pius XI in 1929 by the appointment of a commission of cardinals which was headed by Pietro Gasparri until his death in 1934. In the following years two additional commissions were appointed, one to prepare drafts and the other, composed of scholars from every rite, to collect the sources for oriental law. This work had already been in progress, however, for as early as 1930 the first volume of the collected sources appeared and this was followed in 1935 by a second series, and in 1943 by a third. The series now totals over forty volumes. On 17 July 1935 the preparatory commission of cardinals became the *Pontificia Commissio ad redigendum Codicem Iuris Canonici Orientalis.* As was done in the preparation of the Latin code, the drafts were laid before the hierarchy of the Eastern Churches. Meanwhile, important sections of the oriental *CIC* were promulgated: the marriage laws through the motu proprio *Crebrae Allatae* of 22 January 1949; the rules for judicial procedure by *Sollicitudinem Nostram* of 1 January 1950; the laws for religious and property, and the definition of important terms by *Postquam Apostolicis Litteris* of 9 February 1952; and constitutional law by *Cleri Sanctitati* of 6 June 1957. These were all published in

Latin, though official translations in Greek, Slavonic, Arabic, and Egyptian are provided for.

B. Revision of Older Law

The codification was undertaken in order to replace the confusing variety of source material with a *fons unicus* of canon law. The revision of older law was carried out with the greatest circumspection. In the sphere of customary laws, the *CIC* was concerned only with customs *contra legem* and left those *praeter* and *secundum legem* untouched. Customs contrary to the *CIC* were abrogated insofar as they were expressly revoked in the *CIC;* those not revoked, which were either centuries-old or from time immemorial, could be tolerated. All universal or particular law contrary to the *CIC* was revoked, except where special provision was made for particular laws. All penalties based on custom were abrogated. Other general laws in force up to the *CIC,* which were neither expressly nor equivalently contained in it were abrogated, with the exception of the disciplinary laws in the liturgical books.

The laws which were revoked continue to be of importance for the interpretation of the *CIC.* The following three rules apply: a) canons which embody older law unchanged are to be interpreted in the light of the older law and hence on the basis of the commentaries of the *auctores probati;* b) canons which correspond only in part to the older law are to be interpreted according to the older law insofar as they agree with it and according to their text insofar as they diverge; c) in cases of doubt as to whether a prescription of the *CIC* is a departure from the older law, the latter is to be followed. Continuity is thus assured in a large measure. The older law, though formally abrogated, lives on in substance in the *CIC,* and the conservative spirit of canon law means that the transition from the old to the new is not to be considered as an abrupt change but as a continuous development to meet modern needs. Rights which accrued to physical or juridical persons under the older law, as well as privileges and indults granted by the Holy See and still enjoyed when the *CIC* came into force, remained in force insofar as they were not expressly revoked. The concordat law which was in force at the time of the codification is retained as before and remains untouched by the changes in ecclesiastical law.

C. Analysis

Like the medieval collections of Decretals, the *CIC* is divided into 5 books; the system of division, however, is different. The *CIC* is prefaced with the *Professio Catholicae Fidei.* Book I, *Normae Generales,* contains besides the introductory principles, norms on law, and on custom as a source of Church law, on the reckoning of time, and on rescripts, privileges, and dispensations. Book II, *De Personis,* contains constitutional law and is divided into three sections, *de clericis, de religiosis, de laicis.* Book III, *De Rebus,* covers various matters: the sacraments in six sections including the sacramentals (Part I), holy places and times (Part II), the liturgy (Part III), the magisterium (Part IV), benefices (Part V), and Church property (Part VI). In the first schema the material of Book III was divided into two different books, one devoted to the sacraments. Book IV, *De Processibus,* describes in the first part ecclesiastical courts and the ordinary canonical procedures, and then adds supplements on cases dealing with penalties, matrimony and holy orders, and the rules for estopping legal processes. The second part deals with the process of beatification and canonization, the third with certain proceedings against clerics. Book V, *De Delictis et Poenis,* deals with penal law; Parts I and II may be said to deal with the law, and Part III with specific penalties. The systematization of the *CIC* can be considered on the whole successful, though in individual instances it leaves much to be desired. It is unfortunate, for example, that the laws concerning offices are split into general doctrine on ecclesiastical offices (Book II) and laws concerning benefices (Book III). Similarly, in some of the smaller sub-divisions the systematic order of the material is not always a happy one and often makes it difficult to follow the mind of the legislator.

D. Language of the *CIC*

The consultors were enjoined to use a Latin which would correspond to the dignity of sacred law, as had been so successfully achieved in Roman law. This requirement was largely fulfilled. There is scarcely a trace in the *CIC* of the turgidity which characterized earlier Church laws. Its formulations are usually "clear, straightforward and simple, brief and to the point, sonorous and expressive", and it may well be considered "a classical example of modern Latin" (Köstler, p. 9). The style of the *CIC* sometimes departs notably from classical Latin, less in the form than in the syntax. But this is not a fault and is hardly surprising considering that between classical and present-day ecclesiastical Latin there is a development of nearly two thousand years. Measured against such a span of time the departures are slight. However, the language of the *CIC* also has its defects; these are less a matter of unevenness in style as of a disturbing certainty in terminology. One expects clear and definite decisions from a code, and one of the most important conditions of such clarity is an unwavering adherence to a fixed terminology. The legal language of the Church acquired in the course of time a great number of technical terms which in this epoch had a special sense. This was later partly modified, partly obscured or even completely changed. Nonetheless, outmoded expressions were further employed, so that there was scarcely a single concept for which there were not several expressions, and scarcely one technical term which did not include several concepts. Another difficulty — with which every great legislative work has to contend — was the number of consultors employed, each of whom of course contributed his own colouring to the language. The state of the terminology as a whole is thus not a very happy one. Promising steps towards a clarification of legal language which have been made in some sections of the Codex were rendered ineffective by the use of more antiquated expressions in other sections — and sometimes even in the same section. Almost all technical terms are used now in one sense, now in another, and conversely several expressions are used to designate one and the same thing. One peculiarity of the *CIC* is the number of legal definitions, which often read like the headings in a text-book. This was due to the fact that the legislator, in the face of such terminological confusion, had to begin with a definition of terms to make himself understood. There is no doubt that the law gained in clarity by this practice

and that the technical language of canonists will benefit by it. Unfortunately, the legislator in many instances did not keep to his own definitions, which greatly lessened their value as rules of interpretation. The inconsistency of the terminology forces the canonist to avoid all formalism in his interpretations, and always to take as his guiding-line the spirit and the purpose of the law.

E. The *CIC* and Modern Developments

In order to safeguard the degree of uniformity attained in the *CIC,* the motu proprio of 25 September 1917, *Cum Iuris Canonici,* directed that a pontifical commission of cardinals be set up for the authentic interpretation of the *CIC* (this commission will hereafter be referred to as PCI). The Congregation of Cardinals was to issue no new *decreta generalia* except in urgent cases, and to limit itself ordinarily to *instructiones,* which however, in practice, proved to be more than mere directives for implementation. The commission was also empowered to insert necessary changes or additions into the text of the *CIC.* Except for two alterations, one concerning the requisite form of matrimony (can. 1099, § 2) and the other the penalty for bigamy (can. 2319, § 1, n. 1), the text of the *CIC* has remained unchanged. Nevertheless, the law laid down in the *CIC* has undergone a further development. The greatest contribution came from the authentic interpretations of the PCI, which have become almost as extensive as the code itself. And even in the authentic explanation of individual canons important development can be noted, e.g., in the question of the estopping of the right to sue in cases of nullity of marriage (can. 1971, § 1), and in the admissibility of marriages contracted without a priest in case of necessity (can. 1098). Here the value of the co-operation of theologians and legislators was proved once more, as in the classical age of canon law. The Roman Congregations also had a share in this development, though they are not competent to give authentic interpretations. The judicial procedures laid down for cases dealing with marriage and holy orders by the Congregation for the Sacraments helped the new courts set up by the Code to function, and also contributed to the development of the law. We must also mention the reform of theological studies by the constitution *Deus Scientiarum Dominus* of 24 May 1931, which significantly supplemented the *CIC* in a matter of decisive importance for the life of the Church. On the whole it must be said that the codification of canon law did not impede development, but rather aided it. The science of canon law also derived great benefits from the Codex, partly by learning from the defects of the *CIC* how much work still lay before it. The new emphasis upon the theological bases of canon law and the promising efforts made in the direction of a new systematization have given a new cast to the science of canon law in our time.

F. Reform of the *CIC*

On 25 January 1959, John XXIII announced the convocation of a Roman diocesan synod and of an Ecumenical Council, expressing his desire for a much needed modernization *(aggiornamento)* of the *CIC* which would crown the work of the synods. The *Prima Synodus Romana* (1960) did not give any new impetus towards the reform of the *CIC*, but Vatican II had lasting results. In fundamental constitutional questions decisions of far reaching consequence were made (collegiality of the bishops, the place of the laity, relation to the other Churches and ecclesiastical communities, the principle of religious freedom, etc.). In other questions the Council gave general and also more specific directives for the reform of the *CIC*. The Council was not able to consider all the proposals for reform presented by the bishops. The preparatory commissions and the Council commissions made numerous proposals for the revision of various laws which will eventually contribute to the work of reform. Questions which seemed to be of urgent concern were dealt with, if only provisionally, by papal decrees (jurisdiction of bishops, changes in the structure of the college of cardinals, the eucharistic fast, penitential discipline, mixed marriages, indulgences).

In 1963 John XXIII appointed a commission of cardinals, with Cardinal P. Ciriaci as head, for the revision of the *CIC* (with 21 members); Paul VI added 21 members in 1965 (among whom were 3 patriarchs of the Eastern Churches) and in 1964 appointed to it a group of 70 consultors.

The inclusion of the patriarchs is an indication that the as yet incomplete Oriental *CIC* is also concerned in the reform. The difficulties which some Eastern groups had in accepting the parts of the Oriental code already promulgated were to be seriously considered; for in view of the differences in discipline of the various Eastern Churches it is impossible for them to use a standardized *CIC* based on the Latin model which had in fact been largely used. This led to uniformity but not to unity. It is imperative to give expression to the consciousness of the unity of the Church which was awakened at the Council, by the drawing up of a constitution or basic law which only contains what is essential and characteristic for the entire Church, beyond any differences of rite. Such a basic law is necessary also from the ecumenical viewpoint, as by showing what must be retained for the sake of unity, it reveals the possibility of autonomous legislation in the local Churches. This should also be important for the future development of law in the Latin church.

Future law should therefore emphasize the freedom of the Orientals as regards purely Latin organs of legislation, administration and judiciary. And in general in view of the efforts towards the reunion of the Churches, one can hardly overestimate the importance of separating the administration of the Church Universal from the administration of the Latin Church. With the institution of the episcopal synod and the Secretariats for Christian Unity and for non-Christians, the first steps have already been taken towards the institution of organs representative of the universal Church. The separation of legislative, administrative, and judicial powers should be as complete as possible.

The decentralization accompanying the restoration of episcopal rights requires safeguards at law, and this may be achieved by the establishment of a judicial body (with three courts of appeal: the metropolitan, the episcopal conference or patriarch, the Holy See) for the examination of administrative acts, according to the model of the old *appellatio extraiudicialis* (which was abolished only by the *CIC*). In general, the legal safeguards of the personal dignity of Christians, clerics as well as laity, need to be made much ampler and stronger. Ecclesiastical penalties have to a great extent lost their function of maintaining the social order of the Church, and have become an institution affecting practically only the regions of conscience. The reasons for this lie partly in the change in the relationships between Church and State, in the changes in social relationships generally, and partly in the fact that the distinction between *inner* and *outer forum* which grew out of penitential practice is no longer understood, and is now equated with the distinction between law and conscience. The functional relationship between ecclesiastical penalties and public life needs to be reviewed. *Ad intra* it is a question of whether the Church is strong enough and determined enough to impose such penalties on its members. *Ad extra,* it is the question of how far the Church is competent to enforce effectively its claim on public life, in face of State and society.

See also *Ecclesiastical Law* I, II, *Curia* II.

BIBLIOGRAPHY. C. A. Bachofen, *A Commentary on the New Code of Canon Law*, 8 vols. (1918–22); H. A. Ayrinhac, *The New Code of Canon Law*, 5 vols. (1923–30); S. Woywood, *A Practical Commentary on the Code of Canon Law*, 2 vols. (rev. ed., 1926); A. van Hove, *Commentarium Lovaniense in Codicem Iuris Canonici I*, 5 vols. (1928 ff.); J. Bruno, *Codicis Iuris Canonici Interpretationes Authenticae seu Responsa a CPI a. 1917–35 data* (1935; new ed., 1940); R. Naz, *Traité de droit canonique*, 4 vols. (1946 ff.); S. Mayer, *Neueste Kirchenrechts-Sammlung*, 4 vols. (1953–62); C. Sartori, *Enchiridion Canonicum seu Sanctae Sedis Responsiones* (9th ed., 1954); E. Eichmann and K. Mörsdorf, *Lehrbuch des Kirchenrechts auf Grund des Codex Iuris Canonici*, 3 vols. (10th ed., 1959–64); J. A. Abbo and J. D. Hannan, *The Sacred Canons*, 2 vols. (2nd ed., 1960); S. Sipos and L. Gálos, *Enchiridion Iuris Canonici* (7th ed., 1960); T. L. Bouscaren and others, *Canon Law. A Text Commentary* (rev. ed., 1966).

Klaus Mörsdorf

IV. Church Laws

A Church law is a general norm imposed on the members of the Church. Law is the means whereby the law-giver directs the actions of subjects so that they attain the good of society and their own proper good. The action of all laws is in the line of efficient causality, though not all work in the same way. Some laws make an action obligatory or illicit; others make it invalid; others again do both. There are laws which determine something (e.g., can. 882, 883) without imposing any obligation; others effect some-

thing, e.g., that absolution is valid, though pronounced without the requisite faculties (can. 209). It is in the nature of things that not all laws are equally effective in attaining their goal. Invalidating laws are always effective. Laws which impose an obligation or a prohibition are effective only so far as the subject keeps the law. This depends on his free will and hence on his knowledge of the law. If he disobeys (in good or bad faith), he does not keep the law and hence does not act well. Sometimes a supplementary law exists (punitive sanction) to force the subject to obey the law. The legislator thus succeeds at least in having the law kept as a rule. More is impossible in human affairs.

The Church does not, for the most part, dispose of the powers which are indispensable for the application of the more effective sanctions. And its supreme end, the eternal salvation of souls, also demands that it be merciful and forgiving in the application of its laws. Hence too the many and sometimes easy dispensations.

This should prevent us from deciding too hastily to take an unfavourable view of Church law and its practical application. It is not perfect and of its nature cannot be perfect. There are defects which can be remedied, but not all. Sometimes a defect can be removed only by another law which contains greater defects. It is not easy to foresee the harmful consequences of a law which has yet to be put into execution. Some factors only come to light when the law has been at work for some time. Further, each change in the law has necessary disadvantages. The new laws and their exact meaning are less well known and hence less well kept.

1. *Aim.* The aim of Church law is the supernatural good. Each of the faithful strives for his own supernatural good and co-operates with that of others by keeping divine and human law. In other matters he is free in directing his actions to that end. Where no particular course of action is prescribed by law, he is free. But this does not mean doing just one's own sweet will. Man is always bound to strive for his end. But where in a given situation nothing is prescribed by law (see can. 20) he can and must determine freely what is to be done with reference to the end to be attained. It is

therefore incorrect to interpret can. 20 to mean that in matters not dealt with in any particular precept, canonists may declare as binding a precept which they have deduced from similar laws *(lata in similibus)*. Men, including the faithful, do not need positive laws for everything. Freedom too is an important good. It must be well used, of course, but that does not mean that it always needs a precept to guide it.

a) *Divisions*. Universal laws are laws which are valid for the whole Church; particular laws are those imposed on a section, such as a diocese or a province of the Church.

Particular laws are either territorial or personal. But "lex non praesumitur personalis sed territorialis" (can. 8). A territorial law here means one which affects those for whom it is made exclusively in the territory of the legislator. But it can sometimes mean a law made by the authority in charge of a certain territory (the bishop). The latter type of law can also be personal.

b) *Subjects of a law*. First of all, it is certain that Church laws are not binding on those who are not baptized. But they are binding on all the baptized, even those who do not desire to be members of the Catholic Church. Membership of the one Church of Christ does not depend on the will to be a member, but on the objective fact of being baptized. This doctrine is of particular importance with regard to invalidating laws.

A legislator does not necessarily impose a given law on all his subjects. He can make a law which binds only some of them. This restriction is sometimes expressed by exclusion (naming those who are not bound, can. 1099, § 2; 2230), but mostly by naming those who are bound by the law (see can. 465).

There are some general restrictions: Church laws do not apply to those who have not come to the full use of reason, and to those who are not yet seven years old.

Particular laws are subject to some other general restrictions. As a rule *peregrini* are not bound by the particular laws of their diocese when they are staying outside it, nor by the particular laws of the locality where they are staying. An exception to this last rule is formed by the laws whose transgression disturbs public order, e.g., taking part in Church functions, processions, etc. A law forbidding clerics to go to the theatre does not come under this heading. Universal laws must be kept by all, including *peregrini,* who are staying in a place where these laws are valid, i.e., have not been suspended by a general dispensation.

2. *Special ends*. Each law envisages a particular end. An important axiom is: "finis legis non est lex". This means that what is valid as law does not depend on what is necessary or useful for attaining the end of the law in a given case, but on the law itself, its text, the meaning of the words. An application of this rule is given in the Code itself in canon 21: "Laws whose object is to avert a general danger also hold for particular cases where such danger is not present."

Ignorance of the law mostly excuses from guilt, but does not prevent invalidating laws from taking effect (can. 16).

a) In *dubio iuris* the law is not binding. This means a *dubium iuris objectivum,* which occurs when the law allows of more than one interpretation, none of which can be proved certainly incorrect. In this case, the law itself is the cause of the uncertainty. To affirm that a law is uncertain is to claim good knowledge of the law. Such doubt cannot be removed by further study. A *dubium iuris subjectivum* is different. Here the precise meaning of the law is given in the text, but uncertainty reigns among interpreters and others because they fail to see the correct interpretation. Such a doubt can be removed by further study. The rule given in can. 15 does not hold good for subjective doubt. The two authentic interpretations of can. 1099 form abundant proof of this.

b) In *dubio facti,* the Ordinary can dispense from many laws. A *dubium facti* exists where there is a well-founded doubt, which cannot be resolved, as to whether a certain condition expressed in the law is fulfilled, e.g., whether someone is sixteen years old (can. 1068). If it is an invalidating law, a dispensation should nearly always be sought, in *dubio iuris,* since the risk of acting invalidly should not be taken outside cases of necessity, as for instance the risk of an invalid marriage. If a law only affects the licitness of an action, circumstances must decide what may be done without dispensation. This is a question of moral theology.

3. *Interpretation*. Since a law is a brief, written formula, it often demands inter-

pretation. A law which is of itself certain, but has been wrongly interpreted or declared dubious by some, receives an *interpretatio declarativa*. A law which is of itself ambiguous receives an *interpretatio explicativa* (can. 17). This latter is of its nature authentic. It changes the existing law. The former (given by canonists) can also be unofficial. An authentic interpretation must be accepted by all. The obligation to accept a private interpretation only exists where one has satisfactory grounds for recognizing that it is true. *Valet quod valent rationes.* Its value does not depend on the number of those who proclaim it publicly.

The Pope has set up a commission to deal with the authentic interpretation of universal laws. Such interpretations are nearly always published in the *AAS*. Declarative interpretations do not need to be promulgated and have retrospective force. That which has been now determined as authentic was always valid in law. It cannot be deduced from the fact that an interpretation is promulgated that it is not declarative. Most interpretations are in fact declarative. The others make changes in the law and so are more than interpretations. They are acts of legislative force. Hence they need to be promulgated and have no retrospective force (can. 17). New laws also do not have as a rule retrospective force (can. 10). A priest or pastor may well be justified sometimes in criticizing part of ecclesiastical legislation or in finding it oppressive. But the law as a whole merits our admiration. If one maintains this attitude, the burdens will be more easily borne. Church law also serves the salvation of souls (Pius XI). Not everyone can see this for each part of the law. It is precisely when one does not see it that the law comes into its own. If we ourselves see that something is good, we do it where no law exists. If not, then even a law will not help.

See also *Freedom, Bishop.*

BIBLIOGRAPHY. A. van Hove, *De legibus ecclesiasticis* (1930); G. Michiels, *Normae generales* (2nd ed., 1949); L. Bender, *Legum ecclesiasticarum interpretatio et suppletio* (1961); id., *Dubium in Codice Iuris Canonici* (1962); E. Eichmann and K. Mörsdorf, *Lehrbuch des Kirchenrechts*, I, pp. 94–133.

Ludwig Bender

ECCLESIASTICAL OFFICE

I. In Canon Law: A. Concept. B. Types of Office. C. Meaning and Purpose. D. Conferring of Office. E. The Vacating of an Office. II. Office and Charism.

I. In Canon Law

A. Concept

Ecclesiastical office *(officium ecclesiasticum)* is a permanent institution created by divine or ecclesiastical ordinance for the fulfilment of certain ecclesiastical duties and endowed with corresponding pastoral powers, which can be conferred upon a physical person or a college, for the purpose of exercising, as an organ of the Church, the service prescribed by that office. Ecclesiastical office is the hierarchy of offices rather than the hierarchy of orders. This basic distinction is obscured in the legal definitions of ecclesiastical office (*CIC,* can. 145, and *CIO, De Verborum Significatione,* can. 305); it is stated there that ecclesiastical office brings with it a share in the powers of the Church, whether it be the power of governing or the power of orders. In can. 210 the same idea is found, that the power of orders is bound up with an office or that it can be delegated to a person. But contrary to this is the fundamental assertion with regard to the distinction of both powers, that the power of orders is conferred through the sacrament of orders and the pastoral power (except for the papal authority) through canonical mission (can. 109). The conferring of office is a form of canonical mission (can. 197, § 1) and can thus confer only pastoral jurisdiction but not the power of orders; this is clear from the fact that the power linked with an office ceases with the office. The powers given to a simple priest by the conferring of various offices (cf. can. 294, § 2; 323, § 2; 782, § 3; 957, § 2) for the dispensing of confirmation, tonsure, minor orders and consecrations, are pastoral powers.

In theology one speaks of office frequently in a sense that has nothing in common with the meaning of office in its legal usage, for example, when one speaks of the one office of the Church, or of the threefold office of the Church in teaching, sanctifying and governing, which has become the standard principle of division in the statements of Vatican II. The word most used at the

Council, *munus,* has many shades of meaning. In every statement made concerning "office", one must be conscious of the fluidity of the term.

B. TYPES OF OFFICE

1. According to the type of task and authority which are linked with an office, a distinction is made between ecclesiastical office in the strict sense which confers a share in the sovereign pastoral authority *(iurisdictio)* for the external and internal sphere or merely for the internal sphere; and ecclesiastical office in the broad sense, which confers a share in simple pastoral authority or any other public authority not of jurisdictional type. Only priests can receive an ecclesiastical office in the strict sense; laymen can receive office in the broad sense. The legal definition of office in the broad sense (can. 145, § 1) regulates only the exercise of the office and not the permanent institution of a ministry and thus is outside the legal concept of office.

2. The distinction between primary and auxiliary offices, though foreign to canon law, is characteristic for the structure of the offices of the Church. The primary office serves the structure of the ecclesiastical organization, by providing a spiritual head for the people of God as a whole, as well as for each of its particular communities, so that the faithful and head are joined by it in one community founded by Christ. Typical primary offices are those of the Pope, patriarch, metropolitan, bishop and parish priest. Except for the office of the Pope and of the college of bishops, all the primary offices, because they are bound to particular communities, must be constituted by the proper ecclesiastical authority, and are, as constituted offices, juridical persons even then when they are not beneficed offices (so generally in the monastic realm). With the constitution of a primary office there is always a corresponding ecclesiastical community; they cannot be separated. The auxiliary office, on the other hand, is in the service of the primary office (e.g., the office of Vicar-General, Chancellor, etc.) and is so defined in its relation to a primary office and the circle of people which it serves that it needs no special institution, providing that it is not a beneficed office (e.g., a beneficed

chaplaincy) and thus would need a legally constituted occupant.

3. The necessity of distinguishing between primary and auxiliary offices was recognized in the traditional canonical distinction between beneficed and non-beneficed offices. Although the distinction here is based purely on the laws of property, i.e., the equipment of an office with property whose income is assigned to the support of its occupant (cf. can. 1409), still the idea of the benefice includes something more than is expressed in its legal definition. The basic questions of the ecclesiastical organization of offices, for example, of the erection, changing, and termination of ecclesiastical offices, are treated of under the law of benefices (can. 1414–30); and from this it follows that the benefice has the function of a primary office in present law. At any rate, all the primary offices of the Church among the secular clergy have the character of a benefice, and in addition parishes can be erected without a legal endowment (can. 1415, § 3).

The abolition of the benefice system expected from the reform of canon law will clear the way for defining the notion of the primary office in its pure form.

4. As regards duration of occupancy the distinction is made between irremovable and removable offices; this is not a very fortunate choice of terms as every ecclesiastical office, the supreme office excepted, can be revoked. The distinction refers solely to the degree of removability (see below, E).

C. MEANING AND PURPOSE

The purpose of ecclesiastical office is to confer definite tasks and powers upon a physical person or a college, so that these may exercise, as organs of the Church, the ministry determined by the office. Ecclesiastical office comes about by the fact that certain faculties needed to discharge certain tasks are juridically linked with the tasks in question by law or custom. Some are of divine, others of ecclesiastical institution. Among the latter, the distinction is to be made between canonical institution, i.e., the specification of those tasks and powers bound to an office, and the institution of an office through an administrative act whereby a certain office is here and now established. Only the basic offices by their nature demand to be erected. Even with the office of bishop within a regional Church, a precise definition of its content (tasks and powers) is necessary, without prejudice to its divine institution, as the bishop is part of a hierarchical system that is not sufficiently defined by divine law. Thus the office of bishop also needs ecclesiastical erection.

Ecclesiastical office is a technical legal means of achieving the orderly performance of that service which is defined in the office. If the office is ordained to a college, then it has a permanent occupant, especially when (as in the case of the college of bishops) the college rests upon divine institution. Nevertheless, office and college must be distinguished since the mutual relationship can be abolished in the case of offices which rest upon ecclesiastical institution. The existence of the office independent of the person of the occupant, is evident with regard to those ecclesiastical offices which are to be conferred upon a physical person. The office forms an abiding pole with respect to the coming and going of the occupants, and it is, with certain limitations, even capable of functioning when there is no occupant of the office — not insofar as various auxiliaries are not affected by the vacancy of primary offices (e.g., all judicial officials) or only in part (e.g., the Roman Congregations), but insofar as the primary offices (outside that of the Supreme Pontiff) devolve temporarily upon others in the case of a vacancy (e.g., the bishop's office upon the Chapter of Canons and from these to the Vicar Capitular). These positive legal provisions are based on practical considerations, on the one hand, and upon the function of the office which is independent of the occupant, on the other hand. For that which is legally regulated by means of the power conferred through an office, is active independently of the change of occupant. This continuation of the function of the office is a consequence of the authority present in the office as a lasting institution. Nevertheless, the authority exercised through an office is not less personal than that exercised through delegation, i.e., authority conferred upon a person without the mediation of an office. The difference lies solely in this, that in the office there is a definite content of tasks and powers which is legally established, while with delegation it is necessary to define individually the specific tasks and the extent of authority involved.

D. Conferring of Office

An ecclesiastical office cannot be validly obtained without canonical provision *(provisio canonica)*, i.e., granted by the competent ecclesiastical authority and according to the canons which are applicable (can. 147). In the system of relative ordination which is generally practised in the Eastern Church for the office of the bishop *(CIO* [persons], can. 396, § 2, n. 1) and which is valid for other offices in the law of some regional Churches, the conferring of offices is linked with ordination, i.e., ordination results in a certain office, although conferring of office and ordination are two distinct acts. In the system of absolute ordination, which has been in practice in the Latin Church since the 12th century, the acts are separate, though the inner relation of consecration and office is preserved through the principle that only clerics can obtain pastoral power (can. 118) and especially by the fact that for all ecclesiastical offices to which jurisdiction is joined in the external or internal sphere, namely, for all pastoral offices, the priesthood is required (can. 154). The Pope has power of conferring office throughout the entire Church, and ordinaries within their own territory (can. 152, 1432). Conferring takes place in three stages: a) the choice of the person *(designatio personae),* b) the actual grant of the office *(collatio officii)* and c) in the case of beneficed offices, especially the primary ones of the secular clergy, canonical institution or installation. In the designation of a person the legitimate superior may proceed freely or be bound to a third party having the right to present candidates; accordingly, one distinguishes between free and necessary conferring. Free conferring *(collatio libera)* is normally nomination, but in certain cases (e.g., Pope, Vicar Capitular) simply election (which does not need to be confirmed), the office being legally transmitted by the acceptance of legitimate election.

In the case of necessary conferring *(collatio necessaria)* the superior is so bound to another's proposition that he is legally obliged to confer the office when the nominee is canonically fit and worthy. The proposition can be made on the basis of the right of election or of presentation (or nomination). Office is conferred in the case of an election by confirmation, and in the case of presentation (or nomination) through institution. Whoever has a canonical impediment cannot be elected but may be designated by *postulation;* in such a case conferring of office is an act of grace and favour in the form of *admission.* A properly proposed candidate has the right to be conferred with the office *(ius ad rem)* when he accepts the election or presentation; the office itself *(ius in re)* is obtained with the confirmation or institution. In the case of beneficed offices, and especially with the primary offices of the secular clergy, the right to exercise the office *(exercitium iuris)* is only conferred with the installation, this is, the entry into possession. In the case of the higher offices (e.g., that of bishop) the one upon whom the office is conferred takes possession himself, and in the case of lower offices the official is installed.

E. The Vacating of an Office

Regularly ecclesiastical office is vacated by the death of the occupant, by expiration of the prescribed time, or by retirement. All diocesan benefices and, above all, the primary offices of the secular clergy are conferred for life, so that death is the natural termination of the occupancy (the notion of spiritual marriage). Certain auxiliary offices are vacated by the termination of a specified period of time. Except for the judges of the Rota who are retired at the age of 75 *(Regulae servandae in judiciis apud Sacrae Romanae Rotae tribunal,* art. 2, § 2), canon law recognizes no age limit; retirement coincides in practice with the free resignation of office. The motu proprio *Ecclesiae Sanctae* of 6 August 1966, implementing the decree of Vatican II on the bishops, arts. 21 and 31, invites bishops and other ordinaries, as well as parish priests, to retire from office at the latest at the age of seventy-five years of age. In exceptional cases an office is vacated through resignation, deposition or transfer. Resignation can be either express or tacit.

Express resignation regularly needs to be accepted by the competent authorities, so that the office only expires with the acceptance of the resignation. But in certain cases it needs only to be notified, e.g., by the Pope to the college of Cardinals (can. 221) or the Vicar Capitular to the Chapter (can. 443, § 1). Tacit resignation occurs when the law assumes authoritatively that an office has expired, in view of certain circumstances which are incompatible with holding office (can. 188). Deposition either follows automatically from the law or is the result of a sentence passed by the authorities, which can be either an administrative or a judicial act (can. 192). Deposition by virtue of universal law is always penal, and is then called deprivation of office *(privatio,* can. 2298, no. 6; 2291, no. 10). Deposition and exclusion from the clerical state *(degradatio)* go together as penalties and include deprivation of office (can. 2303, § 1; 2305, § 1).

Deprivation of office by judicial administrative act or purely administrative act as a rule is not penal; in this case one speaks of removal from office *(amotio).* Benefices held by the secular clergy are irremovable and can only be revoked by judicial process, in principle according to the penal provisions of the code. For the sake of the public good, parish priests and other beneficed priests involved in pastoral work can be suspended from office by administrative judicial act (with or without penal measures; can. 2142–85). The previous distinction between irremovable and removable parish priests has been abolished and the procedure will be simplified (Vatican II, Decree on the Bishops' Pastoral Office, art. 71). Non-beneficed offices and benefices of those in religious orders are revocable at will, by administrative act, without recourse to any particular procedure. In the case of transfer to another office, which can be free or compulsory, the first office is vacated as soon as the holder takes possession of the new office (can. 193, 194).

See also *Hierarchy, Ecclesiastical Authority, Pope* I, *Bishop* IV, *Parish* II.

BIBLIOGRAPHY. D. E. Heintschel, *The Mediaeval Concept of an Ecclesiastical Office* (dissertation, Washington, 1956); M. Kaiser, *Die Einheit der Kirchengewalt* (1956); O. Semmelroth, *Das Geistliche Amt* (1958); K. Mörsdorf, "De Conceptu Officii ecclesiastici", *Apollinaris* 33 (1960), pp. 75–87; R. A. Strigl, *Grundfragen der kirchlichen Ämterorganisation* (1960); A. Vitale, *L'Ufficio Ecclesiastico* (1965); K. Mörsdorf, *Lehrbuch des Kirchenrechts,* I (11th ed., 1964); T. Bouscaren and others, *Canon Law, Text and Commentary* (revised ed., 1966).

See also bibliography on *Ecclesiastical Authority.*

Klaus Mörsdorf

II. Office and Charism

It is not seldom that one finds, in the explanation of the nature of the Church, that office and charism are set one against the other. Those in official positions can interpret their task in so rigid a fashion as to take up a more or less uncomprehending attitude with regard to charisms. Likewise, it is not seldom that charismatics are tempted to see in the officials of the Church their born enemies. It has occasionally been put forward on principle that a Church characterized or dominated by offices contradicts the spiritual and charismatic nature of the community of Christ, just as on the other hand a juridically oriented ecclesiology has been too prone to eliminate the charismatic element in its description of the Church. According to Scripture, however, the Church rests "upon the foundation of the apostles *and* the prophets" (Eph 2:20). And we are undoubtedly justified in interpreting the "apostles" as the beginning of that which is later expressed in the Church as office, and the "prophets" as one expression of that charismatic influence from above which together with the office determines the reality of the Church.

The following discussion will be concerned with 1) how office and charism are two essential characteristics of the Church; 2) how their relation to each other must be interpreted as an intrinsic connection; and 3) how there is between them, nevertheless, an essential polarity and tension.

1. To show how office and charism both belong to the life of the Church, it must first be shown how the Church must be both institutional and spiritual, and then it must be shown how office and charism embody these two elements.

a) The Church of the present lives at the intersection of two lines or planes, both of which must be taken seriously in any description of the Church. One line, horizontal, is the historical origin of the Church from the apostles, and hence from Christ its founder. One must understand this "apostolic succession" not only as the sacramental transmission of the spiritual office but as the apostolicity of the Church in general. The Church is not only apostolic because its faith and life correspond to the teaching of apostolic times, but also because they come from them in an unbroken historical line. This horizontal historical line of the institutional existence of the Church is sacramentally founded. In the sacrament of baptism the Church is continuously enlarged throughout the course of history. And in the sacrament of order the office of the apostle is perpetuated for each new generation. This movement of the institutional Church along the horizontal line through the course of history must be understood as a co-ordinate of another line, the vertical or charismatic, for it is at the junction of these two that the actual place and condition of the Church are to be found. The activity of the glorified Lord through his Holy Spirit comes from above to the institution as it makes its way through history, fills it charismatically and really makes it the Church.

b) Office and charism have their place in the Church not only because they both come from Christ — that is, from his historical institution of the office and from his activity from on high in charisms — but also because both of them possess an intrinsic relation to one another. But it is a relation that does not exclude a certain tension. It is based upon the different way in which both represent the same thing; it is a fruitful and necessary complementary interaction. That which is common to both, though in different ways, is the presence of Christ in his Church.

(i) The meaning of the spiritual office is the visible and personal representation of Christ in the social sphere of the Church. Though the spiritual presence of the glorified Lord is, through the Holy Spirit, objectively more real than any physical presence could have been, it has less perceptible reality in the experience of men whose salvation depends upon that presence. This is the reason why Christ instituted the spiritual office within the Church as a visible reality with a social stamp. This is the meaning which St. Paul noted when he said "So we are ambassadors for Christ" (2 Cor 5:20). When the spiritual office is exercised in the service of the word and sacramental worship in the community, the encounter of the glorified Christ with the present Church which occurs in the vertical and charismatic dimension is, so to speak, transferred to the horizontal and social plane. This does not exclude or replace the charismatic element but gives it bodily form and sacramental guarantee.

(ii) The institutional representation of

Christ through the spiritual office is entirely in the service of the charismatic presence of the glorified Lord. Charism must be taken in its largest sense here and not be too hastily restricted to those extraordinary manifestations of the Spirit of God within the Church. By charism is meant the whole sphere of God's self-communication in grace to the Church and to its members. In this sense it includes personal salutary graces — the sanctifying activity of God in the actions of men and the indwelling of God in the state of justification — as well as those special gifts and extraordinary actions of the Spirit of God which are bestowed upon individuals or groups for the good of the community.

2. The fact that office in the Church is conferred through a sacrament is already an indication of the connection between office and charism. The continuation of the Church and its offices in the course of its apostolic succession through history is thus seen to be an abiding and sacramental embodiment of the promise of the Lord, that he would send his Spirit from above to permeate the activity of the office. The relation of office and charism can be expressed in a threefold manner.

a) The function of the office is first of all to effect in the faithful the disposition for the reception of the grace of the Holy Spirit. The official teaching and exhortation move the faithful to open their hearts to the grace of God, and in this sense to his charismatic activity. The activity of the office can even be charismatic in type, insofar as it not merely exerts its authority but adds to it the "prophetic" force and urgency of a charism bestowed by the Spirit of God. Of itself, however, this effect of the office upon the disposition of the believer stands only in an indirect relation to the charismatic life within the Church.

b) But the work of the office in disposing the hearts of the faithful is also itself charismatic in a much deeper sense. The activity of the office in the Church is a sacramental embodiment of the divine activity of grace from above. Where the office of the Church, in virtue of the authority given it, announces the word of God and celebrates the sacramental worship, a sign and an assurance is given of the working of the glorified Lord.

c) But it is not only the activity of the office which is charismatic. The office itself in the Church is charismatic in nature. Its

activity is the pledge of the self-communication of the Lord in grace and charisms, and the spiritual office itself is the representation of the most charismatic of all realities, Christ, who is present in the Church through his Holy Spirit. "In the bishops and the priests who stand at their side, the Lord Jesus Christ, the high-priest, is present in the midst of the faithful", as Vatican II says (*Lumen Gentium*, art. 21).

3. The close relationship and connection between office and charism (the latter in the strict sense), is often experienced as painful tension. Both poles, however, must strive to maintain each other in their purity in the life of the Church.

a) The office, as an institutional element, belongs to the sphere of the world. There is, therefore, a danger that it will take on the form of the world and allow itself to use the rules and instruments of the world, to make an absolute of what should merely serve. Such rigidity and worldliness in the office is then opposed by the charismatic, in the form of the sudden irruption of the Spirit into the life of the Church, with special calls to individuals or communities. Such charismatic supplements or corrections to the endangered office may themselves take on permanent form. Certain charisms in the primitive Church had almost the function of an office in the life of the community (e.g., 2 Cor 8:23; Phil 2:25; Rom 16:1). And in the state of life inspired by the evangelical counsels, charismatic vocations themselves became in fact an institution. In such charismatic activity the glorified Lord asserts himself again and again as the real Lord of the Church.

b) On the other hand, since primitive Christian times, the office has had the charge of watching over the charisms (cf. 1 Cor 1:10ff.; 14:37f.). It must protect the genuine charism against pseudo-charisms and unhealthy phenomena, and maintain the community in the good order which the charisms themselves are meant to serve (1 Cor 14:33). This charge may induce in the holder of the office an anti-charismatic attitude which unduly heightens the tension. But the genuine charism, being of divine force, will also overcome such exaggerations on the part of the office. The office-holder must always remember the warning of the Apostle: "Do not quench the Spirit; do not despise prophesying" (1 Thess 5:19f.).

See also *Apostle, Apostolic Succession, Church* II, *Charisms, Evangelical Counsels, Holy Spirit, Orders and Ordination.*

BIBLIOGRAPHY. Pius XII, Encyclical *Mystici Corporis: AAS* 35 (1943), pp. 193–248; J. Brosch, *Charismen und Ämter in der Urkirche* (1951); H. Schlier, *Die Zeit der Kirche* (1956), E. T.: *The Time of the Church,* in preparation; K. Rahner, *Das Dynamische in der Kirche* (1958), E. T.: *The Dynamic Element in the Church,* Quaestiones Disputatae 12 (1964); O. Semmelroth, *Das geistliche Amt* (1958); Vatican II, Constitution on the Church, *Lumen Gentium* (1964); H. Küng, "The Charismatic Structure of the Church", *Concilium* 1 (1965), pp. 282–90.

Otto Semmelroth

ECCLESIASTICAL PENALTIES

Everybody is aware, however vaguely, that the Church sometimes inflicts penalties on its members; they may, for example, be excommunicated or deprived of Christian burial or, if clerics, may be suspended from the exercise of their functions.

1. *Principles.* It may be objected that such repressive measures contradict the principle of the "holy liberty of the children of God". Nobody, however, will dispute the need for discipline within the Church. The Church's mission is to guide the faithful along the way that leads to salvation. To fulfil this mission it tells its members what they ought to believe and how they ought to behave; it imposes a discipline of faith and morals, a religious discipline. Is it not the living presence of Jesus Christ in their midst? The Church's discipline does not aim at annihilating the will of its members or paralysing their initiative; its purpose is to guide their footsteps so that each may be fully aware of the spiritual import of his or her actions. The liberty of the faithful will then have an object, an orientation. The message of Jesus Christ is a message of love; the Church's discipline reflects the claims that love has upon its members, upon all mankind.

The faithful, moreover, form a community — the mystical body of Christ; all its members are mutually dependent, jointly and severally responsible. Discipline ensures concord within the community, guarantees to each his place and his rights, and entrusts to each his appropriate task. Liberty is,

indeed, the intelligent acceptance of solidarity and responsibilities.

Ecclesiastical penalties are only one aspect — and not the most important one — of this discipline. They penalize infractions of what is prescribed or forbidden by the Church by virtue of its disciplinary power. Like all penalties in all organized communities, they have a threefold object — punishment of the offender, protection of the common good, and reformation of the transgressor. "Religion in spirit and in truth" does not imply the absence of organization, of discipline and of sanctions. It is rather a refusal to degrade organization, discipline and sanctions into a pernickety legalism, a refusal to distort their proper meaning. It implies intense and unremitting effort to maintain organization, discipline and sanctions in the service of their supernatural end, which is the salvation of mankind united in one living community. In order to safeguard this essential liberty which nobody has the right to renounce and which nobody can be deprived of, it is necessary and sufficient that the sanctions shall not be supplemented by physical restraint, such as the prevention of persons from leaving the Church, should they wish to do so. That condition, as it will presently appear, is fulfilled in the Church of today.

The *basis* of ecclesiastical penalties was laid down by Jesus Christ himself (Mt 18:15–18). From the beginning of the Church's history, in fact, we find that penalties are in force. St. Paul does not hesitate to inflict severe punishment on members of his communities who are guilty of some offence (1 Cor 5:5; 2 Cor 2:6; 1 Tim 1:20). As time went on, the Church's penal system developed. For a long time grievous penalties were visited on heretics. We cannot but deplore the excesses of the Inquisition in the Middle Ages. Fortunately those days are over.

2. *Characteristics.* All this does not mean that the Code of Canon Law (1918) which now governs the Latin Church has wiped out all traces of the past. Certain provisions in force today bear the impress of history. They sometimes envisage customs and juridical concepts now out-dated and institutions that have little life left in them. Occasionally, also, they prescribe cumbersome dealings with the Roman Curia.

This, however, is not by any means the

dominant note of the system. Canon 2214 of the Code renews the warning of the Council of Trent to the bishops: "They (the bishops) will remember that they are pastors and not executioners, and must govern their subjects not in any domineering spirit but lovingly as children and brethren; frequently, indeed, benevolence is more efficacious than harshness as a means of correction, exhortation may be more effective than threats, and charity than authority. And so they will temper rigour with mildness, justice with mercy, and severity with tenderness." The Church never rests until it has brought the strayed sheep back into the fold, and it knows it will succeed in doing so through trust, patience and love. This mildness is displayed in various features of the Church's penal system; there is, for example, solicitude for the reformation of the offender, concern that his reputation should be spared, willingness to adapt punitive measures to individual cases, on the principle that it is not the difference of the offences that matters most, but the difference of the offenders. These factors make the system extremely flexible; the law places great confidence in the judge and also in the transgressor. Another result of this is that the Church's penal law, even in its most ancient manifestations, occasionally figures as a forerunner of contemporary secular legislation, which may have just discovered what the Church has practised for many centuries past.

3. *Infractions.* Ecclesiastical penalties are attached to two broad categories of infractions. In the first place there are the *delicta fori mixti,* misdemeanours punishable by both ecclesiastical and the civil authorities. Accordingly, the Church punishes infractions that constitute particularly serious and prevalent deviations from moral principles — for example, suicide, abortion and duelling.

In the second category are misdemeanours which involve only specifically ecclesiastical laws, and may injure the spiritual and religious interests for whose protection the Church is responsible. Their gravity is, therefore, measured by religious criterions. This category is today more numerous than "mixed" misdemeanours. It is not possible to enumerate them all here. The principal are, in descending order of gravity: profanation of the Holy Species, violence to the person of the Sovereign Pontiff, direct

violation of the seal of sacramental confession, apostasy, heresy, impeding the exercise of ecclesiastical jurisdiction, adherence to freemasonry, violation of the enclosure of nuns, participation in the activities of a non-Catholic sect, manufacture of false relics, etc.

The above list gives an idea of the Church's preoccupations and of the dangers it wanted to guard against at the time the list was drawn up. It would be all the better, no doubt, for a little retouching. Duelling is not now among Catholics the scourge it used to be; neither is the manufacture or sale of false relics. In the present ecumenical climate it is easy to imagine that certain cases of "participation in the activities of a non-Catholic sect" would not be punished as severely as formerly — in particular as regards the exchange of matrimonial consent in the presence of a non-Catholic minister of religion. On the other hand, there is a multiplication of purely civil marriages following upon civil divorce, even among those who say they are, and would like to be considered, "good Catholics"; these are not subject to any penalty. This extension of civil divorce is a relatively recent sociological problem.

4. *Penalties.* The memory of the medieval Inquisition was evoked in an earlier paragraph. Its judges undoubtedly handed over parties guilty of the crime of heresy to the "secular arm", but, in doing so, they were well aware that they were sending those parties to the stake. In those days the Church was not entirely averse to punishments of a temporal order. Since then, however, ecclesiastical penalties have more and more taken the form of deprivation of the spiritual benefits dispensed by the Church, and so the essential liberty of the faith has been safeguarded.

There are two categories of ecclesiastical penalties, differentiated in accordance with the main object the Church has in mind. "Censures" or "medicinal penalties" envisage first and foremost the reformation of the guilty party, while "vindictive penalties" are primarily aimed at punishing the delinquent. (To be absolutely complete, the category of "penances" should be added; these provide for the "satisfaction" or reparation accepted by a contrite offender.) Vindictive penalties are usually of fixed duration, while censures have to be removed by a special "absolution", distinct from the sacramental absolution that the offender is entitled to when he has amended. Certain penalties are sometimes vindictive and sometimes medicinal, according to the manner of their imposition. Excommunication, which is the gravest penalty of all and the most frequent, is always medicinal, a fact which stresses the importance attached by the Church to the reformation of the offender. Certain sanctions, moreover, are not always penalties in the precise sense of the term; this is so, in particular, with the deprivation of Christian burial generally enforced in the case of public sinners (concubines and the like), unless they have shown evident signs of penitence. Some penalties are proper to clerics; these include deposition, privation of the right to wear ecclesiastical dress, degradation, and more recently "suspension", which entails privation of the right to exercise certain functions specified in the sentence or prescribed by law — for example, celebrating Mass and hearing confessions. A penalty known as "exclusion from legitimate ecclesiastical acts" notably entails in practice, for lay offenders, privation of the right of sponsorship at baptism and confirmation; it is either supplementary to other penalties or is the principal penalty for certain infractions, such as "suspicion of heresy". "Interdict" is a penalty very closely related to excommunication, which will now be considered.

5. *Excommunication.* From Scripture we learn that excommunication was already in use among the Jews in our Lord's time; anyone who acknowledged Jesus to be the Messiah was expelled from the synagogue (Jn 9:22). The texts of St. Paul quoted in a previous section undoubtedly relate to the first Christian excommunications; the offender is cut off from the Christian community to compel him to mend his ways. This penalty took more definite shape in the centuries that followed. It now operates to separate the delinquent not from the Church, to which he is definitively attached by baptism, but from the communion of the faithful. That is to say, he is deprived of a number of rights, notably, in the case of lay persons, of the right to assist at divine offices (but not of the right to be present at sermons or instruction). He is debarred from *lawful*

reception of the sacraments. (If he nevertheless receives a sacrament he will receive it validly but *unlawfully*.) He cannot participate in the fruits of indulgences or of the suffrages and public prayers of the Church. (But excommunicates may be prayed for privately and Masses may be offered for them privately.) To all these is added the penalty of "exclusion from legitimate ecclesiastical acts", already described. It is this separation from the communion of the faithful that makes excommunication a very grave penalty indeed. It is never final, for, as we have already seen, it is a "medicinal" penalty. The Church never despairs of the conversion of sinners.

Excommunication is the penalty inflicted on the greatest number of misdemeanours particularly those listed above, from the profanation of the Holy Species to the fabrication and sale of false relics.

Excommunication, therefore, is a penalty attached to infractions of unequal gravity, but it is graduated according to the gravity of the offence.

First, however, we must distinguish between the various classes of excommunicates, that is to say, between the *tolerati*, the *notorii* and the *vitandi*. The *tolerati* are those guilty of "secret" delinquencies (committed in private and not likely to be made public), for which no "declaratory" judicial sentence has been added to the penalty of excommunication already attached to the misdemeanour by the specific law concerned. (More will be said of this later on.) The declaratory sentence is pronounced only in the case of particularly serious offences. Excommunicates have no right to assist at the divine offices, but they need not be excluded absolutely. *Notorii* ("notorious" excommunicates) are those who have been guilty of a public and manifest misdemeanour or have been the object of a declaratory sentence; these must be excluded from active, but not passive assistance at the offices, and must be deprived of Christian burial unless evident signs of repentance are forthcoming. Lastly, the *vitandi* must be excluded even from passive assistance at the offices, and the faithful must not communicate with them (hence the designation *vitandi*, i.e., to be avoided), except for a reasonable cause, such as family relationship or professional services. An excommunicate is declared *vitandus* only by a special, express and public decision of the Holy See; such a decision is very rarely given and only in cases of exceptional gravity. The *vitandi* today are very few in number.

A second graduated "scale" also regulates the application of excommunication penalties. Excommunication, as we have seen, is a medicinal penalty, and the offender has a right to absolution when he amends. Now absolution is given by different authorities, varying with the gravity of the offence. Every confessor can absolve minor misdemeanours, major ones have to be absolved by the bishop or the Holy See. Furthermore, when absolution is to be given by the Holy See, certain cases are reserved "very specially", "specially" or "simply". For example, absolution is "very specially reserved" in cases of profanation of the Holy Species and of explicit violation of the seal of confession; it is "specially reserved" in cases of apostasy and heresy. Absolution is reserved to the bishop in abortion cases. These various reservations impress upon the faithful the gravity of the relevant offences. It should be noted that, in case of urgency, and especially if there is danger of death, any priest can absolve from all censures, with the proviso that where the censures are of the most severe class, the penitent is obliged to have recourse to the Holy See afterwards. Certain confessors, too, can absolve from certain reserved censures.

6. *Procedure.* As regards the manner in which the penalties are inflicted, there is a distinction between penalties *latae sententiae* (that is, where the penalty follows automatically by law) and penalties *ferendae sententiae* (where the penalty is imposed by judicial sentence). The latter are subject to the prevailing procedure governing the trial, which takes place before a judge. The former are a special type; a penalty *latae sententiae* is incurred automatically upon infraction of the law; if proceedings are subsequently instituted in such a case, they will not give rise to a "condemnatory" sentence, since the penalty has already been incurred; the sentence will be merely "declaratory". (Sentences of this kind have been referred to in an earlier section.) Excommunication is most frequently a penalty *latae sententiae*. Today, in fact, penalties *ferendae sententiae* are rarely imposed on lay members of the Church.

The automatic infliction of the penalty *latae sententiae* would seem to have the deplorable effect of depriving the offender of the opportunity to defend himself; in fact, this is not so, because the penalty is incurred only if the offender is aware, at least in a general way, that the act he sets out to commit is punished by the Church, if the actual offence is grave in itself, and if its gravity is adverted to by the offender at the time. It is not possible, then, to draw down upon oneself, quite inadvertently, a penalty of this kind, particularly so serious a penalty as excommunication. This procedure, also, has the advantage of compelling the attention of the faithful to the gravity of certain faults; it safeguards the reputation of the offenders insofar as declaratory sentences are only pronounced in the gravest cases; and it obviates overburdening of tribunals.

As regards the penalties *ferendae sententiae,* the procedure is in accordance with the customary rules. The accused has the right to the assistance of an advocate and to information as to the precise nature of the charge etc. He can bring an appeal from the tribunal of first instance (diocesan tribunal) to the appeal judge (metropolitan tribunal) or the supreme tribunal of the Sacred Roman Rota or the Apostolic Signature. In the course of the action, the proceedings can be stopped by the judge who can simply pronounce a "judicial reprimand". When the time comes for sentence to be pronounced, the penalty is sometimes discretionary, and, in the case of a first offence, a suspended sentence is possible. Sometimes the law leaves to the judge the choice of an "appropriate penalty"; sometimes it allows him to increase the penalty normally incurred "if exceptionally aggravating circumstances require it". And after sentence has been passed, remission of the penalty is still possible. The flexibility of the system is obvious, and so is the care taken to adapt the penalty to the individual delinquent.

An administrative procedure, involving appearance before the bishop, can be substituted for the normal judicial procedure; this is more expeditious and more discreet, but it is prohibited in the most serious cases, because the guarantees offered to the accused are less than those available in the judicial procedure.

This diversity of rules occasionally proves somewhat burdensome; some of them, indeed, rarely have a chance to operate. A lightening of the legal load is certainly desirable in order to make it comply with modern conditions. The faithful, too, have grown more lukewarm, more passive, and less actively irreverent than formerly — a sign of the times. But the rules, as they stand, testify to the Church's solicitude for those who are entrusted to its care.

See also *Authority, Church* III, *Ecclesiastical Authority, Ecclesiastical Law* III, IV, *Curia, Clergy, Inquisition.*

BIBLIOGRAPHY. See the text-books and commentaries on canon law; also Pelle, *Le droit pénal de l'Église* (1939); L. de Naurois, *Quand l'Église juge et condamne* (1960).

Louis de Naurois

ECCLESIASTICAL REGIONS

1. *The ecclesiastical territories under the Congregations.* In the *Atlas Missionum* published in 1959 by the Vatican City Press, the map of the world, pp. 3–4, shows the various administrative regions as follows, distributed among the Congregation for Propaganda, the Consistorial Congregation, the Congregation for the Oriental Church and the Congregation for Extraordinary Ecclesiastical Affairs. The reform of the Curia in 1967 did not indicate any changes in this regional distribution of competence, which may, therefore, be presumed to persist fundamentally. The Congregations in question are now re-named "For the Missions", "For Bishops", "For the Eastern Churches" and "For the Public Affairs of the Church".

a) In Africa, Propaganda (an alternative official title for the Congregation for the Missions) has jurisdiction over almost the whole of Africa, with the exception of Northern Algeria, Ceuta, Melilla and Tunisia, which come under the Congregation for Bishops. Egypt, Eritrea and a part of Ethiopia are under the Congregation for the Eastern Churches; Portuguese Guinea, Angola and Mozambique, St. Thomas, the Ile du Prince and the Cape Verde Islands are under the Congregation for Public Affairs.

b) The *Americas* are divided between Propaganda and the Congregation for Bishops. The Propaganda has jurisdiction over the far north and over some of the countries of Latin America.

c) In Asia the jurisdiction of Propaganda extends to more than three-quarters of the whole. But the Congregation for the Eastern Churches has jurisdiction over Afghanistan, Cyprus, Iran, Iraq, the Lebanon, Syria and Turkey.

The Congregation for Bishops has jurisdiction over almost the whole of the Pilippines, except for three vicariates which come under Propaganda.

The Congregation for Public Affairs has charge of the Portuguese territories of Macao and Timor.

d) In Europe, the ecclesiastical districts in general depend on the Congregation for Bishops, if they are of Latin rite, and on the Congregation for the Eastern Churches, if they belong to the various Eastern rites.

Propaganda has jurisdiction over the Balkans, Scandinavia and Gibraltar. The Soviet territories which are a part of the "Church of Silence" theoretically do not depend on any particular jurisdiction. The section of the Secretariat of State dealing with extraordinary affairs has had the main responsibility for these questions.

e) At the present moment the whole of Oceania depends on Propaganda with the exception of the diocese of Honolulu. Australia and New Zealand have a special status because the Church there can provide for its own needs.

Finally we must mention that as a rule ecclesiastical territories or districts are organized according to an ascending hierarchical order: the parish, the deanery which groups together a variable number of parishes, the archdeanery (now rare), heading a number of deaneries, the diocese and finally the ecclesiastical province. Patriarchates really exist only in the East. The functions corresponding to these divisions are those of parish priest, dean, senior dean or archdeacon, bishop, metropolitan and patriarch.

In addition there are more or less permanent assemblies of bishops limited to one or more provinces.

For the definition of these districts and of the functions associated with them, the articles referring to titles mentioned above should be consulted. The precise geographical lines of demarcation as well as the statistics relating to these ecclesiastical territories down to diocesan level are to be found in the *Atlas Missionum* and the *Data Statistica Circumscriptionum Ecclesiasticarum* (Atlas Missionum a Sacra Congregatione de Propaganda Fide Dependentium, Cura Editus Ejusdem Sacrae Congregationis, Ex Civitate Vaticana, Anno Domini MDCCCLVIII) or in the *Annuario Pontificio*.

2. *The function of ecclesiastical districts*. The Catholic Church exercises its jurisdiction through an organization structured both territorially and hierarchically in different grades or levels. Here jurisdiction has for the most part a territorial basis. This is inevitable, for even if the creation or development of the supernatural community does not presuppose a well-defined social group or community, in many cases its outlines have to be adopted. For jurisdiction to be actually exercised the formation of a community is required, that is to say, a group of men conscious of a mutual solidarity and sharing in some common act. Unfortunately, theologians and priests who use this expression "community" do so according to its non-theological meanings whose sociological and psychological content they do not define. Generally the forms that the community takes and the ways of belonging to it are not made clear. In these conditions it is difficult to give it an exact description. Besides, even if one succeeded in showing that the assembly of Christians has special sociological characteristics and that the organization of Christian life has its own territorial requirements, it would still remain important to know the different kind of communitarian connections and social relationships which are established between men at different levels. The function of the sociologist and the geographer then is to help to formulate the notion of community and to define the forms it takes. In the same way, they can show the evolution produced in social relationships on the basis of the formation of groups and communities. They can also indicate to what extent ecclesiastical districts do or do not coincide with the various different forms of human communities, or, quite simply, with other secular geographical districts.

Finally, the sociologist and the geographer help to clarify the part played by the territory in the establishment of communitarian bonds and the creation of communities. For instance, there has been a great deal of discussion about the territorial character of certain districts, such as the parish. In most cases place and territory have been identified. But for the eucharistic assembly to exist before all else it needs a place, not a territory. In other words, the implantation of the parish is always geographical, but need not necessarily be territorial, with the consequence that to come under the jurisdiction of the Church it is not necessary to be attached to any particular territory. Belonging to the Church can be understood in a wider sense which avoids population movements creating problems of competence and responsibility. Belonging to the eucharistic community can be brought about through a plurality of assemblies or groups.

History shows, moreover, that the territorial character of ecclesiastical jurisdiction has been transformed. There was a time when many sacraments could only be received in the parish church, Easter communion in particular. But again many restrictions have been removed recently. For instance in Belgium, jurisdiction for preaching and the sacrament of penance has been extended by the whole of the bishops to the whole of the national territory.

The present state of legislation about territorial districts is, moreover, the cause of many disputes over jurisdiction and allocation, which are often a positive hindrance to effective pastoral care.

No doubt the demarcation of a territory contributes to rational administration and helps efficient supervision.

When a whole territory is properly divided up, responsibilities are well defined, but each division and demarcation can change with the passage of time.

Ecclesiastical districts, like all administrative districts, usually date back a very long time, especially in the older countries of Western Europe where the present districts can be traced back to the end of the 18th and the beginning of the 19th centuries.

It is very probable that at the start the districts followed the real units of common life. But in this matter, as in every human endeavour (and the Church lives in the time of the Incarnation), territorial units have sometimes had to be decided on in virtue of immediate needs and difficulties, such as people's opposition and available financial means, or were modelled on other districts established for quite different purposes by public authority.

Another important factor is that of transport facilities. At times some districts have had to be determined in a particular way so as to facilitate ease of access. But progress in communications and means of transport can, in one generation, completely transform the accessibility of a particular place. On this point we should note that some French administrative units were drawn up around towns in view of the possibility of travelling to the boundaries and back within the space of one day.

In addition, at times the essential needs of religious organization can require certain forms of centralization and co-ordination, and yet at other times favour decentralization and dispersal.

Or again long established districts can be emptied of their population or, on the contrary, experience a considerable increase, and this can effect the whole or only just one part of the district.

Some districts have been created in view of functions which in the course of time have lost their importance or have fallen into disuse.

New services can be developed whose implementation necessarily moves beyond the old established districts or is frustrated by their existence, while more suitable new districts have not yet been practicable. In fact the smallness of some territories can stand in the way of various kinds of specialization and organization of work and services. Men are recruited and retained there who are capable of performing a wide variety of tasks where, all things considered, a specialist or a team of specialists could in the circumstances obtain better results. Many ecclesiastical administrative services would probably be much more efficient if organized on a broader basis, as for example some aspects of financial control and the registration of sacramental acts. Likewise, for the proper supervision of religious life it is now quite clear that the parish on its own is no longer adequate.

It is also obvious that certain people and functions spontaneously go beyond existing spheres of jurisdiction, and that when a number get together to co-ordinate activities between different units, the composition of the group, the methods of reaching decisions and the underlying financial structures can limit the expansion and the development of new forms of organization.

The organization and arrangement of districts can be envisaged either from a geographical or functional point of view, or from both. So working on a restricted geographical basis one can try to organize different ecclesial functions, or again one can adapt and regulate the extent of the territory of jurisdiction taking into account the function that is to be accomplished.

Our modern states embrace in their activities various non-homogeneous geographical units organized on a permanent basis; but for other purposes the territories are defined in each individual case. So there are special regions for administration of justice, and it is the same with the army and with education. Powers and jurisdiction are then limited to the particular function to be performed. All these regions need not necessarily be superimposable, insofar as the particular functions to be exercised are not related to or essentially bound up with others.

So the organization and dividing up of territory can be carried out either on a geographical or functional basis. It seems that in most cases the Church has chosen the first solution. This arises from the way in which powers are divided between different levels of the ecclesiastical hierarchy and the wide variety of responsibilities that are entrusted to them. All the same, insofar as each function corresponds to different technical needs, the second principle, that of functional organization, must be taken into consideration. This is what happens when in a diocese districts for school inspection are decided upon which do not coincide with the ecclesiastical districts on a lower level.

Clearly, the principles we have been discussing here are based on a criterion of efficiency and have nothing to do with the divine order. The judgment of the geographer and the sociologist are restricted to this level.

3. *The adaptation and creation of ecclesiastical districts.* The Church lives in a rapidly changing world, is deeply involved in a human race which has doubled its numbers in less than forty years and lives within a civilization which each day gives to men new ways of expression, communication and action. And so more than ever it sees the need to reform its apostolic organization and territorial districts.

On the other hand, the Church is also a

social organism which must adapt itself to its own development. Many new and complex responsibilities have developed and new methods of co-ordination are needed.

In particular we would mention the need for a better distribution of the diocesan clergy and the need for the pastoral care of immigrants; there are also the problems raised by the renewal of pastoral theology, catechetics and the liturgy and by the co-ordination of Catholic Action; the problems of the exemption of religious in pastoral work, and the sending of priests to other countries, the world-wide organization of charity, the organization of the schools and new methods of pastoral care, as well as the work for the reunion of the Churches and the dialogue with the world and for the continual and ever richer discovery of the message of the gospel and of the socio-cultural environments in which the Church is developing.

The Church then appears as a social organism which on the one hand must be integrated into the societies in which it lives and on the other hand must adapt itself to the demands of its own development. In our day more than ever it must be able to bring about a readjustment of its structures and of its territorial organization in particular.

a) *The problems of divisions within the diocese.* The sociological concept of the parish is no longer a univocal one. It covers very many different situations: small country parishes of 250 inhabitants, city and suburban parishes of 50,000 or more, urban centres, etc. Then more rarely there are national parishes or even functional or personal parishes, as, for example, a university parish.

The parish is the territorial unit which has perhaps suffered most severely from the concentration and evolution of population. The exodus from the country-side has coincided with the development of the towns. These changes took place so quickly that it was too late before countries became aware of what was happening. Towns, as we know them today, whether in Europe or elsewhere, are the products and the evidence of a technological civilization. No doubt there were towns before the 19th century, but few contained more than 100,000 inhabitants. The great modern cities are the product of new systems of production and transport which enable men to be fed outside the agricultural areas. The way they developed

is furthermore directly related to the possibilities of business and trade. The geographical displacement of the population means new parishes. Sometimes this involves an entirely new distribution of the territory. Some central urban parishes can be regrouped, while those on the periphery have to be split up.

But the creation of new parishes and the redistribution of the clergy are not sufficient to solve the problems of pastoral organization in today's towns, and the same is true for the changing country scene.

In fact if the principal sociological characteristic of the parish as an institution has always been that it corresponded to a social group or was a basic element of it, we may ask ourselves whether it still fulfils this role today. At one time the village was the basic unit of country life and to each village there corresponded a religious unity. In the same way the towns of the pre-industrial era were characterized by a social life which was closely organized according to districts. And we can see that the parishes followed the same pattern. No doubt in the country districts and in certain working-class or suburban quarters social relationships are still to a great extent on a local basis. The continuance of such forms of relationship is much greater among the lower-income brackets and varies also according to sex and age, but the general evolution has taken quite a different direction, because a whole series of economic, social and cultural activities are now organized on a much broader scale than before. And this evolution can be seen in the country-side as well as in the towns.

The country areas, often having suffered a relative loss of population, have been greatly transformed during the past fifty years. Even in areas where there has been a decrease in population there are some rural centres where the number of inhabitants has gone up. This simply means that as centres of communication they attract a number of economic, social and cultural establishments, cinemas, businesses and administrative institutions. So the concentration of functions has also taken place in these centres in the rural areas. The result is that today it is the region revolving around these rural centres which forms the social platform for human life and no longer just the village which has lost its unique position.

180

The geography of the towns has also been transformed. Because of the specialization of economic and social life areas have become more functional. Where formerly individual districts included establishments for work, leisure, education and living accommodation, gradually all these have been separated. Men's lives in the towns are no longer centred on one district alone, but rather on the whole agglomeration which is itself subdivided into smaller, more or less organic units. In short, in the rural districts as in the towns the basic unit of the village or district has given way to a completely new conception of organization. Institutions and functions are organized over a much larger spread of territory, serving a multiplicity of formerly independent territorial units, which today together form a region or agglomeration. Social relationships are less and less dependent on people's living closely together. One can understand how under these conditions the parish has ceased to be able to fulfil some of the functions which had previously belonged to it.

On the other hand, many new and important specialized forms of the apostolate have been developed. This in fact corresponds to the birth of new institutions and the different localization of administration, work, leisure, and education. So it can be said that a parish still thought of and actually run as an independent religious structure no longer corresponds to the general evolution. The present organizational structure does not lend itself to the development of group pastoral care.

There are, however, many promising experiments taking place on nearly every continent, tending to the development of inter-parochial and then supra-parochial organizations, since the Rubicon must be crossed. There are also efforts to restore the importance of deaneries, as well as the functions of the dean, the principal dean and the archdeacon which provide structures mediating between the diocese and the parishes.

Because of the existing organization, the planning and initiatives have mostly originated at the level of individual parishes, whereas nowadays secular organization would start from the larger geographical unit and then divide responsibilities and territory according to the particular requirements of pastoral activity. Among the inter-parochial or supra-parochial experiments, we may mention inter-parochial secretariats providing services such as liturgical study, preparation for marriage, reception of new arrivals, centralization and information. These secretariats could in time create the basic organization for urban jurisdictions. Another example is the canonical union of all the parishes in the southern part of Bogotá, under the direction of a committee with a representative of the bishop. The parishes cover the most densely populated areas of the town and the clergy do most of their educational and charitable work as a team. So group enterprises are possible on either a town or area basis.

Supra-parochial activity could also be developed by reviving and adapting already existing structures, such as the deaneries and the archdeanery. These functions and districts at the moment have only an administrative value, except in certain dioceses. New functions have been given to the deans in Cambrai, to the archdeacons in parts of the Paris conurbation and to the principal deans in Tournai.

Sometimes the problem has been solved for the more important towns and the outlying districts of a diocese by the installation of a residential bishop.

These experiments could cater for levels on which pastoral care is sometimes completely absent (for lack of equipment on an urban level, for instance). They could eliminate conflicts between persons responsible for religious structures which are conceived on too narrow a basis. Finally they would contribute to a co-ordination of all the departments of pastoral activity.

b) *The adaptation of diocesan structures and the evolution towards national and continental structures.* Without attaching too much importance to diocesan boundaries, we may say that pastoral efficiency is hampered in a diocese which is too populous, too extensive or too heterogeneous.

The presence of large numbers of faithful and clergy prevents the bishop from having personal pastoral contacts. When one diocese contains many communities or large concentrations of population, some of them may suffer from lack of responsible local direction. The need for local pastoral direction is felt most of all in the large and rapidly developing centres of population where the integration of the people into the religious structures presupposes a group pastorate on

181

a large scale and not just a simple gesture of welcome.

On the other hand the multiplication of dioceses raises the problem of where the sees are to be established. The bishop need not live in the greatest concentration of Catholics, but he must be as close as possible to the greatest number.

Again the creation of new dioceses makes the problem of the redistribution of the clergy more acute than ever, for religious vocations are not always proportionate to the population. So it would be rash to look upon every diocese as autonomous and self-sufficient from every point of view.

For some time now interdiocesan structures have been developed. These can have one or many functions, including even the systematic reapportionment of the revenues of the Church in view of pastoral needs.

An inter-diocesan experiment with only one function is the *Fondation de la Mission de France*, with the Apostolic Constitution *Omnium Ecclesiarum* of 15 August 1954 establishing a *prelatio nullius* whose prelate is the president of the episcopal commission for the *Mission de France*. This is the first example of a seminary being put at the disposal of an episcopate as a result of a particular canonical decision.

One could also imagine the establishment of an inter-diocesan seminary for volunteers for the apostolate in areas where clergy are most needed.

Another inter-diocesan and sometimes inter-provincial experiment culd be attempted by restoring the patriarchates, some of which are still active in the East. Or primatial jurisdiction could also be restored and entrusted to the metropolitan, that is, the bishop responsible for a province.

But perhaps all things considered the tendency nowadays is towards more collective forms of authority. The development of the apostolate in the Church in a changing world has prompted the bishops to assemble at various levels. Besides the *ecumenical council* there are: a) the *plenary council* which is a deliberative assembly of bishops from many ecclesiastical provinces presided over by a legate chosen by the Pope; b) the *provincial council:* a deliberative assembly of the bishops of an ecclesiastical province under the presidency of the metropolitan. In each province a provincial council must be held at least every twenty years, but for some time now

there have been secretariats for the various national hierarchies. These secretariats and the commissions affiliated to them help to co-ordinate apostolic work on a national basis. And finally, there are c) *episcopal conferences,* which are assemblies of bishops belonging to the same country or the same ecclesiastical province, who deliberate in common on problems affecting the direction of the individual Churches. The decisions taken have not the same juridical value as conciliar decrees. In Latin America there is the CELAM, and a similar organization has recently been established in Africa. These are really continental structures seeking to co-ordinate action in different spheres.

See also *Bishop* III, IV, *Diocese, Clergy, Parish.*

BIBLIOGRAPHY. J. Fichter, *Social Relations in the Urban Parish* (1954); M. Pacaut and others, "Paroisses urbaines, paroisses rurales", *5ᵉ Conférence internationale de sociologie religieuse* (1958); F. Houtart, "Les Structures de l'Église", *Qu'attendons-nous du Concile?* (1960), pp. 73–85; J. Remy, "Groups and Personal Relationships in Cities", *Social Compass* (1961), pp. 211–23; F. Houtart, "Pastoral Care in the Cities", *Social Compass* (1961), pp. 659–65; id., "Faut-il revoir le dispositif apostolique?", *Un concile pour notre temps* (1961), pp. 107–33; id., "Les formes modernes de la collégialité épiscopale", in Y. Congar and B. Dupuy, eds., *L'Épiscopat et l'Église universelle* (1962), pp. 497 ff.; E. Pin in *Sociologie de la Paroisse,* Actes du Colloque Européen des Paroisses (1962), pp. 7 ff.; F. Houtart, "Sociology of the Parish as Eucharistic Assembly", *Social Compass* (1963), pp. 75–92.

Jacques Delcourt

ECCLESIASTICAL TRIBUNALS

A. Origin and History

The Church has sacred authority to dispense justice, that is, the power to pass sentence according to law on the faithful who come under its jurisdiction. Conflicts arise which charity alone is unable to resolve — although the Church prefers disputes to be settled by adjustment or arbitration, provided that the public interest is not at stake. But ecclesiastical justice must always strive to reflect divine justice by taking mercy as its norm.

From the beginning of the Church's history, the power of jurisdiction was exercised at various times by the apostles, by the bishops within the communities over which they presided, by the Pope over the entire Church, or by councils over certain regions.

Roman law served as a model, but mitigated by the evangelical precepts.

In the 6th century Germanic customs began to exert an influence in the West that was destined to persist in some institutions such as litiscontestation (see below, D, 3, C).

The revival of Roman law in the 12th century led to its adoption as *ratio scripta,* at least for the principles of ecclesiastical law. Nonetheless, certain institutions became predominant which were more in keeping with the spirit of the Church, e.g., the written form (judicial decisions given only on the basis of written depositions), secrecy, the office of *Promotor Iustitiae,* and, since the decree *Saepe* of 1316, the summary trial, freed from many formalities and reduced to affidavits and the hearing of the parties. This last procedure, with certain modifications to facilitate it, was adopted in essentials by the code of canon law. The code for the Oriental Churches shows that further progress has been made.

B. JUDICIAL POWER AND ADMINISTRATIVE POWER

Side by side, moreover, with the summary procedure mentioned in the last paragraph, an administrative procedure began to evolve from the 16th century onwards, in connection with the setting up of the Roman Congregations. This was defined more clearly by the constitution *Sapienti Consilio* (1908). The procedure thus evolved allows a greater influence to equity. Not only are the rules of law taken into account; the circumstances in which their application can be brought to bear upon the case are also considered. This makes for flexibility and for a better estimation of the interests concerned. It is more expeditious and more equitable than the judicial procedure.

This administrative procedure now holds the most important place in the Church's legal system. In fact, apart from matrimonial cases where judicial procedure is obligatory, litigation is rare, as is evident from the relative fewness of the decisions of the Rota.

C. BASIS AND CHARACTERISTICS OF JUDICIAL POWER

The Church's judicial power is *independent* of that of all civil society. For the historical and theological foundations, see the articles on ecclesiastical authority and jurisdiction.

In the course of a centuries-long development, the judicial system of the Church evolved some features which distinguish it clearly from civil systems.

1. Essentially *one single* hearing is prescribed in ecclesiastical tribunals, with some additions in penal cases and also in matrimonial and ordination cases. The only exceptions to the foregoing are a) the special summary proceedings under can. 1990 where proof of documents is involved; and b) the infliction of minor penalties *per modum praecepti* — an administrative procedure — without a judicial trial (can. 1933, § 4, and 2225).

2. *Adjustment or compromise* and *arbitration* are preferred to judicial procedure.

3. Ecclesiastical procedure is *mixed,* being both written and oral, as well as *secret* with respect to third parties and sometimes even with respect to the parties to the case, at least for the time being.

4. If the public good is involved, the *inquisitorial* principle is followed, because of the overriding interest of the Church.

5. The judges are permitted *wide powers* at least in regard to certain formalities or time-limits that may be laid down by law.

6. The Pope and the bishops in principle possess judicial power but never in fact exercise it, while the irremovability of the judges in ecclesiastical tribunals is relative — they are *ad nutum episcopi.*

D. PROCEDURE

There are various elements, but the procedure is uniform, with slight variations for criminal, matrimonial and ordination cases. Criminal courts may be distinguished from civil proceedings, the former dealing with "delicts" involving penalties, the latter safeguarding threatened or injured rights.

1. *Jurisdictional elements.* a) *Jurisdiction* is the judicial authority which constitutes an essential and inseparable part of the Church's sovereign authority, because, in the Church, the powers are not separate, but only distinct.

Ecclesiastical jurisdiction extends, in the first place, to spiritual cases and to matters connected with such cases, and, in the second place, to persons who have the *privilegium fori,* "benefit of clergy", save for exceptions stipulated in concordats. In a conflict between powers, jurisdiction is determined by the nature of the indictment.

Because separation of powers does not exist, administrative jurisdiction in the proper sense is precluded.

b) The *tribunals* are *ordinary* (diocesan, metropolitan, papal [the Rota and the Apostolic Signature]) or *delegated,* such as a Pontifical Commission.

The public interest is represented by the *Promotor Iustitiae* who is free to take proceedings but must appear at least in penal cases.

The *Defensor Vinculi* upholds the validity of marriages and of ordinations, and intervenes only for that purpose.

A notary is required in all cases.

c) The *competence* of a tribunal is regulated according to the substance of the suit, the status of the parties or functions concerned in it, and territorial considerations. Owing to the spiritual character of the proceedings, the monetary value involved has no part in determining competence.

Because of the nature of the litigation and the dignity of the parties concerned, cases are reserved to the Pope or the pontifical tribunals when they involve, as parties in civil or penal actions, reigning families, heads of state, cardinals, bishops and corporations directly dependent on the Holy See.

Territorial competence is determined by the domicile or quasi-domicile of the parties, the situation of the things in dispute or the place of the contract or of the crime, but a *requisite forum* is imposed in the case of dispossession, benefices, administration of property and inheritance.

Lastly, every member of the faithful can be summoned to Rome, or, if he has been living in Rome for at least a year, he can institute proceedings there. In matrimonial cases, however, the competent tribunal is that of the domicile or quasi-domicile of the respondent or that of the place where the marriage was celebrated; when several cases are interconnected, these arrangements may be modified.

The objection of *relative incompetence* must be raised at the beginning of the proceedings. If it is admitted, the decision of the tribunal cannot be appealed against; if it is rejected, appeal is possible as soon as sentence is pronounced. When there are conflicts, the higher tribunal intervenes.

2. *The parties.* a) Every member of the faithful who is not debarred from suing by some ecclesiastical impediment can institute proceedings. Excommunicated persons, therefore, are debarred and so are the guilty parties in the case of an impediment involving the nullity of a marriage. Corporations may bring proceedings and even *de facto* associations are admitted in certain cases. Parties absolutely or relatively incapable in the legal sense can be represented or assisted by parents, tutor or guardian; in spiritual cases, minors can appear in person.

Collegiate bodies (corporations) are represented by their superior with the consent of their board or council of administration.

Non-collegiate groups are represented by their superior, but, in order to institute proceedings, their administrators must obtain the authorization in writing of the tutelary authority represented by the Ordinary.

b) The parties can institute proceedings personally unless forbidden to do so by special interdict. In general, representation is by agents authorized in writing, unless stipulated by the judge. In penal cases, an advocate must be employed. Advocates and agents must be Catholics and approved by the Ordinary.

3. *Initiation of the case.* A case is initiated by means of three distinct instruments.

a) The *judicial petition* specifies the tribunal to which recourse is being had, gives details of the action, and states the interest of the plaintiff. The petition must be admitted or refused expeditiously by decree. Only in the event of refusal is it possible to appeal to a higher tribunal.

b) The *summons* gives particulars of the case, inaugurates the litigation, determines the jurisdiction and interrupts the period of limitation since the accused ceases to be in good faith. It has to be answered by a specified date.

c) The *litiscontestation* stresses the object of the petition and the plea of the defendant, indicates the limits of the dispute, puts an end to any objections in law advanced by the defendant, and, the judicial inquiry now being regarded as having begun, fixes the time allowed for the making of any necessary appeal.

4. *Conduct of the case.* The next stage comprises three phases, the first of which is separated from the third by the *conclusio in causa*. First phase: This consists of the inquiry or investigation the object of which is to collect the evidence proposed to be presented by the parties, who are required to speak the truth and to reply in person. Admission of evidence by the judge relieves the opposite party from the burden of proof in private cases. The value of any extra-judicial admission of evidence is left to the judge's discretion.

Oral evidence is regulated by the judge as regards the number of witnesses and their examination. The judge has the right to punish witnesses who refuse to reply without legitimate excuse. Certain witnesses are ruled out as *exempt,* for example those who may have been entrusted with information under a pledge of secrecy, those who are incapable because of their office or family relationship, those regarded as unfit (such as mental defectives) or as suspect (whose evidence would be unreliable). Witnesses and evidence can be censured at the discretion of the judge. Experts are admitted, subject to the same rules as witnesses, especially in cases of insanity or non-consummation. Their reports must be presented individually. Their findings are not binding on the judges, but if they are rejected the judges must state their grounds for doing so.

Apart from his right of access to, and admission of evidence, the judge must take account of documents, which may be public (ecclesiastical or civil) or private. Public documents are taken as trustworthy as regards what they attest directly and principally. Private documents have to be recognized by the parties and the judge. Direct or indirect presumptive evidence can also be accepted as provided by law or admitted by the judge on the basis of the facts. Lastly, recourse may be had to declarations on oath, which may be suppletory, estimatory, or decisive.

Points of law may disturb the normal course of the proceedings. They can be put forward in writing or orally, and can be settled by decree or interlocutory judgment, after a brief discussion and an indication of the grounds in law and in fact. Appeal is admitted only in cases where rejection of it would influence the final verdict.

Culpable non-appearance on the part of the accused is considered contumacy and is declared on the petition of the plaintiff, and there is penal sanction where the public interest is involved. The contumacious party ceases to be informed of the course of the proceedings, save where fresh petitions are received or definitive judgment is pronounced, but he can appear before the court before the end of the hearing, taking the case as it then stands unless he is able to justify his absence. If sentence is pronounced, he has three months in which to obtain the *restitutio in integrum* with a view to appealing from the judgment.

Contumacy of the plaintiff is declared only after a second summons has been served. The plaintiff, if still contumacious, forfeits the right to pursue his case, and the defendant has the option of withdrawing from, or going on with, the proceedings. Costs are chargeable to the guilty party.

Intervention by a third party can be *voluntary,* in which event the third party may come forward at any stage of the proceedings prior to the *conclusio in causa;* the case must then continue from the stage it has already reached. Intervention by a third party may also be *necessary* (as distinct from voluntary), in which event it is ordered by the judge at the request of one of the parties or of the official side.

Second phase: This is the *conclusio in causa* which is officially declared after every action or document that may have hitherto been kept secret has been communicated to the parties in the case, and when, in the judge's opinion, the case has been adequately investigated. The effect of the *conclusio in causa* is to prohibit the production of fresh evidence and to initiate the argument.

Third phase: In this phase the argument takes place. Generally speaking, this is a necessary part of the process, although the parties may forgo it in civil cases. In principle it is conducted *in writing,* oral representations being admitted only in order to clarify certain points.

5. *Termination of the case. Interruption* can be caused by death, change of status, or cessation of office, but only up to the *conclusio in causa;* interruption occurs *ipso facto,* however, when an agent ceases to act.

Extinction of an action by discontinuance of the proceedings for the period fixed by law sanctions any defect in legal procedure for a one-year or two-year period, according to the nature of the action.

Renunciation (abandonment of an action) *is made in writing* with the consent of the defendant and of the judge.

Judgment is pronounced by the judge in accordance with the certainty attained, after argument and on the basis of the evidence. In the case of a collegiate tribunal, each judge adduces his findings in writing and their grounds in law and in fact, the presiding judge doing so first and the others following in order of precedence. The judgment opens with the invocation of God's name; then comes a brief summary of the points at issue, followed by a statement of the legal and factual grounds on which the judgment is based together with the pleas of the parties; finally come the terms of the judgment and the giving of costs.

Publication of the judgment is effected by reading it to the parties, by an official statement of its availability in the chancellory, or by a form of notification similar to the summons.

Judgment, however, only has force of law when two similar verdicts have been passed, that is, when two courts have given the same verdict on the same case (except where appeal has not been entered or is renounced or is inadmissible).

Various remedies are available once judgment has been pronounced. They may take any of the following forms. Rectification is available only in case of material error; appeal is available if there is no binding legal precedent, save in the case of judgments pronounced by the Pope or the Apostolic Signature or by a judge delegated *appellatione remota,* and also in cases of contumacy, renunciation and invalid or non-definitive judgments; notice of appeal must be given, within ten days, before the judge *a quo,* and the appeal must be brought, within a month, before the judge *ad quem;* whether the appeal is on general grounds or on a particular point of law, it has a suspensory devolutive effect according to the wish of the parties, i.e., the case goes before a higher court; procedure is the same as that of first instance; fresh submissions are not admitted and fresh evidence is admitted only insofar as it would have been admitted in first instance after the *conclusio in causa* had been declared.

Plea of nullity: nullity can be rectified where there is a defect in the form of the summons or of the judgment, but the plea must be raised at the same time as the appeal or within three months; nullity is irreparable in cases of absolute incompetence, irregular constitution of a collegiate tribunal, incapacity of the parties, want of proper authorization and other substantial defects.

A plea of nullity is heard by the tribunal which has pronounced judgment, except for verdicts of the Rota, which go to the Apostolic Signature.

Opposition by a third party is a remedy that can be invoked when a definitive judgment is prejudicial to the rights of a third party; it prevents the execution of the judgment; it is heard by the tribunal which has delivered the judgment, or by the appellate jurisdiction.

Restitutio in integrum is an extraordinary remedy in cases where judgments have been obviously unjust but have become unassailable by ordinary remedies such as appeal or plea of nullity; it can be invoked on grounds of fact (falsity of documents, fresh and decisive facts, fraud by one party at the other's expense) before the tribunal that has given judgment, and on grounds of law (obvious violation of the law) before the higher tribunal; but this does not apply to judgments of the Rota, which can only be dealt with by the Apostolic Signature.

The execution of the judgment is an administrative act entrusted to the Ordinary of the place where judgment was given in the first instance or, in his default, to the Ordinary of the place where the appeal tribunal heard the case.

See also *Ecclesiastical Authority, Jurisdiction, Ecclesiastical Law, Curia.*

BIBLIOGRAPHY. SOURCES. Before the *CIC* (1917): *Corpus Iuris Canonici; Canones et decreta Concilii Tridentini;* Instructions of the S. Congregations of the Council (1840), for Religious (1880), for Oriental rites (1883), of Propaganda for the U.S.A. (1883); the Constitution *Sapienti Consilio* (1908); *Leges propriae Sacrae Romanae Rotae et Signaturae.* After the *CIC:* Instructions of the S. Congregation for the Sacraments, 7 May 1923, 9 June 1931 and 15 August 1936; *Normae S. R. Rotae* (1934); *De processibus pro ecclesiis orientalibus* (1950); also the Apostolic Constitution *Regimini* on the reform of the *Roman Curia,* 15 August 1967. LITERATURE. L. Wahrmund, *Quellen zur Geschichte des römisch-kanonischen Prozesses im Mittelalter,* I–V (1905–31); D. Lemieux, *The Sentence in Ecclesiastical Procedure* (1934); K. Mörsdorf, *Rechtsprechung und Verwaltung im kanonischen Recht* (1941); A. Esswein, *Extra-judicial Coercive Powers of Ecclesiastical Superiors* (1941); F. della Rocca, *Istituzioni di diritto processuale canonico* (1946); id., *Diritto processuale canonico* (1946); C. Lefebvre, in *Ephemerides Iuris Canonici* 4 (1948), pp. 282–312; E. Jombart, "Délit", in *Dictionnaire de Droit Canonique*, IV, cols. 1084–97; M. Lega and V. Bartocetti, *Commentarius in Iudicia Ecclesiastica,* 3 vols. (1950); C. Lefebvre, "Expertise" in *Dictionnaire de Droit Canonique*, V, cols. 690–702; id., "La juridiction administrative en droit canonique", *L'Année Canonique* 3 (1954–55), pp. 63–74; id., *Analecta Gregoriana* 69 (1955), pp. 435–46; K. Mörsdorf, "De relationibus inter potestatem administrativam et iudicialem in iure canonico", *Analecta Gregoriana* 69 (1955), pp. 401–18; F. Roberti, *De Processibus,* I (4th ed., 1956), II (1926); R. Naz, *Traité de droit canonique,* IV (1958); A. Augustinus, in C. Lefebvre, ed., *Praxis Rotae* (1960); C. Lefebvre, "Pouvoirs de l'Église", *Dictionnaire de Droit Canonique*, VII (1961), cols. 71–108; id., "Rota Romaine", *ibid.,* cols. 742–71; R. Naz, "Procédure", *ibid.,* cols. 281–311; C. Lefebvre, "Procureur", *ibid.,* cols. 324–29; id.,"Remèdes pénaux", *ibid.,* cols. 574–77; id., "Sentence", *ibid.,* cols. 952–62; G. Pellegrini, *Ius ecclesiasticum poenale,* I (1962); A. Jullien, *Juges et avocats du for ecclésiastique* (1964).

Charles Lefebvre

ECONOMIC ETHICS

I

Business ethics pertains to a sphere of economics which only exists in a "social" economy, and one that is organized on a commercial basis. In a "social" economy a social process intervenes between the natural processes of the production and consumption of goods that go on in every economy (even one like Robinson Crusoe's). In the case of a household, or a fully communist society, this intermediate process is an allotment of burdens and benefits: the head of the house assigns each member of the household his task and his share of what is produced, or earned, by common effort; the master plan determines what each factory shall make, where the goods shall be supplied, and how much of what they have produced may be taken by individuals for their own needs. But in a commercial economy the process of distribution intervenes between production and consumption in the form of a contractual exchange of services, and the same happens among producers themselves. Business ethics is the branch of economic ethics that relates to contractual affairs of this kind. Every sort of economic activity is governed by its particular ethics as well as by the general rules of economic ethics, and the larger contract looms in an economy the more importance attaches to business ethics. Since this contractual exchange of services plays an overwhelming role in the present economy of the "free world" — a "commercialized" economy we may call it in the more advanced countries, as very little non-commercial exchange of goods goes on there — and has developed highly specialized forms (credit, insurance, the stock market, and so forth), the range of business ethics widens, constantly posing new problems for solution.

Business ethics engaged the attention of the medieval scholastics, and the later Spanish school did admirable work in this field, much of which is relevant to the problems of our day and indeed substantially coincides with our own view of these problems.

Contracts are systematically dealt with in the tractates *De Iustitia et Iure.* Unfortunately, the authors took over not only the general Roman doctrine of contract, but also all the particular forms of contract which they found in the highly-developed jurisprudence of Rome, thus involving themselves in a speculative jurisprudence based on authority, instead of examining the nature of the various economic transactions. With great logical acumen — sometimes with an exactitude worthy of philologists — they deduced the rights and duties of contracting parties from an analysis of the types of contract treated of by the great Roman lawyers. A classic example is the *contractus mutui,* which — as we are still shown today by unanswerable proofs — entitles the lender to no profit *(auctarium) ex mutuo (sic),* but only to repayment of the loan itself *(tantundem).* They failed to see that conclusions logically deduced from definitions tell one nothing about reality. Ethical evaluations do not depend on a definition, but on the thing defined; in this case, on the economic structure of the transaction intended. This structure can and will change in the course of time, even though we go on calling it a particular kind of contract (such as *emptio–venditio, operae locatio-conductio,* or *mutuum*).

The best scholastic writers are undoubtedly distinguished not only by their juristic brilliance but by the pains they took to inform themselves about business practice (and practices). As often as not, they were able to sift the economic grain from the legal chaff which was often very cleverly misused. Yet these authors looked on the classical transactions and contracts not as human means to an end, changing with the realities of economics, but like Roman law in general as "right reason in writing". Thus they unwittingly helped to exaggerate the autonomy of a voluntarist, individualist private law (no longer controlled, as it was in ancient Rome, by the *ius publicum*) which still influences the jurisprudence of Latin countries.

In the first place, material justice requires that the principle of equivalence be observed: mutual services rendered must have the same value, that is, they must be exchanged only on the proper economic basis. It is for economics to determine what this proper basis is (in a money economy, what prices, or rather what relative prices, shall prevail) and where it shall apply: but this economics can only do with reference to the general end or good, that is, having recourse to principles that transcend the economic domain. Economic or business ethics takes these principles "for granted".

Not only the (principal) service must be taken into consideration, but also the extra services (which are often inadequately recognized), in particular the acceptance of risk. A great many offences against business ethics are committed by burdening, even crushing the weaker party with extra services for which he receives no corresponding benefit, as large firms commonly do by their "general terms of trade" (see below). Business long ago outgrew all the contractual forms and commercial law of antiquity; to a great extent it has either dispensed with contracts or reduced them to a fiction. When a man embarks on dealings with a bank, or takes out a policy with an insurance company, on the basis of the general conditions on which they do business, the two parties do not freely come to terms between themselves; each *submits* to the conditions that have been devised by the company lawyers. In the event of disagreement, there is no question of fact, no enquiry into what the contracting parties intended and agreed to do; only a question of law, how the company's conditions are to be objectively interpreted.

The relations between an employer and an employee (quite apart from the fact that these are largely governed by the general laws of the land relating to labour) are not necessarily based on the existence of a valid contract between them. There may be no more than the fact that employment has been offered and accepted.

Whereas business ethics once had to do simply with *obligationes ex contractu* as contrasted with *obligationes ex delicto,* this is no longer the case. Legal obligations now arise not only from illegal acts (delicts) but also from a variety of legal acts, thanks in particular to the vast extension of legal liability that is inevitable in a modern social economy. The day is long past when, contract apart, a man was only liable if found at fault. In such a situation all one can do is to deduce the rights and duties of all concerned from an analysis of the economic aspect of contractual and other legally enforceable transactions. When disputes arise, a solution that is both just and appropriate must be found in the same way. Small wonder, then, if the number of "undefined legal terms" and "general provisions" in modern legislation constantly multiplies.

In the interests of legitimate business, public confidence in what *seems* to be justice must be fostered, even at the expense of actual justice which is not obvious, and that far beyond the narrow confines of classical *usucapio* and *praescriptio*. Material justice must yield to the demands of legal security on a scale hitherto unknown.

Law simply cannot cope with the volume, rapidity, and enormous diversification of modern business: to legislate for these myriad details and eventualities is humanly impossible. Consequently business depends in very large measure on mutual confidence, and the main concern of business ethics must be to protect this confidence. Quite apart from any binding declarations of intent, the whole attitude of a man who is party to a transaction gives the other party to understand that he interprets the transaction in one definite sense and intends to honour his obligation accordingly. Now the other party must be able to rely on this impression. Neither party must deceive the other, each must justify the other's confidence. Exactly what one may expect in a given transaction depends on "normal business practice" in the circles concerned, the behaviour that is customary, for example, in dealings between merchants or between merchant and customer. This standard, of course, is somewhat fluid and discretionary; it belongs to the realm of "fringe morality". Some business people seek to prosper by operating on the lowest level sanctioned by current practice, a policy that has the effect of debasing commercial standards. What was average behaviour becomes the very best that can be expected, what was barely legitimate becomes average, and underneath a new limit has been established at a cruder level. Since this process may well lead to a general debasement of morality in economic life, there is some truth in the view that a commercial economy such as ours tends to demoralize society. The direct and inevitable result of the lowering of commercial standards is certainly that fairness or consideration which could once be taken for granted on the grounds of customary business practice, but must now be explicitly covenanted. In this respect fringe morality is the concern of the sociology of morals rather than of the ethics of business.

BIBLIOGRAPHY. G. von Mayr, *Die Pflicht im Wirtschaftsleben* (1900); F. X. Eberle, *Katholische Gesellschaftsmoral* (1921); G. Wünsch, *Evangelische Wirtschaftsethik* (1927); O. von Nell-Breuning, *Grundzüge der Börsenmoral* (1928); id., *Aktienreform und Moral* (1930); J. Azpiazu, *La moral del hombre de negocios* (1945); T. Surányi-Unger, *Private Enterprise and Governmental Planning* (1950); A. D. Ward, ed., *Goals of Economic Life* (1953); J. C. Bennet, H. R. Bowen, W. A. Brown, and G. B. Oxnam, *Christian Values and Economic Life* (1954); W. M. Childs, D. Cater, *Ethics in a Business Society* (1954); J. F. Cronin, *Social Principles and Economic Life* (1959); T. F. Divine, *Interest: An Historical and Analytical Study in Economics and Modern Ethics* (1959); B. M. Selekman, *A Moral Philosophy for Management* (1959).

Oswald von Nell-Breuning

II

The ethics of economics is part of social ethics, dealing with the law and order of economics according to moral principles. Ethics and economics are in themselves independent realms with laws of their own in each case. But in any given culture the two orders are closely inter-connected. Economic thinking, the style of an economy, will be the reflection of a given culture and style of life. Hence natural law among Christians is applied in economics mostly in the form of a supplementary code (Thomas Aquinas), that is, as a deduction from the changing circumstances of the development of society.

The notions of work and property are fundamental in the ethics of economics. Their contents are constantly changing.

1. *Historical survey*. Historians of religion are now convinced that primitive man followed clear ethical notions in his economic action. His thought, which was dominated by magico-religious categories, saw higher aids to his weak life in work, hunting, robbery, barter and trade. Property and ownership were felt to be sacred (for himself personally, for his family or community). He saw a relationship between sacrifice and barter; magic and handicrafts were both signs of human "superiority" (G. van de Leeuw), money had a magical origin. Work, however, was part of his very life, for which he had no distinct term or concept (Fourastié).

The agricultural communities which were flourishing over seven thousand years ago had as a rule no doubts about the right of property. Like work it was "part of the substance of life in the world, ethically legitimate and economically excellent" (A. Gehlen). Respect for property, the desire for stability and the readiness to subordinate private to public interests gave rise to the order of law as culture progressed. In the higher cultures of the Greeks and Romans work, except farming, was considered contemptible and hence was the business of foreign settlers *(metoikoi)* and slaves. This was possibly why no technology developed in the modern sense, in spite of high scientific achievements.

In the Christian lands of the West, Roman law, with Germanic modifications, continued in force, but was given new stresses. When Thomas Aquinas said: "Private property is legitimate, but must be used for the common good", he was describing the right to property as an assurance of freedom which brought with it an obligation towards the community (property as a "social pledge"). Work had been respected from primitive Christian times as obedience to the divine order of creation and a means of doing penance. Benedict of Nursia gave it a spiritual value *(ora et labora)* which made it one of the main factors in the shaping of the medieval world.

Thus the agricultural and feudal society,

including ownership of land, was based till well into modern times on the notion of "the legally and ethically admissible" (H. Mittels) and hence ruled by the "natural law". All social structures were rooted, so to speak, on the natural bed-rock. Loyalty on one side meant care and protection on the other. Furthermore, handicrafts, trade and city life in general accepted the notion of an income in keeping with one's state in life. All classes had certain rights and duties by birth, and traditional rights could be defended by revolt if necessary. The difference between rich and poor was regarded (within certain bounds) as the result of the divine order of things. (The system included grave injustices which were felt to be such.)

Hence it was only with industrialization, capitalism and its counterpart, socialism, that the great questions now posed by economic ethics were framed. Industrialization is now often described as the "passing of a second great threshold of culture" in human history (A. Gehlen, H. Freyer), comparable to the transition in the neolithic age to life in settlements. The second great change was of course preceded by gradual developments, such as the secularization of thinking and despotism or absolutism; on the economic level, by physiocracy, commerce, manufacture and banking. These preludes to the great ages of capitalism had their own proper economic ethics. The citizens were to prosper by being formed into a working society. This meant, for instance, a fierce struggle against poverty, begging and idleness. Penitentiaries, workhouses and orphanages were used as training-schools in disciplined work, which helped to create a working class which already resembled a proletariate. The industrial revolution itself (mechanization of spinning and weaving, the steam-engine, the whole manufacturing system) was supported by the principles of "liberalism" which claimed that in view of changed economic conditions "the profits of private enterprise were justified as a service to the community" (J. Messner).

The successors of the classical economists held that equilibrium could only be achieved in a trading economy by the incentive of private profit, which ultimately at least would bring about the harmonization of all interests. Ethics had no place in such economic theory. Its place was taken by the economic law of free competition, which left capitalist enterprise with an easy conscience. The upshot was the reduction of the working classes to the state of a proletariate, living in conditions of misery which were to endure for a hundred years (starvation wages, recurrent waves of unemployment, child labour, widespread in England as late as 1875).

Industrialism also fully re-organized the actual work in the factories by the division of labour, first as between the workers and then between men and machines. Work was regarded as a "commodity", and very often became a soulless repetition of operations (the conveyor belts of the twenties). Factories and business became a "skilful combination of partial human beings" (W. Sombart). The costs of this ethic-less economy were paid a million times over in human dignity. Even the most inhuman hardships were not eliminated for many long years.

The development of industrialization was undoubtedly necessary and inevitable. In barely two hundred years it enabled world population to triple. Standards of living were raised in an undreamt-of way, and its means of communication (travel and news media) were responsible for the present unity of the human race. But it may certainly be assumed that had the human losses, especially those of the classical period of capitalism, been avoided by a just ethics of economics, the progress of industrialization might have been delayed, but would not have been prevented. For modern technology was and is used by the economic system, but is almost independent of it. On the other hand, it is one of the pillars of industry when combined with appropriate economic thinking.

The "social question" provoked by classical capitalism brought mighty forces into play, above all the trade unions and the socialist parties. In addition, voices were raised strictly in defence of social justice or economic ethics, in the Churches or among social scientists. These efforts and the social policies of various States were the real cause of the development of a modern theory of economic ethics. Like the so-called "sciences of relationships", psychology, sociology, political economy and anthropology (previously only in embryo in philosophy and theology), it was a product of the industrialized society of modern times. It may be affirmed that present-day Christian social teaching is based to a great extent on economic ethics and was developed also in opposition to an individualistic and utilitarian view of the world. This throws an enormous responsibility on Christian economic ethics.

The great target of Marxist socialism was liberal capitalism, whose enormities it pilloried fiercely and mercilessly. K. Marx protested passionately against the exploitation of men by the ruling classes, and the "self-alienation" which it brought with it. His doctrine was not aimed, however, at the reform of the class structure, but at its destruction by world revolution. Only the triumph of the revolution and the rule of the proletariate can enable man to find himself once more. This alone will enable him to live well in a being which is of itself well. Marx was fully convinced of the omnipotence of the technological and scientific man, who was to form a society which could not but dominate history and nature and hence redeem itself. His historical materialism and ethical determinism contain no economic ethics strictly speaking. His doctrine is rather a millenarist philosophy of history.

The ethical values presupposed in Marxism were soon recognized by the "revisionists". Hence modern communistic socialism often displays trends towards an ethics of economics and culture. They differ chiefly from the Christian view by regarding human society more or less as a "utilitarian institution without intrinsic bonds" (J. Schaschling).

2. *Present trends in economic ethics.* Modern economic ethics finds it desirable that there should be not merely a wide and equitable distribution of income but also the possibility of acquiring property (housing, savings, part ownership of the means of production). Social security and welfare should not be extended to the point that the will to self-help is lamed. Political economy must aim at a sound balance between a stable currency and full employment, since inflation is at least as harmful as a certain amount of unemployment.

Since freedom is a primary principle of social order, it should also have as much play as possible in economics, e.g., in the choice of calling and place of work, in the spending of income and the encouragement of free enterprise. Property should be restricted only insofar as this is absolutely demanded by the common good (hence, no nationalization merely as an electoral programme).

The two main principles of Catholic social doctrine, solidarism and the principle of subsidiarity, also hold good for economics. Hence on principle the State should not interfere with the initiatives and independence of economic life, and all forms of *dirigisme* are to be avoided, even in the developing countries which are only passing through the critical initial stage of building up capital.

Nonetheless, the needs of the emerging countries are the great social question of today for the Western countries. The income per head in the U.S.A., Canada, Australia and the countries of Central and North-Western Europe is between 500 and 1500 dollars a year. In the whole of South-Eastern Asia and in the majority of African and South American countries it is about or less than 100 dollars. Thirty per cent of the population of the world controls eighty per cent of its riches, while seventy per cent has to do with the remaining twenty per cent. This appalling inequality demands to be evened out, in the name of a genuine economic ethics, by generous aid for development.

See also *Natural Law, Work, Property, Liberalism, Social Movements, Marxism.*

BIBLIOGRAPHY. J. Messner, *Die Soziale Frage* (1928; 7th ed., 1964); A. Müller-Armack, *Genealogie der Wirtschaftsstile* (3rd ed., 1944); R. Tawney, *Religion and the Rise of Capitalism* (1936); O. Schilling, *Christliche Wirtschaftsethik* (1954); J. Pieper, *Justice* (1956); W. Stark, *Social Theory and Christian Thought* (1959); O. von Nell-Breuning, *Wirtschaft und Gesellschaft heute,* 3 vols. (1956—60); H. C. Setts, ed., *Christian Social Responsibility* (1957); J. Messner, *Wirtschaftsethik: Das Naturrecht* (4th ed., 1960); H. D. Wendland, *Einführung in die Sozialethik* (1963); J. Schasching, *Kirche und industrielle Gesellschaft* (1960).

Max Pietsch

ECUMENISM

I. Ecumenical Movement. II. Movements for Church Union. III. Catholic Ecumenism. IV. Ecumenical Theology: A. Controversial Theology. B. Ecumenical Theology. V. Christian-Jewish Dialogue. VI. Christian Denominations: A. Study of Christian Denominations. B. Confessionalism.

I. Ecumenical Movement

The term "ecumenical" comes from the Greek οἰχουμένη which means the inhabited earth (cf. Acts 17:7; Mt 24:14; Heb 2:5). In traditional Catholic usage it refers to a general Council of the whole Church. But its chief use today is to designate efforts on behalf of the unity of Christians. The "movement" in question means here the whole development of inter-ecclesiastical relationships and attitudes of which the goal is the removal of divisions among Christians. Though Catholic faith teaches that the unity of the Church is of divine institution, given by Jesus Christ, and cannot basically be lost, it is also true that the fullness of Church unity cannot be realized and that the unity of Christians was menaced from the start. The NT itself shows how St. Paul had to struggle for it, against dissident elements among the Corinthians and against Judaeo-Christians (Phil 4:2). The problem of unity became graver when notable sociological and national groups broke away, such as Manichaeans, Donatists, Arians, Montanists, Novatians, Monophysites and Nestorians. But large-scale attempts to heal the breaches were first undertaken after the division between East and West in 1054 — efforts which remained fruitless (Councils of Lyons and Florence). The rift within Western Christianity in the 16th century brought up the problem of Christian unity in a still more acute form. Hand in hand, no doubt, with the various divisions, there were always individual efforts to restore unity, above all in the days before the fronts had grown rigid. But it was not till the 20th century that whole Churches threw themselves into the "ecumenical movement". This had been prepared for by the new possibilities of human contact opened up by the 19th century and by the creation of world unions of Churches and denominations. A no less important part was played by the Christian youth organizations, where indeed ecumenical interests were pursued for the first time on a world-wide scale. The history of the ecumenical movement of the 20th century can be divided into three main parts: the period of development, up to the establishment of the World Council of Churches in 1948 at Amsterdam; the period up to the Second Vatican Council; the post-conciliar period, which may be characterized as the period of active co-operation on the part of the Roman Catholic Church.

1. In the period before the establishment of the World Council of Churches, there were may currents and cross-currents in the ecumenical movement. A factor of primary importance for further development was the establishment in Constance in 1914 of an international association for the work of friendship by the Churches, which aimed at contributing to the reconciliation of the peoples by promoting friendship between the Churches. Since no formal profession of faith was demanded, the co-operation of the Orthodox was possible. At a meeting of this association at Oud Wassenaar, Netherlands, 1919, the movement concerned with the relation of the Churches to practical life was founded, under the title of "Life and Work", chiefly at the instigation of Archbishop Söderblom. The first conference of "Life and Work" was held in August 1925 at Stockholm, with 661 delegates present from thirty-seven countries. This was the first time that official representatives of the Churches met in the movement. "Life and Work" sought to further re-union chiefly by co-operation in practical matters. The conference at Stockholm appealed to all Christians to do penance for the grievous harm of division and to make the gospel the decisive force in all regions of life. The work of the conference was continued actively by a standing committee which co-operated with the International Institute for Social Sciences at Geneva and with the Ecumenical Seminar founded by Adolf Keller. "Life and Work" set up its own theological commission (A. Deissmann, M. Dibelius), an Ecumenical Commission for Youth and an information centre with press services. It also undertook various charitable works. The second world conference of "Life and Work" was held at Oxford in July 1937. The theme was "Church, Community and State", and 421 official delegates from 120 Protestant and Orthodox Churches in forty countries took part. The assembly agreed that the goal of the unity of Christians could not be reached without linking up with the movement "Faith and Order", which was concerned with matters of faith and ecclesiastical constitution. It was decided to unite with "Faith and Order" to form the World Council of Churches. The growing interest in theological questions and

the undoubted influence of Karl Barth and the Calvinist Churches of the Continent had much to do with this step.

Christian unity had also been the goal of the movement "Faith and Order", which went back to the World Missionary Conference held at Edinburgh in 1910. There the Anglican Bishop Charles Brent had pointed out that it was impossible to exclude questions of faith and ecclesiology from discussions between denominations. His aim was to set up a council which would keep these matters before the public. He succeeded as early as 1910 in uniting at Geneva a preliminary assembly with 133 representatives from over eighty Churches in forty countries. The Roman Catholic Church was not represented, but the Orthodox Churches assured the organizers of their support. The first world conference of "Faith and Order" was held at Lausanne in August 1927, under the chairmanship of Bishop Brent. There were 394 delegates from 108 Churches. The conference appealed vigorously for Christian unity, and the decisive differences between the Churches were frankly discussed. After the death of Bishop Brent in 1929, the Archbishop of York, Dr. William Temple (later Archbishop of Canterbury), took over the presidency. At the second world conference at Edinburgh 1937, where there were 504 delegates from 123 Churches, it was decided to merge with "Life and Work", to found the World Council of Churches — a decision of fundamental importance.

2. Thus the plan for the World Council of Churches was accepted in principle at Oxford and Edinburgh in 1937. The constitution was outlined at Utrecht in 1938. The implementation was delayed by the War, but in 1948 the World Council of Churches was formally established at Amsterdam. At this first general assembly representatives of 147 Churches from forty-four countries took part. The general theme was "Man's Disorder and God's Design". The notable difference between the concept of the Church in the Protestant and the Catholic traditions was clearly brought out, but this did not prevent the general acknowledgment of the Church as the gift of God, founded by the saving acts of God in Christ. The delegates of the various Churches expressed their determination to remain in contact with one another. The second general assembly was held at Evanston, U.S.A., in 1954, under the title of "Christ, the Hope of the World". The third general assembly was at New Delhi in 1961, where 625 official delegates from 175 Churches took part, along with a large number of observers, including some from the Catholic Church. An important step was the acceptance of the candidacy of twenty-three Churches, including the Orthodox Churches of Russia, Bulgaria and Rumania. Another important step was the decision to integrate the International Missionary Council with the World Council. Thus the World Council was rejoined by a movement which had been one of the decisive factors in its creation, since the ecumenical movement was due to a great extent to the missionary movement. The general title of the New Delhi assembly was "Christ, the Light of the World". The serious efforts to remove points of controversy (through declarations on religious freedom, anti-Semitism and proselytism) showed that the assembly aimed at unity not just for the sake of the name, but as the foundation of a better and more obedient fulfilment of the Christian task in the world of today.

The title of the fourth general assembly, at Upsala, Sweden, July 1968, is, "Behold, I make all things new".

The World Council sees itself as a "fellowship of Churches which confess the Lord Jesus Christ as God and Saviour according to the Scriptures, and therefore seek to fulfil together their common calling to the glory of the one God, Father, Son and Holy Spirit". This is the "Basis", accepted at New Delhi in 1961. The great task is felt to be that of continuing the work of the two world conferences, "Life and Work" and "Faith and Order", and that of the World Missionary Council. The Council aims at making co-operation between the Churches easier, promoting co-operation in the field of studies, and stimulating and strengthening ecumenical and missionary endeavour among the members of the Churches. It keeps up relations with national and regional Christian councils, various denominational "world alliances" such as the "Evangelical Alliance" and other ecumenical organizations. It holds itself ready to convoke world conferences when urgent questions make it advisable. Thus the World Council does not see itself as a super-Church but as an instrument to serve the various Churches of which it is composed. The declarations of the World Council claim no other authority except what they intrinsically possess by reason of their own truth and wisdom. The Council works through the General Assembly as the supreme authority, under which there is a Central Committee and Working Committees as well as permanent administrative offices in Geneva and New York. There is a special secretariat for Eastern Asia. The Commission "Faith and Order" is of particular importance. It enjoys a certain independence within the World Council and has the right to propose that the Council hold special conferences to deal with its interests. Thus at Lund in 1952 there was a third world conference for "Faith and Order", at which it was agreed that the time for comparative study of denominations was over. An appeal was made to the Churches to press on to the unity based on Christ and not only to negotiate but to act together, as far as such common action was not in conflict with principles. The fourth world conference for "Faith and Order" was held at Montreal in 1963, and here for the first time the voices of the Orthodox Churches were given full hearing as well as those of critical historical theology. The dialogue with the Roman Catholic Church was likewise pursued with greater intensity.

At present some 220 Churches belong to the World Council, practically all non-Roman Catholic Christians, in fact. Some Protestant Churches still remain outside, such as the Southern Baptist Convention and the Lutheran Church Missouri Synod. In certain conservative Protestant circles there is a certain amount of opposition to the World Council, based on the fear that it might betray the Reformation.

3. The Roman Catholic Church was slow to join in the ecumenical movement. It was neither theologically nor psychologically well enough equipped. The official attitude was that Catholics should be discouraged from taking up the ecumenical problem along non-Catholic lines. This is the policy which was behind Benedict XV's refusal of the invitations of "Faith and Order" in December 1914 and May 1919; the prohibition of the Holy Office which prevented Catholics from taking part at the Lausanne conference of 1927 (cf. *AAS* 19 [1927], p. 278; *D* 2199); the encyclical *Mortalium Animos* of January 1928 (*AAS* 20 [1928], pp. 5–16); the warning of the Holy Office which included a prohibition of participation at Amsterdam (5 June 1948, *AAS* 40 [1948], p. 257). The Catholic Church took up an attitude of total rejection with regard to the World Council of Churches, where Protestant influence was very strong. Rome showed itself far more favourably disposed towards the Orthodox, chiefly on account of the fact that the Orthodox Churches have the same sacramental and dogmatic reality. Though the Catholic Church insisted on maintaining its standpoint, and offered reconciliation again and again on condition that the primacy of the Roman Pontiff be acknowledged, in the long run the need for mutual information was recognized. The Oriental Institute was set up in Rome in 1927, the Russicum in 1929, while the monastery of Amay (later Chevetogne) was founded in 1925, and in 1927 the Istina centre, for the encouragement of union efforts with the East. But there were no official meetings between the Churches, and no real theological dialogue.

Nonetheless, the ecumenical movement was gaining ground irresistibly in the Catholic Church. Small groups, led by charismatically gifted men, such as the *Una Sancta* movement in Germany, promoted the ecumenical ideal and laid indestructible foundations for the future during the difficult years of World War II. The annual octave of prayer for unity (18–25 January) became more and more popular. The desire for union was reinforced year by year through the multiplication of personal contacts with Christians of other confessions, fresh recourse to the sources (Scripture, liturgy, patristics) which led to extensive inter-denominational work, closer study of Church history and the difficulties caused in the mission fields by the divisions between the Churches. This spiritual ground swell could not but affect in the end the higher authorities. The Roman reaction was first very hesitant, as in the instruction *Ecclesia Catholica* of 20 December 1949 (*AAS* 42 [1950], pp. 142–7), where the many private initiatives were given a firm basis in the Church. In 1952 a non-official "International Catholic Conference for Ecumenical Questions" was founded (Mgr. J. G. M. Willebrands). But the turning-point really came with John XXIII, who made the notion of ecumenism one of the main interests of the Second Vatican Council which he convoked. His motu proprio *Superno Dei Nutu* of 5 June 1960 established a secretariat for the unity of Christians. The Second Vatican Council then became a great ecumenical event. Nearly all non-Catholic Churches were represented at it by observers, who had a real influence on the course of the Council. All the documents of the Council show its ecumenical interests, but these were mainly expressed in the Declaration on Religious Freedom and the Decree on Ecumenism, promulgated on 21 November 1964. Apart from the tangible results contained in the texts of the Council, the many personal contacts and the new spirit which made itself felt at the Council will be of decisive importance. It was symbolic of this new spirit that on 7 December 1965 the Pope and the Patriarch of Constantinople mutually lifted the excommunication which Pope Leo IX and the Patriarch Michael Caerularius had imposed on each other in 1054.

After the Council, ecumenical work within the Catholic Church has been co-ordinated by the Secretariat for the Promotion of Christian Unity, which has become a permanent (curial) institution. Relations between the Roman Catholic Church and the World Council of Churches have become closer and more frequent. There are mixed "working parties" which take in members from the World Council, the Anglican Communion, the Lutheran and the Methodist world alliances. Serious theological work is done by these international commissions and efforts are made to further actual unity.

Up to the present, there has been no official theological dialogue with the Orthodox Churches. Nonetheless, it is impossible to doubt that the Churches are growing closer together, as may be seen from the mutual visits of Pope Paul VI and the Patriarch Athenagoras in 1964 and 1967.

Within the Catholic Church, the ecumenical task is also served by the *Directorium Oecumenicum,* containing the various implementations of the Decree on Ecumenism. The first part of the *Directorium* was published by the Secretariat for Unity in 1967.

We cannot of course discuss here all that is being done on the level of the local Churches. But such efforts will undoubtedly be as important in the future as the many bilateral and multilateral conversations on a world-wide scala. Insofar as the unity of Christians depends on men, much will depend on whether the Churches themselves are ready for real reform and renewal.

See also *Ecumenism* II, III, IV, *Church* II, III.

BIBLIOGRAPHY. H. Brandreth, *Unity and Reunion. A Bibliography* (2nd ed., 1948); G. Baum, *Progress and Perspectives: The Catholic Quest for Christian Unity* (1962); *Internationale Ökumenische Bibliographie* (1962 ff.; 1967 ff.); N. Goodall, *Ecumenical Movement* (2nd ed., 1964); R. Rouse and S. C. Neill, *History of the Ecumenical Movement, 1517–1948* (2nd revised ed., 1967); G. Tavard, *Two Centuries of Ecumenism* (new ed., 1967); B. Lambert, *Ecumenism: Theology and History* (1967).

August B. Hasler

II. Movements for Church Union

A. Origins

Ever since apostolic times the visible unity of the Church of Christ has been endangered and sometimes obscured by schism, heresy and division. The recovery of unity is, however, required of the Church not simply for the sake of a more convincing attestation of its missionary calling but by an explicit command of Christ himself (Jn 17). Even though non-theological motives, e.g., ecclesiastical centralism and political uniformity, have frequently played a major role in concrete efforts to secure unity, the Church has not evaded this command. In the internal Church dialogue of the Councils, with the help of the somewhat fickle patronage of the secular power, it proved possible to check and halt the impetus of the great decisive movements of the first thousand years, considered as historical movements: Arianism, Donatism, Novatianism, Priscillianism, Montanism and Nestorianism have all vanished. Yet even here there was no complete recovery of all those who branched off; Monophysite Churches rejecting the Council of Chalcedon (451) exist down to the present day, mainly in Egypt and Ethiopia. The Armenian Church also goes back to the same origins. Small sections only of these Churches entered into unions with Rome. These separated communities, theologically introverted and culturally isolated, never made any deep impression on the consciousness of the wider Church; only with the severing of relations between the Pope and the Patriarch of Constantinople in

1054 did the division between East and West in the Western Schism begin to assume the character of a lasting form of Church co-existence.

This profound division, with its far-reaching effects in the intellectual and cultural spheres, was the result of a long process of alienation and withdrawal; the patriarchates of Rome and Constantinople had for centuries lived in a latent state of schism which repeatedly took concrete form, most vigorously, no doubt, in the clash between Pope Nicholas I and the Patriarch Photius (864–868). The ultimate breach under the Patriarch Michael Caerularius, responsibility for which was shared by the militant Roman legate, Cardinal Humbert, with his domineering behaviour, had its roots in a complex historical process which the events of the year 1054 simply brought to a conclusion. Objective factors in this process included: the difference between Western Roman and Eastern Greek modes of thought in theology and religion, e.g., controversy over the procession of the Holy Spirit; the difference in their liturgies; and above all the difference in Church structures in East and West. The Eastern Imperial Church readily adapted itself to the patterns of secular authority and regarded the unity of the whole Church as a fellowship of largely autonomous local Churches. But the Western Papal Church was jealous of its independence of secular authority and open to the idea of a monarchical papacy. Subjective factors would include: contempt for the Greeks on the one side, hatred of the Latins on the other. This sense of superiority on both sides inevitably encouraged the hardening of positions and attempts to force them on the other "heretical" side. Developments on both Churches following the breach of 1054 deepened this already wide range of differences.

In the West the idea of the primacy promoted by the Gregorian Reform became the dominant element of Church polity. The 12th-century Decretals made the Pope the source of all authority in the Church, thereby creating a centralizing ideology which was to cast its shadow over all later union negotiations. In the East the concept of an imperial Church was in fact ousted by the concept of autocephalicity, i.e., the independence of the national Orthodox Churches, although the ecclesiological principle of patriarchal autonomy remained

unchanged. The excesses of the Crusades and the political isolation of Byzantium as a result of Turkish encirclement produced among ordinary Church people an emotional shock whose effects have lasted into the 20th century and which has been transmitted to the nations evangelized by Byzantium in the form of a profound distrust of the Latin West; for example, the refusal of the leaders of the Greek Orthodox Church to send observers to the Second Vatican Council. What had meanwhile proved amenable to clarification at the theological level, in negotiations between East and West, was thus at once radically called in question by a counter-pressure from below. Separate theological and religious developments on both sides (Scholasticism in the West, Palamism and Hesychasm in the East) ultimately lessened the chances of reaching agreement on the basis of a common terminology.

B. History of Union Efforts

Only when seen against this complex historical and sociological backcloth does the history of the attempts to achieve unity — and not least their failure — become intelligible. Attempts to achieve unity in the 12th century by absorption of the East failed. In the 13th century the Emperor Michael Palaeologus was driven by mainly political considerations into negotiations with Rome. The union imposed at the Council of Lyons (1274) was, however, not a genuine settlement but "an enforced capitulation of East to West" (de Vries). Rome imposed on the Greeks typically Latin formulas which went beyond the inalienable substance of faith, and also a typically Western concept of primacy. The counter-reaction on the part of the Greek Church was sharp. The union was rejected; the Emperor was exommunicated. The consequence of this failure was a drag on all subsequent conversations. In the 14th century Rome had ceased even to entertain the idea of negotiations at a conciliar level, and simply demanded unconditional surrender. It was only disillusionment consequent on the Western Schism and fear of the danger which Conciliarism represented for the papacy that eventually forced Rome to a more realistic view of the situation and led it to accept the Council so often proposed by the Greeks who admittedly here again were moved by the Turkish menace. At the Council of Ferrara-Florence (1438–39) Greeks and Latins sat down together as equally authorized parties to the negotiations and reached real agreement in the doctrinal question of the *Filioque* but only an apparent agreement in the matter of Church structure. The too hurriedly produced union formula contained, immediately after the recognition of the Pope as the supreme head of the whole Church, the qualifying clause, "without prejudice to all the privileges and rights of the patriarchs of the East". Since each side attached a completely different meaning to this formula, in accordance with its different ecclesiological traditions, the seeds of disruptive conflict were already present. Yet this union — inadequately prepared psychologically — was already doomed to failure at the outset because of the refusal of the people to have any dealings with the West (actual end of the union and capture of Constantinople by the Turks, 1453; official rejection, 1483).

It took the papacy of the Catholic Reform and Counter-Reformation a long time to make up its mind gradually to recognize the right of the East to its own way of life and to draw the appropriate conclusions. Disguised attempts at absorption succeeded in securing a tolerance based on practical considerations; the leaders of the Latin Church had lost any feeling for a measure of genuine autonomy in the patriarchates and for the special character of Eastern spirituality, remaining, down to our own days, prisoners of the idea of the *praestantia* of the Latin rite. Progress was made in the pontificate of Gregory XIII, by the establishment of the Congregation *De Propaganda Fidei* in 1622, by further positive instructions of Benedict XIV and above all Leo XIII. The call to unity addressed by Pius IX to the separated Orthodox hierarchy (1848) met with sharp rejection and went no further than verbal exchanges, because it failed to understand the psychological situation of the East and because the West was not prepared for a sincere appreciation of the distinctive qualities of the East, as the negotiations of the First Vatican Council show. On the other hand, the increasing introversion of the Orthodox Churches of Russia and Greece and their dependence on the State tied the hands of the relevant authorities.

Anti-Roman feeling and political opportunism obviated all possibility of serious dialogue with the West. Efforts to reconcile the Church communities resulting from the Reformation go back to the thirties and forties of the 16th century. So long as the opposing fronts had not yet hardened, discussion was not ruled out but it proved impossible to exploit this relatively favourable situation. The rulers of the Roman Church did not at first realize the depth of the problem, while the Protestant forces, in their eagerness to formulate their confessional position, rejected all compromise and settled down contentedly with their own views. The chances of reconciliation were reduced by the rapid onset of the confessionalizing process, for the issues at stake included not only questions of Church structure but doctrinal matters as well. The absence of any binding doctrinal authority was a major obstacle to dialogue with the Protestants, divided as they were among themselves and continuing to divide even further. Union negotiations at an official level never proved possible, as they had in the case of the Orthodox Church. Contacts were restricted to those between irenical individual members of the clergy and laity. These efforts at union had a precarious, almost amateurish, character. In the 17th, 18th and 19th centuries, Church authorities on both sides seemed no longer interested in them and allowed those who wished to discuss union to do so merely as well-meaning outsiders, unless they entertained hopes of deriving direct strategic confessional advantage from such talks.

In the 16th century, a genuine mediating theology, humanist in origin, sought to heal the breach from both sides. Although it is not difficult from the secure vantage point of post-Tridentine Catholicism to find fault with the inadequacies of this theology (its imprecision, e.g., doctrine of double righteousness, minimizing of doctrinal differences, etc., secular concern for national unity), there can be no questioning its religious earnestness and theological responsibility. Intellectually and theologically its exponents, mostly found on the old Church side, were in the Erasmian tradition. They included the Cologne-born Johannes Gropper (1503–1559), Bishop Julius Pflug of Naumburg (1499–1564), G. Cassander (d. 1566), the lay Cardinal Contarini, and, above all, Georg

Witzel (d. 1573). Secular patriotic motives were more clearly at work in the union efforts of the group around the imperial chancellor Gattinara, continued further by Granvella, Zeld and Zasius. Its great chance came with the religious colloquies started at Leipzig in 1539, continued at Hagenau, and with brighter prospects at Worms in 1541 and at the Regensburg Reichstag. The leading Protestant representatives in the discussions were Martin Bucer and Melanchthon. Agreement was reached on some fundamental points, e.g., on the question of man's original state and free will and even on the question of justification, interpreted as "faith working by love". No agreement was reached in other matters, such as the inerrancy of Councils, confession, the primacy, and transubstantiation. But even the points agreed on were robbed of their credal character by triumphalist self-righteousness on both sides.

After the Council of Trent there was no longer any place for an Erasmian mediating theology, nor did the hardening of opposition during the period of the Wars of Religion provide the necessary conditions for dialogue. On the Protestant side, Georg Calixtus (1586–1656) was an isolated pioneer of reunion on the basis of the *consensus quinquesaecularis* of the ancient Church, comprising the main articles of the Christian faith. His ideas influenced the Conference of Thorn of 1645, which was intended to restore religious unity in Poland though in fact it proved fruitless. Men like Johannes Kepler (d. 1630), the Lutheran astronomer, and Hugo Grotius (d. 1645), the exponent of international law, also showed a deep concern for Church unity. The contacts entered into by Rojas de Spinola, Bishop of Wiener Neustadt, with Protestant court circles, especially Hanover, in the years 1673 to 1683 were mainly diplomatic in character. G. Molanus (1633–1722), the Lutheran Abbot of Loccum, and the philosopher Leibniz (d. 1716), librarian to the Duke of Hanover, were among the parties to these discussions. The exchange of letters between Leibniz and the experienced controversialist theologian Bossuet, Bishop of Meaux, came to grief objectively because of Leibniz's rejection of the Council of Trent but also subjectively because of the Bishop's lack of sympathetic understanding. Many irenical contacts were also cultivated in England,

especially after the return of Charles II to the throne (1660). The Gallican idea of the Church seemed to offer the possibility of reconciliation with the episcopal Church of England. The Franciscan N. Davenport produced a Catholic interpretation of the Thirty-nine Articles, while the Benedictine Robinson discussed the questions of the Real Presence and the validity of Anglican orders. The accession of William of Orange to the throne (1688) was a severe setback, yet renewed union negotiations proved possible under William Wake (Archbishop of Canterbury from 1716).

In Germany, the problem of reunion was not solved by the conversion of many of the princes to Roman Catholicism during the transition period from the 17th to the 18th century. The union plans of the Catholic Enlightenment, by far the most significant of which was the draft of a constitution for a national episcopal Church by the Auxiliary Bishop of Trier, J. N. von Hontheim (Febronius), were reduced to nothing between the opposing fronts. Count N. L. Zinzendorf (1700–1760), the founder of the pietistic *Unitas Fratrum,* enjoyed friendly relations with Cardinal de Noailles. Among the union efforts of the German Romantic movement, those of Franz von Baader have a special importance, aiming as they did at reconciliation with the Eastern Church. There was a further hardening of confessional differences in Germany after 1840 and Catholic-Protestant relations reached a decided nadir in the period of Ultramontanism and Culture-Protestantism. There was no longer any intellectual responsiveness. It was only after his excommunication that I. von Döllinger, who saw clearly that concern for reunion was the special responsibility of German theology, began discussions with the Orthodox and Anglican Churches (Bonn Union Conferences, 1874–75). In England hopes of reunion stimulated by the Oxford Movement were dashed after a few years due to the unsympathetic attitude and inadequate theological equipment of members of the Church hierarchy.

C. Present Situation

Considering the preponderant Italian influence in the Curial administration, which had no experience of Church division in its own territory, it is not surprising that no fresh impetus came from Rome. In the first half of the 20th century, official pronouncements about the separated brethren by the Roman Church were still expressed in terms of the over-simplified ideology of the "Return", even though the tone changed in the course of the years and efforts by individual pioneers for unity were tolerated or even encouraged. The growth of the ecumenical movement within non-Catholic Christendom stimulated Roman Catholic theologians as well to rethink the problems of Church disunity and to intensify contacts with the separated brethren. The renewal of Catholic theology at the beginning of the 20th century, particularly historical and critical research in biblical exegesis, liturgy and Church history, created new bases for dialogue from within. Beneath superficial differences which were children of their times, more fundamental agreements were rediscovered. The theological problems of division were now understood — and this was decisive — in their true context. Catholic unionists were no longer inspired by motives of Church policy but by primarily religious motives. The theological and historical spadework was accompanied by efforts to interest wider circles of Church people in this concern for reunion and to enlist them in the ministry of Christian prayer for unity. The adoption of the Octave of Prayer which had originated in Anglicanism (1908), and the tireless efforts of the charismatic personality, the Abbé Couturier (d. 1953), were important landmarks along this way. The Malines Conversations, which were held between Catholics and Anglicans from 1921 to 1926 under the active patronage of Cardinal Mercier, represented a religious colloquy unique of its kind. Among leading pioneers of the ecumenical idea in French-speaking countries were the Benedictine Dom Lambert Beauduin, who founded the first Union monastery for the study of the Christian East in 1925 at Amay-on-the-Maas (now at Chevetogne), and the Dominican Yves Congar, whose book *Chrétiens Désunis* (1937) represents the first outline of a Catholic union theology. Other important pioneers were the Lazarist Father Portal, Abbé Gratieux and Bishop Besson of Fribourg. In Germany, Max Pribilla, S.J., M. K. Metzger, M. Laros and O. Karrer, communicated, by their lectures and writings, a concern for the *Una Sancta* to clergy and

people, while J. Lortz, developing independently the ideas of his teacher S. Merkle, provided a new basis for a Catholic interpretation of the Reformation and created the indispensable conditions for an unbiased assessment of Luther's personality.

The participation in a common destiny and suffering during the war years increased the contacts between the Christian confessions and this also gave added impetus to practical efforts towards union in ecumenical work-parties. The *Una Sancta* movement which had thus emerged within Roman Catholicism, not without its occasionally severe trials, received striking endorsement under the pontificate of John XXIII by the establishment at Rome of a permanent Secretariat for the Promotion of Christian Unity (1960). The Decree of the Second Vatican Council on Ecumenism (1964) made concern for reunion a matter of conscience for the whole Church. Of theological significance is the decree's recognition of the ecclesial reality of the Churches and ecclesial communities separated from Rome. In the practical sphere mention should be made of its reference to the possibility of concrete joint inter-confessional work and also its recognition of inter-communion with the Eastern Churches. The Decree on Ecumenism inaugurated a new phase in the history of Church movements for unity. Other initiatives on the part of John XXIII and Paul VI have made it clear that this is no ephemeral change of climate but the entry into an authentically new era.

See also *Eastern Churches, Schism* III, IV, *Pope, Reform, Reformation, Conciliarism, Gallicanism.*

BIBLIOGRAPHY. ATTEMPTED UNION WITH THE EASTERN CHURCHES: *L'Église et les Églises. Neuf siècles de douloureuse séparation entre L'Orient et l'Occident*, 2 vols. (Chevetogne 1954–55); J. Gill, *The Council of Florence* (1959); id., *L'accord gréco-latin au concile de Florence: Le Concile et les Conciles* (1960), pp. 183–94; W. de Vries, *Rom und die Patriarchate des Ostens* (1963); B. Roberg, *Die Union zwischen der griechischen und der lateinischen Kirche auf dem II. Konzil von Lyon 1274* (1964). ATTEMPTED UNION WITH THE PROTESTANT CHURCHES: F. W. Kantzenbach, *Das Ringen um die Einheit der Kirche im Jahrhundert der Reformation* (1957); G. Tavard, *Two Centuries of Ecumenism* (1961); R. Rouse and S. Neill, eds., *A History of the Ecumenical Movement, 1517–1948* (1954); Y. Congar, *Chrétiens en dialogue. Contributions catholiques à l'œcuménisme* (1964); B. Leeming, *The Vatican and*

Christian Unity (1965); L. Alting von Geusau, *Ecumenism and the Roman Catholic Church* (1966).

Victor Conzemius

III. Catholic Ecumenism

1. What has to be said under this heading is in substance a repetition of what was said in the Vatican II Decrees on Ecumenism and on the Eastern Catholic Churches. For details, reference may be made to these decrees generally, and in particular to chapter ii of the Decree on Ecumenism. The very fact that the possibility of dialogue and cooperation exists, shows the profound change that has occurred in the Catholic Church's relation to other Christian Churches and ecclesial communities. The Catholic Church of course is conscious of itself, now as always, as the Church in which the one Church of Christ subsists, and in its own understanding of its own nature (as a part of its faith in the whole of the revelation of God in Jesus Christ), it cannot simply concede the same character to the other Churches. Nevertheless, it does not now regard these Churches and ecclesial communities primarily as something which ought not to exist, which has to be abolished as soon as possible by the repentance and conversion of individuals, as heresy and schism to be anathematized. It now regards them primarily as partners in a dialogue and a collaboration between Christians who have more in common than separates them and possess a common task in regard to the "world".

2. The foundation of this dialogue is the realization of what is really common to all or is accepted as a task by all. This includes the common faith in God and Jesus Christ as our only Lord and Saviour; the mutual recognition (as a Christian and human duty) of one another's good will; unconditional respect for one another's religious freedom; the common baptism and common incorporation in Christ; the existence of other sacraments in these Churches; the conviction that grace and justification are found among non-Catholic Christians also; the recognition that the non-Catholic Churches as such have in fact a positive saving function for non-Catholic Christians and that these Churches preserve and live out a valuable Christian inheritance which need not necessarily be found in every respect equally clearly in the Catholic Church as it actually exists in fact; the conviction that the Churches are therefore not separated from one another in every respect, that they are not only "separated brethren"; awareness of *common* responsibility for the division of Christendom, blame for which cannot be attributed simply and solely to present-day Christians, so that we cannot regard the others as formal heretics; recognition that the actual appearance presented by one's own Church, is always in need of penance and reform, and obscures the testimony it bears to its origin in Christ's will to found it; acknowledgment of Christian life in other Churches, even to the point of martyrdom, life which also contributes to the building up of the Catholic Church; and finally the common concern of all for the unity of the Church.

3. A dialogue which is something different from polemics or a direct and onesided attempt at conversion, presupposes that *both* parties assume that they have something to learn from the other and endeavour to learn it. The Catholic can make this assumption. For even though he is convinced that the Church of Christ subsists in the Roman Catholic Church, this does not exclude the possibility and the will to receive and learn from others as well. Nor does this capacity to receive consist solely in the fact that dialogue can provide better information about the attitude, doctrine and Christian life of the non-Catholic partner and the latter's difficulties in regard to the Catholic Church, in other words, knowledge which to a considerable extent is not sufficiently found among Catholics, even among theologians. There is also a capacity to receive because the non-Catholic Christian and his Churches possess a wealth of Christian life and of other developments of the one identical Christianity, of theology, of charismatical impulses, of experience of Christian action in regard to the "world", etc., which need not necessarily be present with the same intensity and clarity in the Catholic Church. Ecumenical discussions of the kind envisaged also have the character of dialogue to the extent that they are not directly concerned with individual conversions to the Catholic Church, though this, if the necessary conditions are presupposed, is a legitimate aim, but one which must be carefully distinguished from ecumenical discussion. They also

have the character of dialogue because even from the standpoint of a Catholic conception of the Church the unity striven for must not simply be thought of as a "return". For the Church of the future which is aimed at, even in its character as Roman Catholic, must also contain the significant Christian past and the treasures of other Churches. In a certain sense, therefore, it will be a different Church from the present Catholic Church in the historically-conditioned form it will bear in that age. Discussion is therefore to that extent a dialogue in relation to an open future. Christians nowadays cannot live side by side in indifference to one another as though their separation were an unalterable fact. A truly Catholic conception of the Church (the Catholic Church as the Church of all) would in fact be unfaithful to itself if it were to take the divisions of Christendom simply as a fact about which nothing can be done. Such infidelity to itself does not happen in theory but does happen very often in practice. Dialogue is necessary and is possible as an open dialogue; this need not forbid any of the partners from pursuing it on their own assumptions.

4. As its object this dialogue has everything which can serve the unity of Christians in belief, Church, Christian life and responsible action for the world. It would therefore extend to mutual information about life and doctrine; improved understanding of one another's theology; the endeavour by each to translate their own theology into the language of the other; the endeavour to overcome real differences in doctrine; agreement for common action (cf. No. 5 below).

5. Dialogue can lead to concrete results and real collaboration even before its ultimate goal is reached. There still exist mutual intolerance and un-Christian forms of competition in the everyday social world, which could readily and broad-mindedly be abandoned. Questions of mixed marriages and denominational schools (and their relations and collaboration) await attention and might be solved in a better way than they have been so far. Concrete organized collaboration in theology would be possible. More translations of the Bible could be made in common, as encouraged by Paul VI. Unfair exploitation of conversions for propaganda purposes by either side could be

tactfully avoided. Agreements should be concluded as to how even now the scandal of a divided Christendom might be avoided in the missions and how, despite the right in principle to pursue missionary activity everywhere, a right which for the Catholic Church is an inalienable one, a friendly, and in view of the shortage of missionaries, realistic division of missionary work or of missionary territories, might be arrived at. Elements actually common to all, in liturgy, hymns and religious customs could be encouraged. Prior mutual consultation could avoid the creation of new obstacles to unity in doctrine and practice, unless these derived from the conscientious belief of each. Everything possible which from the point of view of dogmatic and moral theology is *communicatio in sacris* should not only be tolerated but encouraged cautiously and tactfully, but without undogmatic "irenism". Not everything is possible, of course, but a good deal is, to a different extent it is true in regard to the various Churches. Services can be held in common for prayer and the liturgy of the word without celebration of the Eucharist, and their content need not necessarily only consist of prayer for the reunion of Christendom. With the Eastern Orthodox Churches even a considerable sacramental *communicatio in sacris* is possible, as is expressly stated by the decree of Vatican II on Eastern Catholic Churches (arts. 26 ff.). There is a wide field of collaboration available in the duty of all Christians to shape the secular world in a more humane and therefore more Christian way in the social, cultural, economic, political and welfare spheres. In very many respects the Churches acting in common could be the conscience of secular society. In common they could intervene, even in brave contradiction to egotistical people in their own ranks, in favour of peace, the abolition of racial discrimination, social justice, the eradication of nationalist prejudices, protection of the poor and weak. For all these purposes common institutions could be set up by common action.

See also *Church, Conversion, World*.

BIBLIOGRAPHY. Y. Congar, *Chrétiens désunis* (1937); A. Senand, *Christian Unity. A Bibliography. Selected Titles concerning International Relations between the Churches, and International Christian Movement; from a larger Bibliography* (1937); C.-J.

Dumont, *Les voies de l'unité chrétienne. Doctrine et spiritualité* (1954), E. T.: *Approaches to Christian Unity* (1960); K. Rahner, *Schriften zur Theologie*, III, pp. 356–78, 527–76; IV, pp. 13–33, 46–58, E. T.: *Theological Investigations*, III, IV (1967); U. Valeske, *Votum Ecclesiae*, 2 vols. (1962); Y. Chabas, *De Nicée à Vatican II. Les hommes de paix* (1963); R. J. W. Bevan, ed., *The Churches and Christian Unity* (1963); H. Asmussen and T. Sartory, *Lutheran-Catholic Unity* (1963); P. Gardner-Smith, ed., *The Roads Converge. A Contribution to the Questions of Christian Reunion by Members of Jesus College, Cambridge* (1963); A. Bea, *Unity in Freedom* (1964); Y. Congar, *Sainte Église. Études et approches ecclésiologiques* (1964); id., *Chrétiens en dialogue. Contributions catholiques à l'œcuménisme* (1964); H. Renkewitz, *Die Kirchen auf dem Wege zur Einheit,* Evangelische Enzyklopädie 2 (1964); K. von Bismarck, W. Dirks and I. Hermann, eds., *Neue Grenzen. Ökumenisches Christentum morgen,* I (1966).

Karl Rahner

IV. Ecumenical Theology

A. Controversial Theology

1. *Concept.* Controversial theology does not mean the debating of differences between schools of theology, but the theoretical description of the differences in the expression of the faith which have led to schisms. The notion was developed at the time of the Reformation. The Church had hitherto been confronted mostly with individual heretics, but in the 16th century controversy became theological debate between whole ecclesiastical communities. Its classical representative in the Church was the theology of Robert Bellarmine, and its structural principle was theological contrariety. The opponent's views were examined not to discover what was held in common or how he should be understood, but to formulate oppositions and condemn him. The method still exists today, insofar as the differences between Catholic and Protestant thought are examined. Efforts are made, by means of more and more subtle distinctions, to establish a difference which is not merely within the realm of theological controversy, but actually causes schism. This method can only be based on the theological principle that there is nothing to be learned from one's partner in the dialogue, and that only differences can be demonstrated. Behind it is the claim to sole possession of truth, or at least of the full truth.

There is a danger, on the other hand, of theological discussion becoming so muted that a sort of indifferentism ensues. And in fact the Enlightenment and naturalism did give rise to a certain relativism in theology. Scholars took refuge in purely historical research in order to avoid this tendency towards uniformity. But the real point of controversial theology is again lost in this context.

If the term "ecumenical theology" were used instead of "controversial theology", which is in any case becoming less usual, the term itself would indicate the method and the purpose of the undertaking. Here the emphasis is on unity and mutual understanding, while points of divergence are only dwelt on in order to overcome them.

2. *Methods and principles.* a) The basic presupposition of such theology is the readiness to listen in order to understand. The will to communicate is basic in the dialogue of faith. The will to hear and to open one's mind to the statement of one's partner implies an effort to share the opinions one examines and prescinds from abstract condemnations. This is not the irenism which abandon's one's own opinions. It is rather the will which enables the faith held to be discussed. It is only through sympathetic hearing, which includes personal relationships to the other, that the partners are enabled to voice their own minds. The theological expression of personal faith presupposes the receptivity of the partners to each other, since otherwise language remains on the level of objectivation and loses the relationship to the life of faith.

b) Completeness too in the exposition of faith is only possible on this basis. The possibility is given with sympathetic hearing, insofar as faith can be expressed at all theologically and be embodied in human language. But there must be frank and total ventilation of the confession of faith and the doctrine connected with it, if one is to have a knowledge of the standpoint of others which is not confined to an "objective" list of divergent opinions but can penetrate to the unity of truth which is behind the diversity of true expression. Hence unconditional frankness is a further prerequisite if theology is to become dialogue, to be fully absorbed in it and create there unity rather than opposition. The will to hear and understand means that one is prepared to discuss without prejudice all aspects of the truth, to admit openly, for instance, the discrepancies in biblical as well as dogmatic utterances and make no effort to hide them.

c) In such theological dialogue the utmost commitment is demanded. Beyond the ordinary seriousness with which even abstract speculation must be carried on, the partners must throw themselves personally into the discussion, since they are not talking about debatable opinions of merely relative importance, but about the proper or improper expression of the faith. It is only when the speaker is so involved in the discussion that he himself is called in question that an "understanding" is possible. Hence ecumenical theology demands that the objectivated affirmations be referred back to the life of faith and the experience of faith. Thus a new mode of self-understanding becomes possible for hearer and speaker.

Whatever the outcome of the discussion, whether one accepts or rejects the formulation of faith, this reciprocity of total utterance and hearing is indispensable. Truth can only come about under these circumstances. The partners must understand themselves to be on the same level in the search for the true expression of the faith, if this dialogue is to be pursued in mutual willingness to hear and include the other.

d) This notion of ecumenical theology means that one calls in question one's own utterances and one's own language. The actual theological expression is to be subordinated to the ecumenical dialogue and its truth to be regained in the discussion. The mutual accord brings with it a new understanding and hence the possibility of a new formulation. Here Cardinal Bea writes: "It is well known that the Catholic Church is very conservative in the matter of formulations in which the inherited doctrine has been given expression. But Pope John XXIII himself affirmed at the solemn moment of the opening of the Council that the truth of which the Church is the custodian must be communicated to the world in a new medium of speech, that of modern man, the only language which he understands." Hence the truth must be expounded in terms which are orientated understandingly to the partner in the dialogue, just as every dogmatic definition had a definite relationship to the partner in the debate and the world to which it was addressed. Hence it is the task of ecumenical

theology to refer dogmatic propositions to the new conditions of each age. Hence no linguistic fixation of a dogma is absolutely irreformable.

e) It follows that the formulation, which is a possible expression of the truth, is qualitatively of secondary importance. The primary truth is not comprised in a proposition but is something which can never be fully objectivated. The truth of faith is truth as it determines existence, and hence its basic structure is orientated to existence, as is seen in the encounter of dialogue. Truth in the form of a proposition, on the contrary, is always a partial truth, a fragment of a whole, which cannot be comprehended fully by the abstract thought of man. The act of reflection which precedes each proposition must always fall short of the act of faith itself. Hence on principle man cannot attain full propositional self-expression. What is actually uttered is always qualitatively deficient with regard to the act of faith.

f) Scripture gives us some idea of this understanding of the truth of faith. It contains propositions which contain seeming contradictions in close juxtaposition, with no effort to harmonize them. Here the word of God expresses itself in many ways. Reflection on this revealed word is essential for every theology, and ecumenical interests above all cannot do without this reference of all statements to the Bible. Exegesis and biblical theology have in fact had a large say in the origins and work of ecumenical theology.

The ecclesiastical past divides Christians in many respects, but to look to the root and origin of the faith is the foundation of unity, since the word of God is one in all its diversity. The word of God makes it possible to accept the divisions of the past in a new way and opens in the present the way to a new future; and for the future, which is always newly given by God, there is hope of an understanding ecumenical theology.

3. *The present situation* of (controversial or) ecumenical theology is described in the Decree on Ecumenism of Vatican II as follows. The possibility of agreement transcending differences in expression of the faith is given by the common foundation which is laid in Christ (ch. i, art. 2).

In view of this foundation, the partners in dialogue are to be regarded as children of

God between whom there is a bond in *quadam communione* (ch. i, art. 3). If this mutual relationship is to lead to genuine understanding, the search for the truth in dialogue is necessary (ch. i, art. 4).

This will to dialogue aims at the renewal of the Church and hence of theological expression. "Ecclesia . . . vocatur ad perennem reformationem" (ch. ii, art. 6). The way thither is reflection on the gospel, which must have transformative power on one's own existence (ch. ii, art. 7). Prayer in common is the basic common expression of faith, and without it the theological effort is doomed to failure (ch. ii, art. 8).

All ecumenical action and dialogue must be pursued as between equals (ch. ii, art. 9). Frankness is demanded, but the language used in presenting the faith must be such that it does not provide obstacles to the dialogue and to mutual understanding. And it is above all necessary that ecumenical theology should remember that there is a "hierarchy" in revealed truths (ch. ii, art. 11).

If controversial theology is thus understood as ecumenical theology and so studied in ecclesiastical circles, the understanding of truth will no longer divide, but Christian existence will gain a new understanding of itself through the expression of truth, and in the expression of faith, will find the indivisible unity of faith.

See also *Reformation, Dogma* III, *Heresy* II, *Natural Philosophy, Schism* I, II.

BIBLIOGRAPHY. P. Polmann, *L'élément historique dans la controverse religieuse du XVIe siècle* (1932); L. Lambinet, *Das Wesen des katholischen und protestantischen Gegensatzes* (1947); H. H. Schrey, "Grundfragen einer ökumenischen Theologie", *Theologische Literatur-Zeitung* 75 (1950), pp. 271–9; A. Brandenburg, *Hauptprobleme der evangelischen Theologie* (1957); J. A. Möhler, *Symbolik* (1832), ed. by J. R. Geiselmann, I (1958), pp. 44–54; G. Thils, *La "théologie œcuménique". Notion, formes, démarches* (1960); A. Bea, *The Unity of Christians* (1963); E. Brunner, *Wahrheit als Begegnung* (1963); H. Dombois, "Konfessionelle Auseinandersetzung als hermeneutisches Problem", *Zeitschrift für Theologie und Kirche* 60 (1963), pp. 124–31; R. Gryson, "A propos de 'Théologie œcuménique'", *Collectio Mechlinensis* 48 (1963), pp. 121–34; P. Wacker, *Theologie als ökumenischer Dialog* (1965); K. Rahner, "Questions of Controversial Theology on Justification", *Theological Investigations,* IV (1966), pp. 188–219.

Gotthold Hasenhüttl

B. ECUMENICAL THEOLOGY

1. *State of the question.* The notion of "ecumenical theology" has been in use now for over twenty years in the theological discussion of the various Christian Churches. With the new sense of the contradiction prevailing between profession of faith in the one Church of Jesus Christ and the actual divisions in this Church, the notion of "ecumenical" theology has become the touchstone of sincerity in the theology of all denominations and in all their theological disciplines, and a criterium for the alertness of theological thought in general. For the one gospel of Jesus Christ, which must be preached in dialogue with the world of today — the gospel not merely of conformity with the world, but of the cross and resurrection, that is, of discontinuity with the world in the matter of salvation (since Christ and not the world is our redemption and salvation) — knows nothing of the non-evangelical scandal of this gospel's being preached by divided Churches. On the contrary, it presupposes the unity of Church in faith and love, something that is not merely of secondary relevance to the credibility of the gospel, but is meant to be a sign through which the world may believe. In this perspective, the divisions between the Churches are a scandal running counter to the words of Scripture, and one which all Churches are bound to try to remove. This can only be done if the Churches carry on a comprehensive dialogue with one another in which all questions of their self-understanding and their understanding of the world and the faith can be voiced and treated. There has always been confrontation and debate between the Churches. Hence the dialogue demanded today can be regarded as a continuation or counterpart of the past.

2. *Earlier forms.* The real counterpart of ecumenical theology in the past was the comprehensive polemics carried on by the Churches. The polemical mentality was due to the conviction on both sides that each alone had a monopoly of the truth, while the other was living in error. The salvation of the opponent was in peril, because of the errors of which he was victim. Since this could not be a matter of indifference, every effort had to be made to detach him from his heresy and lead him back to the true

Church. The claim to be the true Church was maintained by the Protestant denominations as well as by Catholics. The conviction of being in sole possession of the truth was formulated in doctrinal articles and propositions. The truths in question were put through a process of fragmentation and isolation in which too little attention was paid to the theological context of each proposition. Controversy, carried on with a religious intensity which regarded all opponents as dangerous heretics, was concerned with defending one's own truth and refuting the adversary point by point. Secondary matters were often treated as essentials, while essentials were often overlooked, so that misunderstandings were bound to arise by the nature of things. It was taken for granted, without critical investigation, that one's own way of thinking was correct, so that one's own theses never came up for discussion and the controversialists never seem to have tried to see things except from their own point of view. This could only lead to a hardening of positions on both sides, to narrow and one-sided views.

But along with controversy, there was always a certain amount of irenism. There were theologians who strove passionately for reconciliation and peace between the Churches and presented concrete programmes for reunion. There are several larger groups which could be named, which can be ranged — though only loosely, no doubt — under the heading of "irenism". There were, for instance, the efforts at union inspired directly or indirectly by Erasmus of Rotterdam. The theologians in question kept mainly before their eyes the picture of the primitive Church, and gave a large place to the distinction between fundamental and non-fundamental truths of faith (Melanchthon, Bucer, Gropper, Witzel, Cassander, Capito, de Dominis, Calixt and Leibniz). But it must be admitted that in doing so they underestimated the historical importance of dogmatic decisions in the teaching and practice of the Churches. This is clear from Erasmus's proposition that the dogmatic claims of the various Churches should be reduced in such a way as to bring about unity.

Among the irenical theologians we must also include the mystical "spiritualists" (such as Franck, Schwenkenfeld, Weigel and Böhme) who thought that a radical spiritualization of the notion of the Church had made room for all denominations and so restored unity. The groups which they formed were early heralds of pietism, though pietism is not a direct prolongation of the thought of the mystical spiritualists. Zinzendorf regarded the confessional Churches as modes and expressions of the one true Church of Christ. Hence all denominations had their legitimate place in his Herrnhuter Brotherhood. This was his way of keeping open, on principle, a link with all Churches, without denying the reality of the Churches. In spite of certain differences, the "Branch Theory" of Anglicanism has certain affinities with Zinzendorf's "Theory of Modes". The Branch Theory held that all Churches — or at least all Churches with apostolic succession of their bishops — were branches of the one Church of Christ.

While irenical theology always had some solution to offer to the question of the unity of the Church, credal theology (comparative "symbolism", from symbolé, creed) went other ways. It was concerned with the understanding, presentation, comparison and estimation of the doctrine of the various Churches. Two procedures may be distinguished here. A purely comparative method concentrated exclusively on study of doctrines, sometimes inspired ultimately only by historical interests. But there was also a "normative" credal theology, which based itself on its own Church to work out criteria for judging the doctrines of other Churches (as in J. Möhler's Symbolik, E. T.: Symbolism).

Credal theology has had a successor in the study of denominations, which is concerned with a comprehensive description of the doctrine and life of other Churches. A purely historical and descriptive type, such as that of K. Algermissen may be contrasted with the dogmatic and normative studies of E. Wolf and K. Barth.

Finally, there is the controversial theology which is concerned with the theological discussion of matters which divide the Churches. Where it presents itself as a basic form of inter-confessional encounter (R. Kösters), the question arises as to whether it does not isolate differences too sharply. When they are seen in the light of the greater whole of what is believed, confessed and thought by all Churches — the primary object of study — the ecumenical goal of overcoming them can be better and more promisingly expounded than when deliberate attention is paid to all that divides. Hence it must be admitted that while controversial theology is an important part of ecumenical theology, its value must not be overestimated.

3. *The theological meaning of "ecumenical"*. Five different meanings have been given to the word "ecumenical" in the course of Church history. All of them have even today fundamental significance for theology and its special role in the preaching of the Church. Ecumenical means (i) belonging to or representing the whole (inhabited) world (originally applied to the Roman Empire — belonging to or representing the Empire); (ii) belonging to the Church universal or representing it; (iii) possessing universal validity in the Church (the ancient Councils); (iv) having to do with relationships between several Churches or Christians of various denominations (the sense which the word took on in the modern ecumenical movement); (v) implying knowledge of Christian unity and the desire to attain it (the ecumenical movement). When these five senses of the word are applied to the nature of theology and the goal it serves, the following points arise.

a) Theology must remain conscious of the fact that the revelation of God in Jesus Christ and its proclamation by the Church is directed to all men. This universal aspect obliges theology not to confuse the findings of Western theology with the revelation in Jesus Christ. Thus the way is open for other regions of culture to articulate their understanding of revelation in their own concepts and their own languages. The way is open to a real pluralism in theology.

b) Such a plurality of theologies would be sustained by the one Church and would be established in the certain knowledge that theology is always a function of the Church and has its living roots there. The plurality of theology was for long the clearest sign of the multiplicity of the Churches, and the bounds of theology coincided with the bounds of the Churches. But the true task of theology is to assimilate comprehensively the revelation which came in Jesus Christ. If it is to do this properly when confronted with the questions of. a highly differentiated modern world, there must be a plurality of several theologies within the one Church,

but not a plurality of theologies of several Churches.

c) In this connection the question of the norm arises, and of the significance of the traditions of the Churches. The questions arise in connection with the normative element in the term ecumenical when used of the validity of ancient Church Councils and creeds. Here the point to be made is the following: in view of the questions put by the modern world and the situation of the present day, the real meaning of Scripture (the gospel, Christ) must be propounded in such a way that it can be heard and grasped. In this process of interpretation, the supreme norm and hence the norm of all other norms is Scripture, of which the inmost centre and central content is Christ and his work of salvation. It is in the light of this central message and only with reference to it that the traditions of the various Churches and even their common tradition are to be interpreted. The dogmatic tradition of the Churches, interpreted in this way and in no other way, but amenable in fact to such interpretation, must be integrated into the new exposition of the truth of the gospel for our own days.

d) The process of re-interpreting the message of the gospel for our own day, into which the tradition of the Churches are integrated, because interpreted in the light of their inmost core, in view of Christ, can only succeed if the Churches are engaged in a comprehensive dialogue with one another. They must allow themselves to be determined exclusively by the word of God and the questions of the present time.

e) This dialogue about the heart of the matter and the effort to solve outstanding questions in the light of the common faith will also help to solve the ecclesiological question of Church unity. Hence an ecumenical theology understood in this sense will not be exclusively concerned with the question of the unity of the Church. It will rather consider itself as a way to unity in the most comprehensive possible sense.

4. *Conclusions*. It follows that ecumenical theology in the sense outlined above is not a new special discipline along with other theological disciplines. It is rather a structural element and a dimension of all theology in all its disciplines. It is impelled by the question of the divisions in faith and their possible elimination. It does not simply

accept division as a fact which it tries to explain by a theology of history. It sees division as a challenge to overcome divisions, "so that the world may believe". Then, ecumenical theology is a theology of fellowship, a theology which has discovered that what is common is proportionally much greater than the differences and divergencies, these being only properly known and estimated in the perspective of the common faith. Thus new possibilities of encounter and openness are created. This new openness makes ecumenical theology a theology of mutual understanding, which is not merely concerned with understanding others, but also strives vigorously to propound its own faith and its own understanding of the faith in such a way that they can be understood by others, in spite of different presuppositions, in the framework of their theology. Further, ecumenical theology is a theology of the sources and the origins. It is concerned with Scripture and its relevant preaching today. Finally, ecumenical theology is a theology of dialogue and is therefore aware of the fact that God is constantly engaged in dialogue with man and that we are addressing in every man the eternal You of God. A God who does not speak is a dead God, and a Church which remains aloof from dialogue testifies only to the death of God, because what it preaches — the word of God, which demands to be heard and answered — would no longer be a living word. This reminds all the Churches that only dialogue among the Churches, carried on in, with and under the word of God, the common dialogue of the Churches with the world of today can really help them to accomplish the true task of the Church in accordance with the gospel.

See also *Church, Ecumenism* I, III, IV A, VI B, *Pietism, Scripture and Tradition*.

BIBLIOGRAPHY. J. R. Geiselmann, *Johann Adam Möhler: Die Einheit der Kirchen und die Wiedervereinigung der Konfessionen. Ein Beitrag zum Gespräch zwischen den Konfessionen* (1940); K. Algermissen, *The Christian Denominations* (1945); J. Weinlick, *Count Zinzendorf* (1956); J. Lecler, *Toleration and the Reformation*, 2 vols. (1960); G. Thils, *La "théologie œcuménique". Notion, formes, démarches* (1960); H. H. Wolf, "Towards an Ecumenical Theology", *The Ecumenical Review* 13 (1960/61), pp. 215–27; P. Bläser, "Ökumenische Theologie", in E. Neuhäusler and E. Gössmann, eds., *Was ist Theologie?* (1966), pp. 385–415; R. Kösters, "Zur Theorie der Kontroverstheologie", *ZKT* 88 (1966), pp. 121–62; J. Brosseder, *Ökumenische Theologie. Geschichte — Probleme* (1967).

Johannes Brosseder

V. Christian-Jewish Dialogue

Jews and Christians possess in common the holy Scriptures of the OT, but are divided in their understanding of it. Jews recognize both oral tradition and Scripture as divine revelation. They cannot therefore allow a difference between moral law and ceremonial law. The Messiah is for them inseparable from the messianic era, when the reign of God is established on earth; since this has not yet been done, Jesus, in the Jewish interpretation, cannot be the Messiah. The primitive Christian community was excluded from the synagogue by Gamaliel II towards the end of the 1st century. Ever since Gentile-Christians outnumbered Judaeo-Christians, the Christian understanding of the nature of Judaism quickly declined. In anti-Jewish Christian literature, the Jew was a sort of lay-figure in the dialogue, which made such polemics rather monotonous. The Jews not only held aloof from Christians, but sought to a great extent to bury the Christian message in silence. Nevertheless a Christian-Jewish dialogue did take place occasionally in antiquity and in the Middle Ages. Conversions to Judaism occurred in the early and late Middle Ages. Conversions to Christianity only began to multiply when the Middle Ages were well advanced. Personal, friendly exchanges between individual Christian theologians and Jewish scholars in the early Middle Ages were replaced, from the 13th century on, by the official religious dialogues promoted by the mendicant orders as a missionary method. The most famous of these dialogues were those of Barcelona (1263) and Tortosa (1412–13).

Spanish Christian apologists, from Ramon Marti (d. 1284) on, made concessions to their Jewish opponents insofar as they sought to base themselves not merely on Scripture, but on the Talmud, in whose haggadic narratives they thought they could find proofs of the Messiahship of Jesus. They championed therefore, in contrast to the University of Paris, the retention of the Talmud. But their proselytizing made friendly dialogue almost impossible. Spain was also the source of a certain influence which

Jewish philosophy exercised on the development of the classical period of Latin Scholasticism. But only Moses Maimonides (d. 1204) was understood by the West as a Jewish philosopher; Avicebron (Ibn Gabirol) was thought to be an Arab. To the Jews he was known only as a poet. The influence of the chief philosophical work of Moses Maimonides, *Dux Neutrorum,* was only effective among those who, like himself, taught that faith and reason were in harmony, especially Albertus Magnus and Thomas Aquinas. Meister Eckhart also used Maimonides extensively, but explained him in terms of his own theology.

Few medieval theologians knew Hebrew well. They learned it from poor and often uneducated Jews. It was only in the age of Humanism that the study of Hebrew led to personal friendship between Christian and Jewish scholars, especially those who sought to find agreement between Christian and Jewish mysticism and tried to found a Christian cabala (among others, Count Giovanni Pico della Mirandola and Reuchlin).

Controversy between Christians at the time of the Reformation and Counter-Reformation led to an accentuation of points of opposition which also proved unfavourable to the meeting of Jews and Christians. Only the Pietists made efforts to establish personal contacts.

In the Baroque age there were so many personal contacts that we might almost speak of "Philosemitism". The last "command performance" of religious dialogue in Germany took place in 1704 at the court of Hanover. At the time of the Enlightenment personal contact between individual Jewish and Christian scholars was pursued, with the aim of surmounting positive religions by a religion of reason. The friendship between Moses Mendelssohn and G. E. Lessing is typical, as also Lavater's open attempt to convert Mendelssohn to Christianity. Under the freer conditions of the 19th century the hitherto predominant position of Orthodox Judaism was shaken. The effort to share contemporary European culture led many Jews to make intensive studies of Christianity. This created the prerequisites for a Jewish-Christian dialogue, which, however, has only taken place to some extent in the present century.

The "quest of the historical Jesus" and the discussion of the relationship of the Jesus of history and the Christ of the Church's faith enabled Jews to consider the possibility of integrating Jesus into the spiritual history of Judaism. Attempts at Christian-Jewish dialogue were made in Germany as early as the end of the 1920s: Martin Buber had public discussions with various Christian partners at Stuttgart. In order to combat a growing anti-Semitism, the "American Brotherhood, National Conference of Christians and Jews" was founded in the U.S.A. in 1928. There followed in England the Council of Christians and Jews. The centre of the "International Consultative Committee of Organizations for Christian-Jewish Co-operation" is also in England. In 1946 the organizations combined in the "International Consultative Committee" drew up at Oxford the theses for religious instruction which received their definitive form in Selisberg in 1947, and influenced Vatican II's Declaration on the Relationship of the Church to Non-Christian Religions. This declaration stresses not only the common heritage of Christians and Jews, but also calls for common studies. An institute of studies directed by Jews and Christians in common has existed in Amsterdam since 1966 (the Beth ha-Midrash).

It is noteworthy that the reform of the Roman Curia brings the relations between Christians and Jews under the auspices of the Secretariat for Promoting Christian Unity, along with the non-Catholic Christian Churches, and not, for instance, under the Secretariat for non-Christians.

See also *Judaism, Curia Romana.*

BIBLIOGRAPHY. G. Hedenquist, ed., *The Church and the Jewish People* (1954); J. Klausner, *Messianic Idea in Israel* (1956); J. Katz, *Exclusiveness and Tolerance. Studies in Jewish-Gentile Relations in Medieval and Modern Times,* Scripta Judaica 3 (1961); P. Schneider, *Dialogue of Christians and Jews* (1967); B. Lambert, *Ecumenism: Theology and History* (1967).

Willehad P. Eckert

VI. Christian Denominations

A. STUDY OF CHRISTIAN DENOMINATIONS

1. It is the primary task of the study of denominations today to describe the contemporary scene, but it must also call on

history insofar as it is the key to the understanding of the present.

The beginnings of such systematic study are found very early in the Church, e.g., in the *Panarion* of Epiphanius and in the *De Fide et Symbolo* of Augustine. The present-day science, however, could only begin after the formation of Churches which used professions of faith to present their understanding of the gospel for theology, preaching and catechesis, and hence to demarcate how they differed from other Churches. As a normative and a descriptive science it began among the Protestant Churches with the introductions to the Lutheran professions of faith and 16th-century polemics among the Reformers, and was made to serve the purposes of controversy. Thus in 1688 B. von Sanden published his *Theologia Symbolica Lutherana,* which proceeded from the confessional theory developed in the Formula of Concord.

Both Pietism and Rationalism tended to obscure or to level out the differences between confessional beliefs. Pietism avoided dogmatic disputes, and the Enlightenment denied all supernatural revelation. The various confessions were treated from a purely historical viewpoint, the purpose of which was to demonstrate "how those who were previously united had become separate . . . The confessions were threatened by the same enemy, whereby the attention was necessarily drawn away from the differences between opposing parties within Christianity and was turned rather to the opposition between Christianity and non-Christians" (Möhler).

Arnold's effort "to present impartially the history of the Churches and heresies" (*Unparteiische Kirchen- und Ketzergeschichte* [1699]) had a wide influence, as had the *Abriss* proposed by G. J. Planck in 1796, the full German title of which may be translated as "Outline of a historical and comparative presentation of the dogmatic systems of the main different Christian parties among us, according to their fundamental ideas, the distinctive doctrine derived from these and their practical consequences". P. K. Marheineke's *Christliche Symbolik* (3 vols., 1810–14) drew on the constitutions, liturgies and Church life of the various confessions, as did K. von Hase's polemic against Möhler's *Symbolik* (*Handbuch der protestantischen Polemik* [1862]). But F. Kattenbusch's comparative study may be considered as the foundation of the modern approach (*Lehrbuch der ver-*

gleichenden Confessionskunde [1891–92]), though it confined itself to Protestant orthodoxy. Kattenbusch sought to see doctrine, liturgy, constitution and spirituality as a whole in each Church, and to compare the Churches on this basis, as did F. Loofs in his *Symbolik oder christliche Konfessionskunde* (1905). H. Mulert's *Konfessionskunde* was the first work to apply such treatment to a comprehensive range of denominations and Churches.

2. For Catholic theology Johann Adam Möhler must be considered the founder of the science of confessions. His *Symbolik* (1832), "a presentation of the dogmatic differences of Catholics and Protestants according to their official confessions", is the most substantial work in the field of confessional science and controversial theology since Bellarmine and Bossuet. The English translation, *Symbolism,* is long out of print.

Möhler was not satisfied to give a merely phenomenological description of the different confessions; besides attempting to present the determining principles and traits of the confessions, he also tried to show how they must be understood in this way and no other. His aim was to discover the driving force behind a given confessional group and to present "the individual propositions of a doctrine in their mutual connections and organic unity", to show how the parts relate to the whole of the system and go back to a leading idea.

Möhler considers the "Protestant principle" to be a one-sided supranaturalism. In a similar manner Vatican II in its first draft of the Decree on Ecumenism tried to show that the ultimate principle of Protestantism was an exaggeration of the transcendence of God, from which proceeded the Reformed teaching on justification and the denial of any true mediatory function of the Church. The decree itself refers to the "very weighty differences not only of a historical, sociological, psychological, and cultural nature, but especially in the interpretation of revealed truth" (art. 19), thus suggesting that Protestantism is a unity composed of various and inter-related individual elements. The decree, nevertheless, avoids reducing all differences to one basic idea or concern; it finally emphasizes the pervading diversity of the interpretations of revelation. It also points out the desirability of a better knowledge of the thought and approach of the separated brethren: "Study is absolutely required for this, and should be pursued with fidelity to truth and in a spirit of good will" (art. 9). The Council recommended for this purpose common research with the theologians of other confessions (art. 11). Thus the task of the study of denominations is outlined, a task which cannot be confined to historical description and comparison but must also face the question of the truth.

An important element in this study is the distinction between revealed truth and its linguistic expression, though the two cannot be completely separated. The Council speaks of "the formulation of doctrine which must be carefully distinguished from the deposit of faith itself" (art. 6). Similar things can be intended by the use of different terminology, Differences in theological expression may be explained as complementary viewpoints rather than opposition of teaching. Such is especially true with regard to the relation between the theology of the Eastern and Western Churches (art. 17). Modern study treats the confessions as seriously as Möhler did those of the 16th century and can relate them to the theology of Luther and Calvin better than was possible in Möhler's time. But scholars will have to remember that most of the Christian Churches do not make definite confessions obligatory for their members. Discussion of doctrine will have to be completed by studies of worship, Church constitutions, Church life, spirituality and missions, which must in each case be viewed as a totality.

Catholic theology developed the modern form of the science relatively late. K. Algermissen's *Christliche Sekten und Kirche Christi* discussed the sects, which had been almost totally outside Möhler's perspective (E. T.: *Christian Sects* [1962]). Out of this work grew his *Konfessionskunde* (7th ed., 1957; E. T.: *Christian Denominations*). This was an effort at a theological understanding of all the Christian communities, by studying their historical development and present state, in the light of biblical and primitive Christian ecclesiology and of the relationship between actual doctrine, worship and practice. "In this way Catholic theology can examine with unwavering honesty and full seriousness the life and teaching of other Christian denominations and thus further

the genuine science of confessions" (Algermissen). It has been rightly said that the study of denominations must start from the internal and external situation of the various Churches and ecclesiastical communities of the present day.

This situation is chiefly determined by the ecumenical movement, by Vatican II, by the dialogue between the Catholic Church and the World Council of Churches, by the rediscovery of the Church among Protestants, by the new relationship among the Western Churches, and by the problems set by the "splinter Churches" and the sects. The relation of the study of denominations to a non-polemical controversial theology and to ecumenical theology must be interpreted anew. The individual Christian Churches and communities have recognized their division as a failing, so that simple contrast and comparison, as undertaken in the study of denominations in the 19th century, is no longer sufficient.

Positive elements in the theology of the separated brethren often result from the treatment of problems which are more or less absent in Catholic theology, e.g., the theology of the covenant, or the biblical aspects of "conversion", the problem of law and gospel. The study of confessions must go back to our common heritage in order to understand certain elements of the theology of those separated from the Catholic Church. It must acknowledge that the method of presentation in Catholic theology can often be the reason why the true face of the Catholic Church is not seen by others. The concrete fellowship of the Catholic Church is not always inspired in its spirituality and theology by the fullness of its faith and its apostolic tradition. Doctrines are stressed which are important for the Christian life of a given period. This may mean that other aspects of the treasury of the faith are neglected. It is also important to consider the philosophical presuppositions of theology and its methods.

Thus Protestant theology in the 19th century was largely based on the philosophy of Kant and German idealism, while existential philosophy is influential at present. Such influences give rise to various notions of "reality" which leave their mark on the whole of theological thinking. Anthropological presuppositions are equally important in the treatment, for instance, of original sin and justification. The study of denominations must also note the reactions of the Churches to the problems of modern man and his world.

Vatican II in the Pastoral Constitution on the Church in the Modern World treats, from the Catholic point of view, this aspect of its mission, which is so closely connected with the nature of the Church.

The attitudes of the other communities in this matter are likewise determined by the ecclesiology proper to each.

BIBLIOGRAPHY. See also bibliographies on *Anglican Communion, Baptists, Eastern Churches, Calvinism, Lutheran Churches, Methodist Churches, Old Catholic Church, Protestantism* III, *Presbyterian Churches.* — K. Algermissen, *The Christian Denominations* (1945); P. Hughes, *A History of the Church,* 3 vols. (2nd ed., 1948); H. Mulert and E. Schott, *Konfessionskunde* (3rd ed., 1956); E. Stakemeier, *Konfessionskunde heute, im Anschluss an die Symbolik J. A. Möhlers* (1957); M.-J. Le Guillou, *Mission et Unité* (2 vols., 1960); J. Jedin, ed., *Handbuch der Kirchengeschichte* (1963 ff.), E. T.: J. Jedin and J. Dolan, eds., *Handbook of Church History* (1965 ff.).

Eduard Stakemeier

B. CONFESSIONALISM

The word "confessionalism" can be used in two different ways: a) It can describe the efforts to bring together Churches with similar creeds, on a national level or in an international association. This sort of confessionalism can be a first step towards ecumenical dialogue. b) More usually "confessionalism" means placing excessive value on one's own limited Church tradition as opposed to the whole Christian heritage which is also present in other Churches, and is therefore a self-sufficient isolation from other Churches. The following observations refer to this second meaning.

1. The Catholic Church does not regard itself as a confession, that is, as one denomination among others, but as the one Church of Christ. If it then holds fast to its doctrine and basic structure, it cannot look on this as a confessionalism which must be overcome, because it is not holding fast to a separate good, but to the heritage of the one Church. It is nevertheless possible and necessary to speak of a Catholic confessionalism.

Even the Church, which regards itself as the one Church of Christ, cannot escape the danger of a particularism in doctrine and life. God's revelation in Christ and the written account of it in the Bible are, according to 1 Cor 13, historical processes and as such provisional. But if the knowledge given to us through revelation comes to us as "in a mirror, dimly . . . in part" (1 Cor 13:12), this is even more true of the Church's confession of faith in this revelation, because here the historical conditioning is carried a step further, since the Church must reply to God's word, but it must translate it into thought and language and present it in ways appropriate to various times and cultures.

At the time of the Reformation "religious parties" were formed, at first within the Church. Then the Reformers began to found their own Churches. This was done on the basis of particular creeds in which they sought to sum up their insights into the Gospel. Thus the actual situation and the mental effort of the believer were of special importance in the formation of these Churches. The consequences of this development go beyond these Churches: however much the Catholic Church might base its life on the complex dimension of objective presentation, it became increasingly involved in this development. Its own position was more and more determined by a negative reaction against the other confessions. Thus its catholicity became narrower in practice and it became itself — not theologically, but in the religious-sociological sense — a "denomination"; this was the next stage in the historical development.

These historical circumstances apply to the profession of faith as a compendium of doctrine, but even more to its sociological aspect: here all sorts of extraneous motives, psychological, social, economic and political, come into it, which are only secondarily divisive factors. It is significant that the Churches emerging from the Reformation first made their appearance as corporations under German imperial law. This beginning has left its mark and in Central Europe the struggle for social parity has never ceased.

These extraneous factors also apply even where the break was not marked by confessional differences as in the schism between the Eastern and Western Churches where these normally secondary factors were genetically primary. Thus the word confessionalism can also be used in this context.

2. When considering possible ways of overcoming confessionalism we must first mention some that are unacceptable.

a) A comprehensive Christian confessionalism, that is, a utilitarian association of expedience, formed by the various Churches for the purpose of gaining some advantage for one's own Church. Here the real sin of confessionalism, satisfaction with oneself, is even more serious than in the naive type of confessionalism.

b) The radical belittling of confessional differences, taking its inspiration from the theology of German romanticism. According to Schleiermacher, every idea loses some of its breadth and depth when put into practice. The rise of confessions is in this view a necessary process, the consequence of which is, according to Marheineke, that not only every culture and every age, but also every individual has the right to form or choose a confession that seems most suitable. This confessional relativism overlooks the fact that the Church did not enter history as an idea but as a reality, and that choice of a confession is not merely a question of the religious individual, but above all of the actual *object* of the faith, Christ and his work of salvation. As the confessions are not simply complementary, but also contain contradictory elements, the decision for or against them is also a matter of the integrity of Christ's work of salvation itself, that is — once the truth has been recognized — a matter subjectively deciding salvation.

c) The Anglican branch-theory which maintains that the confessions are branches, peacefully growing together on the one tree of the Church, takes insufficient account of the seriousness of the break.

d) The fragmentation theory which also comes from Anglican theology does take the break seriously, but fails to consider sufficiently that the mystical Christ must essentially have one body.

3. A genuine attempt to overcome confessionalism can begin by considering the function of a creed. The creed is a subjective effort to grasp the message of salvation, but it must be remembered that the believer is a *social* being (cf. the etymology of *homo*-logia and *con*-fessio). Basically every creed has some ecumenical characteristics: it is intended to proclaim that a certain community is in agreement with all the rest of the faithful. Therefore no particularist restricted Church tradition can be erected into an absolute in the name of a Christian creed.

It is the task of the Catholic Church to make room in its theology and its life for the fullness of spiritual experience which God has given to the other Churches. It can do this because and insofar as the other Churches too have preserved as a common basis the fundamental belief that "Jesus is Lord", for "no one can say 'Jesus is Lord' except by the Holy Spirit" (1 Cor 12:3). Where this fundamental belief has been preserved, the Holy Spirit continues to operate and we can trust him, and his gifts to our brothers of other confessions. On the other hand we shall have to ask our separated brethren whether the content and meaning of this formula — the Lordship of Christ in his Church, in its sacraments and pastoral office, and with regard to the world — are really given their true value in their professions of faith.

The common fundamentals of faith and even more the growing consciousness of a common substance as real Churches — and the documents of the Second Vatican Council do not exclude the other Christian communities from this — provide the possibility and duty for all the Churches to act together before the world in *diakonia, martyria* and *leitourgia*. But confessionalism can only be overcome finally if the Churches share the cross of Christ: whatever is sinful in them, whatever purely human, must die (cf. 1 Pet 2:24). The manifestation of Christ's passion in the body of the Church (cf. Gal 6:17; 2 Cor 4:10) thus becomes a *nota ecclesiae*, a mark of true catholicity.

See also *Church* I, *Revelation, Dogma, Reformation, Schism.*

BIBLIOGRAPHY. K. Barth, *Die Kirche und die Kirchen* (1935); H. Meyer, *Bekenntnisbindung und Bekenntnisbildung in jungen Kirchen* (1953); H. R. Niebuhr, *The Social Sources of Denominationalism* (reprint, 1957); U. Valeske, *Votum Ecclesiae* (1962); H. Carrier, *The Sociology of Religious Belonging* (1965); A. Ahlbrecht, *Die Überwindung des Konfessionalismus in Theologie und kirchlichem Leben,* Una Sancta 20 (1965), pp. 209–15.

Ansgar Ahlbrecht

EDUCATION

I. Basic Education. II. Philosophy of Education. III. Pedagogy. IV. Religious Education. V. Self-Education.

I. Basic Education

1. *Concept.* Formation or basic education is the process by which man acquires the true form of his being as man. The end-product is sometimes known as his culture (the static rather than the dynamic concept of formation). Man is properly such through his "purposefulness", that is, his basic openness and orientation towards a fulfilment which lies before him. He is not "ready-made" like inorganic things of which the essence (basic form) and reality (full presence) are there in their fullness from the start. And his structure is not such that nature and full reality develop surely to their fulfilment as in other forms of organic life. For man is born *tabula rasa;* we might almost say, without a nature and without an existence. Without a nature, because he has yet to find his proper place in the whole scheme of things and take possession of it; without an existence, because he has yet to make his complete presence felt by thus entering into relationship with all other being. In positive terms this blankness is called "freedom", because it is not definitely predetermined either by particular subjective factors (the dispositions and talents of the person) or by particular objective factors (the environment, and anything desirable it may seem to offer). The human person can decide what he wishes to do with his character, gifts, impulses, interests, and desires, i.e., what he wants to make of himself. Similarly he can decide whether he will leave his environment as it is, simply conforming to it, or whether he will resist and attempt to change it.

At the same time this self-determination is not an arbitrary power. Despite the subjective and objective independence we have noted, freedom is restrained by, and is subject to the norm of, the person's interpretation of the universe, the attitude he has decided to adopt towards the basic structures of the world. Consequently, if man is to be able to take free decisions he must face the world, total reality. This power of making present to himself the whole of being, which makes the exercise of human freedom possible, is called spirit (mind) or reason. Thus freedom is rational self-determination, a decision which shapes one's conduct in face of the whole of being.

We term basic education the process whereby the individual enters into relationship with the whole, so that he may be sure that his free decisions are the process whereby he satisfies himself that his world possesses a certain basic structure in which every new experience he has finds its due place. Man is the only being who is capable of such formation, because his mind enables him to confront all reality. Other living beings can only evolve, and possibly be trained; but man besides evolving can consciously develop his own character and abilities. Man's world includes his basic relations — with extra-human nature, with the human community, with society and its history, and finally with God and divine revelation. The educated man knows from what source these relations spring, how they interact, what they entail, how they unify one's life and one's world. In Kant's phrase, he is a "man of the universe": not that he need be a "polymath", with an encyclopedic mind; nor need he be extraordinarily gifted; but he knows where he belongs in the whole scheme of things. His experience of the world, its scale and structure, its purpose and import, enables him to make sound decisions and conduct himself properly. The hallmark of the educated man is not abstract knowledge, nor even the ability to work out the proper course by a process of education from general principles, but an experiential knowledge of the appropriate that has become second nature, imbuing his every act, conscious or unconscious.

Purely speculative knowledge, an abstract presentation of the world, does not amount to a presence which can "educate". To accept such a world, propounded in school or college but never made *present,* remains an act of sheer will-power, ungrounded and therefore ultimately insecure. If "education" secures the free human person his own place in the world, then a system of schooling that teaches a particular world-view clearly fails to educate; instead of education we have a narrow philosophic formalism, and we teach our youth to look for guidance to the oracle of this philosophy instead of making their own decisions in the light of a real knowledge of the world. Such is the gulf between abstract schooling through artificial presentations of the whole and basic education, as formation within the experience of the real world actually present. To be educated is to be moulded by a living world that is present to one in such a way as to govern all one's acts. Thus it may well happen that a peasant in the depths of the countryside, living in close touch with all that enters into the fabric of his existence — God and the Church, the earth and the heavens, his family and village, the landscape and the soil — will be better educated than an intellectual with a vast knowledge of theology, technology, sociology and history by which he has not been formed in depth.

2. *Education and instruction.* Its experiential nature sets basic education apart from every kind of general and philosophic schooling; its global character, from all types of instruction (necessarily specialized), which develop some particular aptitude so as to enable a person to carry out a certain useful function in society, to become an indispensable "functionary". Instruction is either material or formal.

a) Material instruction imparts a certain body of knowledge and, through technical aids and practice, a certain degree of skill in production. Thus the primary school teaches certain knowledge of an objective kind which the common life of men in society necessarily presupposes. Here arithmetic does not serve primarily (like mathematics in formal instruction) to sharpen the wits but to give pupils a mastery of everyday affairs. Similarly, geography and history teach pupils facts about their environment, which must constantly be considered if a harmonious social life is to be possible; and writing is the indispensable means whereby men communicate with one another and acquire further knowledge.

b) *Formal* instruction, on the other hand, seeks to cultivate man's powers (intelligence, reasoning, historical judgment, good taste, technical skill, moral will) so that they may be equal to a variety of duties and situations, often unforeseen. The subject-matter of formal instruction (literature, history, mathematics, physics, ethics, the biblical history of revelation and salvation) is primarily a means of strengthening the native efficacy of the faculty that has to cope with the particular material — of making the student sharpen his wits by using them. Formal instruction always presupposes the material; yet no particular content can be said to be absolutely necessary in formal instruction. Content, being the "occasion", can be endlessly varied. In formal instruction in language and liter-

ature, for example, there is nothing that "one must read", nothing particular one must be able to do, apart from exercising the ability itself.

Apart from religion — which for the Christian believer has an absolute, irreplaceable content — the prior demands of formal instruction over its servant, material instruction, should be recognized in present circumstances. No doubt "classical" (or pseudo-classical) humanism often asserts that ancient culture possesses the same sort of absolute educational value as Christianity claims for its own doctrines. But this primacy of ancient culture is now widely challenged, and where Greek and Latin are still studied it is often only for the purpose of formal instruction.

It will be evident from what we have said that neither material nor formal instruction amounts to genuine education. Neither dutifully absorbing the subjects taught in school nor impressively developing one's talents makes one an educated person. Education makes use of material and formal instruction, organizing them both, but itself fashions a man's relations with the world. If instruction does not place itself at the service of education — which properly relates man to the world and finds him the place where he belongs in the general scheme of things, thus putting him into rapport with the major categories of being and with God himself — then it will simply breed functionaries for society, it will never prepare man to be a person in the world.

3. *The crisis of education.* The present crisis in education has arisen because the enormous increase in human knowledge and skill in particular fields has meant a corresponding loss of the sense of wholeness. Nowhere is the oneness of the world so taken for granted that it can supply the norm for the unity of individuals in a nation, for their knowledge and abilities, for their values and actions. There is no unified whole within which freedom can be really free and not merely aimless. The world-images of religion, history, sociology, ethics, and natural science no longer form a unity. They are more like disparate approaches to something that in itself remains obscure and elusive, so that in effect we are not dealing with real "aspects" of one and the same thing but with isolated "phenomena". The nearer we come to knowing everything on earth and in the universe, and

the better we can compare everything as it were, with everything else, the clearer it becomes that we have lost sight of the key to all comparison — the link that would bind together, order, measure all our knowledge and enable us to judge it. Distance is devoured — seemingly — by the new means of travel, but, the "one" world as the mould of personal freedom recedes into the distance.

Consequently, what is called the "crisis in education" is really a "world crisis", because the "world" as a palpable, present whole has disappeared, has become impossible for us to imagine or experience; this supreme unity, the proper sphere of human freedom, has become a mere postulate. For the ancients, all events were a unity, as nature (φύσις) and unalterable fate (δίκη, μοῖρα); for Christianity, in the saving events made known by revelation — a single historical process, unique and irreversible, which God gradually leads to its appointed end. Both views account for all human acts, giving them all meaning and purpose. But modern man will have none of a purposeful, hierarchical order of nature with a variety of laws and exigencies, duties and rights (cf. the synthesis of all types of law in "natural law"), nor of a single history that brings our future acts into context, giving them meaning, setting them a goal and appropriate standards — a tradition that is authoritative for the individual because its texture has been woven by centuries of common experience.

The present industrialized world takes account of nothing but the technical requirements for the continued functioning of production in its countless specialized ramifications; and nature and history, which should reduce this process to unity, seem but phantoms in comparison with its obsessive reality. Hence Marxism, ignoring their experiential character, dismisses nature and history as "ideologies" sponsored by the ruling class, as ideological "epiphenomena" that have nothing to do with reality of production, which turns the refractory earth into a manageable human environment. The Marxist thesis must be categorically rejected, but this rejection alone will not produce a new experience of an imperative totality in nature or history.

Neither the "natural sciences" nor the history and languages taught in our "educational institutions" can give students any sense that nature is a meaningful whole or

that a single, historical, meaningful world of tradition still forms an imperative framework. "Practical" subjects are as useless in this respect as the humanities: both merely instruct. In the early 19th century education was already being driven into the background by material and formal instruction, as the requirements for entry into the professions became more and more exacting, society forcing this development upon the schools by the continual division of labour. And education has been at a loss to know which world-image to choose since the primacy of the classics, once axiomatic, yielded to contemporary "historicism", and Christianity itself came to be regarded as a historical phenomenon, simply one of the great "world religions". New subjects constantly swelled the curriculum, judged only by the standard of their utility for the student's future work. This situation has left the schools no peace during the past half-century. They have been driven from one reform to the next, none having any relevance to the real problems of education but simply involving new combinations of subjects in view of a subsequent career.

It was always considered the great merit of classical, or humanist, education — the bedrock of all education in the West for centuries past — that it taught "dead" languages for no particular practical reason (such as the reasons for which people study living universal languages like English or Russian, or artificial ones like Esperanto and Ido). It was not merely technical equipment with languages. But the mature perfection of Greek and Latin was by no means useless to the student; by translating and interpreting that literature, familiarizing himself with the shape, the articulation, the genius of those languages, he was able to grasp the nature of language itself, which discloses and gives utterance to a whole world. Thus the classics were and are considered the best means developing human speech in the full sense of the word. But if the educational value of the "humanities" is rated so high, it is principally because the ancient world — substantially preserved in the Greek and Latin languages — was thought to represent the noblest ideal of man (humanity), of art (beauty), of philosophy (truth), of society (law and government). That world as a whole, despite incidental changes, was regarded as the abiding measure of human

215

achievement (especially since the Renaissance and Humanism).

This faith in antiquity (which a Christian, of course, could never fully share with the humanist) was then modified upon the awakening of a sense of history. Greek and Latin do preserve a world to which we owe, to a large extent, our existence, to which we are "bound in natural piety", a world extraordinarily lucid in outline and general structure. But its ideals have formidable rivals to contend with. Nietzsche first raised the question whether the West had not been travelling a false road ever since Socrates and Plato, Jesus Christ and Paul, and ought not now to strike out in a different direction (an idea diametrically opposed to Hegel's, for instance). But real humanism was not content to invoke the unquestionable value of Greek and Latin in formal instruction — where mathematics and certain natural sciences have long been their keen competitors; it roundly affirmed the unique educational value of the whole culture of antiquity — a claim admitted only in quarters where the ancient world is still held to be "canonical", the authoritative pattern for our whole future.

As observed earlier, the present crisis in education is a "world crisis": there seems to be no certainty as to which features of which world are still valid, which principles of which system man should appropriate as a context for the exercise of his freedom; we do not know what kind of world we are to prepare our young people for, how the schools ought to "educate" them. Thus the crisis in education, the world-crisis, becomes a crisis in the schooling and upbringing of youth. A nation that is sure of its bearings imbues its young people with the principles and ideals of its world, chiefly by means of great literature and great art, in which the governing élite are steeped as a matter of course. To make the acquaintance of these works is to sense the purpose of life, the wholeness of the universe, the values that really matter. The answers to these vital questions, thus directly experienced, become part of one's being. The writers who continue to mediate and bring to life a valid world, in whom this world is made *present,* are called the "classics".

Today, great writing can no longer bring us into contact with a valid world, it can only point out the necessity of such a world, the urgency of our quest for it. Thus literature, having lost one of its primary functions in the process of education, is no longer able to hold its own in competition with science and technology; "practical" subjects steadily displace the humanities.

4. *How to meet the educational crisis.* While the proliferation of subjects (hardly distinguishable so far as their utility as means of instruction is concerned) has made any advance towards real education increasingly difficult, it has at least focussed attention on the reason for this difficulty — the disappearance of a single world which accounts for all our experience and with which we are in living contact. The "angry young men" had the merit of bringing the crisis in education to light, showing that young people no longer felt the allegedly valid world of the past to be real or authoritative for them, that it was only a memory to which they clung for the sake of public order. What youth wanted was a new, authentic experience of those totalities which form the structure of the world — nature, hearth and homeland, friendship, the community and the nation, art as a primal experience or wholeness, religion as a sense of communion with the divine. It tried to escape the crushing burden of the endless specialized knowledge young people are expected to absorb, without having to take refuge in an outworn conception of the world. It hoped to find a sound basis for human thought in a new, vital experience of wholeness, by passing from the experience of being to reach the authentic meaning.

Thus it was that reform of the schools took a new turn, and an attempt was made to teach life instead of mere abstract knowledge. In Germany the independent day-schools and boarding-schools which adopted the new approach certainly brought a fruitful influence to bear on the State schools, and yet the real educational crisis was no nearer solution. Even Catholic boarding-schools maintained by religious communities, steeped as they are in the traditional world-image despite its general abandonment outside Catholic circles, have somehow lost their ability to give young people any genuine experience of this Christian world, real though it be. They have signally failed to develop any form of basic education which could be considered their own; instead they faithfully conform in organization, curriculum and teaching methods to the pattern of the State schools, which instruct but do not educate. Obviously, therefore, no vivifying impetus for the State schools could be expected from this quarter.

As for the State schools themselves, their attempts to improve matters by constantly reshuffling the subjects of instruction have done far more harm than good. The fundamental problem, how to preserve the unity of education when such a variety of material must be taught, remains unsolved. "General education" divorced from concrete instruction may indeed be a monstrosity, since it attempts to instil an abstract knowledge of the whole man, but at the same time the aims of education must not be sacrificed to the exigencies of instruction, human personality must not be progressively disintegrated by a purely material absorption of modern culture and technology and by specialized cultivation of certain talents that society considers useful.

By struggling to safeguard the rights of the family in education, to maintain denominational schools, to imbue the whole environment of the young with a religious spirit, the Christian Churches are fighting for true education, and the unity of all things which it conveys, against mere instruction in the void. The issue of the struggle, of course, will depend on whether the Churches offer people a mere system of doctrine and precepts, or genuine religious experience (experience of the holy, of encounter with Christ, of fellowship with Christ in the Church). Only if such experience underlies a religious system can it become the framework of real Christian existence. Again, within the religious sphere itself, there is doubtless a danger that Christian education may be displaced by mere instruction in abstract knowledge of religion.

At the present time the very specialization of science is a constant reminder of the wholeness of which we are bereft, which no one science can capture, which always eludes both hand and mind. The individual sciences are more conscious than ever that they are simply "special" and necessarily presuppose a whole, though one that is not to be attained by any of their own procedures. They realize that they are getting on very well in the world without ever reaching the world itself, which is more than the sum of all the data established by their special research. Thus there is a growing disposition among scientists to consider philosophical and theological questions, without looking for answers from the methods of science — as the 19th century did — and without identifying the world with their own special field. This recognition throughout the particular sciences that theology and philosophy pose genuine questions transcending the field of the specialist entails a new interest in basic education.

It is the business of education to orientate the whole man (intellect, will, and sensibility) in the whole of being, but this cannot be done without religion. Education is tied neither to particular domains (theoretical education, scientific education, education of the intellect, practical education, education of the will, technical education, all of which as such are mere instruction, though each may lead in its own way to education) nor to particular methods (formal education, self-education, education in the school of life). One can be educated anywhere and by any means. Of itself education has no preference for one domain over another (languages, for example, are no more educative than "practical" subjects), one method over another (whether formal education or education in the school of life, self-education or education by others); one may be educated at school or in the midst of life, with or without a teacher, but always it is a matter of moulding one's freedom. Freedom, though unique, is never wholly private and particular. A man is only truly free when he takes possession of his own proper place in the whole scheme of things, and this process educates him, prepares him to live in the real world. Freedom is the only thing that cannot be taught, it can only be brought out. Consequently, a theory of education is always a theory of man.

Education is the issue that most sharply divides personalism and functionalism. Whereas the personalist State seeks to cultivate the freedom of the individual, the totalitarian State fosters the abilities, talents, knowledge, skills of the individual for its own service. Leviathan would breed the ideal civil servant, most useful to society at large when he neither sees it nor senses its presence, who has a place assigned to him instead of finding one for himself. It is for the chosen few of the Central Committee to concern themselves with the general picture, the total context of an individual's work. So that there may be no discontent in the administration, the rest are taught a substitute in school, a complete theory that is enforced by governmental decree. But obviously a fictitious political and philosophical system of this kind cannot do duty for authentic experience of the world and of human freedom.

See also *Man, Freedom, World, Spirit, Nature, Natural Law* I, *Society, God, Humanism* I, *Ideology, Science, Industrialism, Marxism, Language, Occident, Personalism, Christianity.*

BIBLIOGRAPHY. J. H. Newman, *Idea of a University* (1852); T. Litt, *Wissenschaft, Bildung, Weltanschauung* (1928); M. Müller, *Das christliche Menschenbild und die Weltanschauungen der Neuzeit* (1945); M. Scheler, *Bildung und Wissen* (1st ed. under the title: *Die Formen des Wissens und die Bildung* [1925]; 3rd ed., 1947); M. Heidegger, *Über den Humanismus* (1949); R. Guardini, *Grundlegung der Bildungslehre* (1955); J. Castiello, *Human Psychology of Education* (1962); E. R. Hull, *Formation of Character* (1963); G. F. McLean, ed., *Philosophy and the Integration of Contemporary Catholic Education* (1962); H.-G. Gadamer, *Wahrheit und Methode* (1960; 2nd ed., 1965); M. Müller, *Existenzphilosophie im geistigen Leben der Gegenwart* (1949; 3rd ed., 1964).

Max Müller

II. Philosophy of Education

1. *The implications of the word "educate".* To educate is generally taken to mean "to lead or draw out", from the Latin *e-ducare.* Other more or less equivalent words in English are to rear (i.e., to raise) and to bring up. In all cases the notion of education suggests the following elements: a) the possibility of a change in the child; b) a certain direction and purpose in the upbringing; c) the influence of the educator; d) a movement forward and upward; e) a certain intensification of the process. Other languages embody similar elements in the corresponding words. Rearing, upbringing and educating all go beyond the notion of mere material care and nourishment to suggest a sphere of suprasensible personal relationships.

2. *The concept.* What is meant when we say that children must be educated? Or when we say that this or that is a fruit of education?

Or when we speak of a well-educated child, or one that is uneducated, or even badly educated? Do we mean thereby that nature, or an influence operating according to nature, has or has not accomplished its task (Rousseau)? In that case it would still be an open question in what sense we were to interpret "nature". Or do we mean that life itself educates for life (E. Key)? In this case it would be easy to see how the indefiniteness of the concept "life" in such a usage could easily give way to other concepts such as the "state" (E. Krieck), "society" (J. Dewey), "classes" (Ogorodnikov-Schimbirjev), "culture" (Litt and Spranger, to a certain extent), and so on. Or do we mean the development of the individual which occurs under the influence of a community of persons? In this case education takes on the aspect of an interpersonal relationship of a special type. The question about the nature of education thus becomes one about the nature of the educative relationship.

How can we characterize this relation more precisely? Is it to be found on the same level as Eros? But Eros flows from passion and is the effect of inclination and choice, of sympathy and harmony of mind and heart. Thus Eros comprises only part of the other; it does not penetrate to the ultimate kernel of the person. Similarly, in Eros the other person is chosen and set apart from many other possible subjects. The educator, on the other hand, does not choose. He may not do so. He cannot choose to educate one and to leave another. He finds his charge before him and accepts him, regardless of whether he is handicapped or gifted. Education means in the first place acceptance, not exception, because being recognizes no exception. Education means, indeed, that the educator's being is brought to bear effectively upon the being of another, not in order to "make something of" what is "over there" on "the other side" — that would indeed be an exercise of power, a degradation of the will to educate to the will to power. What the educator does is rather to seek out with his own "I" the uniqueness of the other as a person and to awaken it.

a) The first of the fundamental relationships in education begins to take shape. It may be expressed as follows: it is good that this human being is and that he is this human being. This indicates firstly that education is always concerned with "the whole", or rather, the whole person. It is concerned, that is, with man, not in the sense of an object, but as a person; it is concerned not with one or another quality of the person, but with the person in its entirety. This includes the whole sphere of nourishment and care. It implies further that education accepts man in the concrete and therefore with his limitations and failings. But this affirmation includes the third element: education sees man as he is, but it does not want to leave him as he is, whether he be no more than alive, or on the road to full development, or already disturbed and in disorder. The educator is not satisfied with the mere existence of the other. He wishes that the other attain his full development. And this means that the being of the educator must influence the other in such a way that the true self of the pupil be disclosed. Education thus becomes a confrontation of a very special nature. It may be called dialogical confrontation, the chief characteristic of which, according to M. Buber, is the element of "inclusion", which, in turn, is based on the "experience of the counterpart" (see M. Buber, "Education", in *Between Man and Man* [1961], pp. 125 ff.). What is meant by this is the fundamental insight into the soul of the other which grows out of actual "being-for" the other. It is contact with his personal mystery.

b) This points to the second basic relationship. It is expressed in the following sentence: it is good that the other becomes what he should become according to his nature. This desire to see the other become what he should be, to see him achieve the totality of his personal essence, presupposes three things. The first is confidence in the power of growth latent in the child, in its capacity and potentiality for self-fulfilment. More precisely, one must trust the child's will to develop and have faith in its natural capacity to exercise freedom and act responsibly. The second is that the educator wishes to see the pupil become "greater", "better", "nobler" and "purer" than himself. "He must increase, but I must decrease." The third is an attitude of extreme self-effacement, in the sense that the self-realization of the pupil means that he can be helped by the educator, but not that he can be formed, moulded or forcibly bent. Education, no doubt, is essentially an effort to bring "up", to

disclose the latent, to correct the disturbed and disfigured, to provide the pupil with the unavoidably necessary aids to finding his place in the world. But it must not impose itself in any way which would distort the I-You relationship into an I-It one. This would be to dominate rather than to help, to mislead rather than to lead. One must be clearly aware of this possible aberration, because it can falsify the relationship in a way "beside which all quackery appears peripheral" (Buber, *op. cit.,* p. 123). It is here, namely, that even with the purest intentions and highest motives that the pupil is regarded as something that can be manipulated, something out of which one can "make something" or over which one can dispose at will. But when we treat a human being as a thing, we find that "his person slips away from us and that we are left with only an empty shell" (cf. M. Scheler, *Wesen und Formen der Sympathie* [1926], p. 193).

Man is, of course, in many ways a predetermined and "pre-established" being, which at once limits the possibilities of his being "formed" and "moulded". But this is not the question when we speak of the educator's self-effacement or with Buber, of the "ascetical nature of education" (*op. cit.,* p. 123). For we can still call for this attitude while recognizing that man is in fact a very malleable and responsive being — educable, in a word. This is also clear when we note, from the opposite point of view, his imperfection, his fluidity, uncertainty, other-directedness and openness to the world — the last implying his freedom. And it is precisely this which imposes on the educator a self-denial which he often finds painful. His respect for the "You" of the other forbids him to intervene and curtail this freedom. The educator must often look on almost impassively while the pupil goes astray. He must often sadly feel that his best intentions and his best efforts have been wasted. But he must stay there patiently, offering what help he can and giving the greatest thing that he has to give, his love.

c) With this we come to the third basic relation involved in education. We could formulate it in the following manner: it is good that "we" are. This assertion of "being-with" along with the pupil, is not a mere juxtaposition nor a merely accidental association, but a primal metaphysical condition of human existence. Human existence is always an existence in encounter, always "being-with" along with others (cf. K. Barth on basic humanity in *Church Dogmatics,* III/2). Hence the educator goes over entirely to the side of the pupil, that is, he loves him. This is the experience of the truth that the other is a spiritual value intrinsic to our own existence. It is not a matter of sentiment or sympathy, but a gesture whereby the other is held aloft so that the full light of his personal value may shine upon the world (cf. P. Lersch, *Aufbau der Person* [7th ed., 1956], p. 225). With such a close bond between them, the educator avoids the one-sided and hence misguided effort to educate the pupil in a certain mould, to produce a certain type of man. It is possible to renounce such projects, because education is basically not an imposition but an offer, not a demand but a gift. It is, in a word, not possessive. And what is offered is not a "something", not values or good things, knowledge or culture, qualities, talents and virtues, not a definite ideal of man, but what the educator most truly and properly is — a person, himself. For where the educator is both giver and gift, where the fundamental act is the dedication of the educator and the establishment of a situation of dialogue, the interposition of "things" between pupil and educator is excluded. The educator will have to gather and absorb from the world all the forces of the world which the pupil needs for his growth. This is the element of self-education which is always demanded of the educator. He will also bring with him knowledge and values, culture and virtue, talents and qualities and, finally, also a world-image and a human ideal. The educator's union with God will make his ideals serve the growth of the young person. But the primary factor is not this transmission of culture or of values and the like, though such a process is legitimate in teaching, which is precisely given to transmit certain heritages. In education the primary aim is the personal relationship in which the child learns to think in terms of persons and not of things.

In such a relation of giving and receiving, in which one shares with another what is most uniquely his, "being with" is experienced as "grace". It is this which constitutes the special splendour and light which is not dimmed even by the pupil's faults. We cannot and may not disguise and disregard the faults, weaknesses, corruption and evil which slumber even in the child and often enough nullify the efforts of the educator. But genuine love is to see failures and still to love — failures and all. This love must be somewhat one-sided, since the child cannot respond to it, at least adequately. All that remains is that the educator must recognize in the child a summons which makes him experience the child, as a reality to be affirmed and indeed loved, because he is a person with his world and his share in the one existence and ultimately because referred to God.

It should be pointed out that in virtue of such a loving concern by which the educator gives to the pupil what is most his own, namely his self, education takes on a peculiar task: the educator can and should only give "that which is pure and true in his own being" (L. Boros, *Der anwesende Gott* [1964], p. 24). However, every educator, if he is not blind to himself, recognizes his own limitations, weakness, self-seeking, and not least of all his depravity. Thus if he does not wish to run the danger of achieving just the opposite of that which he set out to do — that the other should succeed in embodying the supreme values which are proper to him (cf. M. Scheler, *op. cit.,* p. 187); if he wishes love to grow where he has sown love; if formation in the sense of personal self-realization is to be possible; if the child is to take his essential place in the world as a whole; if the object of love is to be pure, gleaming and unimpaired, the true image of God: then the educator must be careful not to impart the wickedness of his heart as he gives himself. Only the pure, worthy and constructive should be transmitted to others (cf. L. Boros, *op. cit.,* p. 24). Hence the educator needs constantly to purify his love.

Once more the painful boundaries of educative activity make themselves felt. This time not from the side of the pupil but from the side of the educator. He must learn that even there where the truly educative relation begins to develop, the limitations are most in evidence, because his own poverty will then become most apparent. All this is very far from that form of education which "allows things to grow", for such permissiveness is really a rejection of the child. The You is left to itself and allowed to relapse into indeterminacy and helplessness, because the "I-You" relationship has been broken off. To let the child just grow is to let it languish. It is self-alienation. Thus upbringing in the sense explained above is really riches of being in spite of its poverty, because the ontological "being-with" of the educator along with the child bestows on the child that by which it constructs its being.

See also *Education* I, III, *School Systems, Nature, Person, Society* I, II, *Freedom, World*.

BIBLIOGRAPHY. M. Buber, *Dialogisches Leben* (1947), E. T.: *Dialogues of Realization* (1965); id., *Reden über Erziehung* (1956), E. T.: *Between Man and Man* (1965); O. F. Bollnow, *Existenzphilosophie und Pädagogik* (1959); R. Mühlbauer, *Der Begriff "Bildung" in der Gegenwartspädagogik* (1965).

Reinhold Mühlbauer

III. Pedagogy

Pedagogy may be variously defined. The term can be understood to mean formal teaching itself and this signification can then be widened to include the history of change and progress in methods and theories of instruction over the course of centuries and from one culture to another. Pedagogy may also denote both the systematization of general and specific principles governing effective teaching and the study of such systematizations. Pedagogical codifications of this sort include the formulation both of aims and of means for motivating students to achieve these aims as well as elaboration of concrete procedures for making learning as easy, secure and economical as possible. Because its scope is thus so broad, a complete pedagogical theory will involve much of the substance of a philosophy of man, life and value. A good deal may be learned, therefore, about a people's ideology and level of cultural development by examining the techniques they favour in educating their children.

In order to allow for this broader perspective, the term pedagogy has been displaced by the more comprehensive word education in English-speaking countries. In the United States, for instance, departments of education have expanded considerably in colleges and universities during this century. They concern themselves not only with methods of instruction but also with the historical, philosophical, sociological and psychological foundations of education and with all aspects of curricular design, student guidance

and the organization and administration of schools at every level.

In this article, however, pedagogy will be taken in its conventional, limited reference to methods of instruction. The aim will be to underline certain implications that may be drawn from a rapid and somewhat arbitrary survey of the history of pedagogical developments. These conclusions could then be regrouped so as to suggest the tentative outlines of a pedagogy. The focus here is upon the education of intelligence since the basic goal and process of education is treated under I above. It should be understood, however, that these two phases of education are so profoundly interconnected in practice that a perfect precision of one from the other is not possible.

Philosophers interested in education have sometimes dreamt of discovering a general pattern of learning which would point to a basic and universally applicable teaching method. The American philosopher, John Dewey (1859–1952), for instance, believed that all fruitful thinking rises from a problem situation in which one must choose from among a number of alternatives. Such problems, he thought, are best solved by the scientific method which treats the alternatives as practical hypotheses to be tested in action. Even in the elementary school, Dewey would have children's minds developed by involvement in concrete projects, appropriate to their age and interests, which call for use of this empirical technique. Over a century earlier, Rousseau (1712–1778) had advocated a similar pedagogy of learning-by-doing and motivation through interest rather than coercion. On a typical occasion in *Émile,* the tutor, who deprecates verbalism and book-learning, teaches Émile some astronomical principles by pretending to get lost in the woods and then finding the way out from observation of the direction of the trees' shadows.

But whether there is any such universal method of thought and instruction or not, it is clear that every pedagogy needs adaptation to the complexity of the materials and to the age, ability and previous experience of the learners. These learners will belong to one of three groups. They may be very young, preliterate children or older children who are acquiring the basic tools of knowledge but still lack enough mastery of language skills to make the more abstract forms of reasoning and learning possible or they may be persons who possess some degree of adult power and a capacity for self-sustained study. It is only to be expected that specific procedures designed for one of these developmental levels may prove largely useless for another. Socratic questioning, while stimulating for mature students, will not serve to teach factual historical materials to young children

It would therefore be unfair to the great pedagogical innovators to attempt a literal transference of techniques which they devised precisely for one of these groups. For the most part, these pioneers concentrated upon the teaching of young children since this is more difficult in itself and more subject to the danger of unintelligent or fossilized procedures. In the university world, three long-established methods are still usefully employed: the lecture; the discussion (whose forms include the Platonic dialogue, the medieval disputation and the modern seminar) and supervised laboratory or field experience.

Twentieth-century technology has produced variants of these techniques without transforming them essentially. In some vast American State universities introductory courses may enroll a thousand students. These will meet in small groups to watch a pre-recorded lecture on closed-circuit television followed by a brief seminar with a junior staff member. Television thereby extends the range of a senior lecturer without basic alteration of a pedagogical form popular in the medieval university.

In the teaching of young children, however, there have been significant innovations over the millennia. If we survey, at a high level of generalization, the history of these developments, we may distinguish three broad epochs of characteristic emphasis. These eras overlap, of course, and the emphases in question are not strictly confined to a single period. It is rather a matter of some dominant practical approach or of a distinctive innovation which gradually becomes dominant. For in pedagogy, as elsewhere, there is always a gap between the work of the creative pioneers and the established forms which are slow to relinquish their monopoly. Educational reformers of the 16th and 17th centuries, like the Jesuits or the Moravian bishop Comenius (1592–1670), deplored the popular, brutal

pedagogy which preserved the least attractive characteristics of Horace's teacher, Orbilius the Pounder. Comenius called the Latin grammar schools of his day the terror of boys and the slaughterhouse of the mind, but it took several more centuries to achieve a general disassociation of teaching from flogging.

The first of the periods to be distinguished is that of the informal and largely practical pedagogy of primitive, non-literate societies. The second is that of the formalistic and adult-oriented pedagogy of schools in the literate cultures of East and West before the wide dissemination of printed books in the post-Renaissance industrialized nations. The third is that of a *psychologized and child-oriented* pedagogy, the "social movement on behalf of the child" to use Maria Montessori's phrase (1870–1952). This movement, with its concern for the special character and needs of childhood, has developed since the 16th century and particularly since Rousseau. Of each of these approaches one may ask how it views teaching-learning, how it seeks to motivate, and how it conceives of discipline.

We know that pre-historic peoples educated their children, for otherwise neither the children nor the primitive society would have survived. But lacking written records, we do not know what methods these people employed. It may be reasonably conjectured, however, that their procedures resembled those that have been observed by anthropologists studying contemporary non-literate societies in Africa, Oceania, and parts of the Americas. In such cultures two sorts of education occur. For adolescents there generally are puberty rites which may be brief or last several months. This time is occupied with rituals; rote-learning of tribal wisdom; initiation into mythology and religious practice and, particularly for boys, the arbitrary discipline of physical ordeals.

The other, and more important phase of education is informal and practical and extends over the whole period required for bringing infants to adult competency. The parents or other members of the family circle are the teachers. The materials learned are essential or eminently useful and the methods of teaching and learning are concrete. Children learn the characteristics of their physical environment from direct experience. The crucial techniques of hunting, cooking and crafts are learned by imitating adults. Although language is indispensable, teaching is not so much *telling* as it is *showing*. Children learn by doing and acquisitions are not compartmentalized. Thus boys learning to carve ceremonial figures acquire both technical skill and introduction to art and religion. The motivation comes either from natural interest or desire to imitate or from pressure of sheer practical need. Hence, even if an element of coercion is present, it probably appears less arbitrary than it does when there is insistence upon purely formalistic or abstract learning. Discipline can therefore be related quite naturally to the demands imposed by the nature of the learning task itself rather than to such extrinsic devices as punishments, threats and bribes. Primitive education, however, knew little of progress and innovation. Without writing, there was not much accumulation of knowledge. The aims of education were clear but also simple and fixed. The rise of civilizations seems to have been related to the development of writing. Thereupon, in the cultures of ancient China, India, Israel and the Graeco-Roman world there appeared a new kind of education which concentrated upon imparting, through the formal schooling of a small all-male class, skills of a predominantly literary sort. Crafts continued to be learned through apprenticeship, and technicians contributed to the advance of civilization side by side with scribes and statesmen. But it is the work of the school which has occupied the attention of students of pedagogy. That school existed in a culture where the word was powerful but books were scarce. Hence schooling stressed memorization of texts, sacred or profane, and the mastery of rhetoric or exegesis. Programs so verbalistic conceded little to children's natural interests and classrooms were uncomfortable. Hence the motive of fear or of ambition and love of glory were played upon.

The great exponent of this pedagogy of the book was Quintilian whose *Institutio Oratoria* was the acknowledged authority for Renaissance schoolmen fifteen hundred years after it was written. By the standards of this day, Quintilian was himself partially an innovator. He had some knowledge of child psychology, recognized the place of games and outlawed whippings. Still, all his effort is aimed at devising methods which will prepare wealthy boys to be effective speakers and writers in adult life. If one knew only this tradition, one would conclude that the main aim of pedagogy is to help selected students to master, retain and exploit classical literary models.

The political, cultural and technological developments of the past four centuries compelled a reformulation of such educational concepts because universal literacy is a minimum requirement for industrialized nations. The new social conditions were partly responsible for the rise of a succession of pedagogical pioneers: Comenius, Rousseau, Pestalozzi, Herbart, Froebel, Montessori and Dewey are only the better known names. In their theological and philosophical views these figures differed widely but they subscribed, wholly or in part, to a common core of basic convictions about teaching children. This core can be understood as a corrective and supplement of the Quintilian tradition rather than its wholesale rejection.

These educational reformers brought into the school some of the methods which the informal education of non-literate societies or of apprenticeship training had always employed. They also re-affirmed, whether with consciousness of the kinship or not, those values of personality, freedom and kindness which Christianity had long preached to civilizations. Moreover, their view of human nature acknowledged more realistically than the older pedagogy had, man's composite nature and his existential situation in the twofold milieu of nature and society, both of which are pervaded by process.

Each of these leaders was seriously interested in child psychology and wished to organize the educational programme in that light rather than exclusively in terms of what adult society would ultimately require of the students. "The man", said Rousseau characteristically, "must be treated as a man and the child as a child." This attitude has been epigrammatically, if inaccurately, summarized by saying that the school should be child-centred rather than curriculum-centred. From this basic concern for child nature, there flowed four key emphases, i.e., upon concrete sense experience as the starting point for learning, upon purposeful activity, freedom and creativity. It was argued that sound intellectual development requires the development of children's sense powers and this is best done by cultivating their spontaneous interest in their surroundings and extrapolating sophisticated learning from these concrete experiences. Children learn best, it was said, from active encounter with things rather than from passive submission to books.

Since liberty is the requisite for such activity, all the pioneers advocated freedom as opposed to rigidity although they defined differently the limits of this freedom. None defended licence but simply the chance for children to release their creative and imaginative powers, not only through conventional classroom materials but in arts and crafts. If this were done, it was thought that interest in learning and in sharing the life of the student group would provide motivation and ensure good discipline. The natural results of co-operating or not would provide sufficient reward or punishment.

Ideals of this sort clearly require gifted, devoted teachers and in fact the pioneers were often teachers of teachers. The good mother was frequently held up as the archetype of the ideal teacher and, conversely, a Pestalozzi would emphasize the potential of mothers themselves as teachers. Some reformers stressed the notion of the school as a community — like the family (Pestalozzi) or a reflection of the larger society (Dewey). In this community the teacher functions as a guide rather than as a dictator and in any case exercises authority by what Sturzo called the "method of liberty". But to catch the full flavour of the great pedagogical innovators, one must read their own books. These may sometimes appear rudimentary or misguided but their basic message has altered for the better school practice everywhere.

See also *Education* I, II, *School Systems, Universities.*

BIBLIOGRAPHY. Comenius, *The School of Infancy;* Rousseau, *Émile;* Pestalozzi, *How Gertrude Teaches Her Children;* Froebel, *The Education of Man;* Herbert, *The Science of Education;* Dewey, *The Child and the Curriculum;* id., *The School and Society;* Montessori, *The Montessori Method;* William Harrison Woodward, *Studies in Education during the Age of the Renaissance, 1400–1600* (1924); François de Dainville, S. J., *La naissance de l'humanisme moderne* (1940); John S. Brubacher, *A History of the Problems of Education* (1947), pp. 165–248 and 652–4; William Boyd, *The History of Western Education* (1954); H. I. Marrou, *A History of Education in Antiquity* (1956); A. Cremin, *The Transformation of the School: Progressivism in American Education, 1876–1957* (1961); Philippe Ariès, *Centuries of Childhood: A Social History of Family Life* (1962).

John W. Donohue

IV. Religious Education

1. *The notion of religious education* is to be seen against the background of the Enlightenment. It is the scientific analysis of the means and methods to be used in religious and moral upbringing. In the OT, the bonds by which the Israelites were united to Yahweh, strengthened by their constant confrontation with the history of salvation in the liturgy, held good for all stages of men's life. But in the Wisdom literature explicit attention was then given to the education of children and the formation of character. The prophets spoke of God's action in the history of Israel and of the nations. A theology of suffering sometimes interpreted this as God's taking disciplinary measures to educate his people and make them undergo vicarious punishments. Philo tried to link up with Greek culture by showing the spiritual content of the OT and its absolute superiority over Greek philosophy. The Rabbis often unwittingly made religion serve worldly claims. The Torah took the place of Yahweh as teacher. The NT notion has its roots in the OT and in contemporary culture, but all its statements on education have been given a new dimension and purpose.

2. *Christocentric education.* The Christian preaching goes beyond the framework of ordinary instruction. It is based on the message of the coming of the lordship of God and becomes an insistent summons which takes concrete form in re-birth. This imposes the decision, the conversion and faith in which the new moral order is rooted. Its manifestation is the love in which Christians begin to tread the path of the following of Christ.

Life itself is the great educational process which God has instituted for his children (Heb 12:5–11). God the Father comes to meet them, and brings them to share in the eternal, heavenly worship. This fatherly love is revealed in the manifest grace which wills the salvation of all and submits the Christian community to its discipline. Education grows out of the divine salvific will in Christ Jesus and aims at the response of love, peace with God. Those who have been formed by Christ's education will share in the end the same heavenly joy (Heb 12:2), the crown of glory and honour (Heb 2:9) and the solemn, final confirmation of the name of son before the whole heavenly world.

Education in the law of Christ by faith and love. God, by sending his Son, has made us mature and responsible. The aim is to make us be in Christ, like to him (cf. Phil 3:9f.), sharers in his death (Rom 7:4). God's saving act unites men with their Lord, to whom they subject themselves freely. The vocation of the believer is given in baptism, and his education is determined by the fact that he belongs to the Lord (Eph 6:4). Christ's saving action is the restoration and new creation of human nature. It gives education once more the relative independence which was the gift of the creator. The "new creation" (2 Cor 5:17) is now possible – something of which the human educator is incapable — based on love of God and of man. In this new age the educational effort of family and community finds its fulfilment in *agape*.

The child in the plan of salvation. True childhood is being child of God. It means being laid hold of by Christ in the Spirit and thereby becoming the property of the Father and being granted a share in the redemptive work of Christ. The education of the child is the salvific process whereby it is brought into the new people of God and made a member of the fellowship in Christ, as child of God.

3. *Principles of religious education.* Pedagogical principles must be based on the faith as assent and personal decision. The substance and force of the message of salvation must be vividly brought out and shown to be the indispensable truth of faith. In the actual explicit sequence, faith comes first, followed by hope in the glory in Christ which has its definitive fulfilment in the love of God. Hence religious education must prepare for faith, provide it with the chance of growing and taking deeper roots. It cannot mediate salvation. All it can do is help men to find salvation, which it proclaims by presenting the history of salvation and by the words it utters by virtue of the legitimate mandate given by God and the Church. But the means is always the truth or the word of God (1 Tim 2:4; Heb 10:26). The commission to preach means that the obedience of faith must be awakened (Rom 1:5, cf. 16:26). Hence religious education must make the Lord clearly known, and make the encounter with him possible, while God is the real agent and the only educator. The function which man is obliged to discharge is that of putting himself at God's disposition as his instrument and messenger, just as the Church itself is not lord but servant of the word. The message of salvation must be offered in such a way that it can be known, assimilated and put in practice at each age of life. The awakening mind must not only be preserved and shielded, it must be allowed to be itself in a process of self-emancipation. This demands lively understanding, development of knowledge, will and feeling, the transmission of genuine tradition and the strengthening of personal responsibility.

The community of salvation appears as the *corpus Christi mysticum* and the people of God. Christ is the Lord, to whom his creation and institution is subject. There result the charge and obligation to hear, believe, obey and follow, to do penance and to be renewed. The "pilgrim people of God" is set up as the sign of salvation for all mankind. Religious education is less concerned with the cultural force of Christianity than with displaying its vitality and riches as fellowship with Christ in prayer and sacrifice. Before men can take part in the liturgy, they must be called to faith and conversion (see Vatican II's Constitution on the Sacred Liturgy). And then they must be familiar with the use of Scripture, learn to experience the mystery and understand the saving signs. The whole education in the liturgy must be carefully thought out anew.

Man is by his nature the image and likeness of God, but he has this character as a gift which also imposes a task (Gen 1:26). The OT saw this as sharing in the productive activity of God and his rule over creation. In the NT, all becomes Christocentric, since Christ is the true image of the invisible God and thus the first-born of all creation. All things were created through the Logos and formed in his image. The Christian is meant to share the image of the Son in Christ, and thus to be like to God. He must be ready for God's intervention in his life. He must accept his dependence on the sovereign power of God. When he accepts the place assigned to him in creation, he takes his place in the concrete order which is attuned to God's will, and puts his trust in the God of revelation by submitting to God in loyal obedience. He keeps the commandments in which the law is comprised, which is liberation not so much in the sense that he is set free from something, as that he is free for something. In his encounter with his fellowmen he must display the true brotherliness which is the testimony of the good tidings, of the intensity and quality of the basic Christian fellowship. This unifying fellowship can be attained only in the unity which is brought about by the following of Christ.

The tasks of religious instruction cannot be defined one by one in orderly sequence, since there are so many different points of departure. To the essentials belong the proclamation of the event of salvation in its historic uniqueness and the re-presentation of the salvific event, since in it come redemption and salvation to the hearer of the biblical word — the kerygma. In practice, proclamation and education must go hand in hand. In any case, the proclamation must be addressed to the hearer as a person. Here educator and pupil are both challenged by the same claim, and this is decisive for the educational process.

Religious education is only a reality when the pupil is summoned and enabled to consider and examine his whole life in the light of the gospel. His human understanding of the gospel gives him new possibilities with regard to his relationship to God, to himself, to his environment and to the world. He becomes conscious of his Christian existence. With the help of the permanent and variable elements of natural education and on the basis of Christian tradition, the pupil takes over a doctrine and a relationship to the world and thus achieves his initiation into Christianity. In this way the Christian-to-be learns norms, concepts and directives for his life of faith, which will also help him in his doubts and lack of faith. In this way the preaching will be educational, while Christian education will always contain the element of the preaching. While faith displays the reality of man and his world in the light of the gospel, the pedagogical elements must be learned as presupposition, ways and means, and practised as the introduction to a way of life. But here too they will always be given their importance by the gospel and in view of the gospel. This process will have to prove its worth above all by helping the child to find a Christian way of life and to fit into the family and the Church. The more mature and self-reliant a man is, the more clearly must he be able to transform his whole existence into a full life of faith, to find his home in the Church as the people of God, to recognize consciously his orientation to God and his mission to the world and to take full personal responsibility for it.

See also *Faith, Hope, Charity, People of God, Salvation* III, *Creation, Kerygma, Old Testament Books* III.

BIBLIOGRAPHY. J. Collins, *Teaching Religion* (1953); J. Hofinger, *Art of Teaching Christian Doctrine* (revised ed., 1962); G. Sloyan, *Modern Catechetics* (1963); J. Hofinger and T. Stone, *Pastoral Catechetics* (1964); J. Lehmann, ed., *Christliche Erziehung heute* (1964); S. Riva, *Gli orientamenti attuali della catechetica pastorale* (1965); T. Filthaut, *Learning to Worship* (1966); M. Pfliegler, *Pastoral Theology* (1966); W. Langer, *Kerygma und Katechese* (1966).

Leopold Lentner

V. Self-Education

1. *Nature, purpose and aims of self-education.* Unlike what we may term "other-directed" education in which the person who educates ("the educator") and the person who is being educated (the "pupil") are distinct and separate, in self-education the two are identical. Man is at once his own educator and pupil since as educator he "brings up" himself (as pupil) to his higher and true self.

Thus we discover as a basis for the *possibility* of self-education a certain non-identity in the essential structure of human nature, whereby man has an existence extended in the temporal and historical dimension. Man is, of course, always himself, yet never so perfectly or completely that he could not become more himself, never so transparently visible to himself and "at home" with himself that he could not seek and find a further dimension in his potentialities, never so entirely in possession of himself as not to be able perpetually to deepen his hold of himself in a new way. This leads us to the demand to pursue self-education, which is experienced in conscience as the command: "Become what you are."

In this command of conscience, self-education is seen to be not only ontologically possible but morally necessary. For without his own free co-operation man will not become more himself — otherwise the appeal of conscience would have neither meaning nor prospect of success. If even existence itself is an activity, to be performed without any possibility of substitution by the existent being itself (i.e., in this case, man) — and it is significant that the verb "to be" cannot be put into the passive — then it goes without saying that the further actuation must be so regarded. Thus the command of conscience is directed to one's own ego, insofar as it remains latent in its potentialities (*starting-point* of self-education); it calls to it to emerge and seek as a goal (*goal* of self-education) its full personal reality in free conscious self-actualization.

2. *Means of self-education.* Here we already have an indication of the means whereby self-education comes about. Self-education takes place by means of a dialogue with God in conscience, postulating a corresponding dialogue with oneself and finding its concrete setting and opportunity in a dialogue with men and things. In conscience man finds an absolute demand directed at himself and in it (no matter how hidden) the one who makes that absolute demand. In subsequent reflection this person is seen to be the absolute existent being (since otherwise the absolute demand would lack its essential foundation) — and this in a personal sense, seeing that its demand engages man as a person. So the claim experienced in conscience is seen to be the personal call of an absolute person making the demand on man and thus calling him out of himself to self-actualization. He sees himself against an absolute measure which makes plain his own relativity and incompleteness. Now in seeking to measure up to this and to respond to this claim through moral activity, he takes on "respons-ibility", becoming answerable for his disposal of himself. In the measure in which this succeeds, he has experience of himself as being addressed by the Absolute. The Absolute thereby reveals himself as the archetype giving man life and a model for his activity, at once the ground and exemplar for man's responsive growth through self-actualization in freedom.

The personal elevation and development will take place with the help of the archetype. It will proceed through the medium of a self-dialogue in which the person will seek in "creative self-knowledge" to capture, reflect, express (and so grow into) his higher self. He will be impelled to this through his meeting and dialogue with men and things, which as positive (or negative) models will be experienced and accepted (or rejected) in an intimate process of constructive self-development. In this way self-education will carry on its personal dialogue of praise and blame, approving, encouraging and confirming itself in what is positive and condemning, threatening and weakening what is negative. This is the process of self-educative dialogue under the normative power and influence of a hidden dialogue with the Absolute, embracing as well the environment in its entirety.

3. *Forms of self-education.* It is probable that man is not capable of a deliberate methodical or systematic self-education before the awakening of the knowledge of self and of ideals at puberty. In general this express form of self-education is found only occasionally and is contained in a more instinctive "drive" or "functional" form: "A good man in his dark urgings is well conscious of the right way" (Goethe, *Faust*, I, Prologue). Or it has more of an accessory character, i.e., the conscious drive is towards acquiring morally neutral characteristics (such as prestige, prosperity), whereby self-education in the form of personal values (industry, love of order, patience) will be secured indirectly.

See also *Absolute and Contingent, Conscience, Existence* I, *Freedom, Person.*

BIBLIOGRAPHY. R. Allers, *The Psychology of Character* (1933); C. L. Hull, *Principles of Behaviour* (1943); F. J. Sheed, *A Map of Life* (1944); S. Kraines and E. Thetford, *Managing Your Mind* (1946); D. von Hildebrand, *Die Umgestaltung in Christus* (3rd ed., 1950), E. T.: *Transformation in Christ;* H. Kuhn, *Begegnung mit dem Sein. Zur Metaphysik des Gewissens* (1954); R. Guardini, *Briefe über Selbsterziehung* (8th ed., 1961); id., *Die Annahme seiner Selbst* (3rd ed., 1962); T. P. Maher, *Lest We Build on Sand* (1962).

Heinrich Beck

EMPIRICISM

Empiricism is generally taken to be a philosophical attitude based on epistemological preliminaries, which takes experience (internal and external) alone as the foundation of true knowledge and of science. In this sense, empiricism is the opposite of an equally radical *a priori* system where knowledge is based on first principles from which truth and certainty are derived deductively. This current but somewhat conventional antithesis does not, however, render clearly the meaning and aims of empiricism.

Even when the name of empiricism is reserved for the Enlightenment of the 17th and 18th centuries in England, especially for the work of J. Locke (1632–1704) and D. Hume (1711–76), we need to consider it in the context of the history of thought and of the spirit, if empiricism is to be properly characterized. Not every recourse to empirical facts is at once empiricism; yet the tension between the experimental and the ideal pervades the whole of the history of philosophy. Great attention was already paid in antiquity, especially by Aristotle, to experience or sensible perception of beings; and in the course of the Middle Ages in Europe, sensible knowledge, duly tested, became more and more a court of appeal to check the verdicts of metaphysics and the theology of revelation (so, for instance, in nominalism, the school of Chartres, and in such figures as St. Thomas Aquinas, St. Albert the Great, Roger Bacon, William of Occam and so on; Frederick II could make bold to say: "fides enim certa non provenit ex auditu" [*De arte venandi*, c. 1]). But it was only in modern philosophy, strongly influenced by the rapid growth of the knowledge of nature, that reflection on experiment and experience became a systematic programme. Noteworthy here are Francis Bacon's *Novum Organon Scientiarum* (1620), Locke's *Essay concerning Human Understanding* (1690) and the critical writings of Hume.

Whether a thorough-going empiricism ever existed, however, is a question which must be left to future special studies. Locke and above all Berkeley cannot be regarded as representatives of empiricism. Hume comes closest to it. Many motives enter into the basically "empiricist" attitude of Condillac, Diderot, Voltaire, J. St. Mill. This is also true of the so-called *Empiriokritizismus* of E. Mach and R. Venarius. Similar tendencies are to be found in sensism, positivism and materialism: Kant's effort at synthesis in his "transcendental philosophy" did not succeed in overcoming the empiricist climate of modern times and its scientism.

Many ideological currents of the present day display basically empiricist trends: so atheism of a scientific stamp, mechanicist and to some extent dialectic materialism, the exaggerated respect paid to psychology and sociology, especially the sociology of knowledge. The same is true of the rationalist technological approach in general. In the various schools of modern logistics and linguistic analysis the norm of all (philosophically valid) knowledge is taken to be the possibility of verifying a statement on the basis of data furnished only empirically.

The permanent objection against a professed empiricism is that it fails to reflect sufficiently on the conditions of experience. In spite of this necessary correction on the philosophical level, it would be foolish to reject completely the aims and mentality of empiricism. In a "hominization of the world" of Christian intent, the beings of the world must be considered in such a way that their possibilities can be experimentally explored. For the elimination of a divinized or "numinous" world, by reason of the biblical faith in the Creator, has as its logical consequence the "desacralizing" of the world, and hence necessarily implies the fundamental possibility of science and technology in the modern sense. To this extent, the Christian understanding of the world inevitably calls for the application of the empirical method, and so preserves the element of truth in empiricism, without accepting its naive theories of knowledge.

See also *Experience, Knowledge, Materialism, Nominalism, Transcendental Philosophy.*

BIBLIOGRAPHY. J. Maréchal, *Le point de départ de la métaphysique*, II (1922; 12th ed., 1944); R. Reininger, *Locke, Berkeley, Hume* (1922); G. de Santillana and E. Zilser, *The Development of Rationalism and Empiricism* (1941); J. Collins, *A History of Modern European Philosophy* (1954); F. C. Copleston, *History of Philosophy*, V: *Hobbes to Hume* (1959); F. Zabeeh, *Hume, Precursor of Modern Empiricism* (1960).

Heinz Robert Schlette

ENCYCLICALS

1. *Term and background.* Encyclical is a term, derived from the Greek (ἐγκύκλιοι ἐπιστολαί), for an ecclesiastical circular

letter addressed to some or all Christian Churches, for example 1 Pet to the Churches of Pontus, Galatia, Cappadocia, Asia, and Bithynia, or the letter on the martyrdom of Polycarp "to all the communities of the Catholic Church". In the 2nd and 3rd centuries such letters were called catholic letters because of their general destination. This is what Eusebius calls the letters of Dionysius of Corinth (*Hist. Eccl.*, IV, 23). Letters written by Alexander of Alexandria and St. Athanasius to all the bishops (*PG*, XXV, cols. 221, 537; XLII, col. 209) were known in the 4th century as encyclicals. A notable instance is the 5th-century *Codex Encyclicus* containing 41 letters in defence of the Council of Chalcedon by the Emperor Leo I, St. Leo the Great, and many bishops; Evagrius says they come from a collection of "what are called encyclicals" (*PG*, LXXXVI, col. 2532). There is also an important Graeco-Latin encyclical of Pope Martin I written in 649 (*PL*, LXXXVII, col. 119). Many other letters of the first eight centuries are comparable to the foregoing without being called encyclicals.

More recently, Benedict XIV issued an encyclical on his accession in 1740 "to revive the ancient custom of the Popes" (*Bullarium Romanum*, 25, VIII, 3–6), though only seven of his bulls bear the name of encyclical. His six immediate successors gave the name of "encyclicals" to only seven of their documents in the 73 years they reigned. Only with the pontificate of Gregory XVI (1831) does the term encyclical come into general use. Whe have 16 letters of Pope Gregory that are so designated, 33 of Pius IX, 48 of Leo XIII, 10 of Pius X, 12 of Benedict XV, 30 of Pius XI, and 41 of Pius XII. Of the 63 circular letters published by Leo XIII only two are called *litterae encyclicae*: all the rest are *epistolae encyclicae*. A clear distinction between the two is first made under Pius XI and Pius XII. These Popes use *litterae encyclicae* only for a circular letter addressed to the whole Church on an important matter, in which they commonly invoke "the plenitude of their apostolic power".

2. *Authority of encyclicals.* Since the Pope has power "to teach and to govern the universal Church and all the pastors and faithful, they must obey him in matters of faith and morals and also in what concerns the government and discipline of the Church" (Vatican I: *D* 1827). Accordingly we distin-

guish doctrinal encyclicals from disciplinary ones. Much more weight attaches to doctrinal encyclicals on matters of faith or morals addressed to the whole Church: here the Pope speaks "as shepherd and teacher of the whole Church". In exceptional cases, as with Martin I, an encyclical may be "synodal" in character, the Pope promulgating the decisions of a council in his capacity as head of the episcopal college. But normally encyclicals are personal letters to the bishops, motivated as Pius VII says by the Pope's "first and exclusive duty, to strengthen his brethren" (*Bullarium Romanum*, XXXV, 25). The authority of encyclicals derives above all from their essential purpose, "that the whole world may be one in the faith" (St. Leo: *PL*, LIV, col. 799). St. Augustine agrees: "God has entrusted the Chair of unity with the teaching of the truth" (*PL*, XXXIII, col. 403).

A doctrinal encyclical is an utterance of the Pope's ordinary magisterium — addressed, on occasion, not to the Church alone but "to all men of good will" (John XXIII: *Pacem in Terris*) — in which he acts as the "principle of unity, its visible foundation" in the Church.

3. *Obligation.* Pius XII explained in the following terms what obligation encyclicals impose on the faithful (*Humani Generis*, 1950): "Let no one imagine that a Catholic may withhold assent to encyclicals because in them the Popes do not exercise their supreme magisterium. Since they are expressions of the ordinary magisterium, we must apply to them that word of Christ's, 'He who hears you, hears me' (Lk 10:16) . . . If the Popes expressly speak their mind upon a matter which hitherto has been disputed, then it is plain to all that according to the will and intent of the Popes that matter can no longer be freely discussed among theologians." (*D* 2313.)

Thus encyclicals require a positive interior assent (in the sense that no contrary opinion is outwardly defended or inwardly approved) — though not an absolute one —; only the infallible magisterium requires an unqualified and irrevocable assent. The doctrine of an encyclical is ultimately an authentic pronouncement of the magisterium. In theory the Pope could use an encyclical for his infallible magisterium. Four conditions would then have to be verified: a) the Pope would

229

have to speak as supreme teacher of the Church, b) in virtue of his supreme apostolic authority, c) on a matter of faith or morals, d) pronouncing a final and binding definition. An encyclical does not normally fulfill the fourth condition, but could do so if the Pope clearly expressed his intention of defining *ex cathedra*. The Pope decides at his discretion whether to give a "solemn definition", as at canonizations and at the proclamation of the dogma of Mary's bodily assumption into heaven, or a simple one, as is customary in encyclicals. Though encyclicals do not represent infallible pronouncements of the magisterium, they present authentic teaching and have the assistance of the Holy Ghost by which he safeguards faith and morals.

See also *Pope, Magisterium*.

BIBLIOGRAPHY. J.-M.-A. Vacant, *Le magistère ordinaire de l'Église* (1887); L. Choupin, *Valeur des décisions doctrinales et disciplinaires du Saint-Siège* (1907); E. Mangenot, *DTC*, V, pp. 14 ff.; J. C. Fenton, "The Doctrinal Authority of Papal Encyclicals", *American Ecclesiastical Review* 121 (1949), pp. 136–50, 210–20; 125 (1951), pp. 53–62; 128 (1953), pp. 177–98; J. Salaverry, "Valor de las Encíclicas a la luz de la 'Humani Generis'", *XI Semana Española de Teología* (1952), pp. 257–94; id., in Patres SJ, Madrid, ed., *Sacrae Theologiae Summa*, I (5th ed., 1962), pp. 645–9; J. Beumer, "Sind päpstliche Enzykliken unfehlbar?", *Theologie und Glaube* 42 (1952), pp. 262–9; P. Nau, "Le Magistère pontifical ordinaire lieu théologique", *Revue Thomiste* 56 (1956), pp. 389–412; M. Caudron, "Magistère ordinaire et infaillibilité pontificale", *ETL* 36 (1960), pp. 393–431; M. Nicolau, "Magisterio 'Ordinario' en el Papa", *Salmaticenses* 9 (1962), pp. 1–24; Vatican II, *Dogmatic Constitution on the Church* (1964), art. 25.

Joaquín Salaverry

ENLIGHTENMENT

The Enlightenment denotes the most revolutionary of all movements which the Occident has undergone in the course of its history. It has not yet been sufficiently investigated, but it may be admitted that it affected various countries, Churches and generations in different degrees. The historian Troeltsch has characterized it as the beginning of the really modern period of European culture, in contrast to the ecclesiastical and theological culture which had been hitherto predominant.

The Enlightenment originated in the Netherlands and in England in the mid-17th century. Varying considerably in intensity and influence during its expansion throughout almost all of Europe and the Anglo-Saxon and Spanish-American areas of the New World, it reached its high-water mark in French rationalism and materialism (Voltaire, Helvetius, Holbach) and found political expression in the French Revolution. Its richest philosophical and political results (enlightened despotism) were achieved in German territories (Leibniz, Wolff, Thomasius, Lessing, Kant, Frederick the Great, Joseph II). In Southern and Eastern Europe its impact was less widespread and less profound. The 19th century saw the crisis and decay of the Enlightenment (popular rationalism, pseudo-culture) but also a partial success and revival (especially among the working classes). It is represented today in all areas of life by modern scientific rationalism (in particular in materialism, positivism, and communism) and its end is not yet in sight.

The Enlightenment sees itself and presents itself as a goal, a criticism, a function, rather than as an attainment (the state of being enlightened). Lacking any rigid system, indeed self-contradictory to the point of complete amorphousness, yet constantly critical of ignorance, culpable infantilism, intolerance and laziness, it influenced every area of life and culture by its striving for mathematical abstraction, rational clarity *(saeculum mathematicum)*, order and progress. Basic aspects of the Enlightenment are its confidence in reason and scientism, an optimistic view of the world and man, a predominantly and almost pharisaically critical stance ("the real century of criticism" — Kant). From knowledge of the regularity of the natural order and faith in the organizability of human life was derived an enthusiastic belief in progress which banished baroque pessimism and the theory of "decline", rejected the Christian understanding, and strove for a utopian perfectionism as the objective for both the individual and society, encouraging thus the eudaemonism of the age.

For the historian of thought, the Enlightenment is a specific form of modern subjectivism and individualism for which nominalism and humanism paved the way. It adopted their passion for enquiry, their critical stance and laicized culture. It gained stimulus

ЕНLIGHTENMENT

from the intellectualism of baroque scholasticism, and was encouraged by pietism and by the effects of the wars of religion, by the hardening of the social and economic order into absolutism, and finally by the enlarging of man's view of the world (e.g., the discarding of the biblical chronology, discovery of new regions of the world and of new cultures) and the growing importance of the natural sciences and mechanized industry (Newton and Laplace). Nature became the philosopher's book (Galileo); the laws of nature assumed a metaphysical validity; the observance of the laws brings happiness and virtue (C. Wolff); mathematics and natural science, regarded as absolute sciences, become the indispensable bases of philosophical thought (Kant).

Supported at first by the nobility and then increasingly, from about 1740, by the prosperous and educated middle classes, and strengthened by a sense of solidarity among writers, the Enlightenment broke up the aristocratic court society and introduced the bourgeois century. Its social aims often coincided with those of the middle classes, though at the widest extent of its expansion its influence reached beyond them, which was one reason for the emergence of the working classes in the 19th century. The impact of the Enlightenment remained weakest among the peasant class. Freemasonry, semi-religious in character and purely bourgeois in origin, played an important role in disseminating the Enlightenment, as did other secret societies in due course (Illuminati, Rosicrucians, etc.), though the "conspiracy theory" is untenable.

Man and man's fulfilment are the primary concern of Enlightenment thought. The concern is, if not exclusively, at least more centrally than hitherto, with education, *cultura animi,* humanity, civilization. For this purpose supernatural revelation and grace seemed hardly necessary. The Enlightenment's passion for education sought to advance the moral and social welfare both of the individual and of society by the more intensive cultivation of the mind. Relieved of the burden of original sin and anxiety about existence, the anthropocentrism of the Enlightenment strove for the *regnum hominis* (instead of the *regnum Dei*), for equality and for excellence (the élite consciousness) simultaneously, patronizing the "common herd" and aiming at the perfect happiness of mankind (the welfare state of enlightened absolutism). The rejection of the supernatural and the progress of secularization (the latter difficult to pinpoint) varied from country to country and in its effects on the Churches in each period. But we can see unmistakably the tendency to rationalize religion (Kant, *Religion within the Limits of Pure Reason,* 1793), to humanize it as ethical deism, to reduce the confessions to a common denominator of "natural religion", and to dissolve theology into a philosophy of history. Yet despite a growing religious indifference and a hostility to revelation and Church within the Enlightenment, it would be inadequate to stress anti-supernaturalism and irreligion as its main features. The fact that it was tied to the maintenance of a bourgeois Christian and enlightened absolutist order kept 18th-century deism, pantheism, militant atheism and hatred of the Church within bounds. It was only the popular Enlightenment of the 19th century which alienated from the Church the *petit-bourgeois* and working-class masses. It was chiefly in Protestant countries that a distinctive Enlightenment Christianity spread, with its characteristic retreat from dogmas, sacraments and ceremonies, its faith in providence, its obligation to "virtue", its tendency to reconcile Christianity, science and culture; but it happened in Catholic countries too. The Church often came to be regarded in the Enlightenment merely as an institution concerned with morals and education, simply as an auxiliary to the enlightened welfare state. To an anti-curialism and anti-clericalism often merely intensified by the Enlightenment (hostility to the monastic orders, hatred of the Jesuits) were added violent attacks on dogmas and sacraments.

The distinctively Catholic Enlightenment (still insufficiently investigated and everywhere complex) brought about a renewal of Church life as early as the 18th century, particularly in the Catholic states of Germany. Without this renewal — taking the form of advances in positive historical and exegetical methods, improvements in the education, discipline and morality of the clergy, the struggle against superstition and credulity, the decrease in the number of festivals and processions, reform of the liturgy, catechesis and pastoral work, the furtherance of popular education and charitable works — the 19th century restoration (e.g., Clemens

231

Wenceslaus of Saxony, Max Franz of Austria, Franz Ludwig of Erthal) would have been impossible. The Catholic Enlightenment, marked by efforts to establish contact with the development of culture and science which were generally little influenced by Catholicism, and by a longing for tolerance and the reunion of the Church, was not untainted by destructive and heterodox features (rejection of the revelation-based authority of God and the Church, impoverishment of worship, devaluation of contemplation; e.g., E. Schneider, Blau, Eybel, Isenbiehl). The Enlightenment had relatively little influence on Febronianism, which stemmed from late medieval episcopalism, and the traditional demands and grievances of the State Churches. Its connection with the Jansenist movement of opposition and reform within the Church is complex and defies easy summary. The Enlightenment had a lasting influence on the State Churches of later absolutism by its acceptance, reshaping and systematization of the pre-Reformation and Counter-Reformation Church establishment in the Catholic states, with its *iura maiestatica circa sacra*. It considered all aspects of the Church's life to be under State control as a religious society under the jurisdiction of the State. The interventions of Josephinism in Church life, which were partly justified by the need for reform (dissolution of monasteries, amortization laws, parish organization, diocesan controls, etc.) sufficiently illustrate the special problems of the Catholic Enlightenment. They resulted from the interaction and tension between the Enlightenment, efforts at reform, ecclesiastical conservatism and religious decline. Attacked as it was from all sides, the 18th-century Church Enlightenment was incapable of bringing about a thorough-going renewal; the times were unpropitious and its own position was difficult. Yet in many respects its reforms and not a few of its exponents (e.g., J. M. Sailer, E. Klüpfel, G. Zirkel) paved the way for the Church renewal of the 19th century.

See also *Occident, French Revolution, Nominalism, Humanism, Absolutism, Baroque* II, *Pietism, Freemasonry, Secularization.*

BIBLIOGRAPHY. See the articles "Aufklärung" in *RGG*, I, cols. 703–30, and in *LTK*, I, cols. 1056–66; S. Merkle, *Kirchliche Aufklärung im katholischen Deutschland* (1910); B. Fay, *La Franc-Maçonnerie et la Révolution au XVIIIᵉ siècle* (1935); P. Hazard, *La Crise de la Conscience européenne 1680–1717* (1935); id., *La Pensée européenne au XVIIIᵉ siècle de Montesquieu à Lessing*, 3 vols. (1946); E. Weis, *Geschichtsschreibung und Staatsauffassung in der Französischen Enzyklopädie* (1956); R. V. Sampson, *Progress in the Age of Reason* (1956); R. L. Stromberg, *Religious Liberalism in the Eighteenth Century* (1957); J. S. Sprink, *French Free Thought from Gassendi to Voltaire* (1960); A. R. Whitaker, *Latin America and the Enlightenment* (2nd ed., 1961); W. Philip, *Das Zeitalter der Aufklärung* (1963); G. Cragg, *Reason and Authority in the Eighteenth Century* (1964); R. W. Harris, *Absolutism and Enlightenment* (1965); G. M. Addy, *Enlightenment in the University of Salamanca* (1966); H. E. Allison, *Lessing and the Enlightenment* (1966); P. Gay, *Age of Enlightenment* (1966); id., *Enlightenment*, 2 vols. (1966); R. Wines, *Enlightened Despotism* (1966); R. Anchor, *Enlightenment Tradition* (1967); N. Capaldi, *Enlightenment* (1967).

Heribert Raab

ENTELECHY

The term entelechy was first introduced into philosophy by Aristotle who used it in several different but related senses. We shall understand by it an intrinsic tendency within a physical body, by virtue of which it is orientated towards some goal, e.g., the perfection of the individual concerned or of the species to which it belongs. The principle of entelechy is sometimes known as the principle of finality or teleology.

The question whether there is intrinsic finality in the physical world has been much disputed. Aristotle and most of the medieval philosophers held that all physical bodies, whether living or inorganic, have entelechy; this view has also been supported by later scholastic philosophers. Elsewhere, however, the theory that inorganic bodies have intrinsic finality has been generally rejected, chiefly as a result of the growth of physical science which can find no use for final causes within its own domain. In the biological realm there has been less unanimity. Mechanists have regarded living organisms simply as complicated machines subject to the same laws as inorganic matter; some would extend this conclusion also to man. Vitalists, on the other hand, postulate that the organism has a special vital principle which distinguishes it essentially from a machine and renders it capable of genuinely teleological action. At the present time most biologists hold, at least as a working hypothesis, that all vital activity is reducible to the laws of physics and chemistry. Catholic doctrine denies that human acts can be wholly determined by physical law but is not directly concerned with non-human vital activity. In this realm, recent advances in biochemistry make the possibility of complete physico-chemical explanation seem less remote than was formerly the case and this is true also of many aspects of man's vital processes. It is becoming doubtful, therefore, whether one can make a sharp distinction between organic processes which are teleological, and inorganic which are not. Either entelechy is to be found at all levels of being or its existence can be called in question at any level except, perhaps, man. The first of these alternatives has been strongly urged by Teilhard de Chardin. He held that the whole physical world is intrinsically orientated towards the fulfilment of a single divine plan. Thus inorganic matter tends, of its nature, towards the production of living organisms; simple organisms tend to evolve towards the human level; man tends towards an ever closer hyper-personal social unity with his fellow-men. This tendency, elevated to the supernatural order by virtue of the Incarnation, will be finally perfected by the union of man with God in the mystical body of Christ. Teilhard's views have been criticized in some respects but it seems probable that any satisfactory solution of the problem of finality must be along some such lines as these.

See also *Aristotelianism* I, *Evolution*.

BIBLIOGRAPHY. H. Driesch, *Philosophie des Organischen* (4th ed., 1928); Aristotle, *Physics*, revised text with introduction and commentary by W. D. Ross (1936); F. Dessauer, *Teleologie in der Natur* (1949); N. Hartmann, *Teleologisches Denken* (1951); H. de Lubac, *La pensée religieuse du Père Teilhard de Chardin* (1961); G. Crespy, *La pensée théologique de Teilhard de Chardin* (1961); W. Wieland, *Die aristotelische Physik* (1962); K. Rahner, *Hominisation. The Evolutionary Origin of Man as a Theological Problem,* Quaestiones Disputatae 13 (1965); id., *Schriften zur Theologie,* VI, pp. 171–84; L. Polgár, *Internationale Teilhard-Bibliographie, 1955–65* (1966).

John Russell

ENTHUSIASM

1. *Its meaning.* The original Greek word means rapture, being inspired or possessed by a god. Used disparagingly in the 17th century of the religious attitude of the Puritans and in the 18th of that of the Methodists, the English word now has the general sense of passionate eagerness in any pursuit.

2. *Its nature.* Enthusiasm is not something a man "has", but something which he is plunged in. To be enthusiastic means that one's life is caught up in something which, however, is also within man and impelling him on. The other basic trait of enthusiasm is an active outgoing: man is "beside himself", carried away and driven forward by the spirit which intoxicates him. Three co-ordinates ensue. First, the spirit which impels the enthusiast is his primary and indeed unique and unconditional source and impulse. Then there is an equally comprehensive aim: all is grist to the enthusiast's mill, he knows no bounds, shrinks from no enterprise, lays claim to all means of expression, transcends all limits. Finally, the human ego, caught midway between the source and the goal of enthusiasm, is "beside itself", averted from itself, yet by the very fact at one with itself. When enthusiasm blossoms from it, the ego itself achieves a new, more vivid originality: receptive now to all things, it takes possession of all things and of its own being. Enthusiasm takes a person out of himself, to make him one with all things and thereby with himself.

3. *Contrast with ordinary feelings.* Even in his ordinary consciousness, man is secretly "enthusiastic". His spontaneous reaction is not: I see things this way or that — but: This is the way things are! He is instinctively outgoing, intent on the world, and in this very attitude, he affirms the truth: Yes, things are truly so, even apart from me, unconditionally. He only appears as a personal being insofar as the truth dawns with him, in its pristine originality — which is the import of his affirmation. But in ordinary consciousness, the primordial guidance of truth is obscured by the strain of man's anxieties, questioning, assertions and efforts to dominate. Here it is possible that man is not securely at one with the truth. He always gives out what he says as true, and his vital

233

impulse always comes from a "spirit", from the inexorable tendency to interpret the truth and the world. But that it is the spirit of truth is not predetermined. His essence is revealed in enthusiasm as unity with the unconditioned, but his existence is not fully in harmony with his essence. It is not clear that he should exist at all, and it cannot be taken for granted that his existence attains the level of his essence and is "fulfilled". Hence enthusiasm is as essential as it is unusual. It can neither be "produced" nor "preserved".

4. *Criteria of enthusiasm.* Enthusiasm is genuine if its moving spirit is really absolute and universal, is the spirit of truth, and if the ardent ego is simply the instrument of that spirit. Man, being predisposed to exaggerated enthusiasms, is tempted to arrogate to himself the spirit that can only be received as a gift. An unspiritual, counterfeit enthusiasm may intoxicate individuals, even whole societies, serving merely to unleash the ego, to assert and intensify it. Such false enthusiasm is fanaticism. The spirit of truth allows all things to be what they are, its enthusiasm is the other face of its tranquillity and composure: it has one passionate desire — that the absolute shall remain absolute, the relative merely relative.

5. *Theological significance.* There is only one instance of the enthusiasm which corresponds to man's nature and sets up a tension with his existence. It is that which transcends nature and is based on the divine revelation which came in Jesus. Being human means, paradoxically, becoming something more than human: being open to and at one with the absolute source which wells up secretly with each human person and from which each person springs. The mystery of Jesus — Godhead and manhood united in a single person without separation and without confusion — brings about this fulfilment of humanity in a sublime degree, at the same time revealing perfect man as God first conceived of him in grace. Humanity, therefore, finds its fulfilment, human enthusiasm its "redemption", in membership of Christ through the Holy Spirit. The enthusiasm of primitive Christianity thus appears as an initial stage of the Church's being, which, however, in this present age of the world must necessarily be combined with everyday feelings. The cross is the simultaneous presence of enthusiasm and ordinary feelings, the permanent mediator between them and the proof of their authenticity.

See also *Transcendence, Truth* I, *Spirit, World, Religion* I, *Nature, Mysticism* I, *Charisms.*

BIBLIOGRAPHY. A. A. C. Shaftesbury, *A Letter concerning Enthusiasm* (1711); I. Kant, *Critique of Judgment* (3rd ed., 1799), para. 29; R. Otto, *Idea of the Holy* (2nd ed., 1952); E. Fink, *Vom Wesen des Enthusiasmus* (1947); B. Welte, "Das Heilige in der Welt", *Freiburger Dies Universitatis 1948–49* (1949), pp. 141–83; R. Knox, *Enthusiasm* (1951); G. van der Leeuw, *Phänomenologie der Religion* (2nd ed., 1956); W. Trillhaas, "Enthusiasmus", *RGG,* II, cols. 495f.; O. Kuss, "Enthusiasmus und Realismus bei Paulus", *Auslegung und Verkündigung* (1963); J. Pieper, *Enthusiasm and Divine Madness* (1964).

Klaus Hemmerle

ENVIRONMENT

1. *Notion.* By environment we mean the sum of the natural and social factors (the world of things, people, and values) which affect a man (whether he consciously experiences them or is unconsciously influenced by them) and which he in turn affects. By contrast with a man's "social world", which is a whole set type of life, environment is described as "a formless sum total of surrounding conditions without any meaningful inner cohesion" (Nell-Breuning). In a pluralistic society the environment assumes increasing importance, not least because of its power to disrupt and confuse.

We distinguish the natural environment (especially geographical factors like space, communications, climate); the social environment (specifically human, spiritual factors such as standards, ideas, values, and their embodiment in custom, tradition, culture, and civilization, into which young people are drawn by what we call socializing); the local environment (family, school, group, village, town) and the psychological environment (people not in the same place but sharing the same views, like members of a political party or an order).

The content of the term environment (milieu) is ancient: *medius locus.* The term itself was only introduced into sociology by Taine, and thence penetrated other disciplines, especially those relating to youth (environmental pedagogy, vocational guidance, child study, sociology of youth). We find the idea of the environment in pedagogy as far back as Rousseau and Pestalozzi.

2. *Environment and the person.* First of all we must be quite clear that man is not, like animals, the prisoner of his environment, his senses and other organs (von Uexküll), but "open to the world", "not in bondage to environment", "indeterminate". It follows that man determines his environment through his personality (according to his dispositions and time of life). The answer to the problem of dependence as between person and environment is interdependence: just as environment actualizes the person (above all his inherited dispositions), the person shapes his environment. Let us be more concrete:

a) Whether the person (with his inherited character and his freedom) or the environment will prevail depends on the individual and the type of person. The tendency (accentuated by education) is for the early dominance of outward circumstances *(peristasis)* to yield to dominance of the person *(idiostasis)* as he grows older.

b) The personality has certain dispositions which are constants with regard to the environment (generic dispositions such as reflexes, instincts, certain elemental impulses; individual dispositions such as motor activity, sense perception, vitality, temperament: like the build of the body, these are part of the individual's constitution), and others which are variables (workings of the mind, special talents, motives). "The deeper levels of the psyche are inclined to be constants, the upper variables, with regard to the environment." (H. Remplein.) Since character and personal values are variables with regard to environment — the group and the spirit of the age — the importance of environment for education and pastoral work is obvious.

c) Paradoxically enough (assuming that life in general and man in particular can surmount the obstacles environment places in their way) a resistant environment forms a man better (relatively — in proportion to his character, ideals and impulses), since his educative impulses are strengthened by higher demands being constantly made upon them. (Hence the importance of changes of environment, and environmental therapy.)

But the ideal environment lies midway between the too favourable (which breeds luxuriance and precocity) and the too unfavourable (which causes backwardness through alienation).

"Theories of the environment" were developed (first by Comte and Taine) in order to explain certain psychical, cultural, and social phenomena as adjustment to environmental conditions. These theories largely rest on undue generalizations of sound scientific data, and their anthropological assumptions (dependence on Darwin, for example) make them almost worthless, as may be seen from the history of materialism, behaviourism, race theories and criminology.

3. *Environment and pastoral work.* Man, a social and historical being, finds himself in a group-environment in a given age which has a particular spirit. The group-environment and the spirit of the age may either hamper pastoral work or further it. To find the right point of departure for successful pastoral work — something beyond "an otherworldly theology of souls" (V. Schurr) — we must constantly analyze the environment (by sociological research) and establish an environmental typology (the home, for instance, will presumably have more effect on religious practice than the factory or office).

So far the findings of this kind of research show that while a solidly Catholic environment encourages religious practice and makes it the accepted norm, an environment definitely hostile to the Church and the faith notably cuts down religious practice. On the other hand a basically religious-minded environment will encourage religious practice despite a pluralism of religions and outlooks.

Environmental research interprets the present religious crisis as follows: the basically secularized environment of the industrial age, with its pluralism of world-views, "has no arrangements for saviours" (Kindt). It follows that the contemporary environment helps us to understand why religion now tends to be concentrated in smaller groups (the family or an élite) and to be more interiorized, somewhat independent of the environment (Höffner). These trends are making "environmental Catholicism" (Amery) a thing of the past. We still await the emergence of a moral and pastoral theology of the environment which will take the Church in the world seriously.

See also *Person, Education* I, *Pastoral Theology, Marxism* III, *Race.*

BIBLIOGRAPHY. A. Missenard, *In Search of Man* (1949); W. Hellpach, *Sozialpsychologie* (3rd ed., 1951); J. H. Fichter, *Social Relations in the Urban Parish* (1954); id., *Sociology* (1957); G. W. Allport, *Personality and Social Encounter* (1960); id., *Pattern and Growth in Personality* (1961); J. Alberione, *Fundamentals of Christian Sociology* (1962); J. Höffner, *Fundamentals of Christian Sociology* (1965); W. Sterk, *Sociology of Religion: A Study of Christendom,* 3 vols. (1966–67).

Roman Bleistein

EPISCOPALISM

"Episcopalism" is often used to designate the doctrine and organization of the Episcopalian Churches of the Reformation. It is the ordinary English and American usage, adopted by the *Enciclopedia Cattolica,* V, 447, and by the short article *Episcopalismo* in the *Enciclopedia Universal,* XX, 321. But Ettore Rota, in the article *Reforme (Età delle)* in the *Enciclopedia Italiana,* uses the word in a very different sense, a sense which is also that of H. Raab in the article "Episkopalismus" in *LTK,* III, 1959, cols. 948–50. To avoid confusion, we use the term Episcopalism, in the latter sense, now to be described.

In general terms, Episcopalism is essentially that doctrine according to which supreme power in the Church is vested in the collectivity of the bishops, whether they be dispersed throughout the world or, above all, united in Council, and not in the Pope alone (assisted by the Roman Curia). However, in the course of time this current of thought has taken very diverse forms, some of which are unacceptable.

1. *Doctrinal bases.* The doctrinal bases of Episcopalism are to be found in the most ancient documents of the life of the Church and in the NT itself. Christ founded the apostolic college, of which the bishops are the successors; it is on this foundation that the Church is built (Eph 2:20; Rev 21:14). Peter is not outside this college; he is one of the Twelve and their leader: this is why he receives special promises and particular powers, and this as a personal privilege, at least in the sense that he did not receive them from the other apostles but from Christ himself who designated him as the stone or rock on which the Church is built. The authority of the apostolic college is not opposed, therefore, to that of Peter but is rather strengthened and guaranteed by this latter, which gives it its centre of cohesion and direction. The writings of the Apostolic Fathers acquaint us with the exercise of the authority of the bishops, successors of the apostles: the bishop is never isolated, any more than he is strictly limited to the territory which has been given him. He must concern himself with the common good of the whole Church and this responsibility finds expression in many bonds of communion with the other bishops. The theorists of Episcopalism have cited many texts of St. Ignatius of Antioch, of St. Cyprian, of St. Augustine, etc., in this sense.

2. *History.* Despite the action of the reforming Popes of the 11th century, and the unanimous recognition of the supreme and universal power of the Sovereign Pontiff, the Middle Ages preserved a number of currents of Episcopalism: in fact no one succeeded in elaborating a coherent synthesis in which the respective powers of Pope and bishops were harmoniously reconciled. The Avignon papacy, the Western Schism, the conflicts with Philip the Fair and Louis of Bavaria favoured the development of the theory of the superiority of Council over Pope. The need of a reform in head and members by a return to the ancient law of the Church and to its primitive purity was felt vividly. The Councils of Pisa, of Constance and of Basle, the Concordats of Constance (1418) and of the Princes (1447), the Pragmatic sanction of Bourges (1438), etc., were little by little forming the dossier which the partisans of Episcopalism would invoke, such as John of Paris, Marsilius of Padua, William of Occam, Gerson, d'Ailly, etc.

It was above all Gallicanism which was responsible for the spread of Episcopalist ideas. Without really calling pontifical primacy in question the Gallican theologians, against the very excesses of the Ultramontanists, insist on the episcopacy of divine right and sometimes affirm the superiority of Council over Pope and the subordination of the latter to the ecclesiastical canons. The opinions are manifold, ranging from the very moderate opinion of Almain, Tournély, Peter of Marca, and Bossuet, to the frankly heterodox position of Richer.

In Germany it was above all after the

Council of Trent and the Peace of Westphalia that the Episcopalist currents manifested themselves. The Council, while strengthening the position of the Pope, had also affirmed the divine origin of the episcopate, though without specifying the exact relations between the papacy, the episcopate and the Council; in this context J. K. Barthel and his disciples G. Zallwein, P. A. Schmidt and Martin Gerbert must be mentioned. Febronius is the most extreme representative in the 18th century. In the 19th century the Germans discover, beyond that sociological aspect so dear to the Ultramontanists (J. de Maistre, Rohrbacher, Guéranger, etc.) the sacramental aspect of the Church, a community of life with Christ and the Holy Spirit, especially by means of the sacraments; they affirm, as Bossuet had already done, that the analogy with human societies cannot be the point of departure of a manifestation of the nature of the Church, and that a formulation in terms of authority cannot suffice. This leads to a rediscovery of the mystery of the episcopate and of its unity: J. A. Möhler was the principal architect of this renewal.

The eve of the First Vatican Council saw a new awakening of Episcopalism, represented especially by Mgr. Maret and Mgr. Darboy. The Council confirmed in fact a number of their ideas: the divine origin of the episcopate, limits to papal infallibility, and the ordinary and immediate jurisdiction of the bishops who are true pastors.

Vatican II gave new expression to the orthodox element in Episcopalism, and thereby excluded its heterodox forms by declaring that the office of the apostles is transmitted by divine right to the college of the bishops, to which the individual bishops are subordinated: "It devolves on the bishops to admit newly elected members into the episcopal body by means of the sacrament of orders" (*Lumen Gentium,* art. 21). The structure of this college follows the will of its founder, Christ our Lord. Its centre and head is the Roman Pontiff, who exercises the office of Peter. In this way the Church combines both the synodal principle and that of a personal primacy. This structure is most clearly visible in the unity of the (collegial) subject of supreme doctrinal and jurisdictional authority in the Church. This authority is exercised either by the college of bishops or by the Pope alone but functioning *as* head of the college, even in a non-collegiate act.

See also *Gallicanism, Conciliarism, Magisterium, Council, Bishop, Ecclesiastical Authority.*

BIBLIOGRAPHY. See also bibliographies on *Conciliarism, Bishop.* — G. J. Jordan, *The Inner History of the Great Schism of the West* (1930); W. Ullmann, *Medieval Papalism, the Political Theories of Medieval Canonists* (1949); B. Tierney, *Foundations of the Conciliar Theory* (1955); J. M. Morrall, *Gerson and the Great Schism* (1960); R. C. Petry, "Unitive Reform Principles of the Late Medieval Conciliarists", *Church History* (1962), pp. 164–81; K. A. Fink, "Die konziliare Idee im späten Mittelalter", *Die Welt zur Zeit des Konstanzer Konzils* (1965), pp. 119–34.

Joseph Lécuyer

EQUITY

1. *The issue.* Everyone whose moral consciousness has matured to the point where he can form personal moral judgments, faces the problem of how to behave when his personal ethical insight comes into conflict with the demands of the ethos of society. For by the nature of the case no ethos embodied in a society can adequately deal with all the moral problems arising from the constant changes in our cultural situation because of our history and historicity. And, on the other hand, responding to the claims of society is not only a natural impulse but also a high ethical value because man is a social being. This problem comes into sharpest focus when society's claim has been set forth in terms of law sanctioned by the appropriate authorities. Unless society and the authorities suffer from delusions of totalitarian grandeur they must see that it is in their own interest for the citizen to follow them only so far as they have a right to lead. Any ethics, therefore, that aspires to completeness and any system of legislation must consider what should be done when the claims of the social ethos and of positive law conflict with the claims of ethics.

Aristotelian Scholasticism, keenly conscious that the order of being underlies the ethical, sets forth this problem with notable clarity. It does so under the heading of epikeia, a special term basic to the system. Other ethical schools speak of moral emergency, of supra-legal law, of the right or duty of resistance, of "unavoidable sin". Legal systems deal with the problem in their provisions for law and equity, for moral compulsion, freedom of conscience, and so on. The *CIC* (can. 20) makes special provision for the application of epikeia.

2. *History of the term.* In Aristotle ἐπιείκεια means equity, modifying law and legal rights in the light of real justice. Hence epikeia is always the "better justice" (βέλτιον δίκαιον) as against legality. Here he differs from Plato, for whom epikeia means interpreting and applying leniently the law in force. This latter is in itself the better law, but because of our limitations and failings it must be handled with due leniency.

At first the Christian Church solved the conflict between the law in force and real law with the simple principle: "We must obey God rather than men" (Acts 5:29). Since the medieval mind instinctively sought to adjust relations among men by institutional means, our problem specially interested medieval theologians and canonists, and after the reception of Aristotle it was treated under this heading. Thus St. Thomas thinks it right to apply epikeia in a case where literal obedience to the law would injure the common good. He discusses epikeia in connexion with the virtues of community life, relating it to justice. According to whether one considers it legal justice to obey the letter of the law or the mind of the lawgiver, he calls epikeia either part of justice in general or the nobler part of legal justice. Because of his thoroughly anthropocentric view of creation, St. Thomas is convinced that man, though bound to the order of nature, must shape it in accordance with his reason, not simply fit into the pre-established system. Thus he regards positive law as in itself an expression of the order which God wills and therefore obedience to that law is in itself a thing required by legal justice; but given our finitude and our sinfulness, positive law never adequately expresses real justice, so that in a particular case to obey the law may be to offend against justice. Then the virtue of epikeia calls on us to respect justice as distinct from legal justice. Thus, St. Thomas says, epikeia is at once the loftier standard of human conduct and true legal justice, which requires that the law serve the common good.

This idea that man must use his reason to discern what is right has become the central theme of considerations about epikeia since the beginning of modern times, for man is ever more clearly recognized as an experiencing self in the world and so thought increasingly begins with him in that capacity. Suárez, for instance, no longer recognizes epikeia as a special virtue, but says that a man must disobey positive law if obeying it would offend against a virtue which he is bound to practise and which the law itself is often designed to foster. Suppose that the fasting prescribed, meant to foster temperance, proves injurious to one's health: then self-preservation, which God wills, demands that one eat contrary to human law but according to the virtue of temperance. Or if hearing Mass on a Sunday, as required by the virtue of religion, would mean offending against love of one's neighbour, then the latter virtue may require one to break the law. Thus very different virtues may call for the application of epikeia, the main consideration no longer being the abstract common good — which was often conceived of as a kind of static order — but the concrete perfecting of the individual.

With the rise of individualism and the loosening of social ties on the one hand, and the more insistent social demands made upon the individual by expanding legislation in a rising industrial society on the other, epikeia undergoes a further change. It is increasingly taken as the art of prudently interpreting law in the interests of the subject, whose development is unfairly hampered by legislation. Epikeia is prudently judging that positive law does not bind — no longer a particular moral virtue but a general virtue of moral life. It is often taken in so intellectualist a sense as to seem a quickness of judgment rather than an intellectual virtue. Indeed so far from doing justice to its native moral character, people sometimes speak of epikeia as if it were a low cunning.

3. *The present position.* Nowadays ethical theories are trying to remove this slur and secure epikeia a place within systematic ethics worthy of its actual importance in moral life. There is an effort to reconcile individual freedom and social obligation on a broader and firmer basis by stressing personal responsibility, beginning with a more dynamic view of justice and a more functional view of law. The underlying con-

sideration is that a man must discover for himself what is morally right and cannot simply take it for granted that the laws are just. Because we are free, our nature (at once individual and social) and the cultural situation resulting from it are subject to constant historical change, so that there must always be a certain tension between law and right. Seen from this point of view, epikeia is the virtue which always seeks to resolve the tension in favour of right — a function which presupposes an effort to discover true justice and a readiness to satisfy justice even by disobeying positive law. Thus the motive behind the virtue of epikeia is love of justice. In this sense epikeia is a general disposition. Thus the virtue of epikeia may lead one to conclude that a certain law does not bind in a given situation because obeying it would be inequitable. Perhaps the law requires something it cannot fairly require; for example, obeying a traffic regulation when concretely there is no need to do so. Or perhaps the law declares something legal which is unjust; for example, a wage which in the circumstances is not a fair one. In such a case the virtue of epikeia must judge that justice requires more of a man than the law does. Thus it can contribute to the steady improvement of law in times to come. Epikeia will enable one to form sound judgments, on this view, if one has a firm will to give each man his due, the factual knowledge necessary to judge the situation correctly, and grasps the significance of that factual knowledge. Formally, therefore, the virtue of epikeia is love of justice as such. Materially, it is the prudent judgment passed on the law in its relation to the law which transcends legislation.

Thus R. Egenter recently called epikeia "a sense of real justice in the social sphere", a basic attitude of the order of natural justice, something akin to *iustitia socialis*. Similarly J. Fuchs considers it the virtue of obeying law in accordance with the particular situation. He even thinks that epikeia rightly understood represents the legitimate concern of situation ethics. A. Adam looks on epikeia as the virtue of freedom of conscience, which moves man to respect the legal order, which is founded on the order of being, in a manner befitting his freedom. B. Häring goes so far as to pronounce the modern elaboration of the Thomist doctrine on epikeia "the enduring fruit of the great moral controversies about the use of prudential rules", that is, of the moral systems.

Giers modifies and extends this view of epikeia as a general virtue, observing that the subjective persuasion of the individual cannot be the sole criterion of justice in a given situation; because of his social nature, the individual must be guided by the teaching of the Church and the opinion of theologians and experts when dealing with the complex legislation and the demands of justice today. Here the virtue of epikeia is protected as far as possible from individualistic abuse and on the other hand personal responsibility for restraining legalism is kept within bounds.

See also *History* I, *Ethics, Situation, Society* III, *Justice* II, *Individualism, Law* II, III, *Moral Theology* III.

BIBLIOGRAPHY. Thomas Aquinas, *Summa Theologica,* II, II, qq. 120 and 80; F. Suárez, *De Legibus,* lib. VI, cap. 7, n. 11; cap. 6, nn. 5f.; L. Godefroy, in *DTC,*V, cols. 358–61; R. Egenter, "Über die Bedeutung der Epikie im sittlichen Leben", *Philosophisches Jahrbuch der Görres-Gesellschaft* 53 (1940), pp. 115–27; L. J. Riley, *The History, Nature and Use of Epikeia in Moral Theology* (1948); O. Robleda, "La 'Aequitas' en Aristóteles, Cicerón, Santo Tomás y Suárez", *Miscelánea Comillas* 15 (1951), pp. 241–79; J. Fuchs, *Situation und Entscheidung* (1952); B. Häring, *Law of Christ,* 3 vols. (1961–66).
Waldemar Molinski

ESCHATOLOGISM

This article is not concerned with the whole problem of eschatology, but only with the exegetical and theological position which makes the eschatological hope in the strict sense (expectation of the imminent parousia and the end of the present world) the essential element both of the kerygma of primitive Christianity and of the authentic teaching of Jesus. This view has been given currency by three exegetes in particular: J. Weiss, A. Loisy and A. Schweitzer. We shall first summarize their ideas and then describe the reactions which they have evoked. We shall then say why we find their ideas inadmissible and end by suggesting some principles on which the question may be solved.

In 1892 a book by J. Weiss appeared which was to arouse widespread discussion: *Die Predigt Jesu vom Reiche Gottes* (2nd ed., 1900). In opposition to his father-in-law, A. Ritschl, and to liberal Protestants in general, J. Weiss maintained that Jesus was not content to preach the invisible reign of God in souls, but that he borrowed from the prophetic and apocalyptic writings the idea of a sudden intervention of God in history. Jesus did not yet believe himself to be the Messiah; his messianic faith was entirely centred on the future. He awaited the imminent coming of the kingdom of God, not in the form of a progressive and interior development, but as a future phenomenon, sudden and dramatic, which would involve the whole universe, overthrowing the order of the cosmos and bringing about a new world. Jesus first hoped that this coming would take place before his death. This would explain the hasty mission of the Twelve. But later on disappointment and opposition forced him to think that the passion of the Son of Man must intervene before the irruption of the Kingdom. He did not, however, cease to imagine that the Son of Man was to appear in his own generation. Many of the moral precepts of the gospel are impracticable in a permanent social order, and were given only for the exceptional and very brief time which separated the earthly existence of Jesus from the coming of the Kingdom.

In 1902 A. Loisy, who at that time still belonged to the Catholic Church, published his celebrated work *L'Évangile et l'Église*. The book was directed against A. Sabatier (*Esquisse d'une philosophie de la religion,* 1897), and above all against A. von Harnack (*Das Wesen des Christentums,* 1900, E. T.: *What is Christianity?*), who held that faith in the fatherhood of God was the essential element of Christianity. Loisy's answer was that the essential idea of the religion of Jesus was not that which still displayed most vitality, but that which occupied the first place in the authentic teaching of Jesus. But the fundamental theme of his teaching was the imminent coming of the Kingdom, which was to coincide with the glorious coming of the Messiah on the clouds. Jesus thought that he would not be invested with the messianic dignity except at the end of the world. He did not envisage for a moment the prospect of a new religion or the foundation of a Church. He thought only of the eschatological kingdom; it was in fact the Church which came.

Under the name of *konsequente* (thoroughgoing) eschatology, A. Schweitzer gave particularly vigorous expression to eschatologism in his book *Von Reimarus zu Wrede* (1906), re-cast and completed under the title of *Geschichte der Leben-Jesu-Forschung* (1913, E. T.: *The Quest of the Historical Jesus*). Schweitzer accuses W. Wrede (*Das Messiasgeheimnis in den Evangelien,* 1901) of having posed problems which he could not solve because he had made no effort to explain the gospel of Jesus by the Jewish apocalyptic of his day. According to Schweitzer, belief in the imminent apocalyptic coming of the Kingdom was what first inspired the activity of Jesus. This is the secret which he revealed to his apostles in Mt 10:23, when he sent them on their mission: "Truly, I say to you, you will not have gone through all the towns of Israel, before the Son of Man comes." In other words, Jesus believes at this juncture that the parousia of the Son of Man, which for him was identical with the coming of the kingdom, would take place at the end of a quick missionary tour of the apostles. Unhappily, the much longed-for event did not take place. The disappointment marked a turning-point in the whole existence of Jesus. From now on he abandons the crowds to devote himself above all to the Twelve; and he is also convinced that it is his vocation to undergo, by means of his passion, the messianic calamities which are to allow the reign of God to come in power. This is the new secret which he reveals to his apostles at Caesaraea Philippi.

Countless German, French and English works reflect the eschatological theories of J. Weiss, A. Loisy and A. Schweitzer. While Ritschl and Harnack strove to demonstrate the eternal validity of the gospel, these theories lead logically to the conclusion that the gospel message is built entirely on an illusion. To avoid this conclusion, some writers distinguish between the essential thought of Jesus, which is to be preserved, and his eschatological concepts, which were simply a framework provided for Jesus by the Jewish environment in which he lived (cf. in this sense M. Goguel, *Vie de Jésus* [1932], p. 557). This distinction is based on an untenable paradox, because the thought which it puts last in the order of real values is that which was fundamental in the mind of Jesus, that is, the coming of the Kingdom.

To avoid the disastrous consequences of eschatologism, it has often been suggested that we should interpret the eschatological concepts of the NT symbolically, especially those of the gospels. This is the procedure of theologians like E. Troeltsch, M. Kähler and K. Barth. It is also pre-eminently that of the two principle protagonists of form criticism, R. Bultmann and M. Dibelius. According to Bultmann there is only one eschatological reality: the decision which we take at the present moment for or against God. Each time a man takes such a decision, his destiny is irrevocably committed and it may be said that for him the last day has come. Thus, by the answer which he makes to the word of God which is addressed to him, he has attained, as from this present moment, the ultimate realities, salvation or damnation. This interpretation of NT eschatology is to be found in various studies by Bultmann on the synoptics, the fourth gospel and the theology of the NT, as well as in several of the articles published in the collection entitled *Glauben und Verstehen,* 3 vols. (1961–62).

M. Dibelius accounts for the eschatological assertions of the NT in the following way: cf. in particular *Geschichtliche und übergeschichtliche Religion im Christentum* (1925). These assertions are said to mean that Christianity is above this world, independent of it and even to some extent foreign to it. The message of Jesus comes from eternity and tends to take man out of time and implant him in eternity.

What are we to think of all these theories? It would evidently ruin the permanent value of the message of Jesus to maintain, with eschatologism, that it is based on the apprehension of an imminent end of the world which did not take place. But the solution put forward by the protagonists of form criticism is also unacceptable, since it leads to the abandonment of the historical Christ and of the history of salvation of which the Jewish-Christian revelation essentially consists. It substitutes instead a set of abstract concepts with regard to the relationship of men to the other world, which are drawn from the philosophy of religion. But the eschatology of the gospels is something more than a provisional mould in which Jesus thought he was obliged to cast his message, by reason of the Jewish environment in which he lived. This will be readily admitted by those who believe in the reality and objectivity of the history of salvation, which began in the OT and moves to a point fixed by God from eternity. It must, however, be conceded

that when reading the eschatological passages of the NT, especially those of the synoptic gospels, one should make a clear distinction between what is actually and specifically taught and what is merely a process of accommodation to the literary procedures of the times.

With this in mind, we shall now suggest in conclusion certain principles which we think can be of help in interpreting the most obscure eschatological sayings of Jesus.

In the composite discourse into which Mt 10:23 is incorporated, the announcement which made such a vivid impression on A. Schweitzer is linked to the express command given to the Twelve to confine their activities provisionally to Israel (10:6). After the resurrection, however, they will be charged to preach the gospel to all nations (Mt 28:18–20). This can only mean that Christ, while never losing sight of his universal mission, still follows a certain order, and respects the prerogatives of the chosen people in the propagation of the gospel. The meaning of Mt 10:23 then becomes clear: the Jews have the privilege of being the first to hear the message of the gospel, but this privilege has its counterpart in a special judgment.

This special judgment seems also to be envisaged *primarily* in the synoptic apocalypse (Mk 13 and par.). It speaks of the coming of the Son of Man on the clouds as a consequence of the chastisement of the unbelieving Jews, but the declaration of Christ before the sanhedrin as well as Dan 7 show that this coming is to be understood metaphorically. It signifies the complete triumph of the Messiah, as the counterpart to the apparent annihilation of his work, his death or the destruction of the temple of Jerusalem. We may undoubtedly speak of a real announcement of the end of the world. But, as in the descriptions given by the prophets, a concrete event is taken as the stand-point from which the end is contemplated, and this event is made to serve as a prelude to the end, which is less a chronological date than the summit towards which all history moves.

These remarks about the synoptic apocalypse suggest an important consideration. There are undoubtedly certain eschatological statements of Jesus which bear directly and exclusively on the end of time. But even in the other passages, we must be on our guard against overemphasizing the dilemma: judgment on Jerusalem or judgment at the end of time, in texts which of their very nature involve a large measure of obscurity. All through the prophetic and apocalyptic literature of the OT, the graphic descriptions of the end always present us with a *general view* — including judgment and salvation — *in which everything is apparently situated on the same plane.* Differences of perspective with regard to the various phases of the "end" are left to be worked out by the actual experience of the future. The same holds good for the eschatological oracles of Christ. We must reject the one-sided exegesis which applies these texts only to the end of the world. We believe, with J. A. T. Robinson (*Jesus and His Coming* [1957]) and other authors, that Jesus was principally concerned with the approaching crisis within Judaism. But this crisis remained for him within the general framework of the "end", which the decisive intervention of the Messiah had brought very near, to the eyes of faith. Here too the clear distinction between planes and times was reserved for the future.

See also *Apocalyptic, Kerygma, Reign of God, New Testament Ethics, Salvation* III C, *Word of God.*

BIBLIOGRAPHY. C. H. Dodd, *The Apostolic Preaching* (1936); F. M. Braun, "Où en est l'eschatologie du Nouveau Testament?", *Revue Biblique* 49 (1940), pp. 33–54; H. A. Guy, *The New Testament Doctrine of the Last Things* (1948); M. Werner, *Die Entstehung des christlichen Dogmas* (2nd ed., 1953); G. R. Beasley-Murray, *Jesus and the Future* (1954); W. G. Kümmel, *Promise and Fulfilment. The Eschatological Message of Jesus* (1957); id., "Futuristic and Realized Eschatology in the Earliest Stages of Christianity", *Journal of Religion* 43 (1963), pp. 303–14; E. Grässer, *Das Problem der Parousieverzögerung in den synoptischen Evangelien und in der Apostelgeschichte* (1957); P. Prigent, "Chronique bibliographique. L'eschatologie dans le Nouveau Testament (A. Schweitzer, R. Bultmann, C. H. Dodd . . .)", *Église et Théologie* 22 (1959), pp. 26–39; A. Feuillet, "Parousie", *DBS,* VI, cols. 1331–419; id., "Les origines et la signification de Mt 10:23", *CBQ* 23 (1961), pp. 182–98.

André Feuillet

ESCHATOLOGY

This article will not deal with the Last Things in general or in detail. What is intended is a fundamental reflection on the nature of the theological treatise on eschatology. The question is not merely of theoretical and learned interest but has its importance for the proclamation of the Christian message itself. In a world which is now in movement, which is programming its own future, even if only for this world, a great eschatological aspiration is certainly bound up with (though not really derived from) secular goals and hopes of that kind. This undoubtedly makes the proclamation of the Christian hope for the future more difficult than it used to be. Furthermore, precisely in this part of theology the general problem of demythologization recurs in an urgent form. Finally, the preaching of the Last Things presents its own problems. In the course of history this proclamation itself has been strangely concentrated on the individual and this in itself calls for criticism. A cosmic eschatology involving the whole of history has become very colourless and insignificant as compared with a doctrine of the individual immortality of spiritual souls and of their individual destiny. Yet it is quite possible that this *way* of proclamation — valid though its actual content may be — was in fact determined by the conditions of a particular age. It is therefore possible to ask whether that age is not now coming to an end and a new one slowly emerging, one which by its own dynamic orientation towards the future will have a more direct relation to the cosmic eschatology of Christianity which concerns the whole history of humanity.

1. *On the history of this branch of theology.* The history of the revelation of the Last Things down to and including the whole NT, is long and rich, but the history of eschatology is meagre in comparison with that of other sections of dogmatic theology, at least within the limits of ecclesiastical orthodoxy or in contact with this. Since a systematic treatment of the whole of dogmatic theology came into existence, the treatise on eschatology has been placed at its very end. This arrangement can be justified by reference to the creeds and to some extent by the nature of the Last Things. Yet one must at least know what one can hope for before morals can be dealt with as a part of dogmatic theology. And it must not be forgotten, as often does happen, that in substance and even expressly (*D* 16, 86) the creeds directly profess the "expectation" of what is to come.

In other words, they are directly concerned with something present. It is this which must provide the fundamental structure of the whole for the real understanding of what is to come. Conversely, the fundamental structure of our present life can only be understood on the basis of its reaching out towards the future. The treatise on eschatology at the end of dogmatic theology has scarcely had any real history until now. The very unselfconscious course of the very early transition from imminent to remote expectation of the parousia, the slow and imperceptible surmounting of millenarianism and of the doctrine of a real apocatastasis (as a thesis, not simply as a hope open to man), the rejection of a salvation of its nature not open to all in Gnosticism, the refusal of a doctrine of eschatological phases which abolished the absolute, universal and truly eschatological significance of Christ in Montanism and Joachim of Flora, the defence of the grace-given character of beatitude against heretical mysticism (*D* 475), Baianism (*D* 1002–7), German Idealism (*D* 1808) and A. Rosmini (*D* 1928 ff.), the locating of the essence of beatitude in the vision of God, are all particular questions of eschatology which have a history, as are the questions of purgatory, the nature of the beatific vision, the nature of the "fire" of hell, etc.

All these are events in the history of this branch of theology, but do not constitute occurrences of such a kind as to give that history a clear structure and historical articulation, or the content of the treatise on eschatology a systematic self-sufficient form. The only clear and important break which we observe in the history of the treatise so far is Benedict XII's definition that the direct vision of God in the case of the just who are fully purified, and the punishment of hell for those dying in mortal sin, begin even "before" the general judgment (*D* 530f., *Benedictus Deus*). This does not of course establish a balance on the plane of systematic speculative theology between the universal, cosmic, ecclesiological eschata occurring at the end of time in the "flesh", and the individual, existential eschata occurring in each particular case now in the spirit. Yet, since the universal and ancient eschatology remains, it establishes once and for all the inescapability of a genuine and enduring dialectic between these two aspects of fulfilment. Eschatology can never sacrifice one

to the other. Eschatology has therefore become bi-polar, and will so remain and cannot "de-mythologize" fulfilment into the multiplicity of individual eschata. Yet it has to speak of the eschata of individuals and would not do this if it were to speak solely of the end of all. For the rest, as a simple comparison with the history of other branches of theology shows, eschatology has not advanced in theological reflection beyond a relatively superficial arrangement of the statements of Scripture. A gnoseology is lacking and a hermeneutic specially adapted to eschatological statements. The absence of a properly elaborated theology of history and temporality in general and of saving history in particular makes itself felt unfavourably in eschatology as it does elsewhere. The relation between protology and eschatology remains unexamined; that between Christian eschatology and secular utopianism has scarcely yet been considered. The theology of the eschatological attitude of the Christian in his own present life is abandoned to the literature of piety alone. The fundamental terms of eschatology (beginning, ending, fulfilment, orientation of the course of history, time [as a specifically human "occurrence"], future, axiological and teleological presence of what is to come, modes of presence, death, eternity as fulfilling and confirming time as well as suppressing it by raising it to a higher level [as opposed to "continued duration"], judgment, place of beatitude, etc.) are still far from having received the necessary and possible analysis and explicit treatment in a philosophical ontology of human reality, which in the perspective of the present-day view of the world would really facilitate the acceptance in faith of the eschatological message and permit its philosophical synthesis with the conception of existence which modern men hold in other respects.

The treatise on eschatology is still very much at the beginning of its history. What is most concerned with history has had no history in Christian theology. Christian eschatology must come to realize its own nature by thinking out its own implications more thoroughly than it has done so far. This is called for by the situation created by the modern scientific picture of a world in process of becoming; by the unleashing of the will to prospective, planned and rationalized transformation of the whole human con-

243

dition by man as a being who makes himself and his environment; by the possibility of extending the living space of humanity beyond the earth; by the modern militant political world-heresies of secular utopianism, etc. Then it will be possible, for example, to develop the original Christian fundamental conception of the Last Things and to conceive the origin of the "domain" of salvation as resulting from the time of salvation much more clearly than this was possible with the conceptual apparatus of previous eschatology which regarded saving history as unfolding in an already present, spatial domain, static and fixed by nature (the immutable empyrean, etc.). This new phase of the history of eschatology has so far been initiated chiefly among non-Catholics. Liberal Protestant theology (W. M. L. de Wette, J. Weiss, A. Schweitzer, M. Werner) interpreted Christianity and its theology as the history of the parousia which failed to occur. In R. Bultmann's demythologization an attempt is made to existentialize the eschata in the individual instance of each particular believer (similarly C. H. Dodd: realized eschatology). In orthodox Protestant theology either a one-sided eschatologism is pursued or the whole of theology is essentially reconstructed on the basis of a radical rejection of the Calvinist doctrine of predestination.

2. *Themes for an eschatology.* In what follows an attempt is made to indicate in outline the themes of a doctrine of eschatology as it ought to be (and which has for the most part not yet been worked out in the text-books). But an inventory of themes is intended rather than a statement of the systematic arrangement which a treatise of that kind would have.

a) The correct single basic principle for the problem and conception of eschatology would have to be worked out. Eschatology is not an advance report of events taking place "later". That is the basic intention of false apocalyptic as opposed to genuine prophecy. Eschatology is a forward look which is necessary to man for his spiritual decision in freedom, and it is made from the standpoint of his situation in saving history as this is determined by the Christ-event. This situation is the aetiological ground of the cognition. The gaze is directed towards the definitive fulfilment of precisely this human situation which is already an eschatological one. And it is intended to make possible a man's own enlightened decision in relation to what is obscure and open. The aim is that the Christian in that decision may accept his present as a factor in the realization of the possibility established by God in the beginning (*transcendent* return to the "Garden of Eden") and as a future which is already present and definitive in a hidden way. For that future presents itself as salvation now, precisely if it is accepted as God's action, incalculable in its when and how, because determined by God alone. And in that way the stumbling-block presented by the contradiction which still exists between the redemption already present in Christ and the world's sin, the divisions of the nations, the discrepancy between nature and man, desire, death, is endured in patience and hope as a sharing in the Cross of Christ. In other words, eschatology concerns redeemed man as he now is. With him as basis it knows what is to come as something blissfully incomprehensible which is to be accepted in freedom (and therefore in danger of being lost). What is to come (understood in this way) can be evoked in imagery but not described here and now in a report, and it is announced to man because he can only endure his present if he knows he is in movement towards his future, which is the incomprehensible God in his own very life.

b) It would be necessary to create a hermeneutics (theological gnoseology) of eschatological statements. If the above-mentioned basic principle of eschatology is clearly worked out and coherently maintained, definite fundamental norms follow from it concerning the meaning, scope and limits of eschatological statements both in Scripture and in dogmatic theology. These hermeneutical norms also have a basis in Scripture. They are grounded in the fundamental theological teaching of Scripture (unity and uniqueness of history, God's incomprehensibility, unity of spirit and matter in man and his history, salvation as the fulfilment of man as a unity and a whole, etc.). But Scripture also indicates that a real distinction is to be drawn between representation or image on the one hand and reality signified on the other. Scripture freely employs a multiplicity of representative models irreducible to any system — the end as a world-conflagration, as a judgment assembling all together, as a triumphant going out of the saints to meet Christ, etc. Consequently a false "apocalyptic" conception of eschatology is excluded as well as its demythologizing and absolute existentializing. The latter forgets that man lives in a genuinely temporal condition which is directed towards what has really still to come, and in a world which is not simply abstract personal existence but must attain salvation in all its dimensions, even that of the secular temporal process. It must be made clear in theology and preaching that in basic principle what is said about heaven and what is said about hell are not on the same plane. The Church eschatologically proclaims as a *fact* already realized in Jesus and the saints that saving history (in its totality) ends victoriously as the triumph of the grace of God. It only proclaims as a serious *possibility* that the freedom of each individual may operate to his eternal ruin. The theology of hell and the necessary prophetic commination in the Church require, in order to be Christian, always to be kept open in character, since they are statements about our possibilities as they are now, and which cannot at present be superseded. This is in contrast to esoteric knowledge about an apocatastasis and also to anticipatory knowledge of damnation as having already occurred, despite the fact that God's judgment is unknown to us. These principles of hermeneutics can permit an essentially more accurate (even if never plainer) distinction than is usually made between content and mode of expression in the eschatological statements of Scripture and tradition. It is only necessary repeatedly to remind oneself of what has just been said in section 2a. Then it is at once clear that the content of the statements comprises everything which (but no more than) can be understood as fulfilment and definitive condition of that Christian human reality which revelation states to be present here and now. All else is figurative representation of this fulfilment of Christian existence. Because, for example, Christian life as redeemed concerns all dimensions of human existence, the resurrection of the flesh is a dogma of faith, yet we cannot on that account form any precise idea of the glorified body. Because there is a single saving history of mankind as such, its fulfilment cannot be reduced to that of the various individuals.

Yet it is not possible to co-ordinate precisely and in detail the cosmic and individual eschatology or precisely to distinguish them. Because the history of the freedom of individuals, each of whom is unique, is not a mere factor in history as a whole, it is necessary to speak of individual fulfilment (the vision of God), and this history of individual freedom must be held quite open, despite the certainty of the blessed outcome as a whole. Yet it is not possible on that account clearly to mark the occurrence of general and of individual salvation on a common time-scale. This distinction between content of statement and adaptable mode of representation applies above all to the history of the end of the world (before the Last Judgment) and the signs of its coming. The application of these principles to the question of the fate of infants dying without baptism would have to be examined.

c) The actual universal propositions contained in eschatology which precede its various material propositions would likewise form part of a properly elaborated eschatology and would include: the intrinsically limited character of time and its historical configuration from genuine beginning to a genuine irreplaceable end; the uniqueness of each part of sacred history; death, and the "change" effected as an event by God, as a necessary mode of genuine fulfilment of time (since the Fall); the fact that the end has already come with the incarnation, death and resurrection of the Logos made flesh; the presence of this end as constituting the fact of the victorious mercy and self-communication of God (in contradistinction to a double outcome, on an equal footing which would be specified by man's freedom alone); the special character of the time now still unfolding "after" Christ; the persistent character of this period as a conflict (with Antichrist), which necessarily becomes more intense as the end approaches; the question of the convergence of the natural and supernatural finality of man and cosmos (the factors of a "natural" eschatology which involves more than merely the "immortality of the soul"), etc. It is only on this basis that the particular themes usually dealt with in eschatology become really intelligible, because in these the whole inevitably recurs under some particular aspect. Among these particular themes room must be found for a number of things which the theology of the schools scarcely notices, for example the final removal of the cosmic powers of the Law, of death, etc.; the enduring significance of Christ's humanity for beatitude; the positive meaning of the inequality of the glory of heaven; the vision of God as the abiding mystery (the positive meaning of the permanent incomprehensibility of God); the relation between the heaven of the redeemed and the reprobate world of the demons; the positive significance of the persistence of evil and the nature of the latter; the metaphysical essence of the glorified body; the one "Kingdom of God" formed of angels and men; the true nature of the "intermediate state" (between death and general judgment) which must not be regarded as purely "spiritual".

d) Special attention has to be given to the dialectic which necessarily prevails between the statements regarding individual and universal eschata as a consequence of man's Christian being and fulfilment, which comprise all his dimensions. Precisely this dialectic displays the difference between content and mode of representation in eschatological statements. If that dialectic is not taken into account, these statements take on a mythological flavour and consequently are no longer very convincing in the proclamation of the faith. For of course these statements cannot be harmonized, as usually happens, simply and solely by dividing them among different realities which are then treated separately (beatitude of the "soul" — resurrection of the "body"). Nor can it be done by ignoring individual eschatology in favour of universal (simply denying an intermediate state, impossible as it is, of course, to describe this state), or by eliminating universal eschatology in favour of individual as being merely the sum of the latter. For man in body and soul is united into one reality which forms the ontological basis of the dialectical and irreducible unity in duality of the mutually related statements which always concern the totality of his being.

e) Eschatology must always be seen in connection with the other branches of theology, for it concerns what forms the content of other treatises, but in fulfilment. Consequently between eschatology and these other treatises there is a relation of mutual inclusion and they throw light on one another. That is true not only of protology

and the states of man, of the theology of history in general, of the theology of grace (grace as possessed "in hope"), but above all of Christology, soteriology (the definitive acceptance of the world in Christ), ecclesiology (the Church of the last days, willing to be abolished yet raised to a higher plane, into the *basileia* of God; the Church of those awaiting the second coming of Christ in contradistinction to the Synagogue and to religious organizations which regard themselves as timeless), and the doctrine of the sacraments (as *signa prognostica* of definitive salvation).

f) To eschatology there necessarily also belongs the dogmatic (not merely edifying) treatment of the eschatological attitude of the Church and of the individual Christian, and the Christian criticism and redemption of the secular utopias and of the eschatologies of other religions, to the extent that this is not already done by soteriology.

See also *Last Things, Eschatologism, Creation IV, Demythologization, Immortality, Apocatastasis, Millenarianism, Gnosis, Baianism, Idealism, Purgatory, Beatific Vision, Hell I, Hermeneutics, Calvinism, Apocalyptic, Resurrection II, Limbo.*

BIBLIOGRAPHY. See the treatises in dogmatic text-books, e.g., *Sacrae Theologiae Summa*, by Patres SJ, Madrid (1962 ff.), IV, pp. 896–1066 with literature; G. Hoffmann, *Das Problem der letzten Dinge in der neueren evangelischen Theologie* (1929); N. Berdyaev, *Beginning and End* (1946); R. Guardini, *The Last Things* (1966); A. Michel, *Les mystères de l'Au-delà* (1953); J. Daniélou, *Christologie et Eschatologie*, in A. Grillmeier and H. Bacht, eds., *Das Konzil von Chalkedon*, 3 vols. (1951–54); J. Pieper, *The End of Time. A Meditation on the Philosophy of History* (1954); O. Cullmann, *Immortality of the Soul or Resurrection of the Dead? The Witness of the New Testament* (1955); P. Althaus, *Die letzten Dinge* (6th ed., 1956); M. Feuillet, "La demeure céleste et la destinée des chrétiens", *RSR* 43 (1956), pp. 161–92, 360–402; J. Körner, *Eschatologie und Geschichte (in der Theologie R. Bultmanns)* (1957); R. W. Gleason, *The World to Come* (1958); F. X. Durwell, *The Resurrection* (1960); the article "Eschatologie" in *RGG*, II, cols. 650–89; F. Cannarozzo, *La fine del Mondo* (Parma 1961); P. Tihon, "Fins dernières (Méditation des)", *DSAM* V, cols. 355–82; J. Alberione, *The Last Things* (1964); K. Rahner, *On the Theology of Death*, Quaestiones Disputatae 2 (2nd ed., 1965); G. Sauter, *Zukunft und Verheissung* (1965); K. Rahner, *Theological Investigations*, IV, pp. 322–54 (1966); J. Moltmann, *Theology of Hope* (1967).

Karl Rahner

ESSENCE

1. The noun "essence" comes from the verb "esse", "to be", and was formed as if from the present participle, like "be-ing". In German the word for essence, *Wesen,* is both verb and noun. As verb it means to occur, happen, prevail. For Heidegger, for example, the *Wesen der Wahrheit* (essence of truth) goes beyond the "usual concept of *Wesen* (essence)" (*Vom Wesen der Wahrheit,* 3rd ed., 1954, p. 27), and is identical with the *Walten des Geheimnisses* (dominance of mystery) (*ibid.,* p. 24). Behind this stands the *Wahrheit des Wesens* (the truth of essence), where *Wesen,* essence, is being thought of as "be-ing" (*ibid.,* p. 27). This, however, meets us as the "destiny of being" or the unparalleled "event" (*Identität und Differenz,* 1957, p. 72), which unites "man and being in their essential connection" (*ibid.,* p. 31). Because here *Wesen,* essence, always means happening, it is identical with the historicity of being (its undergoing a destiny), or with the ontological history of being, in which the particular factual history of an individual existent has its ground.

2. As a noun, essence has developed from two main points of view. a) In the first place we observe in every existing thing in the world of our experience that it perpetually changes and that it maintains its identity. The individual existent perpetually changes as regards its various appearances, as can be seen, for example, in the growth of living things (egg, grub, chrysalis, cockchafer); it remains the same as regards its inner core which continually unfolds in various external manifestations yet persists in them, as the example of the cockchafer shows. On this basis, essence means what necessarily belongs to a thing and most intimately constitutes it, determining its particular character both statically and dynamically; without its essence a thing would not be what it is. Furthermore, it is possible to speak of the essence even of individual beings, for example the essence of a particular human being, as his own special qualities which characterize him and distinguish him from all others, which manifest themselves in all his behaviour and in which he remains true to himself. In philosophy, we mean by essence the persistent structure in which many individuals agree or resemble one another and in virtue of which they are bearers of the same specific qualities or are of the same kind; this can easily be seen in the case of man. The data just recalled provide the basis for the general concept of essence which by abstraction transcends the particular features which distinguish individuals and retains only the traits or structures in which individuals agree or coincide. The content of the essence obtained in this way is said to be general or universal because it is realized in all the individuals and therefore can be predicated of each individual without in itself designating any individual in particular. The essence is often said to be timeless and changeless; this is true in the sense that its identity persists in the flux of time. At the same time, however, the essence of a thing is the ground of the possibility, and often of the actual realization, of the thing's changing in this or that way, or of its appropriate alterations unfolding in the course of time, as is the case with living things. Nor does the essence exclude, but rather includes, the possibility of one thing's becoming another and so of passing from the domain of one essence to that of another, which is what happens when food is digested, for example. Above all, the essence of man is not rigid and immobile but is precisely the ground of his intrinsically temporal and historical character; in that way the one essence of man is differentiated into many historical forms which persist during an epoch (e.g., men of Greco-Roman antiquity) or a civilization (e.g., men of the Far East). Finally, man's essence or specific nature demands that it find fulfilment in authentic personal self-realization; in other words, essence in the case of man always implies personal existence inasmuch as, in virtue of his essence and under the continual changing summons of being, he realizes himself and actually makes himself by his free acts the person he ultimately is. Consequently, with man it has always to be asked not only what he is but also who he is.

b) The second point of view from which essence is used as a noun has also to be explained on two levels. Each existent in the world of our experience prompts two questions. Because things are in a state of becoming and passing away, the question arises as to whether anything is; because things are distinct from one another in kind, they prompt the question of what something is.

(i) The answer to the first question is given

247

by existence or "there-ness", to the second by "what-ness" or quiddity, which is also often called essence or nature. We should prefer to reserve the latter terms for use on the plane of the second set of problems which will be presented in a moment. There-ness and what-ness refer to the concrete finite being in two different respects; these can be completely separated in thought from one another because in the what-ness actual existence is not comprised and there-ness does not imply this particular what-ness. Since both are found in the individual exist-ent, they are themselves subject to individua-tion; consequently here it is a question of the particular or individual what-ness, this man Peter, for example, viewed in regard to what he is as opposed to the fact that he exists.

(ii) The second plane of problems moves on from the two aspects which characterize already constituted finite beings as a whole, to the two structural factors or principles, the union of which is needed for the constitu-tion of finite beings as a whole. Because the two principles are not aspects of the whole but partial elements of the whole, they are really distinct from one another; here the real distinction is ontological, not one of empirical fact, i.e., the distinction is one between the intrinsic grounds (λόγοι) of a being, not between this being and that as wholes. In precise terms the principles re-present the (ontological) essence or quid-ditative entity *(essentia)* and existence; more-over, the individual existent shares according to the measure of its finite essence in the *per se* unlimited plenitude of being. The essence is necessarily distinct from being because it does not exhaust the plenitude of being. Essence and being stand to one an-other as potency to act; and in this connec-tion the essence is singular or individual, like the "what-ness" referred to above. The two dualities of being-there and being-so and of essence and being correspond to some de-gree to one another, but do not coincide completely because they belong to different planes, as has been explained.

Surveying the various uses of essence as a noun, we observe that "what-ness" is primarily contrasted with appearance, es-sence primarily with being. Above essence and the being which is related to it as its principle and hence limited, is being itself which comprises both as their single ground.

In its whole limitless plenitude it is real as subsistent being, which we call God. As his infinite essence totally exhausts the plenitude of being, it coincides absolutely with the latter. Consequently, since the finite essence, as a way of sharing in being, has its total ground in being, it can only be understood on the basis of being and orientated to it. It fol-lows that metaphysics is most intimately con-cerned not with the essence or "being-ness" of beings (Heidegger), but with being, and cannot be limited to the philosophy of essences as in Rationalism, but is necessarily a philosophy of being. Historically speak-ing, Plato located essence, as the universal or eternal changeless Form, in a place above the heavens and so separated it from indi-vidual earthly things. The latter indeed are related to the Forms or what truly is (ὄντως ὄν) as to their exemplary and final cause, but do not have an intrinsic essence as their own ground. Consequently, despite his theory of participation (μέθεξις), imitation (μίμησις), fellowship (κοινωνία), Plato could never clearly explain their relation to the Forms. In contrast to this, Aristotle found the essence in the individual thing and partic-ularly as concentrated in the essential form (μορφή) actuating matter (ὕλη). The universal concept of an essence is obtained by abstrac-tion from things. Since for Aristotle the immanent essence is not rooted in the tran-scendent archetypal Form, some of his fol-lowers have been inclined to hold con-ceptualist views. Inspired by neo-Platonism, Augustine returned to the archetypal Forms, locating them in the primordial creative mind as God's guiding patterns; yet Augustine too does not do justice to the essence intrinsic to things and for that reason the Forms are known less from things than through direct illumination. Thomas Aquinas accomplished a synthesis of Augustine and Aristotle; in virtue of their essential form, earthly beings are stamped with the likeness of the eternal archetypes in the divine mind and thereby things share in the infinite plenitude of sub-sisting being. Correspondingly man is able to discern their essence in things themselves *(intus legere)* and to grasp this essence in universal concepts obtained by abstraction, which likewise reflect the eternal Forms. Man is only in a position to do this because his active intellect *(intellectus agens)* involves a permanent irradiation of divine light *(Summa Theologica,* I, q. 84, a. 5).

This great tradition was broken by late medieval conceptualism, according to which the universal essence is entirely absorbed by the individual existent and the latter, therefore, provides no basis for an act of abstraction that would penetrate to the essence; consequently the concept of the essence is simply a mental construct which we produce for its practical utility. Influenced by this, rationalism and empiricism took opposite roads which Kant brought together again. According to Kant, the essence intrinsic to the thing in itself is inaccessible to us; the essential structures which we grasp belong solely to the thing as phenomenon and derive from the *a priori* forms of the transcendental subject. In German Idealism Hegel taught that the human mind penetrates to the essence of things, but only inasmuch as it is dialectically one with the absolute mind. At the same time Hegel equated the order of being with that of essence and consequently the primordial reality appears as the absolute idea; in it all other essences are taken up and away, as its finite moments, in the movement of dialectics.

This predominantly essentialist philosophy is offensive to a mode of thought centred on man as capable of personal existence and which, at least as regards man, either denies or minimizes essence as a prior and enduring datum. Such an essence is regarded as incompatible with the freedom and the temporal, historical character of personal self-realization or with the constantly renewed happening of the self-sending of being; according to J.-P. Sartre, personal existence posits its own essence or nature, so that it always is what it makes itself to be. The phenomenology developed by Husserl defined philosophy as the investigation of essences; essence manifests itself in the intuition of essences or ideation (eidetic reduction) when actual existence is prescinded from; essence then appears as the noema related to noesis and as ultimately constituted by the transcendental consciousness. On the basis of his critical realism, N. Hartmann recognized an at least empirical essence of things, which he discerned in realities and analysed as categorical structures. Positivism and neo-Positivism, on the other hand, restrict themselves solely to phenomena and volatilize essence into the regular and empirically observable connections between phenomena.

See also *Truth* I, *Mystery, History* I, *Being, Time, Man* I, *Existence* I, II, III, *Act and Potency, Platonism, Thomism, Rationalism, Empiricism, Idealism.*

BIBLIOGRAPHY. M. Müller, *Sein und Geist* (1040); É. Gilson, *L'Être et l'essence* (1948); P. Capone Praga, *Il mondo delle idee* (2nd ed., 1954); H. Krings, *Fragen und Aufgaben der Ontologie* (1954); C. Fabro, *Partecipazione e causalità* (1960); G. Siewerth, *Der Thomismus als Identitätssystem* (2nd ed., 1961); S. Breton, *Essence et existence* (1962); X. Zubiri, *Sobre la esencia* (2nd ed., 1963).

Joh.-Baptist Lotz

ETERNITY

I. Biblical

1. The OT term for eternity, עוֹלָם, is used for preference to describe the being of God, and given a certain emphasis, but always God's being insofar as it is superior to man and his existence. God was already there before the world of man was created (Ps 90:2; 102:25–29; Job 38:4; Gen 1:1). A thousand years are as a moment in his sight (Ps 90:4). Thus he is the eternal in the first place as "the most ancient God", later, from Deutero-Isaiah on, also expressly called the eternal in the past and in the future (Is 40:28; 41:4; 44:6). As the Alpha and Omega, he comprises within him all history (Is 41:4; 48:12). His years have no end (Ps 102:26 ff.), he is לְעוֹלָם (Gen 21:33) etc. Thus the notion of eternity as applied to God is strongly orientated to human experience of finite time, and rather expresses endless duration than strict superiority to time. Hence too it has a decidedly ethical element, since this eternity emphasizes the absolute reliability of God, of his grace, faithfulness and love, of his decrees, etc. Reflection on the absolute otherness of this eternity with regard to time appears only in late Judaism. Where עוֹלָם is attributed to other beings beside God, this only means an incalculably long time in comparison with calculable periods, and its character varies according to the reality of which it is said.

2. The NT speaks of eternity as a divine attribute (Rom 1:20; 16:26; Phil 4:20, etc.), in the same sense as the OT. Eternity is the contrary of the limited world-period between creation and the eschata. But "eternal" is

also a propriety of the true world of salvation, the eschatological blessings and eschatological ruin. This description of the eschatological blessings as eternal along with God, in contrast to this "aeon", shows that the influence of Hellenism is already at work.

3. What distinguishes the biblical from the metaphysical concept of eternity is the ease with which time or history is merged into it. Just as God is one as triune, so too he is eternal "as he who changes in another" (K. Rahner, *Theological Investigations,* IV, p. 113, note 3). The climax of this way of modifying the eternity-assertions comes with the Incarnation, where we do not merely believe that a human nature was assumed by a God who was left "untouched", but that God himself became man, while remaining eternal God, so that "this event is that of God himself" *(ibid.).* In the light of this truth, this unity in duality of eternity and time, or of eternity and history, points back not only to the history of salvation and of the covenant, but also to the act of creation. The incomprehensibility of these truths explains why a metaphysically orientated theology, fearing the introduction of a wrong notion of time into God, explains eternity in such a way as to do less than justice to the aspect of the "historicity" of God.

See also *Aeon, Creation, Eschatology, Incarnation, History* I.

BIBLIOGRAPHY. H. Sasse, "αἰών, αἰώνιος", *TWNT,* I, pp. 197–209; F. H. Brabant, *Time and Eternity in Christian Thought* (1937); H. Sasse, "Aion", *RAC,* cols. 193–204; O. Cullmann, *Christ and Time* (1951); T. Boman, *Hebrew Thought compared with Greek* (1960); R. Berlinger, *Augustins dialogische Metaphysik* (1962); J. Barr, *Biblical Words for Time* (1962).

Adolf Darlap

II. Theological

1. *General concept.* If one discounts the vague scriptural use of "eternity" to indicate "a very long duration", one can distinguish in general three uses of this concept: a) eternity as unlimited time, which is the way in which the unreflecting mind represents the eternity of God. Yet one also finds this meaning given to it by philosophers (Descartes, Lequier); it represents a constant temptation for philosophical thought. b) Eternity as timelessness (the eternal truths): an eternity of the abstract, which is only preserved from a servitude to the bounds of time because it is not subject to existence — an "eternity of death". c) Eternity as *real duration* which *transcends* time, in that it negates the essential characteristic of time: its division into moments. This is the decisive notion of eternity; it was given classic expression by Boëthius in his definition of eternity as *"interminabilis vitae tota simul et perfecta possessio"* (*De Consolatione Philosophiae,* V, 6: *PL,* LXIII, 858). *Interminabilis* excludes any idea of "beginning and end" and thus preserves what is positive in the popular conception. *Vitae possessio* goes beyond the negative abrogation of time as it is represented in the "timelessness" of the abstract conception.

The most essential element is the *tota simul* which excludes any difference or distinction between individual discrete moments of time. Eternity is not a duration stretching out interminably, but a duration which in its entire "length", as it were, is gathered into one single "moment" — a moment which is permanent because it is identical with being, the *nunc stans* as opposed to the passing moment of our experience *(nunc fluens).* In this sense eternity is only another name for the unchangeableness of God (*D* 391, 428, 1782). In a deeper sense it means that the absolute being transcends the entire order of beings and that it excludes in its unending living density any division, limitation or measure. A being merely absolved from all interior change, but in which earlier and later could be distinguished by its real relation to changeable beings, would be similar to these changing beings. And it would not really be unchangeable, since the relationships could change. If we are treating of a consciousness, it would be contradictory to suppose that it could, without changing, persist in the manner of "before" and "after". The moment B, precisely because it comes after A, cannot be lived in an identical manner. Perfect changelessness in a consciousness demands that there be no transition from "not yet" to "no longer". The completely unchangeable being knows only the present.

Eternity, as a concept, is difficult to comprehend. To go beyond time appears to us more mysterious than to go beyond space, which we do when we combine things which are spatially distinct. Temporality appears to penetrate our thinking in a much deeper way, so that we can only think of eternity in an act which occurs in time. When it is said that the divine duration is *tota simul,* what is apparently meant is that its different elements are fulfilled "in the same instant", for it is in this way that we define simultaneity in our conceptual categories. This would be a contradiction, explained by the fact that one has expounded eternity in terms of time. The idea of eternity, like the other attributes of God, is negative only in the manner in which it is approached conceptually. But is it really something negative in itself? Perception and judgment of time are only possible when one transcends time; even our experience of the present is not a point. It rather occurs as a summation of a certain extent of time within consciousness, an extent of time which, within its limits, is *tota simul* to the consciousness. But the simultaneity of the present is subjective and illusory, for the existence of man, being immersed in time, necessarily includes — whether one is conscious of it or not — past and future. The divine consciousness is being itself, its subjectivity is truth; thus it is *tota simul* in one moment which includes all possible duration. In a deeper sense the spirit transcends time because it has the capacity to think of it and to make judgments concerning it, and also because it seeks to free itself from time by opening itself to truths and values which cannot be destroyed by the passing of time. Rationalist and idealist philosophies have treated of this theme again and again: in terms of the experience of eternity (Spinoza), the eternal present (Lavelle), and so on.

Eternity thus appeared as a characteristic of the most sublime intellective activity. Such ways of speaking include a good deal of rhetoric which is not without its danger: eternity is degraded as soon as it is drawn into the sphere of immanence. What is true in this, is that spiritual self-realization comprises a vertical dimension, an openness towards the eternal even though it is tributary to time. It is precisely this which gives impulse and value to its horizontal development in time. We are not eternal, but there is within us something which points to the eternal and which enables us to conceive of the eternal not merely as negation.

2. *Eternity and time.* Seen from the perspective of a radical dualism, eternity and time have no relation one to the other. They can only be joined together by the doctrine of creation, considered under its aspect of participation, which considers eternity as the origin, ground, and measure of time. Time is contained in eternity not as though it were contained in a longer period of time (like a month in a year), but as in something from which time derives its being and unity, something which "holds together" time (con-tinet). One must be especially careful here to avoid introducing a temporal relationship. Eternity is not "in the beginning" or "at the end" of time. It is both that which gives rise to time and that from which time ceaselessly flows, and also that which bestows upon time its meaning. So too, the "presentness" (or if one prefers, the simultaneity) of each of our moments in eternity is not a "being at the same time", as though they were two periods of time contained within the same duration. It consists rather in this, that the whole order of time and each of its moments receives being through the eternal act. There is here no temporal discontinuity and no simultaneity. From this it follows that things are present to God from all eternity in their temporality: this is the teaching of Aquinas (*Summa Theologica,* I, q. 14, a. 13) and his school, as opposed to thinkers like Albert the Great, Scotus and Suarez, who only speak of an objective, eternal present (in the divine omniscience). According to Aquinas, if it is true that things are because God knows them (and wills them), such knowledge is an eternal vision because the things themselves are eternally in his presence. This only appears absurd if eternity is still unwittingly measured against time.

3. *Conclusions.* a) The true meaning of "eternity" excludes the conception of a God who was lonely *before* he called creation into being. That is, one either imagines an observer who notes that for the moment God alone existed; or one imagines God as noting, at a given moment of his infinite duration that things begin to be, which means that one posits a change in the divine consciousness. Or else one imagines that God sees in eternity the duration of things and conceives of this duration only as a part of his own duration. In this way one would conceive of eternity as parallel to time. The world began, but not at a certain

moment in eternity (which indeed has no moments), and God was *at no time* without the world, for there is nothing temporal before time.

b) Neither should one enquire how it is that God foresees free actions: there is no "preview", but only vision. God does not know the future in its causes (which would only be a type of "probability prediction" with regard to free actions); he knows that which is still in the future for us in his eternal present. The relation between "before" and "after" — as with all other relationships which belong to the structure of created things — only holds good at this level of the created. The question of conditional futures is not thereby solved.

c) The eternal presence of things before God makes it possible to hope that time will be redeemed and restored. "Eternal" life is so called not merely because it will never end, but because in the vision of God men will, in some manner, be immersed in the eternal vision of God whom men will thus know *sicuti est,* and thus will men grasp the whole order of time anew in its supreme truth. In this sense one can also speak of a real participation of creation in the eternity of God.

See also *Time, Creation* IV, *God, Attributes of, Beatific Vision.*

BIBLIOGRAPHY. Thomas Aquinas, *Summa Theologica,* I, q. 10 and q. 14, a. 13; F. Suarez, *Disputationes Metaphysicae,* disp. 50; John of St. Thomas, *Cursus Theologicus,* in primam partem, d. 9; A. Michel, "Éternité", *DTC,* V, cols. 912–21; J. Guitton, *Le temps et l'éternité chez Plotin et Saint Augustin* (1933); L. Lavelle, *Du temps et de l'éternité* (1945); H.-I. Marrou, *L'ambivalence du temps de l'histoire chez Saint Augustin* (1950); E. Brunner, *Das Ewige als Zukunft und Gegenwart* (1953); G. van de Leeuw, *Phänomenologie der Religion,* pp. 434–9 (1954); K. Barth, *Church Dogmatics,* II/1 (1957); J. Mouroux, *Mystery of Time* (1964).

Joseph de Finance

ETHICS

1. *Notion and history.* History of philosophy and philosophy are inseparable, and for ethics history is essential in another sense also. Philosophy, as a deliberate study, takes place within man's history. But it is not the interest of all men. All need a more or less explicit view of the world, but this need not be philosophical. It may be a religious orientation. But men at all times, whether they give themselves to philosophy or not, have to live, that is, they have to give their lives a meaning. Hence they must plan beforehand and then implement their plans, they must choose between possibilities, do this and omit that, take decisions and form habits, adopt attitudes, make use of things, shape their own lives. In this sense man always has an implicit philosophy, but it is precisely this philosophy which always has an ethical dimension, since it is itself determined by an *option fondamentale* of an ethical nature. And this appears most readily (though perhaps only in a rudimentary way), not in the form of theoretical propositions, but as maxims for action — what man is or is not to do, good or evil. Hence man is inevitably a moral being in the original sense of the word — as will be demonstrated more fully in the following. He is responsible for his life, that is, he has to take charge of it and answer for it.

Man is engaged in "creating" himself in the whole course of his life, like mankind throughout its history. This individual and social, but always historical notion is the primary basis of "morality". It means morals in action, not yet based on θεωρία but on πρᾶξις, on self-realization through bringing about reality.

We are concerned, then, first of all, with this moral reality, this realization of a "sketch-plan" for life. But men do not live and act at random. They follow certain patterns. These are first adopted spontaneously and only later become recognized ideals. In general they stem from models and attitudes adopted as historical cultural factors. This is the second sense of the word "moral" here. It means not only the mere "sketch-plan" as the directive for life, but the shaping of one's life in accordance with certain moral directives, that is, certain *mores,* customs. These *mores* are not yet moral philosophy or ethics, which comes later, if at all, and appears as comprehensive reflection on the moral behaviour of men, not as a moral lived out in action. Hence there are three meanings for the word "moral", the first of which was hitherto left outside explicit consideration, in spite of its unique importance. Consciously or unconsciously, moral philosophy always built on the data of an existing moral (in the second sense).

The relationship between moral philosophy and moral life explains the importance of the history of morals. The concept of morals must be extended to take in instinctive reaction to and philosophical reflection on morals. A history of moral philosophy as such, that is, of doctrines and opinions expressed on morality, would be a pure history of ideas, completely cut off from the soil on which these ideas were nourished. The history of *mores* alone, however, would be merely a positivist compilation of material facts.

The history of morals in the full sense has yet to be written. It would take in both the most important findings of social and cultural anthropology and of general history, and also the state of philosophical (and pre-philosophical) reflection. This would demonstrate its understanding of the moral consciousness of a given historical situation. The writing of such a history would be a laborious, but not a difficult task. The ethics of Aristotle, for instance, the first systematic moral philosophy, is almost exclusively reflection on the ethical consciousness of the Greeks. The four cardinal virtues of the *Nicomachean Ethics* represent the virtues striven for and practised in the course of Greek history. Aristotle's effort to provide as it were a handbook of Greek ethics is one last effort to preserve an ethics of fellowship in the City-State. Its failure signalled a new age of political figures who looked farther afield and wielded greater powers, but which was also an age in which Stoicism and Epicureanism offered two different ways by which philosophy could withdraw into the sphere of private, inward reflection and evade the effort to set up a genuine political ethics.

From the point of view considered here, Christianity brought with it a fundamental renewal of morals. Life was given through faith a new meaning which has been hitherto insufficiently noted by moral philosophy. Modern ethics became a mere imitation of the classical, Graeco-Roman ethics and lost touch with the reality of its own times. This unhealthy situation, in which a new set of morals was given no philosophical "translation", lasted till Kant. Kant replaced an ethics based on human nature and aiming at the good and at happiness, by a moral of pure duty, too formal to do justice to the material content of the act. Fichte, however, saw this formalism as a "material formality" — of life, love. Hegel, the Aristotle of his times, since he outlined a philosophical and ethical "Encyclopaedia", considered the ethics of Kant as a mere "moment" of his own ethics. The Kantian "morality" is abstract, out of touch with reality, lofty indeed but completely restricted to the individual and ineffective. It is taken up and away into the "ethical", the objective and supra-individual sphere of the State. Here Hegel anticipated a question which is urgent today, that of a social ethics with its own intrinsic justification and not put forward merely as a corollary to or mere expansion of a general individualistic moral philosophy. The two systems which have had the most lasting effects on the contemporary mind in general are those of Marxism and existentialism. Both derive from Hegel. Marx took over from him the supra-individual, social approach to the function of ethics, while rejecting his idealism. Kierkegaard's approach, however, was personalist, anti-idealist and existential. One of the great tasks of our times is to make a synthesis of the personal and the social, as has already been attempted by the representatives of a humanistic socialism. See the works of such socialist existentialists as Sartre (e.g., *Critique de la raison dialectique* [1960]) and certain contemporary Christian thinkers.

2. *Morality as an anthropological and social structure.* That man has to shape his life means negatively that it does not come to him ready-made. In contrast to the animal's imprisonment in its environment, where its responses are definitely determined by the combination of stimulus and psycho-biological constitution, man is free in his world and capable of various determinations. The stimuli are used by him, through his intellect, with which he derives or elicits possibilities from them, as sketch-plans for his actions. The possibilities may be many, and hence a choice must be made between the various sketch-plans envisaged. Hence human freedom is not bound by a fixed schema of stimulus and response, but can choose between various real possibilities. This process of choice and decision is not of course one single event. It must be constantly repeated. All truly human acts (the *actus humani* of the Scholastics) are decided upon in this way, and life is composed of such acts. The

chosen possibility is realized, not only in my environment, the world, but — what is essential here — in myself. It is integrated into my own reality. Hence all human action must be considered moral action. Man is responsible for his actions because he plans his life freely and executes his plans freely, though with a paradoxical sort of freedom, since, as Ortega y Gasset says, he is "necessarily free". This morality of freedom is expressed in the "sketch-plan", the progressive shaping of actual life. Morality gives a man a "second nature", as Aristotle says, that is, a new reality, the ethos, the moral character or moral personality.

But human action is not determined merely by a set of perpetually new choices between proffered possibilities. The situations which man encounters may be each special and unrepeatable in its own way, but they show nonetheless similarities and point to the past in which other men in similar situations have taken similar decisions. The basis of a civilization or a culture is in fact the comprehensive repertoire of vital responses given at a special epoch. These responses have become consciously articulate and form models and patterns of behaviour. If we consider, not the single act, but human life in its fullness, we have to admit that we confine ourselves for the most part to a choice between various modes of existence and patterns of life — states, professions, avocations — which are offered by the society in which we live.

Thus human behaviour is determined by individual responsibility, by social conditioning and historical cultural traditions. This creates a dependence which is both negative and positive. Some "possibilities" have to be given up as unrealistic, others are multiplied in a way which would have been impossible without these social and traditional conditions. The genuine and not merely ostensible possibilities offered by society vary very widely. Given patterns of behaviour and custom bring about in a society, in spite of the rights of all men, considerable differences and tensions. Groups and classes are repressed or discriminated against. Individuals who do not conform are not always the solely guilty ones.

3. *The indicative and the imperative moment in ethics.* Man is necessarily free, and *has* to shape his life as an individual and as a member of society. It seems, however, that he can shirk this necessity of being free, this perpetual duty of choice, when he finds it tiresome. Hence men readily bow to tyrannies, if conditions are made comfortable enough for them, because there is a certain relief in placing the responsibility for choice on others. To do what "is done", to conform to the general consensus, to direct one's life by the customs and prescriptions of convention, makes things undoubtedly simpler. But it is an illusion to think that man could thus unburden himself of all responsibility, since the initial expression of freedom which leads to complete renunciation of independence is itself an act of decision. And even when an individual renounces completely his political and social freedom — though he thereby strives to destroy what is really human in him — a remnant of personal responsibility survives.

This allows us to distinguish in morality as a principle of structure and order (without going outside this frame of reference) an indicative and an imperative moment, the latter being implicit in the former. What ought to be is already comprised in what is. If man, as we have seen, must plan and anticipate what he desires to be, this is because he is a being which must realize itself at a distance from itself, in the tension between being and ought, in the difference between what it is and what it will be. The imperative of bridging this distance is called duty, the failing in this duty is called guilt. It should be noted, however, that this is not a separation of two realms as in Kant, the ontological and the deontological. The two realms are at one, in a unity in which a distinction is made simply for the sake of clarity. The notion of the "tension of being and ought" is prior to its ethical significance and is the foundation of it. A whole world of anthropological fundamentals — sketch-plan of existence, vocation, the general teleological purpose of existence, moral consciousness, conscience, sense of duty, and, on another plane, phenomena such as discontent, concupiscence, sense of inadequacy and self-pity — all are manifestations of this paradoxical nature of human being.

The imperative moment can be considered from two points of view, either purely formally and structurally, as has just been done, or materially, by considering the concrete content of the imperative. In the latter case, morality is taken as a concept full of content, of which we shall now speak.

4. *Moral formalism and the meta-ethical content of morality.* Hitherto we have spoken exclusively of the conditions by which human action and human freedom are determined. We have not yet discussed what man has to do to be good and not evil. Since Kant, the question of the content has been answered by a formalism according to which morality is measured by *how* something is done, not by *what* is done. The answer is sought in the form and not in the matter, in the structure and not in the content of action. In actual fact, the Kantian and the existentialist formalism conceals more or less effectively a material morality, based in Kant on Protestant principles and in atheism on the notion of emancipation from the supposed tyranny of God, in Marxism on the notion of the emancipation of the exploited classes (see, for instance, Sartre).

It is instructive to compare the supposedly "ethical" formalism of Kant and Sartre. Both derive from historical conditions which are very important from the point of view of religious criticism. In the time of Kant, for the first time in the history of the West, Deism had gained great influence, though restricted to a minority. In the time of Sartre an (anti-theistic) atheism had gained ground for the first time. Atheism and Deism had been hitherto marginal phenomena. It was only after the Enlightenment that they became attitudes which determined action. In both cases the religious element — in reverse — provided the content of morality. Apart from antiquity, the various ways in which Christianity manifested itself have always provided the content for Western morality.

It would be wrong to try to understand the content of a morality uniquely in the light of its religious origins. The secularization of life which had already begun in the Middle Ages and made rapid strides from the Renaissance on, and especially through the Enlightenment, produced a morality which was completely orientated to the world (though even here religious roots have been discerned). Many of its demands, such as the right to work, security in the world, exploitation of natural resources, just distribution of goods, are nonetheless justified. Whether orientated to religion or to social life in general, the prescriptions of a morality are formed, not by philosophical or religious reflection, but by experience, in history. But if the contents of morality are meta-ethical, how can they be adopted by ethics or moral philosophy, if this is not to lose its true character and independence? This brings up the problem of the relationship between ethics and history and between ethics and religion.

Since ethics strives to be a philosophy, it cannot invoke religion but must derive its principles from reason alone. Reason can help to articulate the reality of evil in the world, the contingence of man, the dramatic character of life and the "mysterious" and "absurd" character of death. But these and similar phenomena also show the philosophical inadequacy of ethics and "open" it to religion.

It should be noted that the problem is not restricted to subordinating the philosophical realm of ethics to the meta-philosophical realm of religion. The problem is that ethics, as regards its material, is inadequate in its own realm. The content of a morality is based at least in part on religion. If ethics consists in philosophical reflection on a morality whose content is already furnished by religion, it always comes too late, so to speak. Hence it is not a matter of ethics retracing its steps half-way, till it reaches the point where it finds itself faced with the necessity of opening up to religion. The problem lies deeper. As regards its content, ethics always and necessarily points beyond itself to religion.

As regards the relation of ethics to history and historicity, it must also be remembered that the content of a morality is not given once and for all. Its concrete expression is always a function of history. The conventional ethics here calls upon the notion of natural law. But today ethics is far from being able to offer a systematic and harmonious doctrine of the natural law.

What is the solution of the difficulty that ethics is unable to determine philosophically and master reflectively the content of a morality? If we are working towards a strictly philosophical ethics, there is only one possible solution: to renounce a descriptive set of categories which will be universally valid, and to treat ethics as in this sense a formal or structural science. We have already seen that formalism in ethics is impossible. But the rejection of moral formalism must be carefully distinguished from the possibility — and indeed the philosophical necessity — of an ethical formalism considered as the only possible general schema of the transcendental content of the good. For philosophical reflection can only attain to formal principles, while concrete assertions as to material content can only be made on the basis of experience.

What are the main questions put in this formal or structural ethics? They have already been indicated. With regard to the moral content, ethics has to show: a) its necessity, b) its meta-ethical character; c) its logical possibility — this last being the main problem of Kant and the Anglo-Saxon ethics of the present day.

Finally, we must note the clear difference between the material object of a morality or ethos and the formal object of an ethics or moral philosophy. The aspect which the latter envisages is not just the repetition on a systematic level of the spontaneous experiences of the former. Its effort is to restrict itself to a purely structural consideration of morality. This formalism, this limitation, is the price it must pay if it is to remain philosophy.

Nonetheless, as has already been indicated (and as is particularly stressed in the works of M. Scheler), this formalism is not entirely formal. It is the giving of structure to a content. God, the ultimate ground of all ethos, the nature of man (as spirit, as freedom in eternal life) and the consequent basic demands of ethics are knowable. They allow of, and indeed demand, an ethics which will be not merely formal but also, in a certain sense, though a very open one, allow of material formulation (as concrete duties). By the nature of rational thought, the positive content will be formulated rather negatively than positively — as universally valid prohibitions — which is relevant to situation ethics. But some positive approaches, such as the "golden rule" are not merely formal, because they aim at keeping man open for his transcendence towards God and hence for the absolute value of the person of his fellows.

A further concrete step has to be taken by ethics in each historical epoch. It has to go beyond the transcendental experience of the good to articulate it in the form appropriate to the epoch, and thus formulate valid positive norms of good order.

The ultimate individual concrete formulation, which is, however, decisive, cannot, in the nature of things, be achieved on general principles. The traditional effort in this direction made use of casuistry and epikeia. But the crystallization can only be aimed at in reflection upon the structure and pre-conditions of a "logic of existential knowledge", and in a programme of the practical and theoretical formation of conscience. Ethics can never give the concrete individual directive.

The traditional utterances of the magisterium, on the moral necessity for revelation if the natural moral law is to be known, appear now in a new light, since not only general "principles" but above all concrete "imperatives" have to be addressed to each age and each individual. (See on this K. Rahner, *The Dynamic Element in the Church* [1964].) But still the possibility of a philosophical ethics must be maintained (*D* 1650, 1670, 1785, 1806, 2317, 2320). Ethics remains philosophy but in the sense which philosophy seems to be taking on today, that of anthropology.

See also *Situation, Authority, Freedom, Good, Law, Man, Morality, Natural Law, Person.*

BIBLIOGRAPHY. D. von Hildebrand, *Sittlichkeit und ethische Werterkenntnis* (1922); N. Hartmann, *Ethics,* 3 vols. (1926; 3rd ed., 1949); O. Dittrich, *Geschichte der Ethik,* 4 vols. (1926–32); H. Sidgwick and A. G. Widgern, *Outlines of the History of Ethics* (8th ed., 1931; reprint 1949); H. Bergson, *Les deux sources de la morale et de la religion* (11th ed., 1932); M. Cronin, *The Science of Ethics,* II (4th ed., 1939); D. Ross, *Foundations of Ethics* (1939, 2nd ed., 1949); O. Lottin, *Principes de Morale,* 2 vols. (1947); R. Le Senne, *Traité de morale générale* (1948); T. E. Hill, *Contemporary Ethical Theories* (1950), bibliography; J. Maritain, *Neuf leçons sur les notions premières de la philosophie morale* (1951); H. H. Joachim, *Aristotle, the Nicomachean Ethics,* ed. by D. A. Rees (1951); D. von Hildebrand, *Christian Ethics* (1952); A. Marc, *Dialectique de l'agir* (1954); J. M. Todd, *The Springs of Morality* (1956); J. de Finance, *Essai sur l'agir humain* (1962); P. Engelhardt, ed., *Sein und Ethos* (1963); K. Rahner, *Experiment Mensch: Die Frage nach dem Menschen* (Festschrift M. Müller) (1966), pp. 45–69; M. Scheler, *Der Formalismus in der Ethik und die materiale Wert-Ethik* (5th ed., 1966); J. Pieper, *Reality and the Good* (1967).

José Luis L. Aranguren

EUCHARIST

I. Theological: A. Concept. B. Institution of the Eucharist by the Historical Jesus. C. The Liturgical Form of the Eucharist in the Church. D. Official Pronouncements. E. Theological Explanations. II. Liturgical: A. Various Names for the Mass. B. Early Structure of the Mass. C. Evolution since the Fourth Century. D. Special Features of the Roman Mass. E. The People's Part in the Mass. III. Eucharistic Sacrifice.

I. Theological

A. Concept

Eucharist is the designation for the sacramental meal of the Church celebrated according to the example and the instructions of Jesus, a designation appearing as early as the 1st century and predominating ever since. The word expresses fundamental insights into the nature of the action. The term, which derives from the "thanksgiving" of Jesus at the Last Supper (Lk 22:19; 1 Cor 11:24; Mk 14:23; Mt 26:27) means, as does the root verb εὐ-χαριστ-εῖν, the "proper conduct of one who is the object of a gift", and not only (as in profane Greek) the attitude of thankfulness, but also its outward evidence. This Christian meaning goes back to the Hebrew notion of "blessing" as the praise of God which recalls his *magnalia*. Thanks always presupposes a gracious gift which is in fact only real through the thanksgiving, where alone the gift is effective and present. In the case of the Church's sacramental meal, it is the salvific reality placed therein by Christ, which is Christ himself with his being and work. This reality is acknowledged with praise in the words of a grace at meals uttered over and into the gifts of food. It is thereby actualized and objectified in them and made operative in the words and in the elements of the meal. And so the prayer and also the elements consecrated by it early received the name "Eucharist". Thus we arrive at the following definition: the Eucharist is the actualizing of the salvific reality "Jesus", through the words of thanksgiving uttered over the bread and wine.

B. Institution of the Eucharist by the Historical Jesus

The Church celebrates the Eucharist by virtue of the authority and the commission expressly given to it by Jesus. The institution of the supper by the historical Jesus is decisive for all eucharistic practice and dogma. This conviction is today disputed. A radical circle in Protestant theology denies the institution of the sacrament by Jesus in the way it is presented in the NT and in the liturgy and traces it back to the early Church's understanding of itself and of its sacred meal. The historical fact from the life of the Lord in connection with the Eucharist is simply his fellowship at table with his disciples and sinners, which he understood as an anticipation of the eschatological community. After the death of Jesus his followers continued the "breaking of the bread" together and continued to experience it as an eschatological anticipation, animated by the belief that the glorified Lord was there invisibly in their midst. In the fellowship of the meal the community interpreted itself as the "body of Christ", the "new divine covenant *(diatheke)* in virtue of the blood (the bloody death) of Christ", and gave expression to this self-consciousness in the explanatory words over the bread and wine. It was only the spirituality of the Hellenistic community which linked the presence of Christ materially to the elements of the meal, as may be seen from Mk. The real presence of Jesus in the consecrated elements as thus conceived, is, therefore, only a Hellenistic interpretation which is today no longer possible. The actual last supper of Jesus is, according to this same interpretation, a simple, dogmatically irrelevant farewell meal, which in the NT, however, is described and understood by Mk in the terms of the real presence as the institution of Jesus. This, however, projects back into the life of Jesus, in Christological terms, the meal which was experienced eschatologically by the primitive community. In view of this thesis, which illustrates the tendency to deprive Jesus of messianic character and to demythologize the NT, the institution of the Church's supper by the historical Jesus appears today to be of particular importance.

In support of this — if one prefers not to stress the impossibility of inventing the Eucharist — is the antiquity and origin of the tradition. Its earliest witness, Paul, expressly traces his account (1 Cor 11:23ff.) back to a received tradition, one that ultimately derived from Jesus. This claim is strengthened by characteristics that are typical of Jesus' manner of speech (especially in the so-called eschatological perspective: Lk 22:16–18; Mk 14:25). In the Aramaic turns of speech within all the accounts, their Semitic origin is recognizable, and their date and form can be traced back to the forties. But if this is so, there is scarcely room or time for any gradual spread of a Christologizing activity by the Hellenistic community. A further pointer to the historical Jesus is the fact that both of the extant strands of the tradition, that of Paul–Luke, and that of Mark–Matthew, differ according to formulation and theology but agree in their understanding of the essential meaning of the supper. The difference of the formulations can be traced to the transmitters of tradition; the agreement as to its meaning, however, must be traced to Jesus as the source of the tradition. Finally, there is the added weight of the fact that it is precisely not the excision of the supper from the life of Jesus, but its presence there, and the light thrown on it by Jesus' life as a whole which disclose the true character of the sacrament and which make a consistent explanation possible.

Jesus accomplished the decisive purpose of his life, his task as Messiah, in carrying out the mission of the Servant of God of Deutero-Isaiah, who as God's majestic envoy proclaims and inaugurates a new phase in salvation, and who as martyr takes upon himself expiatory sufferings for the sins of the many. This programme already inspired Jesus at his reception of the "baptism of repentance for the remission of sins" from John (Mk 1:4). Taking on alien guilt meant taking on also the necessity of death. As his life went on, Jesus thought more frequently of his death and spoke more frequently of it to his disciples — a death which was in any case a real danger from the Jewish authorities. It was for Jesus not something that merely happened to him, but a conscious and willed deed to which he assented as a necessity in the history of salvation, and on which he freely decided (Lk 12:50). His total readiness for the death which was the mission of the Servant of the Lord is also expressed in the logion of the ransom (Mk 10:45), and the prophecies of the passion (Mk 8:31; 9:31; 10:32ff.). These are at their core genuine prophecies of Jesus but in their NT form represent interpretative elaborations of the early Church based on

its knowledge of the actual course of the passion. Jesus maintained his obedient yes to vicarious expiation through all outward and inward afflictions, even in the dread of death, torments, and abandonment by God. His death is total dedication and the deepest fulfilment of his being. Besides his death, Jesus also foretold his resurrection — the *Ebed Jahweh* also experiences as the reward for his expiatory death, according to Is 52:13 and 53:10ff., a triumphant rehabilitation and elevation to cultic dignity. In Jesus' prophecies of resurrection we hear the victorious certainty that his death, which he took upon himself purely out of desire for atonement and in eager obedience to the will of the Father, would find recognition before God. This death is the offering of martyrdom. Unlike the cultic sacrifices, there is no separate gift which stands for the offerer and symbolizes his dedication to God. Here the offerer himself functions as gift in his own person and accomplishes the sacrificial dedication by the real shedding of his blood. Jesus must have been sure that God would accept his sacrifice, his body, and hence that God would fill it with new life. Thus the death of Jesus brings with it the resurrection as an inner consequence, as an essential part of it, regardless of the difference in time between the two events. For the fourth evangelist, accordingly, the lifting up of Jesus on the cross already means his being lifted up in glory (Jn 3:14; 8:28; 12:32ff.).

In this readiness for death and in the certain conviction that the sacrifice of his life would be accepted by God and lead to a new order of salvation, Jesus celebrated his last supper and established it as his testament. He summed up in it his whole messianic being and work, gave them concentrated expression in a visible and even edible blessing, and bequeathed them as a sacrament. Hence the supper must not only be explained in the light of the entire life of Jesus, it *is* this entirety in symbolic compression. Its meaning is already partly indicated by its character as a farewell meal (Lk 22:15ff.; Mk 14:25) such as late Jewish Apocalyptic ascribes to the dying patriarchs. There the departing man of God reveals his approaching death, and gives his special blessing into which he puts the whole fruit of his God-filled life. Then, the last celebration of Jesus, according to the synoptics, is the paschal meal, while according to

Jn 18:28 it takes place before the official paschal date. At any rate, its date is near to that of the Pasch, it is influenced by the ritual (the explanation of the foods and the sequence bread-meal-cup), and is permeated by the spiritual atmosphere of the Jewish feast as a cultic memorial of the saving deed of Jahweh. The NT, however, nowhere interprets the Eucharist in the light of the Pasch. A key for the understanding of the supper is given to us by the biblical idea of the prophetic sign *(ôt)* or the prophetic action. This phenomenon is meant not merely as a truth in symbolic dress or the pictorial orientation toward some coming event. It is already the initial realization of a divine decree. An event ordained by God is not merely registered and told of in words, it is brought about and initially realized. The action does not merely represent it symbolically, it anticipates and crystallizes its reality. The prophetic sign is the *signum efficax* of a divine action. Jesus situates his supper within the framework of this specific sphere of divine causality: a) he announces in words the salvific sacrifice of his death; b) he represents it symbolically and makes it present by distributing the food and drink as his body and blood, whereby he c) makes of these elements his person bodily offered up.

a) All the accounts situate the action in the perspective of his death. The primitive apostolic form of the account which is recognizable from Paul and Luke already does this by indicating the time (night of the offering) and by the adjectival phrase at the end of the words over the bread, which is indispensable for the understanding of the action: "given for the many" (ὑπὲρ πολλῶν) instead of ὑμῶν is the original form, reconstructed from Mk 14:24. In a clear allusion to Is 53:12, Jesus' death appears here as the martyr's sacrifice of his person (for σῶμα see below, c), who is the Suffering Servant of God. The same notion is conjured up by the second logion: "this cup is the new *diatheke* in my blood". The predicate "the new *diatheke*" takes up the *Ebed Jahweh* title from Is 42:6 and 49:8, characterizing Jesus as founder of a covenant. He fulfills this task, however, "in his blood", i.e., by shedding his blood. The biblical term "blood" has the connotation of "shed", as the addition "shed for the many" in Mk 14:24 indicates, i.e., instead of, and for the sake of the whole of mankind. This too is dependent on

Is 53:10. The core of the variant Marcian logion over the cup — "this is my covenant-blood" — also conjures up Jesus' violent death, though under a somewhat different aspect. This formula derives from Ex 24:8 and characterizes the content of the cup primarily as the cultic sacrificial element "blood", which is separated from the flesh, then also the death of Jesus as the separation of flesh and blood after the manner of a cultic sacrifice. Thus in all the accounts the death of Jesus is the determinant factor in the Last Supper.

b) The sacrificial death thus announced in words by Jesus was also the object of a symbolic action. He actualized the offering of his person to the Father for men by consecrating bread and wine as his own person and by giving them to be eaten by men. His taking and lifting up of the elements, their blessing and consecration as the body and blood of Jesus, means their transfer to God and displays Jesus' dedication to the Father. When Jesus then gives the food and drink as his body and blood, and gives it to be eaten and drunk by men, he portrays visibly the martyr's death which is the dedication of his inmost life for men, but also its recovery in the resurrection. Moreover, not only the proffering, but the proffering as food and drink reveal how his death, indeed his whole human existence, is for (ὑπέρ) men, in their stead and for their sake. Just as it is the nature of food and drink to be wholly and entirely for men, and just as they give up their own being, to belong to men and to become part of men and thereby build up men's life, so too Jesus is there for men (by the very fact of his incarnation) and belongs to men. So too he gives up his life so that they may live to God. Finally, however, the proffered elements of the meal are not merely an outward means of representing his sacrificial offering on the cross. They are identical with the one and the same sacrificial gift of the cross, this man Jesus. And hence, too, the inner identity of both actions and the actual presence of the bloody offering of himself on the cross is established and finally assured in the unbloody offering of himself in the meal.

c) For by the divine power of his determinative words Jesus changes bread and wine into his own sacrificed person. The term "body" means in the mouth of Jesus, as a rendering of the Semitic expression behind it, not only a part of man, as though his body were distinguished from his blood or soul, but the whole man in his bodily existence. Likewise, the "blood" for the Semites represents the life-substance (Dt 12:23; Lev 17:11,14), and stands for the living being with blood coursing through its veins, especially when it suffers a violent death (Gen 4:10; 2 Macc 8:3; Mt 27:4, 25; Acts 5:28, etc.). It indicates, then, the person in the act of shedding his blood. The adjectival addition to the words over the bread and the cup (Lk 22:19 and Mk 14:24), as also the early apostolic description of the cup as "the new *diatheke*", define the person of Jesus more precisely as the saviour who is the Servant of God. The essential identity of the consecrated elements with the person of Jesus, or (in the traditional language of the schools) the (somatic) real presence of Jesus in the elements of the supper, cannot, however, be based solely on the ἐστίν of the determinative words, as this also has in many biblical phrases a merely metaphorical meaning. It is indicated, however, in the sentence-structure of the blessing which differs from purely metaphorical statements. In the words of consecration we have, in contrast to metaphors, a subject which is of itself colourless and indeterminate, but which is defined by a very concrete predicate. The real presence of Jesus can be better explained from the character of the supper as a prophetic sign in which action and word effect through divine power what they represent. It is supported by the act of distribution which underlines the nature ascribed to the gifts, and also by the fact that they are partaken of. Exegetically, this is ultimately assured by the normative interpretation of the supper in the NT in terms of the real presence, especially in Paul and John. Hence, the bodily person of Jesus is present in the supper, not however in the static manner of being of a thing, but as the Servant of God who in his sacrificial death effects the salvation of us all and more precisely as the sacrificial offering of the Servant who delivers himself up on the cross. The real presence of the person is there to actualize the presence of the sacrificial deed and is united with this in an organic whole. The Eucharist becomes, then, the abiding presence in the meal of the sacrificially constituted salvific event "Jesus", in whom person and work form an inseparable unity.

The inaugurative command τοῦτο ποιεῖτε εἰς τὴν ἐμὴν ἀνάμνησιν gives the Church the power to do what Jesus did. By this command, the re-enactments must be formally similar to the initial supper celebrated by Jesus. It gives them the divinely-effective power of Jesus' supper, and emphasizes and assures their identity of substance with the first supper and with each other. For it characterizes them as the *anamnesis* of Jesus. *Anamnesis* in the biblical sense means not only the subjective representation of something in the consciousness and as an act of the remembering mind. It is also the objective effectiveness and presence of one reality in another, especially the effectiveness and presence of the salvific actions of God, in the liturgical worship. Even in the OT, the liturgy is the privileged medium in which the covenant attains actuality.

The meaning of the logion may perhaps be paraphrased as follows: do this (what I have done) in order to bring about my presence, to make really present the salvation wrought in me.

Besides the narratives of the institution, the NT itself explains Jesus' act in a way which is fundamental and normative for all exegesis and dogmatic theology. Paul affirms the bodily real presence of Jesus when he teaches that the bread which is broken and the cup which is blessed is a sharing (κοινωνία) in the body and blood of Jesus (1 Cor 10:16); when he concludes to the unity of all Christians as one single body (of Christ) from their partaking of the one bread (1 Cor 10:17); and when he points to the unworthy reception of the body of Jesus as explanation of certain judgments of God (1 Cor 11:27–31). Insofar as he places the Lord's Supper in relation to Jewish and heathen sacrificial meals (1 Cor 10:18–22), he presents it as a sacrificial action. A sacrificial meal presupposes and brings with it the killing of the victim. John does not give an account of the institution, but he gives a detailed proclamation of the Eucharist in the great promissory discourse of 6:26–63, which is conceived throughout in the perspective of the sacrament. Its theme is the true bread of heaven. The spiritual reality of this bread – its heavenly origin and its power to mediate life — is there in the historical man Jesus (Jn 6:26–51 b), but the physical reality, as food in the literal sense, is there in his "flesh" (σάρξ) which is intended for the life of the world and which one must really eat ("chew"), just as one must also drink his blood as real drink (6:51c–58). Such partaking, however, presupposes the sacrifice. The surprising term σάρξ, even in connection with "blood", is not a sacrificial element distinct from the blood, but the whole concrete man Jesus, as 1:14 and the personal pronoun (he who partakes of "me") in 6:57 show. In the Eucharist, the descent of Jesus from the heavenly world, his incarnation for the purpose of the sacrificial offering, remain present (6:57f.). But the ascension of Jesus is also effective there (6:62), since the ascension alone makes the sending of the Spirit possible (7:38; 16:7) and hence also our sacramental meal (6:63). For the element which really mediates life there is not the flesh as such but the accompanying Spirit, by which the Godhead in Jesus is meant (cf. 1 Cor 15:45). For John too the Eucharist remains the presence, in the liturgical meal, of the economy of salvation which is "Jesus".

C. The Liturgical Form of the Eucharist in the Church

The essentials of the Lord's Supper were unalterably prescribed for the Church by Jesus, the consecration of the bread and wine to be his body and blood and their distribution to be eaten and drunk. This decisive core was given a liturgical framework which underwent a development. The oldest community celebrated the sacrament (as did Jesus at the institution) in connection with a fraternal repast and in the order which Jesus observed: bread — repast — cup (cf. the indication: "after the meal", 1 Cor 11:25; Lk 22:20). But very soon the sacramentally significant actions with the bread and wine were brought together and placed at the end of the meal, a process reflected in the accounts of the institution in Mk and Mt and also in *Didache*, 10, 1. In the further course of the development, the actual sacramental action was separated from the repast and combined with the morning liturgy of the word. Thus arose the classical form of the Eucharist which is still in use today, the "Mass" which is discernible in Justin's time, *c.* 160 (*Apologia,* I, 67). This liturgical form is an expression of the conviction that the sacrament should only be celebrated in the fullness of faith, which is nourished by the word of God. The Lord's Supper was celebrated at first (preferably) on the Lord's day, the Sunday (Acts 20:7; *Didache,* 14, 1; Justin, *Apologia,* I, 67), and in the 4th century also on Wednesday and Friday, and later daily (first attested by Augustine). The most obvious as well as the most fundamental characteristic of the celebration was that it was a meal. This stood out even more clearly when the participants brought with them, and provided for, the gifts which made up the meal. The Church expresses the meaning of their action in words, in the prayers said at the Lord's Supper. Very early the Church understood their action as *eucharistia,* as the grateful acknowledgment and acceptance of the salvation wrought by Christ, here symbolically made concrete and actual. The great prayer of the canon called down this salvation upon the gifts and asked that it should enter into them. Here the Eastern liturgies in particular dwell upon the whole salvific work of Christ, some more fully, like the liturgy of Hippolytus, the Clementine, the liturgy of St. James and the liturgy of St. Basil in Egypt, others in a short summary form (liturgy of the Apostles and of St. John Chrysostom). In the West, from the 4th century onwards, the Church year took on the form of a historical sequence of events, the redemption was divided up into individual themes and the particular mystery of each feast today was especially honoured in the "preface". The great prayer of thanksgiving culminates in the account of the institution. This places the death of Jesus in the middle of the action and consecrates the elements as the sacrificial gifts of Jesus. Hence, according to the Fathers, *eucharistia* means in effect the same thing as *anamnesis* and both terms signify an essential characteristic of the sacrament. Under this aspect it is the symbolic anamnesis by which the sacrifice of Jesus Christ is made present. Yet the manner in which this re-presentation is achieved does not consist in the liturgical words alone, but also in the action of the Church, namely, in its offering, and this points to a second basic characteristic of the Eucharist. From the beginning, appealing to Mal 1:11f., the Church asserts that in the Eucharist it also sacrifices. It sees in its spiritual thanksgiving which refers all things back to God, and also in the provision and offering of the material elements which make possible the celebration of the sacrament, a sacrifice offered by Christians. But this action of the Church was not intended as the establishment of an independent sacrifice beside that of Christ. On principle and from the start, it was done only to render visible and to appropriate the sacrifice of Christ. For a liturgical offering of gifts, in which the Church also offers itself, is well able to represent the sacrificial act of Jesus. The offering of the gifts is essentially an anamnesis of this, as the liturgy itself affirms as it reflects on the narrative of institution: *unde et memores passionis et resurrectionis . . . offerimus de tuis donis.*

In the framework of the *Eucharistia,* and by virtue of the *Eucharistia,* of which the essential centre is the narrative of institution, the presence of the body and blood of Jesus also comes about, by the consecration and change of the gifts of food. Hence the Eastern liturgies continue the reflection "unde et memores" with the epiclesis for the consecration (change) of the gifts. In explaining the epiclesis we should note that in this whole section the Church is reflecting on its previous action and bringing its character explicitly to mind. Thus the epiclesis, even in the form of a petition, is not what first brings about the consecration. It simply tries to give expression to the consecratory power and purpose of the whole action, especially to the *Eucharistia* which is concentrated in the narrative of institution. The food-offering thus accomplished has its due and necessary conclusion in the sacrificial meal. The nature of the essential sign (the meal) demands that no mass should be without a communion, at least that of the priest who also represents the people. Up to the 12th century the faithful, even in the Latin Church, communicated under both species. Since then, for practical reasons, the practice of Communion under one species has prevailed. It had always been in use for small children, the sick, and in general for all who received Communion at home. The dogmatic justification for it — rather than the real reason for introducing it — was the doctrine then worked out about concomitance. This means that along with *(per concomitantiam)* the body (blood) which is present by virtue of transubstantiation, the blood (body), soul and divinity of Jesus are also present. A new era began with Vatican II, when it allowed Communion under both species in certain cases, concelebration and the use of the vernacular, and indeed by its

reflection on the essential characteristics of the Eucharist.

D. Official Pronouncements

The Church expresses its understanding of the Eucharist most deeply and most comprehensively in the liturgy, which is an important expression of the ordinary magisterium. The extraordinary magisterium has done justice to this perspective in our own day in Vatican II's Constitution on the Liturgy (cf. previously Pius XII, *Mediator Dei*). Earlier Councils, when rejecting distortions and heretical errors, made infallible pronouncements (which, however, also admit of development) upon certain central aspects of the sacrament; as at the 4th Lateran Council, and at Constance and Trent (sess. XIII, XXI, XXII). The Councils for unity, Lyon II (1275) and Florence, formulated the scholastic understanding of the faith for the Eastern Churches. In the early Middle Ages, the symbolism so strongly underlined by Augustine was exaggerated, and the real presence of Christ was reduced to a merely symbolic and spiritual one, in reaction against a too crudely physical view. This was done in a mild and restrained form in the first Eucharistic controversy, by Ratramnus (opposed by Paschasius Radbertus) but in an extreme and heretical form in the second, by Berengarius of Tours (opposed in particular by Durandus of Troarn, Lanfranc and Guitmund of Aversa). After several local synods had pronounced on the matter, the fourth Lateran finally defined the identity of the consecrated gifts with the historical body and blood of Christ, by virtue of transubstantiation, the change of the being of the natural elements into the being of the body and blood of Christ (*D* 430, *DS* 802). This teaching was re-affirmed and made more precise by the Council of Constance against Wycliffe (*D* 581ff., *DS* 1151ff., *D* 626f., *DS* 1198f.) and Huss (*D* 666f., *DS* 1256f.), by the Council of Trent against the Reformers, among whom Zwingli and Calvin denied the real presence while Luther admitted only consubstantiation. In the Eucharist the body and the blood of Jesus is contained not only after the manner of a sign or in its efficacy, but truly, really and substantially by virtue of transubstantiation; only the species of bread and wine remain. Under each form (as already in *D* 626, *DS* 1199), and indeed in each part of them there is the whole Christ, not only for the duration of the partaking but also present and worthy of adoration previous to this and after it. The whole Christ is really partaken of (*D* 883–90, *DS* 1651–8), and in the Latin Church is legitimately received by the faithful under one species only (*D* 934 ff., *DS* 1731 ff.). Against all the Reformers, the dogmatic teaching of Trent (sess. XXII) is that the Mass is not merely a sacrifice of praise and thanksgiving and not merely a commemoration of the offering of the cross, but a real and proper sacrifice in which the priest offers the body and blood of Christ. It is an expiatory sacrifice for the living and the dead, though it is no affront to or encroachment upon the sacrifice of the cross (*D* 948–62, *DS* 1751–5). It is the representation of that of the cross, its memorial and application, as was explained though not formally defined (*D* 938, *DS* 1740). Christ remains the same victim and the same priest as on the cross, though now acting through the priest; only the manner of offering is different (*D* 940, *DS* 1743). This implies the identity of the sacrificial action then and now, which is explicitly affirmed in the *Catechismus Romanus*, II, 4, 74. According to Pius XII (*Mediator Dei, D* 2300, *DS* 3848), the separate presentation of the body and blood of Christ in the consecration represents their separation in death.

The sacrament is effected only by the consecrated priest (Lat. IV: *D* 430, *DS* 802), independent of his personal holiness (Constance: *D* 584, *DS* 1154), essentially in the consecration (Pius XII, *D* 2300, *DS* 3852; Vatican II, Constitution on the Church, arts. 10, 28). Pius XII and especially Vatican II stress the active co-operation of the faithful in the offering of the Eucharist. They offer not merely through the priest but along with him (*D* 2300, *DS* 3852; Vatican II, Constitution on the Liturgy, art. 48), give thanks and receive Holy Communion (Vatican II, Constitution on the Church, arts. 10 and 11). In view of certain modern trends which might fail to do justice to the nature of the Eucharist, Paul VI, in his encyclical *Mysterium Fidei* of 3 September 1965 (*AAS* 57 [1965], pp. 753–74), inculcated once more the real presence (of the body and blood of Christ) by virtue of transubstantiation, calling for the retention of the traditional Church terminology in this matter. He also re-affirmed the continuation of the presence of Christ in the Eucharist after Mass and the rightfulness of adoration by Christians, and also of private Masses. A mere "transignification or transfinalization", by which bread and wine receive a new significance as signs of the self-dedication of Jesus in the Eucharist, are not enough to explain the Eucharist. On the contrary, the new significance and purpose of the sign comes from the fact that it contains, by virtue of transubstantiation, a new ontic reality.

E. Theological Explanations

Theology, which is obliged to seek a deeper *intellectus fidei,* must develop in a systematic way a comprehensive and well-balanced understanding of the Eucharist in all its aspects — one that preserves the richness of its content, grasps its essential structure, explains its many aspects and arranges them properly in the structure of the whole. As the most intimate and most intensive confrontation of the glorified Christ with the Christian still on his pilgrimage, it cannot be adequately treated of in objective and static categories but must also be interpreted in personal and dynamic ones, though mere symbolism and functionalism must be avoided. In it man is confronted by the glorified Lord not in his proper (glorified) form but in another, a symbolic form, which he assumes as the outward expression of his own self, both revealing and veiling himself, in the sacramental symbol of a meal. In this meal the glorified Lord makes present for us and effectively applies to us here and now the self-sacrifice of his own life by which he accomplished the salvation of all once for all. That he presents his sacrifice in the manner of a meal is not a purely arbitrary decree; it rests, rather, upon a certain intrinsic analogy between the two. The connection between them was prefigured in the history of salvation in the OT food-offerings, of which the Roman canon mentions those of Abel, Abraham, and Melchisedech, and in the bloody sacrifice of animals which were concluded by a sacrificial meal. The relation is factually based on the fitness of food to express the self-surrender of an offerer, the giving of himself for others, and his fellowship with them. The meal also receives a directly sacrificial character through the offering of its elements to God — as was practised already in Judaism and by Jesus. Thus the bloody sacrifice of Jesus is fittingly represented as a food sacrifice and as a sacrificial meal, as an offering and a distribution of the elements of a meal. The active character of the Eucharist as a coming of Christ to us is also indicated in the fact that its "presence" suggests not only a passive or static nearness in space, but also Christ's "presenting" himself to us and proffering his saving action to us (compare the relevant verb *praesentare* in the Latin and Romance languages).

The "pneumatic" Christ is present in the celebration of the Eucharist as the *minister principalis,* as the high-priest who offers himself, and as the giver of the feast who gives himself as food. We could define this presence as the "principal actual presence of the person of Christ" (as the sacrificial *subject*). It is mediated and visibly represented by the salvific reality of the Church, which is the earthly mode of the manifestation of the heavenly high-priesthood of Christ, whose "Body" is the fundamental sacrament of redemption. To this Church he bequeathed his bloody sacrifice as an unbloody sacrificial rite (cf. Trent, *D* 938, *DS* 1740). The local community is representative of the whole Church. However, if the sacrifice of the faithful is to be really identical with the sacrifice of Christ, the participants must have a cultic bond with the high-priesthood of Christ. They must really participate in it. This is the "sacramental character" which is conferred in varying degrees of intensity by baptism, confirmation, and orders. It indicates membership of the Church and thereby enables one to participate in worship. The character conferred by priestly ordination justifies the full actualization of the sacrifice of Christ. "Through the ministry of the priest" Christ now offers his sacrifice (*D* 940, *DS* 1743), just as the priest officiates *in persona Christi* (*D* 698, *DS* 1321; Vatican II, Constitution on the Church, art. 28) and *in virtute Christi.* The character given in baptism and (in a stronger measure) in confirmation enables Christians to be co-offerers at the sacrifice, thanksgiving, and Communion. According to Vatican II (Constitution on the Liturgy, art. 48), the faithful also offer the unblemished sacrifice not only through the priest, but together with him, and thereby offer it themselves (*ibid.,* Constitution on the Church, arts. 10, 11).

The celebrating community not only receives the fruits of redemption in the form of a meal, it also actively concurs in and follows out the very deed of redemption, it ratifies for itself after the event the sacrifice of Jesus accomplished previously and without its assistance. The community acknowledges it as something done not only for its good but also in its stead, and appropriates, makes visible and fruitful, this sacrifice of Christ through the symbol of the meal, by offering, consecrating and receiving the elements. The community thereby adds nothing to the value of the work of Christ. Its merit consists in laying hold of the merit of Christ as the only way of salvation. Its real sacrifice is not an attempt at self-salvation nor a repetition of the sacrifice of the cross, but rather its visible representation and appropriation here and now. The Church in this way realizes its nature most deeply in the Eucharist.

But if the faithful are to re-enact the one sacrifice of Jesus Christ, not only must their being receive its essential stamp from the person of Christ as the Saviour (in the sacramental meal), but their activity must receive that stamp from the salvific deed of Christ. This results from the fact that the faithful celebrate the Eucharist principally as the *anamnesis* of the work of redemption. *Anamnesis* here means not only the subjective presence in the consciousness of the participants, but the objective presence, in actual reality in the acts and words of worship. Further, *anamnesis* is not merely a given part of the Mass, but an essential and basic trait which dominates it from the beginning to the end, and is then expressly formulated and reflected upon in various places (especially in the "unde et memores". As *anamnesis,* the Eucharist is the actual presence of the sacrificial deed of Jesus which begins with the incarnation and reaches its culmination on the cross, in the death and the exaltation of Jesus. It is signalled in the Offertory which is modelled on the basic act of worship and in which the Church co-offers its own self, it is invoked upon and into the elements in the words of thanksgiving, the essential being the account of the institution, the constitutive *forma sacramenti.* The priest narrates the institution over the elements, in the words of Jesus himself. Thus officiating *in persona Christi,* he alone appears as fully representative of Jesus and only through his words, supported by the power of Christ, does the sacrificial gift of the Church become identical with the sacrificial gift which Jesus himself is as man. Thus too the sacrificial action of the Church shows itself to be one with the sacrificial action of Jesus. The double consecration, whether understood as Jesus' complete and sovereign disposition of his body and blood, or, according to Mk 14:24, as the separation of both vital elements, at any rate symbolizes and actualizes the death of Jesus by effecting the presence of Jesus as victim, as σῶμα διδόμενον and αἷμα ἐχυννόμενον. The actual presence of the sacrificial deed of Jesus objectifies itself in the (somatic) real presence of his person as the victim (sacrificial *object*) and is rooted in it. The real presence, however, comes about within the horizon of and as a moment of the sacrificial event.

This fact, which is significant for the basic structure of the Eucharist, may also be seen from the following considerations. Acceptance by God is essential to a sacrifice; a real sacrifice is a sacrifice accepted by God. God accepts the sacrifice of the Church because it is the sacrifice of Christ made present. Just as he accepted Jesus' sacrifice on the cross and, as a sign of this, gave his body new life in the resurrection, so too he accepts the sacrifice of the Church which is identical with that of Jesus and fills it with Jesus' life, transforms it into the bodily person of Jesus. The consecration concerns the "substance", which in this context means the meta-empirical, proper, ultimate essential being of the natural sensible elements of bread and wine. This is transformed and translated into the being of the bodily person of Jesus. The outward appearance (species, sight) of the food, however, remains, and signifies the bodily presence of Christ and its final purpose, namely partaking of it. For food is to be consumed. The consecration is thus the preparation for the sacrificial meal in which the sacrificial action is brought to completion. The sacrificial gift, however, stands for the giver and its acceptance by God means in principle the acceptance also of the giver, which (in this order of salvation) is the self-communication of God to the person. In the communion, man enters into closest union with the sacrificial offering of Christ and through it is united with the Father. The somatic real presence of Jesus makes possible the deepest confrontation of Christ with Christians and the Communion, the final end in any case of the symbolic meal, the indispensable act at least of the priest, completes it as an essential, not merely an integrating part (so Pius XII, *DS* 3854) of the sacrifice of the Eucharist. The basic structure, accordingly, is the presence of the sacrificial act of Jesus in a manner through which we can assimilate it and appropriate it, in a sacrificial meal.

If we inquire after the inner reasons whereby a past event can become actually present again, we must first consider the nature of the acting subject. As the actions of the eternal person of the Logos, the saving deeds of Jesus have a perennial quality and are always simultaneous with passing finite time. Besides this, they are also somehow taken up into the glorified humanity of Jesus which, according to St. Thomas (*Summa Theologica*, III, 62, 5; 64, 3), remains the efficacious *instrumentum coniunctum* of the exalted Lord. Those past salvific actions, being taken up into the divine person as also into the human nature of Jesus, can now assume a new spatio-temporal presence — in and through a "symbolic reality". This is an entity in which another being enters and reveals itself, is and acts. The real essence of the symbol as symbol is not its own physical reality, but the manifestation and presentation of the primary reality which is symbolized in it. In virtue of his *potestas auctoritatis,* Jesus so incorporated the supper into his sacrificial act that the sacrificial act is accomplished in and finds its visible expression in the supper.

In the setting and as an element of the presentation and application of the sacrificial act of Jesus comes now the somatically real presence of Jesus as victim. The whole Christ is truly, really and substantially present under both species and in each of their parts, beyond the duration of the Mass, so long as the species, the empirical realities of bread and wine as food remain. The presence of Christ in this manner is worthy of adoration, an adoration that should not, however, lose sight of the connection with the sacrifice of Jesus. The Scholastics, who did not use the terms *corpus* and *sanguis* in the comprehensive biblical sense of a bodily person but rather in the limited sense of the physically separate elements of body and blood, established the totality of the presence of

Jesus with the help of the idea of concomitance (the blood belongs to the body, the soul to both of them, and the Godhead to the humanity of Jesus). Communion under one species results from practical considerations and is dogmatically defensible, though it corresponds less to the ideal liturgical form of Communion. The effecting of the somatically real presence of Jesus has been expressed in dogma since Lateran IV and Trent by the concept (which belongs rather to popularized philosophy) of transubstantiation (change of substance). What is the object of the dogma and what is infallibly expressed by this term, however, is not a given notion of substance and the expression for it as is found in natural philosophy such as that of Aristotle, but only the truth of faith that to the actual somatic real presence of Jesus under the species, there corresponds an ontic situation in which the meta-empirical being of the consecrated elements (that which makes them what they now are) is no longer their previous being as the natural elements bread and wine, but the being of the body and blood of Christ — that the natural being which they have had up to now, has been made over and is changed. How this change is to be explained in terms of natural philosophy depends on philosophical presuppositions which are not defined, i.e., how one is to understand concretely the concept of physical substance and how the empirical appearance of bread and wine is to be understood in relation to it. Explanatory attempts in this direction are but *theologumena* which have their own worth and rights, but which are not those of dogma.

In view of what has been said, the Eucharist appears (in general) as the sacramental presence and application of the event universally decisive for salvation, the sacrifice "Jesus", in the Church's sacrificial meal which he himself instituted. It is the greatest gift of the Lord, the initial transfiguration of worldly things, the inclusion even of the body in the glory of salvation, the bond of the most intimate unity of man with God and of men with each other, through Christ. It is an essential principle of the spatial and temporal catholicity of the Church and its most profound reality.

See also *Sacraments, Communion under Both Kinds, Demythologization* I, *Passover, Liturgy* I, II, *Symbol, Dogma* I, *Theologumenon.*

BIBLIOGRAPHY. GENERAL: *Catholicisme,* IV, cols. 630–59; A. Piolanti, ed., *Eucaristia* (1957); *RGG,* I, cols. 10–51; J. Betz in *LTK,* III, cols. 1142–57 (with older literature); I. Biffi, ed., *Enciclopedia Eucaristica* (1964); "Le Mystère Chrétien", *Théologie sacramentaire,* Iff. (Tournai 1961 ff.); J. de Baciocchi, *L'Eucharistie* (1964). ON SECTION A: J. Betz, *Die Eucharistie in der Zeit der griechischen Väter,* I (1955); J.-P. Audet, "Literary Forms and Contents of a Normal Εὐχαριστία in the First Century", *TU* 73 (1959), pp. 643–62. ON SECTION B: H. Schürmann, *Der Paschamahlbericht Lk 22, (7–14) 15–18* (1953); id., *Der Einsetzungsbericht Lk 22, 19–20* (1955); J. Jeremias, *Die Abendmahlsworte Jesu* (3rd ed., 1960), E. T.: *The Eucharistic Words of Jesus* (1966); P. Neuenzeit, *Das Herrenmahl* (1960); E. Käsemann, "Anliegen und Eigenart der Paulinischen Abendmahlslehre", *Exegetische Versuche und Besinnungen,* I (1960; 3rd ed., 1964), pp. 11–34; J. Betz, *Die Eucharistie in der Zeit der griechischen Väter,* II/1 (2nd ed., 1964); N. Hook, *The Eucharist in the New Testament* (1964); E. Käsemann, *Essays on New Testament Themes* (1964); P. Benoît and others, *Eucharist in the New Testament* (1964). ON SECTION C: J. Jungmann, *Missarum sollemnia,* 2 vols. (1949), E. T.: *The Mass of the Roman Rite* (1951); P. Tihon, "De la concélébration eucharistique", *NRT* 86 (1964), pp. 579–607; J. C. McGowein, *Concelebration* (1964). ON SECTION D: F. Holboeck, *Der eucharistische und der mystische Leib Christi* (1941); H. de Lubac, *Corpus mysticum* (2nd ed., 1948); G. Aulen, *Eucharist and Sacrifice* (1958); R. Schulte, *Die Messe als Opfer der Kirche* (1959); M. Thurian, *L'Eucharistie* (1959); E. Gonzáles, *El Sacrificio dela Misa a la luz del Concilio de Trento* (1960); G. Niemeier, *Lehrgespräch über das Heilige Abendmahl,* Arnoldshainer Thesen (1961); F. Clark, *Eucharistic Sacrifice and the Reformation* (1961); A. Frenay, *The Spirituality of the Mass in the Light of Thomistic Theology* (1963); B. Neunheuser, *Eucharistie in Mittelalter und Neuzeit,* Handbuch der Dogmengeschichte, ed. by M. Schmaus and A. Grillmeier (1951 ff.); E. Mascall, *Corpus Christi* (new ed., 1965). ON SECTION E: I. Filograssi, *De sanctissima Eucharistia* (6th ed., 1957); A. Piolanti, *Il misterio Eucaristico* (2nd ed., 1958); P. Meinhold and E. Iserloh, *Abendmahl und Opfer* (1960); M. Schmaus, ed., *Aktuelle Fragen zur Eucharistie* (1960); F. Wengier, *The Eucharistic Sacrament* (1960); D. Fandal, *The Essence of the Eucharistic Sacrifice* (1961); G. Sola, *Tractatus dogmaticus de Eucharistia* (1961); C. Vollert, "The Eucharist. Controversy on Transubstantiation", *TS* 22 (1961), pp. 391–425; E. James, *Sacrifice and Sacrament* (1962); J. Megivern, *Concomitance and Communion. A Study in Eucharistic Doctrine and Practice* (1963); R. Vossebrecher, *Transsubstantiation et présence réelle face aux problèmes modernes* (dissertation, Freiburg, 1963); P. Pfeiffer, *Die Thesen der Konfessionen zur Anbetung des Altarsakramentes,* Una Sancta 17 (1962), pp. 225–66; L. Lécuyer, *Le sacrifice de la Nouvelle Alliance* (1962); K. Rahner, *Schriften zur Theologie,* II, pp. 191–202; IV (1962), pp. 275–387, E. T.: *Theological Investigations* II, IV (1966); J. Galot, *Eucharistie vivante* (1963); id., "Théologie de la présence eucharistique", *NRT* 85 (1963), pp. 19–39; M. Matthijs, *De aeternitate Sacerdotii Christi et de unitate sacrificii Christi et altaris* (1963); J. Tillard, *L'Eucharistie, Pâque de l'Église* (1964), E. T,: *Eucharist, Pasch of God's People* (1967); O. Müller, "Die Eucharistie als Mahlopfer und Opfermahl", *Gott in Welt, Festgabe Karl Rahner,* II (1964), pp. 121–34; E. Schillebeeckx, "Christus' tegenwoordigheid in de Eucharistie", *Tijdschrift voor Theologie* 5 (1965), pp. 136–73; R. Tartre, *Eucharist Today* (1967); J. Powers, *Eucharistic Theology* (1967).

Johannes Betz

II. Liturgical

The Mass is the celebration of the Eucharist in the various forms prescribed by the Church. These forms enshrine and explicitate something considered in tradition as the command of the Lord: the utterance in thanksgiving of the sacramental words over bread and wine, and the eating and drinking of the consecrated gifts.

A. Various Names for the Mass

The various *names* for the Mass which have been used from the beginning give us an idea of how these forms developed. In the primitive Church, Mass was called the "Lord's Supper" (1 Cor 11:20) or the "breaking of bread" (Acts 2:42, 46; 20:7), since it continued the Last Supper and the act Christ instituted there in bread and wine. Before long we also find the term εὐχαριστία, which is taken from the biblical account of the institution (1 Cor 11:24; Lk 22:19) and stresses the element of prayer. By the end of the 1st century εὐχαριστία was the usual expression and was soon applied to sacramental gifts resulting from the celebration. But the early Latins already began to call the Mass a sacrifice: for St. Cyprian and St. Augustine it is *sacrificium,* for Aetheria and St. Ambrose *oblatio,* like προσφορά among the Greeks. Similarly the Syrians speak of *kurobho* or *korbono:* Mass is the gift, with which one "approaches" the divine majesty. Other names stress the fact that Mass is a celebration for which the community assembles; it is called σύναξις, *collecta; processio* too was used in this sense (Aetheria). The term λειτουργία, which finally prevailed among the Greeks, has the same signification: Mass is the work or service that is performed on behalf of the people or with the people. When we encounter terms like *officium,* (divine) service, High Mass, it is plain to see that set forms are involved. But other names current in the early Church, though they indicate the kernel of the Mass, leave us none the wiser as to its general structure — *dominicum,* "the Lord's" celebration, in the acts of the martyrs, or simply "the holy thing" in the Semitic languages (Arabic *kuddas;* cf. Hebrew *kadosch*). Much the same can be said of *missa,* Mass, which came into use in the 5th century and has been practically the only term in the West ever since (though the old "offering" prevailed in the Celtic Church; cf. the modern Irish "aifreann"). Originally *missa* (= missio = dimissio) meant dismissal. In ecclesiastical usage it meant the closing act of a celebration, which usually involved a blessing. Either the blessing or the celebration itself might be called *missa.* In the end the word was applied only to the eucharistic celebration, to emphasize the blessing for human life which it contained.

B. Early Structure of the Mass

We can only gather from certain hints how Mass was said in the early Church. At first it was associated with a meal, a supper (δεῖπνον, *coena*), since by custom supper was the principal meal of the day in the West. In such a setting Mass was instituted, as St. Paul plainly tells us in 1 Cor 11. No doubt the bread was consecrated at the beginning of the meal, in accordance with the Jewish custom of breaking bread: the father of the family started the meal by breaking the bread and distributing it with a blessing to those at table. Only "after supper" (1 Cor 11:25) was the chalice consecrated, when it was the Jewish custom to pour the third cup of wine and say a solemn prayer of thanksgiving. Between these two acts the meal took its course along the formal lines such as we know from the later *agape* (one spoke, for example, only when addressed by the person at the head of the table), and which were usual at that period (cf. the Qumran texts).

The two sacramental acts must very soon have been brought together, with the result that the Eucharist could be held either before or after the meal, or even separated from it altogether. Analysis of the forms of Mass known to us has shown that the primitive Mass must have comprised seven parts: the taking of bread, a prayer of thanksgiving, Fraction, Communion; taking of the chalice, a prayer of thanksgiving, and Communion. When the two acts were brought together, the seven parts were reduced to four: the taking of bread and the chalice (Offertory), the prayer of thanksgiving, Fraction, and Communion. Dom Gregory Dix, the Anglican liturgical scholar, thinks that a change of such magnitude, universally accepted without demur, can only have been introduced in a place that enjoyed great authority by the end of the 1st century: the Rome of Peter and Paul.

During the 2nd and 3rd centuries the outlines of the eucharistic service become clearly visible. The meal has disappeared. The prayer of thanksgiving is now the chief feature of the rite. Bread and wine are brought out; the prayer of thanksgiving said over them is ratified by the people's Amen; then all present receive Communion. This is the picture of the Mass that we find in Justin Martyr about the year 150. He gives us two descriptions of the Eucharist, one as celebrated after a baptism and one on a Sunday. A text put forward as a model by Hippolytus of Rome about 215 tallies perfectly with Justin and is so instructive that it deserves to be quoted *verbatim*. When the gifts have been brought to the bishop, he stretches out his hands over them and begins: "The Lord be with you." The people answer: "And with thy spirit." "Lift up your hearts." "We lift them up unto the Lord." "Let us give thanks to our Lord." "It is meet and right so to do." The bishop then continues: "We give thee thanks, O God, through thy beloved servant Jesus Christ, whom thou didst send to us in these last days to be our deliverance and our Redeemer and to make known thy counsel. He is thy inseparable Word: through him thou didst make all things and sawest that they were good. Thou didst send him from heaven into the bosom of the Virgin. In her bosom he became flesh and was revealed as thy Son, born of the Holy Ghost and the Virgin. Accomplishing thy will and winning for thee a holy people, he stretched forth his hands in torments to deliver those from torment who should believe in him. And when he was being delivered up to suffer according to his own will, so as to conquer death, to burst the bonds of Satan, to trample underfoot the nether world, to enlighten the just, to set up a landmark, and to proclaim the resurrection, he took bread and giving thanks to thee he

said: 'Take, eat, this is my body which is broken for you.' Likewise the cup, saying: 'This is my blood which is poured out for you. When you do this you do it in remembrance of me.' Mindful, therefore, of his death and resurrection, we offer thee the bread and the cup; giving thee thanks, that thou mayest find us worthy to stand before thee and serve thee. And we beseech thee to send down the Holy Ghost upon the offering of holy Church. Gathering them together in unity, mayest thou grant all the saints who partake of it the fullness of the Holy Ghost, strengthening their faith in the truth, that we may praise and bless thee through thy servant Jesus Christ, through whom be all honour and glory unto thee, the Father and the Son with the Holy Ghost, in thy holy Church both now and forevermore." "Amen."

Though details of the service were left to the discretion of the celebrant, especially the phrasing of the prayers, the whole Christian world must have celebrated the Eucharist in much this form until well into the 4th century.

Here the question arises which has been widely debated for the last twenty or thirty years: what is the basic and permanent structure of the Mass that existed from the beginning, that remained intact through all the subsequent changes, and that must come clearly to the fore in any reform of the Mass we may embark on now? Scripture seems to describe nothing more than a meal, a company about a table with bread and wine that is blessed and distributed. The sacrificial character of the proceeding, central as it is, in no way obtrudes. Yet by Justin's time the celebration has become a gathering for prayer. Bread and wine are still there on the table but those present are not a dinner-party, they have come together to worship God. All later forms of the Eucharist are dominated by the prayer of thanksgiving and the offering of the gifts that logically precedes it. So plainly does the opening *Gratias agamus* refer to this offering that the Mass of the East Syrian rite transforms it into: "Let the sacrifice be offered up to God the Lord of the universe." It would seem best, then, to stress the mention of thanksgiving (εὐχαριστήσας), even in the biblical account of the institution, bearing in mind that a gesture of oblation was certainly made with the cup, and probably with the bread as well: it was the custom for the father to raise the cup a hands-breadth above the table, that is, to offer it. Thus the prayer of thanksgiving said over the gifts emerges as the basic structure.

The Eucharist was celebrated every Sunday (but on few other occasions), attended by the whole Christian community of the neighbourhood, early in the morning (now that it was separated from the meal) before work; Sunday was an ordinary workday for the public.

For the Sunday Justin mentions another element which served as an introduction: "the memoirs of the apostles or the writings of the prophets" were read, then there was a sermon by the president of the assembly, and a prayer for general needs concluded the introduction. This means that part of the traditional service of the synagogue must have continued in use as an independent rite among Jewish Christians, since it was first incorporated into Sunday Mass and then, in the 4th century, became a feature of every Mass. The underlying thought was plainly that hearing the sacred word would best prepare Christians for the sacred action. There are also various indications that the Offertory procession began as early as the 3rd century. Giving the faithful the special role of presenting the material gifts of bread and wine for the Eucharist seems to have been a conscious reaction against Gnosis, which despised material creation and taught that it was evil.

C. EVOLUTION SINCE THE FOURTH CENTURY

With the peace of the Church, the form in which the Eucharist was celebrated began to vary considerably from one country or culture to another, branching out into the various liturgies which are discussed in the article "Liturgy". Here we shall consider how the elements of the original eucharistic rite became diversified in different places. What we shall call the fore-Mass so as to emphasize the unity of the whole proceeding (it is also known as the Mass of the Catechumens, in contrast to the Mass of the Faithful, the Sacrifice), consists principally of readings, and even in St. Augustine's day still began with these. But very early all liturgies developed an introduction to the readings. The *Canones Basilii* (6th century) indicate that the introduction is not yet part of the Mass proper: they say that as long as people are

still coming into church "psalms should be read". But this reading, in the Mass of Byzantium and the East Syrian rite, became a formal office composed of three psalms, which has a certain parallel in the Egyptian liturgies with their three *orationes*. Throughout the East these introductory prayers are themselves preceded at every Mass by a solemn incensation, a consecration of the altar and Church — sometimes of the congregation too —, as a rule amid prayers and hymns. Nor is this all. The incensation is preceded in the Byzantine rite, for example, by the πρόθεσις, a preparation of the bread and wine under the figure of "the slaughter of the Lamb", with many prayers and scriptural quotations, following another series of prayers and rites that accompany the vesting of the celebrant and the washing of his hands. They serve to prepare him for Mass, and to venerate the sacred icons. Only after all these preliminaries comes the ceremonial procession in which the book of the gospels is solemnly borne to the sanctuary, to the accompaniment of the Trisagion, or some other hymn, so that the readings may begin.

The Roman introduction to the readings, on the other hand, is only a short procession, even at Solemn High Mass where it includes incensation of the altar. Basically the ceremony is the same as that observed when a bishop or other prelate enters a church outside of Mass, as for a visitation: the procession is accompanied by singing, in this case the Introit; upon arrival at the altar there is a moment of silent prayer; then a collect (prayer) concludes the ceremony.

Readings from Scripture, the word of God, form the core of the fore-Mass in every liturgy. Hence it is often simply called "the liturgy of the word"; the faithful should be nourished at the table of the word before they are nourished at the sacramental table. Accordingly the ancient Church read the various books of the Bible one after the other and expounded them in homilies, except that as the liturgical year developed, particular texts were assigned to each feast or season: in Lent there were the books of Moses, in Holy Week Job, after Easter Acts, in Advent the prophets. From the Dark Ages onward it was the universal practice to appoint readings for the entire year, in such a way that a portion of the gospels was read at every Mass, preceded by at least one reading from some book of the Bible apart from the gospels. This practice follows the tradition of the synagogue, where each Sabbath there was one reading from the law and one from the prophets. Indeed the Jewish tradition is carried on intact by the Syrian liturgies, which have one reading each from the law and the prophets before the Epistle and Gospel. The Egyptian liturgies too have four readings, but all from the NT: one from St. Paul, one from the Catholic Epistles, one from Acts, and one from the Gospels. Probably the idea behind the Egyptian practice was that readings from the NT were more appropriate to the sacrifice of the NT. The present Roman rite takes this idea into account to the extent that on Sunday the Gospel is always preceded by a reading from the NT; indeed (except on Whitsunday) it is always from an apostolic letter, so that this reading is simply called "the Epistle".

It is only fitting that the congregation should respond, in prayer or song, to what is read to them in the liturgy; and in fact all rites contain such a response. Significantly, every rite has the Alleluia between the second and the last reading — the Gospel — plainly the people's part in a psalm, or the remnant of it. Here again we have a very ancient common tradition based on the service of the synagogue.

In all liturgies, as we might expect, a good deal of solemnity attends the reading of the Gospel: there are candles and incense: the reader is a person of special rank, stands in a prominent place, sings, kisses the book; the congregation stands. Before the Gospel, in the Egyptian liturgies, the book is borne three times round the altar. After the first few centuries and down to our own times we find little mention of the sermon which explains to the people what has been read. All liturgies have the people respond in unison with the Creed, but in most non-Roman rites this happens later in the Mass, just before the eucharistic prayer.

It is an ancient rule that the liturgy of the word should close with prayer. All liturgies have, or once had, a litany at this point for all the necessities of the Christian people. Originally it began, for instance, with a prayer for the catechumens, who were then dismissed; then came the "prayer of the faithful" strictly speaking for the ecclesiastical and civil authorities, the peace of Church and of State, and all temporal and spiritual necessities.

Bread and wine must be set in readiness for the sacrifice of the Mass. It seemed fitting that this action too should be made a ceremony, not only because the people's share in the sacrifice of Christ could be suitably expressed by material gifts from their hands, but also because the East early saw in these gifts a presage of the great King's coming. The former idea led to the offertory procession of the faithful, which was customary practically everywhere by the end of ancient times and in the Roman rite survived another thousand years. The latter idea blossomed richly in the East (if we except the East Syrian rite). Before Mass begins the bread and wine are prepared on a kind of credence table. Where the faithful shared in this ceremony, they had to present their gifts beforehand at the specified place. In the Byzantine rite the gifts are brought in a procession called the "Great Entry" (so called in contrast to the "Little Entry" mentioned above), preceded by acolytes with candles, while ancient hymns sing of the invisible hosts of angels. The procession makes its way through the body of the Church to the altar, where the gifts are set down, veiled, and incensed to the accompaniment of certain prayers. There is usually another preparatory rite, consisting of a symbolic ablution, and all Eastern liturgies have the kiss of peace, stylized in one form or another, which sometimes includes the people.

Now follows the Eucharist, in every rite and with little variation. We might say that the tone is set by the summons in the opening dialogue: "Let us give thanks to (εὐχαριστήσωμεν, hold the Eucharist in honour of) the Lord." The eucharistic prayer, the "Canon", begins. The thanksgiving is also praise and adoration, and in this sense rises to a climax, in every existing rite, at the Sanctus, which every liturgy too would have the people join in the singing. The Byzantine and Syrian tradition normally puts before the Sanctus a simple invocation to all the powers of heaven and earth and the angelic choirs to praise God, waiting until after the Sanctus to give him thanks for the mighty deeds of redemptive history and their fulfilment in Christ. Then follows the account of the Last Supper. The Egyptian and Latin tradition begins the eucharistic prayer with thanksgiving and a panegyrical exposition of the reasons why we must praise God. After the Sanctus (originally) there is a quick transition to the sacramental action: either "Heaven and earth are full of thy glory, and do thou also fill these gifts with thy blessing" (Egyptian liturgies and, substantially, many old Gallican formularies), or — thanksgiving merging into offering — "Wherefore, O merciful Father, we beseech thee to accept these gifts" *(Te igitur)*.

The account of the institution, originally transmitted in pre-biblical formulations, has been reverently supplemented and varies in detail from rite to rite; but today it always closely resembles one of the biblical accounts. While the Roman liturgy has hitherto stressed the holiness of this inner sanctuary, this deepest of mysteries, by saying the whole Canon in an undertone, the Eastern rites convey the same idea by loudly proclaiming the sacramental words. Hereupon the people as often as not cry Amen, or make a formal confession such as that in the Ethiopian Mass: "We proclaim thy death, thy holy resurrection; we believe in thy ascension, we praise thee . . ."

The admonition "Do this in remembrance of me" is followed in all liturgies by the anamnesis: We remember, we do this to commemorate thee. The liturgy can be content with a brief indication of this "memory" here, since the eucharistic (thanksgiving) prayer had to develop it more fully ("thank" and "think" are etymologically akin). The anamnesis now regularly develops instead the description of the sacred act: "we offer". It is remarkable that without any special mention of Christ's sacrifice, all liturgies speak simply of the sacrifice of the Church that is based upon Christ's, asking that God will graciously accept it. The sacrifice of Christ is not in need of acceptance; but the sacrifice of the Church and above all this particular sacrifice is linked to conditions for it to be pleasing.

The close of the eucharistic prayer now introduces the Communion, whereby the faithful partake of the offering — in other words, there is a sacrificial meal — begging God that the communicants may be filled with blessing and grace. Then the eucharistic prayer ends, as it did in the days of Hippolytus, with a solemn doxology.

This straightforward train of thought was early broken up by interpolations. First we have the petitions, spoken by the priest himself at the heart of the sanctuary so as to stress their urgency. From the 4th century onward we find them in every liturgy (except the old Gallican, where they occur only before the beginning of the Canon). They are inserted after the Consecration (Syrian and Byzantine liturgies), or before the Sanctus (in Egypt), or before and after the Consecration (Roman rite). The second interpolation is the *epiclesis* or solemn invocation of the Holy Ghost, which the Oriental rites developed, in the same period, out of the prayer for a fruitful Communion that we have mentioned.

What has been the history of the Communion itself? If not the most ancient, the Our Father is at any rate the most usual element in the preparation for Communion. It was placed here on account of the petition for bread, and also on account of the petition for the forgiveness of sins. In the East, as early as the 4th century, the celebrant said a preparatory prayer of his own and gave the communicants a preparatory blessing (which soon became a blessing of the congregation), crying "Holy things to the holy!" The fraction of the species of bread, coming immediately before or immediately after the ceremony aforesaid, has generally been embroidered with prayers as well. Hardly anywhere has the venerable rite kept its original significance of the distribution of Communion.

First the celebrant and the clergy communicate, then the people, normally to the accompaniment of a hymn. In early times the thirty-third psalm was a favourite for this occasion. After Communion the priest usually says a prayer of gratitude for the heavenly gift. This prayer is especially poignant in the East Syrian rite.

Then the ceremony usually ends rapidly with a valedictory blessing of the faithful (which some Oriental rites elaborate). Purification of the sacred vessels and disposal of any remaining particles commonly takes place after the liturgy proper.

D. Special Features of the Roman Mass

We have Hippolytus's description of Mass (see above) as it was celebrated when Greek was still used in the Church of Rome. The change-over to Latin must have occurred during the 3rd century. It appears that the Canon which we still use comprised the following elements about the year 370: Preface, *Te igitur, Quam oblationem*, the account of the institution with the three prayers that follow, and the final doxology. The text of the present Canon, which was settled by the year 600, and other texts, are preserved to us in manuscripts of the 7th and 8th centuries, mainly the work of Frankish scriptoria. The prayers of the priest survive in the sacramentaries, of which there are three: the Leonine (5th to 6th century), the somewhat later Gelasian, and the Gregorian (compiled by St. Gregory the Great, who died in 604). A special feature of the priestly prayers outside the Canon — an opening Collect, a Secret said over the elements after the Offertory, and a Post-Communion — is that they vary according to the liturgical season (as does the Preface of the Canon), even in the Gallican Mass. In addition both older sacramentaries generally have one or two *orationes* after the readings and before the Secret. Even in the most ancient sources the readings are normally restricted to an Epistle and a Gospel. The celebrant enters (Introit) to the accompaniment of alternating chants — apparently also edited by St. Gregory — which are preserved in the Antiphonary (the "Proprium"). Antiphons are also sung between the two readings (Gradual and Alleluia), and accompany the procession at the Offertory and the Communion. The people continued to answer the exhortations and prayers of the priest and to join in the Sanctus, which concludes the Preface in the West as well as the East from the 5th century onward. *Kyrie, Gloria,* and *Agnus Dei* were also for the people to sing, or for the clerics in choir (not, that is, for the *schola cantorum* who sang the antiphons): they form the "Ordinary" among the chants of the Mass. This form of the Mass, which took shape during the 6th or 7th century, has continued in use down to the present day. The elaborations which began in the Carolingian period left the basic structure untouched, merely filling in gaps.

The first part of the Mass, designed as a ceremonious entrance culminating in the Collect, was now preceded by the prayers at the foot of the altar, of which the kernel is the *Confiteor.* Originally the priest did no more than fall prostrate and wordless before the altar. The *Kyrie* too, vestige of an older litany that has been confined since the 8th century to nine invocations of Christ, should be regarded as the people's preparation for the priestly prayers, like the *Gloria* that is added on feast days.

A special feature of the liturgy of the word is that since about the year 1000 the different rank of the two readings has been made visible by the position assigned to each: if we look at the church from where the *cathedra* used to be and the crucifix now is, the Epistle is read on the left-hand side, the Gospel on the right. Hence the familiar terms Epistle side and Gospel side. Until the restoration of the *oratio communis* by the Second Vatican Council, all that survived of the closing prayer was the one word *Oremus,* for the Secret that is structurally part of it had become a prayer over the offerings. Until the dawn of modern times the Offertory procession of the faithful was basic to the Roman Mass (originally they brought the bread and wine to the altar, later it was money; in the end the procession was only held on a few special feasts). The silent prayers which are still said during the arrangement of the gifts on the altar are a 9th-century contribution from Northern Europe.

As early as the 6th century the principle that the Preface — first part of the eucharistic prayer — should be different for each Mass was grievously breached: henceforth only the great solemnities had special Prefaces, forms of thanksgiving which illustrated redemptive history. Frankish misinterpretation of the name (*praefatio* was taken to mean "introduction" to the Canon instead of delivery in a ringing voice = *praedicatio*) led to further depreciation of the Preface. Petitions interpotalated into the Canon proper had already greatly modified its character as a prayer of offering (intercession for various persons, prolonged during an invocation of the Saints, the *Communicantes;* prayers for various necessities, which St. Gregory cut down to essentials in the *Hanc igitur* we still say today). Now the Carolingian liturgists, wishing to present the Canon as a sanctuary that the priest alone could enter, had it said inaudibly. To compensate in a way for this, the elevation of the host and chalice after the consecration was introduced in the 13th century, in keeping with the adoration of the sacrament then becoming more intensely cultivated. But it is only at the final phrase of the doxology which closes the Canon that the priest resumes contact with the people.

Apart from the general outlines given above (the Our Father and the Post-Communion) and the silent prayers of the priest also interpolated here, practically only fragmentary rites survive in the Communion of the Roman Mass: the fraction of the Host, of which the *Agnus Dei* is part, the mingling of the sacred species, and the call to the Kiss of Peace (now transferred to this position) in the *Pax Domini*. The fact that the Communion of the faithful is not meant to be an exception (it figures only as such in the ordinances of Pius V) and that it should take place at this point, was obscured for centuries, until the days of Pius X and the liturgical movement. Mass ends almost abruptly with the words of dismissal, *Ite missa est*. The late Middle Ages added a substitute for the prayer at the blessing that was once said here (it survives in the *Oratio super populum*) and the prologue to St. John's Gospel.

E. The People's Part in Mass

Pastoral concern lies behind all the developments now going on in the liturgical field. As is obvious from the whole tradition of antiquity and from the actual form of every rite in existence, the Mass was conceived of from the first as a communal service. It assumes that the faithful are present (in whatever strength) and take part: answering the salutation of the priest, making known their assent by acclamations, saying certain of the prayers, singing certain of the chants. The Oriental rites, where they have not been affected by Latin influences, bear striking witness to the communal character of Mass: there is no such thing in the East as a private Mass, and in some rites every Mass is sung. Here too the litany is designed for the people to share: at various points it is prayed by the deacon (by the priest if need be), alternating with the people, in the vernacular.

Parts of the Roman Mass, too, show that the people are meant to share in it: the series of unvarying chants that we call the Ordinary of the Mass — Kyrie, Gloria, Credo, Sanctus, and Agnus Dei. Originally recited by the people, these texts were early allotted to the clergy in choir ("chorale"), and on the rise of polyphony were generally taken over by church choirs, with the result that the people were condemned to silence. Keeping the Mass entirely in Latin had the same effect. At the same time we must bear in mind that Gregorian chant and church music reached their apogee in the post-Tridentine period, notably

enhancing the dignity and splendour of Catholic worship.

Despite its communal character, however, the Roman Mass has also been said privately by individual priests since about the 6th century, chiefly in the form of a votive Mass for the necessities of the faithful (who are not necessarily present). Here the impetratory aspect of the Mass has, as it were, been isolated. After some hesitation it was decided that there must always be a server at a votive Mass. This form of Mass (*missa lecta*) in turn gave rise to another development. In recent centuries the desire to give the faithful an active part in the Mass once more led, especially outside the Latin countries, to the introduction of vernacular hymns, often meant to be a substitute for the Ordinary of the Mass. From the latter part of the 19th century, however, the idea steadily gained ground that only Latin hymns are appropriate at a Sung Mass. Perforce the liturgical movement based its efforts on the Low Mass (*missa lecta*) which grew out of the private Mass and imposed no such restrictions. The Dialogue Mass, calling as it does for a reader and someone to lead in prayer, went far towards restoring the Mass to the people.

From what has been said one will gather that so far we have done little more than lurch from one makeshift to the next. It will be for the reform initiated by the Second Vatican Council to devise a congregational Mass that is both correct in its form and meaningful to the men of our time.

See also *Sacrifice, Liturgy* I, *Liturgical Movement, Lord's Prayer, Sunday, Qumran, Gnosis*.

BIBLIOGRAPHY. F. Brightman, *Liturgies Eastern and Western* (1896); E. Bishop, *Liturgica Historica* (1918; reprint, 1962); J. Quasten, *Monumenta eucharistica et liturgica vetustissima* (1935–37); G. Dix, *The Shape of the Liturgy* (1945); J. Brinktrine, *Die heilige Messe* (3rd ed., 1950); J. A. Jungmann, *The Mass of the Roman Rite*, 2 vols. (1951); id., "The Most Sacred Mystery of the Eucharist" (commentary on ch. ii of the Constitution on the Sacred Liturgy), in H. Vorgrimler, ed., *Commentary on the Documents of Vatican II*, vol. I (1967), pp. 31–45.

Josef Andreas Jungmann

III. Eucharistic Sacrifice

Though the Christian religion is a historical revelation, it does not regard itself merely as a conceptual and doctrinal orientation about the primal event of salvation which took place in the past, but rather as the unbroken handing on of that event across the ages down to the actual present. "The whole point of Christianity is that it is present." (Kierkegaard.) It is only logical, therefore, that the crucial event in the culminating revelation of God in Christ — the Redeemer's sufferings and death on the cross — should become present in Christian worship. Christ himself made such a thing possible by celebrating the Last Supper (Lk 22:19f.; 1 Cor 11:23bff.; Mk 14:22ff.; Mt 26:26ff.) — a salvific, symbolic enactment of his redemptive death — and enjoining the disciples to repeat what he had done (1 Cor 11:24f.), thus guaranteeing that all these "repetitions" would be in substance identical with the exemplar. Accordingly, the Lord called the re-celebration of the Last Supper by his disciples a remembrance of his own person and work (1 Cor 11:24f.) — a notion that conveys all the plenitude of meaning which there is in "commemoration".

In St. Paul the commemoration is already concentrated on the death of Christ. Not that Paul is explaining the Eucharist as a banquet such as those which the Hellenistic world held in memory of the dead; the point of the Eucharist, for him, is that it gives the faithful a share in the death of Jesus, the saving event par excellence. This anamnetic view also conveys the sacrificial character of Jesus' death (Gal 2:20; Eph 5:2; 1 Cor 5:7), of the Last Supper (1 Cor 10:19ff.), and of the cultic re-celebration of the latter, which is already evident from the words spoken over the chalice (Mk 14:24; Mt 26:28), from the association of the Eucharist with the Passover (Lk 22:15; 1 Cor 5:7), and from the many sacrificial terms that are applied to the life and death of Christ (Mk 10:45; Heb 7:27; 9:23, 25; 10:10; 12:14; 13:10; Jo 6:51; 19:34ff.).

Accordingly, we can see why, for all its dislike of the external sacrifices then offered, the early Church nevertheless regarded the Eucharist as a sacrifice fulfilling the OT prophecy (Mal 1:11, 14) of the perfect sacrifice to come (*Didache,* 14, 1, 3). One proof of the fact is the very ancient use of the term προσφορά for the whole Mass. This "early Catholic" conception is not a contradictory one, because the material elements of the eucharistic gifts are regarded as symbols, in accordance with the idea of

anamnesis, and are raised to a spiritual plane by thanksgiving (εὐχαριστία), so that the thanksgiving itself is occasionally called προσφορά. Significantly, the early Fathers take it for granted that the Eucharist which Christ instituted and the Church continues to celebrate, is at once Christ's sacrifice and a sacrifice of the Church's own (the Church being both priest and people). This belief largely held its own even against the allegorical interpretations of Mass that were so much favoured after the 9th century, persisting in the Christian consciousness down to the golden age of Scholasticism, though not worked out in detail like the later theories of Mass as a sacrifice. Such precision only became necessary when the Reformers, reacting one-sidedly against the notion of sacrifice as a "work" in late medieval popular piety, denied entirely the sacrificial character of the Mass.

The Council of Trent laid down in very general terms that Mass is "a real and genuine sacrifice" (in essence identical with the sacrifice of the cross), only offered in a different manner (*D* 940, 948–51); but theologians now had to explain the exact sense of the traditional doctrine. All the theories they evolved to that end try to show that the worship we offer God at Mass is both a *relative* sacrifice and a *genuine* one. These ingenious efforts to safeguard the sacrifice of the NT, which Christ willed to be one and yet to continue in the Church, must not be dismissed as trivial. Concentrating as they did on the sacrifice as such, they certainly contributed more to a profound understanding of the Eucharist than did the superficial symbolism of medieval allegorists. At the same time, these theories (of which we can only discuss certain salient features here) rested on assumptions which obscured the mystery of the eucharistic sacrifice as a whole. Approaching the matter purely from the point of view of abstract dogma (ignoring the liturgical form of the Mass) was an error in method, and was bound to impoverish the understanding of the mystery itself, which ceased to be recognized as the praise and thanksgiving of priest and people. Isolating the element of sacrifice, however, had an even more disastrous effect. During the early controversies with the Reformers, in the pre-Tridentine period, the essentially sacramental character of the Eucharist had still been acknowledged on the Catholic side, but now it was lost sight of. Catholic defenders of the sacrificial character of Mass thus took their stand on the chosen ground of the Reformers — the purely natural conception according to which sacrifice necessarily means expiation in blood *(offerri = mori)*.

Post-Tridentine theologians were forced to suppose that at Mass something natural is done *to* Christ mysteriously present under the appearances of bread and wine. This mistaken idea was most forcefully expressed in what are known as the theories of destruction, which asserted that in some manner or other Christ sacramentally present underwent a destruction, or at least a transformation *(immutatio, immolatio)*. Some (like Lessius [d. 1623]), realizing how difficult it is to entertain the idea that a physical change takes place in Christ who is now glorified, put forward the modified view that the words of consecration merely aimed at separating the body and blood of Christ and so at his death, while the actual effect did not follow, on account of his impassible state. Others (like J. de Lugo [d. 1660] and J. Franzelin [d. 1886]) supposed the element of sacrifice to consist in the state of humiliation brought about by the consecration, where Christ now proffers himself as food to men. Cardinal Cienfuegos (d. 1739) carried this idea to an even further extreme, affirming that Mass is a sacrifice because of the abandonment of the natural life of the senses in Christ at the consecration. What was unsatisfactory about these theories was not merely their ultra-realism, but even more their tendency to postulate an act of sacrifice different from the sacrifice of the cross, which jeopardized the relative character of Mass.

The extreme theories of destruction were countered during the 18th century by the *oblationist* theories. These spiritualized the whole conception of sacrifice, holding that it consisted simply in an interior act of self-surrender, which they attributed either to Christ present on the altar (French school) or the Lord in heaven (Thalhofer). In the latter case Mass was directly and primarily associated with Christ's "heavenly sacrifice" — an explanation which failed to preserve the link between Mass and the cross, quite apart from the dubious idea of a real act of sacrifice taking place in the perfected state that is heaven. M. de la Taille (d. 1933) devised an original variation on this same theme. He suggested that the one sacrifice of Christ was composed of the offering in the cenacle *(oblatio) and* the change of condition on the cross *(immolatio)*, so that in Mass the Church only offered God the sacrifice which had been prepared on the cross. But to say the least of it, he was unable to show that the same subject who offered the sacrifice of the cross offers the sacrifice of the Mass.

Compromise solutions have been attempted in recent years, combining the idea in some theories of destruction that the double consecration at Mass involves only a symbolic death (Vasquez [d. 1604], Perrone [d. 1876], Billot [d. 1931]), with the view of the oblationists that sacrifice, though something essentially interior, also postulates an appropriate outward act. It is gratifying to note that these efforts have also taken the liturgical structure of the Mass into account. J. Kramp (d. 1940), for example, tried to show that the consecration combines the two elements which are regarded as essential to sacrifice — oblation of the sacrificial gift and a change brought about in the latter ("theory of consecration"). But the consecration of the gifts of bread and wine which takes place when they are changed and the offering which the priest makes of them (only after the consecration) involve more than one act of sacrifice — a fact which again obscures the connection between Mass and the sacrifice of the cross.

The multitude of post-Tridentine theories we have had on this matter, each cancelling out the other, is evidence enough that neither a naturalist nor a spiritualized conception of sacrifice will reveal to us the nature of the sacrifice of the Mass. All this astute speculation having produced such scant results, modern theologians are reverting to an essentially sacramental idea of the sacrifice of the Mass, such as the great Fathers and the Schoolmen basically propounded. Thus theological thought has come full circle; but it is not "going round in circles", considering the number of apparent possibilities that have now been eliminated. When the categories of sacramental being are applied consistently to the eucharistic sacrifice, we realize that Mass is "the sacrament of the sacrifice of the cross", in which Christ's redemption becomes present through the ministry of the priest in a memorial which is an image of the reality, without any need of a special and literal act of sacrifice. If the symbolic character of the sacrifice of the Mass is stressed, its strict identity with the sacrifice of the cross will be satisfactorily preserved; furthermore, we can then fully recognize the symbolic character of the liturgical rite, which explains why Mass takes the form of a meal; and finally, it then becomes possible for the Church and the faithful to be organically drawn into the sacramental representation of Christ's sacrifice, for the Church inwardly and actively associates itself with the sacrifice of Christ by positing the sacramental sign that proclaims its assent to the Lord's sacrifice and its own sacrificial dispositions. Thus it not only shares in the deed of Christ but offers itself up in those dispositions, becoming a sacrificial gift along with Christ. This also brings out the significance of Mass as a sacrifice of adoration, praise, and thanksgiving.

Though the "sacramental" theory of sacrifice commends itself for its relative simplicity and its general harmony with the faith of the Church, it does not dispose of every question that occurs to the theologian. Above all, we must still ask what degree of efficacy the sign has: does it merely provide a real image and presence of the *Christus passus* (as has traditionally been supposed), or does it make present the sacrificial *act* of the cross and all Christ's redemptive work in its historical substance, only veiled in symbols (according to the doctrine of mystery in the strict sense as inaugurated by Dom Odo Casel)? Valuable as has been the contribution of the theology of mystery to a deeper, more lively, and more spiritual appreciation of Mass, and even to a sacramental view of Mass, it is still an open question — apart from logical difficulties and the lack of adequate categories to describe the "mystery-presence" — whether admitting the presence of Christ's redemptive act *as such,* veiled in symbols, does not lead us away from the sacramental view of Mass once more; for here the only function of the symbol is to shroud the saving event, which diminishes its own significance. Besides, the equation "offerri = mori" again looms up here, lessening appreciation of Mass as a relative, sacramental sacrifice and allowing the Church no more than an external contact with the sacrifice of Christ. In view of these difficulties the doctrine of mystery has rightly been modified, and is now taken to mean that Christ's deed is efficaciously present by reason of the *virtus divina,* which neither space nor time can limit. This efficacy is not only proper to the glorified Christ but derives from the historical events of his passion, death, and resurrection, as from an instrumental cause. But when all is said and done, we are compelled to admit that no complete, rational explanation of the sacrifice of the NT, in its sacramental image and presence in the Church, can ever be achieved; that in this matter theology will always be en route.

See also *Passover, Sacrifice* I, *Symbol, Sacraments* II.

BIBLIOGRAPHY. M. Lepin, *L'Idée du sacrifice de la Messe d'après les théologiens depuis l'origine jusqu'à nos jours* (1926); M. Alonso, *El sacrificio eucarístico de la última cena del Señor según el Concilio Tridentino* (1929); G. Söhngen, *Das sakramentale Wesen des heiligen Messopfers* (1946); E. Doronzo, *De eucharistia,* II (1948); G. Sartori, "Le Concezioni sacramentali del sacrificio della messa", *Scuola cattolica* 78 (1950), pp. 3–24; E. Masure, *Le sacrifice du Corps mystique* (1950); A. Vonier, *Collected Works,* II: *A Key to the Doctrine of the Eucharist,* etc. (1952); J. Betz, *Die Eucharistie in der Zeit der griechischen Väter,* I/1 (2nd ed., 1963); M.-J. Nicolas, *L'Eucharistie* (1959); B. Durst, *Die Eucharistiefeier als Opfer der Gläubigen* (1960); M. Schmaus, ed., *Aktuelle Fragen zur Eucharistie* (1960); B. Neunheuser, ed., *Opfer Christi und Opfer der Kirche* (1960); A. Piolanti, *Holy Eucharist* (1961); K. Rahner and A. Häussling, *The Celebration of the Eucharist* (1968).

Leo Scheffczyk

EVANGELICAL COUNSELS

When only the canonical meaning of the term was envisaged, the state of the "counsels" as embraced by religious (can. 487) tended to monopolize any treatment of the evangelical counsels. As a consequence, "seculars", who live in the world, seemed deliberately to choose the opposite, namely the state of the "precepts", and the counsels of Christ would have been of little interest for them. But can we say that the religious themselves still recognize the "counsels", as a higher way containing no element of compulsion, in three vows reduced to the absolute minimum binding under obligation? Before discussing the three counsels and the state of life of the counsels, we shall explore the meaning of the evangelical counsels in the Bible and their pastoral implications for all the faithful — as now placed beyond doubt by Vatican II's Constitution on the Church (*Lumen Gentium,* art. 39).

1. *The biblical revelation of the evangelical counsels.* In the Bible the good life always calls for a generosity which goes beyond the exact observance of a code of obligations. Hence, in the divine "law", the ideal of a "whole-hearted" and free service, revealed in its fullness in Jesus, emerges — an ideal to which only the name of "counsel" does justice ("proprio quodam modo", *Lumen Gentium,* art. 39). This view, with its two aspects of the *spirit* and the *object* of the counsel, follows from the twofold revealed nature of the moral life: it is always in relation to God, and God shows himself as love calling for love in reply. In fact, from the very beginning, the good life presupposes the presence of the Lord: "Walk before me and be blameless" (Gen 17:1), an idea which was to attain its *sensus plenior* in the NT, namely, that the value of every good action is constituted by an implicit movement of love which God bestows upon us and which makes the Trinity dwell within us (1 Cor 13; Jn 14:15–23; Eph 5:2; Rom 13:10). Hence the Lord's presence which appears in the "law" and in every good act becomes clearer and clearer and is inseparable from the biblical revelation (*Lumen Gentium,* art. 42). In the OT God already freely grants his people a covenant, in an intimate, personal love, soon to be described as the love between husband and wife, with God demanding in reply a love freely given, a moral commitment, far surpassing the measure of what is strictly due: "You shall love the Lord your God with all your heart" (Deut 6:5). The Israelite is to imitate God: "You shall be holy, for I the Lord your God am holy" (Lev 19:2). The Christian responds to "the goodness . . . and the love" of Jesus (Tit 3:4), he follows the Son. God's friendship invites and woos, but does not compel. It is a summons to love in the sense of a "law" *(iugum meum,* Mt 11:29) whose essence is the effort after the better, the "counsel" (Deut 6:4–13; Jn 14:21–24; Phil 1:10). "One gives orders to one's subjects, but counsel to one's friends" (Ambrose, *De Viduis,* 12: PL, XVI, 256). From this we see the pastoral significance of the evangelical counsels. Christ, his image and his love must be made to shine through the "law" (*Lex Christi,*

Gal 6:2); and in the law the summons to what is better must needs be discovered, and serious obligations (for there is no question of forgetting them) must be given their true meaning as "a necessary love". The burdensome beginnings are overcome by regarding the divine benevolence as the source of all expression of the divine will. The counsel is essentially optional: God's merciful love wishes to bring us beyond the point of safety-first calculations. But a counsel does not imply rigorism. A baptized person esteems all the counsels, but freely chooses those which concern his providential situation (St. Francis de Sales, *Treatise on the Love of God,* 8, 9; cf. *Lumen Gentium,* art. 42). Little by little the spirit of a childlike faithfulness, bringing abundant peace, and growing ever more free ("freedom from slavery", St. Augustine) predominates over the weight of obligations, grave or light, which are, however, never ignored or questioned: "Perfect love casts out fear" (1 Jn 4:18). There is no denial of the fact that Christian perfection "pertains to the precepts" (St. Thomas, *De Perfectione Vitae,* 14), that is, to the two limitless precepts of charity. But the counsel shows "in a special way" (*Lumen Gentium,* art. 42) how they are made realities and given their full symbolism.

Thus, in the "well-beloved Son" (Mt 17:5), we are invited to an attitude of supernatural generosity and giving, which corresponds to what we are rediscovering nowadays in the human sphere of work and economics.

2. *The "Sequere me" and the three counsels.* a) During the first three centuries, Christians were simply taught to follow Christ (which does not mean that the ideal was always realized). Morality was summed up in the simple principle: *Christus sola lex:* the only law is Christ. The good news of Jesus was preached (cf. Acts 5:42), which meant that Christianity was presented in terms of the counsels. It was known from th first that the counsels were free (Acts 5:4; virginity and marriage, 1 Cor 7:25), but *all* were taught the ideal of the eucharistic community, essentially a fraternal unity in *Agape* (Acts 4:32): the *koinonia,* or "sharing of goods" (Acts 2:42–44; Heb 13:16), soon to be called the *vita apostolica.* This was not communism without private property (Acts 5:7), but a practical readiness to share one's goods. All goods

come from the common Father. "No one must be in need"; that was the rule (Acts 4:34). There was a community chest (see "κοινωνία", no. 3, in *TWNT*; cf. Rom 15:27; 2 Cor 8:13). In the 4th century a sect known as the "Apostolics" was reproached with making a precept of a counsel. The same *sequela Christi* which was preached to all was the basis of a voluntary and closer *koinonia* among some Christians, expressed in virginity (Acts 4:32; Justin, *Apologia*, 10, 16; 1 Cor 7:10) and the distribution of all one's goods. This manifold *koinonia* was seen as a decisive criterion of faith (Justin, Irenaeus, Tertullian; cf. R. Carpentier, *Vie Apostolique*, pp. 44–54). Thus the one Church of the first three centuries held consistently to the teaching of the counsels. Christian marriage was also penetrated by the spirit which inspired the state of virginity.

b) Within this one community, rapidly growing groups were formed in the 4th century. Historically, the hermit, the "Christian of the desert", simply continued the *vita apostolica* (as the whole Church saw) when it had become too arduous for the community, involved as a whole in earthly tasks (L. Bouyer, *La Vie de S. Antoine* [1950], pp. 53, 175 and *passim*). Monasticism simply aimed at living to the full the *vita apostolica*: Obedience (to the spiritual father) stemmed automatically from the example of the twelve disciples. This separation poses no doctrinal problems. The call to the desert was charismatic, a substitute for martyrdom, and did not represent an innovation but was profoundly Christian and ecclesial. "Breathe out Christ", said St. Anthony. A phenomenon which can be fully explained by the life and realities of the Christian Church of the time, should not be explained by Jewish fellowships or pagan mysticism (cf. Bouyer, *op. cit.*, p. 51). The problem of jurisdiction does not enter into this article, but the Church always extended its protection to the groups which sought to live out more profoundly the life of the counsels. In the 12th century the triad of poverty, chastity and obedience was established, which gave definitive shape to this signal realization of the *sequela Christi* (*Lumen Gentium*, art. 43; *Perfectae Caritatis*, art. 2).

c) The neglect of the counsel, and especially of the *koinonia*, in general preaching is explained by a shift of emphasis (the demand for a minimum of good will, for the confession of sins, the call to make sure of salvation). The separation of those who followed the counsels from the rest of the faithful also helps to explain it. Ultimately, however, this separation should stimulate all to a greater perfection of love (cf. *Lumen Gentium*, arts. 12, 13, 44, 46; *Perfectae Caritatis*, art. 24).

3. *The ecclesiastic fellowship of the three evangelical counsels*. a) The faith of Pentecost (Acts 1:6) established the people of the promises, characterized as a religious and social entity (κοινωνία). As a new human race where love is the supreme law, it differs radically from the juridical society which men need to regulate their intercourse. This distinction, which explains the seemingly strange contrast between justice and love, alone discloses the true nature of the social imperative of the gospel. This explains the need of a public juridical organization of the counsels (as in the religious orders) where the Church displays itself, to itself and to the world, as a fellowship of love and hence of the glory of God and salvation of human society. This centuries-long experience was assured by the bishops, and then by the Popes, by means of "exemption" (*Lumen Gentium*, art. 45), which does not mean a restriction of local authority, but assures it of the social character of the life of the counsels. The other ecclesiastical institutions based on the counsels are to be viewed in the same way (Secular Institutes).

b) When rightly understood, the legal character of these institutions does not present a difficulty. Certainly the counsels, as a commitment to love, exclude all legalism. But the juridical structure of the Mystical Body is demanded by the love of Christ itself. The social order of the gospel, the kingdom of God, must take shape. Its programme of comprehensive unity must be embodied in tangible law, in organizations with their own rules (*Lumen Gentium*, art. 45).

c) Justice would not be done to the state of the evangelical counsels if their legal obligations were explained without regard for the notion and essence of the counsel. This is true of all Christian morals. The only evangelical counsel is Christ, who is loved and followed for himself alone. The threefold vow, understood as perfect adoration, in the sense of the counsel, consecrates the whole existence and not just three obligations reduced to their minimum (*Lumen Gentium,* art. 44). The vow is only the presupposition for the definitive adoption of the spirit of the counsel: it aims at the "freedom" which goes beyond the law (St. Paul), "triumphant joy" (St. Augustine), the connaturality of virtue (St. Thomas Aquinas).

Summary. Because he is tempted to transgress the divine law, man feels himself under "obligation". He must learn to act more and more through a love which loves God more than self: "Walk in love" (Eph 5:2). Only Christ can make him capable of doing this. He draws him to himself and gives the grace. This demands a pastoral ministry which recognizes duties and precepts, but which tries more and more to set men free of temptation and aims at the generous fulfilment of the counsels. The ecclesiastical state of the evangelical counsels lived out in signal fashion gives permanent testimony to the love inspired by grace which is realized in fraternal fellowship. The pastoral ministry must be fully alive to this testimony, in order to communicate it to the world (*Lumen Gentium,* arts. 44, 46; *Perfectae Caritatis,* art. 24).

See also *Charity* I, *Marriage* I, *Virginity, Obedience, Poverty* II, *Martyrdom, Religious Orders, Vow, Ecclesiastical Law* I, *Law* III, *Law and Gospel.*

BIBLIOGRAPHY. ON SECTION 1: Vatican II, Constitution *Lumen Gentium;* Decree, *Perfectae Caritatis;* J. B. Tse, *Perfectio christiana et societas christiana iuxta magisterium Pii Papae XII* (1963). ON SECTION 2: Thomas Aquinas, *De Perfectione Vitae*; id., *Summa Theologica,* I/II, q. 108, and II/II, q. 184; *DTC,* III, cols. 1176–82; *DSAM,* II, cols. 1592–609; III, cols. 691–4; IV, cols. 1408–22; *RGG,* II, cols. 785–8; *LTK,* II, cols. 1245–50; K. Rahner, *Theological Investigations,* III (1967); G. Gilleman, *The Primacy of Charity in Moral Theology* (1956). ON SECTION 3: M. Viller and K. Rahner, *Aszese und Mystik in der Väterzeit* (1939); R. Carpentier, *L'évêque et la vie religieuse consacrée: L'Épiscopat et l'Église universelle* (1962); id., *La "vie apostolique" mystère de foi: La vie religieuse dans l'Église du Christ* (1964); R. Schnackenburg, *Moral Teaching of the New Testament* (1965). ON SECTION 4: E. Heufelder, *Die evangelischen Räte* (1953); R. Carpentier, *Life in the City of God* (1958); H. Urs von Balthasar, "Gospel as Norm", *Concilium* 1 (1965), pp. 715–22; I. Hausherr, *Vocation chrétienne et vocation monastique selon les Pères: Laïcs et vie chrétienne parfaite* (1963).

René Carpentier

EVIL

1. *The problem.* Evil counts as one of the most distressing questions in theology. It cannot be thought of in itself; it is evil solely as opposed to the good. Being holy, God is also good, and is so of himself, not through participation in a good outside or prior to himself or greater than he. He is the principle and pure source of good, good absolutely as such. Consequently it is impossible for him to be the author of evil; he cannot will evil, and no shadow of evil falls on him. But in that case, how can anything be or happen which is opposed to God and his goodness? To the good belongs the power of good, without which it would not be wholly good. God, therefore, is only absolutely good if his goodness is also absolutely powerful, if he is omnipotently good. If on the other hand God is truly God, the fact of evil, which is contrary to God, points both away from God and back to God. Evil cannot be due to God but he must be responsible for what is responsible for evil. In view of God, evil is evil, but in view of evil, how is God God? A "justification" of God in regard to evil does not exhaust, and in fact does not really touch, the theological question of evil. A clarification of the ground of the possibility of evil is theologically necessary to the extent that it is necessary to think in a way that does justice to God's holiness. The realization of God's holiness in our thought belongs to the coming of his reign, because it prepares the way for it. That is what theology is concerned with. Consequently the question of the ground of the possibility of evil is completed and replaced by the question of the location, overcoming and "end" of evil in God's reign, in his salvific will for man and the world revealed and accomplished in Jesus Christ.

2. *History of the problem.* Pessimism disguises the problem of evil and badness, by denying all meaning to reality: but if it is absurd and meaningless, it is not even open to question. Schopenhauer, who considered the world as the result of blind instinctive will, is the great representative of pessimism. Rationalism and pantheism solve the problem by an optimistic view of the universe. Spinoza, for instance, recognizes nothing as evil, since all finite things are logically

necessary modifications of the one divine substance. Hegel, who gives a dynamic version of Spinoza's view, interprets world history as the dialectical self-explicitation of the absolute spirit and holds that evil is what ought not to remain, but not what ought not to be.

Dualistic systems, from Parseeism, Gnosis and Manichaeism to J. Böhme and the later Schelling, take good and evil (or the grounds of their possibility) as two primordial principles, either as two divine beings in conflict or as tension and division in the one godhead.

The biblical doctrine of creation affirms that the holy, omnipotent God is the author of light and darkness, the Lord of grace and obduracy (or predestination). The free, culpable disobedience of man disturbs the harmony of the original state of things, but man is tempted beforehand by an evil power whose origin is obscure. Nonetheless, it is under the power and judgment of God.

In the process of combining revealed truths with Greek and especially Platonic thought, Origen and Augustine developed the principle which was to become the common heritage of Scholasticism. Evil is not something positive, but negative. It is the lack or deprivation of perfection which should really be present in a free spiritual being. This lack is due to a culpable distortion which the free finite spirit brings about in itself. Origen transposes this cause further back, and regards this world as the place of punishment of souls who sinned in their pre-existence. But he also supposes a general apocatastasis, possibly through the general conflagration, hell, in which the world is consumed. Augustine sees sin as Scripture does and teaches the possibility, and indeed the reality, of the hardening of the wicked decision into absolute definitiveness. His central thinking on evil is less concerned with the philosophical negation of its positive existence than with the doctrine of predestination which was rejected by Catholic theology and only came to the fore again in the Reformation. But even if evil is conceded no being of its own but is referred to God only indirectly through the guilt of man, this is not a positive explanation of its meaning. Harmonizing efforts, based for instance on the aesthetic demands of an order of things which must contain "everything", fail to recognize the absolute contradiction and incompatibility of evil, the absoluteness of man's demand for total explanation, and the full claim of the good and holy as such. This permanent tension between the absurdity of evil and the meaningfulness which the world still affirms of itself — a tension which theology does not resolve, but merely recognizes and endures — makes the problem of evil a mystery.

3. *The phenomenon.* a) *Antithesis to the good.* The immediately striking feature of evil is its antithesis to good. Without good, evil is inconceivable, but good does not in the same way require evil in order to be good. Evil exists in virtue of the good, not vice versa. Yet mere denial of good, absence of good, deficiency, a lesser degree of participation in the good, do not amount to the really direct contradiction of the good which makes evil evil. Evil is "more" than simply what is morally bad, the application of the concept of evil, what is not good, to the domain of moral will. As distinguished from what is bad or inferior, evil means the positing of the contradiction of the good, deliberate denial of the good. Evil is a less extensive concept than bad, but more fundamental. In evil the negation of the good becomes conscious of itself; evil is never merely in fact evil, but is always evil "as" evil, i.e., conscious of the good which it actively contests. An "innocent" evil would not be evil. Consequently, "evil" is predicated of the will or, indirectly, of the mode of being of some existent possessed by a certain direction of the will; the relation to good grasped as such is the essence of the will and of its freedom. Mere weakness of will, therefore, does not reach the core of evil; it is nevertheless evil to the extent that the weak will is identical with its weakness and so makes this weakness an inner and therefore free relation to the good.

b) *Self-contradiction.* Evil is in this way not only antithetical to good, but as such it is in contradiction to itself. On the one hand it is "positive": it is posited, accomplished, affirmed, and this gives it its particular appearance of hard, resistant reality. Yet what is posited, accomplished and affirmed is negative: the refusal of the good, its absence — hence the intrinsic "emptiness" of evil. The refusal of the good, accomplished in this way, discloses a further intrinsic contradiction — the contradiction between good and good within its negation posited by the will. The evil will — and this constitutes its evil — contests the good recognized as such and at the same time claims that what it posits in this contestation is good. It cannot do otherwise. Whatever the will wills, it affirms by that very fact to be good. "Good" after all means: Yes, that is how it should be! And "to will" means to affirm and to posit how, according to the person willing, something should be. Even someone who wants to be evil merely for the sake of being evil thinks it good to revolt, in other words, to be evil. And someone who merely allows himself unwillingly to be overcome by evil wills to have peace and quiet at last; he is tired of resistance and considers what appears to be peace with evil, and therefore indirectly the accomplishment of the evil itself, as preferable and therefore as good.

In this way evil is a conflict of good with good in the will. Something present to the will as good, as something that ought to be, is cancelled by the will and in its place something else is posited as good and as what should be. The formula of the good will is: Because this is good, I will this. That of the evil will is: This is good because I will it. But what is truly good? What makes it genuine? All that is, is permitted to be, admitted to being, is to be in virtue of the primary will. Being itself means what should be; being and good are in that way identical (as transcendentals). Here "being" is not thought of as merely "being there", as bare contingent fact, but as what is affirmed and conceded wherever an existent occurs, the "gift" which properly speaking is in every being, by its existing, that which is always intended by the being of beings, that for which they exist. Good as such is, therefore, the plenitude which comprises and transcends all beings, the one source which confers everything, fulfils everything and so is in harmony with itself.

But the finite will itself is set in being by this unconditional source; it too is something that is willed to be. By its being set in being, something is admitted into being which for its part can affirm itself, actively collaborate with the productive movement of causing being, and accomplish it as its own; something to which it is granted, as it makes its decisions and shapes its own being and that of others, to be the origin of its assent to and agreement with the unconditioned origin. Consequently the activity of a finite will

necessarily involves a duality. It is its own operative source, the centre from which its own being is decided and with it, in consenting and formative activity, everything else, the world as a whole.

But the finite will is only a second cause, only a derivative centre; before it decides itself and everything it must first put itself in harmony with the primordial source which antecedently has determined the finite will and all things. It must, therefore, for its own part accept as good what has already been determined and granted as good in its regard. For the finite will, good consists in the agreement of its own consent to good with the unconditional fiat of God, in consenting obedience. This obedience is not, however, a mere copy, but an active interpretation of the divine will in the world, causing it to come about and to be given shape and form. This agreement is affirmed in each act of the will. By willing, it not only proclaims: For my part this shall be so, but: It truly should be so. For, as will, it is concerned that something should be as it wills it to be; as will it always strives towards being, which has only in part been given and assigned to it, and affirms its accord with its own condition. The affirmation of that accord is nevertheless not itself its own guarantee; there is an intrinsic possibility of discord, and this is the possibility of evil.

c) *Discord within the good.* By bringing something about, the finite will in each case brings something into being, something which should be, in other words, good. Evil therefore cannot have being as its content. What, then, is the content of evil? The evil will denies the good, cancels some good, destroys, deforms or distorts a good content. At the same time it affirms and posits something, some content, therefore, as good. In fact the evil will always wills something good, if only its power of willing which as such is of course good. Even self-destruction posits as good the power by which it can be achieved, the very energy which is good in origin. The evil in evil is, therefore, not something, but the disunity of good with itself, the discord within the good in the will. All that is, to the extent that it is, is good; but it is good in relation to the absolute good and is only good in itself in dependence on that absolute good. It is only in agreement with itself by being in agreement with the whole and so with the unconditional. It is good which sets everything harmoniously in order, and that order is always prior to the moment of finite decision and yet must always be heard anew and brought to new realization by that decision. Evil is the discord of a being with itself and so with the absolute; it is the discord of its will with itself and with the absolute, and ultimately with what it wills, which is not willed by the absolute primordial source in the way the evil affirms it to be.

4. *Evil in the world.* The intrinsic dependence of evil on good excludes a "dualistic" interpretation of the world, as in Manichaeism: the equally primary character of good and evil as two existing principles or at least as constitutive principles operative within the individual being. "Evil" is not something independent, existing in itself, but only in an existing and therefore fundamentally good will. And since it springs from within the will, from its own self-willing, it is not a power above the individual but is located in the individual will itself. As, however, by the very nature of the will, which is always related to the whole, evil brings this whole into disharmony through the person who wills badly, evil has a radiating power capable of bringing into disharmony the world itself and of seductively determining other wills. Through this cosmic power of disharmony and temptation and through the concord of a number of wills in ill-will, evil does attain a secondary, if only apparent, yet effective "independence".

5. *Ground of the possibility of evil.* The question arises all the more urgently: How is evil possible, when only what the omnipotence of the good God is capable of, is possible? The analysis of evil itself indicates the answer. If finite will exists, by nature it is "the same" as good as such: self-transcendence consenting to all being and consequently unity with itself. But because it is finite will, it is not of necessity what it is and its existence stands in the tension of being posterior to its essence. In fulfilling itself, i.e., its essence, it must of itself accomplish what even without it already is. What is most its own, its essence, is "other" than itself, and it must realize this other as its own, i.e., of itself. Therefore it necessarily accomplishes what it accomplishes as good, but what it accomplishes as good, it always accomplishes of

itself and so not of necessity. Ontologically this involves the possibility of a divergence in activity, of disharmony and so of evil. This only occurs through the finite will which is called upon of itself to cancel out its posteriority to the divine will, in order not of itself, but from God, to be "like God", one with him and at the same time quite other than he. God's decision to cause his image, his "nature", to exist in a created likeness, involves the "risk" of the deformation of this likeness. The being of finite mind is the ground of the possibility of evil.

6. *The overcoming of evil.* If evil is the disharmony of the world with itself and with God in the autocratic self-distortion of finite will, the death of Jesus and his resurrection are the overcoming of evil by the free decree of the omnipotent determinative origin. When Jesus became "obedient unto death", he accomplished the act of radical agreement with the will of the Father and so judged and rejected evil, and by this he lovingly assumed the sin and guilt of the world and was "conformed" to it in its likeness on the Cross. Jesus' solidarity with sinful mankind is at the same time the solidarity of the Son's loving obedience to the Father. This new harmony between God and world was revealed and confirmed as the birth of the new man and as the beginning of the new creation by the Easter resurrection. The death and resurrection of Jesus are offered to man as good news to change his evil autocratic self-will by consent in faith, hope and love to God's work in Jesus. The overcoming of evil occurs as the love of God giving his Son as reconciliation, and as the love of the Son which in the one gesture of self-giving embraces both the Father and the sinner, and so links both anew. The Spirit of the Son produces the same love in the redeemed; it overcomes the conflict in the finite will between having to determine itself yet having to allow itself to be determined: love wills as its own, "of itself" what the beloved wills; it is an unbroken, direct union of man with God and his authoritative creative will, with man himself, and with the world produced in being by the loving will of God.

See also *God, Attributes of, Good, Holy* I, *Reign of God, Salvation* IV, *World, Dualism, Rationalism, Nihilism, Apocatastasis, Predestination.*

BIBLIOGRAPHY. Thomas Aquinas, *De Malo;* G. Leibniz, *Theodicy,* ed. by D. Allen (1966); F. Billicsich, *Das Problem des Übels in der Philosophie des Abendlandes,* 3 vols. (1936–59); J. Maritain, *St. Thomas and the Problem of Evil* (1942); A.-D. Sertillanges, *Le problème du mal, l'histoire* (1949); P. Siwek, *The Philosophy of Evil* (1951); M. Buber, *Good and Evil* (1953); B. Welte, *Über das Böse* (1959); C. Journet, *Meaning of Evil* (1963); C. Kerényi and others, *Evil,* ed. by the Jung Institute Curatorium (1967); P. Ricœur, *Symbolism of Evil* (1967).

Klaus Hemmerle

EVOLUTION

I. Anthropological: A. Evolution. B. Hominisation. II. Theological: A. Evolution. B. Hominisation.

I. Anthropological

A. EVOLUTION

By evolution or phylogenetic development the biologist understands that long drawn-out and mighty process which has led, with the passage of the geological epochs, to ever newer and different organic forms, while at the same time guarding the continuity of the stream of life from one generation to the next. Evolution therefore connotes a change or transformation of organic forms with the passage of time. The problem of the origin of life or of the first cell forms a separate question which will be treated separately (see *Life* I). Granted that evolution can be proved, then the properties of the organism will include an inborn power of self-organization and growth which conditions all the stages in the development of an individual from the appearance and maturation of the ovum right up to the highly complex adult form. It includes over and above this individual development an immanent power of evolving into more and more complexly organized forms over the millions of years since the first appearance of life.

In order to justify this concept, the biologist calls on three fundamental facts: a) Living matter arises only from living matter. b) Closely related organisms are essentially similar in their fundamental characteristics (homology). c) Inheritable alterations in plants and animals (mutations) may occur both in the genetic determiners (genotype) and in their outward, visible expression (phenotype). In addition several indirect, so-called suasive proofs drawn from morphology, embryology, physiology, geography and dating techniques, closely inter-connected and completing one another, form a strong argument, supported as they are by the fossil record. Organic forms make their first abrupt appearance in the Cambrian period (which began about 600 million years ago). An abundance of varied and highly organized invertebrate forms appeared which cannot be derived from previously existing forms since practically no fossil remains have been found in the Precambrian. An indescribable richness of fossil organisms has been recovered from all the succeeding geological deposits. These throw light on the vast power of variation possessed by living material which has undergone, on an unimaginable scale, a process in time involving rise and fall, variation and change and self-development.

The evolution of living things revealed by the fossil record appears to be *a periodic process.* Whole groups suddenly enter an "explosive" phase (sometimes after a varying preparatory period) in which their basic plan of construction splits with highly accelerated evolutionary velocity into numerous types of organization. An example of this would be the mammals which have developed, since the early Tertiary, into no less than twenty-five orders and 206 families, well documented in the fossil record. The potentiality latent in the basic plan to develop into different functional forms (e.g., carnivore, herbivore, insectivore; or runner, jumper, climber, burrower, swimming or flying forms) is realized. During the succeeding, much longer period all that takes place is that a vast number of genera and species are differentiated out. A quiet, gradual development through small evolutionary steps occurs in the direction of increasing specialization and frequently, also, of increasing size of the whole body or of individual organs. Towards the end of this phyletic development a shrinkage or even an extinction of the various lines that have been formed takes place in most cases. At many of the transitions from one geological period to another, radical changes in flora and fauna may be superimposed independently on these radiational and explosive phases, with a different temporal pattern for each animal group. At these junctures large sections of world-wide groups of land and sea animals belonging to the most varied lines may disappear; others may decrease to a few relict forms, while others survive the transition without disturbance and still others appear for the first time or begin their explosive phase of expansion. Phyletic development thus unfolds, not in a regular, uniform fashion, but with different evolutionary patterns, velocities and possibilities in each group of organisms.

The evolution of living things seems to be a *discontinuous process;* not in the sense that the continuity of the life stream has been interrupted, but rather in the sense that the higher systematic groups make an abrupt appearance in the fossil record. The twenty-five mammalian orders already referred to arise abruptly in the early Tertiary without a trace of their origins; they arise out of a "vacuum of origin". It is true that as one traces the organizational types back towards their ancestral forms, they seem to converge more and more; but in no case is either a true convergence or a transitional form known. This phenomenon of the absence of true transitional forms in the fossil record is universal, i.e., it has been established without exception for all the major animal and plant groups (e.g., within the reptiles, the Mesozoic and early Tertiary mammals, the flowering plants, etc.). Attempts to explain it have been very varied.

A further characteristic of the evolution of living things is its *directional progression,* not, it is true, in the strictly rectilinear sense, but within a definite margin of variation which is characteristic of all living things. The series leading from the small *Eohippus* of the early Tertiary up to the modern horse *Equus* is well known (Eohippus — Orohippus — Epihippus — Mesohippus — Miohippus — Parahippus — Meryhippus — Pliohippus — Equus). In this evolutionary series a continuous change, parallel with an increase in size, occurs from browsers with low-crowned teeth of simple pattern to grazers with high-crowned teeth with complex pattern; from four-toed feet with pads to one-toed feet with hooves and springing mechanism; from a reptile-like brain to one with large frontal lobes that are covered with a complex pattern of furrows and mask the other parts. Trends like these almost always appear to follow the same direction in whole "bundles" of independent lines developing parallel to one another. They may, however

(e. g., in the changes in lobe outline and shell sculpturing in the Ammonites), repeat the same process several times in periods which are separated from one another in time (iterations). Sometimes they may lead to exaggerated body size or to over-developed organs, to so-called "over-specializations". Since phylogenetic evolution has proved to be irreversible (i.e., not reverting to earlier forms), the evolutionary amplitude or potentiality for developing new patterns is progressively narrowed by specialization, so that eventually new morphological patterns and structures can no longer be formed — or be formed only by devious routes. It is unknown whether an aging of a group, leading eventually to degeneration and extinction, is responsible for these directional processes.

A further character of organic evolution is that it is a *constructive process.* Organic structures are formed, conserved, combined and integrated, further developed or broken down again. This formation of structures occurred not merely in a single or in a few parallel lines, but in numerous lines of the most varied organization and of every systematic rank. They thus created that vast richness of varied forms appearing in the plant and animal kingdom both today and in former epochs. Thus through a repeated self-development and diversification of the lines of descent leading to more novel, and varied expressions, a diversification of the organic world took place along every imaginable pathway, almost exhausting all the possible organic patterns. The "natural system" of plant and animal classification makes it clear that an order reigns within this motley pattern. Because of this order, this graded variety or hierarchical structure, not only are groups of organisms of higher and lower ranks (advanced and primitive) distinguishable, but also smaller units may be included within larger ones, e.g., species are united into genera, genera into families, families into orders, etc. This testifies to the fact that a diversification and perfecting took place not only *within* any given structural pattern but also *beyond* any particular level of organization towards higher levels, e.g., from the level of the jawless fishes (Agnatha), through that of fish with jointed jaws (Placoderma), the true fishes, the amphibians, the reptiles up to the level of the warm-blooded birds and mammals.

This highly significant phenomenon of a "biological ascent" (Anagenesis) is, however, not universal among organic groups. Among the vertebrates it is characterized by increasing differentiation and integration, by an increasing independence from the environment and by individual autonomy. This latter is shown above all by the organization of the nervous system, especially of the brain, and by an intensification of animal interiorization and a higher development of the psychic and conscious elements. The "biological ascent" of an organism reaches a higher point the more its wholeness and autonomy, i.e., its individuality, is realized. The highest point is occupied by man; because of his self-consciousness, i.e., because of his spirituality and freedom, he is not merely an individual but also a person. The causality responsible for these processes has not been explained. So also with the phenomena we have mentioned: the radiation and extinction of groups of organisms, the onset of "explosive" phases and periods of calm advance, the major changes in flora and fauna, the "vacuum of origins" from which the major groups arise, directional evolution in parallel lines, the hierarchically ordered variety and the "biological ascent" — all pose problems and unanswered questions.

No examples of macromutations nor of an accumulation of smaller mutations under the influence of selection and isolation exist among present-day organisms. If they existed, they would give some insight into the causal processes leading to evolutionary transformations or to the creation of plans of organization or of highly complex organs and systems of organs (synorganizations) and of other amazingly "lucky discoveries" of the evolutionary process. The extension or extrapolation of experimental results, especially of genetics (restricted in practice to the intraspecific sphere) to the enormous changes studied in cases of trans-specific evolution, is no more than a working hypothesis. So also is the idea of a deep-reaching, sudden change in the genetic make-up. The large number of hypotheses in existence, their frequent contradictory character and their rapid rate of modification witness to the inadequacy of all causal explanations offered to date; they are no more than attempts towards answering a vast open question. The "family-tree" representation of plants and animals proposed again and

again offer no definitive result, only a temporary picture; i.e., they serve to portray the established or presumed historical relationships between groups of organisms as seen by the present state of scientific opinion; they may be altered at any time by new finds or by new facts. Thus the classical "family tree" of organisms in which the uniform "trunk" is supposed to grow upwards higher and higher in the centre, giving off ascending "side-branches", has undergone fundamental alteration. Now it loses itself in a series of parallel main branches which, it seems, are quite distinct structurally from one another even in the oldest fossiliferous strata of the Cambrian and Ordovician. From this point on they exhibit an independent evolution within the framework of their own amazingly conservative basic structure. The classes of fishes, amphibians and reptiles in vogue up to now are seen to be merely grades of organization through which the individually more or less independent stocks passed (polyphyletically). However, even the modern picture of the "family tree" of organisms makes it quite clear that the history of organisms is characterized by an evolution.

It may now be seen that the concept of *biological* evolution is justified. It allows a vast quantity of various facts to be viewed as a whole and leaves them open to a unified explanation. However, its extension to and use in the essentially different world of human affairs with its historical, cultural, political, ethical and religious phenomena, make too heavy demands on the evolutionary idea and transgress the bonds of the competency of biology. Using an explanatory principle drawn from purely biological evolution and its regularity in the wider context of human affairs effaces the ontologically graded structure of reality with its distinction of levels of being.

See also *Life* I, *Man* I, *Person*.

BIBLIOGRAPHY. C. Darwin, *On the Origin of Species by Means of Natural Selection* (1859); B. Rensch, *Evolution above the Species Level* (1960); T. Goudge, *Ascent of Life* (1961); G. Leeper, *Evolution of Living Organisms* (1962); H. Ross, *Synthesis of Evolutionary Theory* (1962); E. Mayr, *Animal Species and Evolution* (1963); P. Overhage, *Die Evolution des Lebendigen. Das Phänomen* (1963); J. Huxley, *Evolution: The Modern Synthesis* (1964); P. Overhage, *Die Evolution des Lebendigen. Die Kausalität* (1965).

Paul Overhage

B. Hominisation

For a biologist "hominisation" (anthropogenesis) means the phylogenetic processes by which man has developed by continuous transformations from a presumed Primate group of the Tertiary era in his bodily characteristics (upright gait, upper limbs freed from locomotory function, large cranial capacity and brain size, reduced facial region) and also in his psyche (spiritually moulded behaviour, including thought, language, freedom of choice, social institutions and culture). In the investigation of hominisation the object is not only to derive the human type of organization from certain former Primates by comparing similar structural and behavioural patterns, but also to find the effective scientific causal factors. The problem of hominisation arose as soon as the idea of the evolution of organisms took firm root, especially since Darwin's time. Since then, men have sought strenuously to explore by all possible scientific means, the biological and historical origins of mankind.

Since there is no doubt that man is a mammal bearing a close resemblance to the higher Primates, especially the anthropoid apes, the problem of his origins had for a long time been reduced to a zoological and anatomical one. Man was considered to be merely just another species of animal. The problem of hominisation, however, concerns itself with more than the development of a more complex species of *animal*. Even after investigating the origin of this incontestable relationship and the discovery of anatomically intermediate fossil forms (especially the Australopithecines of the early Ice Age), the crucial problem still remains, namely, to account for the development of a completely new type of organism endowed with speech and spiritual behaviour which towers over all other animals because of its historical character and which has achieved a completely new conquest of its environment with the help of a culture. Meanwhile a consciousness of the immense and unique depths that underlie human nature has also awakened among biologists. They realized that any causal theory of hominisation faced an enormously difficult task and so have included the study of behaviour in their investigations. This scientific comparison of man and beast, this search for and discovery of similarities and correspondences in structure and especially in behaviour, does not indicate a desire to paint a purely biological picture of man but is an attempt rather to grasp the field of organic structure and behaviour common to man and beast. By this means one not only sees which human bodily and psychic characters are comparable with those of the beast or are even derivable from them (e.g., the rich instinctive foundations of man's psychic life); one also pinpoints those characters incapable of such a derivation. By demonstrating all the influences of the animal and natural elements, the spiritual element in behaviour is *ipso facto* narrowed down and thus one establishes the degree of evolutionary efficiency and causal dynamism which may be ascribed to organisms as secondary causes. This prevents one from invoking prematurely and without reason extra-scientific factors or even the *Causa Prima* itself in explanation. For many decades now, biological research has been strenuously and patiently carrying out a great number of investigations in various fields (palaeontology, palaeanthropology, primatology, anatomy, morphology, physiology, genetics, behavioural sciences). The aim has been to gain some understanding of that event (hominisation) which occurred in the almost impenetrable obscurity of long ages past.

The following points may be noted as the most important results and discoveries to date:

1. The morphological demarcations between man and certain fossil Primates are beginning to become obscured. Since the discovery of the Australopithecines of South and East Africa (*Australopithecus, Paranthropus, Zinjanthropus*), creatures with upright gait, free fore-limbs, hominid denture, but with small brain and protruding facial area of the skull, the hope has faded of finding an unambiguous criterion for distinguishing man from beast on purely morphological grounds. The more recent discovery of "*Homo habilis*" from Olduvai Gorge has made the distinction even more obscure. Besides, as more and more fossils are discovered, it seems that one can no longer prove a broad "Rubicon cérébral" or discontinuity between the cranial capacities (brain sizes) of human and non-human fossils (*Homo erectus* from Java: 775–815 ccm; "*Homo habilis*": 680–700 ccm; the Australopithe-

cines: 480–530 ccm). As far as one can judge, the spiritual element does not seem to leave an imprint on the morphological characteristics that would be clear enough to enable the scientist to prove empirically in all cases that a given bodily structure is necessarily human.

2. Many of the behavioural characteristics of man may also be found among animals, especially in some of the Primates. These characteristics are traceable to a common mammalian constitution with certain psychical possibilities. Thus, since all vertebrates, including man, have similar neurophysiological structures, it is possible to detect a common behavioural pattern which is modified in each vertebrate class to produce different versions. Here is a list of the numerous, varied achievements of the higher animals in the psychic sphere: a "practical intelligence", i.e., the ability to grasp relationships on the sense plane; the perception of form with a pre-conceptual or "sensory abstraction"; an "indistinct communication of experience"; "central representation of space" with an imagined "manipulation" quite independent of the motory functions; curiosity reactions leading to manipulation of things and an objectivating encounter with the environment; an ability to learn, to create experiences and profit from them; a social structure based on sex; territoriality; family structure; a sense of rhythm; a power of "composing and transposing"; communication through "quantitative symbols", etc. The presence in the higher animals of these and other basic dispositions or pre-requirements of a behaviour stamped by the spiritual, as well as the growing vagueness of the structural boundaries between man and beast, strengthen the conception of an evolution of man's body from a former Primate group. By this inclusion of man within the framework of organic nature and the history of organisms, one approaches some understanding of the elements that man has in common with the beast and also of man's appearance in a definite geological period (Ice Age or Pleistocene) with a definite mammalian body-type. The higher Primates of former times thus seem, both in structure and behaviour, to be "pre-oriented, preparatory stages" (Kälin) directed towards hominisation or as "beings making preliminary sketches of man, preliminary trials on the level of both body and soul" (Conrad-Martius). The world of the living is thus understood as an all-embracing unity governed by the same fundamental principles.

3. All the attempts made to derive abstract, conceptual thought by a continuous evolution from animal "intelligence" have failed. The conscious, reflective understanding and judgment carried out by man is too different from even the cleverest animal behaviour. Likewise, attempts to derive true conceptual counting from "anonymous counting", or conscious learning and the deliberate reproduction of the learned matter from the animals' power of learning have proved unconvincing. One always comes face to face with a qualitative discontinuity when attempting to reconstruct the transition from a creature without culture to man with his culture and social structure. Those modes of human behaviour that are regulated by culture are never an *entirely* natural endowment nor are they *entirely* derivable from the social behaviour of animals. In those successive evolutionary steps that have again and again been proposed to bridge the gap between the emission of sounds by animals and human speech, a discontinuity is always found between an unconscious, spontaneous communication and a conscious, controlled one; between fixed hereditary forms of stimulation and patterns of sounds and a conscious aim to make oneself understood by means of readily available words often specially created for the occasion. Several investigators speak of "a gigantic leap", or of a "enormous evolutionary step" at this point. It is here that Pavlov inserts his "second signal system" — the "signal of a signal", therefore "a new addition" which has "introduced a supplementary principle into the activity of the cerebral area". Many biologists speak of a "turning point" followed by a "solidification of the spiritual element" when referring to the origin of behaviour moulded by spirit; they refer to a "change of state", i.e., of the appearance of "completely new characteristics during the evolution of life", or of a "critical point in organic evolution". These formulations emphasize the discontinuity between animal behaviour and the human behaviour which they would like to derive from the animal, but which cannot be completely so derived.

4. The extraordinary scarcity in the fossil record of the larger Primates of the Tertiary prevents us from establishing a certain evolutionary series of successive fossil forms throughout the Tertiary right up to the men of the early Pleistocene. So also does our complete ignorance of both the time and the nature of the point of origin of the human stock. It was this evolutionary series which opened up the pathway taken by hominisation and influenced its direction, velocity and the morphological stages it passed through. The opinion seems to be gaining strength that man passed through a phyletic line special to himself and separate from that of the Anthropoid apes. In fact, from the whole of the Tertiary, there is only one Primate known which exhibited characteristics typical of the Hominids (*Oreopithecus,* from the Miocene-Pleiocene transition). It cannot, however, be directly fitted into the line leading directly to man. All the remaining fossil forms are of Pongid (higher ape) structure and often exhibit even more primitive characteristics (of the Protocatharinae). Investigators are thus unable to reach any definite conclusions about the Hominids and Australopithecines of the Ice Age. The latter, because of their late appearance and certain morphological peculiarities, cannot have been the direct ancestors of man. At the most they may be considered to provide a rough model of what these ancestors were like. A more likely candidate would be *Homo habilis* (cranial capacity 680–700 ccm), living at the same time as the Australopithecines in the early Ice Age, of which numerous fossil remains have been found since 1963 in the Olduvai Gorge (East Africa). This form which manufactured pebble-tools may probably bring us to the critical phase of the hominisation process or even right into it. The causal factors which transformed the Primate body to the level of human organization cannot yet be analysed with any certainty. The current theories of population genetics, especially when extended (extrapolated) to the major transformations that occurred in the course of the history of organisms, are by no means fully certain. The process of the development of upright gait and increasing brain size with accompanying modifications of the skull have never been satisfactorily explained. The very variety of the hypotheses proposed and their partially contradictory nature prove that the evolutionary process, with its essential characters of alteration in structure and harmonious integration, has not been even approximately analysed, even within specialized fields or in regard to single character complexes. This holds even more strongly for "psychological evolution". Since behaviour can be studied only in living organisms, fossils give us no information on this point. Thus a vast area is opened up to free speculation about the origin and causes of these behaviour patterns and their evolutionary change. This is only too clear from the numerous extant hypotheses about the origin of speech, concepts, abstract thought, human social organization, the manufacture of implements and the origin of culture. None of these hypotheses has been able to bridge the discontinuity in behaviour mentioned above in an illuminating and satisfactory way.

The concept of an evolution of organisms up to the level of bodily organization possessed by man, involving an "enracinement corporel de l'homme dans la nature" (D'Armagnac), is without doubt an inspiring one and one worthy of the Creator. Biologists defend as certain the view that this is really what took place and base their opinion on numerous pieces of circumstantial evidence. Although it is true that scientific research, despite the recent, important and suggestive fossil finds, cannot yet give any valid and certain causal explanation of this evolutionary development, nor any clear picture of the successive stages, still, the fact of hominisation remains *per se* independent of this imperfection of our knowledge. Biologists will never and can never fully reach this goal for which they strive with all the techniques available to research. For it does not seem to be possible, from the philosophical and theological points of view, to reach by means of scientific methods alone an *exhaustive* explanation of hominisation, i.e., of the origin of a new *metaphysical* type of being, such as man is.

See also *Man* I.

BIBLIOGRAPHY. A. Portmann, *Biologie und Geist* (1956); J. Piveteau, *Primates, Paléontologie humaine,* Traité de Paléontologie 7 (1957); L. Leakey, *Progress and Evolution of Man in Africa* (1961); W. Howells, *Ideas on Human Evolution* (1962);

P. Overhage and K. Rahner, *Das Problem der Hominisation* (2nd ed., 1963); M. Bates, *Man in Nature* (2nd ed., 1964); K. Rahner, *Hominisation. The Evolutionary Origin of Man as a Theological Problem*, Quaestiones Disputatae 13 (1965); P. Overhage, "'Homo habilis'", *Theologie und Philosophie* 41 (1966), pp. 321–53.

Paul Overhage

II. Theological

A. EVOLUTION

1. *The unity of the world of mind and matter.* Philosophical and theological reflection proceeds on the assumption that the fact of evolution is established by natural science. With the resources of theology or philosophy this can neither be proved nor rejected as impossible.

a) Since according to Christian philosophy and theology every created being, because finite, is in a state of becoming and changing and is part of the unity of the world which is directed towards a single goal of full accomplishment, the concept of evolution can be employed to describe, in a general and comprehensive way, what characterizes all the reality, distinct from God, which lies within the horizon of our experience. That concept would then of course have to be differentiated as variously and as analogously as the notion of becoming. As compared with the latter, however, it has the advantage of bringing out more clearly the directional progression of change.

b) In this "evolutionary" world of becoming there are, however, essential differences between the various beings and therefore their evolution is itself intrinsically heterogeneous. Natural history, the history of mind or spirit, of the person, of human societies, of salvation, all display essentially different kinds of "evolution". It would be a philosophically and theologically false evolutionism to claim that the categories of biological evolution can be transferred in precisely the same sense to the "evolution" of man as such, to history in the proper sense, and to claim that this history can be adequately interpreted and explained on the basis of such categories. Any evolutionism would be unacceptable from the philosophical and theological standpoints, and would have to be rejected as objectively heretical, which affirmed, not within the limits set by scientific method but in an apodictic statement extrapolated so as to refer to the whole of reality,

that there are no essential differences within the empirical world. This would imply that man himself is entirely a "product" of the pre-human world, that he does not result from a creative act of God which is terminatively special. It would deny that man is essentially distinguished from all other things that exist in the empirical world around him by a direct relation to God in his spirituality and freedom, because it would imply that what he is and signifies amounts to nothing but a momentary existence in the physical, biological sphere. It would deny that there is any change of an evolutionary kind which requires for its possibility the dynamism of transcendent causality operative in the world. The philosophical and theological proof of the falsehood of evolutionism understood in this way will be outlined partly in what follows and partly in the articles *Man* I–III and *Soul*.

c) The irreducibility of sub-human living things to what is purely material, in the sense of b), may well be a legitimate, well-founded thesis of natural philosophy, and it will be freely assumed in what follows. But the affirmation of an ontological difference in essence between the purely physical world and the biosphere is not, strictly speaking, a theological affirmation.

d) Provided this is clearly and unmistakably presupposed, it is legitimate to speak, though with due caution, of the evolution of the one world. Matter and finite spirit are intrinsically related to one another, even though the relationship is different in each case and differs with each degree of being. They both spring from the creative act of the one God; matter has no meaning except in a world of personal spirit; at least in man it is a necessary condition of mental activity and the scene of personal history and co-being; each in its own way, matter and mind have a single goal in the one plenitude of God's kingdom. The angels too do *not* have to be thought of as beings which by their very nature stand in no relation to the world of matter, even if they have no "body". The "history" of matter must therefore be the "history" of making mind possible, and finds in the incarnation of the Logos and the transfiguration of the universe in the resurrection of the flesh (the two are connected) its own culmination in the perfect fulfilment of the created spirit in God, in the beatific vision and end of man.

e) The unity of the world in spirit and matter, envisaged as the unity of a history, can be thought of as an "evolution", i.e., as development from within towards what is essentially higher, provided "becoming" (in the full sense of the word) is conceived as a being's "self-transcendence". It is possible to do this, for what we call God's conservation and *concursus* in regard to the existence and operation of a finite being must not be regarded as an occasional intervention of God from without, but is an enduring and most intimate intrinsic condition of the being and activity of the creature. It activates the very becoming of beings and can therefore make the immanent or transitive effect of becoming contain more "actuality" (even of a substantial and essential kind) than the finite agent itself possesses. And God's transcendent causality enables the creature *itself* actively to *effect* this supplement and not merely passively to receive it. Such a concept of self-transcendence naturally does not imply that from anything at all anything whatsoever can come. In cases where something essentially new comes into existence from and through something lower (for example, a being which is spiritual as well as biological from a mere living creature) the divine impulsion to such self-transcendence fully realizes the strict concept of "creation".

f) On these assumptions the one world (which from the start is a material world but equally from the start is under the cosmic dynamism of those created spiritual "principalities and powers" which we are accustomed to call "angels") can be thought of as moving from its material beginning towards its spiritual and personal fulfilment, in an evolution under the dynamism of its divine ground which confers self-transcendence and orientation. At all events the great stages of its history need not be thought of as a series of supplements added from outside to its original constitution.

2. *The intrinsic unity of the biosphere.* a) If there is evolution, and if it is possible (for this has not been demonstrated) to assume an ultimately monophyletic evolution, at least as a working hypothesis in biology, then the temporal unity of the biosphere is implied. This supposition may be risked here as a hypothesis because there is such a thing as evolution in general, because hominisation presupposes as its condition a leap to a higher plane (self-transcendence), which is not less than what would have to be postulated in the hypothesis of a monophyletic evolution; and because the metaphysical economy-principle demands that if possible, a new initiative by God within the one changing world, should not be postulated unnecessarily. It follows then that if a monophyletic evolution is assumed, the whole world of living things appears as a real unity linked together in time, and based on, and incorporated in, the temporal unity of matter which itself is one.

b) Such a view, as well as other considerations, leads to the question of the ontological unity of the biosphere. In the first place the ontological unity of the *material* world must not be overlooked. In ontology, what the Scholastics called *materia prima* is not a reality multiple in itself and of itself, occurring many times as an "intrinsic" element in the many things of experience. It is the one, real, substantial principle of the spatio-temporal dispersion of what is materially multiple, the ontological principle of what is partly observed and partly presupposed as the single fundamental field or domain of all concrete phenomena and of physics. The biosphere of course also shares in this ontological unity of space-time. It is comprised within the material world's single space-time manifold, which is its ground, not the subsequent outcome of mutual causal influence. The question whether above and beyond this the temporal unity of the biosphere as such points to a spatial unity of a quasi-substantial kind, leads to the further question whether in this sphere the substantial formal principle (the ground of the spatio-temporal configuration of a living thing) must be thought of both specifically and individually as plural, as "multiplied", or not (the human spiritual person being always excluded). Everyday experience and traditional natural philosophy always answered the question in the first sense. As many really distinct substantial forms were directly assumed to be present as distinct "individuals" of different living "species" were observed.

But this everyday experience is not conclusive. On closer examination the limits of biological individuals very often become vague. (Cf. the phenomenon of the "runners" at first connected with the mother-plant and then separated from it; the fluid transition between various plants and animals which appear to be one; the germ-cell inside and outside the parent organism, etc.) Living forms which present what are apparently very great differences in space and time can ontologically have the same morphological principle, so that enormous differences of external form can derive from the material substratum and chance patterns of circumstance without change of substantial form (caterpillar — chrysalis — butterfly). A true physical "continuum" (beyond the unity of the physical "field") is not necessary as material for a substantial formal principle of living beings. What for us is a plurality of living things visibly manifested by spatial discontinuity, is therefore no proof of an ontological plurality of living things in respect of their formal principle. The same holds good of the antagonism among living forms, for this is also found within living beings which everyone regards as one and the same. The biosphere would perhaps therefore be more correctly, because more simply, envisaged, if we were to think of it as perpetually based on *one* substantial formal principle. This latter would have a tremendous potentiality of ways of manifesting itself in space and time and would realize these possibilities in space and time in accordance with the conditions of physical matter actually present, even though these conditions themselves receive direction from that formal principle. This picture on the one hand would match the development of physics, which reduces (or seeks to reduce) the plurality of "specifically" different natural substances to the space-time variation of one and the same matter. It would also bring out more clearly the formal ontological difference between biosphere and the "noosphere" of personal minds. Only in the latter would there be individuals simply and substantially distinct from one another; individuals that are no longer the increasingly complex modifications in space and time of the fundamentally one and evolving biosphere.

3. *Theological and ontological problems regarding the causes of evolution.* a) (i) The question of the "mechanics" of evolution is a scientific question. It concerns the "genetic" conditions, inner and external, of a material kind (modification of genes etc.), under which something biologically "new" arises. In principle they are physically producible conditions susceptible of explanation in terms of function. And natural science by its very method can restrict its attention to that question.

(ii) Because of the unity yet essential intrinsic differentiation of the world, only a certain number of formal structures can and must be named as characterizing this one evolution: a tendency towards a growing complexity of the various individual beings, towards greater "interiority", towards greater specialization combined with greater openness towards the whole of reality, orientation and irreversibility of evolution. On that basis man, together with other beings possessing self-consciousness, freedom and dynamic transcendent orientation towards God, appears as the goal of cosmic evolution. Since he is material and since his materiality is a factor in the material unity of the whole universe as "field" and since he can manipulate himself physically and morally, in this world and in relation to the "other world", it is quite legitimate to affirm that the world becomes aware of itself in man and attains a direct conscious encounter with its ground, God.

(iii) The free gift of God's grace, God's communication of himself, was incorporated in the world from the beginning (for the angels possessed it from the beginning, and man as the goal of the world was intended by God from the start as man divinized); consequently, world evolution really, and not merely in the divine "ideas", moves under the dynamism that is directed towards the "kingdom of God". The history of nature and the world becomes the history of salvation and revelation when man is reached, for man, aware of his supernatural teleology, historically objectivates that orientation. Its "omega point" is in fact Christ, in whom created matter, finite spirit and the divine Logos in whom all things subsist, are united in one person and this unity is manifested in history.

b) (i) The metaphysical question of what actually happens in evolution from the ontological point of view, i.e., with regard to the totality of operative causes, must first of all be analysed in such a way that it is clear that the answer will differ according to the differing ontological relation of the "new" that has come about, to the mundane cause (antecedent) that preceded it. If the new is substantially new or even something essentially higher, i.e., if numerically an additional substantial principle appears or even a being which by its very character cannot in principle be understood as a purely space-time modification of the data already present in its antecedent, but has an irreducibly higher ontological position in relation to the very nature of being as such (even though this does not preclude a cosmic causal derivation), then the question must on principle be framed differently from when what is "new" can be understood as a different but physically producible space-time pattern of data already present. In the first sense the question arises with theological and philosophical certainty only in regard to the "evolution" of man and with some philosophical certainty in regard to the transition from the purely material to the biosphere. Within the biosphere itself the question does not necessarily have to be raised in that way. Yet it soon becomes clear (cf. below) that from the ontological point of view, this correct and enduring distinction in objective reality and in mode of stating the question is not so important, theologically speaking, as it might at first seem, provided that in general the coming into existence of something new is correctly understood.

(ii) Intramundane becoming as self-transcendence. If and where something really "new" comes about and yet derives from a cause within the world (and supposing that mere occasionalism is rejected on philosophical and above all on theological grounds), its cause "goes beyond" itself; it posits more "reality" than itself is and possesses. According to the metaphysical principle of causality, this self-transcendence, which must at this point still be thought of in a quite general way, is only possible in virtue of the dynamism of the absolute Being which is at the same time what is most intimate to the mundane cause and yet absolutely distinct from the causally operative finite being. The absolute Being constitutes active beings (by conservation and *concursus*) not merely as something static, but in their active self-transcendence whereby they both accomplish their own nature and posit what is "new". The "new", being more than the agent, is at once the effect posited by the mundane cause and by the transcendent causality of the absolute Being. In the mind's transcendent experience, the dialectic of this relationship is directly present: the absolute Being, as asymptotic goal of the movement of mind or spirit is always what is "beyond";

it posits the finite spirit as separate and absolutely other than itself and yet at the same time it is what is most intimate to it, the basis of the ontological movement of becoming in the finite spirit. The latter moves in virtue of that Being's opening itself to it, and does not merely strive towards a horizon which in the last resort would simply be an "object" pursued in virtue of the intrinsic capacity of the knowing subject itself. Since in this transcendental experience the ontology of a being is an immediate datum, there is found there as an actual ontological occurrence a self-transcendence towards what is more, in virtue of the absolute Being. Self-transcendence can therefore be shown here to be a valid metaphysical concept.

(iii) If the ontological concept of active self-transcendence is once metaphysically established, the idea of evolution and its compatibility with divine causality no longer offers any insuperable difficulties from the ontological point of view. Causal dependence within the world and ontological difference of kind between a mundane effect and its cause are not mutually exclusive but inclusive. Corresponding to the various ontological differences (mere spatial and temporal rearrangements of matter, modifications of a field, repetition of the identical, accidental but stable change, the production of what is essentially new), the divine dynamism which supports the change in question can and must be affirmed as different in respect of its "term". Consequently the concept of a creative intervention of God will only be employed where it is a question of what is essentially new. But this creative intervention, as distinct from the perpetual positing of matter in the world generally, must not be conceived as a supplementary intervention from outside, adding something new to something that exists, with the latter remaining purely passive. It must be understood to bring about the self-transcendence of the mundane antecedent of what is new. Because, however, divine dynamism is understood to be ontologically necessary in *all* real becoming and therefore in *all* evolution (though this dynamism is not an object of natural science), the question where an *essential* self-transcendence is present and where not, is not so urgent. We know that it is present in man's coming to be, whether ontogenetically or phylogenetically. And it is decisive for man's understanding of himself to know this. But self-transcendence is directly accessible in the transcendental experience of subjectivity and freedom. And so man knows himself (in his unity and totality) as created by God *and* as the product of mundane antecedent causes. With this concept of self-transcendence, and if we attribute full weight to the strict substantial unity of man (matter and "soul" being substantial principles, not independent beings), and if full meaning is given to the role of the parents in procreation, which is to beget a human being, not a biological entity, then the statement that in evolution God creates the "soul" of man, while evolution produces the body, needs careful understanding. Both causes have as their term the one human being, because they do not operate side by side, but as mutually implicated, because the divine causality constitutes the ontologically transcendent dimension of created causal efficacy.

4. *Man within the evolving biosphere.* a) If man as a spiritual person derives from the biosphere by evolution, then he still belongs to it, if only as the term into which the material world and the biosphere rise above and beyond themselves. Man's derivation from the material and biological world is an enduring one. And in that respect in every human being the entire cosmos attains anew a unique self-possession. Every human being is in dialectical unity both a portion of the cosmos, rooted in the cosmos, and a unique appropriation of the whole cosmos. For the problem whether phylogenetically man's origin from the biosphere occurred once or several times, see the article *Monogenism*.

b) This insertion of man into the material world (which goes further than a mere mutual efficient causality, for at the very least it is also based on the unity of matter, in other words, ontologically, prior to any mutual influence), raises in a new way the old question of the "plurality of forms in man". Does the origin of man from the biosphere signify that in him, the biosphere principles which determine its spatio-temporal unities (or the *one* new principle prevailing in it; see above), are still present? The formal concept of self-transcendence expresses nothing certain either positively or negatively on this point. The account given in traditional theology, that the spiritual soul

is also the principle of vegetative and animal life, does not exclude, it would seem, the possibility that this could take place through a hierarchy and teleology of partial realities of the substantial order belonging to the biosphere as such (the "vestigial organs", embryological false starts from the beginning of ontogeny which are perhaps human, etc., seem to point in this direction). The relation between spiritual soul and these subordinate "forms" can itself be thought of in different ways, so that what is meant by it need not necessarily contradict the real meaning of the Thomistic doctrine of the unicity of form in a new being which is substantially one: the single higher form itself produces out of its own polyvalent ground, and according to the formal principle of its antecedent, the earlier partial form, and can discard this latter once more. If such a plurality of forms of spatio-temporal configurations within man can perhaps be thought of as a legacy from the biosphere, then the old problem of the plurality of forms in man is new and urgent, because through biochemistry and genetics (with all the problems they raise), we are now slowly arriving at the possibility of forming a concrete idea of these "forms" and their manifestations.

c) On that basis the problem arises whether in man's actual shape and form, in his physiological automatisms etc., there were once or still are, features which, though of course compatible with the nature of man, nevertheless do not yet represent that full accomplishment towards which man, still in process of development, is still moving; in other words, the question whether the history of the biosphere in teleological relation to man is still continuing *within* man as he at present exists. If it is firmly held that the proper nature of man as a personal spirit open to infinity, cannot *per definitionem* be further exceeded and has already reached its absolute culmination in grace and the Incarnation, nothing in principle can be objected to the idea of a further history of man in his biosphere (and not merely in personal spirit and the products of its self-objectivation in civilization). Such a history is actually taking place in what we can empirically observe as races, race-mixture, and so on. And if the necessary moral conditions of respect for man were observed, even a deliberate manipulation of this history by man himself would be conceivable. Such a question might also involve consequences for moral theology.

See also *Man, History* I, *Salvation* III, *Spirit, Soul, Matter, Creation, Life* I, *Causality*.

BIBLIOGRAPHY. P.-M. Périer, *Le Transformisme. L'origine de l'homme et le dogme* (1938); M. Flick, "L'origine del corpo del primo uomo alla luce della filosofia cristiana e della teologia", *Gregorianum* 29 (1948), pp. 392–416; E. Ruffini, *La teoria della evoluzione secondo la scienza e la fede* (1948); J. Marcozzi, *Evoluzione o creazione? Le origini dell'uomo* (1948); J. Ternus, *Die Abstammungslehre heute* (1949); J. Kälin, "Evolutionstheorie und katholische Weltanschauung", *Divus Thomas* 27 (1949), pp. 5–16; A. Bea, *Il problema antropologico in Gn 1–2. Il transformismo* (1950); P. Denis, *Les origines du monde et de l'humanité* (1950); J. Carles, *Le Transformisme* (1951); J. Marcozzi, *L'uomo nello spazio e nel tempo* (1953); P. Teilhard de Chardin, *Le phénomène humain* (1955), E. T.: *The Phenomenon of Man* (1959); J. Kohn, *Evolution as Revelation* (1963); K. Rahner, *Hominisation. The Evolutionary Origin of Man as a Theological Problem.* Quaestiones Disputatae 13 (1965).

Karl Rahner

B. HOMINISATION

1. *Preliminary remarks.* a) Philosophy as transcendental reflection on the nature of man cannot make any statement about the precise mode of origin of the first human being. It can have no objection to the possibility of an intra-mundane causal nexus through a "qualitative leap" between two beings which are essentially different from one another. The concept of an active self-transcendence, under the dynamism of divine conservation and *concursus* as the immanent ground of the active mutability of the creature, seems a difficult one, but not contradictory, and the facts appear to demand it. On the other hand, metaphysical anthropology establishes with certainty a radical difference of nature between man and brute. Consequently a causal origin of man from the world around him, even if it is thought of as active self-transcendence, within the requisite dynamism of the divine concursus, has at the same time quite definitely the character of a new, direct creation by God.

b) In theology it is customary to distinguish between "soul" and "body", and to attribute the origin of the former to "creation" and of the latter to evolution. But it must not be forgotten that soul and matter signify substantial principles of an individual being, not two complete beings subsequently combined. Soul and matter form a strictly substantial unity. If this is kept in mind, "creation of the soul" can only mean that the whole man is directly created by God in the sense that as a corporeal spiritual person he essentially differs from the brutes and consequently is not simply and solely the product of the "biosphere", and is not merely on its level. In that case, evolution of the body can only mean that the whole man takes his origin from the world around him. The two statements made simultaneously about the same man are conceivable because the concepts of becoming and causal dependence do not exclude but rather (usually) include a "qualitative leap". The latter is possible as something posited by a creature through the divine dynamism which supports from within its active becoming.

2. *The teaching of the Church.* a) According to the Church's teaching, it would be heretical to declare that man as a spiritual person is in that respect a product of infra-human reality according to its own natural laws. For the First Vatican Council defined (*D* 1802) that there is a difference of nature between matter and spirit; and man, at least "as regards his soul", is directly created by God (*D* 170, 533, 738, 1185, 1910, 2327; according to Pius XII: "animas enim a Deo immediate creari catholica fides nos retinere iubet").

b) Nevertheless the Church's magisterium, provisionally at least, does not reject the scientific thesis that man, as far as his body is concerned, stands in historical connection with the animal kingdom; the question may be freely discussed (Pius XII in an address in 1941 [*D* 2285] and in *Humani Generis* [*D* 2327]), but this freedom does not extend to the question of monogenism (*D* 2327).

c) There are no further official ecclesiastical pronouncements on the compatibility of the two affirmations. We must be careful not to think that the question is fully solved merely by applying the first proposition to the soul, the second to the body. The spiritual soul which results from one direct creative act of God of necessity also signifies a transforming specification of the bodily component, even if this creative act occurs in living matter. And so the doctrine can and must be maintained that Scripture speaks of a *peculiaris creatio hominis*, as the decree of the

Biblical Commission in 1909 (*D* 2123) teaches.

3. *The teaching of Scripture*. God's revelation in Scripture envisages man always and everywhere as one corporeal and spiritual being. And in contrast to everything else met with in the earthly world of human experience, man in his bodily reality is the spiritual and moral partner of God, spoken to by God. In this reality, which is in unique contrast to all else, man is represented as originating in a special creative initiative of God aimed directly at man and producing the image and likeness of God which until then had not existed. It is certainly not possible to deny that so much at least is contained and asserted in the first three chapters of Genesis. And since tradition has always drawn the doctrine from the Genesis account of the creation of man, it is binding on us (cf. *D* 2123). On the other hand it must be said that the Genesis account is not intended to be an eye-witness report of exactly what took place. In other words, what is involved is a statement (probably a historical aetiology), which expresses what it really means in popular terms by the use of vivid imagery. We are not only permitted, but commanded, to take this *genus litterarium* into account, for the Church not merely tolerates such a view but itself teaches it (*D* 2302, 2329).

If this is admitted in principle, however, it follows that Scripture in Genesis 1–3 contains nothing beyond what has been said which, in respect of our present problem, could with certainty be affirmed to belong to the content asserted and not to the mode of presentation. The formation of man from the dust of the earth can and must be taken as a way of expressing the fact of creation. If this *genus litterarium* is taken into account, no argument against transformism can be drawn from Eve's formation from "Adam's rib". It cannot be proved that this image expresses more than a relation of congruity between the first human being and the second, and the unity of both (a view held as early as Cajetan, and at the present time by H. Lesêtre, W. Schmidt, J. Chaine, H. Junker, J. de Fraine, etc.), even if reference is made to *D* 2123. For if the "formatio primae mulieris ex primo homine" which is there defended as historical is soberly interpreted in the light of *D* 3202, all that is asserted is that in this narrative too we have

to acknowledge the affirmation of a historical event; it is not thereby denied that any figurative element is to be found in it. And so on the basis of Scripture too we must affirm what the Church's magisterium declares on the present question.

4. *Tradition*. a) It must be admitted that before the 19th century the general interpretation of the Genesis account (leaving aside evanescent suggestions of a more subtle conception) was that God created man's corporeal nature from non-living matter. Yet Christian tradition was aware from the beginning that in the accounts of the world's first origins more than in other passages of Scripture, figurative modes of expression are to be reckoned with. Our present-day question did not arise. It is true, of course, that revelation and tradition, objectively speaking, can answer a question which was only explicitly propounded at a later date, yet in the present case it must be said that tradition does not contain an explicit or formally implicit rejection of a bodily link between man and the animal kingdom. And this is because what tradition certainly intended to affirm with the absolute character of a statement of the faith, namely the special position, and therefore special creation, of man, is still just as true today on the assumption of moderate transformism. But it cannot be shown that this absolute character of a statement of the faith must also be attributed to the modality under which earlier tradition imagined the event in question to have taken place, but without being able either expressly to distinguish that mode from the actual content affirmed or expressly to include it in it. Such absence of a distinction, however, is not necessarily an implicit denial of the possibility of the distinction, if it was not possible, in view of earlier historical conditions, to raise the question of the possibility of such a distinction.

b) The first explicit ecclesiastical pronouncement of an official kind was made at the local synod of Cologne in 1860 (*Collectio Lacensis*, V, col. 292). Here even the moderate theory of descent was rejected. In 1871 the Catholic St. G. Mivart proposed a moderate transformism ("Mivartism"). In 1895, M. D. Leroy, O.P., had to retract the view he had expressed on moderate transformism ("L'évolution restrainte aux espèces organiques"; cf. *Civiltà Cattolica*, XVII, 5 [1899], pp. 48 f.). In 1899, P. Zahn for the same reason had to withdraw from commerce his book *Dogma and Evolution* at the command of the Holy Office (*ibid.*, pp. 34–39). No objection was raised to later works defending moderate transformism by Teilhard de Chardin, F. Rüschkamp, P.-M. Périer, E. C. Messenger and others. Nevertheless even until quite recently such moderate transformism was rejected by the great majority of theologians as contrary to Scripture and open to theological objection. In the 19th century it was still regarded as heretical, for example by G. Perrone, C. Mazella, B. Jungmann, J. Katschthaler. Since Pius XII allowed free discussion, the number of Catholics who positively support transformism has considerably increased (C. Colombo, P. Leonardi, J. Marcozzi, P. Denis, J. Carles, B. Meléndez, J. Kälin, F. Elliott, etc.). Yet even now there are theologians who reject transformism even in its most cautious form, because they do not think it scientifically proved and because theological reasons still seem to them to militate against it, even though usually now they do not risk assigning any theological note of censure. So, for example, E. Ruffini, J. Rabeneck, I. F. Sagüés, Ch. Boyer, M. Daffara, C. Baisi. This development of doctrine has not yet been the subject of more detailed theological reflection. At all events it shows that the Church is always learning and that appeal to the unanimous agreement of theologians is an argument that must be handled cautiously.

5. *Systematic treatment of the problem.* If we assume that the doctrine of hominisation through evolution is correct (positively to decide this is not in itself a matter for theology), the following can be said.

a) God supports most intimately, from within, the creature as a mutable being in its becoming, in its movement of self-development and self-transcendence. Becoming ultimately means active rising beyond self, in which God so moves the mover that it receives its own self-movement (and not merely a movement passively undergone), from God (as ground) and as directed towards him (as asymptotic goal). Any other conception of becoming leads in the last resort to occasionalism or to change without cause. What we call matter (and especially when it is already animate and sensitive), has an intrinsic affinity to consciousness, imma-

nence, spirit, because it originates by creation from God the absolute personal spirit, and is the potential intrinsic substantial co-principle of a personal created spirit (man).

b) Since the one universe (even in its material reality) has a single goal, its salvation, transfiguration and accomplishment in the kingdom of God, it is directed and impelled by God from the start towards that goal: the full accomplishment of created spirit, which integrates matter into its final perfection.

c) Consequently the becoming of the material world can certainly be regarded as orientated from within by God, in dynamic self-transcendence towards man, in whom the world achieves immanence, subjectivity, freedom, history and personal fulfilment. Hominisation designates that occurrence in nature in which the universe finds itself in man and is consciously confronted with its origin and goal.

d) When man is in question (whether from the phylogenetic or ontogenetic point of view), God's rendering possible a self-transcendence of the cosmic causal antecedent in the direction of man denotes the same thing as what theology calls immediate creation (*D* 2327). God's transcendental causality in making such self-transcendence possible must be characterized on the basis of its term. If therefore something substantially new arises which *in se subsistit* (i.e., despite its function as the principle of a space-time configuration, always exceeds this function, precisely as spirit), then the divine enablement which is directed precisely to that term, is "creation" and it is "direct". For from God as source something is constituted which involves a new independent being. The example of human procreation (human ontogeny) shows that in such an account, the concept of *immediata creatio* can be used. For the language customarily employed by the magisterium applies this expression to the coming into existence of the whole human being (although the matter involved already existed), yet without any intention of denying that the parents are the cause of the human being in question. That God makes possible a mundane causal efficacy does not, therefore, exclude the concept of direct creation, provided that something substantially new and really independent comes into existence and that the divine causality (as is the case as a matter of course), directly terminates in it. In the case of phylogeny that is even more patently so, because the mundane causal antecedent is then specifically inferior to man.

See also *Man* II, III, *Body, Soul, Monogenism, Form Criticism* II.

BIBLIOGRAPHY. F. X. Mayr, *Woher der Mensch? Das Ende der "klassischen" Abstammungslehre* (1954); P. Teilhard de Chardin, *The Phenomenon of Man* (1959); id., *The Future of Man* (1964); K. Rahner, *Schriften zur Theologie,* I (1954), pp. 253–322; V (1962), pp. 183–221, E. T.: *Theological Investigations,* I (1961), V (1965); id., *Hominisation. The Evolutionary Origin of Man as a Theological Problem.* Quaestiones Disputatae 13 (1965); P. Teilhard de Chardin, *Appearance of Man* (1966); id., *Man's Place in Nature* (1966); L. Polgár, *Internationale Teilhard-Bibliographie 1955–65* (1966); H. de Lubac, *Teilhard de Chardin: The Man and His Meaning* (1967); R. Overman, *Evolution and the Christian Doctrine of Creation* (1967).
Karl Rahner

EXISTENCE

I. Concept of Existence: A. Introduction. B. The Different Epochs. C. Philosophical Articulation. II. Philosophy of Existence and Existential Philosophy. III. "The Existential": A. Philosophical. B. Theological.

I. Concept of Existence

A. INTRODUCTION

The word "existence" has become one of the signs of the times in modern thinking, having also given its name to one of the predominant trends of philosophy.

It should, however, be noted that even in existentialism the term is understood so differently by such figures as Heidegger, Jaspers, Sartre and Marcel that what they have in common is hard to define briefly, in spite of the general accord of their interests. It may, however, be affirmed that in this philosophy existence means the actuality of human existence. Thus it is not the same as the scholastic *existentia,* which, as opposed to *essentia,* was the actuality of any essence, not just that of man. But even in Scholasticism the concept had varied. In Thomism, for instance, it crystallized another whole concept of reality than in Suarezianism. Thus the history of the concept from its first appearance in Marius Victorinus (d. *c.* 362)

to the present day must be envisaged. It can be shown that the variations in meaning are not accidental, but correspond to the changes in metaphysical self-understanding. But it would be wrong to confine such an analysis to the periods in which the term undergoes such changes, since the thing itself, self-understanding as understanding of existence, was always there. For a full history of the interpretation of existence, all epochs would have to be examined, even where the self-understanding effective in all action and thinking was not expressly articulated. It would cover all the fundamental aspects of life — myth, religion, art, law, politics, philosophy, technology — and would coincide with the determination of the spirit of each age. All that can be attempted here is to show briefly that human consciousness does not always interpret itself in the same way. Its variations give rise to epochs in the history of the spirit which have a quality of their own in each case, which can easily be lost sight of by the readiness with which one's own type of self-understanding is taken for granted. Though it cannot be directly grasped, the spirit of an age, embracing the main aspects mentioned above, is clearly seen in its relation to history and its trend, and in the resulting philosophy of the times.

B. THE DIFFERENT EPOCHS

1. The Greeks are the founders of Western history as well as philosophy. Nonetheless, the main interest of the Greeks was in nature and its ultimate, permanent causes. Philosophy at its highest was only interested in the permanent substratum of all beings which underlies all changes. History, as that which comes to be and passes away, was not knowable and ultimately not worth knowing. Even a thinker as open-minded and comprehensive as Plato thought of his ideal State as isolated from its neighbours and even from its own past. It was so detached from time that once founded it would remain always the same. Aristotle was interested in contemporary politics and gathered much historical material, but for his self-understanding, strictly speaking, only the cyclic and permanent was valid — reason with its eternal laws. Implicit or explicit, even in the great historian Thucydides, was the basic conviction that nature, including the nature of man, would never change. The self-under-

standing of the Greeks was drawn up basically on the pattern of nature. The concrete course of events had at most the significance of a paradigm from which the nature of things could be deduced. But there was little notion of possible development and real change, and hence little interest in the future and in history in general. The Roman mind differed only in emphasis, the duration and extent of the Roman empire giving a somewhat different perspective. In common with the Greeks they had a great sense of the permanent, either as the eternal form of all reality or the inevitable necessity of facts. Plato even reached the concept of love and the good as the reality which could provide deliverance from the prison of history. But the perspective of a great future in which history was to attain its fulfilment was unknown to antiquity.

2. The self-understanding of Israel was very different. Israel had little interest in science, art and culture, and little scope for them; but it was supremely alert to the human. If we compare Deutero-Isaiah and Herodotus, who were almost contemporaries, the difference between Greek and Jewish self-understanding stands out vividly. But the mind of Israel was not formed by theoretical knowledge and research. Its self-understanding came from repeated reflection on its own history. It learned from its memories and reflection that it was a people with one God who was very close to his own, demanding from his people loyalty and faith in his promises. This is a completely new dimension of self-understanding. Reality is not the cyclic repetition of nature, but the creation of God. But faith in creation is faith in the promises, the promises of a future made possible by loyalty to God (covenant). The ground of all historical reality, both as its beginning and its end, is a person. This stress on the personal element, including the notion of decision and freedom in history, was unique.

3. Thus existence was no longer determined by fate, as among the Greeks, where even the world of the gods was so determined and thus underlined the rule of fate. Israel's experience was taken up by Christianity, especially in the preaching of Paul and John, where self-understanding was fully conscious of the reality of freedom as a creative, though not identifiable power. This untrammelled grasp of freedom, by virtue of which alone could the reality of guilt and sin be accepted, was not the result of a natural process. It was based on confidence in the God of Israel who became man in Jesus of Nazareth and through him offered salvation to all men. Faith in the incarnation made the early Christians take man as seriously as God, and reinforced the dialectic and dynamism of the OT, as the event of cross and resurrection shows. This brought about a self-understanding which did not fear death, because it had experienced the creative force whose power and fullness it expressed by the word Pneuma. In spite of the intenser confrontation with sin and death, the Christian mind, characterized profoundly by faith, hope and love, had the courage to believe that all history and the whole cosmos, now that God had entered in, was to attain an ultimate salvation. This self-understanding which reconciles and unites nature and history, sin and redemption, man and God, is unique both as the expression of man's actual experience and as the adumbration of a future salvation.

4. Reflection on these basic experiences gave rise, in the Fathers, and especially Augustine, to a self-understanding which took in all history for the first time. It was this sense of man as a whole, and of his whole history as a salvific process which determined the nature of the Middle Ages and of modern times down to the present day, in spite of many deviations and much secularization. In the Middle Ages this heritage was transformed in the course of reflection on classical antiquity. The history of salvation, with its primordial sense of freedom, was comprised in an order of creation where heaven and earth, past and future, had a remarkably finished look and where even the notion of God as part of the comprehensive hierarchical order, static and permanent, led to legalism and nominalism. The understanding of self tended to approximate to the understanding of things. The modern age tried to counteract this tendency. The Renaissance and Reformation looked back once more to antiquity and primitive Christianity, initiating a new discussion between the biblical experience of salvation and the classical notion of culture. Then the elimination of the cosmology of Aristotle and Ptolemy threw man once more back on himself, but at the same time opened up the way to a self-understanding in a

cosmic framework. The epochs of Humanism, Baroque, Enlightenment, Romanticism, Classicism and so on followed. The two possibilities of self-understanding offered by the history of the West were made more radical and total, but at the same time relativized. The resulting mentality, in all its practical, intellectual and technical endeavours is more and more conscious of its historical evolution and setting. It thus aims at a social, scientific and technological control which will assure it absolutely of the future.

C. Philosophical Articulation

Once the two sources of Western self-understanding, Greek and Jewish, had come together, as outlined above, and developed and changed, a change in philosophical theory also ensued. The classical and medieval metaphysics is essentially different from the type of thinking which began with the transcendental philosophy of Kant. This was continued in the systematic philosophy, of the dialogue or dialectical type, of Fichte and Hegel, according to the two basic forms of Western metaphysics. Finally, after Kierkegaard, came the phenomenology of Husserl and the existential or ontological thinking of Heidegger, and also the dialectical materialism of Marx. Both of these deliberately gave up all systematic philosophizing, to help man to an authentic self-understanding. The question of beings *qua* beings had been put by the classical metaphysics, on the basis of Plato's analysis of the difference between becoming and the true being of the form (between ὂν γιγνόμενον and ὄντως ὄν), which became a metaphysical discipline in the hands of Aristotle and was re-stated by Thomas Aquinas. This basic question tries to see beings not from any particular aspect, their usefulness or acceptability, for instance, but from the aspect which it is as itself — namely as a being. This "ontological" question does not separate beings from their essence, which is to be themselves, i.e., beings. But the "cause" which identifies each being with itself, that is, makes it be itself being, must be a supreme totality in which are contained all differentiation and demarcation — and that is being. Hence the basic trait of this metaphysics is to ask after the ground and origin of beings in being. This mediation, for Aristotle and for Thomas, is accomplished by the "active intellect" (νοῦς ποιητικός,

intellectus agens). Nonetheless, this metaphysics fails to note that the origin of beings in being is not to be thought of as a sort of cosmogony, on the analogy of a natural ontogenesis, but is once more essentially mediated in the consciousness of man. This relationship to the consciousness which was not entirely neglected in classical metaphysics, became fundamental and systematic with Kant and led to the new "transcendental" approach. Here for the first time the principle that all understanding of reality is self-understanding was clearly envisaged. The principle that infinite being was the ground of all beings, the absolute truth and goodness, which had been *per se nota,* intrinsically evident, to classical metaphysics, was now called in question. Kant could find no way of justifying the possibility of ontological knowledge, which he therefore held was beyond the limit of human possibilities. Being became consciousness, essence became category and beings objects. Man, deprived of contact with metaphysical reality of an absolute and universal nature, was thrown back on himself and so knew himself in another way, that is, as subject for objects.

If classical metaphysics had lost sight of its true nature in the myth, so to speak, of ontogenesis, this transcendental changeover (not a denial but a transformation of metaphysics) reminded it that all understanding of reality is likewise self-understanding. Nonetheless, there still remained, even though on a higher level, a fundamental process of objectivation: being becomes the consciousness of the subject with regard to the object. Self-understanding is not complete and authentic.

Fichte eliminated the alienation by envisaging for the first time the personal relationship as the interplay of subject and object, in which the subjective consciousness of Kant now became a mediating element. This medial consciousness is seen as the light and life (truth) of the whole personal realm. It makes the Kantian object mediate between persons and so appear in itself. In contrast to classical metaphysics there has been a mediation, but the meaning of being becomes nonetheless once more infinite, absolute, life and light. And beings cease to be mere objects for subjects and are transformed into independent media. Self-understanding becomes once more complete or absolute, but in a radical interplay of immanence and transcendence. And more clearly than ever before, the question of being or light is posed, in the distinction between the light and the source of light (God). Fichte's philosophy of absolute freedom became in Hegel the philosophy of the absolute spirit. For Fichte, self-understanding is absolute mediation in freedom and hence also in history. It is just as absolute a mediation of the spirit in Hegel, but now necessary, in a necessary process of history. It seemed impossible to go beyond the stage of total reflection on self attained in German idealism. Nonetheless, in spite of the inclusion of history and historicity, this philosophy reflected self-understanding merely as a system. A new question was adumbrated by Kierkegaard and Marx and then posed expressly by phenomenology: the meaning of existence prior to any mediating system — a meaning not to be attained by way of mere reflection. The question had not been unknown to Fichte and Hegel, and especially to Schelling. But a new effort was made to clarify it by means of the so-called phenomenological analysis, applied to the region of immediate experience of the proper nature of being and not to any proprieties arrived at by deduction.

Heidegger's thought in particular strives to grasp being as the ground which, though the force behind all attempts at systematization, is itself unattainable through reflection. His effort is therefore to describe the experience in pre- or non-philosophic terms. Self-understanding is the medium in which "being" makes itself known as event. The historical or existentialist experience of this event cannot be demonstrated, but only expounded or interpreted (hermeneutics). This "being" has itself a history, which determines the changing self-understanding of man in each different epoch. "Being" impinges on each epoch as a different sense of human existence.

As regards the Christian self-understanding, the question now arises as to whether there is not something similar going on, inasmuch as the self-disclosure of the Logos varies from epoch to epoch. It seems true at any rate to say that antiquity understood itself in terms of nature and cosmology, and that the Middle Ages still remained tributary to a sort of ontogenesis. But the transcendental changeover of modern times brought with it a more anthropological self-

understanding, totally systematized in German idealism. It was transformed from system to experience in the turn to existentialism, though even here, as must be noted, full justice is not done to self-understanding as historical *and* social. The reason is that this self-understanding basically views history in the light of its origins rather than as something heading for its destiny. Hence if an outline of philosophy is to be drawn up on the basis of the true Christian experience and the self-understanding which it implies, it must be primarily a transcendental philosophy of freedom which is at once ontological and "dialogue-centred", thus preserving the heritage of tradition. It cannot be bounded within a formal system. Since it takes seriously the non *a priori* nature of the historical experience as a matter of freedom and of dialogue, it must try for a hermeneutics which will be a "phenomenology" of the Incarnation. This means that history is to be made visible as also the history of God (history of salvation). It is only on this basis that the future can be grasped and moulded — in hope — in all its technical, scientific and social manifestations. This will make possible a self-understanding both inspired by revelation and orientated to a future history which moves towards its own absoluteness.

See also *Existence* II, III A, *Pre-Socratics, History* I, *Salvation* III A.

BIBLIOGRAPHY. M. Heidegger, *Sein und Zeit* (1927), E. T.: *Being and Time* (1962); K. Jaspers, *Philosophie,* 3 vols. (1932 ff.); G. Marcel, *Homo Viator* (1945); J. P. Sartre, *L'être et le néant* (1943), E. T.: *Being and Nothingness* (1957); C. Fabro, *Dall'essere all'esistente* (1947); H. Blackham, *Six Existentialist Thinkers* (1952); J. Owens, *The Doctrine of Being in the Aristotelian Metaphysics* (2nd ed., 1957); K. Jaspers, *Reason and Existenz* (1956); G. Siewerth, *Das Schicksal der Metaphysik* (1959); H. Barnes, *Humanistic Existentialism* (1962); F. Copleston, *Contemporary Philosophy* (1963); M. Müller, *Existenzphilosophie im geistigen Leben der Gegenwart* (3rd ed., 1964);. W. Barrett, *What is Existentialism?* (1964); H.-G. Gadamer, *Wahrheit und Methode* (2nd ed., 1965); J. B. Lotz, *Sein und Existenz* (1965); B. Welte, *Auf der Spur des Ewigen* (1965).

Eberhard Simons

II. Philosophy of Existence and Existential Philosophy

1. *The term.* The term "Existentialism" covers various forms of present-day philo-

sophical thinking which all have one thing in common: existence is not the actualization of an essence, as the Scholastics understood *existentia,* but the actual being of man and, above all, the active realization of man's existence, which is in each case an individual act. This way of thinking is centred on man as the irreplaceable individual. Hence the philosophy of existence is not purely theoretical. It tries, on the contrary, to break down the automatism and self-deception of everyday consciousness, to achieve real selfhood. (On Heidegger, see below; but for the moment, and in any case according to the way his thought has been understood and his influence felt, it is true also of him.)

2. *Origins.* There have always been thinkers inspired by this goal throughout the history of Western philosophy, such as Socrates, St. Augustine and Pascal, to name its foremost representatives. Romanticism sought to give effect to this impulse, against the rationalistic metaphysics of the 18th century. Act, ego and freedom were the key-words of J. G. Fichte, life, fact, freedom and existence those of F. W. J. Schelling. G. W. F. Hegel, whose original impulse was the same, arrived at a philosophy of the spirit and a system of absolute idealism which was already subjected to decisive criticism in the later philosophy of these two thinkers. But this is only now being seen in its proper perspective. The criticism which was effective was that of S. Kierkegaard and the neo-Hegelians of the left, principally L. Feuerbach and K. Marx. Feuerbach opposed the doctrine of the absolute spirit by presenting man as essentially body and senses, as the being whose nature it is to be a *genus* in the original sense — a begetting or production. In this sense Marx took over Feuerbach's conception, to extend and apply it on the economic and social scale. In contrast to these thinkers, S. Kierkegaard opposed systematic thought from the religious point of view, affirming that such systematization, like the corresponding way of life of liberalized Churchmanship, excluded the existence of the individual, masked the anxiety of freedom left to itself, and falsified the claim of the incarnate God to the obedience of faith by turning the scandal of the paradox into the rational perspicuity of universal structures. Philosophy and science, ecclesiastical institutions and Christianity itself were attacked by F. Nietzsche, who denounced all universal truths and values in favour of the will to live and the claim to power asserted by the individual great man.

3. *Growth and influence.* These impulses had at first no wide effects on philosophy. But with the disturbance and indeed the collapse of the old order of things brought about by the First World War and its consequences, a new spiritual situation was created, as could already be clearly seen in art and literature, especially in the work of R. M. Rilke und F. Kafka. And along with the reaction of "life-philosophy" and of a "dialogical thought" (E. Rosenstock, M. Buber, H. and E. Ehrenberg, V. von Weizsäcker, F. Ebner and — closest to Heidegger — F. Rosenzweig), existentialism now appeared as an answer.

a) The philosophy of existence had already had a profound influence through the teaching activity of its founders, when it was given its decisive expression in *Sein und Zeit* by M. Heidegger (1927), E. T.: *Being and Time* (1962), and in *Existenzerhellung* ("clarification of existence"), the second volume of K. Jaspers's *Philosophie* (1932). Beyond the circle of their disciples strictly speaking (K. Löwith, W. Bröcker, H.-G. Gadamer, W. Schulz, R. Berlinger, H. Arendt; with G. Siewerth, M. Müller and J. B. Lotz, coming from the Thomistic school), the two philosophers have exercised a notable influence over the whole field of scholarship, as in psychology (L. Binswanger), philology, (E. Staiger, B. Allemann), ethics (E. Grisebach), education (O. Bollnow, T. Ballauf) and especially in theology, first and most markedly among Protestants (R. Bultmann, F. Gogarten, F. Buri, G. Ebeling, E. Fuchs, H. Ott), but also among Catholics (R. Guardini, K. Rahner, B. Welte).

b) Though philosophy was then silenced in Germany by the pressure of events, the philosophy of existence came in the forties to have a lively influence in France, under the name of existentialism. The main product of the movement was *L'Être et le Néant* of J.-P. Sartre (1943), E. T.: *Being and Nothingness: An Essay on Phenomenological Ontology* (1957). Other exponents were S. de Beauvoir, A. Merleau-Ponty and A. Camus. The "Christian existentialism" of G. Marcel and the "personalism" of E. Mounier formed a contrast to this predominant trend. In both forms French existentialism has been strongly influenced by Heidegger and Jaspers, though for the most part it has not been expressed in the technical terms of philosophy. It has chiefly appeared in the literary form of the drama, novel and film, which was, however, the form in which it in turn influenced Germany after the war.

c) Representatives in Italy are N. Abbagnano and L. Pareyson, and in Spain X. Zubiri and M. de Unamuno, who has interpreted Don Quixote as the embodiment of "the tragic sense".

4. *Forms.* a) Heidegger rejects the interpretation of his thought which would make it an existence-philosophy or an existentialism — above all, in the atheistic interpretation of Sartre. His early works have in fact been generally read and accepted as anthropological analyses. But in the intention of the author, they were already orientated towards a philosophy of being. His description of existence by means of its "existentials" — his term for the categories of existence, whence the name "existential philosophy" for this stage of his thought — was meant only as a "fundamental ontology", which was to provide the guiding lines for an understanding of being itself, accessible only through the understanding and self-understanding of man. Man is the being who is always ahead of himself in his basic characteristic of concern *(Sorge)*, because his past comes upon him as his future. This means that he is inevitably concerned for himself, for his capacity to be and to be himself, in all situations, including the ultimate possibility offered by death. Since this is the structure of man's life and existence, the fundamental principle of interpretation must be time or temporality, which forms the "horizon" within which alone being can become present.

In this way both the findings of phenomenology (E. Husserl, M. Scheler) and the insights of W. Dilthey and P. Yorck von Wartenburg into the historicity of man have been given ontological relevance in existential philosophy. But the plan of which *Sein und Zeit* was only part of the first part was not carried out in full. Since the thirties, Heidegger has been striving, by means of the experience of the nothingness of all beings, allowing himself to be led by language, "to

think (of) being itself". To present this undertaking is strictly speaking outside the scope of this article, since here Heidegger leaves existential philosophy behind, which is still akin to metaphysics, in spite of all contrasting attitudes. But just as metaphysics needs to be overcome if its true nature is to be arrived at, so too "thought of being" completes existential philosophy.

This "reversal" is not a disavowal of what went before. It is rather its logical complement, which adjusts it from the one valid standpoint: it is, for instance, as the background of the historicity of existence that the unfathomable "fate" of being itself is revealed — which determines existence. As Heidegger explains in various comments on the history of Western philosophy, the whole of ontology is to be regarded as the disaster of "forgetfulness of being" — inculpable because "fated" — and must now be overcome and "won over". It considered being only from the point of view of beings and in their interest; it falsified its truth by turning it into a correctness which could be at men's disposal; and finally, impelled by this will to conquest, unmasked itself most fully in Nietzsche's "will to power" and crystallized itself most vividly in modern technology.

The being spoken of here is not "a" being (*Seiendes* — present participle of "to be"), but is distinguished from all beings by the "ontological difference". Hence, too, being is not the supreme being, God. "God" as represented in metaphysics is in any case "dead" — inactive and ineffective. This, according to Heidegger, is not to postulate a sort of atheism. But there is as yet no way of speaking properly of the true and "divine God". And being too is not identical with this true God: being should rather lead to a consideration of the holy, and so be a preparation for pondering the nature of the godhead, the only possible prelude to speaking of God. Hence being is not a mode of being of man, any more than it is of God: it is not, for instance, the "authenticity" which is to be attained by "existentiell" effort. Being is "itself"; it cannot be expressed in technical terms; it is only thinkable in "recollection". Hitherto, like the holy, being could best be deciphered through art (though always into a new concealment), especially through poetry — and here principally in the work of the poet F. Hölderlin. But like the destruction of previous metaphysics, the interpretation of the poetic word is merely meant to prepare the ground for a future metaphysics, which, however, cannot be thought out deliberately, forced into existence, as it were. It must be waited for, till its hour strikes in the history of being, till the "event" of it occurs. And then it will come from still deeper within the region of what is not yet definable: from where time and being "are given".

b) In contrast to the existential philosophy of the early Heidegger, K. Jaspers does not examine existence for the sake of being, but for its own sake. His thought, tributary above all to Pascal, Kant, Kierkegaard and Nietzsche, is strictly a philosophy of existence. It is concerned with existing man, who is in the midst of "encompassing" being, and becomes conscious of it in his failure in the "limit situations" (death, suffering, struggle, guilt), though unable to gain more than an indirect knowledge of it, "in ciphers". Thus Jaspers's "clarification of existence" (*Existenzerhellung*) is not a fundamental ontology but, like the "orientation to the world" which precedes it, and the "metaphysics" which builds upon it — and, indeed, like the whole work of the philosopher — an attempt to articulate the "summons" to one's fellow-men. This is done in existentiell communication, by living out loyally one's historicity and transcending oneself by virtue of one's freedom, without letting this upsurge harden into social and political intolerance or any sort of dogmatism. The "openness" of "philosophical faith" will be maintained in view of the "transcendence", and this openness, keeping its distance in love, will allow for the different possible realizations of other existences while refusing to subject its own way to any conditions.

c) J.-P. Sartre links up directly with Heidegger, though his philosophy is, like Jaspers's, that of existence, while going back ultimately to Hegel and phenomenology. In contrast to the compact world of the thing "in itself", consciousness finds itself "condemned" to freedom. It is there "for itself", fearful of the nothing of radical indeterminacy, but always locked in mortal combat with others, whose very look is an effort to determine in their own way its indeterminacy — and whose own necessary reaction is one of defence against being

determined by the person they look at. Nonetheless, Sartre holds that the self-determination of the I must take place with a sense of responsibility towards all men. The long-promised ethics, which is to present existentialism as "humanism", has not yet appeared. (But see his *Critique de la raison dialectique,* I, 1960.) Such responsible freedom must fend off the gaze and the grip of others (and can only experience material reality, where it intrudes unasked, with a sense of "nausea" — and can accept it only as a challenge to active, creative intervention and re-shaping). Hence it must logically reject a creator planning it beforehand and drafting for it an obligatory order of being. Belief in God is explained as a type of *mauvaise foi* (that of a cowardice and dishonesty where the I refuses to be aware of its freedom), as an end-projection of the *passion inutile* which man is, because in spite of (and as) being "for himself" and as being "for himself" he tries to reach the sealed-off placidity of the thing "in itself". Instead, he is always called upon to become what he is — and is not as yet, because estranged by ignorance, convention and halfheartedness — absolute freedom.

d) A. Camus starts with a vision of the estranged of man's "Sisyphus" existence and comes to a view of the dignity and meaning of man. This inspires a "revolt" against his humiliation and leads to an ethos of moderation, as already appears in the nature-epiphanies of the early travel essays, which is a "holiness without God". G. Marcel, on the other hand, represents a "Christian existentialism" — the title of the book of studies in his honour edited by É. Gilson. Like the critics of Hegel, above all Schelling, he sees idealism as his primary philosophical opponent, and in particular the theoretical attitude of the *cogito ergo sum*. He starts instead from the everyday experience of the whole man and finds him always being "committed" in new ways. Self-recollection in face of this "commitment" (*engagement*) leads out of the realm of "having" which can be surveyed, controlled and calculated, to the realm of "being", which is not a problem to be solved but mystery, man's perpetual setting, of which he grows aware in recollection. He is faced with the decision of refusing its summons in despair, or surrendering to it in "openness". In saying Yes, man chooses the only possibility by which he can truly be himself, and this means brotherliness, loyalty, obligation towards those entrusted to him, fidelity and obedience towards the mystery that guides him — and may lead him to the revelation in Christ — since he is *homo viator* in hope.

5. *The present day*. Though produced by one particular situation, the philosophy of existence has been expounded in so many highly diversified responses that no one name can really cover them all. And with the passing of the original situation, the philosophy of existence has lost its predominant role. In France it has been replaced by the Marxist *engagement* or by the "pure theory" of structuralism. In Germany analytical philosophy is coming to the fore, along with a philosophical critique of society. Even in Heidegger the philosophy of existence has become, in his famous "reversal", the thinking of being. Traditional thinking is less concerned with the philosophy of existence than with this "post-metaphysical" thinking. Here it finds itself faced with the task of reaching a new understanding of the meaning and limitation of the *concept,* of absorbing reality, person and history more profoundly into its thought (in a thinking of "the name"), of becoming a philosophy of "participation, symbol and representation" — in other words, a "new metaphysics" (M. Müller, pp. 219–59). Hence instead of an assessment and critique of existential philosophy, the reader is referred to the articles *Existence* I, *Freedom, History* I, *Metaphysics, Ontology, Person, Being.*

See also *Being, Categories, Existence* I, *History* I, *Holy* I, II, *Language, Man* I, *Person* II A, *Metaphysics, Romanticism, Transcendence, Technology.*

BIBLIOGRAPHY. ON SECTION 3: E. Mounier, *Introduction aux Existentialismes* (1947); J. Benda, *Tradition de l'existentialisme* (1947); K. Douglas, *Critical Bibliography of Existentialism: the Paris School* (1950); H. J. Blackham, *Six Existentialist Thinkers* (1959); J. Collins, *Existentialists, A Critical Study* (1959); F. Copleston, *Contemporary Philosophy* (1963); M. Müller, *Existenzphilosophie im geistigen Leben der Gegenwart* (3rd ed., 1964); J. B. Lotz, *Sein und Existenz* (1965); W. Barnes, *Existentialism* (1967). ON SECTION 4a: M. Heidegger, *Existence and Being* (2nd ed., 1956); H. Lübbe, *Bibliographie der Heidegger-Literatur, 1917–55* (1957); id., *Identität und Differenz* (1957); id., *Nietzsche,* 2 vols. (1961). ON SECTION 4b: K. Jaspers, *Man in the Modern Age* (2nd ed., 1951); id.,

Reason and Existenz (1955); P. A. Schilpp, ed., *The Philosophy of Karl Jaspers* (with bibliography) (1958); K. Jaspers, *Faith and Revelation* (1967). ON SECTION 4c: J.-P. Sartre, *Critique de la raison dialectique* (1960); id., *L'existentialisme est un humanisme* (1946), E. T.: *Existentialism and Humanism* (1948); A. Manser, *Sartre: A Philosophic Study* (1966). ON SECTION 4d: A. Camus, *Le Mythe de Sisyphus* (1942), E. T.: *Myth of Sisyphus* (1955); id., *L'homme révolté* (1951), E. T.: *The Rebel* (1953); G. Marcel, *Être et avoir* (1935), E. T.: *Being and Having* (1965); id., *Homo Viator* (1945), E. T. (1962); id., *Existentialist Background of Human Dignity* (1963).

Jörg Splett

III. "The Existential"

A. PHILOSOPHICAL

The term "existential" or "existentials" was introduced by M. Heidegger in his *Sein und Zeit* (1927; E. T.: *Being and Time* [1962]). Since then, it has been used in many different senses, in Protestant theology, for instance, by Bultmann, Fuchs and Ebeling, in their existential interpretation of the NT, in Catholic theology by K. Rahner, with his concept of the "supernatural existential". Heidegger himself did not make use of the term in his later work. But in his *Being and Time* he gave a precise account of the meaning of "existential": "The question (of the ontological structure of existence) aims at displaying what constitutes existence. We give the name of existentiality to the interconnection of these structures" (*Sein und Zeit,* p. 12; cf. E. T., p. 12). "Because the (ontological characteristics of beings) are determined by existentiality, we call these characteristics existentials. They must be sharply distinguished from what we call categories, which are the determinations of beings insofar as they are not related to existence." (*Ibid.,* p. 44; cf. E. T., p. 44.) "The question of existence can only be clarified by existing. The self-understanding which leads to this we call existentiell ... The interconnection of the structures (which constitute existence) we call existentiality. Their analysis is in the nature of an existential understanding, not an existentiell one." (*Ibid.,* p. 12; cf. E. T., p. 12.)

In contrast, therefore, to the categories, which are regarded as determinations (ontological) of beings within the world, the existentials are the determinations (ontological) of man in his understanding of himself as "existence". Thus Heidegger, having recourse to the origins of Western metaphysics, which had fallen into philosophical oblivion, posed once more the problem of the difference between "being there" and "being something", "is-ness" and "whatness", *existentia* and *essentia*. The problem was traditional in metaphysics, but remained unanswered as long as the real question of the meaning of being was not put. In working out his "analytics of existence", which adumbrate the meaning of being, and begin thereby to throw light on the meaning of the "categories" of beings, Heidegger defines the "existentiell" as that which directly affects the concrete existence of man — imminent death, for instance. This is distinguished from the "existential", which determines the ontological structure of existence — the character, for instance, of being doomed to death (the being-for-death) which permeates all elements of existence. In Western metaphysics, the understanding of being was based solely on beings as objects in the world — this because of the fated "oblivion of being". Existence and essence were attributed, analogically according to degree, to all beings. It was an attribution (κατηγορεῖν) which veiled the primary nature of truth in being, which is that of event, to concentrate on the thought and representation of the "subject". This metaphysics was re-traced when appropriated by the modern notion of existence, which, however, was enriched with theological content since Schelling and Kierkegaard, though more and more restricted to subjectivity in its terms of reference. Hence the modern notion of existence, being in the strictest sense of the term the *out*-come, i.e., the departure *from* the various interpretations of being which had dominated in the course of history — ἰδέα, ἐνέργεια, *substantia, actualitas, subjectum* — had to be primarily existential. It had to be achieved in the light of the forgotten ontology of the primal relationship between being and man grasping being, since man as the "thereness" of being is the only possible foundation of any metaphysics of essence-existence. In this way the priority of essence over existence or of existence over essence was no longer determinative for the existence or "being there" of man — Heidegger thus differing from J.-P. Sartre and K. Jaspers and other existentialists, and from the traditional ontol-

ogy of the West in general. And human existence, as grasp of being, was contrasted with all categorized "beings", whether conceived of as immanent or transcendent, since it was "ek-sistence", that is, the finite human being "standing out" into the fated yet freely-happening openness and security of being (which bring about this outgoing).

Thus the existentials — such as "being thrown there", "being in the world", "being exposed", "being with", "happening to be thus somewhere", understanding, purpose, sketch-plan, care, anxiety, being-for-death, "historicity" — cannot be deduced from a supreme principle of thought, like a systematic table of categories. The existentials could only be markers along the way of a historically engendered and hence always incomplete and non-terminable understanding of being. Hence a categorized interpretation of beings and of man, in the light of the specifically Western notion of being, is to some limited extent legitimate, and indeed necessary, say in the construction of a general or regional ontology. But there can be no exclusion on principle of a different type of experience of being and its past or future articulation by humanity.

As the Western metaphysics of being and its implications are more and more fully appropriated, its "absoluteness" — hitherto conceived of metaphysically — can no longer be the final valid exclusion and hence relativization of another understanding of being. It can only be the existentially minded self-emancipation (always newly available and imperative in history) of the fixed categorical thinking of a culture or epoch or system, under the challenge of the total human experience of being yet to come as a necessary existentiell which must be freely accepted. And, of course, the ever increasing weight of the past to be assimilated is an intrinsic element of the onset of the future. Hence Heidegger's assertion, that "existential analytics is rooted in the existentiel (*op. cit.,* p. 13; cf. E. T.) is decisive. The future of philosophy must be thought of in terms of man's being claimed in the process of history by being which is always still more in the future and hence absolute. And the self-understanding of theology must be that it is uttered to one and all, in the historical word of revelation, and yet that it is still not (eschatologically) uttered to the end. Hence theological critique of the concepts of an objectivating thinking derived from a philosophy or science will be the ceaseless task of propounding and proclaiming the mystery of God as it calls forth the primordial (existential) understanding of man and his primordial (existentiell) freedom.

See also *Being, Categories, Man* I, *Demythologization* II.

BIBLIOGRAPHY. See bibliography on *Existence* II; also O. Pöggeler, *Der Denkweg Martin Heideggers* (1963); W. J. Richardson, *Heidegger, through Phenomenology to Thought* (1964); M. King, *Heidegger's Philosophy* (1965).

Franz Karl Mayr

B. THEOLOGICAL

1. *In general*. The ontological and not merely factual superiority of man to things which, according to Christian faith and its doctrine of man, characterizes him, justifies in principle an inquiry into his existentials. It provides good reason for refusing to make the mistake of classifying them from the start among the categories which are supposed to apply to every finite being but which in fact are derived from material things.

2. *Supernatural existential*. The term existential can also be used in a special way in theology. There can be no doubt about the following truths, though their further theological interpretation can be left open. Even prior to justification by sanctifying grace, whether this is conferred sacramentally or outside the sacraments, man already stands under the universal, infralapsarian salvific will of God which comprises within its scope original sin and personal sin. Man is redeemed, and is permanently the object of God's saving care and offer of grace. He is under an absolute obligation to attain his supernatural goal. This situation, "objective justification" in contradistinction to its subjective application by sanctification, is all-inclusive and inescapably prior to man's free action, which it determines. It does not exist solely in the thoughts and intentions of God, but is an existential determination of man himself. As an objective consequence of God's universal salvific will, it of course supervenes through grace upon man's essence as "nature", but in the real order is never lacking to it. This alone explains why, even if he rejects grace, or in perdition, a man can never be ontologically and personally indifferent to his supernatural destiny. Until recently the Catholic theology of the schools had generally held, despite occasional protests such as those of Ripalda and Vásquez, that a real offer of supernatural grace for a salutary act only occurs when a human being encounters the explicit preaching of the gospel, or when revelation as a historical tradition is present in some other way, e.g., transmitted from "primitive revelation", or in the OT. Now Vatican II considers that there is a possibility of salvation for (inculpable) atheists and polytheists (*Gaudium et Spes*, art. 22; *Lumen Gentium*, art. 16; *Ad Gentes*, art. 7), though they also need real faith, and hence the grace of faith (*Ad Gentes*, art. 7). Hence there can be no serious doubt that all men permanently stand under the offer of grace really operative in them. This permanent and ever-present offer is always accepted in their moral activity, unless they shut themselves to it by their own moral guilt. Through the supernatural formal object which is involved in grace itself, the primary feature of revelation, and therefore the possibility of faith, is already present. That man is really affected by the permanent offer of grace is not something which happens only now and again. It is a permanent and inescapable human situation. This state of affairs can be briefly labelled "supernatural existential", to prevent its being overlooked. It means that man as he really exists is always and ineluctably more than mere "nature" in the theological sense. The precise relation of the supernatural existential to nature, to original sin *(simul iustus et peccator)*, freedom, and justification requires more detailed investigation.

See also *Man* I–III, *Person* II, *Categories, Salvation* I, *Nature, Original Sin, Freedom, Justification*.

BIBLIOGRAPHY. See bibliography on *Demythologization* II, *Faith* I; also: A. Röper, *Die anonymen Christen* (1963); H. Ott, "Existentiale Interpretation und anonyme Christlichkeit", in E. Dinkler, ed., *Zeit und Geschichte, Festgabe R. Bultmann* (1964), pp. 367–79; B. Welte, *Heilsverständnis* (1965); A. Darlap, "Theologie der Heilsgeschichte", *Mysterium Salutis,* I (1965), pp. 1–156; H. de Lubac, *Le mystère du Surnaturel* (1965); J. B. Metz, "Unbelief as a Theological Problem", *Concilium* 1 (1965), pp. 484–92; K. Rahner, "Theology of the Incarnation", *The-*

ological Investigations, IV (1966), pp. 105–20; id., "Die anonymen Christen", *Schriften zur Theologie,* VI (1966), pp. 545–54; J. Alfaro, "Faith", *Concilium* 3 (1967), pp. 24–30.

Karl Rahner

EXPERIENCE

1. *Introduction.* Experience is one of the most enigmatic concepts of philosophy. It is ordinarily taken to be a source or special form of our knowledge, deriving from the immediate reception of the given or of the impression, in contrast to discursive thought, mere concepts, authoritatively accepted opinions or historical tradition. When experience presents itself, its presence means a special kind of supreme certitude of irrefutable evidence. Since the human spirit is primarily "in potency", and hence needs the knowledge which takes in what it perceives, human knowledge and experience are profoundly identical.

Transcendental experience is that which man has by the fact that he has his being, prior to all concrete modes of existence, out of the unlimited spiritual horizon, however this be understood — indeterminately, for instance, as limitless openness in general, or intuitively and abstractively as "being" (G. Siewerth), or again, as the happening of the meaning of the world and truth in historical process. Particular experience *a posteriori* is essentially linked with sense perception and representation, or to the psychological self-consciousness of the soul. External experience is in regard to corporal objects, directly through the natural senses, indirectly through the extension lent them by technical aids. Inner experience is that of one's own states of mind and soul (representations, imaginations, etc. in the direct mental processes, self-consciousness in reflection). Extrasensory perception is the hypothetical object of parapsychology. Specific differences are made between aesthetic, hermeneutic, historical, mystical, personal, religious, prescientific and scientific experience and so on. Experience is also used to designate the knowledge and sense of reality gained from direct intercourse, in contrast to a "book knowledge" which remains external. Such experience can be attained by deliberate effort: it is the power to adapt to the future gained by the prudent mastery of many spheres of life; or it can be insight which accrues rather by accident (from what is undergone). Experience in this sense, in spite of the mastery which it confers, reveals the openness of experience for new and unforeseen though not wholly unexpected "experiences". No historically acquired experience can be transmitted or represented externally in the full immediacy of its self-attestation.

2. *History and analysis.* In Aristotle, experience is linked directly to the immediate presence of the individual object, but the combination of a number of repeated memories are necessary to give the mastery of a single experience which corresponds to "science" (ἐπιστήμη) or "art" (τέχνη). Every experience is the differentiation of an indeterminate proleptic knowledge which must be confirmed by induction as a true universal. (Induction is therefore not a subsequent generalization on the basis of a collection of facts.) Even the individual fact is already seen in the light of a universal. Aristotle does not contrast experience with thought as do the moderns. Thought is the completed experience of objects which are already determined from every aspect by thought itself. But since experience does not grasp its own unity, and remains completely embedded in production, practice and knowledge, it is still only a material element ("source") in the direction of a fixed body of knowledge which surpasses experience.

The transcendental method of Kant envisaged the constitutive elements of experience, the overplus with regard to all that is given in experience. Elements enter into our empirical knowledge which derive only from ourselves. Experience is only possible by means of certain *a priori* principles. The categories do no more than help us to decipher the phenomena and spell out experience to ourselves. Since Kant's experimental method of thought begins by affirming that "reason only has insight into what it produces itself according to its schema", we have a Copernical revolution in thought which throws light on a basic trait of modern experimental science. Only the successful experiment can prove that nature conforms to thought. Experimentation proceeds methodically by stating the terms of reference ("the horizon") within which observations are made. Beings are not envisaged in their total subsistence but only from certain aspects and in definite perspectives. Then comes the identification of the "object" with a general law or concept under which the individual case falls. This deliberate procedure according to a definite method undoubtedly means that the original thing and the world of life to which it belongs have been to some extent denatured and dissolved. This alone is enough to show that empirical research is not a straightforward reproduction of reality in the sense of a reduplication. The facts have first to be methodically denuded, since even in their pre-scientific state they bring with them an interpretation. The findings of scientific research which can be checked by everyone and are as remote as possible from the realm of the subjective necessarily involved a certain alienation of the "thing". Though modern empiricism subjects itself to a severe mental discipline, recognizing the limitations and the provisional nature of its science, striving for the openness, self-denial and realism of the inductive method, it should not be allowed to obscure the priority of the "world of life", even in a necessarily scientist civilization.

Experience is given a new dimension in early German idealism. Consciousness, antithetically at first, strips itself of all that is objective, in order to realize the direct intuition of self which is demanded in practice by the infinite Ego. This intuition is produced by freedom and becomes thereby — since the unconditioned can never be an "object" — the most immediate of experiences, the "intellectual intuition". Since the one act of self-consciousness can only be realized in the endless conflict set up by opposing activities, it cannot come about in one moment, but only in the development which comprises the individual acts. There must therefore be a "transcendental history of the Ego", "a pragmatic history of the human spirit". Experience only comes to self-awareness in history. This "experience", too strongly centred on subjective reflection, was then opened up by Hegel to a confrontation with the concrete reality of the historical process. The life of the spirit is not withdrawal but recognizing itself in otherness, finding its own in the alien, dissolving and reconciling the positively resistant. Such history-centred work of the spirit is inspired by the experience that absolutely nothing exists except what is produced by the spirit. The experience emphasized in such speculation is not a mere

narcissism of the spirit or the merely formal elimination of self-alienation through dialectics. However, it does not meet the objection that the reconciliation may be extorted by logic but is not verified in reality. The criticism of the post-idealist era was to the effect that experience cannot be simply transposed into problems of consciousness and is not exhausted in concepts or judgments (cf. Marxism on "praxis").

The phenomenology of Husserl and the early Heidegger seek to avoid all speculative constructions, haphazard data and only apparently verified concepts, and to go back from the derivative judgment based on the evidence of intuition to the immediacy of experience. "The knowledge which sees is reason aiming at bringing understanding itself "to its senses" (i.e., to reason) (Husserl). Experience is not merely the description of immediate facts. In the exclusion of false preconceptions, in the accentuation of unnoticed permanent prolepses or references, and in the critical return to the understanding of the world crystallized in the use of language, the true self-attestation of beings comes about in their real immediacy, which, however, always includes our relationship to phenomena. Thus phenomenology tries, while rejecting objectivism, to take the "world of life" ("the natural world") as its explicit theme and hence regain the native place of experience.

Criticism of Husserl is chiefly directed against his taking transcendental experience as an achievement of subjectivity and the active positing of being as alone constitutive (in spite of the concessions made to elements of passivity). Thus he fails to recognize the constitutive originality of a transcendental experience which is prior to all division into subject and object. But it is the (always historical) medium of disclosure of the world and truth. It is prior to all activity of knowing and all empirical experience. It is at once the supreme potentiality (receptivity, passivity) of man and his supreme achievement, because man must hold out under the immense breadth and depth of the realm from out of which beings can encounter him and summon forth from him and transform a statement of meaning.

In Heidegger, experience is "a search without anticipations, a search which implies pure discovery". Such experience, which is not constructed by the subject and is also not an abstraction derived from beings, opens the way to a reality which is revealed as such only in this experience itself. Subjectivity is not simply to be taken as the opposite to objectivity, since such a notion of subjectivity would be an objectivation of the subjectivity itself.

It is also of the essence of experience to be intrinsically open to further experiences. Progressive experience gains better knowledge of its previous knowledge. The nothingness of "vain" efforts and the negativity of painful experience have a fertility of their own. The perfection of experience consists of an undogmatic openness for new experiences and not in the watertight security of absolute knowledge where consciousness and object coincide totally. The force of Hegel's thought was that he saw speculative dialectics in the light of the nature of experience, but the limitation of this philosophy of reflection was that it took up a basic standpoint which from the start had left behind the intrinsic historicity of experience as such: it strode forward as the irresistible power of eternal reason and its principles. As long as experience is treated merely as an element in the formation of fixed concepts or the setting up of a pure theory, it is robbed of its native mobility, and its proper productivity and transformative power are repressed. Since it is of the nature of experience to disconcert empty concepts and thwart set hopes, it constantly widens the scope of real and so leads men to recognize and learn about a region of life which cannot be easily demarcated. In such tranquil listening man really learns for the first time, and tries, for instance, to tell of his experience in fresh and unworn words.

The basic problem which remains is the relationship between experience understood in this way and authentic reflection. Reflection is necessary because it renders the genesis and structure of experience perspicuous and hence calls in question the certainty of practical life which is always so questionable. It too is the only force which can also reject the false claims of experience, to prevent its being confused with arbitrary feelings or unclear opinions. Reflection is condemned, no doubt, to be always secondary, but in its backward look it can also develop a tremendous critical force to which all experience must be exposed to some extent. The priority of experience has been made clear. But it would be pernicious to play off reflection and experience, scientific empiricism and experience, against one another. The relationship between these terms is urgently in need of clarification.

3. *The notion of experience in theology.* There can be no doubt of the legitimacy and importance of the notion of experience (as sketched above) in theology: see the articles on *Religious Act* and *Religious Experience.* The following points may be noted here.

a) The significance for salvation which is implied in a theological truth can only be adequately demonstrated when man's receptivity for such truth has been investigated. The truth of God is also the truth of our existence and its meaning, so that the fact that the Christian message is the *scandalum crucis* does not exclude but rather demands that the intrinsic connection between the mystery of revelation and our human existence be explored.

b) The full nature of religion and faith cannot be based theologically merely on experience and its certainty, since the reality of faith which is offered and bestowed in grace is a deed of God which penetrates and embraces man more thoroughly than anything which can be reflected in concrete experience. Experience is by the nature of things never adequately rendered.

c) In a secularized world, the roots which every direct or scientific truth of faith has in religious experience and the realm of the holy must also be demonstrated with the proper hermeneutics, to preserve the unique nature of faith, and to resist both abuses which would make it the victim of ideologies and the tendencies which would submit it to the critique of ideologies. The theological use of the notion of experience demands to be radically explored.

See also *Knowledge, Dogma* I, *Dogmatism, Tradition, Aristotelianism* I, *Kantianism, Idealism, Phenomenology, Existence* II, *Dialectics, Reflection, Empiricism.*

BIBLIOGRAPHY. R. Lenoble, *Essai sur la notion d'expérience* (1943); A. J. Ayer, *Language, Truth and Logic* (2nd revised ed., 1946); G. Picht, *Die Erfahrung der Geschichte* (1958); M. Müller, *Expérience et histoire* (1959); H. Urs von Balthasar, *Herrlichkeit,* I (1961), pp. 211–98; W. Adorno, *Drei Studien zu Hegel* (1963); M. Oakshott, *Experience and its Modes* (1963); M. Heidegger, *Hegels Begriff der Erfahrung: Holzwege* (4th ed., 1963); H. Bouillard, *Logique de la foi* (1964); H. G. Gadamer, *Wahrheit und Methode* (2nd ed., 1965).

Karl Lehmann

F

FAITH

I. Way to Faith

1. *Theological presuppositions.* a) As a result of God's universal salvific will and the offer of the supernatural grace of faith as an abiding feature of man's mode of existence as a person, every human being, even previous to the explicit preaching of the Christian message, is always potentially a believer and already in possession, in the grace that is prior to his freedom, of what he is to believe (i.e., freely accept): God's direct self-communication in Christ. It is quite possible, in fact, that the person whom the preacher of the faith encounters is already justified (because he was obedient to the dictates of his conscience, to the extent this had made itself heard), and therefore already believes, in the theological sense, even if what he explicitly believes is very little. In both respects, therefore, faith may always be assumed to be present. Bringing someone to the faith will mean the endeavour to develop this already existing faith into its full Christological and ecclesiastical, explicit, social, consciously professed form. This endeavour can and should link up with all the elements of faith already present. It must therefore show that the Church's Christian faith is the historically and socially complete form of what the person to be converted already "believes". Consequently, the starting-point which is always present (the condition which may be assumed), never consists merely in a human being's "natural reason". This in fact is already historically determined and bears the stamp of the human being's actual situation and of his personal experience. Furthermore, it is already supernaturally "elevated" and orientated towards the explicit, conscious knowledge of faith.

b) Conversion to faith is always a process with many stages, and these need not necessarily follow the same course in every individual. Nor can it be presumed that if the whole explicit content of the faith is presented in an objectively sufficient way, it can only be due to personal (subjective) guilt in every individual case, whatever the particular situation and limits of time, if in fact all these stages in the genesis of faith are not accomplished. The messenger of the gospel can therefore rightly ask himself what stage in a gradual history of faith has been reached by the collective or individual *kairos*. He can then try to lead as far as that point, i.e., to indicate the ways of access and for the rest patiently leave God to bring about a situation where further progress will be possible. Otherwise he would perhaps waste too much human and ecclesiastical effort.

c) An approach to faith presupposes that a human being who is to be led to faith already has a starting-point, and that from it and from the very nature of that starting-point, there exists a transition to the further reality of faith in whole or in part. The first point has already been dealt with above, section (a). The second implies that the realities and truths of faith are really interconnected, and that there is therefore a connection also between what is always a prior datum and what has to be believed anew and expressly. Faith is never awakened by someone having something communicated to him purely from outside, addressed solely to his naked understanding as such (as, for example, the statement that the chemical formula of water is H_2O). To lead to faith (or rather, to its further, explicit stage), is always to assist understanding of what has already been experienced in the depth of human reality as grace (i.e., as in absolutely direct relation to God). The connection between what has already been experienced (in faith or, it may be, in incredulity), and what has to be accepted anew in explicit faith need not and cannot of course always be of the kind that links conclusions to premises in logical inference. There are connections of meaningful correspondence. And for this kind of connection it is sometimes quite sufficient to show that to some particular question there is only one answer in the concrete and historically speaking, even if several answers are theoretically conceivable. The intrinsic homogeneity of the whole of dogma in relation to one ultimate primordial question experienced by man elevated by grace would need to be worked out much more clearly in dogmatic theology (and then in the instruction of converts) than is the case nowadays when positive theology predominates. Then the multiplicity of propositions formulated for belief would give a much clearer impression of being something people could make something of, rather than of a mere exercise of formal obedience to propositions which God has of course revealed, but without which it would be quite possible to imagine even the fully explicit accomplishment of salvation. A full understanding of what is meant here is therefore only possible on the basis of a unity of fundamental and dogmatic theology in which — without materially curtailing the Church's teaching, as Modernism did — the whole "system" of doctrines of faith would appear as the one complete answer to the inescapable primordial question of human existence regarding the relation between the absolute mystery (called God) which forms its ground, and that existence itself. The answer would then be that this sacred mystery forms the ground of human existence in the absolute, merciful intimacy of radical self-communication, that this self-communication found its irrevocable historical manifestation in Jesus, that

around him there is a community (called the Church), deriving from him and given its structure by him, of those who believe in the self-communication of God in him and who explicitly profess this in historical and social form, and who, believing and hoping, await the revelation of this self-communication at the end of history (of the individual and of the world).

2. *Ways of approach to faith*. a) The primary approach to faith is a man's direct confrontation with himself in his whole nature as free and responsible and thereby with the incomprehensible ground of this human reality, called God. For many people this, of course, is "taken for granted", but must be perpetually re-awakened and accomplished if faith is to be elicited in a really radical way, breaking the crusts of custom formed by its institutionalized formulations. The person who is to act as stimulus to awaken and confront someone with this way of approach must nowadays be able to perceive and bring to full awareness the comprehensive question set to man by the transcendence of his commitment. He must be able to show that man cannot evade himself as an all-embracing question; that he still affirms the question's existence even when he declares he will leave it as unanswerable; that total commitment cannot be evaded, that the sceptical judgment on man as conditioned and determined, is itself an experience of freedom, an act involving freedom, that God is not an object among other objects of experience which under certain circumstances one may fail to discover, but is necessarily affirmed in the accomplishment of man's intellectual and moral activity, even if he is explicitly denied, or not named, or is met with under quite different conceptual modes of expression. This can provide the basis for inquiring whether a man would not really be interpreting his own concrete experience more accurately, at least in its highest moments and as it finds typical objective historical expression in the highest events of religious history, if he were to take it to be the experience of a supreme, most radical, saving and forgiving presence of the mystery of God communicating himself absolutely. Courage to trust in the possibility of the highest fulfilment of meaning, readiness to believe, is needed. And the experience can be the hidden ground of

apparent despair at the groundlessness and experienced absurdity of human reality in "Nihilism".

Such experience of grace, for that is precisely what it is, can in fact occur in the most varied forms from individual to individual. The spiritual guide in encouraging explicit faith will have to observe what actual form the experience takes in the particular catechumens he is dealing with. It may, for example, be indescribable joy, unconditional personal love, unconditional obedience to conscience, the experience of loving union with the universe, the experience of the irretrievable vulnerability of one's own human existence beyond one's own control, and so on. On the same basis he would then have to explain what is really meant by God, grace and even by God's "Trinity". At such a point the *perichoresis,* the *circumincessio,* of fundamental and dogmatic theology is apparent. Fundamental theology can never be purely formal, in the sense of furnishing solely a proof of the "fact" of revelation in abstraction from any content of that revelation, while dogmatic theology always appeals to grace-given divinization and what this involves: the light of faith and the experience of grace, which actually comprise the reality conceptually represented in the truths of revelation.

b) On the basis of such faith in God as incomprehensible and intimately present, it would have to be shown that corresponding to man's historicity, in all the dimensions of his existence, including the religious, his transcendental divinization necessarily expresses itself historically, is manifested as an historical and explicitly formulated human datum. This would have to lead to an understanding of the history of revelation, of the history of redemption, individual and collective, and of the vital necessity of religion not in the sense of non-historical reflection on the individual's own "religious need" (which in such a non-historical form is only apparently possible), but in the form of trust in, and insertion into, a historically concrete religion with a social organization. Consequently, the question can only be *which* is the actual historical and social form of religion to which a man must trust himself in order to practise his personal religion in a truly human way, i.e., in actual history and in society. This would be the starting-point from which to interpret people's present-day knowledge of the multiplicity of religions and their history, so as genuinely to overcome the danger of relativism arising from that knowledge. (Frank admission that the history of salvation, of revelation and of faith takes place everywhere in history and society by reason of the universal salvific and grace-giving will of God; concept of a "legitimate" religion outside the history of the Old and New Testament revelation; combination of culpable degradation of religion with grace-given and revelational elements in the non-Christian religions; eschatological surmounting of the plurality of legitimate religions, including that of the OT, by the absolute coming of salvation in Jesus Christ, etc.; these are the keys to such interpretation.)

c) The approach to a confession of faith in Jesus Christ would have to be sought in a "transcendental Christology", i.e., from the "idea" — even if, historically, this can only appear with Christianity itself — of an absolute, historical mediator of salvation in whom God's self-communication to his creation in grace finds its highest and irrevocable historical manifestation. It would have to be shown that the very concept of such an absolute mediator of salvation involves the authentic doctrine of the hypostatic union in its correct, i.e., non-Monophysite, meaning. That doctrine must be presented very precisely, so as to avoid any appearance of mythology, which would be quite unacceptable nowadays. Christ must be shown as a true man with a created consciousness and an active human centre of freedom. In other words, he must appear as the very question which man *is,* and which the hypostatic union "answers" ontologically (and not by a merely factual link of an objective, substantial kind), and which that answer actually validates and posits (*ipsa assumptione creatur,* as Augustine noted). Of course it will then have to be shown also that that "transcendental Christology" is actually realized in Jesus Christ, so that the sacred history of redemption has already entered its eschatological phase. For this again, appeal will be made to the idea (quite familiar from ordinary life), that in order to fulfil his nature, man everywhere has to enter into concrete historical relationships which he can never justify with full theoretical certainty. It must also be noted that in fact nowhere else in history apart from faith in Jesus Christ has even the claim been made to realize the highest transcendental idea of human fulfilment such as is found in the God-man. That has its importance; there is a legitimate question which, though it may have many conceivable answers, has in fact only received one. It has positively to be shown that where a *saving* reality is concerned, the circle linking historical reality (miracles, Jesus' resurrection) as ground of faith, with faith as the sole mode of knowledge of, and testimony to, such a reality, is legitimate. This is the only antidote to present-day scepticism in regard to extraordinary "historical" events. It has to be emphasized that even on a very cautious "historical" interpretation of the gospels (as evidences of faith in Christ and only in that way as reports on Jesus' life-history), Jesus' claim to be the absolute mediator of salvation is sufficiently established — and that includes what is really meant by metaphysical sonship of God.

d) If there is once courage for the act of faith in Jesus as the historically eschatological manifestation of God's absolute self-communication, the next step, grasping the significance of the Church, will no longer be too difficult. If it is seen that the Church was not merely founded from outside by a purely juridical enactment, but is the abiding presence of the eschatological Christ-event, then the existence and meaning of many of the Church's characteristics (e.g., doctrinal infallibility, the *opus operatum* of the sacraments), become much more intelligible. It must also be indicated that among Christian denominations (prescinding from the Orthodox), only the Roman Catholic Church has the courage unambiguously to claim to be, in constitution and doctrine, representative of Christ historically and as a Church. Protestantism does not have this courage. It can only regard itself as constituting conditional and human forms of organization of individual Christians. Furthermore, the Roman Catholic Church is the "old" Church, with the most tangible historical links of every kind with the early Church. Consequently there is at least a presumption that it is the Church of Christ, and this could only be annulled if it were plainly proved that it has unmistakably fallen from the gospel of Christ and laid an obligation on its members accordingly. But that cannot be done. Such

an approach to an understanding of the Church as the necessary historical presence of the interior divinization of mankind by grace, of the Church as "fundamental sacrament", facilitates access to ecclesiology for men of the present day. They can take the Church seriously without identifying it with what it exists to serve.

See also *Salvation* I, III A, *Freedom*, *Faith* II, *Modernism*, *Nihilism*, *Trinity of God*, *History* I, *Religion*.

BIBLIOGRAPHY. H. Urs von Balthasar, *Die Gottesfrage des heutigen Menschen* (1956), E. T.: *The God Question and Modern Man;* H. de Lubac, *Discovery of God* (1960); A. Röper, *Anonyme Christen* (1963); F. Jeanson, *La foi d'un incroyant* (1963); K. Rahner, *Hörer des Wortes* (2nd ed., 1963); H. Bouillard, *Logique de la foi* (1964); Q.-A. Rabat, *Vérification religieuse. Recherche d'une spiritualité pour un temps de l'incertitude* (1964); J. B. Metz, "Unbelief as Theological Problem", *Concilium* 1 (1965), pp. 484–92; K. Rahner, *Theological Investigations,* V (1965).

Karl Rahner

II. Faith

1. *Dimensions of faith.* God has revealed himself to man in his Son made man (Heb 1:1; Jn 1:14–18; Mt 11:25–27); revelation is the mystery of God who draws near to man in the human word of his eternal Word. Man's response to God revealing himself in Christ is called faith; faith, therefore, is as supernatural as revelation itself, and together they constitute the mystery of God's encounter with man in Christ. In this encounter it is God who makes the first move; his inward call enables man to receive the divine word. Man freely decides to submit to the absolute claim of divine revelation. Faith is indissolubly both a gift of God and a human act, both grace and freedom. Faith is a compact act of many different aspects. No doubt these may be analysed, but they form an organic whole and are therefore unintelligible unless studied in their organic interrelation. Modern exegetes are agreed that faith includes knowledge of a saving event, confidence in the word of God, man's humble submission and personal self-surrender to God, fellowship in life with Christ, and a desire for perfect union with him beyond the grave: faith is man's comprehensive "Yes" to God revealing himself as man's saviour

in Christ. The magisterium of the Church teaches that the act of faith is a complete surrender of man to God, one which includes acceptance of revealed doctrine, voluntary submission to grace, and trust in God's promises (*D* 798, 1789, 1791; Vatican II; Constitution on Revelation, art. 5). Theologians, recognizing the complexity and intrinsic unity of the act of faith, distinguish in it the following basic dimensions: faith as knowledge of revealed truth (believing in God who reveals himself in Christ: *"fides quae creditur"*); faith as trusting obedience to God and as a personal encounter with him: *"fides qua creditur"* (believing God, the formal structure of faith): in this sense faith is the disposition for justification and ordination to final salvation in the beatific vision, that is, to participation in the life of the glorious Christ (the salvific and eschatological dimension of faith). Thus Christ is the centre, the foundation and the final goal of faith (the Christocentric and Christological aspect of faith).

2. *Faith as knowledge.* Trust in God's promises and obedience to his commandments are the most obvious features of faith in the OT, but it usually implies knowledge of God's salvific intervention in history, whether this has already happened or is yet to come (Gen 15:2–6; 16:11; Exod 4:1–9, 28–31). The whole history of Israel revealed the God of the covenant as the only saviour, with the result that monotheism became the fundamental dogma of Judaism: "I, I am the Lord, and besides me there is no saviour" (Is 43:10–12). The "knowledge of God" which the prophets preached involved professing faith in the one God (Hos 2:20; 4:1; 5:4; 13:4; Is 45:5, 22; Jer 24:7; Ezek 6:7, 10, 13; 7:27; Joel 2:27; Deut 4:39; 7:9) in certain fixed formulae (Deut 6:20–24; 26:5–9; Jos 24:2–13; Ps 78; 106; 135; 136).

The event of Jesus' death and resurrection caused the aspect of "kowledge" in Christian faith to be particularly stressed. The great profession of faith of the primitive Church was: "Jesus has risen: God has made him Lord and Saviour, according to the prophets" (Acts 2:44; 4:4; 8:13; 11:21; 13:48; 17:2). To believe, according to St. Paul, is to accept the resurrection of Christ and its meaning for salvation as a reality (Rom 10: 9, 10; 1 Cor 1: 1–19; Phil 3:10–11; 1 Thess 4:14). Faith and its message to each other as the statement and its content: the term πίστις (faith) is used to mean the actual content of the apostolic preaching (Rom 10:8; Gal 1:23; 3:2, 5; Eph 4:5; Acts 6:7; 13:8, 12). By faith one attains to "knowledge of the truth", because the gospel is "the word of truth" (2 Cor 6:7; Col 1:5; Eph 1:13; Gal 1:6–9; 1 Tim 2:4; 4:3; 2 Tim 3:7).

In the Johannine writings "faith" and "knowledge" have the one object, the divine Sonship of Jesus (Jn 8:24, 28; 14:12, 20; 17:21, 23), and each implies the other (Jn 4:42; 6:69; 8:31, 32; 10:38; 17:8; 1 Jn 4:16). To believe is to recognize Jesus as him whom the Father has sent (Jn 17:3), to accept the truth of the testimony he gives of himself (Jn 3:11–13, 31–36; 8:14, 18, 24, 30–32, 40–46), to confess that he is the Son of God (Jn 11:27; 20:31; 1 Jn 4:2, 3, 15), to profess his "doctrine" and to persevere in it (Jn 7:16, 17; 2 Jn 7–11). To be a Christian (Acts 11:26; 26:28) is to accept the truth of the mystery of Christ (the death and resurrection of the Son of God) and its meaning for salvation (Acts 16:31; 26:23; Phil 2:5–11; Gal 4:4; Rom 1:3–5; Jn 1:1–18; 20:31; 1 Jn 5:20).

From the very beginning the Church has expressed its faith in special formulae (1 Thess 1:10; 4:14; 1 Cor 1–8; 12:3; Rom 1:4; 10:9; Phil 2:5–11; Acts 8:37; 1 Jn 2:23; 4:2, 15; 2 Jn 7). Profession of faith in Christ and the Trinity was of basic importance in the baptismal liturgy; in order to belong to the Church, the community of salvation, one had to believe in the mystery of Christ in which man shares through baptism and faith indissolubly united.

It is not difficult to see why the act of faith includes acceptance of the content of revelation as true. Man can only be saved by participation in the saving event of Christ (Acts 4:2; Rom 1:16; 3:22–28; 6:1–9; 10: 9, 10; Jn 3:14, 16, 36; 20:31); but it is impossible to share in this event without believing in its reality. The cognitive character of faith is an expression of the reality of the mystery of Christ; one cannot be maintained without the other. "If Christ has not been raised, your faith is futile" (1 Cor 15:14, 17); which means that faith apprehends the death and resurrection of Christ as real. Faith lives by the reality of its object, which is God's saving intervention in Christ. But for this reality the act of faith would have no content; it would be reduced to a purely subjective act. If the event of Christ is not real in itself, neither can it be real for me and it would be impossible to live it as a reality (Gal 2:20; Rom 4:24, 25; 2 Cor 5:15).

God has definitively revealed himself in the ineffable religious experience of Christ. The man Jesus was conscious of being the Son of God. But this ineffable experience (the repercussion, in Jesus' human consciousness, of the mystery of the Incarnation) could only be conveyed to men through human signs, symbols, metaphors, concepts and words. The message of Christ conceptualized and objectified the non-conceptual experience in which God manifested himself to Christ as his Father. In the incarnate Word the human word was used to give utterance to God's ineffable self-communication to his Son, the man Jesus. So too the divine person of Christ, the Father's eternal Word, reveals himself to men in human words.

That the human word can be made an expression of the divine Word, corresponds to the possibility of man's body-soul nature being personally assumed by the Son of God. This potentiality is identical with the basic structure of the finite spirit which is radically open to the Absolute within the limitless horizon of being; and hence this limitless openness, the proper character of which is displayed in the absolute affirmation of the judgment, could be taken into personal union by the uncreated Word of God. Man's spiritual nature, as openness to being and as conscious self-possession, constitutes the basic potentiality *(potentia obedientialis)* for the Incarnation, grace, revelation, and faith. This concept of man, which any attempt to explain God's supernatural self-communication to man and man's personal encounter with God must logically presuppose, implies the doctrine of the analogy of being.

If God's revelation in Christ is validly expressed in human language, acceptance of this revelation by faith must involve an assent of the intellect; only by this means will it be possible to apprehend the message of Christ and in it the actual reality of God revealing himself. Doctrinal propositions objectify the mystery of Christ, but through the doctrinal message faith attains the revealed reality.

The intellectual nature of faith is inseparable from its ecclesial character. Unity of faith is essential to the Church (Eph 4:5), which would not be the community of believers without their common participation in the same reality of faith; such common participation is impossible without the sociological transmission of revelation, which must be expressed in definite concepts if it is to be preached. Thus the ecclesial kerygma, as the bond of union in the Church, must be accepted as true in the faith of Christians. The Church would not be visible as the community of believers if the act of faith did not include an intellectual assent.

3. *Faith as Christocentric.* At the heart of faith we find Christ, the Son of God made man and the saviour of the world. OT revelation coincides with the history of salvation of the chosen people and is ordained to the universal salvation to be revealed in Christ; NT revelation, especially in the Pauline and Johannine writings (Col 1:15–20, 26–28; Eph 1:10; 3:9–11; Gal 4:4–6; 2 Cor 5:18–20; 1 Tim 2:3–7; Jn 1:1–18; 3:16–17; 17:3; 20:31; 1 Jn 4:9–10; 5:11, etc.), presents Christ as the centre and principle of creation and the supernatural order of salvation. Patristic theology, both Greek and Latin, was aware of the historical development of revelation and its culmination in Christ; the liturgy shows Christ unifying the history of salvation in himself as its last end.

In the mystery of the Son of God made man the personal, immanent mystery of God — the Trinity — and the mystery of the Church — which is humanity called in Christ to a divinizing union with the divine persons — have also been revealed. Faith is theocentric and ecclesial because it is Christocentric. All revelation is summed up in these three fundamental mysteries implicit in the incarnation of the Word, who reveals the Father, sends the Spirit, and saves mankind. Whatever its actual content may be, every act of faith is ultimately ordered to the mystery of Christ.

Thus the religious value of faith in its intellectual aspect is clear. Because the act of faith includes an intellectual assent, the believer attains the actual reality of the saving even which is Christ, and is able to share in it; the personal appropriation of salvation takes place in the inward conviction that God has saved us in Christ. This assent requires that man submit the autonomy of his reason to the transcendence of divine grace and aim at the mystery of the divine life itself, in which he has already begun to share through the Word of God.

4. *Believing God.* The mystery of God who saves us through Christ can only be known insofar as God discloses his divine consciousness to man by giving testimony to himself. "Believing God" formally constitutes faith: this term, which frequently occurs in the OT and is also found in the NT (Gen 15:6; Ex 14:31; Num 14:11; 20:12; Deut 1:32, etc.; Acts 16:34; 27:25; Rom 4:3; Jn 5:24), means the attitude of one who assents to and relies on God's word and promises: believing God, man entrusts himself to him. NT faith looks at what God has done in Christ but also what God will do through him at the end of time, and therefore it is united with hope (Eph 3:12; Rom 5:1; 6:8; 1 Thess 1:3; 4:14; Heb 11:1–40). The fourth gospel uses the expression "to believe Christ" (πιστεύειν with the dative: Jn 4:21; 5:38, 46; 6:30; 8:31, 45; 10:37; 14:11), that is, to accept the witness which the Son of God bears to himself, in which the Father too gives testimony of himself (Jn 8:14, 18; 12:49, 50; 14:10, 24). Faith rests on the human word of the Word of God, so that its ultimate guarantee is the veracity of God himself (Jn 3:32–34; 8:26; 1 Jn 5:10): it is theological to the extent to which it is Christological.

To believe is, formally, to know reality through the knowledge which another person has of it and which he communicates by his testimony; between faith and reality there intervenes the person of the witness, who communicates his knowledge so that the believer may share in it and thereby attain to the reality itself. Testimony is essentially the communication of knowledge and the communication of consciousness (the witness's consciousness of his own veracity); faith is essentially sharing the knowledge and consciousness of another person.

Divine revelation is formally the communication of God's self-knowledge and self-consciousness so that man may rely on God's infallibility as the final guarantee of truth; in revelation, the veracity of God is engaged, that is, he commits and communicates himself in his word. This communication is absolutely supernatural, because no intellectual creature as such can have any claim to God's infallibility as the formal basis of his assent.

When he believes God, man knows revealed truth through the infallible knowledge God has of himself and consequently shares in the divine consciousness; faith is a divinizing, supernatural participation in the very life of God (Thomas Aquinas, *De Ver.*, q. 14, a. 8; *In Boet., De Trin.,* q. 2, a. 2; *Summa Theologica,* I, II, q. 62, a. 1 ad 1; q. 110, a. 4; II, II, q. 1, a. 1; q. 17, a. 6).

Revelation and faith are supernatural by reason of their formal structure. Revelation is formally the personal self-communication of God to man through his word; faith is formally the personal self-dedication of man to God who addresses him. Believing God, man relies on the divine veracity and by that very fact puts his trust in the God of truth; faith essentially entails confidence in the divine testimony, that is, a confident surrender of man to God who reveals himself to man and thus saves him. Like the Incarnation, revelation is in itself a saving event. By the very fact of speaking to man God draws near to him as his saviour, and man experiences this nearness of God, present in the divine word, as his own salvation. Revelation and faith essentially involve a mutual gift on the part of God and man. God communicates himself, and man, by his acceptance, gives himself to God. It is a personal encounter: God offers man his friendship by disclosing the secret of his divine consciousness, and man enters God's intimacy. Faith is fellowship of life shared by man with God. This personal encounter and fellowship of life between man and the self-revealing God takes place in Christ. By faith Christ dwells in the heart of man (Eph 3:17) and man lives by Christ's own life (Gal 2:20; 3:26; Rom 6:4–10; Jn 10:14, 26–28; 17:20–23; 1 Jn 2:23–24; 4:7, 15, 16; 5:1, 20).

5. *Faith as a gift of God.* It is only by the grace of God that man can believe God (Eph 2:8–9; Jn 6:44, 65). The prophets describe what God does to the believer as creating a "new heart", as infusing a "new spirit", that is, as a spiritual transformation in man's inmost thoughts, feelings, and purposes (Jer 24:7; Ezek 36:26–28; Is 54:13). This idea of the interior transformation wrought by grace is further developed

in the NT. According to St. Paul, conversion to Christianity radically renews man's interior structure in relation to God. The Spirit (πνεῦμα) inwardly enlightens the heart of the believer with a new knowledge and filial love of God (Eph 4:17–19; Col 1:21; 3:9, 10; 2 Cor 4:4–6; Gal 4:8; 9; Acts 16:14). Only when moved by the Spirit can man accept the mystery of Christ; and if the Christian grows in the knowledge of that mystery, this is also due to the vivifying presence of the Spirit (1 Cor 1:23; 2:10–16; 12:3; Eph 1:15–19; 3:14–19; Gal 2:20). According to Jn 6:44–46 and Mt 11:25–27, the preaching and miracles of Christ do not of themselves enable a man to believe in him. God must also draw the man to himself by an interior revelation. One of the central statements of John is that the "knowledge" of God and Christ that faith involves is a special effect of the presence of grace within man. To "know" and confess Christ one must be "born of God" and "abide" in him, that is, remain in fellowship of life with him (1 Jn 2:3, 5; 3:6, 9; 4:6–8, 15, 16; 5:1). Faith stems from a supernatural faculty of "knowledge". This is plainly stated in 1 Jn 5:20: ". . . the Son of God . . . has given us understanding (διάνοια), to know him who is true (God)." The word διάνοια has always been rendered as faculty of knowledge (J. Alfaro in *Verbum Domini* 39 [1961], p. 90).

We must therefore conclude that according to the NT God himself creates the interior dispositions in man which are necessary if he is to be related to him by faith. The Fathers, particularly from St. Augustine on, envisaged the work of grace in the act of faith as an inward illumination. This concept was embodied in certain documents of the Church's magisterium (*D* 134, 141, 180, 181, 1791; Vatican II, *Lumen Gentium,* art. 12; *Dei Verbum,* art. 5). Under the influence of this Augustinian doctrine the theologians of the 13th century (notably St. Thomas, cf. J. Alfaro, "Supernaturalitas") worked out the first systematic explanation of the supernatural character of faith. God inwardly draws man towards an immediate union with himself, by giving him a new dynamism ordered to the beatific vision, thus enabling him to accept the transcendent credibility of the divine word — that is, to rely on God's word as being of itself absolutely worthy of credence. Grace raises man's spiritual powers above the limitless horizon of being and orders them to a supernatural end, to God in himself.

Occam's extrinsicism, on the other hand, developed a conception of grace entirely opposed to that of the previous century: grace, a created entity infused into man by God, does not affect the natural orientation of man's spiritual powers and their acts. The natural powers of man can accept divine revelation with an assent identical with the act of supernatural faith. From the 14th century down to our own day these antithetical opinions have continued to divide Catholic theologians. Owing, however, to closer study of the NT and the Fathers and keener appreciation of the transcendence of the formal motive of faith and of the vivifying effect of interior grace, there is a marked tendency among contemporary theologians towards the Thomist conception of supernatural faith.

By faith man knows God and his mysteries through the knowledge God has of himself. This sort of knowledge essentially surpasses man's natural powers which can only reach God by rising from the creature to the Creator (Wis 13:1–9; Rom 1:20; *D* 1785). Consequently, man cannot believe God unless his spiritual powers are intrinsically raised to a higher plane by the supernatural light of faith *(lumen fidei),* just as he cannot see God unless he is intrinsically elevated by the *lumen gloriae.* Hence the act of divine faith, in its formal structure, is a super-creaturely participation in the life of God and therefore it essentially involves a transformation of man that divinizes him. The finite intellect cannot base itself on the divine veracity (that is, on the consciousness of God) unless God inwardly draws it to himself. God must mysteriously become present in the depths of man if man is to come into real contact with the word of God, which is God himself. If one reflects that to believe God is to rise above one's own reason and base one's life on the divine word, it will be obvious that this is impossible without a personal invitation from God to enter into confident fellowship with him.

Grace raises man to a participation in the very life of God. This implies the elevation of man as a spirit, as a being capable of conscious self-possession. This dynamic elevation gives one's supernatural acts their specific character as consciously tending towards God in himself (which orientation is experienced in the consciousness in the strict sense, that is, in the non-objectivated self-possession of the person, in its acts). Through grace man experiences himself in the very depths of his consciousness as a being called to intimate fellowship with God.

The believer already possesses "eternal life", which tends to its eschatological fullness in direct union with God in Christ (Jn 3:16, 36; 4:14; 17:3; 1 Jn 3:2, 15; Rom 8:23; 1 Cor 13:10–13). This supernatural orientation inevitably makes itself felt in the mental life of man as the new experience of being attracted by God himself. If grace did not act upon man insofar as he sets up a relationship to God, it would remain wholly extrinsic to man's religious life, something there by mere juxtaposition, not a force that brings about an interior transformation. Consequently it must be admitted that grace elevates the spiritual dynamism of man to relate it to God himself. Man is thereby enabled to enter upon a personal relationship with God in faith.

The inward illumination of grace has no objective content. It simply enables man to accept the content of revelation (presented to him from without in the preaching of the Church) as the word of God (2 Thess 2:13). Grace operates as a non-conceptual attraction to God in himself, which is prior to the free act, and thus God becomes mysteriously present in man's depths as God, that is, as personal transcendence. God reveals and communicates himself to man by no other intermediary than this attraction to himself, and man knows God non-conceptually through the experience of the actual ordination to God. As man becomes conscious of this ordination or dynamism, he thereby becomes non-conceptually conscious of the goal of this dynamism, God. There is no vision, no direct experience of God, only the experience of the tendency towards God in himself, in which God is attained non-conceptually. God is not directly present in himself, but in the created dynamism orientated towards himself.

The existence of this supernatural ordination to God in himself is not known through introspection but through theological reflection. The experience of this invitation to divine intimacy cannot normally be an object of reflection in such a way that man can discover there God in himself as the goal of this invitation. The psychological repercussions of grace in man are too obscure, as a rule, to offer certainty of one's vocation to faith; the external signs of revelation are the normal basis of this certainty. Interior enlightenment by grace prefigures the act of faith, implying as it does an obscure, preconceptual presence of God (communicated, and manifested as salvation, by his attraction to himself), and hence ordering man's spiritual powers to a personal encounter with the transcendent You, first in the mystery of faith and finally face to face in eschatological salvation (1 Cor 12:10–13; 2 Cor 5:7; 1 Jn 3:1–3). Hence the operation of grace dynamically anticipates the character of the act of faith itself, disposing the depths of man's being to accept divine revelation freely, and thus to express the mystery of God's salvation in Christ in conceptual terms. The preconceptual and the conceptual are both essential to the act of faith, each requiring the other. Without the non-conceptual divine presence in the supernatural attraction towards God, man would be unable to give his unqualified assent to God's word in reliance on its transcendent credibility; if the content of divine revelation were not affirmed in conceptual terms, man could not reach God his saviour by a genuinely human act.

6. *Faith as a fundamental human choice.* By faith man freely submits to God's salvific love. For the OT, unbelief is rebellion and faith is obedience to God's word (Num 14:9, 11; Deut 9:23; Pss 78; 105; Is 2:2–24; 25:6–8; Jer 16:19). For St. Paul, faith is obedience to the gospel, that is, man's willing submission to the salvific economy that God has established in Christ (Rom 1:5; 10:16; 15:18; 16:26; 2 Cor 9:13; 2 Thess 1:8–10). According to St. John, faith is rooted in the very heart of human liberty, when man sacrifices his own glory, sincerely seeks the truth, and listens in loving docility to the inward voice of God (Jn 5:44; 8:43–47; 10:26, 27; 15:22–24); faith is coming to Christ, following him, accepting his witness to himself — in a word, a radical and total decision for the person and mission of Christ the Son of God (Jn 3:32–36; 5:38, 43; 6:35, 37, 65, 68; 7:37-38; 8:12–24; 10:4,5,27,37; 12:37, 48).

The freedom of faith (D 797, 798, 1786, 1791; Vatican II, *Dignitatis Humanae,* art. 10) corresponds to the supreme gratuitousness of revelation and salvation. God's word confronts man with the mystery of Christ, which cannot extort the assent of reason because it transcends reason. On the other hand, the demands of Christianity (its absolute character, the imitation of Christ based on the law of love and the cross, the eschatological orientation of Christian existence) demand of man the most radical decision of his freedom. Christ demands faith in himself that shall be an irrevocable decision (Lk 11:23; 8:22; Mk 9:43–47; Mt 5:1–48). Faith is not so much an act or a series of acts as a basic and total attitude of the person, giving life a new, definitive direction. It comes from depths of human freedom, where man has received the interior invitation of grace to enter the intimacy of God; it embraces his whole being — intellect, will, all that he does (submission to the mystery, the love, and the law of Christ). By accepting doctrine, faith accepts the revealed reality itself, the person of Christ with its claim on total dedication in love and obedience. Faith is at once an assent of the intellect and a consent of the will, which finds its true fulfilment in action.

Faith is born of desire for eternal life and is thus inseparable from hope, without which no one can wish to be saved. In its formal structure ("believing God"), faith implies trust in the divine witness and submission to the absolute authority of his word. It is a defined doctrine of the Church's magisterium that the loss of God's friendship through sin does not necessarily extinguish faith: man may be a believer and a sinner at one and the same time (D 808, 838, 1791, 1814). But it does not follow that faith can exist without a longing for charity; faith is not possible without the desire for salvation, which begins when the sinner is reconciled with God and is fulfilled in perfect friendship with God in glory. Even in its most imperfect form faith is ordained to friendship with God, and only reaches its perfection (even as faith) when charity has made it a living faith. Absence of charity deals a mortal wound to the life of faith itself. The believing sinner is torn by a radical inward antinomy: his faith is a constant call to reconciliation with God, while his sinful state draws him towards apostasy from faith. This contradiction tends to resolve itself, either by a return to God's friendship or by a total separation from God in unbelief.

The element of freedom is essential in the act of faith, for the activity of the intellect is subordinated to the will. Thus its assent is a prolongation of the free movement of the will towards the God of revelation. Since intellect and will are rooted in the person, who is actuated in them, in the last analysis it is man who by his free assent lays hold on revelation and salvation. It is the business of the will to unify man, whom God calls upon to decide freely what his own eternal destiny shall be, either accepting salvation as the gift of God's love or imprisoning himself in his own sufficiency. Faith sinks its roots in the very depths of human freedom, that is, in the fundamental and permanent choice by which man opens himself to, or rebels against, the Absolute as grace; here the ultimate meaning of human existence is decided.

7. *The certainty of faith*. God's word demands man's unqualified assent (Acts 2:36; Rom 4:19–21; Gal 1:9; Lk 1:18–20; Heb 10:22; 11:1). It is not possible to believe God as God, subject to certain limitations. The Church's professions of faith breathe an absolute certainty (D 40, 428, 706, 1789, 2145) which is based on the infallibility of God's witness (D 1789, 2145) and springs from the interior work of grace (D 1797). Thus the *absolute* certainty of faith is supernatural. It stems from the supernatural character of its foundation (divine revelation) and its principle (divine grace), which correspond to one another. Faith is infallible because it shares supernaturally in the infallibility of God; its absolute certainty excludes actual doubt, but not the psychological possibility of doubt or denial. The certainty of faith is entirely different from the certainty proper to philosophic or scientific knowledge; it is a special kind of certainty, based neither on the obvious truth of (essentially mysterious) revelation nor on any obvious rational proof of the *fact* of revelation (otherwise faith would not be free). Paradoxically, faith is absolutely certain and essentially obscure. The believer does not accept divine revelation, because he sees the truth of the mystery, or knows from rational evidence that God has spoken, but because under the guarantee of the external signs of divine revelation and the impulse of grace within him, he freely decides to rely on the word of God, who of himself is absolutely worthy of credence.

The assent of faith is both absolutely

certain and free. Hence all theologians conclude that this assent cannot result from a process of reasoning; for in such a case it would either follow from evident premises, and so be fully certain but not free, or it would not stem from the evidence of the premises, and so would be free but not absolutely certain. True, this does not altogether explain the *absolute* certainty of faith. The question still remains: if this certainty is not the result of evidence, then where does it come from? It is not enough to recall the influence that the will has over the intellect. The will can move the intellect to assent, but cannot of itself produce an unqualified intellectual assent (which in the natural order only evidence can do). The absolute certainty of faith can only be explained by the inward illumination of grace, which enables man to rise above his natural mode of knowledge and rely on the transcendent credibility of God's word.

8. *Faith and salvation.* The role of faith in salvation is fundamental (*D* 801). By faith man recognizes the reality and the absolute gratuitousness of God's initiative in saving sinful humanity through Christ (Rom 10:9; 3:22–30; 4:16; Gal 2:16; 8:22, 24; Eph 2:8–10). Man can only be saved by sharing in the mystery of Christ's death and resurrection, which means that he must first of all affirm the reality of this mystery (1 Cor 15:12–16) and freely accept the economy of salvation that God has established and revealed in his Son (Rom 10:16; 2 Cor 9:13; 2 Thess 1:8). Thus faith is man's basic response to God revealing himself as man's saviour. It is an attitude which accepts salvation as sheer grace, renouncing all pride in one's own works (Rom 3:22, 24, 27; 4:2, 20; 1 Cor 1:29; 4:7; Gal 2:16). Man's response to the absolute gratuitousness of God's saving intervention is faith. Hence faith confesses the grace of God. To believe is to consent to be saved by God; it is to accept God as the pure gift of himself, as grace. Faith revolves about God's inscrutable, absolutely gratuitous design to save us in Christ (Eph 1:3–14; 2:5–10; 2 Thess 2:13; 2 Tim 1:9); but it is fulfilled in deeds (which express its vitality) and is perfect, proximately disposes to justification, only when joined with charity (Gal 5:6; 6:15).

From God's universal salvific will (Mk 10:45; 14:24; Rom 5:12–20; 1 Cor 15:20–22; 1 Tim 2:1–6; 4:10; Jn 1:29; 3:14–17; 1 Jn 2:2) and the absolute necessity of faith for salvation (Heb 11:6; Jn 3:16–21; *D* 801) it follows that God calls upon every human being to make the fundamental choice of faith, that is, to decide freely the meaning of his existence by accepting or rejecting grace. Theologians today are agreed (and are confirmed in their view by Vatican II, *Lumen Gentium,* arts. 2, 13, 16) that all men receive an interior invitation from the grace of God. But there remains the problem of how an act of faith is possible for men who through no fault of their own are unaware of the content or even the fact of revelation. Attempts to solve this problem have been numerous, but unconvincing. There is, however, a promising trend in contemporary theology towards a new solution based on a profounder sense of the illuminating function of grace as self-communication and manifestation of God, in non-conceptual terms, in his drawing men supernaturally to himself. The proper effect of grace in man is an interior invitation to familiar fellowship with the Absolute. Through this invitation (not objectified conceptually but experienced in the ordination to God in himself) man experiences himself in his non-objectified consciousness as called to a free and loving acceptance of the Absolute, who gives himself as sheer grace. Man's free response (acceptance or rejection), preformed in the experience of this ineffable call, is radically a decision of faith, in that it either welcomes or repels God communicating and supernaturally manifesting himself in the obscurity of his non-conceptual presence. Since this decision does not grasp divine revelation in conceptual terms, it does not have the full quality of an assent of faith. In this sense it is essentially deficient as an act of faith. But it is a decision which in the manner of a vital act includes an embryonic and not merely virtual faith. It is rooted in the inexpressible depths of human freedom (whose choice may transcend the conceptual knowledge which conditions its exercise), but merely has not yet attained the corresponding expression in categories. It is a faith which is lived but is not (yet) conceptually grasped, because its full development is hindered by circumstances outside the human will. In such a decision, man's life and choice go beyond his objective conscious knowledge. If he could tell himself in conceptual terms the real meaning of his free response, conditioned and preformed by his experience of the attraction of the Absolute, then he would realize that he has (or has not) believed God. This decision implies the *fides qua creditur,* but not the *fides quae creditur.*

This solution does not seek in any way to minimize the conceptual aspect of faith, which is absolutely necessary for man to grasp the content of divine revelation; an act of faith which is properly such will contain both elements, conceptual and non-conceptual. The basic gospel message (God as salvation of men) expresses in conceptual terms the very reality which man apprehends non-conceptually in his experience of grace. Thus without a corresponding knowledge of the objective content of revelation, the decision of faith lacks the appropriate human expression; only the Gospel enables man to understand himself, that is, to understand the meaning of his decision and of his whole life. By the decision that he makes in the supernatural existential situation (in response to the experiential call of the transcendent You to a personal encounter with himself) man opens himself or closes himself to grace, that is, God giving himself and revealing himself in the gift. Such a decision, in its existential aspect, is equivalent to the decision of faith.

9. *The eschatological nature of faith.* The conception of life and fundamental attitude of the Christian are essentially eschatological. Faith looks beyond the world and death in eager expectation of eternal life in the encounter with the risen Christ (1 Cor 1:7–8; 1 Thess 1:10; Rom 8:23–25; Phil 3:20; Tit 2:13; 2 Cor 5:1–10; Phil 1:19–26). The believer already shares in the saving mystery of Christ, yet not fully as he will at the end of time, when the Lord will impart to men and even the material world the glory of his resurrection (1 Cor 13:10–13; 2 Cor 5:6–10; Phil 1: 21–23; 3:20–21; 1 Thess 4:17; Rom 8:19–23; Heb 11; Jn 3:36; 17:3, 24; 1 Jn 3:2). Faith is eschatological because it is Christocentric. Because faith is centred on the mystery of Christ, which will only be fully revealed at his second coming, it is dynamically ordered to the perfect union of man with Christ in glory and in him with the Father and the Holy Spirit. In the obscurity of the divine word the believer already knows the personal mystery of God (Incarnation, Trin-

ity) whom it will one day be his eschatological fulfilment to see face to face.

By its formal structure ("believing God") faith already tends towards the vision of God. Through revelation God discloses the mystery of his divine consciousness to man; through faith man enters God's intimacy and begins to share in his divine life. This intimate personal encounter between God and man, which revelation and faith entail, seeks its own fullness in a perfect union. Grace, being God's drawing man to himself, directs the act of faith towards the vision of God. True, the assent of faith, expressed as it is in human concepts, is necessarily bound up with a mediate knowledge of God by analogy and in this respect does not transcend the horizon of being. But its tendency does transcend that horizon, being ordered to God in himself, who makes himself present non-conceptually but without any intermediary other than the experiential attraction he has for himself. The final goal of the supernatural dynamism of faith is immediate union with God. Since the act of faith expresses the totality of man as soul and body (assent to the content of revelation inevitably involves concepts, images, and the like) and eschatological salvation will fully glorify man as man (resurrection of the body), man tends through faith to a perfect union with Christ in glory, and thereby to the vision of God and his personal mystery, the direct revelation of the Father, the Son, and the Holy Spirit. Just as Christ is the centre and foundation of faith, so he is also its last end; man believes God in Christ so as to reach the vision of God in Christ (J. Alfaro in *Gregorianum* 39 [1958], pp. 222–70; in *Catholica* 16 [1962], pp. 20–39).

Christian existence runs its course within history and time; but God's supernatural call gives that existence a new direction destined to transcend time by participation in God's eternity in direct union with the glorified Christ. Through faith man experiences and possesses himself in a new dimension; his consciousness of being present to himself is now set within the *a priori* horizon of ordination for eternity. The believer, in time, is on pilgrimage towards eternity, that is, is on the way to meet the Lord.

See also *Faith* III, IV, *Hope, Charity* I, *Revelation, Mystery, Word, Grace, Salvation* I, III A,

Absolute and Contingent, Potentia Oboedientialis, Analogy of Being, Supernatural Order.

BIBLIOGRAPHY. P. Rousselot, *Les Yeux de la foi* (1913); J. Bainvel, *Faith and the Act of Faith* (1926); A. Schlatter, *Der Glaube im Neuen Testament* (4th ed., 1927); M. C. D'Arcy, *The Nature of Belief* (1931); R. Guardini, *Vom Leben des Glaubens* (1935), E. T.: *Life of Faith* (1961); P. Antoine, "Foi", *DBS,* III, cols. 276–310; K. Rahner, *Hörer des Wortes* (1941); J. Mouroux, *Je crois en Toi* (2nd ed., 1948), E.T.: *I Believe* (1959); J. Dupont, *Gnosis. La connaissance religieuse d'après S. Paul* (1949); G. des Lauriers, *Dimensions de la foi* (1952); J. Guillet, *Thèmes bibliques* (2nd ed., 1954); B. Douroux, *La psychologie de la foi chez S. Thomas d'Aquin* (1956); A. Weiser and R. Bultmann, πιστεύω, πίστις, *TWNT,* VI, pp. 174–230; C. Cirne-Lima, *Der personale Glaube* (1959), E. T.: *Personal Faith*; J. Alfaro, "Fides in terminologia biblica", *Gregorianum* 42 (1961), pp. 463–505; id., "Cognitio Dei et Christi in 1 Jn", *Verbum Domini* 39 (1961), pp. 82–91; E. O'Connor, *Faith in the Synoptic Gospels* (1961); J. Pieper, *Belief and Faith* (1963); J. Alfaro, "Supernaturalitas fidei iuxta S. Thomam", *Gregorianum* 44 (1963), pp. 501–42, 731–87.

Juan Alfaro

III. Motive of Faith

1. *God reveals himself in Christ.* According to the OT to believe God is to rely (הֶאֱמִין = hiphil of אָמַן = to be firm) on his word (Gen 15:1–6; Exod 4:15, 28–30; 14:31; Is 43:1, 10; Jn 3:1–5). St. Paul adopts this concept when saying that faith accepts the Gospel as the word of God (2 Thess 2:13). While Heb 1:1 declares that God has spoken to us in his Son, the fourth gospel outlines a theology of God's testimony (μαρτυρία) through Christ as the foundation of faith: Christ reveals God because he is the Son of God made man; the personal mystery of God is known only to the Son, who alone sees the Father; the human testimony of Jesus is the testimony of the very Son of God and that of the Father as well; consequently to believe Christ is to believe God, trusting in God's own veracity (Jn 1:14–18; 3:11–13, 31–33; 6:46; 8:12–55; 12:44–50; 14:6–11, 24; Mt 11:27; 1 Jn 5:10). Thus the christological nature of faith is a consequence of the Incarnation: the divine person who is the Word speaks to men with human words. Since faith rests ultimately on the person of the witness, when man believes Christ he enters into a relation with the person of the Son of God himself. The formal foundation of faith is Christ, that is, God himself as revealing himself in Christ.

The object of faith is the mystery of God who in Christ calls men to participation in his divine life. This mystery exceeds the native powers of the human intellect — it can only be known by men through the divine testimony. This doctrine, familiar to the Fathers, has been confirmed by the Church's magisterium: the motive of faith is the authority of God's word, his truthfulness and infallibility (*D* 1789, 1811, 2145; Vatican II, *Dei Verbum,* arts. 2, 4).

The signs of divine revelation (miracles and the like), as known solely by the light of reason, are not the motive of faith. Since the assent of faith is absolutely certain and free, it cannot spring from a process of reasoning. Hence it cannot be formally based on the motives of credibility which are the point of departure for a rational proof that a divine revelation exists (*D* 1799, 1813). Faith presupposes the signs of credibility but they are not the formal motive of faith; they are a condition of faith, not its cause.

The teaching authority of the Church's hierarchy is the infallible and obligatory norm of faith, but not its formal motive. The Church, the community of believers, is entrusted with divine revelation, which it proclaims in its preaching and witness. It is the primordial sacrament of the glorified Christ, living by his Spirit, the channel through which men draw the supernatural life of faith; yet it is not strictly the motive of our faith. This can only be Christ, because he alone is the Son of God made man, the personal revealer of God.

2. *The motive of faith as the object of faith.* The fourth gospel represents Christ's testimony as testimony to himself. Christ is always both revealer and revealed, the revealer manifesting himself as such; he demands that one believe his testimony to himself, and he testifies that his testimony is worthy of credence. This absolute demand that one believe what he says of himself, and for the simple reason that he says it, springs from Christ's consciousness that he is the Son of God, and is the exercise of this Sonship. Faith is accepting Christ's testimony to himself, at once believing him and believing in him — believing that he is the Son of God the revealer, and believing him as God's

Son and as the revealer (Jn 5:16–18, 38, 40, 43; 6:29–30; 7:25–31; 8:14–20, 25, 28, 30–31, 45; 10:24–39; 11:25–27; 14:2, 10, 11). This is to say that the motive of faith is also its object; the act of faith includes above all its own formal motive; by one and the same act a man believes what God has revealed in Christ and also believes that God has revealed himself in Christ.

Since the 13th century this has been the view of all theologians who recognized the decisive role played by the inward illumination of grace in the act of faith: when interior grace draws a man towards God, he enters confidently into contact with personal and transcendent truth; by a single act he believes God revealing himself and believes that God does reveal himself. The essence and expression of the act of faith is: God has spoken, God has revealed himself, in Christ.

St. Thomas insists that the person must be primary in the act of faith: a person's word is believed. He holds that the formal aspect of faith consists of the fact that God is believed (*Summa Theologica,* II–II, q. 11, a. 1; q. 2, a. 2; etc.). In the act of faith man enters into a personal relationship with the God who speaks to him. This is the kernel of faith, which is therefore essentially religious. When submitting to the divine word and confiding himself to it, man gives himself to God, who communicates himself to him and reveals himself and draws him to himself by an inward illumination. The human response includes the affirmation of the existence of divine revelation (even though the believer is not always conscious of this).

Faith does not merely accept the gospel, but accepts it as God's word (2 Thess 2:13). The content of revelation deserves credence because God himself attests it, and since the divine testimony includes the reason of its credibility, it is credible in itself. This is the sovereign, transcendent and immediate character of the divine word: God cannot speak otherwise than as God and therefore his word necessarily affirms its own credibility and demands belief of itself. (If Christ had not declared his self-witness to be absolutely valid, he would not have revealed himself as the Son of God.) It would be as absurd to try to base the credibility of God's word on something outside that word, as to seek the source of God's being in something other than that being itself — God is believed as

God only if he is believed on the sole authority of his own word. Faith achieves its fulfilment when it declares (giving voice to man's total response): *God has spoken.* The theological opinion which holds that the act of faith merely affirms the content of revelation (the view of those theologians who deny the illuminating function of grace), deprives the act of faith of its formal aspect (that which makes faith faith, believing God), the personal relationship of the believer to the God who speaks to him.

Thus the first thing which the act of faith lays hold on *(primum credibile)* is the actual existence of divine revelation, the fact that God has spoken in Christ. This priority is not one of time (an act of faith necessarily affirms some definite truth contained in revelation) but one of credibility; the primary object of faith is God the author of revelation, because of the supernatural attraction by which God draws men to himself. Man is able to accept the divine word as supremely credible of itself because God communicates himself and discloses himself non-conceptually in the interior call, being himself present in the supernatural tendency towards him. The inward illumination of grace enables man to rise above his natural mode of knowledge and enter into relationship with the transcendent Thou. Through God's non-conceptual presence (not a direct intuition of God but a new contact with God through the sole intermediary of the vital tendency towards him) man is inwardly addressed by divine revelation, and enabled to grasp it in its transcendent character. The ultimate motive of faith, then, is the divine testimony, which man is able to grasp thanks to an interior illumination from God. The structure proper to faith and also the special character of the knowledge which it imparts are here apparent. Faith, like the beatific vision, gives man a share in the knowledge which God has of himself in the divine life; hence the supernatural and mysterious character of faith and vision.

Even though human reason cannot comprehend the intrinsic credibility of God's word (any more than it can comprehend the aseity of God's being), the act of faith still remains a free human act, one therefore that reason can reflect upon. Man must be able to explain to himself his attitude of faith by justifying the free decision of his faith at the bar of his own reason. The act of faith is not unreasonable, because it presupposes the signs of credibility and their rational comprehension — the preambles of faith.

See also *Faith* II, IV.

BIBLIOGRAPHY. A. Gardeil, *La crédibilité et l'apologétique* (2nd ed., 1912); A. Lang, *Die Wege der Glaubensbegründung bei den Scholastikern des 14. Jahrhunderts* (1931); R. Garrigou-Lagrange, *De Revelatione* (1945); E. Mori, *Il motivo della Fede da Gaetano a Suárez* (1953); R. Aubert, "Questioni attuali intorno all'atto di fede", *Problemi e Orientamenti di Teologia dommatica,* II (1957), pp. 655–708; R. Tucci, *La sopranaturalità della fede per rapporto al suo oggetto formale secondo S. Tommaso d'Aquino* (1961); J. Alfaro, "Supernaturalitas fidei iuxta S. Thomam", *Gregorianum* 44 (1963), pp. 501–42, 731–87; K. Rahner, *Theological Investigations,* V (1965).

Juan Alfaro

IV. Preambles of Faith

1. This expression refers to an aspect of the theological problem of "reason and faith", which is ultimately the problem of "nature and grace". It is God who of his good pleasure reveals himself and creates in man an ability to receive the divine word; but it is man who freely believes and enters into vital contact with the God of revelation. What is necessary for man to satisfy himself that his free decision to believe God is not an arbitrary choice? How can each of us justify his personal faith at the bar of his own reason? In its formal motive, which is the authority of God himself, faith transcends reason; but faith as a *free choice* must be subject to a man's control, and he can do no less than ask himself the reason for his own decisions: no one may use his freedom in disregard of his intelligence.

From the time of its first appearance in 13th-century Scholasticism, the term "preambles of faith" (*praeambula fidei, antecedens fidem,* etc.) has had two meanings. Principally it means a number of metaphysical truths (the existence of a personal God who is the Lord of the world and of man; the intellectual nature of man as openness to the Absolute, his ability to know truth, and his freedom; the validity of the underlying principles of being and the moral law; etc.) which reason can establish and which revelation presupposes — not precisely in the sense that these

natural truths must precede faith by a priority of time but in the sense that if they were denied the falsehood of revealed doctrines would logically follow, and that without them the mysteries of faith would lack internal credibility. The business of the preambles of faith is not to prove the fact of divine revelation but to make intelligible the content of revealed doctrine in which they are themselves implicit. But for the ideas and knowledge which make up the preambles of faith, man could attain no understanding at all of revealed mysteries (*D* 1650, 1670, 2305, 2320). Though demonstrable by natural reason, there is nothing to prevent the preambles of faith having been revealed by God and forming in themselves an object of faith (*D* 1785, 1786, 1807, 2305). Since the 17th century some of these metaphysical truths have been held to be necessary assumptions in apologetics (*D* 1799).

2. The term preambles of faith, or some synonym, has also been applied since the Middle Ages to the fact of revelation insofar as that fact can be known by reason through external motives of credibility such as miracles. Both Old and New Testament accept the evidence of the signs whereby God attests his revelation (Exod 4:2, 5–16; 14:5–31; 19:9; Mk 2:10–11; Mt 11:2–6; Jn 2:11, 23; 3:2; 5:36; 10:25, 37; 11:45–47; 15:22–23; 20:30–31). It is defined by the First Vatican Council that the divine origin of Christianity can be proved from such signs (*D* 1813, 1812, 1794, 2305). That definition confirmed a theological conclusion (nothing is said in Scripture of any natural knowledge of the signs of revelation) which was admitted by all Catholic theologians: that *if the free decision to believe God is to be consistent with the rational nature of man, it must be possible to prove the fact of revelation by means of external signs of credibility.*

God's revelation demands of man an unqualified, irrevocable "yes" which gives his whole life a permanent orientation: human freedom is at its most intense in the attitude of faith. Man may not take or abide by so grave a decision without being certain that it is his duty to accept the Christian message as the word of God ("practical judgment of credibility"). Therefore he must be able to determine whether or not his duty to believe is an illusion, something purely subjective: for this he must have criteria at his disposal which guarantee his knowledge of this obligation. Grace may well act within a man in such a way as to prove its own divine origin beyond any doubt; God can call one to the faith through the interior sign of an extraordinary religious experience (in defining the validity of external signs the Vatican Council did not deny the value of interior signs, which Catholic theologians have always admitted: *D* 1812). But experience has shown that in the case of most believers the interior action of grace is not sufficiently clear to establish the certainty of the obligation to believe; as a rule, it is impossible to transform personal religious experience into an unquestionable sign that God is inviting one to believe. Unless we wish to admit that the decision of faith is blind, we must hold that the external motives of credibility offer sound enough evidence of our duty to believe (*D* 1790; apologetics shows the validity of these signs, which are appropriate to the nature of revelation as embodied in an ecclesiastical society. Christ and the Church are the supreme sign of divine revelation). Knowledge of the signs of credibility precedes the act of faith (since the certainty of the obligations of faith is founded on them): this knowledge is a rational inference (a passing from the sign to the thing signified), and therefore an act of the intellect ("speculative judgment of credibility" — *the signs prove that revelation exists*). The act of faith presupposes a conviction that one must believe, and this in turn presupposes that one is able, by some means or other, to uphold the duty of faith at the bar of one's own reason — a thing not normally possible without rational knowledge of the fact of revelation. In actual practice, this rational knowledge is seldom formulated as such, but will usually be implied in a person's concrete realization of his duty to believe, insofar as that realization is produced by the influence of the signs.

3. The signs, and his rational knowledge of them, give man control not of the intrinsic credibility of the divine word but of his *own knowledge* of the duty to believe and of his *own free decision* to believe, which otherwise would be blind. The signs and reason take one only as far as the practical judgment of credibility, not onto the sacred ground of the act of faith itself, which arises solely from the testimony of God interiorized by the

divine impulse, and from human freedom. To introduce any rational element into the actual assent of faith would be to destroy its absolute certainty, since full rational evidence of the fact of revelation is not (as a rule) to be gained from the signs of credibility. The possibility of rational knowledge of the signs of revelation is merely a condition of the uprightness of the free decision which man takes to believe God. It is not necessary to suppose that in fact rational knowledge of the signs is the work of human reason alone; God offers man the supernatural light of grace along with the signs of credibility (*D* 1789, 2305). The signs that God has spoken are not presented to man simply as objective data but as proof of a divine intervention in the world that gives human life a new meaning: in these signs God draws near to man and summons him. Before this summons human liberty, and therefore also divine grace, comes into play. In the concrete, realization that one has a duty to believe derives from a rational factor (knowledge of the signs) and a suprarational factor (supernatural light), organically fused in one summons that is both outward and inward. Reason enables us to perceive the divine signs; but grace makes us see in them a personal call to faith (St. Thomas, *Summa Theologica*, II, II, q. 1, a. 5 ad 1). The inward light of grace transforms our rational knowledge of the signs into a realization that *"God is calling me to believe in him"*: the "practical judgment of credibility" involves an element that is personal, unutterable, incommunicable, the resonance in our consciousness of the divine call. Inwardly drawing man to itself, Personal Truth gives him a knowledge *per connaturalitatem* in which he vitally experiences an invitation to rise above creatures and trust in the transcendent credibility of God's word.

See also *Apologetics, Fundamental Theology, Miracle.*

BIBLIOGRAPHY. M. D'Arcy, *The Nature of Belief* (1931); F. Schlagenhaufen in *ZKT* 56 (1932), pp. 313–74, 539–95; R. Aubert in *RHE* 39 (1943), pp. 22–29; A. Sohier in *Gregorianum* 28 (1947), pp. 521–25; A. Horbath, *Divus Thomas* 25 (1947), pp. 29–52, 177–91, 395–408; E. Seiterich, *Die Glaubwürdigkeitserkenntnis* (1948); R. Aubert, *Le problème de l'acte de foi* (2nd ed., 1950); G. de Broglie, *Gregorianum* 34 (1953), pp. 341–89; E. Waldschmidt, *The Notion and Problems of Credibility in St. Thomas and the Major Commentators* (1956);

A. Gaboardi, *Teologia fondamentale. Il metodo apologetico: Problemi e orientamenti di teologia dommatica* (1957); L. Monden, *Le Miracle, signe de salut* (1960), E. T.: *Signs and Wonders;* A. Lang, *Die Entfaltung des apologetischen Problems in der Scholastik des Mittelalters* (1962).

Juan Alfaro

FAITH AND HISTORY

A. The Problem

The unity and difference in which faith and history combine have been thrown open as a problem only by the modern forms of thought which have made their explicit articulation possible. But the tension between faith and history in a general and fundamental sense is a basic characteristic of Christian existence in general and is therefore as old as Christianity itself. Indeed, in and through Jesus Christ it points back to the history of faith and salvation in the OT.

With the modern opening up of the historical dimension of existence, to some extent in the wake of Christianity, a transcendental horizon of consciousness has been disclosed which makes the Christian event discernible in the phenomenal character which is proper to it.

Theologically speaking, man, as an individual and as a society, must be described as the historical coming of the free, supernatural, absolute self-communication of God which is eschatologically present and manifest in Jesus through his incarnation and resurrection. Faith is historically mediated in Jesus and is itself the free, historical grace-inspired acceptance in confidence of the sovereign disposition of existence in this event. From all this it is apparent that faith is inextricably linked with history. And since man is always freely accepting or rejecting transcendence and reality as a whole, and thereby himself, in a decision which he can never fully analyze (since reflection is afterthought, an effort to illumine and explicitate the living act) it follows that the *a priori* condition of faith, readiness to believe and its actuation, already are constitutive structures of human existence. But this is not the autonomous achievement of the subject; it is a matter of a common interpersonal act, in union at once with the self-realization of other historical freedoms (in society and in language) and with the active acceptance of the freely-bestowed grace which makes the act possible. Thus faith, in the broad sense of readiness to believe, is essentially historical in a three-fold sense: it stems from the history of the "I", of the other and of the bestowal of grace. This must be the starting-point for the discussion of the problems which are posed by the concrete relation to history which is intrinsic to the Christian faith.

B. Modern Perspectives

The problem felt most keenly by modern thought was that faith in the theological understanding of the term was based on the definite historical reality, on historical testimony and not on metaphysical truth. The question, therefore, was how the freedom and originality of the act of faith and its supposedly universal validity could be maintained in view of this basis.

Does this not imply a direct and inexplicable transition from the dimension of the historical to that of the absolute assent of faith (cf. G. E. Lessing)? How is the gap between the contingence of a historical truth and the absoluteness of the act of faith to be filled? It cannot be within the power of historical thinking to close the gap, since a "qualitative" decision cannot be attained by "quantitative" means (Kierkegaard). It would also be contrary to faith to consider it as the prolongation of historical knowledge. Lessing sought to bridge the gap between the historical and the absolute by a "leap". Kierkegaard tried to express this leap in positive terms by describing it as "decision", since on the plane of the "objective" the synthesis between history and faith could only be a paradox. "Subjectivity" was the only possible meeting-point of the two. If paradoxical decision alone is able to mediate between faith and history, existence itself is then a paradox.

Lessing's schema for the interpretation of the relationship between faith and history supposes that the historical element is a random one, lying outside all that is essential to the self-understanding of man. And the schema for relating faith to history is that of the subject and the object. But this approach fails to recognize that history and the historicity of the self and its relation to the world are constitutive elements of the existence of man. But if man in his faith and his freedom is a historical being and essentially so, as regards his understanding of being, world and self, it follows that the relationship of faith and history must be mediated by this interpersonal historicity of man.

If what is at stake for man in his relationship to history is his own very self, this relationship is such as to found and permeate his existence. Then, since historical relationship implies at once historical understanding, the latter is not a subsequent extrinsic addition to man's act of faith. If existence itself is the medium in which faith and history are mediated, and if faith is an act of historical existence, it follows that with this mediation a plane has been attained on which alone the identity and difference of faith and history can be consciously discerned.

C. Faith and Historicity

The relationship of man to history by which he understands and interprets it has a primordial and permanent character, inasmuch as man is always history's target prior to all his questioning of history. Hence understanding of history is always self-understanding: as man is to history, so is he to himself. Understanding of and relationship to history form a primordial unity with self-understanding and selfhood, and this unity is a unity of encounter to such a degree that it is valid in both directions. But the relationship to history is prior to all historical "factual" interests, that is, it is of an ontological character. It is only if the relationship of man to history is so primordial that it is the key to his self-understanding that man is referred once more in his search for himself to the *a posteriori* of history which cannot be logically deduced.

But then history, in spite of its *a posteriori* character, has also the *a priori* character of the existentially significant. This means that what is essential for man can also be historical and that the historical can likewise be essential. Hence the function of the historical understanding arising from the confrontation with history is not to allow man to dispose of himself, but to make man totally responsive, with regard to a possibility of selfhood which is a primordial question of man.

Hence historical understanding always has the formal structure of the act of faith. For man has always lived his historical existence and assimilated it before he reflects consciously upon it. But this reflection is not confined to generalities. It is concrete, that is, performed in a way which involves objectifiable elements of a definable "material"

nature, and hence "history" in the sense of records of the past.

Hence (contrary to Bultmann, at least as generally understood) the explicitation in terms of the records of the past is of the essence of historical understanding and hence of the self-understanding of faith. History is misunderstood both where it is watered down to a merely objectivated record of past facts and where it is made lose its historical reality, existentialized or ideated.

It is only when history and the record of the past are envisaged in their unity of structure that this concrete character of historicity and history is safeguarded. It is only then that faith can give an account of its foundation. Hence man's being referred to history is not a special case in the sphere of the religious self-understanding of man. It is not simply a *de facto* condition arising *a posteriori* out of the traditional understanding of faith. It is antecedently and fundamentally clear that it must be so, by virtue of the openness of man (in his metaphysical *a priori* condition) to the factual realm which founds his existence. It follows that faith's being history-centred, as regards the historical free act, is only the supreme instance of this basic condition of human existence, in which man always finds himself as a dialogal-historical reality.

D. The Self-Justification of Christian Faith

Thus Christian faith is always within the framework of the articulate history-centredness of "faith" in general. But it is not a mere instance, not even merely the supreme instance of such historicity. It also sees itself as at once the judgment upon history and the incalculable fulfilment which surpasses history's trend. Hence it cannot be content to regard itself as merely one way among others of rendering articulate such readiness to believe. It finds itself commanded to communicate itself to all. But for this very reason the problem of historical self-justification becomes most tryingly acute for faith.

Nonetheless, the structure of this justification does not differ from that which has been outlined above. It is a personal justification, which does not mean giving individual feelings and prejudice free rein, but it is of a personal, objective and historical nature. Take for instance the actual ("historical") relationships of contemporaries. Their openness for each other, and its justification, can be seen to be a combination of direct "personal evidence" and deduction from things done and said — a combination which is absolutely intrinsic to such contacts. The peculiar nature of such personal evidence with its combination of direct and indirect factors cannot be adequately described by the word "paradox". For at least insofar as paradox affirms an antagonism between the two factors and hence turns the difference into opposition, it fails to do justice to the essence of the personal which manifests itself precisely by self-communication by means of works, things and words. And then again, the special nature of such personal evidence is not properly understood if it is treated as rational verification and logical proof, since this would be to misunderstand the essential difference between the two spheres. The difference is of course admitted, and indeed gives rise to the very problem in question, namely, how even a fully valid proof on the basis of "facts" cannot be the foundation of the strictly personal assurance. But then the error is made of demanding for this personal assurance a proof which would be on principle of the same nature.

Even a personal relationship where a period of time intervenes is characterized by the two-fold structure of its self-enlightenment. It differs, no doubt, from a relationship with contemporaries, but we must bear in mind that the contemporary relationship is not merely "subjective", direct, but also "objective", even in the sense of being determined by things and works; and that the historical relationship (to a figure in the past) is not merely historical, in the sense of involving also the records of the past, but also — inasmuch as a matter of history and records — direct, personal and "contemporary". This structure can be verified for the relationship established through the various degrees of mediation to the founder of the faith himself, and it also holds good for the channels of this mediation. These channels are witnesses whose testimony is given with probative force: with proofs personally and objectively "verifiable", just as the self-revelation of the founder himself is given in the power of the Spirit and of signs. While it is true that man is always predisposed to the experience of faith when thus addressed, his expectation is not simply the norm or law for such an utterance. The revelation fulfils

his hope by going beyond it, and by doing so modifies it. In consequence, the Christian faith can point to the general structure of belief and the relevant reality justifying this readiness to believe in each case, when demonstrating against unbelief that its faith is reasonable. Nonetheless, it cannot strictly speaking justify its absolute claim and its validity in the eyes of others, since this claim of the reality to which the believer appeals can only be experienced by virtue of the reality itself and of the encounter with it (which, however, must be mediated through the testimony — a testimony once more both personal and embodied in things).

Thus the foundation of faith for the believer himself (and its justification as hope [1 Pet 3:15] with regard to others) must be distinguished from the "missionary" justification of the call to faith which he addresses to others. Nonetheless, this distinction is only a minor one in the framework of the problems envisaged here. In both forms of justification, the Christian must allow the factually historical its full rights and uphold its permanent significance for the faith (as against a merely "existential interpretation"). But then again, this factual history is only "probative" as a moment in a total personal relationship. This unity of the factual and personal is not confined to faith or the believing subject. It is also there, and functioning as the foundation, on the side of revelation — as the unity of the God who speaks in history and his *incarnate* Word. And these two aspects again, faith and revelation, must not be considered separately, but as moments of the identity-in-difference of the comprehensive event of grace in which God both imparts himself and enables man to respond to his self-communication. Hence in this complex event of revelation and faith, what is personal in the event comes about only through and in the fact, while on the other hand the "literal text" of the facts are at once read and understood in the "Spirit" — the Spirit who is both the spirit of the believer and the Spirit of God who frees and sustains him, who searches the depths (1 Cor 2:10), who is the Lord (2 Cor 3:17). In the light of his experience of this Spirit, the believer can now in fact go beyond the "justificatory" foundation of his own faith to "impose" on others the "missionary" foundation of his faith, since his faith gives him the conviction that this revelatory event — the structure of which has been described above — has already included all others within its scope, in a very fundamental way, in keeping with the universal salvific will of God.

From another point of view, the complex structure of the event as here revealed can again be demonstrated by the relationship between the *fides qua* and the *fides quae creditur*. The two acts are not to be opposed to one another but must be regarded as two intrinsically combined moments, not only in the individual believer but also in the social realization of these acts. This means that it would be wrong to contrast an existenti*el*-individual *fides qua* with some supposed opposite which would be a *fides quae* as a fixed deposit preserved by the Church. The personal and the ecclesiastical quality is proper to both these moments and in this way to faith as a totality. In consequence, the task of the justification of the Christian faith in its own eyes is never either merely the affair of the believing individual, nor again just that of the Church in its magisterium and (fundamental) theology. It is the common task of "both". This is true of the analytical, speculative foundations, of the self-justification of the truth which comes about as one "does" it (Jn 3:21) and of its attestation to those outside by means of mutual love (Jn 13:35). In this three-fold self-justification of the faith, more is manifest than just the believer or the community of believers in the attestation of faith. He who is believed is also attesting himself, not just as the object of faith, but as once more himself the source of faith. In this testimony he is directly at work to convey his historical summons and to bring about the historical response of the believer in faith and in history.

See also *Salvation* I, III, *Jesus Christ* II, *Christianity. Incarnation, Resurrection* I, *Transcendence, Freedom, Language, History* I.

BIBLIOGRAPHY. See bibliography on *History* I; *Faith* III, IV; also: G. E. Lessing, *Theologische Streitschriften* (1777), E. T.: *Theological Writings* by H. Chadwick (1957); S. Kierkegaard, *Abschliessende unwissenschaftliche Nachschrift* (1846), E. T.: *Concluding Unscientific Postscript* by D. Swenson and W. Lowrie (1941); J. H. Newman, *An Essay in Aid of a Grammar of Assent* (1870); P. Rousselot, *Les Yeux de la Foi* (1910); H. Krumwiede, *Glaube und Geschichte in der Theologie Luthers* (1952); R. R. Niebuhr, *Resurrection and Historical Reason* (1957); R. Aubert, *Le problème de l'acte de foi* (3rd ed., 1958); J. Mouroux, *I Believe* (1959); C. Cirne-Lima, *Personal Faith* (1959); M. Buber, *Two Types of Faith* (1961); A. Weiser, *Glaube und Geschichte* (1961); M. Seckler, *Instinkt und Glaubenswille nach Thomas von Aquin* (1961); J. Pieper, *Belief and Faith* (1963); W. Pannenberg and others, *History and Hermeneutic* (1963); K. Rahner, *Hörer des Wortes* (2nd ed., 1963); J. Robinson and J. Cobb, eds., *The Later Heidegger and Theology* (1963); H. Bouillard, *La logique de la foi* (1964); B. Welte, "Vom historischen Zeugnis zum christlichen Glauben", *Auf der Spur des Ewigen* (1965), pp. 337–50; J.-B. Metz, "Unbelief as a Theological Problem", *Concilium* 6, no. 1 (1965), pp. 32–42; A. Darlap, "Theologie der Heilsgeschichte", *Mysterium Salutis*, I (1965), pp. 1–156; H.-G. Gadamer, *Wahrheit und Methode* (2nd ed., 1965); M. Blondel, *Letter on Apologetics* and *History and Dogma* (1965); G. Ebeling, *Theology and Proclamation* (1966); id., *Problem of Historicity in the Church and its Proclamation* (1967); K. Jaspers, *Philosophical Faith and Revelation* (1967); G. Noller, ed., *Heidegger und die Theologie* (1967); K. Rahner, *Belief Today* (1967); id., *Ich glaube an Jesus Christus* (1968).

Adolf Darlap

FAITH AND KNOWLEDGE

The relation between faith and knowledge is frequently formulated as follows: to believe means the same as not to know, or to know only provisionally, partly or superficially. This is not only an indication of the difference between the two spheres, but represents a definite characterization of faith as inferior. If knowledge is taken to mean well-founded and certain understanding, and if understanding indicates mental assimilation of that which is, and if the substantiation and certitude of understanding rests upon one's own insight and experience, then faith would appear to be hopelessly inferior to knowledge. Faith would then expressly mean the renunciation of one's own experience and insight and the acceptance of assertions and opinions on the basis of the authority and the testimony of another; it would appear that faith would then be greater the more it refused to see, the blinder it was. And finally, it would seem that the reality with which faith is concerned — especially faith in God and Christian faith — is the sphere of the invisible (cf. Heb 11:1), the inaccessible and the non-verifiable: all that which seems to border on the unreal.

For an individual in such a situation, however, there remain (we are told) but two possible ways of acting. He can practise a sort of double book-keeping in which truth would have two forms, or in which he would attempt so to separate faith and knowledge, both in the act and in the object, that a bridge between them would be impossible. The other and more cogent possibility (we are again told) consists in this, that one should attempt to elevate that preliminary and inferior understanding which faith offers to a knowledge based upon insight, and that one should relinquish all the assertions and claims of faith that are not capable of this or conflict with such knowledge.

1. *History of the problem.* It is significant that in the Bible, and especially in the NT, there is no evidence of such an opposition between faith and knowledge, in which the latter is taken to mean well-founded or certain understanding. On the contrary, faith and knowledge as they are represented in the Gospel of John, for example, are one; both concepts are alternately used and are interchangeable.

In the first centuries of Christendom, those Christians who came to the faith from philosophy understood faith as the true philosophy (Justin), or as the only proper knowledge. The theological thought of the Middle Ages formulated the proximity and inner unity of faith and knowledge in the well-known sentences: "I believe, that I may understand (comprehend)", and "I understand, that I may believe". Thomas Aquinas, who was sensitive to the difference between faith and knowledge, included them both in the unity and entirety of truth — truth cannot contradict truth — anchoring them both in God, the source and goal of faith and knowledge.

As this unified and ordered picture was more and more blurred toward the end of the Middle Ages and at the beginning of the modern period, and as tragic and painful conflicts broke out between theologians and the representatives of the new advance of the natural sciences (Galileo), the way was prepared for the mutual alienation and division between both. This division was decisively deepened and encouraged by the philosophy of early modern times oriented as it was toward the autonomy of reason. This was even more the case as knowledge and science in the strict sense came to be considered by philosophy to be possible only in the realm of experience, mathematics and the natural sciences, and as the natural sciences

(and later also history) put forward "certain" findings as contradictory to the assertions of faith and of revelation. The programme of the critical philosophy of Kant, to limit knowledge "to make room for faith", expressly formulated, rationalized, and made effective use of such a dualism between faith and knowledge. Similar to this, though from other motives, was the intention of Jacobi, who wished to remain a heathen in his intellect, and a Christian in his heart. The philosophy of German Idealism (especially Hegel), on the contrary, attempted to achieve complete speculative penetration of the Christian faith and to "sublimate" it in the form of knowledge and understanding. There were not a few theologians of this period who accepted this programme and who tried to support it from revelation. In the course of the 19th century, the separation, or at least the dualism, between faith and knowledge was upheld especially among the upholders of the theory of science, which claimed that knowledge is only possible in the spheres of mathematics and the natural sciences. Here eventually the natural sciences expanded to a scientific world-view and claimed to have the answer to any question. This was especially accentuated when a definite philosophy added its weight to these claims, or where the Christian faith was characterized as an ideology furnished with myths.

Our own day has seen a change in this approach insofar as natural science, through its foremost representatives, no longer claims to be a totally comprehensive view of life, and expressly recognizes its limits. Scientists claim competence only within that part of reality which is covered by the instruments and methods of science, and admit that science leaves room for an answer and, indeed, looks out for one, which it cannot of itself give.

No doubt, the answers to these questions are denied the character of true knowledge: they are relegated to a realm of faith distinct from scientific knowledge, or to that of a metaphysics which is discounted as merely subjective opinion. Present-day philosophy, especially existential philosophy and personalism show ever more clearly what place and what importance is to be given to faith. From these points of view, however, Christian faith is again called in question as one kind of faith opposed to philosophical faith (K. Jaspers) and a new dualism of incompatibility is asserted because both are concerned with the ground and totality of existence.

2. *The notion of faith.* To see clearly in this matter, it is well to expound the genuine concept of faith. The basic form of faith is indicated in the statements: I believe you; I believe in you. To believe some*thing* is but the secondary form of this. From this it is clear that faith is primarily and properly not a relation of man to things, propositions, or formulas, but a relation to persons. And this relation is directed in particular to knowledge of the person. Faith is the manner and means by which we gain an understanding approach to a person. This is so true that without faith the reality and the mystery of the person remains closed in its most profound and real sense.

A person is not really known as he is by being taken under control and analysed by tests or experiments — such knowledge would remain more or less peripheral and superficial and could never lead to what is most significant: the person and his own unique existence. Knowledge of a person on the lines of mathematics or the natural sciences is inappropriate because such methods are inapplicable. A person in his true nature, in his very self, is only known if he allows himself to be known, if he discloses himself.

Faith opens the way to knowledge of the person. The one who believes shared in the self-disclosure of another, in his life, in his thought, in his knowledge, understanding, love and desire; he shares the manner and the way in which another sees himself and the world of things and of men. The "I believe you" necessarily includes certain particulars, in the form of: I believe what you say, what you ask, what you promise. Thus, faith implies also a faith in assertions, a faith in the sense of "holding to be true" certain statements and propositions of a very definite and concrete kind. But this belief in "truths" and "propositions", in "something", is not an isolated and unrelated belief; it is encompassed and sustained by the person who is believed. Whatever its particular object is, any related statement of the kind "I believe that . . ." is based upon the competence and the authority of the person at the centre of this belief, and upon the assurance derived from these.

Faith is therefore not a preliminary, partial, or approximate type of knowledge. It is authentic knowledge; it is understanding in that realm which is primarily not concerned with world, things, and objects, but with the person. Faith is not an unsure and unfounded type of knowledge. It is certain and well-founded: but it bases itself in the competence and trustworthiness of the one who is believed, and it is based on his insight and knowledge. From this it is clear how one-sided it is to consider knowledge as certain only there where one's own experience and insight can reach. With such a limitation, important areas of the reality of our knowledge would be eliminated or closed: the sphere of the person and of persons — consequently of men and of all that is human.

The discrediting of faith as a type of knowledge could only occur where reality was restricted to things, and these reduced to quantity and phenomena. This blindness to the reality of the person also occurred where knowledge was accepted only in the form of logic, mathematics, and the natural sciences. It is only possible to set faith and knowledge in opposition or contradiction when one is blind to the diversity and multiformity of what is, and when one lacks the realization that to the diversity and multiformity of what is, there corresponds not one but a multiformity of methods, of ways and approaches to knowledge.

Faith is not a compelling type of knowledge, though it is one that is thoroughly well-founded. It is founded on an act of confidence and dedication with regard to a person, who through his self-disclosure offers fellowship and participation with himself. But this act of trust must itself be grounded on something. It is grounded upon the credibility of the one to whom belief is given, on the extent and the manner in which he legitimates his authority and competence. He must justify his claim to be believed. The evidence of credibility is the condition and presupposition of faith and of the knowledge which it implies.

3. *Faith and knowledge in theology.* With this, the basic characteristics of faith are indicated and these apply also to what is called faith in a special sense — faith in God and Christian faith. This must be so if this faith is also to be a human act, as it claims to be. It is also true of Christian faith, and true in a particular way, that it is not primarily and originally a

relation to things and propositions, but a personal act, a confrontation between the human "I" and the divine "You". Its primary formula also runs: "I believe you." This faith in God is definitely put forward as knowledge of the reality and of the mystery of God. There are indeed traces that lead from the world as a created reality to God himself. They lead to his existence and give knowledge of attributes of his nature. But, properly considered, these traces do not lead into the inner mystery of God himself, for the world is not God but only his work. And, what is even more important, creation is already and essentially a kind of revelation and self-disclosure of God (Rom 1:18). Faith is thereby already invoked as the manner in which we acknowledge in creation not only rational order and laws, but the very word of God.

If, over and above that, it is possible and essential to arrive at a knowledge of God as he is in himself, a knowledge of the inner being of God, of his life, his mystery, his eternal designs for our salvation, of what it means for man that God is the ground and last end of his existence — then this is only possible if God reveals and discloses himself other than in the way in which he does in creation. It is thus that we must understand the statement that is so important for the analysis of faith in God: God is not only the object and goal of faith, but he is, through his very self-revelation, its principle and ground.

If the revelation of God culminates in Jesus Christ, then faith as Christian faith means fellowship with the person of, and in the knowledge of, Christ. Faith is a pre-eminent way in which the biblical words are fulfilled: "It is no longer I who live but Christ who lives in me" (Gal 2:20). Christian faith is knowledge and understanding in the most eminent and elevated sense of the word: it is access to the reality of God who has spoken his ultimate word and accomplished his unsurpassable act of revelation in Jesus Christ. The Christian faith discloses a new reality for which a "conclusive" knowledge, which controls and checks on the basis of individual insight and experience and after the manner of mathematics and the natural sciences, is improper and incompetent. It is a reality which can neither be attained nor contradicted by such knowledge. To renounce or to exclude the knowl-edge which is heard and accepted in faith, would mean that man robbed himself of his highest potentiality — and precisely with reference to knowledge. He would be barred from the supreme realization of his existence and personality and lose the possibility of expecting an articulate answer to the question of the principle and goal of existence.

In this act of faith the true existence of man is represented and realized: his existence as a created being capable of being addressed, as obedient, as a hearer of the word, and as man before God. From this one can form a definition of man: he is the being who is capable of faith. Faith describes the manner of human existence, the primary attitude of man before God, of the man who exists only through God. Only as a believer does man find himself.

If it is true that the confrontation of persons which is represented in the formula "I believe you" includes faith in certain assertions, it is true especially with reference to faith in God. It is all the more apposite in this case as the fragility, the limitation, the finitude and imperfection which are intrinsic to all men, even the greatest and noblest, are precisely what make possible, found and justify the unconditional and unhesitating character of faith. Faith considered as the acceptance of propositions is founded — and this is especially so of the truths of the Christian faith — upon the person who is believed. And in this way it does not have the isolated character of impersonal relations, the neutral and (non-existential) "it". Such truths are but a concrete and particularized form of how God expresses and communi-cates himself in revelation. From this it fol-lows that faith in revealed truths is not founded primarily on the fact that they form a unified system and a structured whole which would be shattered by the denial of one of the statements, but on the fact that such a denial really signifies a mistrust and a non-acceptance, indeed, a rejection of God. It would call in question the basic act of faith represented in the form "I believe you".

If the presupposition of faith in general is the credibility of the person who is believed then it is necessary likewise to establish the credibility of the Christian faith. The whole question culminates in the question which runs through the whole event of revelation: "What do you think of the Christ? Whose son is he?" (Mt 22:42.) Is Christ one among many, or is he the unique revelation of God in his person, the Son of God in the exclusive sense — the Word made flesh who said of himself: "He who has seen me has seen the Father" (Jn 14:9), of whom John said — and this is important to situate the question: "No one has ever seen God; the only Son, who is the bosom of the Father, he has made him known" (Jn 1:18). Jesus Christ not only asserted the claim which is founded on the mystery of his history and his person, but rendered it credible. He did this through his life, through his destiny, through his word and work — and above all, through his death and resurrection to which the NT gives the testimony of faith and of history, and finally through his work in history up to the present day: the Church. Thus the question, "Who then is this?" (Mk 4:41), is answered, and the Christian's "I know whom I have believed", is given not a compelling proof, but a trustworthy basis and sufficient certitude. This still leaves room for the free decision of men to believe or not, and it demands — for the sake of faith — total commitment.

4. *Faith and science.* The question of faith and knowledge is especially acute and difficult with regard to the Church's pronouncements on faith and doctrine, and the conflicts with the assertions of the sciences which have actually arisen in the past and which in principle are always possible. Here we must note the following: the Church must not be separated from the revelation of God which culminates in Jesus Christ. The Church belongs to the concrete and particular element of revelation, it is part of the work of God who reveals himself in Christ and it is an object of the Christian faith. The Church is the work of Jesus Christ. In it Christ, through the Holy Spirit, is present and active in the world and in history in a new way. In the Church, the word and work of Jesus Christ are represented, actualized, and mediated in a new way in each age, so that men of every age may be contemporaneous with the revelation of God and with Jesus Christ. Christ promised to this Church that it would abide in the truth which he revealed to it, and that this his truth would abide in the Church. This enables us to recognize that faith in the comprehensive sense is made possible and mediated by the words and works of the Church. If the Church is all that is said of it here, then clearly it is above all the believing

Church, indeed, the real subject of faith, and its pastors and teachers must be first and foremost listeners and believers. To try to attain revelation outside of the Church, whether it be simply without it or against it, basically rejects the concrete work and will of the God who reveals himself, and rejects the total dedication of faith.

It is also clear what the function of the Church is with regard to revelation. It has no new revelation to proclaim: it has rather to believe the revelation transmitted to it, to keep it, to guard it, to defend it. The Church must propose revelation and expound it anew in each age of history. In carrying out this task and performing this duty, the Church and its magisterium in the face of uncertainty, doubts and disputes, must express itself again and again in an authoritative way and articulate its pronouncements in the form of dogma. Such clear decisions are demanded of the Church and are part of its most essential tasks. It is also possible, nevertheless, for the Church as a whole to grow in the faith and in the understanding of the faith, to be led ever deeper into all truth in fulfilment of the promises which were made to it and to give testimony to this new understanding.

But when the believing and teaching Church proposes its doctrine, it is not lording it over or claiming to dispose at will of revelation and faith. It is a service in obedience to its Lord who called the Church to that activity and empowered it to carry it out. In the Church's obedient service of faith and revelation, which consists in its conservation, development and exposition, Christ himself continues his work: he keeps the Church true to himself and guarantees that the Church is the pillar and the ground of truth, against which the gates of death will not prevail. But because men carry out this work, and because Christ has entrusted his cause to men, this service will always fall short of its possibilities and will always be less than fully performed.

It is also especially true of the faith which the Church proposes for belief that such faith means both knowledge and understanding. It is the knowledge and understanding of that life and that reality which is opened up for us by the revelation of God in Christ for the sake of our self-understanding and salvation. It is also true here that between the faith and teaching of the Church, and the knowledge of natural reason and the sciences, there can be no final and insoluble conflict. If it nevertheless has actually arisen and threatens continually to break out anew, then the reason can only be that the perspective and different nature of the question in each sphere is not properly observed; it must be due to misunderstandings or trespasses with regard to the boundaries of faith or knowledge. In the case where conflict between the two has actually materialized, what is demanded is clarity concerning the real nature of faith and knowledge. It is necessary to examine whether or not the particular question is a genuine question of faith and revelation (here, for instance, the actual intention of the statements of Scripture are to be determined, the literary form and style, the difference between content, mode of representation, and means of expression). Likewise, it is necessary to examine whether or not knowledge in such a case is really knowledge or only a hypothesis or opinion.

In principle, the conflicts can all be resolved, and the actual conflicts of past history could have been resolved. Burdensome though the past may be, it is a part of the way of faith and the way of man and of the Church. But there is a way out that leads to a possible solution and answer — and it is in the direction that we have tried to indicate here. Within the terms of the relations between faith and knowledge as they have been described here, a whole series of problems is eliminated from the very start, especially those that result from an inadequate conception of faith, or from a narrow and one-sided conception of knowledge, from a stunted conception of reality and above all from disregard of the person and personal activity. Problems are avoided which result from failure on one side or the other to observe the respective limits and spheres of competence. Finally, the problems are avoided which proceed from an incomplete or false understanding of what revelation is and of what faith intends to express in a particular and definite instance.

See also *Knowledge, Experience, Gnosis, Truth* I, *Science* II, *Ideology, Existence* II, III, *Personalism, Church* II, *Dogma* I, II.

BIBLIOGRAPHY. J. H. Newman, *Fifteen Sermons Preached before the University of Oxford between A.D. 1826 and 1843* (1843); id., *The Idea of a University* (1853); R. Guardini, *Faith and Modern Man* (1952); K. Heim, *Christian Faith and Natural Science* (1953); id., *The Transformation of the Scientific World* (1953); E. L. Mascall, *Christian Theology and Natural Science* (1956); E. Coreth, *Grundfragen des menschlichen Daseins*, I (1956); J. Mouroux, *I Believe* (1959); H. Fries, *Glauben — Wissen* (1960); J. Abelé, *Christianity and Science* (1961); G. Ebeling, *The Nature of Faith* (1962); P. Chauchard, *Science and Religion* (1962); J. Brodrick, *Galileo: The Man, His Work, His Misfortunes* (1964); H. Urs von Balthasar, *Science, Religion and Christianity* (reprint, 1964); C. F. von Weizsäcker, *The Relevance of Science* (1964); H. Bouillard, *La logique de la foi* (1964); K. Rahner, *Hominisation. The Evolutionary Origin of Man as a Theological Problem*, Quaestiones Disputatae 13 (1965); H. Fries, *Aspects of the Church* (1966); K. Rahner, "Intellektuelle Redlichkeit und christlicher Glaube", *Schriften zur Theologie*, VII (1966).

Heinrich Fries

FASTING

1. *In religious history.* Fasting is abstention from food for ethico-religious reasons. Historically, fasting in primitive as well as in more advanced societies is based on the experience that while food provides strength for the spirit by giving physical strength, man disturbs and destroys the inner order of spirit and body, if he fails to control the amount he eats and drinks. The phenomenon of fasting also rests on the notion that a meal is an occasion and expression of joy. Historically one must therefore differentiate between fasting as a help towards an attitude of mind and a fast of mourning; commemorative fasting may have developed out of the latter. There is also a difference between fasting and abstinence from certain types of food and drink, particularly meat (often from certain animals) and alcoholic drink. The universal experience, which is the basis of the phenomenon of fasting, is manifested in the view of archaic religions that fasting is a defence against taboo powers and a means of obtaining mana.

2. *In the Bible.* a) *Old Testament.* The primitive concept of fasting, as outlined above, can also be found in the beginning of the OT, where fasting is part of common vigilance in the service of Yahweh, the God of the tribes (Lev 16:29 ff.; 23:27, 29; Jg 20:26; an echo of this in Est 4:16). In an individualized and spiritualized form it can still be seen in Exod 34:28 where Moses pleads for his people through his fasting. According

to the prophets, fasting must be an expression of a comprehensive, radical turning of man towards God and his commandments, particularly love of one's neighbour; otherwise it is without value (Is 58:3ff.; Zech 7:3ff.; Ecclus 34:30f.).

b) *New Testament.* According to Mt 4:1ff. and Lk 4:1ff., Jesus began his public life with a forty days' fast in the desert, but as Mark's older account (1:12f.) shows, Matthew's and Luke's stylized version of a forty days' fast designates the beginning of Jesus' work as that of a prophet. It is probably a motive taken over from Exod 34:28 and 1 Kg 19:8; nor can we find any pronouncement of Jesus on fasting in Mk 9:29, for καὶ νηστεία is an insertion in later manuscripts. It is only in Mt 6:17 that it becomes clear that Jesus valued fasting as a personal expression of piety: "thy father ... will reward thee." Jesus also seems to have observed the prescribed collective fasts, otherwise Mk 2:18, which is the most instructive statement on his attitude towards fasting, would be incomprehensible: fasting has nothing to do with the μετάνοια which must follow the arrival of the kingdom of God in his person, but it is a sign of mourning to mark the departure of the "bridegroom". Jesus' sovereign attitude towards fasting corresponds with the rare mentions of the observance of fasting by the very early Church (only in Acts 13:2f. and 14:23; mention of fasting in Acts 10:30 and 1 Cor 7:5 was inserted in later manuscripts).

Probably due to the influence of ancient dualism and a revival of OT legal thinking, fasting was gradually accorded greater significance in early Christianity and was used as a kind of penance (under the influence of Celtic penitential practice).

3. *In theology.* a) As fasting is general to mankind, a theological approach must start not from concupiscence, but from the fact that man must, through fasting, dispose himself (even materially) to allowing his neighbour to share his property in spite of the just claims of self-love. The unconditional demands of love are based, theologically, on the example of Christ and his identification with his neighbour (Mt 25:35–40). Pope Paul VI stressed the connection between fasting and love in his Apostolic Constitution *Paenitemini* of 17 February 1966 (*AAS* 58 [1966], pp. 177–98): "Nations who enjoy economic plenty have a duty of self-denial, combined with an active proof of love towards our brothers who are tormented by poverty and hunger."

b) Further, fasting retains in principle the valued position in the Christian life which tradition has accorded it within the sphere of man's relationship to himself, that is, in the integration of his body (according to Paul) into the whole life of faith.

4. *In canon law.* The regulations about fasting and abstinence are contained in can. 1250–1254, with further particulars in Pope Paul VI's Apostolic Constitution, *Paenitemini,* on the penitential discipline of the Church.

The *law of abstinence* requires abstinence from meat and soups made from meat. The *law of fasting* allows only one full meal each day. Detailed regulations are given each year by episcopal notification. Abstinence is obligatory on all who are seven years of age, fasting between twenty-one and sixty.

Pope Paul's Apostolic Constitution, *Paenitemini,* authorizes bishops' conferences to modify the laws of fasting and abstinence to suit modern conditions and to substitute prayer and works of charity for abstinence and fasting.

See also *Asceticism, Penance* I, *Dualism, Judaism* I, *Ecclesiastical Law* I, *Religion* II B.

BIBLIOGRAPHY. F. Wasserschleben, *Bussordnungen der abendländischen Kirche* (1851); H. Schmitz, *Busse und Bussdisziplin,* 2 vols. (1883–98); Billerbeck, IV, pp. 77–114; J. T. McNeill, *The Celtic Penitentials and their Influence on Continental Christianity* (1923); A. J. Maclean, "Fasting (Christian)", *Encyclopaedia for Religion and Ethics,* V, cols. 765–71; J. Behm, "νηστεία", *TWNT,* IV, pp. 925–35; A. Guillaume, *Jeûne et charité dans l'Église latine des origines au XIIe siècle* (1954); B. Häring, *Law of Christ,* 3 vols. (1961–6).

Marcellino Zalba

FIDEISM

As A. Lalande notes in his *Vocabulaire technique et critique de la philosophie* (1962), pp. 348ff., Fideism is a theological expression, which applies to a trend of thought found in a number of writers who are inclined to restrict the power of reason with regard to knowledge of truths of the moral and religious order, in particular in establishing the credibility of faith. Fideism characterizes the kind of mind which spontaneously reacts against anything that appears to diminish the supernatural and gratuitous character of faith. In this sense, Montaigne, Pascal and Huet could have been accused of being Fideists. It should also be noted that the word has a special meaning when used in French Protestant theology. Here (cf. E. Ménégoz, *Publications diverses sur le fidéisme,* 5 vols. [1900–21], and A. Sabatier, *Esquisse d'une philosophie de la religion* [1897]) it means the adherence to the content of salvation ("the saving truth") through a faith exclusively determined by the emotions, paying no attention to doctrinal beliefs whose value is only symbolic. This position is due to the influence of Kant, Schleiermacher, etc.

As used nowadays, the expression Fideism is principally reserved to describe a movement of thought which developed in France at the beginning of the 19th century as a reaction against rationalism and in close liaison with the traditionalism of Bonald and Lamennais. Its main champions were Mgr. Gerbet, the Abbé Bautain and Bonnetty. Mgr. Gerbet advanced his views in his work *Des doctrines philosophiques dans leurs rapports avec les fondements de la théologie* (1826) which drew a sharp rejoinder from Rozaven de Leissèques, S. J., in 1831, under the title: *Examen d'un ouvrage intitulé: des doctrines . . .* Bonnetty developed his ideas in the *Annales de philosophie chrétienne* which he founded in 1830 and which he edited along with Gerbet and Salini up to the time of his death in 1879.

Here he also attacked a scholasticism which he judged to be too rationalistic. In 1855 he was forced to subscribe to four propositions presented to him by the Congregation of the Index, of which the most important is this: "the use of reason precedes faith and leads men to faith through revelation and grace" (cf. *D* 1649–52).

But the description of Fideist is most properly applied to the Abbé Louis Bautain (1796–1867), professor of philosophy (1816), superior of the minor seminary (1830) and dean of the Faculty of Letters at Strasbourg (1838), honorary doctor of theology of Tübingen, proposed by J. A. Möhler; then director of the college at Juilly (1840) and professor at the Sorbonne (1853). A disciple of Cousin and strongly influenced by Baader, Hegel, Schelling and Jacobi, in 1819 he

rediscovered the Catholic faith of his childhood under the influence of Mlle. Human, an Alsatian mystic. From then on, in reaction against his former rationalism, he held, like St. Augustine, that "philosophy which is the study of wisdom is none other than religion". This is the basic theme of his book *L'Enseignement de la philosophie en France au XIXe siècle* (1833) which he took up again in the two volumes of his most important work, *La philosophie du Christianisme,* 2 vols. (1835). He appealed to Rome against a condemnation pronounced by his bishop, Mgr. Le Pappe de Trevern, and after successful negotiations with Roman theologians, in particular with G. Perrona, S. J., he subscribed to a declaration rejecting as erroneous the two following statements: reason alone cannot prove the existence of God; reason cannot establish the motives of credibility of the Christian religion (*D* 1622–7). (On this and on the meaning of the other statements subscribed to in 1834, 1835 and 1840, see P. Poupard, *Essai.*) The First Vatican Council in its dogmatic constitution *De Fide Catholica,* session III, 24 April 1870, chapter III (*D* 1781–1820) explicitly affirmed the power of reason with regard to natural knowledge of God and the rational preambles of faith.

The Fideists, especially Bautain, whose Fideism was rather an attitude than a system, were led by their disparagement of reason and defective definitions of faith to view faith from what was in fact an existential attitude. The soul, they held, had a disposition which enabled it to see the light of God and recognize his signs, while a more rational apologetics demanded logically a preparatory stage. For this logical preamble, based on what the Fideists called an "ineffective experience", they substituted as the foundation of faith the conditions which enable the word of God to be heard fruitfully. Convinced of the deficiencies of the traditional proofs, they were inclined to deny intrinsic value to all the preambles of faith. They exaggerated the effects of sin in fallen nature, which necessarily retains, after all, the "points of insertion" for grace. This grace, while it integrates man in the supernatural economy of salvation, does not, however (in the sphere of historical proofs), compensate for the lack of certainty intrinsic to all human testimonies, but restores to the will the consciousness of its power of intellectual decision, in spite of the difficult consequences which such a decision brings with it (see the introduction to *Humani Generis, AAS* 42 [1950], pp. 561f.). The Fideists were justified in insisting on the originality of the supernatural certainty of faith, and on the freedom of this certainty. But they were wrong in excluding its rational foundations, to which the magisterium has constantly called attention. Further, they eliminated the distinction legitimately made between the explanation of knowledge of God and the foundation of faith. Faith is not a logical deduction, but it still has a "logic" of its own, the logic of "the free, rational assent to the mystery of Christianity. It is the demonstrable and freely acknowledged harmony between the message of the gospel and the logic of human existence." (H. Bouillard.)

See also *Faith* I, III, IV, *Traditionalism*.

BIBLIOGRAPHY. J. H. Newman, *An Essay in Aid of a Grammar of Assent* (1870); R.-P. Laberthonnière, *Essais de philosophie religieuse* (1903); E. Le Roy, *Dogme et critique* (1907); P. Rousselot, *Les yeux de la foi* (1913); J.-V. Bainvel, *Faith and the Act of Faith* (1926); S. Harent, "Foi", *DTC*, VI, cols. 171–237; C. Butler, *The Vatican Council* (1930); F. Hocedez, *Histoire de la théologie au XIXe siècle*, 3 vols. (1942–52); P. Poupard, *Un essai de philosophie chrétienne au XIXe siècle, l'abbé Louis Bautain* (1961); id., *Journal romain de l'abbé Bautain* (1964); H. Bouillard, *Logique de la foi* (1964).

Paul Poupard

FORM CRITICISM

I. Form Criticism. II. Genus Litterarium.

I. Form Criticism

Contemporary scientific views on the literature of the Old and New Testaments are to a large extent based on the results of the form criticism of our own century. This state of affairs makes it incumbent upon all who intend to adopt a responsible attitude toward the Bible to acquire a basic knowledge of the "methods of form criticism", as well as of the results achieved by means of them for the "history of forms" in biblical writings. The official teaching of the Church lays upon scholars the task of scientifically investigating and interpreting sacred Scripture in order "that as many ministers of the word as possible may be equipped to impart the nourishment of Scripture to the people of God in a truly beneficial manner". It enumerates a series of "suitable methods" by which this task is to be accomplished, and in particular the method of form criticism (cf. Vatican II, *Dei Verbum*, arts. 23, 12). For our understanding of the synoptic gospels the form-critical approach is the "indispensable key". It may be said without exaggeration that "unless we begin by determining the form and history of the individual units of tradition in the synoptic gospels, we can achieve no understanding of them whatever" (*I. Herrmann,* p. 64).

1. The place of form criticism in the history of biblical scholarship lies between the period which was dominated by literary criticism and the new phase which has opened, characterized by the "history of redaction". About the turn of the century a certain "discontent with mere literary criticism" (H. Zimmermann), together with a new awareness of the linguistic aspects of the biblical texts, which were derived for the most part from religious and popular traditions, led to a preoccupation with the pre-literary stage of tradition. NT scholars followed the trail which OT scholars (especially H. Gunkel and his school) had already blazed. These NT scholars adopted a new approach, investigating the texts from the aspect of oral tradition, the form in which they had initially been transmitted, and the marks of which they still bore. This approach was used especially in research into the synoptic gospels.

a) At the beginning of the present century J. Weiss declared explicitly that the investigation of the literary forms of the gospels and of the individual groupings of material in them was one of the "tasks for contemporary scientific research into the NT" (*Aufgaben der neutestamentlichen Wissenschaft in der Gegenwart* [1908], p. 35). But his predecessor, J. G. Herder, had already "recognized for the first time the problems involved in form-critical research into the gospels" (W. G. Kümmel, p. 98). Another predecessor towards the end of the previous century was F. Overbeck, who had called for "a history of the forms" of "the primitive literature of Christianity" (*Historische Zeitschrift* 48 [1882], p. 423). Before the First World War two classical scholars, P. Wendland (*Die urchristlichen Literaturformen* [1912]) and E. Norden (*Agnosthos Theos. Untersuchungen zur Formengeschichte religiöser Rede* [1913]), set in motion form-critical researches into the NT in certain important directions. After the War, the period of the form-critical approach really began.

b) K. L. Schmidt paved the way to the analysis of forms in the individual pericopes with his work on the "framework of the history of Jesus" (1919). This work showed that the gospels were edited compilations of previously isolated pieces of tradition, and also of earlier partial compilations which had been handed down either orally or in writing. Next the methods of form criticism were perfected, especially by M. Dibelius (*Die Formgeschichte des Evangeliums* [1919; 4th ed., 1961]) and R. Bultmann (*Geschichte der synoptischen Tradition* [1921; 6th ed., 1964], E. T.: *The History of the Synoptic Tradition* [1963]). By these means an attempt was made to establish the laws of oral tradition by which the individual units of tradition had been developed and had acquired their distinctive shape. "To trace these laws back, to make the emergence of those small units comprehensible, to work out and explain their characteristics, and in these and similar ways to arrive at an understanding of the tradition — this is what it means to investigate the gospel form-critically." (M. Dibelius, p. 4.) R. Bultmann, whose approach is more strongly influenced by comparative religion and historical criticism, formulated the truth "that the literature in which the life of a given community, even the primitive Christian community, is reflected, springs out of quite definite social conditions and needs, which produce a quite definite style and quite specific forms and categories" (cf. E. T., p. 4). In the past fifty years the methods of form criticism have been tested over wide areas of Old and New Testament texts. Today reliable instruments are available to the practitioners of form criticism in the manuals of K. Koch (*Was ist Formgeschichte? Neue Wege der Bibelexegese* [1964]; this work is orientated more strongly towards the OT) and H. Zimmermann (*Darstellung der historisch-kritischen Methode* [1967]). Both authors provide full and detailed accounts of the "history of redaction", which currently appears as a supplement to the form critical approach, and which enquires into the literary form and theological meaning of the final redaction of the gospels or other NT writings.

2. The following points may be mentioned as instances of the most important *aspects and results* of the work of form criticism today. For the understanding of biblical literature, of the process by which it emerged, of its transmission and its content, a knowledge both of the smallest units ("formulae") and the slightly larger ones ("forms"), as well as of the larger literary forms which embrace these ("types", literary genres) is indispensable. Once light has been thrown upon the history of the genres as well as on the "form" of the smaller units, the possible or probable *Sitz im Leben* ("social setting", actual community background) of these can be determined, and this in turn lead to a reconstruction of the history of their transmission, and thereby to a history of the development of the biblical writings as a whole.

a) In OT research the study of types of psalms, for instance, has led to a deeper understanding of the praise of God offered by the people of the old covenant. Once we have established that these chants belong to the various ceremonies of Israelite worship, to royal feasts or to the sapiential tradition, we learn to understand the situation of the psalmist in each case, the atmosphere surrounding him as he prays and other points. The prophetic writings can be more effectively interpreted if we pay attention to the various forms of discourse which are employed (messenger-sayings, narratives in the first and third person, reproaches, threats, exhortations, promises, etc.). We can gain a deeper insight into the transmission of ancient Israelite law if we notice the various forms (including those used by other nations) in which they are couched (for instance, apodictic or casuistic formulations).

b) In the treatment of the NT writings the form-critical approach has also proved fruitful. Among the four categories of NT writings (gospels, acts, epistles, apocalypse) two are of Christian origin: "gospels" and "acts of the apostles". The individual synoptic gospels are actually considered by the more recent exponents of the "history of redaction" as each belonging to a particular genre of its own (Mt: βίβλος; Mk: εὐαγγέλιον; Lk: διήγησις). There is some hesitation as to how form-critical methods should be applied to the Johannine writings (the most important applications are to Rev with its hymnic, prophetic and apocalyptic forms), but side by side with this goes more intensive work on the *Corpus Paulinum* (epistolary forms, thanksgiving, autobiographical passages, ancient formulae, proofs from Scripture, doxologies, hymns, lists, etc.; cf. B. Rigaux, *Saint Paul et ses Lettres* [1962]). This has yielded copious information, so that a comprehensive form-critical account of the Pauline writings has become a real *desideratum*.

c) Up to the present it is the traditional material of the synoptic gospels that has been most clearly defined. This material has been divided into the two basic categories of sayings and narrative tradition. In the transmission of sayings a distinction is drawn, e.g., between prophetic sayings, wisdom sayings, legal sayings, parables, "I" sayings, "Imitation" sayings, and also composite sayings. In the narrative tradition one distinguishes paradigms, controversies, miracle stories, historical narratives, the Passion narrative, and also composite narratives (cycles, summary narratives, etc.). The basic insight that it is real life (i.e., as regards the tradition of the primitive Church, the complex forms of life in the early Christian communities) which creates the variety of forms permits us to deduce from the distinctive kind of form its *Sitz im Leben,* though admittedly it is not always easy to determine this, especially as it may have changed several times in the early stages of transmission, e.g., when an isolated unit of tradition was subsumed under a more comprehensive category, or even as soon as a saying of Jesus was made to serve the early Christian preaching. Today in general a threefold *Sitz im Leben* can be deduced for the "Jesus" tradition: Jesus himself, the tradition of the primitive Church, the gospel redaction. Again for each individual *Sitz im Leben* various factors corresponding to the forms can be recognized. For instance, in the case of Jesus one may think of a dispute with his adversaries or the instruction of his disciples. In the case of the tradition of the primitive Church one may think of its missionary, catechetical, disciplinary or liturgical interests. In the case of the evangelists one may think of the literary and theological aims which they set themselves, these again being also determined by the needs of the ecclesiastical region in which each evangelist lived.

d) For the historical reconstruction it is important that one should carefully trace one's way back from the most recent *Sitz im Leben* to the earliest (which can be established at times not only for the evangelists and the Church tradition, but even for Jesus and his immediate disciples). Here the distinction between the literary form and the historical testimony it contains must be strictly observed, especially as the tradition has been shaped more by theological interests than by historical or biographical ones. The question of the historicity of the material handed down is rendered neither superfluous nor impossible by the form-critical approach to the text, but is assigned its proper place as the last question. In view of the kerygmatic interests of tradition, the historical question is not the most urgent theological one.

e) Form criticism has shown that the NT writings as a whole documentate the preaching Church and are the testimonies of faith. Thus by their very nature they demand to be investigated for their preaching message, for the faith to which they bore witness. Form criticism can sketch at least in broad outline the history of early Christian preaching and early Christian witness to the faith. Thus it contributes not only to our understanding of the NT (like the OT) writings but throws light also on the beginnings of the community of believers which produced these writings and is responsible for guarding them to this day. In this sense it also contributes to the Church's present understanding of itself.

BIBLIOGRAPHY. E. Fascher, *Die formgeschichtliche Methode* (1924); M. Dibelius, "Forschungsberichte", *Theologische Rundschau* 1 (1929), pp. 185–216; G. Iber, in *Theologische Rundschau* 24 (1956/57), pp. 283–338; V. Taylor, *The Formation of the Gospel Tradition* (2nd ed., 1935); K. Grobel, *Formgeschichte und synoptische Quellenanalyse* (1937); E. B. Redlich, *Form Criticism, Its Value and Limitations* (1939, 2nd ed., 1948); F. M. Braun, *DBS,* III, cols. 312–17; G. Iber, in *Theologische Rundschau* 24 (1956/57), pp. 283–338; H. Riesenfeld, *The Gospel Tradition and Its Beginnings* (1957); G. Schille, in *NTS* 4 (1957/58), pp. 1–24, 101–14, and 5 (1958/59), pp. 1–11; A. Wikenhauser, *New Testament Introduction* (1958), pp. 253–77; G. Bornkamm, "Evangelien, formgeschichtlich", *RGG,* II, cols. 749–53; id., "Formen und Gattungen im NT", *ibid.,* cols. 999–1005; E. Käsemann, "Liturgische Formeln im NT", *ibid.,* cols. 993–6; C. Kuhl, "Formen und Gattungen im AT", *ibid.,* cols. 996–9 (with bibliog. for OT); R. Schnackenburg, "Formgeschichtliche Methode", *LTK*, IV, cols. 211–13; H. Schürmann, "Die vorösterlichen Anfänge der Logientradition. Versuch eines formgeschichtlichen Zuganges zum Leben Jesu", *Der historische Jesus und der kerygmatische Christus* (1960), pp. 342–70; I. Hermann, *Begegnung mit der Bibel* (1962); A. Feuillet and A. Robert, *Introduction to the New Testament* (1965); A. Vögtle, *Das Neue Testament und die neuere katholische Exegese,* I (3rd ed., 1967).

Rudolf Pesch

II. Genus Litterarium

1. *Definition.* The problem of the *genus litterarium* of a writing is not confined to biblical exegesis. In French literature, for example, in the 17th and 18th centuries, the theory of the *genres littéraires* and of the distinctions between them occupied an important place. In this context lyrical, dramatic, epic, comic and tragic *genres* were spoken of. The "classicists" attempted to lay down exact rules, against which the "romanticists" protested. Today an attempt is being made to reach back beyond the literary to the "social phenomenon". The *genus litterarium* is regarded as "a collective form of thinking, feeling and self-expression which reflects a whole civilization" (A. Robert). Thus it corresponds somewhat to style in the plastic arts, which is a function of a whole complex of circumstances (materials employed, predominant conception, etc.) which every architect, painter or sculptor must necessarily take into account if he is not to meet with incomprehension. The genre evolves with the life of the milieu with which it is so closely linked. When a work belongs to a civilization other than our own, it is dangerous to pass judgment upon it in terms of the literary genres which are familiar to us and it becomes very necessary to determine the laws which govern the genre in question.

2. *History of the question of literary genres in biblical exegesis.* No exegete has ever questioned the existence of various *genera litteraria* in the Bible: lyrical, didactic, historical, etc. No one has ever denied that the truth of a poetic composition, a parable or an allegory is one thing, while that of a historical narrative is another. Many scholars have set themselves to determine the laws of these different genres among the ancient Semites. It has been noted, for instance, that the psalms contain chants of various kinds, which are subject to rules determining their style,

structure and content, rules which are also found more or less universally throughout the ancient Near East. In the same way the legal texts, the covenant formulae or the preaching of the prophets follow norms which are more or less fixed, the study of which is indispensable to exegesis. Certainly biblical revelation very often breaks out of this basic structure, but it is precisely when we compare biblical forms with the others that the originality of the former are thrown into relief (cf. J. Harvey in *Biblica* 47 [1962], p. 195), the more so since "views which are very different in themselves can lie concealed under external forms which are identical", or better, perhaps, "almost identical" (Robert – Feuillet, I, p. 138).

3. *The magisterium of the Church.* a) *Before the encyclical Divino Afflante Spiritu.* In practice among Catholics the question has been put forward principally, if not quite exclusively, in relation to the books which are presented in the Bible in the form of historical narrative. Formerly certain exegetes appealed to the literary genre to assimilate a number of biblical narratives to "myths" in the sense of the term then generally understood, or to fables devoid of any historical value. The magisterium of the Church at first showed itself extremely reserved; yet as early as the encyclical *Providentissimus Deus* Leo XIII (1893) had promulgated the principle by which Catholic exegesis was to be guided. St. Augustine had provided an excellent formulation of it long before. On the subject of the manner in which the Bible speaks of the "shape of heaven" he explains that "the sacred authors have omitted to treat of these problems of the scientific order because they do not impart to those who recognize them any information which is useful for the life of blessedness". More precisely, Augustine admits that the hagiographers know these things but says that "the Spirit of God who spoke by their mouths did not wish to teach men matters the knowledge of which could not be in any way profitable for salvation" (De Gen. ad Litt., 1, 9, 20; *PL,* XXXIV, col. 270; *Enchiridion Biblicum,* no. 121, recalled by *Divino Afflante Spiritu, Enchiridion Biblicum,* no. 539, and by Vatican II in *Dei Verbum,* ch. III, no. 11, n. 5). The point of importance here is not so much the particular application as the reason which is adduced; according to

the still clearer formulation of St. Thomas, "The Spirit did not wish to tell us through the authors whom he inspired any other truth than that which is profitable for our salvation" (*De Ver.*, q. 12, art. 2 corp., likewise adduced by Vatican II, *ibid.*). Certainly there is no question (though this has sometimes been alleged) of restricting scriptural inspiration to certain privileged parts of the Bible. The point is rather to define exactly the end which God had in mind when he inspired the hagiographers, and in consequence the sense of Scripture as a whole. In technical terms the "formal object of revelation defines the object of the teachings provided by Scripture" (P. Grelot). This was in the very nature of things to point to one of the essential characteristics of all inspired Scripture precisely as inspired, and to define in some fashion what might be called, if the expression were not equivocal, the "inspired *genus litterarium*". (The formula comes from L. Billot, *De inspiratione Sacrae Scripturae theologica disquisitio* [4th ed., 1929], p. 166. By this he meant to rule out any recourse to the *genera litteraria* in order to interpret the narratives of the Bible.)

In 1905 the Biblical Commission visualized a possible application of this to history: in certain rare cases, not to be admitted as such except on the basis of solid proofs, the hagiographer could perhaps not have intended to relate history truly and properly so-called, but rather a parable, an allegory under the form and appearance of history, or rather to give his narrative a meaning which was far removed from the strictly literal or historical sense of the words (*Enchiridion Biblicum*, no. 161). Again in 1909 the Biblical Commission admitted, for instance, that in the narrative of the creation the sacred author had presented not scientific teaching as the "concordist" explanations supposed, but rather a popular description *(notitiam popularem)* adapted to the intelligences of the men of that period (*ibid.*, no. 342).

The expression *genus litterarium* had not yet been coined. It appeared for the first time in the encyclical *Spiritus Paraclitus* of Benedict XV (1920). Certainly the passage in question is intended directly to exclude "the *genera litteraria* which are incompatible with the full and perfect truth of the divine word"; but the encyclical only condemns an "abuse"; when it recognizes explicitly the "justice of the principles, provided that they are contained within certain limits" it seems to have in mind among others the principle of the *genus litterarium* (*ibid.*, no. 461).

b) *Pius XII and the encyclical Divino Afflante Spiritu.* The whole question was to define those limits, and specifically the extent to which the Catholic exegete could have recourse to the *genus litterarium* in interpreting a historical narrative. It is this problem that the encyclical of Pius XII (1943) *ex professo* investigates: the official introductions in introducing the passage actually employ a significant sub-title: "The importance of the *genus litterarium,* above all in the case of history".

After having defined what it called "the chief law of all interpretation", which is to "recognize and define what the writer intended to say" (*ibid.*, no. 557), the encyclical states that "in order to determine what the authors of the ancient Near East intended to signify by their words" it is not enough to have recourse to "the laws of grammar or philology, nor merely to the context". It is "absolutely necessary for the interpreter to go back in spirit to those remote centuries of Eastern history, and make proper use of the aids afforded by history, archaeology, ethnology and other sciences in order to discover what literary forms the writers of that early epoch intended to use, and did in fact employ" (*ibid.*, no. 558). The reason for this is also given: "To express what they had in mind the writers of the ancient Near East did not always use the same forms and expressions as we use today; they used those which were current among the people of their own time and place." Now the encyclical goes on to explain that it intends to refer not only to "poetical descriptions" or to "the formulation of rules and laws of conduct" but also to "the narration of historical facts and events" *(ibid.)*. Nor does the encyclical hesitate to make this "investigation into the *genus litterarium* employed by the hagiographer" one of the most important tasks, and one which "cannot be neglected without great detriment to Catholic exegesis" (*ibid.*, no. 560).

c) *From the encyclical Divino Afflante Spiritu to Vatican II.* This directive, however, which has been called "one of the most striking innovations of the encyclical" (J. Levie), was deliberately confined to affirming the principle. In 1948 the Biblical Commission made an initial application of this principle to two problems, which were disputed at that time: the Mosaic authorship of the Pentateuch and the historicity of the eleven first chapters of Genesis. In this they took up and made more precise the replies given in 1909, which were concerned only with the three first chapters. In this connection the Commission declares that "the literary forms of these chapters do not correspond to any of our classic categories, and cannot be judged in the light of the Greek or Latin *genera litteraria,* or those of modern times". In consequence "their historicity can neither be denied nor affirmed *en bloc* without making an inappropriate application to them of the norms of a *genus litterarium* under which they cannot be classified" (*ibid.,* no. 581).

Two years later — and, moreover, in the course of referring to these declarations — the magisterium made a declaration which was still clearer and gave encyclical authority to its declarations (*Humani Generis,* 1950). With regard to these same eleven first chapters it declared: (i) that they "do not correspond in any strict sense to the concept of history upheld by the authorities of our own time"; (ii) that "at the same time they do belong in a true sense to the category of history"; (iii) that this sense "still remains to be explored and determined more precisely by exegetes" (*ibid.,* no. 618).

Thus for the OT, the question of principle, and one of its most delicate applications, was virtually solved. But up to the present no application had yet officially been made to the NT. Many even denied explicitly that this principle could be applied to it. Hence the instruction of the Biblical Commission of 14 May 1964, *De historica Evangeliorum veritate,* begins by recalling the duty of the Catholic exegete concerning "the investigation of the *genus litterarium* employed by the sacred writer". It explains that this statement of Pius XII enunciates "a general rule of hermeneutics which must be observed in interpreting the books both of the Old and of the New Testaments, given that the writers in composing their works had used modes of thought and writing which were current among their contemporaries". It then applies to the gospels the positive results which Catholic exegesis has achieved by using with due prudence the method of "form criticism".

It shows in particular how at each of the three stages of the transmission of the gospel message one has to take the *genus litterarium* into account. In fact even "when he was expounding his teaching by word of mouth the Lord followed the modes of thought and speech appropriate to his own time, and adapted his words to the mentality of his hearers". The apostles in their turn "bore witness to Jesus" and "faithfully related the events of his life and his words" but "with the fuller understanding which they themselves had enjoyed after having been instructed by the glorious life of Christ and enlightened by the light of the Spirit of truth". Furthermore they too, like Christ, "taking the condition of their hearers into account in their manner of preaching, adapted to that condition the terms in which they interpreted the words and actions of Christ". Thus, as the instruction says, they had recourse to various "modes of expression" *(variis dicendi modis),* some of which it enumerates: "catechesis, narratives, testimony, hymns, doxologies, prayers and other literary forms of this kind, which sacred Scripture and the men of that time were accustomed to use". Finally, the third stage, "this preaching, at first orally transmitted, was subsequently committed to writing in the four gospels for the good of the Churches according to a method adapted to the particular end which each evangelist had set before himself". For "the teaching and life of Jesus were not simply related merely for the sake of preserving the memory of them. They were preached in order to provide the Church with the foundation of its faith and the basis of its moral teaching".

Under these circumstances the exegete finds himself faced with the following task: his first duty will be to "investigate what the intention of the evangelist was when he related a given episode or recorded a given saying in a particular way, and again when he set these in a particular context, for the meaning of a statement also depends upon the context in which it is placed". It would be difficult to throw into stronger relief the importance of studying the *genus litterarium* in order to arrive at an accurate interpretation of the gospels.

d) *Vatican II and the constitution Dei Verbum.* This is the doctrine which the Council has recently confirmed in its Dogmatic Constitution on Divine Revelation, in ch. III with regard to the inspiration and interpretation of Scripture and in ch. V with regard to the historicity of the gospels.

The first passage treats *ex professo* of the *genera litteraria* of the Bible, and the terms in which it does this are particularly striking and clear. Having recalled the traditional doctrine concerning "the truth of Scripture deposited in the books of the Bible for our salvation" (art. 11) the constitution enounces the principle which the encyclical *Divino Afflante Spiritu* called "the chief law of all interpretation" and which precisely gives rise to the necessity of taking the *genus litterarium* into account: "Since God speaks in sacred Scripture through men in human fashion, the interpreter of sacred Scripture, in order to see clearly what God wanted to communicate to us, should carefully investigate what meaning the sacred writers really intended and what God wanted to manifest by means of their words" (art. 12). Now it would be impossible to establish what this intention of the writer was without "among other things having regard for the 'literary forms'". It is in fact not only clear that "truth is proposed and expressed in different ways according to whether it occurs in a historical narrative, a prophecy or a poem", but the constitution speaks explicitly of "texts of history of one kind or another" *(textibus vario modo historicis),* thus affirming that there were many ways of relating a "historical" event. In other words, there were several historical genres. The controversy which had long set certain Catholic exegetes in opposition to one another on this point was solved.

It follows that the interpreter must "investigate what meaning the sacred writer intended to express and actually expressed in particular circumstances as he used contemporary literary forms in accordance with the situation of his own time and culture", and the reason for this is likewise given: "For the correct understanding of what the sacred author wanted to assert due attention must be paid to the customary and characteristic styles of perceiving, speaking and narrating which prevailed at the time of the sacred writer, and the customs men normally followed at that period in their everyday dealings with one another."

Finally the last paragraph (art. 13) discloses the ultimate basis on which this doctrine rests: it is a corollary of the mystery of the incarnation of the Word of God himself, an incarnation which took place at once in human nature and in human words: "The words of God expressed in human language have been made like human discourse just as of old the Word of the eternal Father, when he took to himself the weak flesh of humanity, became like other men."

In ch. V the constitution applies these principles to the gospels, taking up what is essential in the instruction of the Biblical Commission on the historicity of the gospels, a résumé of which we have given above. The Council asserts their historicity unambiguously, but at the same time it explains the sense in which it intends this term to be taken: for the evangelists are not content to record mere facts; their purpose was to show at the same time the significance of those facts as they themselves had perceived it most of all in the light of the event of Easter: "What Jesus said and did the evangelists handed on to their hearers with that clearer understanding which they themselves enjoyed after they had been instructed by the events of Christ's risen life and taught by the light of the Spirit of truth." (Art. 19.) Further, "they have selected some things from the many which had been handed on, reducing some of these to a synthesis or developing some in view of the situation of their Churches, always in such a fashion that they told us the honest truth about Jesus". Thus the Council defines to some extent the essential characteristics of the literary genres of the gospels.

4. *Conclusion.* While therefore the constitution *Dei Verbum* envisages a study of the literary genre chiefly in its bearing on the inerrancy of Scripture (art. 12) or on the historicity of the gospels (art. 19), nevertheless it goes beyond the strictly apologetic attitude with which the problem had usually been approached up till then. In fact the exegete's reason for having recourse to the literary genre is not simply that he wants to solve the difficulties to which certain historical narratives in the Bible can give rise. In reality the study of the literary genre has a contribution to make to the exegesis of the Bible as a whole, that of the psalms, for instance, which occasioned the researches of Gunkel and of the prophetic or sapiential books or again the legal texts in the Pentateuch, and of course the Song of Solomon. Furthermore, a given book does not usually present only one literary genre, but is com-

posed of elements which fall under widely different genres, to each of which special attention should be paid.

If, then, the meaning of words or formulae is always more or less conditioned by the literary genre of the passage in which they are found, as recent research has shown more and more clearly to be the case, it can be understood that the exegete, anxious as he is to obtain an accurate grasp of what God wished to say to us through the medium of the inspired writer, counts the study of the literary genre as one of his primary duties (*Enchiridion Biblicum,* no. 560). His faith in the inspiration of Scripture, the Word of God, far from deflecting him from such a task, makes it still more incumbent upon him.

See also *Bible* III, *Biblical Exegesis* II, *Biblical Historiography, Demythologization* I, *Form Criticism* I, *Jesus Christ* II, *Old Testament History, Preaching* I, *Inspiration.*

BIBLIOGRAPHY. F. Hummelauer, *Exegetisches zur Inspirationsfrage* (1904); H. Gunkel, *Reden und Aufsätze* (1913); id., *Die Gattungen der religiösen Lyrik Israels;* id., *Einleitung in die Psalmen* (1933); A. Robert and L. Vénard, "Historique (genre)", *DBS* IV (1949), cols. 7–32; A. Robert, "Littéraries (genres)", *ibid.,* V (1952), cols. 405–12; R. Bloch, "Midrash", *ibid.,* V; A. Gelin, "Genres littéraries de la Bible", *DTC* Tables, fasc. 8 (1959), cols. 1790–94, 1263–81; R. E. Murphy, "A New Classification of Literary Forms in the Psalms", *CBQ* 21 (1959), pp. 83–87; *Géneros literarios en los evangelios. Semana bíblica Española,* XIII (1959); L. Alonso-Schökel, "Genera litteraria", *Verbum Domini* 38 (1960), pp. 1–15; J. Harvey, "Le *ríb-*pattern réquisitoire", *Biblica* 43 (1962), pp. 172–96; F. X. Léon-Dufour, *Les Évangiles et l'histoire de Jésus* (1963); id., *Études d'Évangile* (1965).

Stanislas Lyonnet

FORUM

The notion of a forum, as a special place, goes back to the early days of civilization. As a juridical term, it comes from the usage to which the place which it designated was put (e.g., the Forum Romanum), in an age when religion, political life, and law intermingled. Etymologically, the word implies a fencing which both protects and separates. So having first meant a place, the word became associated with a court of justice. It became a formal term in juridical language, meaning primarily the court as an institution and in a stricter, forensic sense, a sphere of competence. Since the formal term has different meanings, the sense in which it is to be understood will depend on the context in which it occurs. The different meanings are correlative, the poles of an interlocking system.

1. *Evolution of the term.* The distinction between the external and internal spheres goes back to the *forum poenitentiale* and *forum iudiciale* of the earlier 13th century, which meant respectively the confessional and the courts. *Forum poenitentiale* was the term which first appeared (Robert de Courson, d. 1219), meaning what the Church does in the process of penance as contrasted with God's invisible rule. Here we must note that the term did not designate any particular penitential practice, but embraced both private penance and the public penance which was still practised at that time. *Forum ecclesiae* was also used in the same sense (William of Auxerre). A bare twenty years later we then find *forum poenitentiale* contrasted with *forum iudiciale* (William of Auxerre, Alexander of Hales, Philip the Chancellor). At that period there was still no clear-cut division between the penitential and judicial practice of the Church, and in making the distinction these men no doubt felt that the two domains formed one comprehensive whole — as indeed they did before penance became a thing apart. The distinction drawn was one between two ways in which the Church did its forensic work, two parts of its activity *(forum ecclesiae)* as contrasted with God's invisible rule. Before there could be a separation of penitential from judicial practice, it was necessary to distinguish between crime and sin, so that the cause in question could be assigned to one sphere rather than the other. So the contrast between law and morals played a part in demarcating the two spheres of competence, but only as a basis for assigning cases to one or the other of two quite different institutions.

In the *Summa Theologica,* III, q. 96, a. 4, St. Thomas asks whether the *lex humana* binds a man *in foro conscientiae.* Here *forum conscientiae* does not mean an external institution but the same thing as *iudicium conscientiae* and *conscientia* itself. Human law and conscience — or to put it more generally, the respective spheres of law and conscience — are contrasted. The new terminology also entered into St. Thomas's doctrine on penance, but here acquired an institutional sense. In *IV Sent. dist.,* 17, 18, he uses *forum poenitentiale* and *forum conscientiae* in the same institutional sense. In the other sense, alongside *forum iudiciale* and with the same meaning, he speaks of *forum contentiosum, forum exterius, forum iudicii, forum publicum exterioris iudicii,* and *forum causarum.* Thomas's expressions *forum exterius* and *forum conscientiae* influenced the development of aur terminology.

The decisive impulse in establishing a non-sacramental internal sphere was given by the bishops at the Council of Trent (sess. 24 de ref. C 6) when they granted faculties to dispense from irregularity and suspension incurred by a secret delict and not yet brought before the *forum contentiosum;* and to absolve *in foro conscientiae* from all secret delicts incurring censure. These faculties were used outside the sacrament of penance as well. Accordingly it was perceived that *forum internum* (or *forum conscientiae*) was not identical with *forum poenitentiale,* but meant a juridical effect both *in sacramento* and *extra sacramentum,* with the particularity that the act of jurisdiction in the internal sphere had no efficacy *in foro externo* (cf. Sanchez, *De Matrimonio,* VIII, disp. 34). These ideas won general acceptance and gave currency to the term *forum internum,* which in the writers of that day was the counterpart of the *forum exterius* or *externum* (= *iudiciale*), a term established in usage at an earlier date. *Forum internum* was more accurate than *forum conscientiae,* with its various senses, as a term embracing both the sacramental and the non-sacramental domain.

2. *The present law.* The *CIC* (cf. can. 196) contrasts *forum internum* and *forum conscientiae* in the traditional way applying them respectively to the domains of law and conscience with certain nuances, indeed, but so consistently that we may say that it is the doctrine which predominates widely. This doctrine interferes with a proper understanding of the distinction. The forum of conscience is a man's direct relationship with God and must not be confounded with the internal forum, which as contrasted with the external forum means a different way the

Church has of exercising jurisdiction. An ecclesiastical sentence pronounced in the external forum, provided it is sound and just, binds in conscience no less than a sentence in the internal forum. The difference between the external and internal forum is that in one case the Church acts publicly and in the other secretly, a secret act in the sacramental internal forum being set apart by the seal of the confessional from a secret act in the non-sacramental internal forum. What is public knowledge or will presumably become such, should be dealt with in the external forum; what is secret and will presumably remain such in the internal forum. Having two alternative procedures, thanks to the distinction between external and internal forum, helps to lessen friction between the person and society, because the embarrassment involved in public proceedings is confined to matters which are already public knowledge.

3. *Efficacy of an act of jurisdiction.* a) *The external forum and the non-sacramental internal forum.* According to can. 202, § 1, an act of ordinary or delegated jurisdiction granted for the external forum is also efficacious in the internal forum, but not vice versa. This rather imprecise formula means that an act done in the external forum in the exercise of jurisdiction granted for the external forum, is also efficacious in the internal forum, whereas an act of jurisdiction done in the internal forum has no efficacy in the external forum. At the same time, an act done in the internal forum does not merely quieten conscience; it has a juridical character. The same kind of matter will be dealt with now in the external, now in the internal forum; in both spheres the Church acts compassionately. In either case the sentence the Church hands down in one forum or the other definitively settles the matter that was at issue. For example, a matrimonial impediment from which a person has been freed in the internal forum is really eliminated, and a penalty remitted in the internal forum is really remitted. If a matter hitherto secret becomes known to the public, it may be seen in a false light. An act of jurisdiction in the external forum has only one advantage over the same act in the internal forum: it ensures that the matter cannot be seen in a false light. Thus it sometimes happens that a matter already settled in the internal forum

has to be settled again in the external forum to give it full publicity.

b) *The sacramental internal forum.* Decisions in the sacramental internal forum are as definitive as those in the non-sacramental internal forum, where favours of the same sort are concerned. Sacramental absolution of sins, however, poses a special problem. Following the Council of Trent, the *CIC* holds that for valid absolution a priest must not only have the power of order but also *potestas iurisdictionis in poenitentem* (can. 872). Recent theologians have pointed out the mediating role which the Church as the visible storehouse of salvation plays in sacramental confession: sacramental absolution, like the ancient rite of reconciling the penitent which it has replaced, also directly reconciles the penitent with the Church; *pax cum ecclesia* as a constituted and efficacious sign *(res et sacramentum)* becomes a sacramental cause of *pax cum Deo.* The sacramental sign is primarily concerned with bringing the sinner back to the bosom of the Church, which, canonically speaking, is an act of jurisdiction on the part of the Church whereby the sinner is juridically restored to ecclesiastical fellowship and to enjoyment of all his rights as a member of the Church. Thus we can see why *potestas iurisdictionis in poenitentem* is necessary for valid absolution and why this requirement is no mere matter of outward discipline but follows from the very nature of the verdict.

4. *Ecclesiological significance of the distinction.* There is only one ultimate purpose behind the distinction between penitential and judicial practice and the later division of the internal forum into acts within and acts outside the sacrament of penance: and that is to eliminate or at least lessen friction between the human person and society. Built up by God's word and his sacraments, the Church as a spiritual community nevertheless rests essentially upon the upright loyalty of its members. So it cannot confine itself to the merely external juridical order. It must seek their free consent, always bearing in mind that outward behaviour depends on the inner frame of mind. The rulers of the Church, therefore, whose task it is to cope with dangers arising from the personal sphere, must strive to order the visible structure of the Church in such a way that its outward appearance corresponds to its real

being. The perfection of this would mean candid confession before the community and public reconciliation, which is what the primitive Church demanded (cf. Acts 5:1–11) and the ancient Church made considerable efforts to achieve, especially by developing canonical penance. But precisely its experience of canonical penance taught it that it asked too much of human nature. Because of this realization it was laid down (in the reforming synods of the early 9th century) that secret sins should be dealt with by secret penance and only public sins by public penance. In this way, the Church did what was urgently needed for salvation and at the same time laid the groundwork for separating the confessional from the courts and distinguishing accordingly between their two spheres of competence. But the Church makes it perfectly clear to this day that it considers the two spheres one, especially by prescribing that one who has gravely sinned, whether the offence was secret or public, cannot approach the common eucharistic table until he has been absolved from his sins in the sacrament of penance (can. 807, 856).

See also *Ecclesiastical Authority, Ecclesiastical Law* I, *Penance* II, *Conscience, Law* II, III, *Jurisdiction.*

BIBLIOGRAPHY. P. Capobianco, "De ambitu fori interni in iure ante Codicem", *Apollinaris* 8 (1935), pp. 591–605; id., "De ambitu fori interni in iure canonico", *Apollinaris* 9 (1936), pp. 243–57; id., "De notione fori interni in iure canonico", *ibid.,* pp. 364–74; W. Bertrams, "De natura iuridica fori interni ecclesiae, *Periodica* 40 (1951), pp. 307–40; B. Poschmann, *Paenitentia Secunda* (1940); K. Mörsdorf, "Der hoheitliche Charakter der sakramentalen Lossprechung", *Trierer Theologische Zeitschrift* 57 (1948), pp. 335–48; B. Poschmann, *Busse und letzte Ölung* (1951), E. T.: *Penance and the Anointing of the Sick* (2nd ed., 1968); K. Mörsdorf, *Lehrbuch des Kirchenrechts,* I (11th ed., 1964); T. Bouscaren, *Canon Law Digest,* 5 vols. (1960 ff., with annual supplements); T. Bouscaren and A. Ellis, *Canon Law: A Text and Commentary* (1966).

Klaus Mörsdorf

FRANCISCAN THEOLOGY

1. *Historical outline.* St. Francis of Assisi was against the life of study, seeing in it a threat to devotion. Learning, he said, leaves

the heart arid and does not serve love. But his Testament shows that he thought highly of genuine theology: "We must esteem all who are learned in the things of God and honour them as men who dispense spirit and life." Despite some initial resistance, Franciscan studies were flourishing remarkably early. By 1250 the Order already had some 30 schools. Franciscans were soon among the most celebrated doctors. They did not succumb to the dangers St. Francis had feared, but were able to combine great learning with deep piety and Franciscan simplicity. It was a milestone for Franciscan theology when the Order set up its own houses of studies at Paris and Oxford, then the leading universities for theology. Alexander of Hales (d. 1245), who was teaching at Paris, entered the Order there in 1236, thus securing the Franciscans the first chair they occupied in the University. Most eminent of all at Paris was St. Bonaventure (d. 1274), who probably best represents the spirit of Franciscan theology. As General and "second founder" of the Order he ensured studies a permanent place among Franciscans. He is the "prince of mystics" (known as the Seraphic Doctor). At Oxford the Franciscans set up their own house of studies in 1229. Its first teacher, Robert Grosseteste (d. 1253), a former secular priest, left his stamp on this school, which taught Scripture, Greek, as necessary for studying Scripture, mathematics and physics. The Franciscan house quickly became the most important school in Oxford University and the most influential of all Franciscan schools.

Chronologically speaking we must distinguish a) the older Franciscan school, comprising the first generation, that is, the contemporaries of St. Bonaventure (whose particular doctrines are Augustinian: *materia spiritualis, rationes seminales, pluralitas formarum,* knowledge in uncreated light, non-accidental character of the soul's faculties; but Aristotle is not absolutely rejected — hylemorphism, for example, is admitted); b) the middle Franciscan school, to which the theologians from Bonaventure to Scotus belong (basically Augustinian but moving closer to Aristotle), and c) the later Franciscan school, which derives from Duns Scotus (d.1308) and is called the Scotist school. Scotus remained faithful to Augustinianism but also had a high regard for

Aristotle and Avicenna. A great speculative thinker *(doctor subtilis),* he critically examined the intellectual patrimony of tradition and still had the resources to produce an original system of his own. None of the important theologians among his pupils and adherents reached the eminence of Scotus. "So in fact the great Franciscan theology ends with Scotus." (Dettloff.) Franciscan theology was not spared amid the general decline. Speculation about the *potentia Dei absoluta* was dominated by over-fine distinctions. God's sovereign freedom, so greatly stressed by Scotus, was no longer seen in its connection with love and degenerated often into arbitrary power.

2. *Spirituality.* There is no real system of Franciscan theology, so we cannot describe it in terms of theses which Franciscan theologians generally maintain. It is characterized not so much by a doctrine as by a particular spirituality which expresses itself in certain interests and certain attitudes. Much of this, indeed, is to be found outside Franciscan theology, but there it does not enter — at least to the same extent — into the structure of theological thought. Blossoming in the golden age of Scholasticism, Franciscan theology drew on two chief sources — Augustinianism and, above all, the personality of St. Francis. The two leading schools of the Order, at Paris and Oxford, were steeped in Augustinianism by their first masters. If more and more Aristotelianism was absorbed as time went on, the original Augustinian approach persisted in essentials. It was no accident that most of the medieval Augustinians were Franciscans, for Franciscan spirituality and Augustinianism are closely akin; whereas the leading exponents of Aristotelianism are St. Thomas and his school. Far more important than Augustinianism, however, the characteristic theses of which mainly relate to philosophy, is the spirit with which St. Francis imbued his Order. This spirit, as we best see in St. Bonaventure and Scotus, shapes Franciscan theology in the following basic respects:

a) Franciscan theology thinks primarily in existential and personal terms as well as in terms of Scripture and redemptive history. St. Francis has at heart the following of Christ, hence the Christian life that brings salvation. He preaches only the full following of the gospel, no particular kind of piety. He demands only what Scripture demands. This attitude is reflected in the attitude of Franciscan theology towards philosophy, which is not studied for its own sake but in view of theology. Philosophical problems are dealt with under their theological aspect. This is because philosophy cannot lead to salvation. "Apud philosophos non est scientia ad dandam remissionem peccatorum." (St. Bonaventure.) Theology should not only convey knowledge about salvation but also lead to salvation itself. So its chief goal is not so much knowledge as action and the sanctification of man ("ut boni fiamus" — St. Bonaventure). It is a science but also, and much more, wisdom. Accordingly, Franciscan theologians think in more personal terms than the other theologians of the time. Hence the precedence they assign to the will over the intellect, the stress laid on freedom in God and creatures, the primacy of love. Against St. Thomas, for example, Scotus defends the freedom of man even in the beatific vision, and holds that the essence of beatitude is love, the highest form of personal encounter. Preoccupation with the scriptural history of redemption is seen in the crucial importance attached to Scripture. For St. Bonaventure theology is primarily the study of Scripture. Exegesis is a basic interest at Oxford. This attitude shows itself most clearly in the choice of points of departure for thought. In the question, for instance, of the cognitive capacities of man, there is little or no interest in man as such; what matters is man as he concretely exists, as we meet him in Scripture, man fallen and redeemed. Speculation serves only to shed light on the actual economy of salvation.

b) God is pictured above all as love and transcendence. Here too we find the spirit of St. Francis, who in his Song to the Sun calls upon God with the characteristic words, "Most high, almighty, compassionate Lord". St. Bonaventure tries to explain the mystery of the Trinity in terms of the outpouring of generous love. On the basis of the Platonic principle *bonum diffusivum sui* he sees the immanent divine life as a giving of itself in love. For Scotus not only the Holy Spirit but God *simpliciter* is *formaliter caritas* and *dilectio per essentiam.* Thus there is nothing in God not really identical with love. Love is the deepest motive for all God does. Giving his love freely, God desires man to be his partner in love.

God's transcendence is reflected in the awe felt before his incomprehensibility, in St. Bonaventure's *docta ignorantia,* and Scotus's insistance on God's freedom. Creatures owe their goodness to God's free will: "God does not will creatures because they are good, they are good because he wills them." The same sovereign power is seen in the doctrine on acceptation: "Nihil creatum formaliter est a Deo acceptandum." But if God is free, he is not arbitrary; for God is love, bound in his free acts by the goodness of his nature. He can only act according to his nature, that is, lovingly.

c) A further characteristic is a very modern-sounding positive attitude towards the things of this world. In the Song to the Sun St. Francis greets them as his brothers and sisters. This Franciscan love of nature is not sentimentality; it springs from an ability to find God in all things. Franciscan theologians take the same attitude, especially in their exemplarism and in St. Bonaventure's idea of symbolism. Creation is a book in which with the help of Scripture we can recognize God and meet him.

d) Franciscan theology is christocentric. The Lord's person is the centre of life for St. Francis, drunk with love. No school of theology has so exalted the primacy of Christ as the Franciscan. For St. Bonaventure Christ is the *tenens medium in omnibus,* the centre and mediator of all theological knowledge, the centre of Scripture and of the universe. Scotus demonstrates the same central position of Christ by his doctrine of Christ's absolute predestination, which he did not invent but which he worked out so decisively that it rightly bears his name. Since his day only Teilhard de Chardin has made a comparable attempt (on a scientific basis) to establish Christ as the centre of all creation.

e) Franciscan theology insists in a special way upon the humanity of Christ, here again following in the footsteps of St. Francis, who honours especially the mysteries of the Lord's humanity (building the crib at Greccio in 1223; the stigmata, 1224). Franciscan theologians preserved this tradition, especially Duns Scotus. In his Christology he "goes to almost impossible lengths to defend the reality and completeness of Christ's human nature" (Dettloff). This concern underlies many Scotist theses: for example, the negative determination of the human personality, two *esse existentiae* and two sonships in Christ, denying that Christ's merits are strictly infinite because the human nature in which Christ suffered is finite. Closely bound up with attachment to the humanity of Christ is veneration of his Mother. It is not by chance that Scotus, one of the two greatest Franciscan theologians, bears the title *Doctor Marianus* for his services in explaining the doctrine of the Immaculate Conception.

See also *Augustinianism, Scholasticism* II C.

BIBLIOGRAPHY. C. R. S. Harris, *Duns Scotus,* 2 vols. (1927); É. Gilson, *Theology of St. Bonaventure* (1938); F. Copleston, *History of Philosophy,* II: *Augustine to Scotus* (1950); É. Gilson, *Jean Duns Scotus: Introduction à ses positions fondamentales* (1952); F. Copleston, *Medieval Philosophy* (1961); H. Urs von Balthasar, *Herrlichkeit,* II (1962), pp. 265–361 (Bonaventure); W. Dettloff, "Franziskanertheologie", in H. Fries, ed., *Handbuch theologischer Grundbegriffe,* I (1962); J. Bougerol, *Introduction to the Works of St. Bonaventure* (1964); E. Gössmann, *Metaphysik und Heilsgeschichte* (1964); A. Schafer, *Position and Function of Man in the Created World according to St. Bonaventure* (1965); F. Wetter, *Die Trinitätslehre des Johannes Duns Scotus* (1967).

Friedrich Wetter

FREEDOM

I. Biblical. II. Philosophical: A. On the General and Philosophical Notion of Freedom. B. Social Structure of Freedom. C. History of the Concept in the West. III. Theological.

I. Biblical

It would be a mistake to take a philosophical notion of freedom as the starting-point for an investigation of the biblical texts, on the assumption that though there was no literal equivalent for it, the "thing itself" was there. For we find that a number of senses in which the word freedom is used are not to be found in Scripture. Thus LXX translates חָפְשָׁה by ἐλευθερία, while both חָפְשִׁי and חֹר (noble, freeborn) are rendered by ἐλεύθερος, there being no Hebrew equivalent for ἐλευθερόω. The use of παρρησία is also to be considered when our notion of freedom is in question.

1. *Old Testament.* "Free" is the opposite to "being a slave". Hence in legal texts and in Jer חָפְשִׁי is found almost exclusively

where there is question of emancipating a slave, mostly in connection with the emancipation of debtors of Israelite stock after seven years (e.g., Exod 21:2). These regulations, which are influenced by the social and humanitarian principles of Deut, aim at a just and equal division of social goods among all the people, which presupposes a brotherly attitude of love towards all who are thus considered "neighbours". Here freedom is an important element in the fulfilment of the promise, in the general framework of equal justice for all. But Israel's exodus from Egypt, the "house of bondage" (Deut 7:8), is not considered as emancipation, though Philo interprets it in this way (*De Migr. Abr.,* 25: θεός εἰς ἐλευθερίαν ... ἐξείλατο). The lateness of this interpretation indicates that the OT thought of freedom only in an economic and social sense. So too חֹר designates social standing. There are no traces in terminology of any reflection on "inner freedom". The transition from the OT notion of freedom to the wider Greek sense is marked by the additional clause in the LXX at Prov 25:10a, "Love and friendship give freedom", i.e., they are things which safeguard a man's social standing. Ecclus 10:25 affirms that external freedom has only a relative value compared to wisdom, even that of a slave. Philo goes a step further in *De Confusione Linguarum,* 94, where he says that the most secure freedom is the wise man's observance of the law. In all these texts we can see the influence of the ordinary philosophy of the Greeks, as it appears in particular in Epictetus (*Diss.,* IV, 1). Here slavery is not a matter of social standing, but exists wherever something is imposed on a man against his will. Social differences disappear in face of the fact that only the "wise" are free, and that no one who does wrong (ἁμαρτάνει) can be called free (*Diss.,* II, 1, 22f.). This Greek notion of freedom is turned into a theological concept in Hellenistic Judaism, where Philo, for instance, speaks of freedom in connection with redemption (*De Conf. Ling.,* 94; *De Migr. Abr.,* 25; *Quis Rer.,* 124), remission of sins (*Quis Rer.,* 273) and perfection. According to *Quis Rer.,* 275, there are two races of men, one of which is engaged in warfare and doomed to slavery, while the other, the τέλειοι, are in possession of peace and freedom. In apocalyptic, freedom is mostly designated as the possibility of deciding, in the present time to which the preaching is addressed, before the coming of judgment (*Syriac Apocalypse of Baruch,* 56, 11; 85, 7). In *4 Esdr.,* 8, 4f., this time is restricted to the brief span of life.

2. *New Testament.* In the synoptic tradition, the term ἐλεύθερος is found only in the episode of the temple tax, Mt 17:24–27. Jesus refuses payment, on the ground that kings collect tribute and taxes from strangers, not from sons. Sons are therefore free of the obligation (a consequence which is not applied in the miracle which follows). In the original tradition, the fact that Jesus and Peter are sons (of the "king" God) leads to the concrete conclusion that they are free from taxes. The kingship proclaimed by Jesus is conceived of as so real and effective that sonship in it has political consequences with regard to earthly rulers — though this eschatological truth is not now fully manifest in practice. The pericope is in fact part of the Matthaean traditions about Peter which contain other far-reaching statements on the present dignity of Peter and the Twelve, which is legitimated by its eschatological character.

According to Jn 8:31, to continue in Jesus' word makes men disciples, and this gives knowledge of the truth, and this again gives freedom. Hence to continue in Jesus' word is the basis and presupposition of freedom. The Jews fail to understand that Jesus is speaking of "true" freedom: how have they still to be set free, since as children of Abraham they are already free? Nonetheless, real freedom is to be free from ἁμαρτία, as only those are, according to 8:31, 36, who are united with the Son. That the Jews have freedom in an earthly sense, as children of Abraham, is not denied. The point of Jesus' answer to their argument is the notion of δοῦλος τῆς ἁμαρτίας. For the slave is not only contrasted with the free man, he is also contrasted with the Son, when their positions in the household are considered. The freedom which the Jews possess is the freedom of men who are slaves to sin. Hence they share the characteristic status of the slave that no permanent abode is assured them. The reality of freedom depends therefore on its permanence. The opposition between slave and free man becomes in 8:35b, after the transition in 8:35a, that between slave and

son. Since the slave has no permanent standing (8:35a), and permanence in the household is confined to the circle of the Son. It is only because Jn used two contrasts to slavery that both permanence and freedom are linked with the Son. In this way the fact that the Jews are slaves of sin is used to prove that true freedom is only to be had in the Son.

In the letters written by Paul or under his influence we find a notion of freedom which has its origin in the theological use made of Greek notions by Hellenistic Judaism. There are three main headings under which the Pauline notion may be summarized.

a) Baptism eliminates all differences between slave and free man in the line of redemption. According to Gal 3:26–29, all who have been baptized have put on Jesus and so have become one, none other than Jesus himself. The solution that all are now one in him is here used to answer the pressing question about the relationship of the one heir to the many heirs. All are Abraham's seed, and thereby heirs to the promises. The equivalence of Jew and Greek, slave and free, is also found in 1 Cor 12:13. All have become one body through the one Pneuma. This notion appears in another form in Col 1:11, where the catalogue is lengthened and the Christology developed. In Eph 6:8 there is a similar elimination of the difference between slave and free, though here merely in view of the coming judgment (cf. Rev 19:18). The eschatological event brings such a universal change that all social and national differences disappear. That Paul speaks of slave and free as well as of Jew and Greek is not merely due to the circumstances of his time. It is also part of the theological concept of the Apostle.

b) The possession of the Spirit frees Christians from sin, death and the necessity of using the law as a way of salvation. Thus in Gal 4:21–31 the story of Hagar and Sarah is used to prove against the Judaizers that possession of the promise sets Christians free from the law, that is, because they have received the Pneuma. Christians are free from the law because they must be regarded as children of Sarah, that is, of the free woman. The decisive point is that Isaac was born from a mother who was free, and that mother and son represent the relationship between freedom and having the promises. In 2 Cor 3, glory, the new covenant and freedom from the law go hand in hand. Here too freedom is associated with possession of the Spirit (v. 17). The way of salvation offered by the law is here depicted as past slavery, in contrast to present freedom. No one should relapse into such slavery (cf. Gal 2:4; 5:1; Rom 6:20). The Apostle's own freedom is particularly important, since it is this alone — his having been redeemed — that enables him to co-operate in the deliverance of his communities (1 Cor 9:1). The same line of thought appears in 1 Cor 10:29, for the freedom of the strong stems from the fact that once they are redeemed they are free to disregard all cultic considerations of a merely human nature. The NT contrast between slavery and sonship is used by Paul in Rom 8:21 to depict the relationship between the old creation and the new and imperishable one. The hope of Christians is to attain the freedom of the *doxa* of the children of God, which is primarily freedom from death and all that is passing away.

c) But the freedom bestowed by the possession of the Spirit really means being bound by a new type of "slavery". In contrast, for instance, to Epictetus, freedom is not an ideal to be pursued for its own sake. It is only "the converse of a new service". Statements to this effect are found in Paul whenever he has to affirm that being redeemed in principle does not free men from the permanent obligation of observing moral commandments. The new slavery is therefore nothing else than being under the law of Christ (Rom 8:2). Freedom from the sphere of the *sarx* and sin is not freedom to return to them again. The "vacuum" is to be filled by loving service of one another (Gal 5:13 f.). And just as this love is a gift, so too this freedom is a call: in baptism, man has been set free by God to be able to fulfil the law. Rom 6:18–22 in particular identifies this freedom from sin, lawlessness and death as serving as a slave under the new righteousness. Thus unlike John, Paul is not concerned to emphasize "true" freedom but simply makes use of the concept to speak of a radical transition from one sphere to another — from one slavery to another. The repeated mention of its fruits in Rom 6:18 ff. stresses further that this freedom is an obligation to certain achievements, precisely because it is a gift. Such affirmations were occasioned, no doubt, by a certain libertinism in the Pauline communities which was sup-

posed to be justified by the possession of the Spirit, as is clear, for instance, from 1 Cor 7: 20–24. The question in Corinth was whether all slaves were now free, enjoying the earthly freedom promised in the OT as an eschatological blessing. Paul gives his usual answer to the question of the moral consequences of a "realized eschatology". The slave's bondage and the free man's liberty are minor elements in view of the fact that all who have been set free by the Lord are still servants of Christ. For "you were bought with a price" (1 Cor 6:20), i.e., the fact that they belong to Jesus is represented as the consequence of being purchased as slaves. This new servitude makes all human differences merely relative. But it is also used to show that the life of the individual is a calling. No upheavals are on the way, since one and all are slaves and summoned to service, like the Apostle himself (1 Cor 9:19). Thus Paul counters the tendency in his communities by referring the freedom of Christians back to the process of their redemption. This bars the way to libertinism and links the freedom of Christians with the redemption through Jesus Christ.

This Pauline solution is then reflected in 1 Pet 2:16, though the soteriological aspect is now lacking. The same moral arguments and the same contrast between freedom and slavery are used in 2 Pet 2:19, which affirms that the libertines who promised true freedom are in fact "slaves of corruption". This is first couched in Hellenistic terms, but v. 20 links up with the redemption of Christ, though the key-word freedom does not occur in this verse. The meaning of the "perfect law of liberty" in Jas 1:25 and 2:12 must be left an open question. It may be freedom in general as one of the blessings of salvation, a concept which occurs elsewhere in early Christianity. Or it may be the law which man can still fulfil before judgment, a concept which occurs in apocalyptic. Both texts are in the context of rewards to be meted out (i.e., at judgment). Or it may be a law connected with freedom from circumcision. Perhaps it is an echo of the Pauline solution, insisting that the law must be fulfilled, but by free men, i.e., by men who are and know themselves redeemed.

Like ἐλευθερία, the term παρρησία also comes from the political sphere and characterizes democratic freedom as the right of free speech, as frankness and courageous candour, while it also means the familiar confidence with which strangers can deal with each other. In the Cynic philosophy of NT times παρρησία like ἐλευθερία designates moral freedom. In the LXX there is the additional element of candour before God (Job 27:9f.), a boldness which appears in particular in the prayer of the just and finds its fullest expression in joy. Hence according to Philo, courage and candour are only to be found in the just and the wise. In the NT *parrhesia*, boldness, is a characteristic of the missionaries of the kingdom of God when they come before men — of Jesus himself in Jn, of the apostles in Acts, of Paul who speaks of his "boldness before God and man" (cf. 2 Cor 3:12; Phil 1:19; 1 Tim 3:13). Elsewhere the word means the free access which the just now have to God (1 Jn; Eph 3:12), which means that they can freely pray to God and that they will survive unscathed on the day of judgment. In Heb, *parrhesia* is the free access to God made possible by Jesus. Unlike therefore, *parrhesia* is not contrasted with slavery, but designates the granting of untrammelled intercourse with a person. And this free access to God enables Christians to face the world of men boldly.

See also *Justice* I, *Law* I, III, *Salvation* II, *Apocalyptic*.

BIBLIOGRAPHY. J. Weiss. *Die christliche Freiheit nach der Verkündigung des Apostels Paulus* (1902); O. Schmitz, *Der Freiheitsgedanke bei Epiktet und Paulus* (1923); M. Müller, "Freiheit", *Zeitschrift für die neutestamentliche Wissenschaft* 25 (1926), pp. 117–236; H. Schlier, "ἐλεύθερος", *TWNT*, II, E. T.: pp. 487–502; S. Lyonnet, *Liberté chrétienne et loi de l'Esprit selon S. Paul* (1954); F. Nötscher, "Schicksal und Freiheit", *Biblica* 40 (1959), pp. 446–62; D. Nestle, *Eleutheria. Studien zum Wesen der Freiheit bei den Griechen und im Neuen Testament, I: Die Griechen* (1967).

Klaus Berger

II. Philosophical

A. On the General and Philosophical Notion of Freedom

1. The concept of freedom is an analogous one, predicated in different ways of beings of very different types. The various forms of attribution all agree, however, to a certain extent, not by defining the same specific content, but by indicating a formal relation which remains the same. This relation can be put negatively or positively. Negatively, freedom means "being free from", i.e., the relation of not being bound (to a given being or law), of being independent from something and of not being determined by a given principle of determination (*libertas a coactione,* freedom in the sense of not being forced). This negative concept is also a relative one, because every finite being belongs to a world and is related to other beings in the world. It may be free from direct relationships to this or that, but only because their places are taken by others. Beings, for instance, which are not inserted into civilization and history, which are therefore "free" from these relationships, are all the more fully involved in nature and the universe. Men who are free from links with the past are all the more fully absorbed by the demands and goals of the present. A being fully free in the negative sense could not be a being in the world: without relationships, fully isolated, it would be based on nothing and be nothing. Negation is always relative and presupposes a positive. If relative, negative freedom were conceived as an absolute, such a fully indeterminate being would be without a world and reduced to nothingness, or its complete indetermination would have to be replaced by full self-determination. If negative, relative freedom is thought out to its logical conclusion, it becomes the mere obverse of positive, absolute freedom; and such a being would be God.

2. Thus in contrast to the negative, relative concept, there is a positive, absolute concept of freedom. A being is positively free insofar as it is in possession of itself and possesses in this relationship the sufficient condition for all its being and relations. Here freedom means self-possession, being completely present to oneself, complete self-sufficiency. This was called by the Greeks autarky, the condition of having within oneself one's principle and goal, one's beginning and end. The Latin *libertas,* as *dominium in actus suos, dominium super se ipsum,* corresponds to the Greek autarky.

The decisive point is that autarky, not mere independence, but a positive relationship to self, is now the basis of selfhood and self-determination in the sense of being fully at one with oneself. It then becomes distinctive for the concept of person, which was developed in Christian thinking to designate this condition. A being is a person inasmuch as it is in possession of itself and is not possessed by another. For the Greeks, the freedom of autarky was a sign of the divine — that which, "thought of thought" (νόησις νοήσεως), thinking itself, is its own sufficient reason and end and hence is fully "blissful". Among the non-divine, man approaches this state most closely in "theoria", the pure state of blissful contemplation which is its end in itself. In Christian thought this mode of freedom was described by "hypostasis" and "persona". Thus freedom and personality can be primarily predicated only of God, but secondarily of man as the being who in spite of being finite has a certain possession of himself and so participates to a certain degree in absoluteness. In this freedom of self-possession he is the *imago Dei*.

3. Human freedom is clearly neither merely negative and relative *(libertas a coactione)* nor fully positive and absolute *(dominium super se ipsum)*. Man has some dominion over himself *(dominium super actus suos)* and so also over parts of the world. But he is nonetheless inserted into the world and dependent on the beings among which he finds himself, upon which he exercises his faculties and dispositions, while he is also dependent on the laws of the world to which he remains subject in all his lordship.

Thus freedom — which may also be attributed in a certain negative and relative sense to infra-human beings, while as positive and absolute is proper only to the infinite person of God — is an analogous concept in general. But so is the concept of human freedom in the strict sense. Here too it has many senses, which are again united by the double relationship — the negative one of a certain isolation with regard to other beings and to oneself, and the positive one of a certain dominion over other beings and oneself. This combination of isolation and power, being "free from" and "free to" constitutes human freedom in its many different aspects.

4. The basic mode of human freedom may be called *libertas transcendentalis,* transcendental freedom, which is the fundamental propriety of man by which he alone can say "is". He can contrast all things with himself as "beings" and so comprehend them "in being", while he can also contrast himself with all things and comprehend himself as this other who is contrasted with all beings. Man has the faculty of "distancing" all things from himself and himself from all things and even from himself. He can objectivate all things and even himself. This universal distance is at once transcendence, "being over and beyond" every individual being and even himself qua individual. It is the possibility of absolute reflection, a possibility which presupposes a footing in the absolute. Such freedom is identical with man's being as spirit. This freedom or spirit is the "light" by which man can illuminate all things, including himself. This light means that in finite man there is a formal absoluteness, which is called *participatio quaedam infiniti* by Thomas Aquinas. This formal, that is, empty transcendence of man is the fulfilment of negative freedom in a positive, though merely formal sense. This empty distance does not overcome or eliminate man's material bondage, but it gives it a new meaning.

5. It follows that man can never be deprived of this transcendental freedom, which is part of his "equipment" as man. But its emptiness and impotence points on to another mode of freedom.

Man is not simply there, he does not simply grow: he has "to be", he is a task absolutely imposed on himself, he has to decide to be himself or what he will be and there is no way in which he can evade this decision. Man has to move out of the distance of transcendental freedom and give himself, out of this distance, his own concrete form. This mode of freedom is called *libertas arbitrii,* freedom of decision (or "existentie*l* freedom").

How does decision take place? Man "is" in as much as he acts, posits actions for which he might have posited others. None of the actual acts is necessary, that is, none is determined by definitely assignable causes and explicable only by their effects. Each act proceeds from a state of indifference. This state has also been termed "freedom"; *libertas indifferentiae* indicates a state in which man must always act (by deed or omission) but in which several possibilities of action are offered, with regard to which man is indifferent.

6. This is the point taken up by polemics against the freedom of the will. Determinism maintains that such "indifference" does not

exist. Like every other being, in every moment of his being man is totally "determined", and for every transition from a given state to another there is a sufficient reason — an adequate "motive" or some other "cause".

Indeterminism maintains, on the contrary, that there is real freedom of action *(libertas actionis)*. Man is not merely the product of preceding and concomitant, conscious or unconscious "efficient" or "final" causes. He is also, conditioned though he may be, unconditioned initiator. Freedom qua initiative is called spontaneity. Hence indeterminism explains freedom of action by having recourse to *libertas spontaneitatis*. But since everything in the world of space and time is within the series of cause and effect (nothing is simply first) and hence explicable through its preconditions, man, when understood as free, is inexplicable on principle and supra-mundane though existing in the world. In his *libertas spontaneitatis,* man is seen once more as the image of God, reflecting the Absolute as first cause. Hence freedom seen as spontaneity is not an intramundane factor. For Kant, it is not a "phenomenon" and hence not a possible object of scientific enquiry. It is prior in nature to the world, unconditioned — what Kant calls "noumenal". Hence it cannot be attained by scientific, objectivating knowledge, though it can be experienced and evident in the exercise of the act *(praxis)*.

But when the freedom of the will, freedom of action and of choice, is thus reduced to *libertas spontaneitatis,* the structure of the actual choice, the actual decision in favour of certain actions, is not sufficiently explained. Man has merely been shown to be at once conditioned and unconditioned, a being at once of the world and outside the world or absolute, at once contingent and non-contingent, or in Kantian terms, phenomenal and noumenal.

7. Freedom of choice and action, which transforms the state or indifference of freedom into the act of self-differentiation, could not be called freedom if it were merely arbitrary and random when spontaneity determines itself and the empty distance is filled. An arbitrary freedom would be no freedom: a man "free" in this sense would be leaving his actions at the mercy of mood, whim or chance. The freedom of a libertarian liberalism is baseless. It stems without any intrinsic necessity from the empty distance of transcendental freedom and from the power of a spontaneous initiative, but between these and the actual action lies the gulf of random wilfulness. However, the necessary derivation of the free act, if it is to remain free, can only mean a necessity of meaning, a consequence in meaning.

8. The choice falls upon a particular object because it is seen as valuable and preferred to other valued objects. But a value is always "valuable to": when we allow our choice to be motivated and explained by something "valuable" — and determinism is right in affirming that even the free choice is always reasoned, never baseless — this value is valuable and a "motive" for us, because we realize ourselves in it, and hence our essence. Hence the choice of actions and of the beings towards which these actions are directed is preceded by a basic choice, the only one which we can call decision in the strict sense: the choice of what we really will to be, the sketch-plan of our own essential form.

It is only within the horizon of this prior decision that anything at all is allowed in as a motive. By "essence" or "basic form" we mean the fundamental meaning, the fundamental attitude of man in the totality (on which see *Education* I). This totality, the only possible situation within which essences limiting each other can exist (Plato: an εἶδος is only an εἶδος in the κοινωνία τῶν εἰδῶν), is what we call the "world". It is the scene of constant changes. But we only say that the world changes when the structure of the basic meanings of beings, the basic structure of values, changes.

Hence affirmation of essence is also affirmation of the world for the time being in which this essence has validity and meaning. The existenti*el* decision for one's own being and purpose is therefore decision for one's own basic form (essential or eidetic freedom as choice of basic mode of life); and it is also decision for the world for the time being, for a form within the total order of being (ontological freedom as prior choice of world and acknowledgment of a given total order of being).

Thus the free act is fully determined by its motive, but the motive is only a motive in the pre-determination which is given by the basic choice of free decision. This freedom of decision enshrines the real personal freedom in which man's transcendental superiority to the world and his spontaneous priority to the world become concrete in active moulding of the world by means of free affirmation of the world and of essence. Freedom is only freedom in the concrete sense when all these freedoms are combined.

B. Social Structure of Freedom

1. Since freedom is transcendental distance and transcendent spontaneity, it is essentially part of man. But this "primordial" freedom is still only the basis for "existential freedom", the realization of man as person; it is not yet this personal being in actual reality. Transcendental and transcendent freedom are actuated only in the decision of existentiel freedom for its own essence as basic form (essential or eidetic freedom) and for the world as total order and order of being (ontological freedom). But the reality of world and essence is given only in the individual acts, whose accomplishment ("ontic" or "external" freedom) is subject to a number of conditions imposed on the individual by society. This corresponds to the way in which the more internal freedom of the existentiel affirmation of the world and essence depends on the knowledge had of them through a "basic education" transmitted by society. It follows that freedom is indivisible. Universal distance (transcendental freedom) cannot be separated from basic spontaneity (transcendent freedom), and both are actuated only in the decision for the world as offered by education (ontological freedom) and for the essence as experienced and conceived (eidetic freedom). In this last aspect the voice of conscience tests a given action for its aptitude to fulfil the essence. But the concrete action, in order to be real, involves things (as provided by nature and culture) and knowledge of their use (as provided through general technical education in the most general sense). This principle of indivisibility or totality proceeds necessarily from the analogous unity of the notion of freedom. A mere inner freedom or a purely transcendental or transcendent one is impossible, just as a merely external technical command of things cannot be called freedom, if it does not proceed from and return to that inner relationship to self of which we have spoken.

2. It follows that human freedom can never be a simple state of man or a specialized propriety; but neither is it simply the actuation of selfhood, pure act without history like the divine freedom. On the contrary, human freedom is history by its very nature: transition from indeterminate distance to decision with regard to world and essence, transition from decision to concrete act, the productive act, that which produces works. Action makes use of technical procedures to produce technical works in our environment. It brings out the intrinsic connections of things in truth as the work of science and of knowledge; or it transforms them in beauty as the work of art. Out of the possibilities of life together the free actions of man produce the works of fellowship, marriage and the family, society and state; from the God-given possibility of standing before God man becomes "Church". Thus actions are ordained to the works of truth, beauty, human unity and social links and so on, and in this ordination they are wholly regulated by what is to be produced and achieved, that is, by the objective laws of action. Man is wholly claimed by the works to be done and the states to be achieved. He becomes truly a person by going freely out of himself to throw himself into the work to be done. Hence the first step in the realization of freedom must be alienation. But since self-possession is the essence of human freedom, the "objectivation" of freedom in work must be followed by a further movement: the return which is the fetching in of the work in the act. All works and objectivations can only be said really to "be" insofar as they are modes of life, vital acts, absorbed into a life of freedom which has become through them more than a merely individual life. It is a life in which person and work, selfhood and world, have attained one and the same existence. Hence apropos of human free acts Thomas Aquinas speaks of a *redditio completa in se ipsum*, a complete return upon one's self. Return presupposes going out: the *conversio ad phantasmata* of Thomas Aquinas, man's turning freely to the sensible world.

Thus human freedom is not a state, as it is in things (freedom from this or that compulsion), nor is it as in God a pure act of self-consciousness. It is this history of outgoing and return, which was later described dialectically by Hegel and Marx (each in his own way) as extrapolation, alienation and conquest of extrapolation and alienation by return or synthesis. Hence the second basic principle of freedom is its history and historicity. If there is only freedom *as* history, it must be always *in* history, that is, the modes in which freedom is realized as history of union with the world and of absorbing the world and its works, must take on forms determined by the total history of the human race.

Metaphysically speaking, the principle of identity is latent in the principle of historicity as regards freedom: action and effect, person and work are the same thing. Action takes place in the effect, work "is" only a mode of being which fulfils the free man (by being re-absorbed). It is the one and the same act (not two acts) by which I am posited in the work and the work in me. Note the gnoseological formulation of this truth in Aristotle and Thomas Aquinas: *cognitum in actu et cognoscens in actu sunt idem*.

3. From the principle of historicity, the third basic element of freedom may be deduced, the principle of sociality. Most works could never be done by one man alone — truth in philosophy and science, beauty in art and literature, mastery in techniques, society and State, etc. Where free persons unite — simultaneously or generation after generation — for a common purpose, a task that can be done only by division of labour (in historical succession and in simultaneous association), freedom is the integration of a multitude of free achievements. The mode of co-operation, however, cannot be brought about by compulsion, if freedom is to remain freedom and the person a person. Freedom without permanent alienation is only possible in common consent to the acknowledged need of common action. Hence the principle of sociality does not lead to a doctrinaire and mechanical socialism but to solidarity.

4. Work, then, is always the common work in which a generation, a people, a number of generations find themselves. Nonetheless, the essential agent in freedom is always the individual person who freely disposes of himself. The proper and ultimate subject of freedom is the free individual, as Kierkegaard maintained again and again against Hegel. For freedom is the history of a person's "coming to himself", which culminates in fully conscious self-possession. In the strict sense, only the individual is with himself: self-possession can be predicated only analogously of a community or a people. Mastery over nature or foreign peoples may be exercised by a community. Mastery over self can be exercised only by the individual, and it is by reason of this self-possession that the individual is called a person. Hence we may speak of a principle of substantiality or personality as regards freedom.

5. All these principles recur in the principle which regulates the mode of realization of freedom: the principle of subsidiarity.

Freedom in act is identical with the personality of the person: it is the person's mode of being. This mode of being is at once individual and supra-individual, conditioned and unconditioned. Conscious selfhood, as an act feasible only to the self, makes the individual unique as a person. He does not merely exercise a function on behalf of the supra-individual, he brings back the supra-individual to what matters throughout: the individual person is the absolute why and wherefore of all action. The common works of the realization of the person — science, art, technology, economics, politics, etc. — are not merely helps and means towards the self-realization of freedom and the person. Such a view would render them valueless. These common works are modes of self-realization, of the reality of freedom and the person. But as such modes they are forms taken by freedom, and they retain their meaning and purpose only by being referred back to the person and its reality. The free person can never be a means to something else. He is always the end of all else, and hence absolutely an end in himself. This is what constitutes the inviolable dignity of the person, as both Thomas Aquinas and Kant affirm. The principle of subsidiarity acknowledges the person not only as the real subject, origin and goal of freedom, but also as the primary agent in freedom, which must itself act to fulfil itself, in spite of all the helps provided by society, State and Church. What the person can do as an individually free being may not be taken over by the community; what the smaller unit, in which the individual still acts as his own man, can do, may not be taken over by a larger community. And what can only be done by the largest community — the State as *societas perfecta* — must always be carefully referred back to the self-realization of the individual person. It may not be seen in isolation as "functioning" on its own behalf. The individual as such necessarily has a function in society. But man is not just an individual and a "functionary". Working does not absorb his whole self, but his works are modes of his being, realizations of his freedom, and as such are inserted into the historical process in which he returns to himself. Since the outgoing action of achievement is also under the law of the homeward return, the principle of subsidiarity is absolutely valid.

These five principles of Christian social philosophy are the consequences of a notion of freedom based on all the elements here discussed and not confined to any one of them. In the light of the foregoing, the rights of man are seen to be the rights of freedom, which apply not to the individual but to the person, who only realizes his selfhood in the historical process of involvement in his works. The rights of man are personal, not individual. So too the basic duties can be deduced from personal freedom, but not from individual. They are not negative restrictions on the individual (demanded by the formal truth that it has to allow for the existence of the freedom of others) but positive means of the achievement of the person, deriving from its basic structure. For personal freedom can only be real in the service of the common work, in which it returns to itself.

The principle of subsidiarity does not indicate one of the structural components of freedom itself (like the first four principles) but is a guide-line to its realization indicated by the personal structure of freedom. This guide-line is always subject to the historical process in the actual distribution of tasks and rights to individuals, the freely-formed smaller units, the family, society, State and Church. What an individual or a small unit can really achieve, what they have to renounce or what would be a blameworthy weakness if they renounced it, always depends on the historical situation.

C. History of the Concept in the West

1. *The Greek notion of freedom.* It is to be noted that the Greeks did not think of free-dom as the freedom of self-decision or the freedom of the will, but as the freedom of the State or of its citizens. The ἐλεύθερος was the free citizen, ἐλευθερία was political freedom. The freedom of the State was its "autonomy", the fact that a civic community could regulate its life in common by its own rules, decided upon in view of the common good of the citizens. And the individual member of the community was only positively free in relation to this community, in which he found his fulfilment, as it in him. To be free "from" the State was a misery — the lot of the felon or exile. The freedom of the individual was quite compatible with his being thoroughly bound up with society as a whole, the determining factor in all education and each way of life. The Greek was not free under a tyranny, where State and citizens ceased to be one, and freedom only perished when the two were sundered.

Freedom as autonomy is a reflection of the metaphysical notion of autarky. The πόλις is principle and end, origin and duty. The Greeks knew nothing loftier than this very fact of common life in which all individual lives surpassed themselves and found themselves.

In Aristotle this thoroughly political notion of freedom became a theological one. Freedom was the autarky of the divine. God the only truly free being who, having no goal and no ground outside himself, is absorbed in blissful love of self and though loving nothing outside himself is "loved" by all, that is, longed for as the perfect.

2. *The Christian notion of freedom.* A very different notion of freedom appears in the revealed religions of Judaism and Christianity. Elements occur, apropos both of divine and human freedom, which have given such a distinctive stamp to the Western notion of freedom that nothing comparable can be found in the other great civilizations. The Jewish-Christian heritage has made the freedom of the West unique.

As regards divine freedom, the God of the OT and NT is not merely free in the sense of Greek autarky. His freedom goes out of itself in the act of creation, where it works unhampered by anything prior, creating out of nothing. This combination of freedom and creativity is absolutely new. Freedom is seen as the absolute power to initiate and set in motion, as the supreme mastery which begins by calling its subjects into being and thus justifies its absolute claim to lordship. Another notion also appears. When God creates, his creatures are not the necessary consequences of his being and nature, and they are not created merely in the order of creation, but also in that of redemption. When man "falls" — freely renouncing the fulfilment of his being in God, choosing instead a fulfilment of his being in himself: a basic choice with regard to essence and world, such as had been undreamt-of in Greek antiquity — God bestows on him a new potentiality which does not stem from the nature of creation or from the nature of God. The freedom of God in which he makes himself the partner of man, summons the existentiel freedom of man to try to find itself through and with God. In the OT, this possibility is bestowed on a freely chosen people which had in no way merited the choice, while in the NT it is bestowed on all mankind. "History" in the true sense begins for the first time in this interplay of divine and human freedom. It is the free decision of essential freedom confronted with absolute claims and absolute offers of help, uninterruptedly, a decision for or against but always in partnership with the absolute freedom of God. This notion of history as the history of the two freedoms was given its most magnificent expression by Augustine in the light of the Old and New Testaments.

Thus human freedom, in spite of being unconditioned, is finite in a double sense. It is always a response to the absolute freedom of God, which it is in need of as the goal of its free decision. And throughout history human freedom has always failed in the encounter with God. From the Jewish-Christian point of view, the beginning of history was original sin. Human freedom is fallen freedom. The fallen and sickly freedom of man cannot heal itself. The remedy offered by God in the OT was the covenant characterized by the "law", in the NT it is God himself in his Son Jesus Christ in whom God's free love is incarnate. But man cannot accept this offer without the grace of God: the decision of fallen man's failed freedom can only become free again with the help of the freedom of God himself.

There are three conclusions to be noted as regards the Christian view of freedom:

a) Even if we bear in mind the basic structure of freedom and its acts, we shall miss its full reality if we fail to note the religious dimension of freedom: that it is fallen freedom needing the help of grace. Man's freedom alone necessarily falls a victim to slavery. The conviction of the wounding (*vulneratio*) and the sinfulness of human freedom is the only preservative against utopian dreams of Christian freedom, and strictly divides the Christian view from that of liberal humanism.

b) The view taken of human freedom in the historical Fall — whether it was destroyed (*libertas destructa*) or only wounded (*libertas vulnerata*) — whether grace heals and helps or must simply create man anew — marks the deepest difference between the Catholic notion of grace and freedom and that of the Churches of the Reformation. But here too the theologies of all the faiths have a problem which cannot really be solved by the powers of human thought: for if the freedom which has been enslaved is to be free again, it must take up God's free offer as it actually comes. But of itself this enslaved freedom is incapable of giving its assent to its salvation. Only those who have received prevenient, helping grace, for the free assent to the grace which makes freedom free once more (*gratia sanans, gratia efficax*) can actually perform this act of dedication and remain healed in it and become holy (with the help of further grace, *gratia sanctificans,* which enables us to keep the moral law consistently and love its author in unwavering natural love). But this prevenient grace is given by God prior to all merit, in an unfathomable free act. "So then he has mercy upon whomever he wills, and he hardens the heart of whomever he wills" (Rom 9:18). Hardening comes upon those who have not received the prevenient grace for the assent to redemption. The mystery of "predestination" in relation to freedom arises here. Since the later Augustine Christian theology has been struggling here with the question of the (sinful) *servum arbitrium* and the (healed) *liberum arbitrium* — how it is that freedom itself is not free enough to liberate itself from the slavery into which it has fallen; how it is that only God can enable freedom to be itself, through the grace of his mysterious choice.

c) It is the freedom thus healed and restored through Christ and in Christ which is meant when Christian theology speaks of freedom in the strict sense, as was done most clearly by Paul, who called it "the freedom of the children of God". Sin was for Paul the real slavery, by which man was at the mercy of the "world", "this world" or aeon, seen as the sum total of what is here below. The free man is the man at one with God. Only if he abandons himself to God does he receive himself back as his own personal possession. Otherwise he is held captive by his "works" and the activities directed to them. When he is thus given back to himself, he receives all things and all is subject to him, everything is "open" to him. It is now true to say: "Dilige et quod vis fac!" — "Love, and do what you will" — because the man who loves God is governed by no outside law, his freedom being identified in love with the freedom of God.

3. *From antiquity to the Renaissance.* The concepts of freedom which were dominant till the Renaissance were either varieties of the two concepts which had been most highly developed historically, that of Greek antiquity and that of Jewish-Christian faith, or syntheses of them.

In the Stoic philosophy of late antiquity the ancient politically-orientated concept of freedom lost its political character. The positive assertion of autarky became a renunciation of the world, a withdrawal into isolation and a negative attitude. The key-terms were *apatheia,* impassibility, and *ataraxia,* impassiveness, and Stoic freedom became freedom from the world through a retreat into the inmost spiritual kernel of man. This was to ignore the principle of historicity, that the spirit can only be really itself by going out into the world and fetching it in to itself.

In the greatest days of the Middle Ages, Thomas Aquinas tried to synthetize the various concepts of freedom, using the schema of the different types of movement to describe the degrees and realms of beings as degrees and realms of various types of freedom. The lifeless object is moved only from without, but plants have a spontaneous organic motion from within. The animal has more freedom of movement, not being bound to a particular place, and can follow his instinctive purposes by moving around. Man is the one being in the world who goes beyond the free spontaneous outward movement to return within himself. In all his movements he comes back to himself. He is the first being capable of a *reditio completa in*

se ipsum. The movement of the angels, however, and in a supremely pre-eminent sense, the self-moved movement of God do not pass through the process of outgoing and returning. Their presence to themselves is not dependent on outside factors but is a "self-sufficient circumincession" without any previous self-alienation. The free act by which God goes out of himself in creation produces created reality according to his own image. But this image is the Son, the Logos, the *verbum per quod omnia facta sunt.* This is the *intellectualism* characteristic of Thomism: knowledge is higher than all will and action, and here it is God's self-knowledge in the Son which is the ground and norm of all his action. With Scotism and the nominalism of Occam trends appear which could be called metaphysical and theological voluntarism. God's freedom is conceived as the *potentia Dei absoluta.* There are no norms for his creation and his act of creation, so it is no longer necessarily a reflection of the essence of God. All that can be still deduced from its contingence is the fact that it has been willed. The order of essences, the natural law and so on give way to world orders which merely reflect *de facto* decrees. It then becomes possible to affirm with Luther that the "harlot reason" cannot decipher the will of God from the cosmos. It can only be accepted by faith from revelation. The differences between metaphysical and theological intellectualism and voluntarism (or nominalism) are among the decisive factors in accepting or rejecting knowledge of the natural law (a law proceeding from the nature of freedom and absolutely regulating in turn this freedom). The strict Lutheran notion of freedom is based entirely on the religious conditions to which the Christian is submitted, entirely ignoring the possibility of genuine freedom outside this realm in which the relationship to God is restored by Christ.

4. *Secularist views of freedom.* The views taken of freedom since the Renaissance are no longer Christian in the strict sense, though after fifteen hundred years of Christianity they cannot be pagan. A new period began in which an effort was made to interpret in a purely immanent "secular" sense many phenomena of "Christian freedom". One could show that the Christian interpretation of freedom affected the fundamentals of the

359

theory of knowledge in the *Meditationes de Prima Philosophia* of Descartes. In the fourth meditation, error is attributed to sin, to the infinite and absolute presumption of our will which trespasses beyond the bounds imposed on our knowledge and tries to assign to man an absolute essence and knowledge which does not pertain to him. The pagan Socrates had ascribed all faulty actions to errors in knowledge, but here all faulty knowledge is ascribed to the basic decision of the free will, which has been wrong since original sin. In contemporary English philosophy discussion was based only on the negative notion of freedom, sometimes on the notion of every man's hand being against everyone else in the unbridled egoism of self-assertion. This primitive freedom was then said to have imposed limits on itself by the foundation of the State as a free, rational consensus. This notion influenced even the *Contrat Social* of J.-J. Rousseau.

No major philosophy of freedom was proposed again till Kant. In the "*a priori* feeling" of "awe", the non-objectivated, scientifically unknowable, noumenal freedom of the will in action experiences itself in the action as its own law-giver and as an end in itself not dominated by other ends. Will is the will to will, freedom is freedom for freedom and it can only be attested as morality, in the elimination of all heteronomy. In such autonomy man's life is spontaneous and non-conditioned (not inserted into the causal sequence of the world), based on absolute spontaneity — which is ultimately the true "in and of itself". Fichte based on this his distinction between the thing done *(Tatsache)* and the action of doing *(Tathandlung)*, envisaging the latter as the true being of man and the world since it was freedom realizing itself. For Hegel, world history is the history of freedom coming to (consciousness of) itself, the transition from slavery in the world of nature to absolute knowledge as identity of knowledge of self and of the world, as identity of possession of self and of the alien. Hegel's concept of the principle of historicity is applied magnificently to freedom, but the human person is just as consistently made the servant of the universal spirit, for whose freedom countless persons and peoples have had to sacrifice themselves and perish.

Marx objects against Hegel that in his system reconciliation after self-alienation does not take place in reality, but only ideally, in knowledge and consciousness. The self-fulfilment of man only takes place really in the common mastery of nature by a collective achievement organized according to a division of labour. In capitalism, one class alone enjoyed the fruits of the victory won by man the worker. But the products must go back to the producers. All goods must be at the free disposal of all in a classless society. Man will then be free — his being, work and his existence will be identical — but not as a single individual, only as a species, since it is only as a species that he succeeds in transforming nature into a world at his disposal. The concept of freedom as mastery *(dominium)* is erected into an absolute, while the other meanings of freedom are completely lost sight of. The work which man tries to fetch back is here simply the work of society and technology as producers, while all the works of the true, beautiful and good are reduced to "epiphenomena". Culture is regarded at best as a means to happiness, not as a mode of life. Further, in Marx the individual person has no subsistence as the agent of freedom. Freedom is exercised only by the human species in its organization as "society". And society, in the historical attainment of its freedom as societal freedom, is itself not free, being at the mercy of the laws of dialectical and historical materialism.

See also *Creation* III, *Person, Power, Transcendence, Knowledge, Spirit, Decision, Meaning, Essence, Education* I, *World, Existence* II, *Society* I, II, *Conscience, Natural Philosophy, Natural Law, History* I, *Social Movements* IV, *Marxism.*

BIBLIOGRAPHY. Aristotle, *Nicomachean Ethics,* tr. by J. Burnet (1900); St. Augustine, "De Libero Arbitrio", *CSEL,* LXXIV (1956); M. Luther, *Bondage of the Will,* tr. by J. Packer and O. Johnston (1943); E. Kant, *Critique of Practical Reason,* tr. by T. K. Abbott (2nd ed., 1900); H. Bergson, *Time and Free Will* (1910); É. Gilson, *La liberté chez Descartes et la théologie* (1913); M. Planck, *Kausalgesetz und Willensfreiheit* (1923); M. Heidegger, *Vom Wesen des Grundes* (1929; 4th ed., 1955); J. Auer, *Menschliche Willensfreiheit im Lehrsystem des Thomas von Aquin und Johannes Duns Scotus* (1938); O. Lottin, *Psychologie et morale au XII*e *et XIII*e *siècles* (1942); G. Siewerth, ed., *Thomas von Aquin: Die menschliche Willens-Freiheit* (1954); J. de Finance, *Existence et liberté* (1955); T. Ballauf, ed., *Fichtes Freiheitslehre. Eine Auswahl aus seinen Schriften* (1956); C. Bay, *The Structure of*

Freedom (1958); M. Clark, *Augustine, Philosopher of Freedom. A Study in Comparative Philosophy* (1958); J. Adler, *The Idea of Freedom,* 2 vols. (1958 f.); G. Lunati, *La libertà. Saggi su Kant, Hegel e Croce* (1959); R. Guardini, *Freedom, Grace and Destiny* (1961); S. Hook, *The Paradoxes of Freedom* (1962); A. von Spakovsky, *Freedom, Determinism, Indeterminism* (1963); H. Thielecke, *The Freedom of the Christian Man* (1963); H. Vorster, *Das Freiheits-verständnis bei Thomas von Aquin und Martin Luther* (1965); M. Pohlenz, *Freedom in Greek Life and Thought: The History of an Ideal* (1966); R. Guardini, *Focus of Freedom* (1966); J. Splett, *Der Mensch in seiner Freiheit* (1967).

Max Müller

III. Theological

1. The elaboration of the ecclesiastical and theological notion of freedom was carried on from the start in a dialogue with the philosophical notion of freedom throughout its history. To a great extent the two concepts were almost indistinguishable, and they always acted and reacted on one another. For the moment, however, the influence of modern thinking on freedom — in the debate between metaphysics and "after metaphysics" — has only been felt here and there.

In the documents of the magisterium, freedom is usually understood as man's psychological and moral freedom of choice in general, but with particular attention to matters of sin and justification where it is regarded as the ground of responsibility before God. The precise nature of this freedom is not described but presupposed as known. The documents stress, however, that freedom does not merely mean absence of external coercion, but also absence of inner compulsion (cf. *D* 1039, 1041, 1066, 1094). Its existence can be known by the light of natural reason (*D* 1650; not a defined doctrine).

Accordingly, the Church regards freedom of choice as an inalienable and essential part of man's nature (*D* 160 a, 348, 776, 793, 815, 1027 f., 1065 ff., 1094, 1388). The early Church condemned the determinism and fatalism of the Gnostic and Manichean systems, and any form of predestination in which God moved man to an evil act by suppressing his human freedom (cf. *D* 160 a, 200, 300, 316 ff., 321 f., 348, 514). The Church solemnly defined that even under the influence of original sin man was in principle free, that he had to assent freely to the salutary grace which was both necessary and prevenient, and that he could

really resist this grace, even where it was sufficient (*D* 792, 797, 814 ff., 1039 ff., 1065 f., 1093 ff., 1291, 1298, 1359 ff., 1375, 1521, 1791, 2305). At the same time, the notion of freedom as (moral or psychological) autonomy with regard to God was excluded, and also the notion that freedom in fallen man was the power to act by virtue of an untrammelled and unthreatened self-mastery. Freedom is subject to the impulses of concupiscence, and is said to be diminished, weakened and wounded (*D* 160 a, 174, 181, 186, 199, 325, 793). Furthermore, without the gratuitous grace of God this freedom is absolutely incapable of salutary acts (*D* 105, 130, 133 ff., 181, 186, 199 f., 300, 317, 373, 811 ff.). Hence, though man remains responsible for himself by his freedom, his freedom is only enabled to perform the action in which it is most truly itself when it is set free for it by the free grace of God, to which man has absolutely no claim, since he is a mere creature and a sinful one. This gracious liberation of the will is regarded both as the gift of the possibility of the free act and — where it actually takes place — as the gift of the act itself (cf. *D* 177, 182, etc.). But it is precisely the gift of the free act to freedom itself.

How God can create natural freedom in spite of its radical dependence and how the salutary act can be given as a free act by the grace of God — such questions are left to be freely discussed in the schools.

2. For a systematic theology of freedom which will go beyond the framework of the post-Tridentine systems of grace and free will, only preliminary suggestions are provided by modern philosophy. The basic principles of a theological anthropology will point the way to a deeper grasp of freedom. Just as in created being dependence on God and degree of being grow in equal and not inverse proportions, and the possibility of the creation of such being demands the unique intervention of divine power, so too with created freedom. It is a transcendental note of being in general which appertains to various beings in proportion to their degree of being. It is simply called freedom where the degree of being proper to the spiritual person is reached. It is responsible self-mastery, even in face of God, because dependence on God — contrary to what takes place in intra-mundane causality — actually means being endowed with free selfhood. In

the present order, this created freedom is by God's decree the vehicle of the personal free self-communication of God to a personal partner in free dialogue of the covenant. But it exists truly in the mode of a creature, whose finiteness is known in its history and historicity, in its bodily nature and in its being subject to limitations by the force of power.

When freedom is seen as the free love of God in dialogue with the partner necessary to such freely given love, it appears as the essential dignity of the person. This view of freedom must be the foundation of the doctrine of a rightly understood freedom of conscience and of the right of freedom to room for its concrete realization in face of undue restrictions laid upon it by State or Church.

In such a concept of freedom, it would be seen to be in need of interpretation by God. It cannot "judge itself" because it is historical and hence while its process is still going on it can never be fully present to reflection. This interpretation by God must be seen as a verdict of guilty and a verdict of gracious acquittal passed upon guilty freedom. It will then be seen that the freedom of choice (of the Greek notion) stands in the same relation to Christian freedom, by reason of the liberating grace of God, as nature stands to grace. The former, while retaining its nature, is still frustrated of its true sense where it is not elevated and redeemed by the freedom of the children of God.

Hence the proper attitude of man to his freedom must be defined as thankfulness. It is a welcome gift which he gladly accepts, not something to which he is "condemned". And because his individual deeds and basic choice are in principle not amenable to full and certain cognizance, it is only by hoping in God that he can accept it without being plagued by scruples or threatened with self-righteousness.

Hence in theology freedom is understood as having its source and goal in God (who is its "object" and the "horizon" of all possible objects). In this way it is total dominion over the self, aiming at the definitive. It is self-mastery bestowed on man in the dialogue with God, where he is called to the finality of love's decision. Freedom always finds itself fettered in an irremediable situation of disaster and as it accepts this verdict in faith, always finds itself the recipient of liberty through Jesus Christ. But in this way — at

a level on which the systematic theology of freedom must cancel itself out by finding itself safely on a higher plane — freedom is a mystery to itself and all others. It is mystery as the primordial dialogue, as freedom liberated from bondage and called into the absolute mystery.

See also *Responsibility, Man* I–III, *Gnosticism, Manicheism, Predestination, Grace and Freedom, Concupiscence, Conscience, Nature* III.

BIBLIOGRAPHY. H. Rondet, *Gratia Christi* (1948); A. Rzadkiewicz, *Philosophical Bases of Human Liberty according to St. Thomas* (1949); L. Oeing-Hanhoff, "Zur thomistischen Freiheitslehre", *Scholastik* 31 (1956), pp. 161–81; F. Bourassa, "La liberté sous la grâce", *Sciences Écclésiastiques* 9 (1957), pp. 49–66, 95–127; H. Rondet, *Essai sur la théologie de la grâce* (1961); K. Barth, *Church Dogmatics,* IV/3 (1962); K. Rahner, *Theological Investigations,* II (1964), IV (1967).

Karl Rahner

FREEMASONRY

1. *History.* a) *Period of workers' Masonry.* Freemasonry has been credited with many fantastic origins (for example, Solomon's Temple, the mystery religions of antiquity, the Knights Templar, Rosicrucianism, and others). In fact it derives from the medieval builders. The name comes from England, where "free mason" means one who works in freestone (sound stone), as opposed to a "rough mason". Freemasons had certain secrets concerning their technique and their organization (words, signs, grips designed to safeguard the monopoly in the hiring of labour that was enjoyed by qualified craftsmen). All this made up the celebrated "masonic secret", sealed with an oath. The idea that something esoteric was involved — alchemy, perhaps — is modern guesswork and has not been substantiated. The spirit of these workers' "lodges" was Catholic (patron saints: St. John and the Four Blessed Crowned Martyrs). To them we are indebted for the building of the cathedrals. (Workers' masonry must not be confused with the medieval guilds, quite another matter.)

b) *Transitional period (16th to 17th century).* When Gothic art ceased, the workers' bodies also generally disappeared; but they managed to survive in England and Scotland by *accepting* honorary members (*Accepted*

Masons). These British masons went on taking the archaic oath to keep the "Secret" — an empty gesture since the Secret was no more.

c) *"Speculative" period (since 1717)*. In 1717 four lodges combined to form the Grand Lodge of London, which in 1723 adopted *Anderson's Constitutions*. Thenceforward the spirit of the institution was totally different. "Architecture" acquired an allegorical sense. Instead of stone cathedrals, the brethren were to build the human Cathedral, ideal Humanity, "to the glory of the Great Architect of the Universe" (God); the Tools (square, compass, etc.) were given their present symbolic meaning. The *Apron,* emblem of labour, was still worn in the lodge; women were still excluded, since the workers' freemasonry had no female practitioners; and the brotherhood kept the three degrees of Entered Apprentice, Fellow Craft, and Master Mason. During the 18th century Freemasonry spread through Europe and America, but it did not play the part that has been ascribed to it, either in the encyclopaedist movement and the philosophy of the Enlightenment or in the genesis of the French Revolution.

Napoleon tamed Masonry in France. After 1815, except in Great Britain, the *Carbonari* and others, hostile to the settlement of Europe made by the Congress of Vienna, found the lodges a useful retreat in which to conspire against religion and monarchy. From this period we may date the breach between traditionalist, "regular" Masonry and the "irregular" types of Masonry. For the latter, the unification of Italy called for the ruin of the papacy and of the Church itself. Freemasonry in France was responsible for the anti-clerical laws of the Third Republic. In Spain it contributed to the ephemeral Republic of 1931–36. Regular Freemasonry has always condemned such aberrations. When the Grand Orient of France, in 1877, deleted reference to the "Great Architect of the Universe", all regular Grand Lodges withdrew from association with that body. In 1929, invoking its great prestige, the Grand Lodge of England imposed a fundamental document on all Grand Lodges throughout the world: eight "Basic requirements for recognition as a Grand Lodge", the chief of which is "belief in the Great Architect of the Universe and His revealed Will".

Freemasonry was outlawed in Fascist Italy and Nazi Germany. It is still banned in Spain and Portugal, and also in the Communist countries, which consider it reactionary and "bourgeois".

2. *Aims.* Here the distinction between regular and irregular Masonry stands out most clearly, for contrary to the belief of many people the Craft is by no means a monolith, but rather a body riven by divisions. It is neither a religion nor a system of philosophy, and it would be a great mistake to speak of it in ecclesiological terms such as orthodoxy or a magisterium. Freemasonry teaches its members no doctrine: it offers them symbols which convey a certain ideal of work, "Work on crude Stone"; that is to say, a moral improvement, designed to form crude Stone into "square Stone". *Initiation* is not a matter of intellectual knowledge. It is an inward enlightenment, represented by the "blazing Star". (✳. — "G" stands for Geometry.) Masonry, then, is an asceticism leading to a gnosis, a gnosis that can be conveyed neither in words nor in concepts. That is why the Masonic Secret cannot be divulged, even though many books have been written in order to make it known. They have only revealed the "exoteric", not the "esoteric".

Three "Great Lights" must be present in every lodge of regular Freemasonry: the *Book of the Sacred Law* (the Bible), the *Compass,* and the *Square.* Non-Christians may substitute the holy book of some other religion for the Bible; for example, the Koran. Only atheists are debarred. Freemasonry forbids any interference in politics. All Freemasons are brothers and owe one another support and assistance. Regular Freemasonry respects all faiths and Churches — indeed it advises members that it is the part of a good Mason to be assiduous in the practice of whatever religion he may profess — and is loyal to all legitimate civil authority. The irregular types of Masonry have disregarded these maxims, plunging into politics and at times even proclaiming themselves "the Counter-Church". But it is ridiculous to accuse them of Satanism or of holding obscene and sacrilegious ceremonies, as a whole special literature has done since the days of the notorious charlatan Léo Taxil (1887), whose lies are sometimes repeated even now.

3. *Organization, rites and hierarchy*. a) *Organization*. A group of Freemasons is called a lodge, and a number of lodges form an Obedience, or often a Grand Lodge. The president of a lodge is a Venerable, that of a Grand Lodge, a Grand Master. Obediences correspond to countries. Masonry has no supreme head and there is no international directorate. To become a Mason one must be twenty-one years old, "freeborn, and upright". Women are admitted only by certain irregular bodies, such as English "Co-Masonry" and the *Droit Humain* founded at Paris in 1893. Members are at perfect liberty to resign. The fraternity reserves the right to expel the unworthy. In practice many Masons cease to be members within a few years of initiation, through failure to pay their dues.

b) *Rites*. Masonic rites vary from Obedience to Obedience: the Emulation, the Ancient and Accepted Scottish Rite, the Improved Scottish Rite, etc. There was a tendency in the late 19th century for the irregular Masonic bodies to "rationalize" the rituals by eliminating all reference to religion. Then a reaction set in, led by the great symbolist Oswald Wirth. In a limited sense the Masonic Ritual may be said to represent for the Craft what the liturgy does for the Church. Masonry even has its "liturgical" music, some of it by Mozart, an ardent member, whose *Magic Flute* simply puts the Ritual upon the stage.

c) *Hierarchy*. "St. John's pure and genuine Masonry" consists of three degrees, called "symbolic" or "blue": Entered Apprentice, Fellow Craft, and Master Mason. The latter is "complemented" by the Royal Arch, a ceremony inspired by the Bible. But in addition to this triad, Anglo-Saxon Freemasonry has Side Degrees and other rites with Higher Degrees (six in the Improved Rite, thirty-three in the Ancient and Accepted Scottish Rite. The rite of Misraim, now extinct, had as many as ninety-six). Most of these are outdated accretions and some are puerile. One degree, that of Knight Kakoch (thirtieth degree of the Ancient and Accepted Scottish Rite), has been denounced by Masons themselves. Devised by certain 18th-century ritualists who credited the foolish fable that the Knights Templar survived in the shape of Freemasonry, it administers oaths of hatred and vengeance originally directed against those who suppressed the Order, Clement V and Philip the Fair; but anti-clericals soon regarded the two men as the embodiment of "spiritual Despotism" and "Tyranny". Many Masons, particularly in Germany, repudiate the whole idea of Higher Degrees. American Masons, on the other hand, are devoted to them, especially the thirty-second degree, which makes one a "Prince of the Royal Secret".

4. *Freemasonry and the Catholic Church*. Workers' Freemasonry never caused the Church any disquiet, despite its "secrets", for it has always accepted the legitimacy of the professional secret. Under the *Ancien Régime* papal bulls acquired juridical force only if they were registered by the civil authorities (in France, the *Parlement*). Since the 18th-century bulls were not registered, many churchmen became Masons — seculars, regulars, even bishops.

Clement XII's bull *In Eminenti* was the first condemnation of Masonry. It was confirmed by Benedict XIV in the bull *Providas* (1751). These documents did not condemn the Craft as heretical, nor because of any false doctrine it taught, but because of its secret. An enigmatic passage in the bull, "Aliisque de justis ac rationabilibus causis Nobis notis" ("and on other just and reasonable grounds known to Us"), suggests that besides the reason given for the condemnation there may have been a covert one connected with the cause of the exiled Stuart dynasty at Rome. (Cf. my study, *Nos Frères séparés, les Francs-Maçons* [1961].)

Subsequently Freemasonry was condemned by a number of papal acts, the most recent being Leo XIII's *Humanum Genus* (1884). This encyclical shows how much Freemasonry appeared to be infected by all the errors (naturalism, indifferentism, etc.) catalogued in the Syllabus of Pius IX.

Can. 684 and 2335–2336 of *CIC* contain the Church's present legislation on Freemasonry. The duty which Catholics formerly had to denounce its leaders has disappeared, but can. 2335 (interpreted by an instruction of the Holy Office of 10 May 1884) envisages "those who join a Masonic or other sect which conspires against the Church or lawful civil authority". It follows that where this offence is not committed — *a fortiori* where it is positively excluded — the relevant censure is not incurred, since can. 2228 provides that "the penalty appointed by law is incurred only if it is certain that the offence has been committed in the strict terms of the law". Accordingly it is at least doubtful whether the penalty provided by can. 2335–6 (the major excommunication *latae sententiae*) has been incurred in those cases where the statutes and public utterances of a Masonic Obedience expressly declare that that Obedience allows its members nothing which could be considered "conspiracy against the Church or lawful civil authority". Furthermore, the Code provides that when any doubt attends a law, the law is not binding *(non urget)*. One may well ask, therefore, whether those Obediences like the National Grand Lodge of France, the *Vereinigte Grossloge* of Germany, or the *Grand-Orient* of Haiti (the latter even sent a petition to the Second Vatican Council), which have publicly taken steps to avoid the canonical censures, are still excommunicated. The question can even be put in the case of the Grand Lodge of England, which has not gone so far but has always repudiated irregular Masonic bodies. Be that as it may, the faithful are obviously not empowered to pass judgment in the matter, which the Church alone must settle. Inevitably, the post-conciliar commission set up by Pope Paul VI to revise the *CIC* will have to consider the problem, since can. 2335–6 are to be examined on the same basis as the rest. Dr. Mendez-Arceo, Bishop of Cuernavaca (Mexico), officially raised the question at the Council.

Were the Church to follow such a course as we have intimated is possible, regular Freemasonry would still have to take into acount can. 684 *(De fidelium associationibus in genere)*, and that in the name of its own principles, which forbid it to receive Catholics who are in revolt against their Church. Can. 684 says, "Let the faithful avoid secret societies, and those which are condemned or seditious or which try to evade legitimate supervision by the Church." Regular Freemasonry is not a *secret* society. (In Great Britain it scrupulously obeys a law requiring it to provide the Clerk of the Peace with its membership list.) It is not seditious. And when it ceases to be "condemned" depends entirely on the Church. But what satisfaction can the Craft give in respect of "legitimate supervision by the Church"?

BIBLIOGRAPHY. J. Anderson, *The Constitutions of the Free Masons* (1723); J. H. Mounier, *De l'influence attribuée aux philosophes, aux franc-maçons et aux Illuminés sous la Révolution française* (1801); A. Calvert, *The Grand Lodge of England, 1717–1917* (1917); O. Lang, *History of Freemasonry in the State of New York* (1922); A. Wolfstieg, *Die Philosophie der Freimaurerei*, 2 vols. (1922); M.-G. Martin, *Manuel d'histoire de la Franc-Maçonnerie française* (1926); A. G. Mackey, *Encyclopaedia of Freemasonry*, 2 vols. (1927); D. Knoop and G. P. Jones, *Genesis of Freemasonry* (1949); B. Jones, *Freemasons' Guide and Compendium* (1961); A. Mellor, *Freemasonry* (from the French, 1961); id., *La Franc-Maçonnerie à l'heure du choix* (1963); id., *Christianisme et Franc-Maçonnerie* (1965). — The London Lodge "Quatuor Coronati" publishes a periodical annually for private circulation, called *Ars Quatuor Coronatorum,* which is an indispensable source of information.

Alec Mellor

FRENCH REVOLUTION

One of the most momentous events in European history, the French Revolution, ushers in the "modern world" of Europe and the particular problems that world raises for the State and society, Catholic life and cultural life, indeed the individual's whole existence.

1. *Causes and occasion.* General trends in thought, society, and politics combined with special conditions within France paved the way for revolutionary change which would spread from France all over Europe. When the wars of religion came to an end, the philosophers of the Enlightenment took to criticizing monarchical absolutism, the practice of imposing an established Church on the whole population, and the privileges enjoyed by a hereditary aristocracy. A new rationalist, utilitarian, and eudaemonist approach answered the claims of traditional authority with demands for a new "natural order" of human affairs which was to be worked out by autonomous reason (Locke, Montesquieu, Rousseau). It was not only the rising bourgeoisie but also sections of the nobility and clergy that echoed the "philosophers'" criticism of abuses in 18th-century France under the *ancien régime*. Discontent was stimulated by the American War of Independence and the crisis in the finances of the French State under the well-meaning but incapable King Louis XVI (1774–92). The Crown, proving too weak to carry out a thorough reform of the State, was first confronted by a "revolution of the privi-

leged" (Assembly of the Nobles, 1787). Then in 1788 when the Estates General were convoked (for the first time since 1614) under the imminent threat of national bankruptcy, the failure of the absolute monarchy was plain.

2. *The Revolution to the fall of the monarchy (1789–92).* Electoral agitation and the election and assembly of the Estates General (from May 1789) were in view of the establishment of a constitutional monarchy. Catholicism seemed in no danger at all; much was made of it as an element of cohesion in the new national community. But proceedings at the opening of the Estates General revealed that the political and social change which had set in had a momentum of its own; the Third Estate (which had twice as many members as the nobles and clergy) demanded individual voting instead of voting according to Estates. Considerable support was forthcoming from the ranks of the First Estate, where the lower clergy — more numerous by far — threw off the control of the bishops, most of whom were of noble rank. This "rebellion" of the lower clergy, whom a social gulf divided from their wealthy prelates, soon led to the *de facto* dissolution of the First Estate. Liberal-minded groups among the nobility likewise supported the Third Estate. The Crown attempted to keep the Estates separate, but finally ordered their amalgamation for common consultation. Now the bourgeoisie had the initiative. The Estates General had become the National Assembly. A new situation was created by organized mob demonstrations (storming of the Bastille, 14 July 1789), spontaneous disturbances among the rural population, and the King's irresolution. On the night of 4 August the National Assembly, led by representatives of the nobility and clergy, announced the abolition of all feudal rights and dues, all personal, regional and communal privileges. The Declaration of the Rights of Man and the Citizen, 4 to 11 August, meant that the National Assembly subscribed to the ideas of social equality and national unity. Thus it gave effect to the principle of the free movement of persons and goods, basic to bourgeois capitalist society, but it confined the principle of equality to the juridical sphere by maintaining the right to private property. (This soon gave rise to socialist criticism of

the "half-measures of the bourgeois revolution".)

Now the constitutional and legislative work of the Assembly was devoted to mobilizing further the radical bourgeoisie and limiting the Court's freedom of movement. By the constitution proclaimed on 2 September 1791 the King was left only a suspensive veto against decisions of the elective Chamber. The treatment of ecclesiastical matters in 1790/91 shows us the helplessness of the Crown and the exceedingly rapid change which had come about in the attitudes and forces at work. Along with the constitution, the laws dealing with the Church determined the destiny of the revolution, "since they led to a clash between widespread traditional religious loyalties and the philosophic dream of a purified religion with the secularist State in absolute control of the Church" (H. Herzfeld). Late in 1789 the National Assembly had decided to place all Church property "at the disposal of the nation" to relieve the financial crisis. In compensation, the clergy's salaries were to be paid by the State. Opinion was divided among the clerical deputies, some of whom inclined towards Gallicanism.

The turning-point in the relations between the Church and the Revolution came with the "Civil Constitution of the Clergy", July 1790, which reduced the 135 dioceses to 85, provided that bishops and parish priests be elected by assemblies of citizens, suppressed religious orders and associations, and reduced relationships with the papacy to a formal minimum. No previous understanding had been reached with Rome, later attempts at conciliation failed, and the State required the clergy to accept the Civil Constitution on oath. Thus a rift opened between the non-jurors and the "constitutional" clergy. In a brief of 10 May 1791, after being silent for too long, Pope Pius VI condemned not only the Civil Constitution of the Clergy but also the general principles of 1789, especially religious liberty. Meantime the schismatic "constitutional" Church was formed in France, with the help of the State, and took over all clerical offices. The non-jurors (about 55%) were extruded, soon persecuted, and many exiled. Religious conflict, trouble in foreign affairs, and renewed financial crises exacerbated the internal situation. Constitutional deliberations ended (September 1791) and new elections to the legislature brought the Girondists to power. They pressed for completion of the Revolution and had war declared on Austria (20 April 1792, "crusade to liberate the peoples"). Following a violent upheaval in Paris (Danton) and the attack on the Tuileries on 10 August 1792, the King was deposed.

3. *The reign of terror (1792–94)*. While the first wave of public terror inspired by military reverses and fear of counter-revolution was claiming its victims (September Massacres), the newly elected "National Convention" decided to abolish the monarchy. Introduction of a new calendar reflected the dechristianization of public life. The constitutional Church declined, but the nonjuror clergy were split by royalist attempts "to make religion a means instead of an end" (M. Emery). Louis XVI was condemned to death and executed (21 January 1793). The National Convention adopted emergency measures for internal and external security: revolutionary tribunals, committee of public safety (executive organ of the Convention), universal conscription (producing mass-armies for the Revolution). Terror reached its zenith from the autumn of 1793 to the summer of 1794, with civil war (La Vendée) and the execution of "suspects". At the same time cultural and religious life was made to serve revolutionary and anti-Christian propaganda; many churches were closed and attempts were made to set up a substitute religion, non-Christian and national. A new constitution adopted by the Convention in June 1793 signified the triumph of a lower middle-class, egalitarian democracy over the class distinction of the liberal bourgeois State of the 1791 constitution; it did not take effect because the Jacobin Robespierre ruled for a year with his terrorist dictatorship. While his significance for the maintenance of the Revolution against traditional forces in Europe is unquestionable, his rigidly doctrinaire figure is still the subject of discussion. Robespierre fell on 27/28 July 1794, as successes in war and foreign policy were bringing about a relaxation. People were sick of terror: the Revolution stood at the cross-roads.

4. *The Directory and the end of the Revolution (1795–99)*. For the next few years moderate republicans, in growing reliance on the army, steered a middle course between royalist reaction and continuing radicalism, trying to consolidate the achievements of the Revolution in a bourgeois class-society. With the end of the Convention, the constitution of 1795 entrusted power to a five-man Directory. A *corps législatif,* chosen by indirect suffrage, acted as a parliament. But despite impressive military successes the Directory was unable to halt civil war in the Vendée and overcome economic, social, and ecclesiastical disintegration. The anti-Catholic policy of the Convention continued, with only a brief respite in 1796/97. Then an attempt was made to negotiate a settlement with Rome, but military and political events in Italy had the opposite result: the revolutionary armies occupied Rome, in February 1799 Pius VI was taken in captivity to Florence and thence deported to France, where he died on 29 August. At Paris, thanks to the weakness of the Directory, General Bonaparte succeeded in his coup d'état of the eighteenth of Brumaire (9 November). He set up a provisional government to draft a constitution. Thus the revolutionary era ended in a military dictatorship and the way was opened to the Concordat of 1801, which took into account the steadfast vitality of the French Church and was the first attempt at a *modus vivendi* with the Church in post-revolutionary society.

5. *Conclusion*. The French Revolution and the Catholic Church came into "tragic conflict" (A. Latreille), with extraordinarily profound and lasting consequences for the Church's relations with the modern world born of that Revolution. Whereas the general attitude of Catholics towards the French Revolution was long one of extremely hostile and undiscriminating criticism (e.g., Cardinal Hergenröther: "The France produced by the Revolution was not Catholic; the only Catholic France was that which fell victim to the Revolution"), a more differentiated view has recently asserted itself, pointing out the Christian roots of the declaration on the rights of man and the contingent character of the actual course of events. A comprehensive re-interpretation of the French Revolution in the light of Vatican II (human dignity, religious liberty, pluralist society) is now due. It must do justice to the defensive reaction of the Church as a force in history and also to the ensuing dialectic

of Church and world. And it must also examine the whole process of modern secularization from the standpoint of secular history and ecclesiology alike.

See also *State, Society, Social Movements* II, *Enlightenment, Absolutism, Gallicanism, Rights of Man, Secularization.*

BIBLIOGRAPHY. H. Belloc, *The French Revolution* (2nd ed., 1911); J. M. Thompson, *The French Revolution* (2nd ed., 1944); A. Latreille, *L'Église catholique et la Révolution française,* 2 vols. (1946–50); J. Leflon, *La crise révolutionnaire 1789–1848* (1949); R. R. Palmer, *The Age of the Democratic Revolution. A Political History of Europe and America, 1760 to 1800,* 2 vols. (1959–64); G. Lefebvre, *The French Revolution. From its Origins to 1793* (1961); H. Maier, *Revolution und Kirche. Studien zur Frühgeschichte der christlichen Demokratie 1789–1850* (2nd ed., 1964); G. Lefebvre and others, eds., *The French Revolution. From 1793 to 1799* (1964); J. Godechot, *France and the Atlantic Revolution of the Eighteenth Century, 1770–1799* (1965).

Heinrich Lutz

FUNDAMENTAL THEOLOGY

Fundamental theology is the word now used for what used to be called apologetics. This does not mean that the subject-matter and goal of apologetics have been abandoned, but that they have been made part of a more comprehensive theological reflection, primarily a positive one, where apologetics plays a decisive role but is not the whole of fundamental theology.

If we start from the words themselves, fundamental theology means the investigations of the foundations in the realm of theology. These foundations are not artificially constructed like an ideology and they are not extrinsic elements. They are presupposed by theology and hence form part of it.

1. *Notion and object.* Theology, as the science of faith or of God's revelation to men, has various foundations. Fundamental theology does not claim to consider them all, but its approach is nonetheless definite and decisive. It may be described as a transcendental theology, inasmuch as it considers the nature and event of revelation as such, prior to all special theology or branches of theology. The question is: What is the basis and presupposition of all theology in each of its departments and what is its "overriding" determinant? What is the principle which provides beginning or end, according to the perspective chosen? What is the master-key which opens the way to each department? A theological science based on such considerations takes a place corresponding to that of ontology in philosophy and in the general scheme of thought.

The revelation of God who communicates and discloses himself is the foundation and principle and likewise the all-embracing truth which takes in all elements of revelation and hence all theological disciplines. Revelation supplies the premises and impulse for all theological argument. Its content is made explicit in the detail of its individual elements, but revelation as such, as the "transcendental" condition of possibility of theology, is presupposed, and cannot be interrogated in detail. J. S. Drey, the founder of the "Tübingen School", put the problem as follows: "Revelation, as the condition and determinant principle of all particular revelations, as that which mediates revelation into particulars, cannot appear as an object among the objects to which it has given rise: that is, the doctrine *de revelatione* cannot appear as one dogma among others. It is at the basis of them all as their presupposition." But this is precisely the object of fundamental theology as the theological science of foundations or basic science: revelation as the origin and heuristic principle and overriding unity of all branches of theology. In this sense, fundamental theology is basic and formal theology, postulated by theology itself, the result of its profounder reflection on itself. It is a constitutive and structural element of theology. Hence its central question is: What is the revelation of which the various branches of theology speak and which both founds and comprises all particulars of revelation? How does it appear, how is it to be understood? What are its structures and categories, how does it come about, how is it communicated?

Here the fundamental theology in question does not start from a general concept of revelation. It bases itself on the theological concept of revelation, as given, for instance, in the pregnant formula of Vatican I: "Deus se ipsum revelavit et aeterna voluntatis suae decreta" (*D* 1785). It is set the same limits by historical experience and transcendental *a priori* reflection to which the spirit is elsewhere subject as a being in history. Man accepts spontaneously a historical experience which is never fully amenable to reflection and investigates the *a priori* conditions of possibility of such actual experience, which is the only way to gain a real understanding of this experience. The question thus posed as to the nature and possibility of revelation has a number of implications which fundamental theology makes explicit: the absoluteness, the supreme power, the sovereign freedom, the personal nature of God.

This question entails another (whose purpose is to ask how the proofs can be given in articulate and methodical detail): Has revelation, as so understood and as so presenting itself, actually taken place? It is the question of the *de facto* occurrence of revelation. Are there proofs, reasons, credentials and testimonies for the revelation which came at a certain time and place? Are there proofs which can be tested? Are there testimonies which will satisfy the questing, questioning spirit that revelation is credible by nature, and as a happening and a reality? Have men reason to accept revelation in faith, so that they are intellectually justified in doing so and obliged in conscience to take this step?

Thus the task of fundamental theology is to describe the nature of revelation and to demonstrate its *de facto* existence by pointing to the criteria of revelation and the signs of its credibility. This is what gives this theological science its special character. It considers the basis for the various branches of theology and its own special perspective: the question of the credibility of revelation and the justification of faith which this contains. It has to show the justification of faith, in the act of faith itself, which here above all is a faith calling for insight: *fides quaerens intellectum*. It is the problem of the *credibilitas rationalis*.

Thus the legitimacy and the necessity of fundamental theology stem from the fact that God has disclosed himself for the world and man in his revelation, that this revelation concerns man, the question of whose salvation is posed and decided by it. But this is only possible if revelation of itself appears in this way, if it gives testimony before men, if it justifies and accredits its statement, if it is capable of meeting and addressing man in his inmost self, if it corresponds in some way to the potentialities of man, world and

history, if it can fairly meet and persuasively answer the questions, objections and doubts which it raises.

The NT documents, in the form of living preaching, the revelation of God which culminates in Christ. But since it is testimony and proclamation about God's word and work, it is also testimony for men, and presents itself as such, arguing, explaining and substantiating its claims. It presents itself as a credible and well-founded answer by pointing to the credentials which the claim to revelation offers. These credentials, according to Scripture, are the "signs", the "works", the purpose of which is clear. The summary which forms the conclusion of St. John's Gospel expresses this intention clearly: "Now Jesus did many other signs in the presence of his disciples, which are not written in this book; but these are written that you may believe that Jesus is the Christ, the Son of God, and that believing you may have life in his name." (Jn 20:30f.)

Like the preaching of Jesus, the apostles' preaching about Jesus Christ is always centred on and impelled by two components, as it were: God who has disclosed himself in his word, ultimately in the Word who is the Son (Heb 1:1), and man, who is to come in faith to this God of revelation, for whom the way must be made ready, who must be able to justify his faith.

These unquestionable and essential truths, attested by Scripture, which make it kerygma and not a mere formal record, justify fundamental theology and make it necessary. For it does justice to the situation involved: revelation — God disclosing himself to men — men confronted by God revealing himself — men confronted with revelation. Hence comes the specific method of fundamental theology. If it is to substantiate and justify revelation as such and faith, by the demonstration of credibility, it cannot argue from the truths of revelation and from faith. It cannot use dogmatic proofs. It must have recourse to rational, philosophical and historical argument: to metaphysical thought for the nature and criteria of revelation, to historical thought for the fact of revelation. Fundamental theology cannot use revelation as a middle term in its proofs, since revelation is the goal of its efforts and the source of its inspiration. Its efforts must be rational in nature. It appeals to the verdict of insight. Hence, for instance, fundamental theology cannot draw proofs from Scripture or the doctrinal decisions of the Church by virtue of their inspiration or infallibility, since the inspiration of Scripture and the infallibility of the Church have still to be demonstrated and cannot be assumed. Scripture and Church teaching are to be treated as documents and sources to be investigated by the methods of philosophy and historical criticism, insofar as the sources in question can throw light on the nature, fact and credibility of revelation as such philosophical and historical thinking demands. The Church is an essential theme in fundamental theology inasmuch as it has a transcendental dimension for theology. The Church is mediator and depository of revelation, and also *the* believer. Hence the Church is *the* condition of possibility of theology. This dimension and its claims must be explained and justified in fundamental theology as an intrinsic part of the whole.

2. *Methods and application.* But there is still another special sense in which fundamental theology has to be an investigation of foundations and a basic theological science. When it enquires into the conditions of possibility of revelation, it must consider how revelation, which is "not of this world" is to come forward as revelation entering this world; how revelation, which as God's word is beyond space and time, can take place in space and time; how revelation, which does not stem from the mind and words of men, can still be word and event for men and their minds and their capacities as beings of this world and of history. Hence as science of foundations and basic theology, fundamental theology has also to consider whether divine revelation which presents itself in a certain way is possible in the world of beings and for man. The question can and must be put, whether the world in which man finds himself a being, and man's own existence and nature, are such that there is room, openness and possibility for revelation from God. For this must be a freely given revelation, beyond what is already given and recognizable by nature. And it must be such that it is acceptable by men as "revelation" in the world, in words and in history, while still remaining God's own most proper word. It must not come under the creaturely *a priori* of the finite spirit, under pain of ultimately not differing in quality from "natural revelation" given through the world

and man's mind. This presupposes man's openness for revelation, without prejudice to the freedom of God in revealing himself, and without laying down beforehand inadmissible rules for the how and what of revelation. Then, the word of God himself only escapes being reduced to a word from God about God, in the *a priori* mental constitution of man, if God is himself a component, in the grace of faith (as "uncreated" grace), of the hearing of the word of God — which of course can only exist as heard and believed.

Clearly, in this sense too and in these perspectives there can be a basic science of theology as a fundamental theology. It will be guided by ontological and anthropological principles and it will furnish an indication of the credibility of (a possible) revelation which is most important by reason of its ontological, anthropological and existential roots — its reference to the components and structures of existence. Since revelation comes to man in the world, space and time, the world, space and time, and above all man himself and all that determines him, must contain the presuppositions and prefigurations which make revelation possible and are therefore produced beforehand by revelation itself. These very elements must be brought to light and expounded in a theological science which aims at being a principle and foundation; otherwise it would not make good its claims: it would not be "fundamental" enough.

We can therefore see in what sense fundamental theology is the foundation of theology. It would be too much to claim that the questions and answers of fundamental theology are the sole foundation of theology as a science of faith and revelation, or the sole foundation of faith itself. It might possibly be so, if faith in God the revealer followed with logical rigour or psychological compulsion from insight into the grounds of credibility, like the conclusion from the premises. But such is not the case. Hence the notion of foundation in fundamental theology needs to be qualified. Faith in the true sense in the divine revelation as a definite concrete reality is a new act and a new decision on the part of man, posited because of the authority of God who reveals himself. The authority of the *Deus revelans* is the real motive of faith which produces the act of faith and its real ultimate foundation. Knowledge of the credibility of revelation and of the faith which corresponds to it, in the two ways described above, creates the conditions and presuppositions whereby the assurance of faith can be explicitly possible, justified and demanded. Insofar as these conditions and presuppositions are a foundation, fundamental theology is the foundation of theology. This was summed up by Augustine in the pregnant words: "Nemo crederet, nisi videret, esse credendum." The "videre esse credendum" is concerned with the broad ring of truths which have been spoken of apropos of the justification of faith and are ordinarily called the *motiva credibilitatis.*

The questions dealt with in fundamental theology, seen from the standpoint of supernatural faith, are preliminaries and not the main questions. But from the standpoint of the human being who is to be the site, recipient and partner of a possible revelation, they are in fact decisive. If they are not asked or if they are dismissed too quickly, then — as it is instructive to note — when man is trying to penetrate explicitly the grounds of its existence, revelation is out of the question; it does not appear as a question worth putting, as a possibility, as an invitation, as an obligation. And man does not "dream" of going into the matter of revelation. But by the believer who reflects on his faith and explores its presuppositions and possibility — for the sake of the wholeness of his faith — this question and above all its possible answer must be taken with the utmost seriousness. These presuppositions and conditions may well determine the destiny of a man's faith.

3. *The kerygmatic character of fundamental theology.* Discussion of the foundations and presuppositions of theology and faith brings out further aspects when the effort is made to apply fundamental theology to practice. There is first the missionary aspect.

Fundamental theology can become missionary theology, addressing itself primarily to men outside the faith or on the threshold of faith. Then, as the science of the encounter of revelation and man, it takes man as it finds him in his human nature, situation and existence and tries to put him in contact with revelation. It calls his attention to something within him which is open to the word of God which transcends him, and addresses him without stemming from him,

for the work of salvation offered him in that word of revelation. It shows him how truly he longs to hear it, how safely it can fetch him home, how receptive and ready he is for it, and how much he depends on it. It tries further to remove the difficulties which stand in the way of seeing and hearing God's revelation. In unfeigned solidarity, honestly trying to encounter and communicate, it enters into the situation of questing man. It asks his questions and pushes them further, and thus tries to go beyond man and his perhaps too hastily drawn boundaries and inadmissible restrictions. Its effort is to expound the word of God's self-revelation as the answer to man, as the full and definitive disclosure, illumination, fulfilment and realization of man, in the sense of the words: "What you worship as unknown, this I proclaim to you." (Acts 17:23.) It works on the theological principle of the theology of existence: "To speak of man is to speak of God, to speak of God is to speak of man."

It may be said of "missionary" fundamental theology that it is theology in the form of pastoral care, and pastoral care in the form of reflection (E. Brunner). It is the response to the command: "Always be prepared to make a defence *(apologia)* to anyone who calls you to account for the hope that is in you." (1 Pet 3:15.) Hope is characteristic of Christian existence, while "being without hope" is characteristic of existence apart from Christ. The account given of this hope to one who asks for it should be so revealing that the questioner can be gripped, moved and perhaps won by this hope and its setting. The approach recommended in the same text, "Do it with gentleness and reverence, since your conscience is clear" (1 Pet 3:15f.), is still valid today. It is incumbent not only on the faithful but on the theologian reflecting scientifically on his faith, and it is an encouragement to him. The goal of such efforts is described by Paul as "taking every thought captive to the obedience of Christ" (2 Cor 10:5).

Along with the missionary element, there is also the apologetic, in the strict, original sense of the word. In 2 Cor, a very personal letter, Paul speaks of the "warfare" which he has to conduct, and of the weapons of this war. The weapons of God "have divine power to destroy strongholds. We destroy arguments and every proud obstacle to the knowledge of God." (2 Cor 19:4f.) The first letter of Peter, having called for the Apologia of the Logos of hope, affirms confidently that those who revile the Christian life will be put to shame by the Christian answer. This does not amount to a biblical foundation of apologetics as a theological science. But it affirms unmistakably that defence against and above all offensives against hostile positions, accusations and distortions are among the functions and tasks of the Christian faith and its preachers. If this is so, it is a matter which must be carefully considered in the science of faith.

Hence apologetics as an aspect of fundamental theology is concerned with the defence of revelation as such, of its nature, existence, possibility, claims and credentials, against all that is brought up as objections, doubts, misgivings and attacks. Such misgivings are voiced in the name of man and human reason. There is hardly any position which has not been invoked, right down to the present day, to reject and combat revelation. To be silent or to surrender one's weapons would be a sign of weakness and faint-heartedness. There is a duty of defending the faith by giving the answer of faith, and this is best done not by grappling at close quarters with each attack, but by discovering its presuppositions, analysing its nature and trying to win it over.

At the present time, efforts are being made to draw up a programme of a "new fundamental theology" (K. Rahner), which as a basic theological discipline and an integrating element of dogmatics aims at raising to an articulate level the pre-scientific understanding of the faith. Its aim is therefore to produce evidence for the inner credibility of the truths of revelation and to investigate the conditions under which these truths can be accepted by men existentially at any given moment of their existence. The effort is not directed towards the explicitation of the content of revelation in all its manifold aspects, but to concentrate it in the "mystery of Christ".

See also *Apologetics, Theology, Revelation, Ideology, Ontology, Tübingen School, Transcendental Theology, Experience, Reflection, Kerygma, Faith* III, IV.

BIBLIOGRAPHY. J. S. Drey, *Die Apologetik als wissenschaftliche Nachweisung der Göttlichkeit des Christentums in seiner Erscheinung,* 3 vols. (1838–47); M. Blondel, "Lettres sur les exigences de la pensée contemporaine en matière de l'apologétique", *Annales de Philosophie chrétienne* 66 (1895–96); E. Brunner, *Revelation and Reason* (1946); H. Brillant and M. Nédoncelle, *Apologétique. Nos raisons de croire et réponses aux objections* (2nd ed., 1948); G. Söhngen, *Philosophische Einübung in die Theologie* (1955); H. Fries, "Newman und die Grundprobleme der heutigen Apologetik", *Newman-Studien,* III (1957), pp. 225–47; L. Linden and W. Costello, *Fundamentals of Religion* (1956); T. Corbishley, *Religion is Reasonable* (1960); H. Urs von Balthasar, *Herrlichkeit,* I (1961); Y. Congar, *La foi et la théologie* (1962); K. Rahner, *Hörer des Wortes. Zur Grundlegung einer Religionsphilosophie* (2nd ed., 1963); G. Ebeling, *Word and Faith* (1963); H. Bouillard, *Logique de la foi* (1964); A. Dulles, *Apologetics and the Biblical Christ* (1964); M. Blondel, *Letter on Apologetics and History of Dogma* (1965); K. Rahner, *Schriften zur Theologie,* VII (1966), pp. 54–76.

Heinrich Fries

G

GALLICANISM

The term "Gallicanism" in the sense of a certain doctrine and practice which persisted during various periods was coined by the historians of the 19th century. There are two aspects to be noted. One is the historical manifestation of a French nationalism in Church affairs, including the reaction of the monarchy to the centralism of the papal Curia, which, however, allowed the French State many rights in the ecclesiastical sphere. The other is the theory of canon law, compounded of conciliarist, episcopalist and nationalist elements, which was formulated towards the end of the Middle Ages, on the basis of the historical position of the French monarchy, and was given political expression in the "Declaration of Gallican Liberties" under Louis XIV (1682).

The *de facto* and *de jure* status of the French monarchy with regard to the Church (including rights of patronage and regalia) had been built up in the early Middle Ages by the notion of the sacredness of the kingship. The anointing of the monarch gave him a semi-official standing in the Church. In the Frankish kingdom he was "King of the bishops". King and episcopate worked together at provincial councils and thus there grew up a sense of collective responsibility, while at the same time the episcopate received certain privileges from the king as the first *ordo* in the State. This epoch left legendary memories. The theoretical basis of the later Gallicanism, formulated in the 16th and 17th centuries in many books on Church history and canon law (P. Pithou, P. Dupuy,

P. de Marca, E. Richer) appealed to the notion that the Gallican freedoms were the universally acknowledged freedoms of the primitive Church — which had been preserved without taint of heresy only in the Gallican Church.

It was further maintained that the French monarchy had always been a safeguard of the Church and the Pope (under the Merovingians and Carolingians). The close connections between king and Church (as outlined above) then became the main argument for the claims of the French king to a national Church. The resistance of the Curia to the interventions of the French king brought about a decided reaction. After the Gregorian reform, Gallicanism saw itself as opposed to Roman centralization and the doctrine of the *plenitudo potestatis in spiritualibus et temporalibus*. The conflict came to a head in the clash between Boniface VIII and Philip the Fair. The historical consequences were grave, because the King's triumph was complete, and the theological results showed themselves in countless controversial books, which conjured up the conflict, and Philip's appeal to public opinion. The royal claims (to certain prerogatives) were put forward in such a way as to reject the papal claim to the *plenitudo potestatis* (P. Dubois, P. Flotte, G. de Plaisans, John of Paris). Practical measures were taken by the Crown lawyers to restrict the rights of the Church. In the name of the King, they continued to claim jurisdiction in matters of liturgy, canon law and episcopal election.

The Great Schism brought these different tendencies out into the open. At the same time that it disqualified the Pope from governing the Church, it made the King the supreme court of appeal. The withdrawal of obedience in 1396 gave to the Church of France a real autonomy. More important again was the work of the universities. The theologians of the day rethought the whole treatise on the Church and thus came to assert the superiority of a General Council over the Pope. And so now claims of a political complexion were backed up by theological reasoning. From now on there was to be also a theological Gallicanism.

Assemblies of the clergy took place under Philip the Fair. In 1561 they became an institution which continued to develop its own internal organization, meeting at regular intervals and so helping to form a less individualistic episcopate imbued with reforming and pastoral zeal.

When appealing against the Pope to the King, the Gallicans did not realize that they were substituting one kind of absolutism for another. In the 17th century this royal absolutism was to lead to a renewal of Gallicanism which by then appeared as a consistent and coherent teaching. Louis XIV called an assembly of the clergy in 1682 with the express purpose of intimidating the Pope over the question of the *regale* (the right of the French kings to receive the revenues of vacant bishoprics). Bossuet succeeded in reducing the influence of the parliamentary Gallicans, and in his Four Articles set forward a Gallicanism of the bishops: the independence of the crown in temporal matters, the authority of the decrees of the Council of Constance, the maintenance of Gallican liberties (the royal prerogatives) and the rejection of the personal infallibility of the Pope (his authority depending on the assent of the Church).

This charter is a summary of what we might describe as "classical Gallicanism": a conscious and coherent attitude, loyal to the past and seeking to make its own standards and point of view prevail in the future. It was an anachronistic return to the Fathers, to a pre-Gregorian and pre-scholastic Church, to a Church more theological and mystical than canonical and political. But this also involved a repudiation of the doctrinal and disciplinary developments of the last six hundred years and a reserved attitude to the papal invitation to the national Churches to rid themselves of the burden of their own individual history

and prejudices. One can easily see why the Holy See demanded that the Four Articles should be withdrawn (Alexander VIII, 1690; D 1322–6).

Now that French Gallicanism appeared to be of universal and lasting validity, it soon found its imitators in Josephinism and Febronianism. Though abandoned in theory by Napoleon, it reappeared in the *Constitution civile du clergé* as later on in the *Articles Organiques*. One can also see, according to an age old pattern repeated through the centuries, that this doctrinaire and aggressive Gallicanism led directly to a reaction by the ultramontane party represented in the 19th century by Joseph de Maistre and Lamennais. The *Syllabus* appeared as a culmination to this critical offensive by condemning many of the fundamental tenets of Gallicanism. The proclamation of papal infallibility was directly opposed to two of the Four Articles.

Gallicanism may now seem only a matter of past history, but it is still active in the modern mentality.

See also *Episcopalism, Reform* II C, *Schism* IV, *Conciliarism, Josephinism, Absolutism.*

BIBLIOGRAPHY. L.Pastor, *History of the Popes*, 40 vols. (1891–1953); *DTC*, IV, cols. 185–205, VI, cols. 1096–157, XI, cols. 1878–96; V. Martin, *Le Gallicanisme et la réforme catholique* (1919); J. Rivière, *Le problème de l'église et de l'état au temps de Philippe le Bel* (1926); J. Lecler, "Qu'est-ce que les libertés de l'Église gallicane?", *RSR* 23 (1933), pp. 385–410, 542–568; 24 (1934), pp. 47–85; V. Martin, *Les origines du Gallicanisme,* 2 vols. (1938 f.); J. McManners, *French Ecclesiastical Society under the Ancien Régime* (1961).

Émile Delaruelle

GNOSIS

1. *Definition and typology.* Gnosis designates both an essentially non-Christian religion of redemption in late antiquity, represented in various associations, and the central concept of that religion, which appeared more or less at the same time as primitive Christianity and spread over Samaria, Syria, Asia Minor, Egypt, Italy, North Africa, etc. Gnosis soon came in contact with Christianity, and made use of its doctrines in strange exaggerations and distortions. This form of Gnosis, beside which a pagan Gnosis also existed, was considered as a Christian heresy ("Gnosticism")

and combated as such by the Church as a dangerous rival. The conflict between the Great Church and Gnosis had already been signalled in certain texts of the NT, where there are hints of early forms of the Gnostic sectarianism which reached a high point in the 2nd century. Gnosis succumbed in the end, though not before it had established itself in the form of Manichaeism from North Africa to Central Asia. An Eastern branch of the Gnosis of late antiquity still exists today, especially in Iraq, as Mandaeism. Traces of the survival of Gnosis can be found in the doctrines and practices of some medieval sects, such as the Bogomils, the Catharists and the Albigenses. Gnosis is often used in a broad sense to designate a notion of religious or philosophical knowledge which appears in many forms in the phenomenology of religion, in philosophy, in Christian theology and ideological criticism. But as the central concept of the Gnosis of late antiquity, Gnosis is religious knowledge with the following characteristics.

a) Gnosis is knowledge of the spiritual self of the Gnostic, and of the divinity which is consubstantial with this self. This knowledge appears as recognition of the origin of the spirit-self, of the cause of its enslavement in the world of darkness and of the ascent by which the spirit escapes into the heavenly realm of light. Hence it is knowledge of this realm of light and of the genesis, nature and destiny of matter, the world and the creators of the world. b) Gnosis comes from divine revelation and is mostly given through redeemers or envoys. c) The knowledge of the Gnostic is of direct soteriological and ontic value. Once the spirit-self has been awakened by divine revelation, the Gnostic is enabled to distinguish good and evil (light and darkness) as ontic realms and can thus make a decision which in its ethical execution (in practical life and very often in cultic acts and sometimes magic) leads to a division of these realms and hence to a division of the cosmos which comes to a climax in a universal eschatology. The themes of the "Gnostic myth" are described as follows by the Valentinian Theodotus: Gnosis is "the knowledge of who we were, what we have become, where we were, whither we have been cast, whither we hasten, whence we are delivered, what is birth and what is re-birth" (Excerpts from Theodotus, 78, 2 [in Clement of Alexandria]). Though the extremely diversified objectivations or conscious myths of Gnosis are not easily reduced to any system, a basic common form may be illustrated by means of a paradigm which allows us to combine under a common denominator the various ideal types which can be derived from the writings of the Gnostic communities.

The basic structure of the myth is a dualism which displays two aspects.

a) There is a dualism between the good, spiritual Godhead beyond the cosmos, with its divine sphere (pleroma) and its beings of light ("aeons") and the ignorant, lower demiurge, the creator of the cosmos, with his archons (the spirits of the planets etc.), matter, the cosmos and the world of men. The distinction between the supreme Godhead and the inferior demiurge is always essential in Gnosis, though the various systems have different concepts of him. He is either (more or less) evil, ignorant and hostile to God, or he is a degenerate being of light which finally finds its way back to the realm of light, as in Mandaeism. The demiurge has sometimes a less extreme position, as among the Valentinians, where he attains a certain salvation after the end of the world. But a more favourable view of the demiurge does not mean that the existence of evil, hypostatized in many forms, becomes a less acute problem.

The Gnostic attitude to the demiurge, mostly identified with the creator God of a despised or rejected OT, and the radical distinction between the demiurge and the supreme God, makes it impossible to include esoteric Judaism (often called "Jewish Gnosticism") under the heading of Gnosis. Such Judaism remained faithful to monotheism. But Manichaeism is a Gnosis, even though its demiurge is a godhead of light who establishes the cosmos, at the command of the good God, in order to sift out the light swallowed by the darkness.

b) There is another dualism, a necessary consequence of the former, between the divine spirit-self of man (or of the Gnostic) and the demiurge along with his Powers and their creations (the cosmos, matter, bodies, fate and time).

(i) The Powers of the demiurge produce both the human body, in which divine light is imprisoned as its spirit-self, and a power (often called ψυχή but also given other names) which is implanted in man to bemuse the spirit-self and so retain it in the world.

Hence there is often a trichotomy in Gnostic anthropology. Man (or the Gnostic) is composed of the spirit-self ("spiritus", "humectatio luminis", "anima", etc., in Greek and Coptic πνεῦμα, νοῦς, ψυχή, etc.), the body, and the demonic power often termed the ψυχή. Behind this three-fold division a two-fold one may be discerned, since the demonic planetary ψυχή belongs rather to the darkness than the light. Since the spirit-self is often called ψυχή in the texts, in contrast to the documents where the mystifying power is given this name, the meaning of ψυχή must be sought in each case from the context.

(ii) The imprisonment of the light in matter is usually explained by a series of notions which outline the pre-history and genesis of demiurges, the world and man. In Gnosis of the "Syro-Egyptian" type, a divine being falls from the realm of light and so brings into existence the creative Powers, the world and man. Thus evil proceeds from the realm of light by an emanation which takes the devious route of a tragic fall. The fallen being is either a male figure (ἄνθρωπος, "Man" or "Primordial Man" ["Urmensch"], as in the Poimandres of the Corpus Hermeticum or among the Naassenes), or a female hypostasis, like the Sophia of the Valentinian and similar systems. The cause of the fall is ignorance or passion. The figure in question is a cosmological principle, since it is cause of the genesis of the world, and an anthropological principle, since it constitutes the spirit-self of man, which is a fragment or a production of the fallen light. In the "Iranian" type of Gnosis, darkness or evil is not an emanation from the realm of light, since light and darkness are primordial independent kingdoms opposed to one another. The prelude to the imprisonment of light is an attack by the darkness. In the case of the Manichaean Urmensch (or of his elements of light), the cause of his descent, however, is the desire of the light to overcome darkness by struggling with it or by self-sacrifice. This schema also appears in combination with the "Syro-Egyptian" type. While the sparks of light imprisoned in the world are often considered to be "portions" of these hypostases of the light, the hypostases contribute in various ways to the work of redemption — a point which is over-simplified by researchers when they try to express it by the paradigms of "the myth of the redeemer", "the myth of the primordial man as redeemer" — the salvator salvatus or salvator salvandus. The fallen light which has to be delivered is often variously located in the different systems. It is thought of for preference as enclosed in human bodies, but sometimes also exists outside men in the archons and in nature, as in Manichaeism.

(iii) There is no consistent answer in Gnosis to the question of whether all men have a spirit-self and hence can be redeemed, or whether this spiritual element and hence redemption is confined to a part of mankind. In one group, all men possess a spark of the light, though the systems vary as to whether the entirety of the fallen light will be saved or not.

Another group divides men basically into those in whom the light is embodied and who can therefore be saved (the "pneumatics") and those who contain no spark of light and therefore perish (the "hylics"). In the system of Valentinus, however, another intermediate category is introduced, that of the "psychics", who are capable of some sort of salvation if they keep the precepts of the main Church. The transmigration of souls is a feature of many of the systems in both groups, it being important for the successive sifting out of the sparks of light. The fallen light is roused to Gnosis by the call of Gnostic revelation to the pneumatics, and this awakening is the initial phase of the ascent in the myth's view of individual (and universal) eschatology. As regards morals, the conduct of the Gnostic is basically determined by two extreme positions. One is that of a radical rejection of the world in asceticism, the other is an equally radical rejection of the world in an antinomian libertinism — though rejection of the law need not always be libertinistic, as Marcion shows. The notion that actions are indifferent is an intermediate position which is rather rare. These ethical attitudes are based on the dualism between matter and spirit in Gnostic anthropology, which is consistent with the rejection of the demiurge and his creations. This rejection enables the Gnostic to assert a freedom which makes him superior to the world, though the roots of his freedom are all negative.

The eschatology of Gnosis gives priority to the individual's destiny, which is seen as definitive deliverance. The myth describes it as the ascent of the soul after death through the planetary spheres, a journey which can be prepared for by rites and magic.

But individual eschatology remains in the context of the general hope, which envisages the ultimate re-integration into the pleroma of all the fallen light which can be saved. After the re-integration comes the end of the world, which is the definite separation of the divine from the non-divine. The irreversible process by which the last stage is attained is the eschatological orientation of Gnosis. The Gnostic dualism of matter and spirit excludes the hope of an eschatological renewal of the world and of a bodily resurrection.

2. *Origin and essence.* The very complex phenomenon of Gnosis is explained in very different ways, and its relations to primitive Christianity are also viewed in widely different lights. Most specialists have abandoned the "heresiological" standpoint of the ancient Church, for which Gnosis was a deformation of Christianity. The discovery or the closer study of original sources in the 19th and 20th centuries enlarged the concept of Gnosis and enabled it to be regarded as predominantly a specifically independent religious phenomenon which displays a new mentality throughout all the well-known components from the Hellenistic and Oriental world which it adopted into its system. Scholars are mostly concerned with the history of themes. The highly diversified phenomenon of Gnosis can generally be given an adequate explanation by assigning the manifold themes to the backgrounds to which they seem to belong — "Greek", "Hellenistic", "Oriental", "Christian", "Jewish", "Iranian", etc. — though these spheres themselves are often variously described by the scholars in question. The origin and essence of Gnosis is then explained, according to the line of research adopted, as a combination of various elements from the various spheres — or of the phenomena which are supposed to be characteristic of the various spheres, such as certain philosophies or religions. In such schemata, certain components are mostly taken to be predominant in each case, and hence to supply the key to the origin and essence of Gnosis. Thus A. von Harnack, for instance, described Gnosis as a "radical Hellenization of Christianity", a view also upheld by E. de Faye, F. C. Burkitt and H. Langerbeck. For H. Leisegang Gnosis was a distortion of Greek philosophy, while R. McL. Wilson describes Gnosis in the narrow sense of the term as "the product of a fusion of Christianity and Hellenistic thought". For H.-H. Schaeder it was the Hellenization of ancient oriental religions. A mainly "Oriental" genealogy was proposed as early as the 18th century by J. L. Mosheim, for whom it was a *philosophia orientalis*. This is also the view of such scholars as K. Kessler ("Babylonian"), W. Anz, W. Bousset and in particular of R. Reitzenstein. Reitzenstein regarded Gnosis as a form of the religion of ancient Iran. G. Widengren is a more recent upholder of this view, on which the criticism made by C. Colpe is highly relevant. In the discussion of "oriental" or "hellenistic" origins, Jewish components (cf. B. K. Sturmer) or "heterodox Judaism" were often considered important. But authors like M. Friedländer, G. Quispel, J. Daniélou and R. McL. Wilson (apropos of the pre-Christian origins of Gnosis) hold that the Jewish elements are actually the main constitutive ones, as also in Mandaeism.

The pre-Christian origin of Gnosis is maintained in particular by the supporters of "oriental" and "heterodox Jewish" origins. Along with the historical derivation of themes, psychological and sociological explanations are offered in particular by G. Quispel, who describes Gnosis as "the mythical projection of the experience of the self" (after C. G. Jung) and by R. M. Grant, who sees the main roots of Gnosis in the collapse of Jewish eschatological hopes after the fall of Jerusalem, A.D. 70. Some scholars, e.g., U. Bianchi, also combine explicitly the historical method with a phenomenology concerned with the affinities of various types. The philosophical interpretation of H. Jonas, however, who regards the Gnostic "attitude to existence" as basically novel, is determined both by the philosophical problems posed by the early Heidegger and by the difficulties of the history of themes and the psychological and sociological approaches. He does not make use of his interpretation to give a historical analysis of the causes of Gnosis. R. Bultmann, who accepts to a great extent the findings of the students of comparative religion, also discusses Gnosis in terms of an existential and ontological analysis of existence. He also makes the origins of Gnosis pre-Christian, and holds that this initial stage of Gnosis and Christianity influenced each other.

3. *Gnosis and the New Testament.* There are two main problems of method here. a) As is well known, all our documentation for a fully-fledged Gnosis is from the 2nd century A.D. and later. These documents, which often vary widely in time and in structure, are used to construct show-models of Gnosis — especially of a Gnostic "Myth of the Redeemer" and an "Urmensch-Redeemer-Myth", cf. H. Schlier, E. Käsemann, R. Bultmann. This is often done without a correspondingly critical check on the findings of the "school of history of religions", whose categories were to a great extent decisive in the construction of the models in question. Little attention was often paid to the fact that these models minimized and smoothed out important differentiations in the sources, so that the problems of the theme of redemption in Gnosis ceased to be seen in all their acuteness and artificial spring-boards were laid for the following stages of research. Such antedated models were then compared more or less extensively with certain NT writings, and similarities in terminology were used to prove the influence of (proto-) Gnostic tendencies on NT authors — an influence conceived in various ways according to the varying interests of the researchers. Another result of this method was that errors combated relentlessly in the NT, and often defined in very different ways by scholars, could now be classified as (proto-) Gnostic.

b) As a historical phenomenon, Gnosis has a "pre-history" to which the patristic tradition offers pointers and for which the designation "Early" Gnosticism or "Pre-Gnosticism" is admissible, though there is a difficulty in using this category because the presence of Gnosis can only be definitely ascertained when *all* the essential concepts are connected up in a whole. Hence when only individual themes crop up, it is often begging the question to consider them as reflecting a constituted "Gnostic myth" or a prototype of Gnosis strictly speaking as it appears later. Sometimes such themes are only elements of a non-Gnostic frame of thought. It is with these sorts of reserves in mind that one should approach the suggestions of links with Gnosis or a Pre-Gnosis in the fragmentary indications of the NT.

It seems hazardous to accept the existence of a (Pre-)Gnosis among Paul's opponents at Corinth. The discussion of Wisdom in 1 Cor 1 and 2 hardly suggests a Gnostic myth of "Sophia" as redeemer. Other themes, such as the verdict passed on sexuality, 6:12–20; 7:32–34, 38, the contrast between ψυχικοί and πνευματικοί, 2:14f.; 15:21, 44–49, the "pneumatic" sense of perfection, 4:8, and the denial of the resurrection, 15:29–32; 2 Cor 5:1–5, may seem to present apparent analogies with Gnosis. But in spite of ingenious reconstructions, the general frame of thought in which these themes are supposed to be connected remains ultimately obscure, and the heretics in question (cf. 2 Cor 10–13) cannot be identified with certainty. They may well fit in to the general but rather vague framework of a "pneumatic enthusiasm". The heresy at Colossae (veneration of the στοιχεῖα τοῦ κόσμου, Col 2:8, 20, which are called ἀρχαί and ἐξουσίαι at 2:10, 15 and identified with the ἄγγελοι at 2:18) is mostly regarded as a form of Gnosis, the στοιχεῖα etc. being supposed to be the Gnostic Archons or the Gnostic world of light. In the first instance, Gnosis can be excluded, because it is against the mind of Gnosis to worship the evil Powers of the demiurge, and in the second instance because the aeons of light in Gnosis cannot be identified with cosmic powers. The notion of the "Body of Christ" which is so strongly emphasized in Col and Eph is often explained as the reflection of a Gnostic Anthropos-Myth of a redeemer, and statements which seem to imply it (Col 1:17f.; Eph 4:13; 5:23; descent and ascent of the redeemer, Eph 4:8–10; heavenly building, Eph 2:20f.; wall of partition, Eph 2:14–16) are treated as critical Christianizations of Gnostic thought. But there is greater heuristic value in the efforts to find the religious background in the ambience of early Judaeo-Hellenistic speculation of the type of Philo. The "Gnosis falsely so called" of the Pastoral Letters (1 Tim 6:20; sexual and food taboos, 1 Tim 4:3; myths, 1 Tim 1:4; 4:7; 6:20; Tit 1:14; 3:9); the resurrection already accomplished (2 Tim 2:18) may be regarded as reflecting an early form of Gnosis, even though the features indicated remain disconnected and are rather meagre. Acts 8:4–25, the pericope dealing with Simon Magus ("that Power of God which is called Great", 8:10), provides a link with early Gnosis.

The denunciations of Rev 2:6, 14–16, 20–24 may possibly be directed against an early form of Gnostic libertinism. In Ephesus

(Rev 2:6) and Pergamum (2:15) there are heretics called "Nicolaites", probably to be identified with the heretics of Thyateira, 2:20–24, but their connection with the later Nicolaites (Irenaeus, *Adv. Haer.*, I, 26, 3) remains obscure. It is possible that the denunciations of Jud (cf. 2 Pet 2:1–22) are directed against Gnostics of a similar type. They despise the angelic powers (Jud 8), give their lusts free rein (vv. 8, 16, 18) and are described by the author opprobriously as ψυχικοί (v. 19).

It is highly questionable that 1 Jn contains polemics against early Gnostic heretics ("Antichrists", 2:18, 22) who contested the incarnation (4:2f., cf. 2 Jn 7) and denied that Jesus was the Christ or the Son of God (2:22; 4:14; 5:5). The Gnostic Christology (cf. Cerinthus in Irenaeus, *Adv. Haer.*, I, 26, 1) re-constructed by some scholars with the help of 1 Jn 5:6 in particular, is simply an interpretation, which remains open to doubt.

Research into the background and interests of Jn allots a large place to the paradigm of the "Gnostic redeemer myth" (for which texts from Mandaeism in particular are adduced), since this schema — which, however, finds less and less favour today — might seem to make the Johannine Christology more easily understandable. It is no doubt possible that Gnostic schemata had some influence, at least on the metaphors of the descent and ascent of the redeemer (Jn 3:13; cf. Phil 2:6–11). But such analogies cannot be the key to the essential meaning of the Johannine assertions, according to which salvation appears in the historical Jesus. At any rate, Christ is not represented in Jn as the "Urmensch-Redeemer" whose task is to awaken the "spirit-selves" of the Gnostics, consubstantial with himself but buried in matter.

See also *Gnosticism, Manichaeism, Mandaeism, Catharists, Theological Methodology* I, *Aeons, Dualism.*

BIBLIOGRAPHY. GENERAL: For the sources, see bibliography on *Gnosticism, Manichaeism, Mandaeism.* — F. C. Baur, *Die christliche Gnosis* (1835); M. Friedländer, *Der vorchristliche jüdische Gnostizismus* (1898); W. Bousset, *Hauptprobleme der Gnosis* (1907); A. von Harnack, *Dogmengeschichte,* I (5th ed., 1914), E. T.: *History of Dogma* (reprint, 1958); R. Reitzenstein, *Das iranische Erlösungsmysterium* (1921); R. Reitzenstein and H. H. Schaeder, *Studien zum antiken Synkretismus aus Iran und Griechenland* (1926); F. C. Burkitt, *Church and Gnosticism* (1932); H. Jonas, *Gnosis und spätantiker Geist,* I (1934), II (1954); K. Stürmer, "Judentum, Griechentum und Gnosis", *Theologische Literaturzeitung* 73 (1948), cols. 581–92; G. Quispel, *Gnosis als Weltreligion* (1951); J. Daniélou, *Théologie du Judéo-Christianisme* (1958), E. T. (1964); H. Jonas, *The Gnostic Religion* (2nd revised ed., 1963); R. McL. Wilson, *The Gnostic Problem* (1958); R. M. Grant, *Gnosticism and Early Christianity* (1959); C. Colpe, *Die religionsgeschichtliche Schule* (1961); H.-M. Schenke, *Der Gott "Mensch" in der Gnosis* (1962); R. Haardt, "Das Universaleschatologische Vorstellungsgut in der Gnosis", in K. Schubert, ed., *Vom Messias zum Christus* (1964), pp. 255–79; U. Bianchi, *Le origini dello Gnosticismo* (1967); R. Haardt, *Die Gnosis — Wesen und Zeugnisse* (1967); H. Langerbeck, *Aufsätze zur Gnosis* (1967). GNOSIS AND NEW TESTAMENT: H. Schlier, *Christus und die Kirche im Epheserbrief* (1930); L. Cerfaux, "Gnose préchrétienne et biblique", *DBS,* III, cols. 659–702; E. Percy, *Untersuchungen über den Ursprung der johanneischen Theologie* (1939); R. Bultmann, *Das Evangelium des Johannes* (1941; 17th ed., 1962); id., *Das Urchristentum im Rahmen der antiken Religionen* (1949), E. T.: *Primitive Christianity* (1956); J. Dupont, *Gnosis: La connaissance religieuse dans les épîtres de St. Paul* (1949); R. Bultmann, *Theology of the New Testament,* 2 vols. (1952–55); C. H. Dodd, *The Interpretation of the Fourth Gospel* (1953); R. P. Casey, "Gnosis. Gnosticism and the New Testament", *Studies in Honour of C. H. Dodd* (1956), pp. 25–67; W. Schmithals, *Die Gnosis in Korinth* (1956); G. Quispel, "Gnosticism and the New Testament", in J. Hyatt, ed., *The Bible in Modern Scholarship* (1965), pp. 252–71; R. Schnackenburg, *Die Johannesbriefe* (2nd ed., 1963), E. T. in preparation; id., *Das Johannesevangelium* (1965), E. T.: *The Gospel according to St. John* (in preparation); R. Haardt, "Gnosis und Neues Testament", in J. Sint, ed., *Bibel und zeitgemässer Glaube* (1967), pp. 31–158.

Robert Haardt

GNOSTICISM

Gnosticism, a category which is often applied very inconsistently, mostly designates the Gnosis rejected by the early Church (sometimes called "Christian Gnosticism" and often summed up by the misleading term of "Christian Gnosis"). Gnosticism is sometimes used for early forms of Gnostic thinking, including then very often the pagan Hellenistic Gnosis which had remained apart from Christianity. The term is even used at times to designate the whole phenomenon of the Gnosis of late antiquity. Structurally, most systems of Gnosticism are of the "Syro-Egyptian" type of Gnosis. Though patristic literature often seems to use the terms Gnosis or Gnostics for particular Gnostic communities (the Carpocratians called themselves "gnostici", Irenaeus, *Adv. Haer.*, I, 25, 6), Irenaeus himself also uses the two terms to designate the whole phenomenon of Gnosticism, e.g., in the Greek title of *Adv. Haer.* and in *Adv. Haer.*, I, 23, 4 (cf. 1 Tim 6:20), II, 13, 8. It is highly probable that with Simon of Samaria (Acts 8:4–25) we have a testimony to pre-Christian Gnosis in the first half of the first century. His disciple, the Samaritan Menander (*c.* A.D. 100) influenced Saturninus (Satornilos) of Antioch, who propounded a "Christianized" form of Gnosis in Syria, and probably also Basilides, who was teaching in Alexandria (with his son Isodore) in the first half of the 2nd century. In Asia Minor, Cerinthus was a contemporary of Polycarp of Smyrna. But it was above all in Egypt that Gnosis took firm foothold. The most eminent of all Gnostics, Valentinus, taught at Alexandria. He came to Rome about 140, where he was soon excommunicated and founded a school of his own. Marcion of Pontus, who has a place of his own in the history of Gnosis, since he does not speculate on aeons, suppose the existence of a "spirit-self" etc.; reached Rome in 139 and was excommunicated in 144. Marcion founded his own Church.

Elsewhere Gnosticism formed schools, and associations for the celebration of the mysteries, but Marcion had a Church with a hierarchical constitution and its own canon of the NT, Lk and ten letters of Paul, all in an expurgated edition.

Valentinianism in particular, divided into a Western, Italian school under Ptolemy and Heracleon and an Eastern under Theodotus and Marcos (not Bardesan) whose followers were known to Irenaeus in Southern Gaul, spread rapidly and widely, as did the Marcionite Church, over nearly all the Roman Empire. Some groups were named after the heads of the schools, such as the Simonians, Satornilians, Basilidians, Valentinians, Marcionites and Nicolaites (no historical connection with the Nicolaus of Acts 6:5). But there were many groups, not always easily distinguished from one another, who took their names from various other sources: the Ophites or Naassenes (from the Greek ὄφις and the Hebrew נָחָשׁ respectively, "serpent"); the Barbeliotes (from the goddess of light, Barbelo);

the Archontics (from the Archons); the Cainites (from the biblical Cain); the Carpocratians (from the Egyptian god Harpocrates or Horus, rather than from a historical person named Harpocrates, as in Irenaeus, *Adv. Haer.*, I, 25, 1). There were still communities of Gnostics some centuries later, such as the Valentinians in Egypt in the 4th century and the Marcionites in Syria in the 5th. Till original sources (preserved in Coptic) were discovered or exploited at the end of the 19th and especially in the 20th century, scholarship had to rely on the works of anti-Gnostic authors, whose accounts included many quotations and sometimes large portions of Gnostic writings. There were important fragments of the works of Theodotus, Valentinus, Basilides, Heracleon, Ptolemy, etc. The most important original sources are the *Coptic Papyrus Berolinensis 8502* and above all the Coptic papyri from *Nag Hammadi* (Chenoboskion). This literature goes back mainly to the Sethite, Barbelo-Gnostic and Valentinian groups. The *Evangelium Veritatis* of the Jung Codex (Cod. I of *Nag Hammadi*) shows traces, like the *Gospel of Philip,* of Valentinianism. It cannot be proved that Valentinus was the author of this Coptic gospel, nor that it is identical with the gospel of the same name mentioned by Irenaeus, *Adv. Haer.*, III, 11, 9, which is not known otherwise.

The controversy with Gnosticism was a fruitful source of the development of dogma in the Great Church, to a great extent because basic problems such as that of the Creator-Redeemer and that of the relationship of cosmology to soteriology were eliminated by Gnosis, whereas the Great Church saw itself challenged to give a solid and systematic solution. Thus Gnosis helped the Great Church to see the problems in their full acuteness. Nonetheless, controversy with Gnosis was not the main source of the development of dogma, in spite of the large place allotted to Gnosticism in recent discussion. The development of dogma is intrinsically connected with the historicity of the Church and its recognition of itself as eschatologically orientated. But special forms and trends of dogmatic development derive to a great extent from the pressure imposed by the problems of Gnosis. The claim of Gnosis to offer redemption became in the Alexandrian school the occasion for theological reflection on the relation between

Pistis and Gnosis. The systematic development of trinitarian doctrines was furthered by Gnostic speculation on the aeons and its separation of the supreme God from the demiurge, to which the Great Church reacted in the opposite direction. In particular, against the docetism of Gnosticism, which accepted Christ as a redemptive hypostasis, to which it applied various Christologies, mostly docetic in character, the Great Church affirmed the doctrine of the incarnation, the integrity of the human nature of Jesus and the salvific character of the crucifixion. In contrast to the spiritualization of the notion of the Church in Gnosticism and its appeal to secret traditions, the organization and apostolic tradition of the Great Church took on firm and stable forms and determined the canon of the NT. One connotation of the dogmatic doctrine of the resurrection of the body is that it is an answer to the treatment of matter as demonic in Gnosticism. In the development of the doctrine of grace, the controversy with the ethical positions of Gnosticism was important.

See also *Gnosis, Alexandrian School of Theology, Docetism, Canon of Scripture.*

BIBLIOGRAPHY. sources: Pagan Gnosticism: Tractate "Poimandres", in A. D. Nock and A.-J. Festugière, eds., *Corpus Hermeticum* (2nd ed., 1960). Christian Gnosticism: secondary sources: Justin, Irenaeus, Hippolytus, Clement of Alexandria, Origen, Epiphanius, etc.. Plotinus, Porphyrius. Cf. W. Völker, ed., *Quellen zur Geschichte der christlichen Gnosis* (1932). Writings not strictly Gnostic which contain traits of Gnosticism include the Acts of Thomas, the Odes of Solomon, the Pseudo-Clementine Recognitions. See also Hennecke – Schneemelcher – Wilson. Primary sources: "Pistis Sophia", "The Two Books of Jeû", "Unknown Gnostic Work" (with German tr.), ed. by W. Till, in *GCS*, VL (3rd ed., 1939); English tr. of the third work by C. A. Baynes (1933); "The Gospel of Mary", "The Apocryphon of John", "Sophia Jesu Christi" (*Pap. Kopt. Berol.*, 8502) ed. and tr. by W. Till (in German) (1955). From *Nag Hammadi* (so far published): "Evangelium Veritatis", ed. and tr. by M. Malinine and others (1956; supplement, 1961); "Gospel of Thomas", ed. and tr. by A. Guillaumont and others (1959), cf. "Secret Sayings of Jesus" by R. Grant and N. Freedman (1960); The "Unknown Gnostic Work", ed. and tr. by A. Böhlig and P. Labib (1962); three versions of the Apocryphon of John, ed. and tr. by M. Krause and P. Labib (1962); "De Resurrectione", ed. and tr. by M. Malinine and others (1963); two Apocalypses of James, Apocalypse of Paul, Apocalypse of Adam, ed. and tr. by A. Böhlig and P. Labib (1963); "Gospel of Philip", tr. and ed. by W. Till (in German) (1963); E. T. and commentary by R. McL. Wilson (1962); "The Hypostasis of the Archons", text in photocopy by P. Labib (1956), German tr. by H.-M. Schenke in *Theologische Literaturzeitung* 84 (1959), cols. 5 ff. LITERATURE: General: E. de Faye, *Gnostiques et Gnosticisme* (1913); A. von Harnack, *Markion* (2nd ed., 1924); L. Cerfaux, "La gnose Simonienne", *RSR* 15 (1925), pp. 489 ff.; *ibid.,* 16 (1926), pp. 5 ff., 265 ff., 481 ff.; F. M. Sagnard, *La gnose valentinienne et le témoignage de Saint Irénée* (1947); A.-J. Festugière, *La Révélation d'Hermès Trismégiste* (4 vols., 1950–54); E. Haenchen, "Das Buch Baruch", *Zeitschrift für Theologie und Kirche* 50 (1953), pp. 81–98; C. H. Dodd, *The Bible and the Greeks* (1954); H.-Ch. Puech, *Plotin et les Gnostiques,* V (1957); A. Orbe, *Estudios Valentinianos,* 5 vols. (1955–61); A. D. Nock, "Gnosticism", *Harvard Theological Review* 57 (1964), pp. 255–79; On *Nag Hammadi*: see *Elenchus Bibliographicus*, Biblica. General information: H.-Ch. Puech, *Les nouveaux écrits gnostiques, Coptic Studies in Honour of W. E. Crum* (1950); J. Doresse, *The Secret Books of the Egyptian Gnostics* (1960); H. Ch. Puech, "Gnostic Gospels and Related Documents", in Hennecke – Schneemelcher – Wilson, I (1963), pp. 231–361; W. C. van Unnik, *Newly Discovered Gnostic Writings* (1960); R. Haardt, "Zwanzig Jahre Erforschung der koptischen-gnostischen Schriften von Nag Hammadi", *Theologie und Philosophie* 42 (1967), pp. 390–401. Special studies: H.-Ch. Puech, G. Quispel, W. C. van Unnik, *The Jung Codex,* tr. and ed. by F. L. Cross (1955); J. Leipoldt and H.-M. Schenke, *Koptische-Gnostische Schriften aus den Papyrus-Codices von Nag Hammadi* (1960); R. McL. Wilson, *Studies in the Gospel of Thomas* (1960); K. Smyth, "The Gospel of Thomas", *Heythrop Journal* 1 (1960), pp. 189–98; K. Grobel, *Gospel of Truth* (1960); B. Gärtner, *The Theology of the Gospel of Thomas* (1961); R. Haardt, "Das koptische Thomasevangelium und die ausserbiblischen Herrenworte, in K. Schubert, ed., *Der historische Jesus und der Christus unseres Glaubens* (1962), pp. 257–87; J. E. Ménard, *L'Évangile de Vérité* (1962); id., *L'Évangile selon Philippe* (1964); id., "La 'Connaissance' dans l'Évangile de Vérité", *RSR* 41 (1967), pp. 1–28.

Robert Haardt

GOD

I. The Divine. II. Knowability of God. III. Proofs of the Existence of God.

I. The Divine

1. *Revelation and the question of God.* Man as he finds himself includes a dynamism towards an absolute in being, meaning, truth and life. Christian belief in revelation has always designated this absolute by the term "God". The reality which it denotes is in the Christian view a primary transcendental datum of the

human spirit which must be firmly maintained, even though in the history of religion the empirical derivation of the idea of God remains an open question. Here a purely evolutionary theory which assumes primitive origins still confronts the theory of an original monotheism (belief in a High God). Neither of these theories can give an exact account of the genesis and development of the idea of God, though in favour of the theory of primitive monotheism it may be said that an explanation of belief in God drawn from nature, magic and animism does not appear convincing. Belief in a primitive revelation, in which man was given the (unanalysed) knowledge of a personal divinity, is not a matter which falls within the scope of the methods of comparative religion. These can neither prove nor disprove it.

Christian thought is not absolutely tied to the findings of the history of religions, which always have to some extent an ambivalent character. Christianity is convinced that in the OT revelation a completely new and underivative awareness of God appears, even though in the historical emergence of what was new, the links with the old ideas of God can be traced, so that it is possible to speak of a "development" of OT monotheism.

For man to speak about God at all represents in reality an "impossible task", for according to the statements of revelation as well as the experiences of the profoundest religious minds of humanity, God is precisely the inexpressible, impossible to conceptualize and objectivate. On the other hand, man must undertake this task, because it is impossible to pass over in silence the question of God. Man's own personal existence intrinsically involves that question, which is precisely what makes human reality problematic. Even contemporary militant atheism must acknowledge this. Its denial of God testifies to the impossibility of ignoring the question of God, and so on the Christian side does the extreme "Death of God" movement, which replaces an allegedly unacceptable personal idea of God by referring to the normative consciousness of human freedom which appeared in Jesus and which must serve as a norm. Even the deliberately intramundane philosophy of modern times was not able to exclude this question, even when it disdained the term God and replaced it with the principle of the universe (G. Bruno), the absolute spirit (G. W. F. Hegel), life

exulting in itself (F. Nietzsche) or the supra-worldliness of the power of being limiting man (M. Heidegger). Even J. P. Sartre's resolute atheism has to raise the question of God in order to make intelligible the titanic human decision in favour of absolute freedom.

An explanation of this question of God which is involved in man's very existence as a person is only possible by reference to man's constitution as partner in a dialogue. Fundamentally, man stands under God's call, and his primordial orientation is towards hearing God's word.

Purely theoretical philosophical thought will, it is true, never be able to make it perfectly evident whether this call really proceeds from something outside man, from an absolute, or is merely an echo of the voice of human reality moving with its finitude and fragility in an inescapable circle of immanence and endless monologue. Consequently man is ultimately certain about God only through acceptance of a revelation in which God discloses himself to man perfectly freely and by his own power, and thereby opens man's destiny to a partnership between God and man.

It is true that the assumption of the occurrence of a divine revelation of this kind, which brings the relation between God and man into the pattern of events of history and temporality, sets a new problem. Why does God still appear to man to be questionable and problematic in his action and being? This is connected with a right conception of revelation. Revelation, whether regarded from the side of the absolute God or from that of finite man, cannot bring about a complete disclosure of the mystery of God. Even for the prophets and the apostles, the actual witnesses to revelation, the revealer remains shrouded in the hidden character of his nature. And so the hidden character of the God of revelation has been a constant theme of all thought about God based on revelation, since the Greek Fathers and the "negative theology" which they inaugurated, through Augustine, German mysticism, Nicolas of Cusa (*Dialogus de Deo abscondito*) and Luther, down to Pascal and Newman. It is notable that the very nation chosen by the God of revelation could raise the question of the *name* of God. This was not done out of intellectual curiosity, but from longing for assurance that God was near with active help in the darkness of faith and the hazards of history, to which the immutable God, despite his most intimate proximity, must always remain transcendent (cf. Exod 3:1–15).

2. *Proofs of the existence of God and God's mysterious character.* Man's turning from God in sin, and the consequent clouding of his knowledge (cf. Rom 1:18–21; see also *Original Sin*) is the ultimate reason why he will always experience God's mystery as a kind of absence, and has to raise a question about him. But this clouding is not so radical that there is no receptivity left for the call of God which comes from the order of creation. This receptivity is also indispensable when "supernatural" revelation occurs (because it guarantees personal responsibility for acceptance of the Word of God). It must not, however, be declared to constitute a way of natural knowledge of God side by side and on an equal footing with the revealed knowledge of faith (*D* 1785).

These various reasons for the non-self-evident character of God also explain why human thought has always been concerned with the natural demonstrability of God's existence, and why conscious inquiry of this kind was taken over and sanctioned by Christian theology in the form of the proofs of the existence of God. These "proofs" have become problematical in some respects for people nowadays, even for people concerned about religion. Yet no less a person than Hegel (on the basis of his own philosophical conception of God, it is true) regarded a feeling of repugnance for proofs of God's existence as "acquired intellectual prejudice". Such persistent prejudice is also largely explained by a misconception of the particular structure and purpose of these proofs. In the details of their historical formulation (cf., for example, the *quinque viae* of Aquinas, *Summa Theologica,* I, q. 2, a. 3) they are certainly open to objection. But fundamentally they cannot be abandoned because they make clear the unconditional which lies at the basis of all contingent phenomena of the world and which is particularly apparent in man's awareness that an absolute claim is made on him. Otherwise the Christian belief in God would be exposed to the suspicion of illusion, and theology would dishonestly evade the ultimate question of truth in regard to its highest "object".

3. *The theological problem of atheism.* The hidden and non-evident character of the God of revelation, in conjunction with the clouding of human knowledge and the brittle orientation of the will towards the perfect good, also provides a basis for judging the phenomenon of denial of God, atheism. This deformation is nowadays frequently attributed to failure in the Christian proclamation of God and to the absence of persuasive testimony to God given in people's lives. It is, of course, never possible to dispute such failure of practical belief in God, but it is clear that the problem is very superficially envisaged if atheism is regarded solely as a consequence of failure to give practical effect to the idea of God. If that were so, atheism could only be interpreted as a misunderstanding of theism, as criticism of an idea of God out of harmony with the age, and therefore as aiming in reality at a more genuine act of faith. This possibility may be conceded where people deny God externally, in words, but hold fast to an absolute principle or value, even if in doing so they merely endow something derivative and relative with the character of an absolute. And certainly such a possibility can be admitted when, as in some Eastern forms of religion, for lack of an explicit conceptual theology, the absolute which is affirmed and honoured is not given a doctrinal basis. In these cases it is not really possible or appropriate to raise the question of theism or atheism at all.

This conception also accords with the observation of Vatican II that even in non-Christian religions there is "perception of that hidden power which not infrequently implies knowledge of a supreme God or even of a Father" (Declaration on the Relationship of the Church to Non-Christian Religions, *Nostra Aetate,* art. 3), even though what is meant is not given adequate expression in personal terms. A corrective to the apersonalism which is maintained in theory is often found in the actual practice of popular piety, which develops a cult of gods and spirits and so creates a substitute for the monologue of an apersonalism which is unsatisfying for man as a person. For an attitude to be regarded as "veiled theism", one would also have to inquire whether it produces a total dedication of the will and the acknowledgment of absolute ethical norms. And do these find realization in an attitude to the world and in a spirituality which affects man in the very centre of his being and prompts him to an attitude of adoration? That will not be the case with an atheism which has reached the highest degree of intellectual self-awareness, and which, like the "postulatory atheism" of N. Hartmann, considers that the existence of an absolute "centre of values" must be rejected precisely because of the dignity of the moral person. Nor is it possible to explain as misunderstood theism that virulent modern atheism which, drawing on Hegel's dialectic of "master and servant", regards all theism as expressing an intolerable heteronomy of the "unhappy consciousness", which can only be abrogated by acknowledging the divine humanity of the mind in its development.

A transcendental deduction may demonstrate from the fundamental principle of a theoretical and self-conscious atheism that the very denial of the unconditional and absolute implies its affirmation as one of the conditions of its denial. Such atheism is therefore in contradiction with itself. But from the subjective point of view of the person concerned, atheism must be regarded as an accomplished fact. That also applies even though from the standpoint of the Christian belief in God it must be admitted that no logical argument for the non-existence of God is possible, and consequently that any subjective conviction to that effect can only be apparent. In general, of course, a proof of the non-existence of some being will only be conclusive if the contradictory character of the alleged existence can be shown in the form of a *reductio ad absurdum*. From the Christian standpoint, atheism is objectively without foundation. It cannot, therefore, annul the objective, ontological constitution of man with his orientation towards God and his condition of image and likeness of God. But to try on this account to speak of atheism being impossible, would fail to recognize that man by his very condition as a finite being and by a decision of his finite freedom is able to deny the objective order from which he cannot in fact detach himself. And this provides a sufficient basis for atheism.

It must also be remembered that it is never a question of an intellectual judgment alone, but also of a decision of the will. Atheism is not an exclusively intellectual problem. If it were, this would ultimately lead to the theory of a mere error of the understanding and therefore in fact the very possibility of formal atheism would be disputed. Since a moral failure is also involved, rooted in man's shutting himself off in himself and making an absolute of his own finitude, denial of God must be regarded as a wilful "suppressing" (Rom 1:18) of the idea and experience of God which press upon man. Its character as sin and guilt must therefore be taken seriously. This does not mean that the element of guilt can be affirmed and determined from outside in each individual case.

4. *The problem of speaking about God.* The purpose of theological endeavour, however, is not to inquire about God, but to speak correctly about God, and this is also a fundamental purpose of God's call. Such speech, however, aims at intimate personal converse with God as the absolute personal partner, and this in turn is to find its perfect accomplishment in the direct vision of God. Consequently the problem of inquiry about God turns into that of correct speech about him and to him. This problem arises from the fact that our words and our concepts with their limits and essential relation to finite objects, are not capable of grasping the divine, which by its very nature is unlimited and unobjectifiable, prior to every determination and as the "divine" God, is the primordial and comprehensive factor in all thought and speech *about* him. Early Christian theology (as we see particularly vividly in the Pseudo-Dionysius) on the basis of living experience of the absolute otherness and nonobjectifiability of God, came to recognize a real inexpressibility of God, and only admitted negative statements about him. Behind this was the Augustinian principle that God is more known and acknowledged by non-knowing than by presumptuous human curiosity which can only lead to a human simulacrum of God. But this programme of a "negative theology" has never been carried out because, if pursued strictly, it would lead to complete silence about God. This would contradict the teleological character of the question about God inherent in man.

The same must be said of a modern form of negative theology which will only consider statements about God if they take the form of existential self-interpretation of the believer. This position may be based on a hidden agnosticism or on an extreme actualism and existentialism. In an indirect mode of statement of this kind, though God is still acknowledged, for example, as the force at the root of my preoccupations (H. Braun), God is no longer regarded as existing in himself. And this is where the demand is expressly made to forget the very word "God" (P. Tillich) and to formulate this word, as well as the demands of theistic religious feeling, in a new and "unreligious" way for modern man. Underlying this programme is the genuine problem of the relation between God's immanence and transcendence. In an unreflecting kind of faith, there was a one-sided tendency to the second pole of the dialectic, and the problem was over-simplified. But in the radically new approach, the dialectic between the "worldliness" and the transcendence of faith is once again unbalanced. Theology as speech about God threatens to turn into a "pistology", i.e., a doctrine of man's concern with faith, and into an existential interpretation of man. And it is impossible to say whether the latter has any further need for the objective reality and genuine partnership of God, or whether it ever reaches the point of acknowledging a personal God.

The same thing applies to attempts to think of God as only found in actual reality in the course of human personal relationships. Those who think in this way do not want to speak in so many words of a personal God (J. A. T. Robinson). Behind this is the objection that even the category "personal" is not appropriate to God; it is said to conceive God on the lines of a "highest being" *above* man and his world. The self-contradiction of this line of thinking will perhaps be clear from the substitute solutions proposed. The experience of God is said to be man's "being accepted" or as the experience of the obligatory force of the unconditional seen in the light of whole-hearted love for the world and the neighbour. Such sense of "being accepted", whether as an experience of the human person or of the unconditional, presupposes a person who accepts man and imposes the condition. Consequently for man, since he is himself a person, God cannot be less than a person, unless man wants to exalt himself into being the only absolute reality he will acknowledge.

The biblical testimonies, though they do not use the term "person" as such, make it clear that human thought about God is obliged to use the category of the personal. But it is fully represented and its place taken by the idea of the "name" of God and by the use of the divine name sanctioned by God himself (cf., e.g., Exod 3:14; 6:3; Is 42:8). Holy Scripture makes it clear on the one hand that God cannot be designated and grasped under a single name. Tradition develops this in the idea of God being "many-named" and even "nameless" (cf. *D* 428). On the other hand Scripture shows equally clearly that the God of revelation makes himself known by his name as a determinate subject and individual reality, as an "I" of supreme concreteness and dignity, and that as such he enters into a personal relation with men. From the ontological point of view this relation is what ultimately makes possible the phenomenon of human personality and personal relations. God's personal character finds expression above all in the personal pronoun "I" which is applied to him innumerable times in Scripture. Reluctance to apply the category of the personal to God identifies such a procedure too readily with reification of God. But no such danger is present if we recognize that when God is said to be "personal", the term is not a univocal designation and that it does not involve any limitation of God. It does not mean he is a stronger but limited "I", and that we are fixed in a static relation to him. It points to God as the all-comprising, transcendent ground of all personality, the total reality of autonomy, self-possession and responsibility. Understood in this way, God as personal is also the transcendent pole and more comprehensive reality which includes the human I-Thou relation to God. He therefore means more than the mere function of providing the absolute ontological ground of men's personal lives and of their mutual personal relations.

5. *The ways of speaking about God.* The difficulties that arise here are those of correct thought and speech about God. Traditional scholastic theology sought a solution in the doctrine of the analogy of all statements about God. This presupposes that God is quite different from what our concepts and words are capable of grasping. On this negative basis, which of course itself involves an implicit awareness of God's special character,

the mind is impelled to the further step of articulating the positive cognitive element in concepts of God. By their very nature these concepts can represent the divine only in a way which is both dissimilar and similar to it (cf. *D* 432). Yet they nevertheless direct our statements towards God's mystery, and consequently give them a genuinely meaningful content. Thus statements about God as personal or about his attributes refer to and attain a genuine reality in God, but because of their dissimilarity in similarity they cannot capture and express the mode of the reality they point to. If this were not so, language about God would be completely pointless and meaningless. This would amount to a thorough-going agnosticism, and as regards God, such agnosticism always leads to atheism. But even with its proper mode of dissimilar similarity, analogical thought has a tendency to specify God too precisely and by univocity and one-sidedness to circumscribe the all-inclusive or to delimit parts in what by its very nature is indivisible. Consequently, analogical thought requires a complementary kind of language about God, the language of dialectical statements. These do not envisage the divine solely from one angle and under one aspect but, because of its illimitedness, address it from many, even opposite points of view and under various aspects. Analogical thought itself of course includes a dialectical element by its emphasis on similarity *in* dissimilarity. As a consequence, dialectical statements about God, which, for example, think of God's divinity both as hidden *and* manifest, as transcendent *and* immanent, as absolute *and* as a factor in history, and which proceed both theocentrically and anthropocentrically, cannot dispense with the analogical element in each of the particular designations they employ. Recognition of this would lead at the same time to a better realization that statements about God always belong to a particular thought-form and are therefore inadequate. They would then be kept open for supplementation by other thought-forms.

6. *The history of revelation as warrant for speech about God.* Thus even if man can only think of God mediately and can only speak of him in a fragmentary way, this possibility exists and is even obligatory through the primal word of God uttered in revelation. By this utterance, God himself has entered into human language and has permanently empowered it to express him. And so the scandal which dialectical theology still takes at language about God founded on the analogy of being, is removed by showing that there is an *analogy of faith* in which God himself from on high chooses and sanctions created language as a symbolic expression of his mystery. The high claim implied in this affirmation of the possibility of appropriate language about God, ought not to be countered with the objection that God is thereby anthropomorphically distorted and diminished. Serious consideration ought rather to be given to the fact that by his creation and endowment with grace man is a "theomorphic" being called to speech about God and with him.

But if such speech is not to fail in its purpose in regard to the absolute God, it must follow the path by which God himself came down to man in revelation itself, i.e., it must be in accordance with revelation. The God of revelation is not an abstract idea or the supreme being. He is the Lord who turns to man in history, giving him grace and saving him. For statements about God to be in accordance with revelation, it is not sufficient that all Christian speech about God should be based on the norm provided by the revealed testimonies of holy Scripture, which themselves find an expression appropriate to their epoch in dogma and the magisterium of the Church. It is necessary, in fact, that such speech should not give the first place to statements about God's metaphysical being in himself and their speculative deduction from a root metaphysical concept. That place must be taken by an account of the saving actions done for man. In these the God of revelation shows himself with his care for the world, his love, holiness and justice as man's "pro me", powerful on man's behalf. But the complete form of God's concern for the world, God's true "being along with us", has revealed itself in the incarnate Son, in Jesus Christ. Consequently, language about God which is in accordance with revelation must always remain centred on God's highest concrete expression which took place in the coming of the God-man. The light of the revelation of Christ must always shine on any idea of God that accords with revelation. What God's love, truth, holiness or justice is, in language in harmony with revelation, must shine forth "in the face of Christ" (2 Cor 4:6), and must be learnt there.

7. God's being in himself and for us: the idea of God. This of course raises for the thoughtful believer the question whether statements about God's being in himself, and therefore any use of metaphysical language about God in ontological categories, are not impossible and therefore to be rejected. Here what Scripture itself has to say should serve as a warning of the need for caution. Scripture in fact indicates that God's *action* in regard to the world also reveals a divine *being,* which a fully conscious (theological) faith certainly can and must take as the subject-matter of statements. For God does not consist solely of his relation to man in revelation or of his significance for man. A purely functional concept of God of that kind which sought wholly to eliminate God's intrinsic being would ultimately make God a human simulacrum. The God of OT revelation is not merely his nation's helper in its life and survival. Here and there in Scripture use is made of God's so-called absolute attributes, which cannot be inferred solely from his relation to the world but truly transcend it (cf. Num 23:19; Ps 102:28). Such investigation of God's being is not intended solely to protect God's relation to the world, and his benignity towards man in history, from the danger of an anthropomorphic interpretation which would make the personal God a mere higher demiurge or superior world-spirit. It also promotes recognition and worship of the deepest mystery of God, which does not consist solely of his gracious merciful action for the world, but is in his being, which is not exhausted or exhaustible by that action.

It is indisputable nevertheless that Christian discourse about God in accordance with revelation, will prefer to speak of the active attributes manifested in God's history with mankind rather than to determine the metaphysical attributes of God's essence. Consequently it will speak chiefly of God as Lord, of the events of the creation and the covenant, of his glory, holiness, fatherhood and love, as they impressed themselves on biblical man. Of course the expression of the attributes which have a biblical basis and which are relative "ad nos" in revelation gives rise to the hermeneutical question whether their relevance to human existence can still be made clear to people of today in a changed sociological situation. Is it possible to bring out the individual relevance of the content of the theological message? Here translation is indispensable. But it will respect the conditions of genuine translation which are fidelity to the original and recognition of an inalienable identity of spirit. In ontological terms this means that such a translation cannot deviate from the principle that God himself does not alter even though human thought changes. Even if the concept of God changes with a new world-picture and understanding of being, it contains an immutable element, and something constant in man himself corresponds to this. If this assumption is not made, and it is asserted with D. Bonhoeffer, for example, that modern man has become formally godless and no longer acknowledges any religious *a priori,* there is no point of reference in man for those "absolute" attributes of God and a translation is impossible. All understanding of the original language has been lost. In that case, however, it is not only superfluous to "smuggle in" God as a "stop-gap" into extreme human situations from which there is no escape (Bonhoeffer); it is also impossible to confront man with God at man's "strongest point", i.e., "in the midst of life", in his "health, strength, certainty and simplicity". For according to this conception man is conscious of his maturity in a transcendental and radical sense and therefore can no longer stand in need of God. If intellectual honesty in the Christian "proclamation of God" is understood in this way, and if it remains logically coherent, it will finally be compelled to draw the conclusion against itself and completely eliminate the truth of God from man's mind.

When the inadequacy of such enthusiasm for the negative is once recognized, it becomes possible to indicate the existential context of the biblical concepts in the new world-picture. Then the God who reveals himself in the history of the Covenant as Lord does not entail man's tutelage and enslavement. He reveals man's vocation to a partnership in which equality of rights does not indeed prevail, but in which man, precisely by his awareness of infinite distance, experiences his own greatness which consists in transcending himself towards the infinity of God. Then God's holiness becomes intelligible to man in relation to man himself, as the plenitude which manifests man's need, as the grace which judges him but also raises him from his sinfulness, as the power which obliges him to profoundest reverence. It is then impossible to misunderstand God's fatherhood as if it meant setting up an external heteronomous authority. It is seen to point to a transcendental living dependence which is the ground which makes human freedom and dignity possible and makes man, as God's mandatary in the empirical domain of this world, grow to his full stature as a creature.

The unique love of God which is revealed in his fatherhood and which, according to 1 Jn 4:8, can even be understood as the decisive NT definition of God, can then be taken generally as the essence of the divine action in regard to the world, which has its supreme revelation in the Son's sacrifice as victim for sin (Jn 3:16). This also manifests directly the relation to the world of this essential attribute of God, which the Gospel deduces from God's act of revelation just as it does God's power over man. The very form of this merciful love, accepting and overcoming death, throws light on the fundamental enigma of human existence, that of evil. God in his merciful love here effects something higher than love of esteem or love of friendship (the distinction between eros and agape being duly noted). This is evident from the power with which love penetrates the dark mystery of sin and throws many points of light into its darkness, even if it does not illuminate it fully. This holds good not only in regard to the objective disposition of the order of salvation but also to the subjective experience of the redeemed human being. He experiences most profoundly the power of God's love when he is in the situation of the prodigal son (Lk 15:11–32).

God's love only appears in its full magnitude through the resistance of sin. But it seems, however, to lose its superior power at the end of history, where the mystery of evil flows into the mystery of reprobation. Here the love of God appears not to prevail over sin, and the highest purpose of God's active reality is apparently curtailed. The assumption of a double divine decree, predestinating some to salvation, the rest to perdition, as in Calvinism, would at once detract from the genuineness of God's all-embracing love. On the other hand it would be no solution to re-edit the doctrine of apocatastasis and regard evil as swallowed up in the end by divine power. K. Barth sees here an actual danger of curtailing the freedom and gratuitousness of divine love and of naturalizing it into a cosmic power. Certainly a faith which is convinced of the omnipotence and purposefulness of God's love which is so resplendent in revelation cannot discuss the phenomenon of reprobation by bypassing this love and taking no account of it. It will rather note that the freedom inherent in this divine love cannot nullify the decision of freedom even in man and the sinner, but can only keep on inviting it afresh. The mystery of the loss of the goal of beatitude cannot be attributed to the lack or lessening of divine love for particular human beings but only to a love which always respects created freedom and which bears and tolerates the sinner's self-hardening. Thus in the mystery of definitive loss of God, God's love shows itself to be a love which permits man's totally free decision and endures its resistance, just as the love of Christ on the cross not only overcame the sin of those who were converted but also endured the sin of the unrepentant and obdurate. Consequently even the mystery of reprobation is comprised within divine love, though this can only manifest itself to the reprobate in the dark glow of his own disordered self-love and obduracy in the misuse of his freedom.

Some light is thrown on the darkness of this mystery by the historical experiences which man has of God's love. He can recognize that in the revelation of God's love, justice also is achieved, the justice with which the Holy One must cast from himself the evil to which man clings, and which God must leave to its own futility. Even the divine justice, which according to the strong expressions of the OT is revealed in the wrath and jealousy of God (Exod 32:11; 34:14, etc.), must not, theologically speaking, be regarded as a by-way of the divine paths, running alongside but unconnected with the universal mainstream of divine love, even though its complete conceptual integration is impossible to human understanding. It is possible for us at least to recognize that God must measure and judge finite human love and its defective manifestations by the measure of his own love. All earthly love requires the observance of measure and order, and God's love is the universal standard for the love which is required of man, the standard by which its absence or defective forms can be recognized. Man experiences the non-fulfilment of the standard required of him as God's justice and punitive verdict. At the same time it must be remembered that for man in his condition as pilgrim, as the history of salvation supremely demonstrates, every such judgment given by God always includes an offer of salvation. Consequently the biblical concept of God's justice can also signify the constancy with which he asserts his saving and loving will in the world and obtains his "rights", that is, causes his grace to prevail. At the same time this means that, as its obverse so to speak, the divine justice which bestows salvation brings into operation the diacritical function also. This is displayed as judgment and condemnation when man resists divine grace and holds fast to this decision. Consequently God's justice itself may be regarded as an element of his love directed towards the world and therefore set up for man as a standard. Viewed in this way, love always remains the all-inclusive and guiding principle of God's action in the world. Those who earnestly seek their salvation can therefore be convinced that God's justice can never stand *against* his love and that the greatest love possesses the greatest clarity of judgment.

Love as a warm affection for a beloved person only attains its full identity if it is welcomed and reciprocated by the beloved. Consequently even God's love which is intrinsically perfectly free from desire and need, objectively seeks the response of the creature's love. This is aroused and evoked by God's love itself, and while it consists primarily in the act of love of God it is inseparably linked with love of the neighbour (cf. Mt 25:40; 1 Jn 4:20). The reason for this unity does not lie only in the dynamism inherent in genuine love of God, which necessarily extends to all that God has created. It has even deeper roots in the social character of the individual human being, whose self-development is only possible through personal relations with his fellowmen. The perfect love of God as the highest act of human self-fulfilment can therefore only be exercised in conjunction with love of the neighbour, and is impossible without the latter. A purely existential, anthropological interpretation of the love of God is therefore excluded. The human act of loving God is not identical with love of the neighbour, and love of God is not only accomplished in love between human beings. L. Feuerbach's transposition of the Johannine sentence (1 Jn 4:16) into "Love is God" turns God's inaccessible subjectivity into an attribute of man and leads to a purely horizontal religious spirit. Coherently developed, this can no longer maintain the reality of God and soon dispenses even with the name of God. Fundamentally it also destroys the special quality of Christian love of the neighbour. The source of this love is that prior to any human love, God gives himself to man in incomprehensible grace. This alone is what enables man to love his neighbour in a way which far transcends any consideration of utility or any humanistic motives. Only those who have first known God's love in Christ can love their neighbour as God's image unselfishly and without reserve.

A purely horizontal interpretation of God's love which is identical with a total reduction of God's transcendence to human immanence, is excluded for Christian thought for another reason which points to the mystery of the Trinity. God's love for the world must not be regarded as a natural, necessary movement towards the creature, otherwise God will appear to be an indigent and dependent being. This impression is only to be avoided if the divine being is believed to be a movement of love even independently of any relation to the world and in itself. But this is only possible between persons. And so the recognition of God in his essence as love, independently of the world, leads to the assumption that there are personal relations within God, which constitute the mystery of the Trinity. Of course it is only possible to make this conceptual connection on the basis of a positive divine revelation of the three persons in God, such as is found in the history of salvation. The NT above all makes it clear that God's being in its relation to the world and as bestowing salvation finds its perfect revelation in Jesus Christ the Son of the Father, and that this revelation becomes in the Holy Spirit a permanent reality in the world which lays hold of man and fills him. Thus the revelation-event itself exhibits a personal linking of God's action with the unoriginated abyss of love in the Father, the perfect generation of this love in the Son, and its spiritual interiorization and its perpetual actualization in the Holy Spirit who as truth (Jn 14:17), love (Rom 5:5) and holiness (1 Pet 1:15) permanently transmits revelation as principle of life. In this sense belief in the Trinity would be genuine biblical kerygma, even though it could not be demonstrated beyond all dispute by trinitarian texts. A fundamental trinitarian awareness, expressed in many triadic formulas, is a very definite feature of the NT (cf. 2 Cor 13:13; 1 Cor 12:4ff.; Eph 1:3; 1 Pet 1:2). In it the plenitude of revelation present in Christ unfolds both (backwards) into the source of revelation hidden from us, and (forwards) into the presence of the revealing power dwelling in us in the Holy Spirit. Regarded in this way, the mystery of the Trinity is not a *mysterium logicum* merely imposing submission on the understanding. It is the mystery of perfect redemption in which the mysterious "God above us" (the Father) becomes "God with us" (the incarnate Son) and "God in us" (the Holy Spirit in grace).

It is true that such an account of the Trinity which follows the course of the testimonies of revelation in the economy of salvation, might give the impression that the true personal nature of the principles of the economy of salvation is not preserved and safeguarded. In fact, such safeguards are only possible in discussing the "immanent Trinity" if ontological terms (substance, relation, propriety) are also used. This doctrine, which took form in the Christological and Trinitarian controversies of the patristic period, is not a mere external addition to a kerygma of the NT essentially expressed in terms of the history of salvation (cf., for instance, *D* 39, 40). That is why even the early Trinitarian controversies had a soteriological purpose. It can be seen that a triadic economy, if not rooted in the immanent relationships of the three divine persons and their essential unity, would soon have had to be reduced to a merely apparent triad and the mere semblance of an economy. The triadic structure of sacred history and of the reality of redemption (which is not to be regarded as merely a temporal succession in the operation of the three persons), unless anchored in firm faith in an immanent Trinity of three essentially equal persons, could only be regarded as an appearance of the one God

in various forms. Such a "modalism" in the economy of salvation could never support the weight of reality and salvation contained in the events of creation, redemption and eschatology effected by the Father, Son and Holy Spirit. Realizing this, Origen drew the conclusion: "(The believer) will not attain salvation if the Trinity is not complete."

The perfection of salvation and its intellectual justification is finally explicitated in the question of the indwelling of the Trinity in the justified. At the present time this is answered more and more often on the lines that a genuinely personal relation links the three divine persons and the grace-endowed human being. Thus the mystery of the intrinsic being of God over and above the transmission of the divine saving action to the world, truly find its perfect counterpart in man, who is sealed with the life of the Trinity. Here the mystery of the infinite God is continued in the mystery of finite man, "theology" becomes "anthropology", without one cancelling the other or being in any way incompatible with it.

See also *Absolute and Contingent, God* II, III, *Monotheism, Trinity of God, Jesus Christ* III, *Holy Spirit* I, *Religion* I B, C, III, *Atheism, Spirit, Revelation, Existence* II, *Transcendence, Calvinism.*

BIBLIOGRAPHY. A. E. Taylor, "Theism", in *HERE*, XII, pp. 261–87; H. M. Féret, *Connaissance biblique de Dieu* (1955); C. de Moré-Pontgibaud, *Du fini à l'infini* (1956); R. Guardini, *The Living God* (1957); J. D. Collins, *God in Modern Philosophy* (1959); H. de Lubac, *Discovering God* (1960); I. Trethowan, *Basis of Belief* (1961); G. Vahanian, *Death of God* (1961); K. Rahner, "Theos in the New Testament", *Theological Investigations,* I (1961), pp. 91–167; E. L. Mascall, *He Who Is* (1962); Y. Congar, *La foi et la théologie* (1962); J. A. T. Robinson, *Honest to God* (1963); P. van Buren, *Secular Meaning of the Gospel* (1963); J. C. Murray, *Problem of God* (1964); H. Gollwitzer, *Existence of God as Confessed by Faith* (1965); E. L. Mascall, *Secularization of the Christian Gospel* (1966); K. Rahner, "Remarks on the Dogmatic Treatise 'De Trinitate'", *Theological Investigations,* IV (1966), pp. 77–102; J. Feiner and M. Löhrer, eds., *Mysterium Salutis, Grundriss einer heilsgeschichtlichen Dogmatik,* II, chs. 1–5 (1967).

Leo Scheffczyk

II. Knowability of God

When the question of the knowability of God is consciously posed, it is seen to be inseparable from that of the proof of the existence of God, but not identical with it. It has the prior task of defining the framework within which alone a rational proof of the existence of God can be possible.

1. *In the Bible.* The texts which speak of a universal possibility of knowing God, even in non-Christians and pagans, are Wis 13:1–9 and Rom 1:18–21. Wis 13:1 ff. affirms that God may be known from the greatness and beauty of visible good things, as Lord of all creation. Men's failure to acknowledge God as Lord of creation is understandable but inexcusable. Paul writes in the same vein Rom 1:18 ff., "For the wrath of God is revealed from heaven against all ungodliness and wickedness of men who by their wickedness suppress the truth. For what can be known about God is plain to them, because God has shown it to them. Ever since the creation of the world his invisible nature, namely, his eternal power and deity, has been clearly perceived in the things that have been made (ἀόρατα . . . νοούμενα καθορᾶται). So they are without excuse; for although they knew God they did not honour him as God or give thanks to him, but they became futile in their thinking and their senseless minds were darkened." In conjunction with Rom 2:14 ff., where it is said that the conscience of pagans and their words of self-accusation or excuse give testimony to the law written in their hearts, according to which they act by nature, we have here a clear indication of the universal knowability of God. But the knowledge is hardly meant as theoretical and conceptual. It is to grow out of man's conscience in his contact with the things of this world, which is a sort of medium through which it is obviously discernible. Being a practical and existential knowledge of God, it is not threatened by stupidity or deficiencies on the intellectual or rational level, but by the moral attitude, the refusal of truth, injustice. Whatever be the exact translation one adopts for these passages, one must be careful not to read into them philosophical principles which cannot be intended. The fact that they affirm that the godhead of God appears and is obvious through the medium of the created world need not be taken to mean an indirect knowledge of God through causality or deduction. Quite apart from the suppositions which can hardly be justified historically, this would be systematically to disregard the immediacy

which — according to the text — must be displayed in whatever mediums are used, if one is to speak of the manifestation of the godhead of God in creation.

2. *In the magisterium.* The universal knowability of God, which was constantly presumed or propounded throughout the tradition of the Church, was first formulated as a definition at Vatican I, against positivism, agnosticism and an increasing tendency to traditionalism. It was defined that "the one true God, our creator and Lord, can be certainly known by the light of natural reason, through created things" (*D* 1806; cf. 1785; *DS* 3026, 3004). The actual process by which such knowledge is arrived at is not defined — how, for instance, we are to explain the mediated nature of this knowledge ("through created things") or whether and how it can be enunciated in the form of a rational proof. However, from earlier doctrinal pronouncements (against Bautain, *D* 1622, Bonetty, *D* 1650, and Froschhammer, *D* 1670; *DS* 2751, 2812, 2853), it appears that a *ratiocinatio* is meant, in the sense of a knowledge which is attained through conceptual proofs. On the other hand, the Church has insisted, against all exaggerations of Gnosticism and rationalism, on the necessity of the "moral" assistance of God, if he is to be really known in the concrete by individuals (*D* 1786; *DS* 3005).

3. *In systematic theology.* The Bible and the magisterium are not merely concerned with the possible knowledge of God in the sense of a theoretical and rational proof of his existence, but also and above all with the moral and existential knowledge of God which means acknowledgment of his godhead. Hence theology must distinguish clearly in each case how the knowability of God is understood: as (purely) theoretical or as existential. They are by no means the same thing, as will be seen.

Since patristic times, theologians have constantly been preoccupied with the problem of the rational proof of the existence of God. Two traditions, which sometimes cut across one another, may be distinguished. One is the proof of the existence of God, on the lines of a "clarification of the truth", which goes back to Augustine and ultimately to Plotinus or Plato. The other is that of Thomas with his famous "five ways" which are based on

Aristotelian principles. The Augustinian tradition is concerned with the condition of possibility of all spiritual and moral life, a consciousness of truth which as life and light is the deepest *a priori* of all knowledge and will, a primordial source welling up within the inmost core of the human spirit and prior to all man's thoughts and deeds, of which it is thus the explanation just as it is the force and guide of his desire of God. Through all the variations, the general structure of the Thomistic proofs is to demonstrate, on the basis of empirically existing beings and their contingent actuality, that transitory contingent beings cannot be their own sufficient reason. This provides the metaphysical principle of causality ("that which does not exist of itself must exist through another"), which is then used to conclude to a first cause. After further analyses, this first cause is identified with God. What makes this type of proof problematical is that, on principle, all proofs of the existence of God must demonstrate God as a personal being or show that the relationship between man and God is personal. But this means a relationship between (at least) two "freedoms" or two "I's", and not between some other sort of *things*. But the astonishing thing about freedom is that it must to some extent be its own sufficient reason, otherwise freedom would not ultimately be responsible for its own decisions. It is likewise true that consciousness must also be in a certain sense its own sufficient reason, otherwise consciousness could not always be self-consciousness. This relatively self-explanatory personal freedom and consciousness still remains contingent, and there is the question of how we are to think of its being based on a reality outside itself, and indeed of what we are to think in general of the relative independence of the free spiritual reality. But it seems certain at any rate that to explain the relationship between man and God some principle of personal existence is necessary to show how freedom can be called to be and consciousness generated. The production of the person as freedom and consciousness cannot be the same type of causation as gives rise to facts and things. But if the person and its independence cannot be brought about in the same way as a material thing, the contingence of the person cannot be subsumed under the contingence for which the metaphysical principle of causality

is valid, even when considered precisely as metaphysical and not physical. For if we do not find a new principle to explain the origin of freedom, the grounds of freedom or of the person would still be considered after the pattern of causality, even when metaphysical, and there would be no advance in the theological problem. Hence a complete justification of the Thomist proof seems to call for an examination of its traditional structure as a whole, to see how the contingence of finite beings can be grasped as the personal contingence of the free consciousness. One should then show how the person is founded on God's summons and how from this summons God may be proved to exist personally and absolutely. Whatever particular forms this transcendental reflection may take, it is clear from the start even in the ideal case of a fully thought out proof of the existence of God, we should have attained only a theoretical knowledge of God, which is logically secondary. If we refuse to admit that such theoretical knowledge is enough as the fundamental justification of human existence — as if we only had to "transpose" rational knowledge into life — then there must be a primordial way of knowing God, given immediately in the historical process along with man's very existence. This historico-existential knowledge must precede all merely rational and secondary mediation, but must, nonetheless, proceed from a truly mediated knowledge, since consciousness of God is not always clearly present as soon as existence is encountered. This primordial mediation of consciousness of God, which man himself brings about in his historical existence is in fact a reality — in personal love or dialogue. The dialogue which takes place in truth and love is the mutual apprehension of the "I" and the "You", where the "I" and the "You" come to consciousness of themselves, and also of their common ground, the love and the truth which becomes event in the encounter.

In the concrete reality of love between two persons, given and received, each loves the other — who loves the other. They love each other by loving their mutual love. Thus they not only love the reciprocity of their love, but much more — as the medium and basis of their reciprocity — love itself. In love as an actual event, both love this love in its intrinsic genesis just as love loves itself. Thus they experience love as origin in themselves. Thus in love there is a consciousness of existence in which the I and the You come to themselves and to each other as to their origin. The transcendence of freedom and consciousness which is "lived" by every "I", being the ultimate *a priori* of human existence, is not *ipso facto* an object of knowledge. But when this transcendence comes "from without" to meet the "I" in the "You", primordially and, as it were, "objectively", and fulfils itself in the encounter, that is, communicates itself in its own being, then, through the dialogue, it is both actual as historical event and consciously known as it primordially is. Where love is real and true as dialogue, the reality of freedom and consciousness in the "I" and the "You" is truly and consciously orientated to its transcendence, that is, to the love which as the light of all consciousness and the life of all freedom displays and attests itself as self-originating. The dialogue is the reflection of existence at its most original in the historic process, and it is also a revelation of transcendence. In this conscious apperception of existence as the act of transcendence, man at last understands what transcendence really is. For it is only in such an act that one grasps the unique quality of transcendence which can never be communicated on the level of theory: the power of love to bring about freedom and insight, the love which approves (or condemns untruth) and grasps existence in its profoundest depths, to ratify and justify it irrevocably in the supreme majesty of love. This is the only way to arrive at an existential knowledge of God. There what is immanent in reciprocal love is disclosed as absolute transcendence, which gives itself a name in its absoluteness and historically speaking can be termed God.

This is a clear demonstration of the value of existential knowledge of God in contrast to all merely theoretical or rational proofs of his existence. We can see why abstract rational proofs must be without effect on the immediate living of life. They lack the majestic conviction which only shows its power in the light coming with love. Rational proofs are inadequate to sustain the confidence of existence, but the existential proof of the dialogue, being actual event, can carry with it conviction from this basic experience. We can also see why sin and guilt are fundamental factors, because the revelation cannot

come about where the truth is not willed in the dialogue. This does not mean that men who do not, or think they do not know God must be considered bad in philosophy, and treated for the moment as "psychological cases". The historical condition of the atheist can be shown to be determined by his being open or closed to the truth in the dialogue in question. When we know that true knowledge of God comes about in sincere encounter, we see that the existential force of the theoretical proof of God need not be exaggerated. At the same time we see that the all-sustaining knowledge of God needs to be actuated by man in historical dialogue, and hence that it is largely dependent on the historical situation and traditions in which each man develops. Whether grace is necessary for the apperception of existence which as an act of transcendence implies the knowledge of God may be left an open question, historically speaking. Even if — theologically speaking — grace must be supposed, the universal possibility of existential knowledge of God is not ruled out, since the theology of grace allows us to suppose that the universal salvific will of God is a determining factor and a force in the personal history of every man.

The knowability of God thus appears as the *a priori* condition of possibility of abstract rational proof and as identical with the act of existence as it takes place in the historical dialogue of personal encounter. The knowledge of God implicit therein may be further analyzed as regards its conceptual structure, but its true and unique quality can only be known in the experimental proof which every man must set up for himself in life in the boldness of personal encounter.

See also *God* III, *Creation* I, *Positivism* I, *Agnosticism, Traditionalism, Freedom, Consciousness, Transcendence.*

BIBLIOGRAPHY. Thomas Aquinas, *Summa Theologica*, I, q. 12, a. 12; Bonaventure, *I Sent. dist.*, 3, 1f.; M. J. Scheeben, *Die Mysterien des Christentums*, II, para. 61 (3rd ed., 1958), E. T.: *The Mysteries of Christianity; DTC*, IV, cols. 757–87; H. Lennerz, *Natürliche Gotteserkenntnis* (1926); P. Descoqs, *Praelectiones Theologiae Naturalis*, 2 vols. (1932–35); M. Blondel, *L'Action*, 2 vols. (1936–37); K. Rahner, *Hörer des Wortes* (1941; 2nd ed., 1963); M. Blondel, *La Philosophie et l'Esprit chrétien*, 2 vols. (1944–46); J. Dupont, *Gnosis. La connaissance religieuse dans les épîtres de St. Paul* (1949); A. Marc, *Dialectique de l'agir*

(1954); M. Grison, *Théologie naturelle ou théodicée* (1959); C. Tresmontant, *Essai sur la connaissance de Dieu* (1959); M. Schmaus, *Katholische Dogmatik*, I (2nd ed., 1960), paras. 30–37 (biblio.); J. A. Boekraad and H. Tristan, *The Argument from Conscience to the Existence of God according to J. H. Newman* (1961); W. Brugger, *Theologia Naturalis* (2nd ed., 1964); E. Simons, *Philosophie der Offenbarung* (1966); H. U. von Balthasar, *God Question and Modern Man* (1967).

Eberhard Simons

III. Proofs of the Existence of God

The proofs of the existence of God are the rational terms in which man states why and how he reaches the natural conviction that he can legitimately affirm the existence of a personal Absolute. A "natural" conviction is not based on an explicit verbal revelation from God.

1. *Catholic doctrine.* Unlike Protestant thought, which in Karl Barth goes so far as to repudiate the *analogia entis,* Catholic theology, consciously taking its stand on God's revelation in Jesus Christ, does not repudiate but rather demands (at least the possibility of) a natural theology centred upon proofs of the existence of God, just as Christian faith presupposes a basic natural knowledge of God (though not precisely a proof) which makes faith reasonable. The doctrine that it is possible for reason to prove the existence of God, virtually defined by the First Vatican Council (*D* 1785, 1806) against fideism and strict traditionalism, was formally included in the anti-modernist oath (*D* 2145) by Pius X; and both documents explicitly cite Rom 1:18–32 in its support. To affirm that possibility is not to say whether such a thing has ever happened in historical fact. Vatican I itself acknowledges (*D* 1786) that "it is due to revelation that the truths concerning God which are not of themselves inaccessible to reason can in mankind's actual circumstances be *readily* known, *by all, with solid certainty,* and *unmingled with error*". Pius XII (*D* 3005) actually holds that this text affirms the *moral* (relative) necessity of revelation. What the Catholic thesis means, in a word, is that logically speaking and in themselves the proofs for the existence of God are natural, even though history testifies that in fact they have been correctly worked out only within Christian thought, and here too always under the influence of grace.

2. *Presuppositions.* a) The proofs for the existence of God presuppose at least the basic fact of man's spiritual life (as a tendency and an affirmation), and in that sense cannot be purely *a priori* (an argument that attempts to start from the mere idea of God is ineffectual). But it would be naïve to try to argue from nothing more than the fact of the world's existence or our experience of it; the rational principle which enables us to argue coherently that God exists is only to be found in man's own structures, as an *a priori* of human experience.

b) We see, then, that man always bears within him, in germ, the proofs for the existence of God, always lives them, in germ, in all his spiritual life: they need only become explicit. At the spiritual level every striving of human life is always sustained by the Necessary, open to the Infinite, illuminated by Absolute Understanding, summoned by Creative Love. Man may turn a deaf ear to that call; he cannot destroy the antecedent knowledge and the antecedent love of God, which is his very self.

c) And so the sense of religion is the deepest of the elements that make up human life. Without using the rational formulae which are the proof for the existence of God, it normally issues in an affirmation of God that is charged with emotion. Explicitly working out the proofs for the existence of God brings about conscious certainty, but to base the religious life exclusively on this mental process would destroy religion itself.

d) There is another point we must bear in mind. Perfectly sound though the proofs for the existence of God — or any other metaphysical argument — may be in themselves, it does not necessarily follow that they will convince any given individual. Metaphysics cannot verify a fact with the compelling certainty of mathematics or physics. It fails us when we are faced with a choice that will commit a whole human life. Hence pastors should make a prudent preliminary study of the individual's emotional nature, particularly fostering his humility in the presence of mystery (especially as regards the problem of evil, the mystery of sin); for he must be brought to a responsible acceptance of the transcendent dimensions of life, in the context, for instance, of the experience of love and other "limit situations". The metaphysical affirmation of God might legitimately be called "philosophic faith", so as to indicate that in the concrete it is both religious and free.

e) The conditions of validity for a proof of the existence of God can be stated thus: (i) If the term of the argument is to be God (a religious concept), it must attain him as at once personal and absolute. Today we can no longer rest content with the quick conclusion of St. Thomas's five ways ("this being everyone calls God"), nor even with the sheer demonstration of the *Ipsum Esse Subsistens;* many would still deny its personal character. (ii) On the other hand the proof for the existence of God must truly attain the Absolute (the Necessary and Infinite), not simply a first cause which as such would be part of the world, or a finite spirit which would explain the order of the world. So those proofs will always be metaphysical ones. Even if we follow tradition and divide them into physical, moral, and metaphysical proofs, not even the first category can be considered physical or scientific in the modern sense (it would be better to call them cosmological). And a systematic natural theology will yield preference to the more properly metaphysical proofs (with their indispensable moral basis).

3. *Cosmological proofs.* Because these are based rather on experience, the scientifically-trained mind finds them especially congenial and persuasive, whereas the philosopher has difficulty making them lead unambiguously to God. Some of the physical proofs that are offered really prove no more than that the dynamism observable in the world must have had a beginning, which ultimately *suggests* that God created it.

The law of entropy in thermodynamics (when changes in energy occur, the total amount of energy in the universe remains constant but there is an increase of entropy, or energy which cannot be further transformed) was much invoked to that end in the late 19th and early 20th century. Today we have the more direct appeal to the remarkable consensus about the age of the earth that scientists have reached from a variety of approaches (the radiation of the still radioactive elements; the steady expansion of the universe, etc.). Everything combines to indicate that the world is some 5000 million years old. As we cannot here discuss the evidential value of these data (the hypothesis of cyclic dynamisms

must be excluded), we pass on to the best known and most popular of the proofs for the existence of God, that drawn from the order in the world.

This argument, already in use among the Apologists, has been continuously used in Christian tradition; it is St. Thomas's fifth way. It takes us back to an intelligent ruler of the universe, who is then identified with God. There are two steps: first observing an order (a teleological one) in the world, then excluding a non-intelligent cause of that order. Contrary to the impression given by some text-books, the first step is not difficult when the proof is drawn from living reality. It is an insufficient explanation of the vegetable and animal world — whether we examine individuals in their dynamism (orientation in response to stimuli [tropism], the vital equilibrium, instinctive behaviour, functional adaptation in ontogenesis) or as an evolving whole (natural selection, adaptation to environment, above all the fact of hominisation) — to suppose that everything has arisen through a purely fortuitous combination of physical and chemical elements (considered only in their own energy). Neo-Darwinists themselves will not dispute this straightforward thesis. It is the second step that causes the difficulty: the recognizable teleology does not at once exclude an explanation through a non-intelligent cause. Nowadays it is said to be the work of a kind of instinctive force (called entelechy, or the soul, in individuals; or the power of evolution, or dialectical law, in the whole). Left to itself, the common sense of mankind sees in nature something analogous to our technical achievements; but this may be discounted on the ground — as Kant put it — that nature, unlike technological production, posits itself by an immanent power, so that it would be unjustifiable anthropomorphism on our part to assume that the world must be ordered and ruled by an intelligent being. If we reply that any kind of teleology presupposes an end envisaged and intended from the first, something only an intelligence is capable of, our opponent will say that we are begging the question, since he finds a non-mental pre-existence of the end, "in an instinctive way", sufficient. But if the essential superiority of intelligence over instinct is admitted (even supposing the latter to be of immediate driving force in the individuals), the order which so supremely surpasses the technical achievements of human intelligence cannot be ultimately ascribed to a non-intelligent cause. And so we can prove the necessity of an Intelligence that orders and governs the world.

To go on to identify it with God, we must show that the modern scientific attitude forbids us to separate the ordering principle of nature from that which produces it formally as ordered nature itself. If this is conceded, there will be less difficulty in regarding this Intelligence as the creator in the strict sense, even of material things. In this way we attain the Absolute. Those who do not follow this line of argument can confine themselves to the more metaphysical proofs.

4. *Moral proof*. A variety of attempts have been classified under this heading: the argument from the universal conviction of mankind, from the experience of the divine (especially in mystics), from the desire for happiness; and finally the deontological argument — the argument from conscience. It is not hard to see that the first two arguments are not very solid. We take up the deontological argument, which as we shall see is interwoven with the metaphysical proof, and indeed forms an element of the latter. Though it is deeply rooted in tradition, we find the deontological argument explicitly formulated only in neo-Scholasticism, no doubt unconsciously influenced by Kant, with his primacy of the practical and of the will. Though that primacy led in the 19th century to religious emotionalism and various forms of irrational vitalism, ending in Nietzsche's atheistic life-philosophy, the *Critique of Practical Reason* nevertheless set forth a real proof for the existence of God as the ultimate postulate of moral action. Its validity was recognized by Fichte.

In general, the deontological argument runs as follows: man is aware of obligation; but obligation makes no sense unless one admits the existence of God; therefore one must admit the existence of God. Of course what the argument means will vary according to the various ideas of obligation. It would prove nothing to a man who held that obligation arises only from explicit knowledge of God and his preceptive will; for him the argument would beg the question. But even a man who held that obligation arises from precept only could consider the deontological argument an explicitation of

knowledge implicit in the awareness of obligation and its absolute claim. For a eudaemonist, the argument would come down to the desire for happiness, the final object of which — always sought implicitly — turns out to be God alone. Seen more profoundly, obligation is the indefeasibility of the Good in itself, which cannot as such be rejected. Man, whose goodness as a person is the core of his being, is radically open to the totality of good (here is the essence of his freedom); obligation is the necessity (born of openness and to be accomplished freely, without physical compulsion) of respecting every other personal realization of good and of loving it as one does oneself. A person who accepts this necessity as absolute (a fundamental datum of morals) cannot satisfactorily account for it apart from the deep attraction of an Infinite Good, at work in our moral judgments and in the free decisions of our love — the only thing that can explain the good that we are and that other personal beings are; an ultimate centre in which we are all rooted, to which we are all open, which absolutely transcends us, yet is not alien to us ("closer to me than my inmost self, raised above everything I am": St. Augustine, *Confessions*, 3, 6, 11); which must be essentially personal. Formulated in this way, the argument is really another form of the metaphysical proof. And the metaphysical proof, in whatever form it may be put, can never abstract altogether from obligation and love if it is to defend the transcendent and personal character of the Absolute against pantheism and deism.

5. *Metaphysical proof*. Ends are the deepest study of metaphysics, and so the first basic form of metaphysical proof for the existence of God will be one that seeks God as our last end. It will start from two facts: man's tendency towards good, and what St. Augustine calls man's restlessness (always wanting something beyond any concrete end that he achieves), which reveal a horizon or ambit of infinitude and argue that what attracts us through that horizon is an Infinite Being. Though what is primarily considered is the Good-in-itself and its indefeasibility (as in the deontological argument, or the argument from love), one must also consider the aspect of the good-for-us which is always present in value judgments and in the pursuit of good

(the truth of the argument from the desire for happiness). Another form of the argument which looks quite different but is closely akin will follow St. Augustine, St. Anselm (Monologion), and St. Thomas (the fourth way) and explore the vision of the universe in terms of value — different degrees of truth, goodness, and beauty — which man has through his unlimited openness to good; concluding that those degrees are explicable only if they culminate in a *Summum Bonum,* a Supreme Good.

At any rate, besides first remarking upon a radical human experience (restlessness, conscience, love, desire, admiration), the proof uses a truth which is justified by human reality and which may be formulated as the principle of the reality of the good: what human nature itself is radically ordered and drawn to cannot ultimately be unreal. Blondel, Jaspers, Maréchal, Scheler, and Marcel variously use this insight in our day. Those who reject it (for reasons difficult to sustain) have had to pronounce man himself an absurdity ("passion inutile"); and the pronouncement is repudiated by life itself. There is another way of formulating this experience in articulate concepts, based on a strictly metaphysical understanding of the principle, "impossibile est desiderium naturale esse inane".

A second basic enunciation of the metaphysical proof results from a precise examination of efficient causality. It attains God as the first principle, above all as the Necessary Being, which must accordingly be perfection in every respect (infinite) and unique. St. Thomas's first three ways, which blend Aristotle (first mover) and Avicenna, are typical examples of it (somewhat too simple in structure). It strikes one spontaneously as the most objective proof, and many prefer it even today. But one must not forget that the reality of the world, from which this proof claims to start, is a reality which is attained by man in a judgment the point of which is to posit the world as a being (as something that *is,* that participates in being in one way or another); so even here a human act — spiritual knowledge — is the indispensable point of departure. So too it is within himself (implicit in the validity of the judgment and thereby justified) that man finds the truth which alone, as a rational principle, can make his first perception fruitful.

This is the principle of the ground of being (Leibniz's principle of sufficient reason): beings cannot ultimately be there without a ground. This leads to what is generally called the metaphysical principle of causality: the contingent (an entity which does not contain the ultimate ground) ultimately depends on the non-contingent (necessary being). Since contingency displays itself in the very structure of the judgment (which attributes being to an object) and in the beings which are its proper object, the ultimate non-contingent ground cannot be affirmed univocally but only analogically, by dialectically transcending the contingent structure of our judgment, as *Ipsum Esse Subsistens* (Being that subsists of itself), in St. Thomas's apt expression, as the ultimate boundary which cannot be represented but can be clearly designated, where the tension between beings and being ceases. In order to identify the Necessary Being with God, we must first show that it is infinite and unique; and conversely that the Infinite (to which the first form of our proof led us) necessarily exists. If we distinguish, as above, between beings and being and then transcend the distinction, the problem has hardly been set before it is solved. But it became acute once more with those writers after St. Thomas's time who did not make this distinction.

Duns Scotus, basing himself on the univocity of being, sought for a way in which to prove that the necessary being is infinite. Occam thought it impossible to prove that there is a single, infinite Being. Suarez attempted the proof anew: Necessary Being cannot be multiplied, because its very notion includes existence, and existence belongs only to the individual; and that which is necessary and unique is all-perfect, being the sole source of all real perfections. Descartes tried to establish the inference by working in the opposite direction: from an analysis of the idea of the Perfect Being (fifth meditation; in the third, he gives the question a more anthropological turn, starting from its origin within ourselves), he concludes to the necessity of its existence. Like Descartes, Leibniz proceeds from the idea of the Perfect Being (which is possible, because it does not involve a contradiction) to the necessary existence of that Being; and at the same time, from the Necessary Being — admitted to exist because something real exists (or can exist) which would not have a sufficient reason if it were entirely contingent — to its uniqueness and perfection, as Suarez does.

This synthesis, formalized and emptied of content by Wolff and Baumgarten, was sharply criticized by Kant in his *Critique of Pure Reason*. He calls the argument of Descartes and Leibniz the ontological argument and declares it invalid because it does not retain the slightest relation to experience (it starts from concepts or from a purely logical possibility) and wrongly goes on to make existence as a perfection a concept (thus Baumgarten, and probably St. Anselm in ch. II of the *Proslogion*). So far as Kant is concerned, the cosmological argument (Leibniz's second, which we have propounded earlier) proves the existence of a Necessary Being, but we relapse into the ontological argument if we try to conclude that therefore the most Perfect Being exists. These two objections are sound: it will not do to argue from an idea or define existence as a perfection. We must also admit that the illation from the Necessary to the Perfect is of itself reversible, but the interchangeability of the arguments does not entail the unacceptable consequences blamed by Kant. There can be a real proof (which may indeed be called ontological) which demonstrates (without assuming it) the real possibility of the infinite as goal of human activity (as in the first form of the metaphysical proof); and establishes further that necessary existence must be proper to that Being (since contingency is an imperfection). The second form of the argument, having proved the existence of the Necessary Being, must show that it is all-perfect and infinite; either by the more arduous method of Scotus, Suarez, or Leibniz, or preferably by recourse to the profound Thomist notion of being and its roots in the structures of human judgment; contingence as well as finitude is displayed in them, inasmuch as being (which of itself means unlimited fullness) is restricted to this or that determination (essence) in all beings. Finitude and contingency coincide in the proper object of human judgment. And conversely, in *Ipsum Esse Subsistens* both contingency and finitude are transcended; so that Necessary Being is thus seen to be identical with the Infinite, and by that very fact essentially unique.

We see how the two forms of the metaphysical proof form a unity and complement each other: for the first ground is the last end, the unique Absolute. If it is difficult to prove that the Necessary Being as such transcends the world, as against Spinoza's monist view (that the world is a modality of the one necessary Substance), infinity proclaims its own transcendence; for the Infinite admits of no modalities; and on the other hand the conception that finite things are dialectical moments within the evolution of the Infinite (Hegel) does not square with genuine infinitude. The metaphysical ascent is certainly dialectical — one, however, which is *open* and reaches a synthesis beyond all finitude in *Ipsum Esse Subsistens*. It substitutes for the monist (pantheist or panentheist) view of the universe a view that is participationist in the right sense: finite reality (man and the world) shares in the perfection of the Infinite as a likeness He has created. While using the different types of extrinsic causality (exemplary, efficient, and final), we must take care not to lapse into a shallow extrinsicism: the Infinite can never be brought under the same common denominator as the finite, though the Infinite is always "closer to it than its inmost self", as St. Augustine says. Thus the Infinite is the ground of all finite realities, above all, of the spiritual.

This consideration is necessary if the metaphysical proof is really to take us to God as a personal being.

As St. Augustine showed in his proof of the existence of God as truth, and as the basic intuition of post-Kantian transcendental Idealism has reaffirmed, if the primal human fact of judgment is to be fully accounted for (and that is what the second form of the metaphysical proof has in view), the Absolute himself must be intelligent (*Ipsum Intelligere Subsistens,* to use a dialectical analogy). And as the analyses of Blondel, Bergson, Scheler, and Marcel have particularly stressed in our day, if the primal human fact of restlessness (love, conscience, freedom) is to be fully accounted for, which is what the first form of the proof has in view, then the Absolute must also be *Ipsum Amare Subsistens,* a Being essentially free and personal. Describing the Absolute by spiritual predicates does, no doubt, raise difficulties, because it seems to exclude the perfection proper to matter. But these are resolved if we regard being as spiritual of itself and matter as *deficient* being, which is essentially the way to spirit and its prelude. Such a view, which is supported by the concepts of physics and biology today, as Teilhard de Chardin has shown, can be considered sound in our context, though only as a postulate in a consistent explanation of the primal fact of man's spiritual life. What is insufficient and inconsistent with the self-experience of man is a philosophic faith which denies the personal nature of the Transcendent. In view of all this — and also in view of a "death of God" theology which is not clear about its foundations — the validity and the limitations of the proofs for the existence of God should be clear.

See also *God* II, *Natural Theology, Knowledge, Analogy of Being, Principle, Absolute and Contingent, Necessity, God-World-Relationship.*

BIBLIOGRAPHY. Plato, *Symposium,* 210e–211d; *Republic,* 505–520; Aristotle, *Physics,* 7–8; *Metaphysics,* 12; Augustine, *De Libero Arbitrio,* 2; Anselm, *Proslogion,* 2 (E. T. by M. Charlesworth, 1965); Thomas Aquinas, *Summa contra Gentiles,* I, 13; 32–34; *Summa Theologica,* I, q. 2, a. 3; q. 13; I. Kant, *Critique of Pure Reason,* ed. and tr. by N. K. Smith (new ed., 1965); A. E. Taylor, *Faith of a Moralist,* 2 vols. (1930); E. Gilson, *God and Philosophy* (1941); A. E. Taylor, *Does God Exist?* (1945); W. Bryar, *St. Thomas and the Existence of God: Three Interpretations* (1951); J. Defever, *La Preuve réelle de Dieu* (1953); H. Bouillard, *Karl Barth,* III (1957); B. Lonergan, *Insight* (1958), ch. xix; J. Collins, *God in Modern Philosophy* (1959); H. de Lubac, *Discovery of God* (1960); J. de Langlade, *Le Problème de Dieu* (1960); J. Nugent, *Fundamental Theistic Argument in the Metaphysical Doctrine of Saint Thomas Aquinas* (1961); F. van Steenberghen, *Hidden God* (1963); C. Desjardins, *Dieu et l'Obligation morale* (1963); B. Welte, *Heilsverständnis* (1966); K. Jaspers, *Philosophic Faith and Revelation* (1967); H. Ogiermann, "Causa Prima. Metaphysische Gottesidee und Kausaldenken", *Theologie und Philosophie* (till 1966: *Scholastik*) 42 (1967), pp. 161–86.

José Gómez Caffarena

GOD, ATTRIBUTES OF

1. *The problem of treatment.* If revelation in sacred history is God's self-communication in word and deed, it is also the self-revelation of his living and giving, his "truth" (in contrast to any creaturely mediation and the knowledge which is thereby given), which are traditionally designated as the nature and

the attributes of God. These topics are dealt with in the tractate *De Deo uno* (separately from the theology of the Trinity), though they are also treated under the headings of creation and grace. Insofar as revelation is not concerned with the imparting of metaphysical statements about being to a purely receptive and speculative reason, but rather with the evocation of the knowledge, freedom and faith which direct men toward God, the theological elucidation of the attributes of God is not so much concerned with a theoretical explanation of certain themes, as with the demonstration of the summons contained in these assertions (in spite of its being possible to misunderstand them in an objectivating sense). The treatment of the attributes of God should therefore not follow an abstract metaphysical principle (as in fact it generally does), but the progressive self-revelation of God in sacred history. In this method of presentation, nevertheless, it must always be made clear that all experiences of God, including those of the OT, must be related to the experiences which Jesus had of God and are to be interpreted in the light of his experience. All the experiences of God which are recounted in sacred history are to be viewed against this horizon.

The question of the attributes of God cannot be answered, therefore, by a metaphysical sketch-plan of the idea or the "nature" of God, which (as a *norma normans et non normata*) would decide in advance who and what God "could be". The answer can only be given by God himself in the form of his own free and characteristic decisions in the events of revelation. That which occurs in the course of sacred history is not an instance of some natural law which must ever act in the same fashion; it is primarily an incalculable free act of grace. Nevertheless, the historical action of God has as a whole an inner relationship to the world and represents thereby a revelation of his "nature". Thus, the OT and the NT display a unity of action and an identity in the attributes of God. Yet this identity throughout the history of revelation must not be reduced to the necessity and static nature of a metaphysical image of God. God is the same according to both OT and NT, not because both ascribe to him a necessarily changeless being, but because the whole of sacred history represents the progressive revelation of how a free and historically active God chose to act in regard to his creation, and of whom he showed himself to be.

However, this revelation of God who is active in history addresses a world from which he was already not "far away" (Acts 17:27) but to which he had always revealed himself in "natural revelation" (and this revelation is known by Christian faith to have a supernatural orientation). Theology, as a reflection upon the revelation in Jesus Christ, thus includes in its understanding of this word the "preparatory word" of God concerning himself and explains it by means of a questionable pre-Christian natural theology. It is called upon to give such an explanation not only by the revelation in Christ, but by this natural theology itself. But this call can bring with it the temptation to make that "preliminary understanding" of the natural knowledge of God the criterion of his historical self-revelation. This unavoidable ambivalence of call and temptation is the basis of the legitimacy and the limitations of theological assertions about the attributes of God.

2. *The traditional teaching on the attributes of God.* By the attributes of God the traditional scholastic teaching understands the divine perfections which are really identical with one another, which make up the "physical nature" of God and which are founded in the "metaphysical nature" of God as the ultimate ground of the divine being from which the attributes can be said to follow as from a logically prior being. The nature and the attributes of God are completely identical by virtue of the absolute simplicity of God. The distinction between the individual attributes is only virtual. As God is ultimately absolute mystery, all the assertions which theology can make concerning his attributes are much more disproportionate than proportionate. This incomprehensibility of God is itself, according to Lateran IV, one of the attributes of God. "We firmly believe and profess with sincere hearts that there is only one, true, eternal, incommensurable and unchangeable, incomprehensible, omnipotent, and ineffable God." (*D* 428.) These affirmations are repeated by Vatican I in a somewhat more expanded form: "There is one, true, living God, Creator and Lord of heaven and earth, omnipotent, eternal, immense, incomprehensible, infinite in intellect

and will and in every perfection. As he is one unique spiritual substance, wholly simple and unchanging, we must acknowledge him to be really and essentially distinct from the world, totally blessed in himself and of himself and ineffably elevated above all things which are and can be thought of apart from him." (*D* 1782.) Theology generally arranges these attributes according to negative and affirmative, communicable and non-communicable, absolute and relative, static and dynamic. The necessity of a doctrine of the attributes of God is founded on the nature of human thought which is incapable of adequately including and comprehending in one act the whole of a "higher" being in its unity and simplicity. When speaking of the attributes of God we must always remain conscious of the inadequacy and limitations of human expressions with respect to the divine mystery.

3. *The attributes of God and the biblical concept of God.* The scholastic teaching concerning the attributes of God can claim to be founded on the testimony of the Scriptures. Nevertheless, the extent of this testimony is very limited, for the teaching on the attributes of God is in the end the product of scholastic philosophy and not of biblical thought. Biblical thought is not concerned with a metaphysical knowledge of God. The question about an ἀρχή, an ἰδέα, a last and final unity, is not asked in the OT or the NT and therefore questions about the nature or the attributes of God are not posed. The existence of *(one)* God is spontaneously assumed in the Scriptures: there is no need to prove that God is, for he reveals himself to his people in the faithfulness of his interventions. Thus, the Scriptures do not ask *who* God is, but only *how he shows himself* in his actions with men. One can only conclude to the nature of God on the basis of his actions with men, and the Scriptures speak primarily about these actions of God in the history of salvation.

God revealed himself *gradually* to Israel in the institutions and promises of the covenant. This absolutely free and sovereign revelation and the knowledge of God which it imparts are given in history, i.e., this revelation contains surprises, new horizons, and developments. It was awaited by the men concerned in hope and openness for the future, that of God and their own. The definitive revelation in the history of God's self-disclosure is the revelation of the Father in his servant Jesus. Through his obedience Jesus has become the way to all knowledge of God.

As God revealed his countenance gradually in concrete historical actions, the biblical image of God is a dynamic one. Naturally, many statements of Scripture about the mode of God's actions can be taken as indirect statements concerning the attributes of God. The Scriptures themselves understand these statements, however, as the personal active revelation of the divine freedom. According to the Scriptures, it is only to a limited extent that this can also be verified in "natural" ways on the basis of the world and its structures. But even here assertions such as those concerning the eternity (Rom 16:26), immortality (Eph 6:24; 2 Tim 1:10), and invisibility of God (Rom 1:20 etc.) take on new significance in the light of God's redemptive action. They lose their abstractness and are experienced in concrete relations. For "the knowledge of the glory of God" shines "in the face of Christ" (2 Cor 4:6) and reveals itself in the Spirit in whom man is able to call God "Father". Hence divine predicates such as ἀόρατος (Rom 1:20; Col 1:15, etc.), ἄφθαρτος (Rom 1:23; 1 Tim 1:17), μακάριος (1 Tim 1:11), ὁ θεὸς φῶς ἐστιν (1 Jn 1:5) are less characteristic of Scripture than such as "the faithful God" (1 Cor 1:9; 2 Thess 3:3, etc.), the "God of peace" (Rom 15:33; Phil 4:9, etc.), "of patience" (Rom 15:5), "hope" (Rom 15:13), "trust" (2 Cor 1:3) and "love" (2 Cor 13:11), or, in Johannine terms: "God is truth" (Jn 3:33). It is also said that God is merciful (Lk 1:72, 78, etc.), kind (Mt 19:17 etc.), forgiving (Mt 6:14; Mk 11:25), loving (Jn 3:16 etc.), the "saviour" (Lk 1:42; 1 Tim 1:1; Tit 1:3, etc.). This is a language which, in spite of its affinities with possibly similar assertions of a metaphysics or natural theology, is in the end only intelligible in faith.

See also *Revelation, Faith, Trinity of God, Monotheism, Salvation* III, *Natural Theology, Analogy of Being, Covenant.*

BIBLIOGRAPHY. L. Lessius, *De Perfectionibus ... Divinis* (new ed., 1881); R. Garrigou-Lagrange, *Les perfections divines* (1920); J. H. Newman, "The Mystery of Divine Condescension", "The Infinitude of the Divine Attributes", *Discourses to Mixed Congregations* (1849; new ed., 1929), 14, 15; id., *An Essay in Aid of a Grammar of Assent,* I (1870), ch. v; R. Jolivet, *Études sur le problème de Dieu* (1932); M. Wundt, *Die deutsche Schulmetaphysik des 17. Jahrhunderts* (1939); X. Le Bachelet, *Dieu, Sa Nature d'après les Pères, DTC,* IV, cols. 1083–94; H. Smith, "The Operational View of God", *Journal of Religion* 31 (1951), pp. 94–113; G. L. Prestige, *God in Patristic Thought* (1952); K. Barth, *Church Dogmatics,* II/1 (1957), sections 28–31; M. Schmaus, *Katholische Dogmatik,* I (6th ed., 1960); C. Heris, *Le Mystère de Dieu* (1960); K. Rahner, "Theos in the New Testament", *Theological Investigations,* I (1961), pp. 79–148; A. Dondeyne, "L'athéisme contemporain et le problème des attributs de Dieu", *ETL* 37 (1961), pp. 462–80; F. Genuyt, "Le mystère de Dieu", *Le Mystère Chrétien,* I (1961).

Edward Sillem

GOD, GLORY OF

The phrases, "the glory of God", "give glory to God", "act for the glory of God", are part of accepted Christian usage but they need to be properly explained. Understood in too anthropomorphic a way, they fail to do justice to the divine transcendence and hence to the absolutely free and disinterested love of God in his dealings with the world.

1. Scripture. Radically, the scriptural notion of the glory of God, in the general sense of the "bright majesty" of God, goes back to the Hebrew כְּבֹד יהוה, which is translated as δόξα by the LXX. Through this translation, it clearly determines the usage of δόξα in the NT. In the Latin Vulgate כָּבוֹד and δόξα are translated by *gloria*. Both δόξα and *gloria* mean more than the English "glory". In many cases it would be better to translate them by "majesty".

a) *The Kebod Yahweh in the OT.* The original meaning of glory in the OT is not, as among the Greeks and the Romans, that of a repute which demands admiration and praise, an honourable fame (cf. Cicero, *Rhetoric,* II, 55). Glory is primarily the real value, the measurable power, the weight of power (כָּבֵד, "to be heavy, weighty"). This meaning goes hand in hand with the classic sense of the majesty of fullness of light, of wisdom or beauty, which are worthy of honour and praise. Yahweh both reveals and conceals his *kabod* in the cloud and in consuming fire (Exod 16:7f.; 16:10; 24:15–17; 40:34f.; 40:38; Deut 5:24), a fire as bright and powerful as thunder and lightning, testifying to the powerful, inaccessible and terrible majesty of God. For those who experience it, this manifestation of Yahweh means punishment or gracious help (Lev 9:6, 23f.; Num 14:10; 16:19, etc.), which inspire adoration and praise: Exod 15:1, "I will sing to the Lord, for he has triumphed gloriously"; Exod 15:7; Ps 29:1–9. As well as by the marvels, the *kabod* of Yahweh is also revealed by the natural course of the world, and it summons all peoples to the praise of God, Pss 57:6–12; 145:10–12; 147:1.

b) *The doxa in the NT.* The majesty of God has become visible in Jesus Christ. He is the radiance of the *doxa,* the image of God's being (Heb 1:3). The *doxa* of the Father is revealed in the incarnation of his Word (Jn 1:14). Hence the gospel is the glad tidings of the *doxa* of Christ (2 Cor 4:4). Through Christ, God has illumined men's hearts with "the light of the knowledge of the glory of God in the face of Christ" (2 Cor 4:6).

The invisible presence of the δόξα in the tabernacle or temple of the ancient covenant (Exod 25:8), for the sanctification of men, is replaced by the incarnation of the Word of God, the personal and tangible presence of God among men (Jn 1:14, 16; 1 Jn 1:1–4). Just as the majesty was once concealed by the cloud, so too now by the humanity of the Word. The δόξα shines forth during the earthly life of Jesus only in "signs" and manifests itself only to believers (Jn 2:11; 11:40). In his state of lowliness, the Son "glorifies" the Father, consummating the work of redemption, and the Father "glorifies" the Son (Jn 12:28; 17:5). For Paul, the risen Lord is the "Lord of δόξα" (1 Cor 2:8). In the parousia, the heavenly δόξα of Jesus will be revealed to all (Mt 24:30). Peter, James and John experience a foretaste of this glory at the transfiguration (Lk 9:32), as does Paul before Damascus (Acts 9:3).

The glory of the Son is shared by the children of God, whom he "leads to glory" (Heb 2:10), as partners of his glory (1 Pet 5:1–4). According to Paul, the justified already participate in the eschatological glory (2 Cor 3:18; 4:17), though in a hidden manner and essentially in hope (Rom 8:18). The whole creation longs and groans for this glory (Rom 8:19–23).

When Jesus appears in this world, the angels proclaim "glory to God in the highest, and on earth peace among men with whom he is pleased" (Lk 2:14). It is the will of God that the Father should be glorified in the Son (Jn 14:13; Phil 2:11), and that the Son should be glorified in men (Jn 17:1–6). The glorification of God, of Christ and of men go together (2 Cor 4:15), as the fruit of the growing love which comes to completion on the "day of Christ" (Phil 1:9ff.; 1 Pet 1:7; 2 Pet 3:18). In the heavenly kingdom of God, the liturgy will be in the form of adoration and thanksgiving in Jesus Christ (Rom 16:27; Jude 1:24f.; Rev 1:4–7; 5:13).

2. *Systematic theology.* God created the world "not to increase his blessedness or to acquire it, but to manifest his perfection" (Vatican I, *D* 1783, 1803). His glory is primarily his intrinsic ontological perfection and his loving possession of himself in his holiness. The creation in which he manifests himself is ordained towards this holiness and glory, and this manifestation is of itself at once the "external" glory of God, "objective" or *materialis.* But creation would be meaningless if there were not also beings who go beyond this "objective" or "external" glory to respond to the revelation of the majesty of God through their knowledge and free love. The "objective" glory of God is only really glory insofar as it is a summons to spiritual beings to honour God "formally" and subjectively. Thus man would deny his own being if he tried to restrict himself to the "objective" glory of God, that is, to the fact of his human existence as such. But when he gives glory to God, he fulfils himself and finds his own glory in participating in God's glory. Thus, on Prov 16:4, Aquinas says: "The Lord made all things, to communicate himself" (*Summa Theologica,* I, q. 44, a. 4). Irenaeus says: "To those who see God, his glory gives life . . . participation in the life of God is the vision of God and the enjoyment of his blessings . . . the glory of God is the living man, the life of man is the vision of God." (*Adv. Haereses,* IV, 19; *PG,* VII, cols. 1035–37.)

a) Hence, the external glory of God means primarily the subjective attitude of adoring acknowledgement of the majesty of God. It is an act of adoration before the absolute mystery.

b) This act is directed to God's self-revelation, insofar as it manifests the majesty of God in its power and splendour. This self-revelation takes place in and through creation which through its being and through its response reveals God's glory and finds its purpose there. The unsurpassable eschatological revelation takes place in Christ Jesus, as the climax of the history of salvation.

c) The manifestation of the glory of God in history is again based on his fullness of being, his intrinsic power and majesty, as known and affirmed by God himself. This cannot be impaired, extrinsically or intrinsically, and hence constitutes his holiness.

See also *Transcendence, Charity* I, *Parousia, Hope, Reign of God, Liturgy, Worship, Beatific Vision, Creation, Salvation* III, *Holiness.*

BIBLIOGRAPHY. ON SECTION 1: I. Abrahams, *The Glory of God* (1925); J. Schneider, *Doxa* (1932); G. von Rad, "δόξα", *TWNT,* I (2nd ed., 1966), pp. 238–42 (OT); G. Kittel, ibid., pp. 247–55 (NT); L. Brockington, "The Septuagintal Background of the NT Use of Doxa", *Studies in Honour of R. H. Lightfoot* (1955), pp. 1–8; R. Bultmann, *Theology of the New Testament,* II (1955), pp. 49–59. ON SECTION 2: Along with the text-books "De Deo Creante", see P. Donnelly, "Saint Thomas and the Ultimate Purpose of Creation", *Theological Studies* 2 (1941), pp. 53–83; id., "The Vatican Council and the End of Creation", *ibid.* 4 (1943), pp. 3–33; Z. Alszeghy and M. Flick, "Gloria Dei", *Gregorianum* 36 (1955), pp. 361–90; P. De Haes, "Deus Omnia Creavit ad gloriam suam", *Collectanea Mechlinensia* 28 (1958), pp. 139 to 142; G. Padoin, *Il fine della creazione nel pensiero di S. Tommaso* (1959); A. Queralt, "El fin ultimo natural en Luis de Molina", *Estudios Eclesiásticos* 34 (1960), pp. 177–216; M. Schmaus, *Katholische Dogmatik,* II/1 (5th ed., 1955) with bibliography.

Humbert Bouëssé

GOD-WORLD RELATIONSHIP

1. The relationship between God and the world can be understood in various ways: as a relationship of knowledge or being, between God and the world or between the world and God. In each case the significance and our certainty are different. The central problem today is the relationship of being (the real relation) between God and the world. The introductory remarks about the other relationships lead up to this.

a) *The relationship of knowledge.* In contrast to theology, philosophy is constituted by the fact that its knowledge ascends from the world to God. Basic notes of the deficiency, the contingency of the world or the transcendence of man in its tension between the finite and the infinite point to the Absolute and Infinite which gives meaning and purpose to the world and to man. Its divine nature is envisaged, strictly speaking, by philosophy only insofar as the interpretation of man's being and activity in his world demands this perspective, and hence makes it possible. In Christian revelation, however, which is the source of theology, the movement of knowledge takes the opposite direction. God reveals what could not be deduced from the ontological structures of the world, his sovereignly free gracious will to impart his own life to men in Jesus Christ, at the same time giving us knowledge of the profound mystery of his triune Godhead. The knowledge "from above" through the word of God criticizes and surpasses with liberating clarity and inexhaustible significance the knowledge "from below", what men learn from the divine works.

b) *The relationship of being,* by which the world is referred to God, is the basis of the relationship of philosophical knowledge between the world and God. There is a relationship of being, a real relationship, in the strictest sense of the word, since the being of the world in its entirety was not just brought about once and for all at its origin, but is produced and sustained by God in continuous creation throughout its continued existence. The being of the world *is* intrinsically a permanent relationship to God, and it is constituted at each moment by this relationship. But the efficient causality is not everything. The world-constitutive relationship should rather be considered for the most part in terms of its finality, by which it is ordained to God. The origin of the world is elevated and surpassed by its future. God freely makes the world exist for the ever greater bestowal of his own excellence and goodness. Its goal (the cause of causes, in the old doctrine) is the primary and ultimate dynamism in the ontological relationship of the world to God. This constitutive relationship, recognizable in philosophy, also concerns the Christian faith, with its message of grace bestowed on man, of which the centre is the personal union with God in Jesus Christ. For it is the fundamental presupposition and outline of the final end which is but general and unfulfilled.

What has been said hitherto about the relationship of knowledge, philosophically and theologically, and about the relationship of being, as between the world and God, is in substance common ground among Catholics. But as regards a real relationship appertaining in itself to the order of reality, between God and the world, i.e., relating God to the world, philosophy — and traditional theology for the most part — hold that this must be denied. Today, however, theological reflection is inclined to maintain the reality of the relationship of God, the God of grace, to man and the world.

2. We shall now try — without claiming to give a complete solution — to propound or indicate the grounds for and against, a) in philosophy, b) in theology, and c), take up a middle position which will be necessarily very fluid and open.

a) The philosophical reasons against a real relationship aim at preserving God's absolute independence as regards all that is not God, and the immutability thereby involved. A relationship to the world would change God, because it would add something real to his being, like an accident. For all change and increase would imply potentiality and hence contingency and finiteness. To take an example from human experience: husband and wife become through generation and conception ("fundament of the relationship") subjects or bearers of the relationship to their child ("term of the relationship"), and as such subjects they are called parents. The relationship is accessory to the already existing "absolute" being of the subject, and is really distinct from it, which is the characteristic of real "predicamental" relationship. This implies that it is impossible in the infinitely simple, unchangeable being of God. God's absolute independence excludes the second type of relationship, the "transcendental", in which a being or a principle of being is of itself (without any additional predicament of relation, and hence transcendentally, that is, in a way pervading and surpassing all predicaments or categories) related to its term of relationship, without which it can neither be nor be thought of (cf. W. Brugger, p. 302). Such a relationship, which is really identical with its subject, exists reciprocally between finite substance and its accidents, or between body and soul; and the real relationship of the creature to the creator is now generally included under this head. The philosophers who reject the real relationship of God to the world (cf. Brugger, p. 306, on A. Brunner, pp. 177 f.) consider that a transcendental relationship implies dependence of the subject on the term even when (as in creation) the term only comes to be through the free decision of the subject. Hence in a transcendental relationship God would not be dependent on the world in the sense that the world was (partial) cause of his relationship to it. But a real relationship of God to the world would be dependent on the reality of the world as the necessary condition of the relationship. Hence God would not be the Infinite Absolute, utterly independent of all that is not God.

But the stringency at least of the argument may be questioned. The real relationship of God to the world would be conditioned by and dependent on the world (which would react, so to speak, on God himself) only if the world, as fundament and presupposition of the relation, were a real factor in the setting-up of the relationship (which would then be conceived as static). But would God be conditioned by and dependent on the world if his creative will, the free decision whereby he really and effectively wills from eternity that the world should be in time, is so purely dynamically and purposefully referred to the world that the world is, of itself, only consecutive to, and not constitutive of, the real relationship of God to the world? If freedom with regard to the existence or non-existence of the world is an intrinsic perfection in God, the necessary eternal exercise of this freedom, the free eternal self-determination, of which the immediate consequence is the existence of the world, is also a perfection. No doubt all this is absolutely identical with the one, simple, unchangeable, infinite will of God, which is his being. But does it follow that the creative will which constitutes the world must only be *considered* by us as a relationship to the world, though it *is* not really so? Even though it is the supreme instance of real self-reference, that is, the most primordial and totally creative? If this "instance" does not fit into the scheme derived from finite relations (especially the words re-lation, "bringing back to"), the terminology must be examined. Strictly speaking, the distinction between transcendental and predicamental relationship is that in the former there is real identity of the relation and its subject, and in the latter case there is not. But it is not simply true (even in *sensu diviso*) that the subject of every transcendental relationship "can neither be nor be thought of" without its term, which is not a constitutive note of transcendental relationship as such. God can truly exist without the world. He only cannot insofar *(in senso composito)* as he is the eternally free creator who wills the world to be real. This creative will as act is absolutely and really identical with God's being in, of and by himself. God in himself does not become different by this willed act (even if we suppose that it contains a real relationship to the world — which is the question).

b) The theological affirmation of the "reality of the relation of God to his creatures" (Schillebeeckx, p. 45; cf. pp. 43–52, 69f., 90) is now based principally on the personal character of the encounter between man and the Creator-God of free grace. The dogma of grace means real "intersubjectivity" between God and man, a living fellowship of love, not two "one-way streets", but a common current to and fro. That the relational can exist, without being relative in the sense of the imperfect, is attested by the revelation of the Trinity in God. Love is essentially a relational reality, and creation and grace are acts of love. Hence God really loves us, "and for that very reason God's mode of being, with regard to really existent men, is a transcendental relationship of love in a real partnership" *(ibid., p. 83).* Thus God's anger with sin, his joy at men's goodness, would not merely be ways of speaking of effects brought about in sinful or good men, but would be a real activity in God himself. The "absolute newness" of God would react really to human freedom in its history, to the prayer of petition, for instance. The focus of such encounter between God and man, in action and reaction, would be Jesus Christ: "To maintain that the change or becoming is entirely on the side of the humanity of Jesus ... would be as much as to say that we are dealing with an 'impersonal humanity', not personalized by the Son of God himself." *(Ibid., p. 49.)* An authentic theology, which does not take refuge from the discomforts of metaphysics

in a mythologizing vagueness, knows very well (as does Schillebeeckx) that the supposition of a real relationship to the world may not affect the absolute independence of God; that his "reaction" to the actual exercise of men's freedom takes place in sovereign transcendence, which includes man's freedom to set himself free for himself; that, therefore, the "partnership" between God and the world cannot be an interchange on the same level. Otherwise God would not be God and man would not be man (for man, as a relative being, finding himself referred to God, implies intrinsically the absoluteness of God). But the immutability of God must not be confused with frozen rigidity. The mystery of the way God is immutable surpasses human understanding.

But here again a question may be voiced. Do we preserve the divineness of God's being-for-men in creation and grace if we imagine, too anthropomorphically, that God proposes something, then carries it out and finally waits for the actions of his creatures to react to them? God's willing of the world — eternally necessary as an act, eternally free as regards its being terminated in finite objects — identical with his being, has in itself no finite purpose for the world. It has simply an immediate result, arrived at without any finite mediation immanent to the divine will: the very reality of created nature and grace, down to its very core, the humanity of Jesus Christ, produced by its personal assumption by the Son-Logos (for the formal structure, see W. Brugger, p. 344). God's Yes to the fellowship in love with man, insofar as it is distinct from God's own being, *is* nothing else than the being of man and the world, including the ultimate reality of the most free decision of the creature. Such immediate production of the "other", down to its selfhood and its own activity, is the most sovereign and efficacious, and also the most selflessly free, self-surrendering, self-abandoning affirmation of the "other" in love, purely for his own sake. Because the creative will of God, without the world as prior intrinsic term of relationship, causes world and man to be directly, man and the world, as creatures, belong to God (the more so, in grace, and most of all in Jesus Christ), as the "other", without which God would not be what he is, that is, he who thus loves man and the world. Thomas

Aquinas says of God: "amat nos tamquam aliquid sui" (*Summa Theologica*, I, 30, 2 ad 1). Hence God becomes and changes, by creating the world and man with all the changes of his free history, and above all by himself becoming man (without its being necessary to ascribe to him a real relation to the world).

c) A real relation of God to the world cannot be the secondary combination of realities otherwise separate. Once it was misunderstood in this way, silently and commonly but nonetheless to some extent, it had to be rejected by philosophers for the sake of the sovereign independence of God, but it had to be accepted by theologians on account of the reality of God's fellowship in the incarnation and grace with his opposite, man. Whether or not one retains the term (properly understood) of a real (transcendental) God-world relationship, the intermediate position may be put as follows, in the terms now available: God changes because he becomes man; he becomes something else and exists otherwise by becoming and being man. But God, the Absolute, Infinite and Simple, cannot change intrinsically. Hence he changes, not in himself, but in something else belonging to himself. He becomes different, not in himself, but "only" in the otherness of himself. To put the emphasis in this way does justice to the element of truth in the philosophical denial of a real relation of God to the world. Nonetheless, God changes — in his own self's otherness. This does justice to the element of truth in the theological affirmation of a real relation of God to the world. God does not change in his being as it is for himself, but in his being for "the other". God's changing for others and in others does not imply any strict addition (in creation) or diminution (in the incarnation, as self-emptying). It is identical with the infinite living reality of God's own being. In a word, one could say that God changes in that which is other — not God. "God can become something, he who is changeless in himself can be changeable in something else." (K. Rahner, IV, p. 147; see also p. 116, note 15, pp. 148 ff., 295; I, pp. 194–206; cf. F. Malmberg, pp. 61–65.) "He changes when in producing the derivative 'other' he himself becomes the derivative, without having to undergo the process of becoming in his own originating and original self." (K. Rahner, IV, p. 148.) God, the "self-determining subsistent" (Schillebeeckx, p. 44), determines himself to becoming man and to creating the world, and becomes and is creator and man: he himself, in the otherness of himself, bringing this other continually to be, through himself, through the subsistent freedom which is his being. "Deus est in se, fit in creaturis." (F. Baader, after Scotus Eriugena, *Werke,* II [1851], p. 145.) Such a solution should not be considered as the mere juggling with words of a feeble dialectics. The two partial affirmations — God himself changes, but not in himself — cannot fall into place for us in a comprehensible — that is, Hegelian — synthesis. Since we cannot comprehend the internal possibility of incarnation and creation, the real solution of this problem of knowledge in our regard is only possible through its being absorbed into the mystery of the love of God, who answers the love of man, which man has because he is loved (1 Jn 4:10).

See also *World, Knowledge, Absolute and Contingent, Transcendence, Being, Creation, Grace, Trinity of God, Incarnation.*

BIBLIOGRAPHY. L. Billot, *De Deo Uno et Trino* (7th ed., 1926); A. Krempel, *La doctrine de la relation chez S. Thomas* (1952); K. Rahner, *Theological Investigations,* I (1961); W. J. Kane, *The Philosophy of Relation in the Metaphysics of St. Thomas* (1958); F. Malmberg, *Über den Gottmenschen* (1960); J. B. Lotz, *Ontologia* (1963); W. Brugger, *Theologia Naturalis* (2nd ed., 1964), esp. pp. 301–7, 339–46; E. Schillebeeckx, "Die Heiligung des Namens Gottes durch die Menschenliebe Jesu Christi", *Gott in Welt,* II (1964); P. den Ottolander, *Deus immutabilis* (1965) (in Dutch); K. Rahner, "On the Theology of the Incarnation", *Theological Investigations,* IV (1966), pp. 105–32.

Walter Kern

GOOD

1. *Introduction.* The good is "the end which is the object of all desire", according to Aristotle, who puts this description forward as traditional (*Eth. Nic.,* I, 1–1094a). Scholasticism took over the definition (e.g., Thomas Aquinas, *Summa Theologica,* I, q. 5, a. 1). The primordial reality of the good allows of definition as little as does the notion of desire. It can only be described on the basis of the experience of the good, that is, on the basis of the self-experience of desire,

and classified in the frame-work of this description. The philosophical tradition has found two perspectives important. One envisages the type and degree of desirability, and divides the good into the *bonum utile* (the useful and helpful), the *delectabile* (that which contents and delights) and the *honestum* (that which is valuable in itself, that which ought to be). The other envisages the reality or the realization of the good, and divides it into *bonum onticum* (or *naturale,* the goodness or appetibility which goes with being) and the *bonum exercitum* (attained, actualized or realized goodness). The latter in its purest form (that which is knowingly and freely willed) is called the *bonum formale* (the good in the strictest sense). The two aspects, the ethical and the ontic-ontological, do not coincide, but they are most intimately connected. The precise determination of their relationship, that is, the question also of their unifying original ground, from which the good first addresses us, so that our desire and reflection can respond, brings us to the history of this experience and the nature of its self-understanding.

2. *History of the concept.* Scholastic metaphysics makes *bonum* one of the transcendentals, along with *unum* and *verum.* Whatever is, is — according to its degree of being — of itself good for itself, and by virtue of common being also good for others. The degree in which being is possessed determines the degree of goodness. On the analogy of substance and accident, and on the analogy of the substantial entities themselves, which range from the *paene nihil* of *materia prima* to the *summum ens, esse ipsum,* goodness is also ranged in degrees up to the *summum bonum,* the supreme good. Goodness does not add a new determination to being. It merely explicitates one aspect of its intrinsic relationships, the reference to the faculty of desire (the will).

This concept gave rise to two controversies. There was the question of the relationship of *ens* and *verum* to *bonum,* in other words, that of knowing and willing. There was also the question of the possibility and reality of the bad, especially of evil. Appealing to Plato, the Augustinian and Franciscan schools attributed a priority to the will which made it the foundation of knowledge. The possibility and power of evil stood out all the more clearly. This is less

clear in the Aristotelian and Thomistic school which emphasized the priority of knowledge. And though the primordiality and power of freedom, and the proper character of the good itself were definitely noted and thoroughly thought out, they also stood out less clearly.

This was the occasion of the real disappearance of the proper reality of the good in rationalism, which culminated in Spinoza's conception of the *amor intellectualis.* But it also gave rise to an irrational philosophy of values, which especially in its modern form separates *esse* and *bonum,* knowing and willing (or "feeling") in a dualistic way and never envisages the antecedent unity in being as well as in consciousness. The appeal to a merely irrational "feeling" is a simple rejection of a positivist denial of the objectivity of the good, but has no way of demonstrating its claim. It was in this type of controversy that the Aristotelian position was built up, in its endeavour to establish the ontological foundations of the good, in opposition to the Sophists. But the controversy also had the effect of restricting the general perspectives. The character of challenge or claim which the good presents was obscured by the description of the objective finality of the real, in terms of potency and act. This was then followed by an ethics for which the common sense insight of the cultured was normative — insight into the relationship of end and means, for the attainment of happiness in the achievement of the perfect.

Thus in the Aristotelian-Thomist conception, the good is envisaged in the light of the *appetitus,* and regarded as that which fulfils, while the ethical perspective remains secondary and derivative. One can see how it may give occasion to the aberrations of hedonism and rationalism. In Plato the good is envisaged more authentically, and one might say that the ethical perspective is prevalent, if ethics is taken in a more primordial and comprehensive sense than in the Aristotelian system. In Plato the good is the ultimate principle of the κοινωνία τῶν ἰδεῶν, principle of being as well as of truth, of reality as well as of the response to reality. It is illustrated by the metaphor of the sun which gives light and life. All reality is considered a participation of this good, and hence (like the good itself) not only is or wills to be (in the *appetitus naturalis*) but is *rightly* so and wills to be what it *ought* to be (*Republic,* VI; VII;

Philebus). The proximity to the Hebrew and Christian (biblical) experience is obvious. But the question comes up of the material object of the good, its concrete realization on the various levels of participation. The question is also relevant in subsequent forms of Platonism, as when Augustine lays down the principle "Love, and do what you will" (*In Jo.*, 7, 8: *PL,* XXXV, 2033). For its precise application he has, however, to call on theological data, such as he envisages when he says, "Love, but give heed to what love merits" (*Enarr. in Ps,* 31, 2, 5: *PL,* XXXVI, 260).

Consequent to the new approach of Descartes and Cartesianism, this view was given an "epochal" effectiveness by Kant. His basic principle, that nothing "can be considered good except the good will" (*Grundlegung zur Metaphysik der Sitten,* I [Academy Edition IV, 393], E. T.: *Fundamental Principles of the Metaphysic of Ethics,* tr. by T. Abbott [10th ed., 1955]) recalls the *bonum formale* of tradition — especially when one remembers that the latter should not be restricted to the "objective". In willing its object the will primarily wills itself; freedom chooses itself when it makes its choice. Kant takes the *bonum formale* in a more precise sense, since he does not mean what is *de facto* willed but what is rightly willed, what ought to be willed. His polemical situation forbade him an adequate grasp of the unity of the theoretical and practical reason, and he did not go beyond a formalism of duty — which explains the attacks of Hegel and of the proponents of the philosophies of value, though it does not justify the radical opposition of the latter. Here Fichte intervenes, to synthetize systematically the formal and material elements in Kant (the latter being quite adequately present), as well as the theoretical and the ethico-practical. Modern research has shown that it is as wrong to brand Fichte's (later) system as "subjective idealism", as it is conversely to label the Aristotelian-Thomist (and Hegelian) doctrine as ultimately a non-moral justification of the *de facto* process, supposedly taken as the norm.

After the descriptive efforts of the phenomenology of values, and the challenge of existential philosophy, M. Heidegger deliberately renounced all ethical assertions. This was not because he denied that being presented itself as good and as challenge, but because he is aware of the inadequacy of the modes available to express this fundamental experience, which determines unmistakably his ontological thinking.

3. *The problem.* As it affected the thinking of an epoch, this basic experience was expounded in various ways, with the emphasis now on the ontic, now on the ethical, now on the value-laden character of reality, or again on the claim of the "ought". In none of the major forms of thought (that is, the ontological and transcendental) was a given aspect stressed to the exclusion of the other, but nowhere was justice done to both aspects at once. The same is true of the approaches which stressed the objective or natural and the subjective.

The good, as a transcendental and challenging reality is at once that which rightly is and that which ought to be. As such, it cannot at once be visualized or sensed objectively and unconditionally, in a simply theoretical contemplation. It can only be experienced, in a radically willing opening of the person, which is less *desire* and striving than obedience and surrender. This does not of course constitute the good — since these responses are both demanded and evoked by the good — but in its concrete form they go to make up the moral "event". Just as in the case of truth the event is the common actuation of the knower and the known, so too the good is the event in each case of the one act of call (destiny) and response — in the individual and in the epoch — in the interpenetration of the rule of the good and of autonomy. Can this complex relationship be expressed without giving the impression of a relativism conditioned by external processes or of a mythologization of reality or simple facts, of some type of humanism or the formalism of an empty "decisiveness"? Perhaps this embarrassment signals the intrinsic difficulty of thinking and speaking of the good — not that this makes the attempt any the less permissible or imperative. For as such, the good can only be willed and done, "loved" as it wills to be. Hence the good, as properly experienced — an experience which has been described above as both active and passive, since it is a laying hold of by allowing oneself to be laid hold of — can by its very nature be only partially and inadequately articulated. The experience of the good is fundamentally less amenable to full explicitation than even the experience of truth, knowledge or decision.

The "experience" of the good is the starting-point and constant guide of reflection. It is brought about both by the appeal of the good and by him who opens his heart to it. The two factors make it clear that this experience can have a history, though the good always remains the good. Being freedom in act its concrete form cannot be deduced in any particular case or positively defined — except in general as "love", which remains love in all categories of realization and may not become hatred. Negatively, it may be defined as excluding certain attitudes or acts.

Efforts have been made to define the good more precisely, chiefly from two points of view. One sees it as perfection or happiness, which of course for the free spirit implies love and goodness — not as means to the end, but as essential constituents. The other sees it as dedication and love, which for the free spirit means fulfilment — not as an end to be achieved in isolation, but as "accepted" and completed love. Behind these efforts lies the great reality which is not only the object of actual desire, but which *ought* to be accepted by virtue of its own majesty and splendour. It is that which is "good for me" but which is only so because it is incalculably "good in itself". It summons man to this response and enables him to make it, while holding him sharply and inexorably at a distance because of the inadequacy of his answer. "No one is good . . ." (Mk 10:18.) But since it is the good — and not merely the "ought" — it comes, as men know, once more to aid this weakness. It reveals itself gratuitously and unforeseeably as grace, in the full sense of all experience which claims "meaning" — from the simplest and vaguest assurances to the great testimonies of religious history. But here the good points on beyond itself to the holy.

See also *Transcendentals, Experience, Evil, Rationalism, Value, Principle, Cartesianism, Kantianism, Knowledge, Decision, Situation* II, *Grace, Meaning.*

BIBLIOGRAPHY. A. C. Ewing, *Definition of Good* (1947); B. Häring, *Das Heilige und das Gute* (1950); G. Siewert, *Die Freiheit und das Gute* (1959); E. Weil, *Philosophie Morale* (1961); J. Pieper, *Reality and the Good* (1967). See also bibliography on *Transcendentals.*

Jörg Splett

GRACE

I. Biblical. II. Theological: A. History of Doctrine. B. Systematic. III. Structure of *De Gratia.*

I. Biblical

1. *The Old Testament background.* The prehistory of the theological concept of grace is to be attached to the terms חסד and חן in the OT. Both appear as χάρις in the LXX. They do not signify proprieties or entities, but, like the OT concept of justice, a social attitude, and its deployment in action rather than merely the mental disposition. Hence the concepts of תם, צדקה and ישר are closely connected with them, as is also שלום. Hence, in contrast to our notion of grace, חסד may be attributed to both partners in the relationship between man and Yahweh. For it must be remembered that חסד is the unfailing duty of reciprocity which exists between relatives, friends, sovereigns and subjects, and above all, between the contracting parties in a covenant, since the covenant implies the obligation of חסד (1 Sam 20:8). Here חסד is often used in combination with a second term such as truth (loyalty), love, justice, rights or mercy. The relationship to God called for by the covenant is described in Exod 20:6; Deut 7:12; Hos 6:4 as חסד. Hence, particularly in later texts, the God-fearing are called חסידים. The way is really paved for the Christian concept of grace in the texts which speak of God's relationship to Israel in the covenant (1 Kg 8:23; Is 55:3; Ps 89:29, 50; 106:45). Here the covenant bestowed by God is in fact identical with the "חסדי" which he has promised. Man can ask God to remember his favours or to act in keeping with them, that is, he can appeal to Yahweh's loyalty to his covenant (Ps 6:5; 25:6f.). This occurs above all when man has violated the covenant and asks Yahweh to remain faithful in spite of the breach. Hence stress is laid on the close connection between Yahweh's חסד and the keeping of the commandments (1 Kg 8:23), while חסד takes on more and more the meaning of mercy (Is 63:7; Jer 16:5; Hos 2:21), as the failings of the people are stressed.

This is true not only of the prophets but also of later times, since LXX mostly translates חסד by ἔλεος. Where Yahweh's חסד is seen as a blessing to be hoped for in the future, its theological basis is sought in the past, either in the promises to David (Is 55:3; 54:8) or to the fathers (Mich 7:20); or man begs (in the Psalms) for God to act "according to the חסדי", that is, in keeping with his salvific actions in the past. No such historical roots are attached to the word חן (except in 2 Kg 13:23), which does not stem from the realm of social ethos but simply means "favour". In the Pentateuch it is used only by the Yahwist (except Deut 24:1), and is practically confined to the phrase "to find favour in someone's eyes". Thus it is often used apropos of the patriarchs. As the phrase is used in ancient narratives (1 and 2 Sam) to speak of subjects finding favour with the king or a wife with her husband, the application to the relationship with Yahweh is a transfer from the realm of the profane. It means no more than that someone is pleasing to Yahweh. In the case of Abraham, the phrase was first given a theological sense by St. Paul (Rom 4:1). In the OT, חן is seldom used in the theological sense, that is, of favours bestowed by God; see Ps 84:12, where it is a protective gift of God along with glory, Prov 3:34, where God bestows his favours on the lowly. The verb חנן is found more frequently in the theological sense (to be kind, gracious, merciful), sometimes in connection with the "face of God" which man sees or which shines upon him when he has found favour in God's sight and is blessed by him (Gen 33:10f.; Num 6:25). When חסד is used, more stress is laid on the sovereignty of the liberality of God than in חן (Exod 33:19 and the psalms of petition in the first person singular). Hence חסד is closer to compassion and consideration for weakness than to the notion of loyalty to a covenant. Hence too the prayer for חן occurs more often in formulas where the individual appears rather than all Israel (but contrast 2 Kg 13:23; Amos 5:1; Mal 1:9).

The LXX translates חסד by χάρις only in Est 2:9, 17; Ecclus 7:33; 40:17, which is, however, the standard translation of חן. Hence in the theological language of Septuagint Judaism χάρις, except on very few occasions, only means the favour which man finds in God's sight. But God's saving action, in his fidelity to his deeds and promises at the beginning of history (חסד) is translated only by ἔλεος (of which there is an echo in Lk 1:72). In spite of this LXX usage, the NT writers used χάρις very widely to render the sense of חסד.

2. *New Testament beginnings of a theological concept of grace.* The fact that χάρις (with χαρίζεσθαι, χάρισμα) is practically confined to Lk, Paul and the epistles of a Pauline character shows that the term was a key concept for the salvation brought by Jesus only in certain sections of early Christianity. Since the usage is very frequent in comparison with the Jewish and Greek backgrounds, it must be regarded as a technical term from a certain type of missionary activity which was developed in particular by Paul. We can see at once that χάρις became a sort of slogan, if we compare the expanded form of greeting used at the beginning of the epistles ("grace to you and peace") with the normal opening of a letter. The Pauline usage is "the Christian community's transformation of the Jewish opening blessing" (H. Schlier; but see the opening of the letter in the Syriac Apocalypse of Baruch 78:2, "Mercy and peace be with you"). One of the characteristics of χάρις in the NT is that it stands in general for the whole salvation freely bestowed by God in Christ. The precise theological content of it is not indicated, nor its place in the history of salvation. What is in the foreground is the notion that God, in his freely-bestowed love, has made good the relationship between man and himself. But in profane Greek χάρις already meant both the condescension of the giver and the thanks of the favoured, as well as beauty or winsomeness. Thus it pointed to a joyful openness for one another, freely given, unenforceable. When applied to the relationship between God and man it meant both the salvation granted by God and the thanks offered by man. The freedom of χάρις in contrast to wages or reward is already brought out by Aristotle (*Rhetoric,* 1385a).

In the synoptic tradition χάρις and χαρίζεσθαι are found only in Lk. Hence the terminology of Mt and Mk offers no points of departure for the development of a doctrine of grace. In Lk 6:32–34 we have the pre-Lucan usage of Q (par. Mt 5:44ff.: the specific μισθός) where χάρις is the heavenly reward, hence a salvation yet to come; in Lk 1:30; 2:52 (cf. Prov 3:4) the OT usage still survives. But in Lk's own style, χάρις is the salvation wrought by God since Jesus, particularly through the words of the gospel. The offering of this salvation to men through the preaching plays a special role (Lk 4:22; Acts 14:3, 26; 20:24, 32), so that χάρις, as in Paul, implies above all the act of believing (Acts 4:33; 11:23; 13:43). Here χάρις functions as a force given by God, as the combination with "power" and "signs" shows (Acts 6:8; cf. Lk 4:22; Acts 4:33; 7:10). This force is a special characteristic of missionaries (Acts 14:26; 15:40). In some very typically Lucan texts χάρις appears as an independent active force, the salvation of God itself expanding in place and time (Acts 4:33; 11:23; 13:43; and especially 20:32 — the constructive work of the word of grace as it confers the inheritance). The salvific grace of Christians is linked with the person of Jesus only in Acts 15:11. But even there it is only the grace of the Lord in general, which according to Lk 2:40 is simply "with him". It seems on the whole that the terminology of Lk is not derived from Paul but reflects a wider tradition which is partly pre-Pauline.

We find Paul reflecting at length on χάρις for the first time in Romans, and here too the element of gratuitousness is brought out in particular. But the usage is already so well worked out that χάρις means the whole salvation bestowed through Jesus Christ, the blessings in general to which the Church is called (1:6). But χάρις indicates in particular the saving power by which the Apostle was appointed to his task (1:15) and the legitimate apostolate itself (2:9; cf. Rom 1:5; 12:3). Thus the Christians addressed by Paul can be called partakers in the grace of the Apostle in Phil 1:7. Hence the action of God in his χάρις is not confined to the general sanctification of all the baptized, but is an economy of salvation with a diversified inner structure.

It follows that χάρις has basically the character of salvation, in contrast to a past ruled by sin, and especially in contrast to the vain effort to attain justification by works done under the law (Gal 2:21; 5:4). In the realm of χάρις justice is attained through the Spirit and because of faith (Gal 5:4, 5). But this grace is not given at once to all, but only to those who are called and chosen to receive it (Gal 1:6, 15; Rom 11:5). And even here it does not come to all in the same way, but appears as charisms of various types.

The office of apostle in particular is a special mode of working of the divine χάρις,

which elsewhere signifies in a very general way the divine act of mercy extended to man. Here χάρις appears, as early as Gal, as a region or realm, comparable to that of the law (Gal 5:4; cf. the notion of justification), and is therefore opposed to all that is ungodly, all that belongs to the realm of *sarx,* death and sin (2 Cor 1:12). This realm is opened up in Jesus Christ (1 Cor 1:4). To turn back to the law for salvation (Gal 2:21; 5:4) or to return to sin in general (2 Cor 6:1) is to offend against this gift of salvation. But the concept of χάρις has still further connotations in Paul. It also means thanksgiving to God and the loving gifts of the community — applications of the term which are not to be isolated from the meaning already given (cf. 2 Cor 8:7, 9; 9:8, 14, 15). Because of the χάρις of Christ, the community can and must bring about a χάρις, and because of the χάρις which God gave, χάρις is due to him (Rom 9:14, 15). This is not a play upon words, since χάρις is a relationship to another in loving compassion. The relationship is set up by God's mercy in the salvation which came in Jesus Christ. This is the basis and model for human compassion, and also the motive for thanksgiving. Thus the usage of the term χάρις shows that thanksgiving is the action corresponding to grace in this relationship. In 1 Cor in particular attention is paid to the embodiment of grace in charisms. Paul makes use of the different individual embodiments of grace to try to solve the problems of community discipline and ethics. The multiplicity of charisms is contrasted with the unity of the Pneuma (1 Cor 12:4). In Rom, Paul stresses the fact that grace is given through baptism, as a gift (3:24), which contrasts it with the works of the law as a way of salvation, since under the law rewards are calculated, while in the order of χάρις the fulfilment of the law is a gift bestowed in the charism of love. In the important text Rom 5:12–21, the fall of Adam and the grace which came (χάρισμα) in Jesus Christ are not simply opposed, for the efficacy and riches of the latter far exceed the former. Grace is greater than sin, and its conquering march cannot be held back by sin. Thus the multiplication of sin in the time of the law only served to demonstrate all the more forcibly the riches of grace (Rom 5:20). But this truth is no reason for abiding in sin to allow grace to display its riches more abundantly (Rom 6:1). Sin and grace are successive aeons or reigns. Transition from one to the other is made when one dies with Christ to the power of the ancient (Rom 6:2), which happens in baptism (Rom 6:3 ff.). But the way of salvation which grace substitutes for the law does not mean new freedom to sin. It means being laid hold of by a new power (Rom 6:14 ff.). What therefore has Paul done for the concept of grace? He did not describe the full theological concept, but linked its function indissolubly to the death of Jesus Christ in his notion of the history of salvation; then, he situated it for believers in the process of justification and baptism; and finally, he interpreted this χάρις as a call to special moral or apostolic service.

In the rest of the Pauline literature, these concepts make themselves felt above all in Eph, where we find similar stress laid on the richness of grace (cf. Rom 5), the special grace of the apostolate and the individuality of the gifts of grace (Eph 4:7) and on the notion of a divine dispensation of grace (Eph 3:2). As in 2 Tim 1:9, grace is contrasted with works in Eph 2:8. But these are not now the works of the law, but simply human action as distinct from the divine plan of redemption (2 Tim 1:9). In many places, χάρις appears beside δύναμις, and the dawn of the day of salvation is described as its epiphany (Tit 2:11). In Heb, χάρις is the salvation granted in the new order of worship centred on heaven which must never be abandoned (Heb 12:15).

Like Paul, John opposes grace to the law (Jn 1:17) and in 1:16 we meet the key-word of the fullness of grace, which is interpreted in vv. 14 and 17 as the salvific blessing of "truth" (an obviously Johannine mode of expression, which reflects, however, the OT combination of חסד ואמת. The term is used in a variety of ways in 1 Pet. It is important to note, for instance, that at 2:19 f., the sufferings of Christians appear as grace. 1 Pet shows how wide the concept of χάρις was in the Hellenistic missionary area before, during and after Paul's work. If 1 Pet 4:10 reflects pre-Pauline tradition, the division of grace into a number of charisms could no longer be regarded as an original achievement of Pauline theology. In 1 Pet, grace can also be used simply to indicate Christian salvation as a totality (1 Pet 1:10, 13).

See also *Justification, Covenant, Charisms, Sin* I.

BIBLIOGRAPHY. J. Köberle, *Sünde und Gnade im religiösen Leben des Volkes Israel* (1905); J. Moffat, *Grace in the New Testament* (1931); A. Pujol, "Caritas in Novo Testamento", *Verbum Domini* 12 (1932), pp. 38–40, 76–82; W. F. Lofthouse, "Chen and Chesed in the Old Testament", *Zeitschrift für die alttestamentliche Wissenschaft* 51 (1933), pp. 29–35; J. Wobbe, *Der Charisgedanke bei Paulus* (1932); N. Glueck, *Das Wort Chesed im alttestamentlichen Sprachgebrauch* (1927; 2nd ed., 1961); R. Bultmann, *Theology of the New Testament,* I (1952), pp. 288–92; C. R. Smith, *The Bible Doctrine of Grace* (1956); G. Farr, "The Concept of Grace in the Book of Hosea", *Zeitschrift für die alttestamentliche Wissenschaft* 70 (1958), pp. 98–107.

Klaus Berger

II. Theological

A. HISTORY OF DOCTRINE

The doctrine of grace propounds the theological problem at the heart of Christian faith, insofar as faith reveals man's understanding of himself, the world and God. The task of human life in the world is here displayed in all its tensions: the doctrine of the divine choice, call and election which integrate human responsibility into the order of a world regulated by the goodness and holiness of God; the doctrine of the redemptive work of the God-Man Jesus and of the divine Spirit in the Church, which makes justification the work of the triune God; the ensuing doctrine of the forgiveness of sin, and the healing of natural man by the gracious gift of God's love (Rom 5:15; Rev 22:12), so that man's personal decision and whole nature are re-installed in the sphere of God, man's creator, Lord and Father.

1. The treatment of these problems in the NT was primarily in the Jewish categories of a universal history of salvation (Synoptics, Acts), an eschatological mysticism (Jn) or a theology of redemption and salvation (Paul). In the early Church, the revealed doctrine had to be defended and developed against an excessive emphasis on ethical effort (inspired by Phariseeism or Stoicism) and against a (Platonizing) spiritualization (cf. *Didache, Barnabas, 1 Clement, Letters of Ignatius, Hermas*).

2. The defence of the mysteries of the Christian faith was particularly necessary in the 2nd and 3rd centuries, against the pagan,

Jewish and ecclesiastical Gnosticism of late antiquity. Against its doctrine of man's self-redemption through a special salvific knowledge and the interpretation of Christ as a demiurge, the first great theologians of the Church (Irenaeus, Tertullian, Origen) proclaimed Christ crucified as the one redeemer (the *anakephalaiosis* of Eph 1:10). Against its dualistic contempt for the world they affirmed the goodness of creation and the grace of human freedom. Clement of Alexandria gave the Platonic doctrine of the divinization of man (*Theaetetus,* 176 AB) a Christian interpretation (cf. 2 Pet 1:4), in particular by the doctrine of the indwelling of the Holy Spirit (Rom 8:11; 2 Tim 1:14).

3. The inner change in man through the gift of sonship of God (1 Jn 3:1 f.) was given profounder theological expression through the dogmatic development of the doctrines of the incarnation and Trinity in the 4th and 5th centuries at the Councils of Nicaea, 325, Constantinople I, 380, Ephesus, 431, and Chalcedon, 450. Athanasius and Gregory Nazianzenus appealed above all to the work of Christ ("God became man so that man might become God"), while Didymus the Blind and Basil stressed the indwelling of the Holy Spirit and Cyril of Alexandria that of the triune God (after Jn 14:23, 26). Under the influence of the philosophy of neo-Platonism (Plotinus, Proclus), a Christian mysticism, of which Origen had been a precursor, came into being, chiefly through the writings of the Pseudo-Dionysius (*c.* 520) and his commentator Maximus the Confessor. It taught the possibility of a consummation of the earthly life of faith in a supernatural, ecstatic vision and love of God even on earth, within the framework of ecclesiastical spirituality. This theology of grace has remained a major influence in the Orthodox Eastern Churches to the present day.

4. In the Roman Church of the West, the struggle against a view of sin and grace which made them merely external to man, in Pelagianism, occasioned the development of the special treatise on grace by Augustine. Basing himself on St. Paul, he emphasized the universal causality of God in justification, sanctification and predestination, and also the reality of grace in man. But for the Jewish perspective of the history of salvation in St. Paul, he substituted an anthropological approach in keeping with his own Roman thinking and the Germanic (or Celtic) thought (of Pelagius). His doctrine, expounded in many copious works between 412 and 430 ("The Perfection of Man", "Nature and Grace", "Grace and Free Choice" "Grace and Original Sin", "Predestination of the Saints", etc.) was ratified by the Roman Church in the Indiculus of Pope Celestine I (*D* 129–42).

5. Certain theologians of the 5th century such as Lucidus Presbyter and (possibly) Arnobius the Younger, who did not, like Augustine, understand grace as an outcome of God's love, but rather as the exercise of God's omnipotence, put forward the erroneous view that man was not free under God's predestination and reprobation ("Predestinationism"). Monastic circles in North Africa (Hadrumetum) and South Gaul (Lérins) put forward the doctrine afterwards known as Semipelagianism, which held that at least the "beginning of faith" and final perseverance were the work of man alone, and not of grace. Both heresies were rejected at several Councils, especially at the Second Council of Orange in 529 (*D* 178–200). Here the doctrine of Augustine (with restrictions as regards his notion of predestination) was given definitive ratification by the Church.

6. His doctrine of predestination was discussed again in the Carolingian theology, when the mistaken notion of Isidore of Seville about a "double predestination" (*gemina determinatio*) was taken up by the monk Gottschalk of Orbais. This led to a comprehensive debate, which came up at the synods of Quierzy, 849, Valence, 855, Toucy, 860, etc. with Hincmar of Reims representing the Church. Some rational light was thrown on the obscurity of the Pauline doctrine (Rom 9:18) and new stress laid on human freedom. In his monograph, "On the Harmony of Divine Knowledge, Predestination and Grace with the Free Will", Anselm of Canterbury transmitted the new doctrine to the Middle Ages. The first comprehensive theologies of the Middle Ages, from 1100 to 1250, treated of grace either in the tractate on faith and charity (Anselm of Laon) or in the tractates on the sacraments (Abélard, under baptism) or in Christology (Victorine mysticism).

7. In the Roman Church the doctrine of grace was given its markedly anthropological attitude in the late 13th century, when the metaphysics, ethics and psychology of Aristotle had been made the key to the study of the theological problems. Here the Dominicans led the way (Thomas Aquinas and his school), till, from *c.* 1280 on, and especially after Duns Scotus, the Franciscans too developed their more Augustinian theology with the help of the categories and principles of Aristotle. In opposing in particular Peter Lombard's view that grace was simply the indwelling of the Holy Spirit (*Sent.,* I, dist. 17), Thomas Aquinas had developed his description of grace as a "supernatural *habitus* of the human soul" (*Sent. Comm.,* II, 24–28; *Summa Theologica,* I, q. 110–14), while the Franciscans (William de la Mare, Duns Scotus and his followers) identified grace with the supernatural virtue of charity. Thomas Aquinas and his school regarded grace as the sufficient reason for a possible *meritum de condigno* ("merit by worthiness") of man before God, while the Franciscan school maintained that man could have only a *meritum de congruo* ("merit by equity"), and at the end, not a due reward, but only free acceptance by God *(acceptatio).* Some nominalists like Peter Marsh and John Bassolis held that God could refuse this *acceptatio,* even with regard to man in the state of grace.

8. This late medieval doctrine of grace, with its tendency to seek holiness through works inspired by the fear of God, was rejected by the Reformation. Luther taught that the justice of God (Rom 1:17) imputed the redemptive work of Christ to the believer (Rom 3:22) without works on his part, precisely because he was a sinner (Gal 3:13). Besides this justification by faith, Calvin also stressed again the change wrought in man by repentance and rebirth and a Christian life of faith (*Institutiones,* III, 3, 11–18). The attitude of the Council of Trent, 1547 (*D* 792a–843), to these doctrines was inspired by Scholasticism as it had developed particularly in Spain (Andreas de Vega, Francisco de Vitoria, Dominico Soto, G. Seripando). It interpreted and condemned the doctrine of the Reformation and gave its own a more biblical expression.

9. The same mentality gave rise to the great controversy between the schools of Thomists (Dominicans) and Molinists (Jesuits) about the role of grace and human freedom in the genesis of meritorious works. It was ended by the Church in 1607, though not decided, and flared up again in the 20th century (G. Schneemann, A. Dummermuth, etc.). Thomism was primarily concerned with maintaining the sovereignty of the creator God as *causa prima* (by a *praemotio physica*), while Molinism sought to maintain the freedom of man as well as God (by a *concursus simultaneus*). The Reformation doctrine of the total corruption of man by sin, revived by Baianism (*D* 1001–80), Jansenism (*D* 1092–6, 1295–303) and B. Quesnel (*D* 1351–90), was rejected by the Jesuit theologians of the day with the help of newly developed concepts such as the *desiderium naturale, potentia oboedientialis* and *natura pura.* In the 19th century, the question of grace was of importance in particular in the problem of faith (as in the controversy between J. von Kuhn and C. von Schälzer), while M. Scheeben used the concept of life developed in the Romantic movement to expound more fully the Thomistic doctrine of grace.

10. Since 1920, the "eventful" *(heilsgeschichtliche)* character of grace has once more come to the fore (in the "mystery theology" of the sacraments), and also its personalistic character (as the self-communication of God; cf. R. Guardini, K. Rahner). The *Church Dogmatics* of K. Barth (German, 1932 ff., E. T., 1949 ff.) (cf. H. Küng, *Rechtfertigung* [1957], E. T.: *Justification* [1964]) and H. de Lubac's *Surnaturel* (1946) (cf. G. de Broglie, L. Malevez) stimulated a new interest in the question of the supernatural order. In view of the ecumenical spirit of Vatican II and the central importance of the doctrine of grace in Christian life, the present great historical hour of the Church demands that the many possible starting-points and stand-points for the doctrine of grace should be surveyed comprehensively by Christians, in mutual understanding and no longer in hostile opposition, so that justice may be done to the rich deposit of revelation.

See also *Predestination, Justification, Gnosticism, Pelagianism, Habitus, Grace and Freedom, Baianism, Jansenism, Calvinism, Sacraments* II, *Revelation.*

BIBLIOGRAPHY. See bibliography on Grace I; also: H. J. Iwand, *Rechtfertigungsglaube und Christusglaube* (Luther) (1930); N. Merlin, *S. Augustin et les dogmes du péché originel et de la grâce* (1931); F. Stegmüller, *Francisco de Vitoria y la doctrina de la gracia en la escuela salmantina* (1934); J. Gross, *La divinisation du chrétien d'après les Pères grecs* (1938); T. F. Torrance, *The Doctrine of Grace in the Apostolic Fathers* (1948); J. Auer, *Die Entwicklung der Gnadenlehre in der Hochscholastik* (1941–52); H. Brosch, *Das Übernatürliche in der katholischen Tübinger Schule* (1962); R. Gleason, *Grace* (1962); H. Rito, *Recentiores theologiae quaedam tendentiae ad conceptum ontologico-personalem gratiae* (1963); W. Dettloff, *Die Entwicklung der Akzeptations- und Verdienstlehre von Duns Skotus bis Luther* (1963).

Johann Auer

B. Systematic

1. *Introduction.* This article, which presents the Church's doctrine, biblical theology and systematic reflection in a single unified account, must on principle be read in conjunction with others which deal with the doctrine of grace from other points of view: *Man (Anthropology), Salvation, Order* III, *Justification, Faith, Hope, Charity, Holy Spirit, Holiness, Charisms, Merit, Religious Experience, Mysticism, Beatific Vision, Sin, Concupiscence.*

The question arises from the start as to what is the right basis for such a survey. The customary post-Tridentine division of the treatise into actual grace and habitual grace will not do, because it makes questionable assumptions. The starting-point must be a theological statement about man in the unity of his whole nature. This must be the source from which the distinction between nature and grace and possible distinctions within the concept of grace itself are drawn, and which will themselves serve as principles on which a treatise of this kind can be composed. In this sense we are starting from the theological proposition (of dogmatic anthropology) that the human being who is a Christian believer must understand himself to be called in history to God's own most intimate life, by the effective word of God's free and absolute self-disclosure; and that he is so called in his character as creature, and despite it, and despite his recognition of himself as a sinner by his very origin.

The decisive feature of this proposition is that God does not bestow merely a certain kind of saving love and intimacy, or a certain kind of saving presence (such as ontologically is necessarily implied even by the abstract concept of a relation between

Creator and still innocent creature). God does not confer on man merely created gifts as a token of his love. God communicates *himself* by what is no longer simply efficient causality. He makes man share in the very nature of God. He constitutes man as co-heir with the Son himself, called to the eternal life of God face to face, called to receive the direct vision of God, called therefore to receive God's own life. Here we really reach the heart of the Christian conception of reality. The true and complete relation of the Absolute and of what we experience as ourselves and our world and know to be finite and contingent is not a relation of identity or of necessary connection in which the Absolute unfolds and attains its own plenitude as in the various forms of pantheism. But neither is it the simple relation of an absolute efficient cause to its effect, which remains external to that cause. It is rather the free relation of the Absolute communicating himself. And this relation by creative, efficient causality posits the recipient of the Absolute's outgoing self-communication, in order to be able to communicate himself in the mode of free personal intercourse in dialogue, and by the incarnation and grace to set the created world free for its own history.

The Christian doctrine of grace (with its highest realization, when the divine Logos becomes a creature) is the genuine means of transcending pantheism and deism. For the latter may be philosophically surmounted but is not really overcome by postulating that God is merely concerned about the *machina mundi* which he has set in being and motion. And the Christian doctrine of grace transcends these two systems of the relation between Absolute and contingent, each claiming to be metaphysically necessary, even though it is a doctrine of freely bestowed love. And this love shows itself thereby to be the real essence of the absolute reality. The "necessary" structures of absolute reality do not determine freedom as if the latter were something secondary, but are the formal structures of free and absolute love itself. This love itself turns towards the contingent. Yet it need not, except by the "necessity" of freely-bestowed love.

2. *"Supernatural" grace and nature.* On this basis it is possible to establish in the first place the distinction between nature

and supernatural grace and the character of the latter.

a) *The official teaching of the Church.* The doctrine of the supernatural character of grace (as God's self-communication) is *expressly* mentioned for the first time in an official pronouncement of the Church when in the Council of Vienne the vision of God is attributed to the (grace-given) *lumen gloriae* (*D* 475). It is then propounded expressly, and the term *supernaturalis* is employed, against Baianism, Jansenism and semi-rationalism (*D* 1017, 1021, 1023f., 1026, 1385, 1516, 1669, 1671). It is taught by Vatican I (*D* 1786, 1789) as the reason for the absolute necessity of revelation and as a characteristic of faith. Pius XII (*D* 2318) stressed the importance of not weakening it (in contesting the abstract possibility of a "pure nature"). It is only this supernatural character of grace which ultimately explains why in the Church's teaching grace is declared to be gratuitous, impossible to merit by man's own powers, so that of himself man can neither positively prepare himself for it nor obtain it by prayer (*D* 134f., 141, 176f., 797, 813, etc.). The fact that man is sinful cannot of itself be the total reason for this.

b) *Systematic theology.* (i) God's self-communication in his own divine life, both as given, and as accepted by man, is essentially God's free, personal, uncovenanted favour. In itself it is a free gift in relation to man, not merely insofar as he is a sinner (i.e., someone who culpably shuts himself to God's offer of himself and to God's will as this is expressed in the whole of human reality), but even prior to this. On the one hand for the creature to be endowed with God in a personal love which communicates God himself is an unmerited favour on the part of God himself. It is essentially a freely bestowed favour if a person discloses his own self. And on the other hand the spiritual creatures (even if we assume them to be already constituted) cannot receive this favour as posited or promised by their own (innocent) nature, but apprehend it as consisting of a genuine dialogue in time and history which therefore presupposes the existence of the person addressed. Consequently the spiritual creature cannot regard it as identical with its character as creature or as posited by this with ontological necessity. If through its acceptance on the part of finite man (in

accordance with the essence and measure of a finite creature) this self-communication by God is not to be reduced to an event which remains in the domain of the purely finite (which would contradict God's self-communication as such), the acceptance precisely as such must have its ground in God in the same way as the gift itself. The self-communication as such also effects its acceptance; the actual and proximate ability to accept is itself a supremely free grace. That is very clear as regards faith. If revelation when heard is to remain truly *God's* word, and not to become a divinely-inspired word about God, known as such — the two are *not* identical — by falling into the created, finite *a priori* frame of reference, then God himself must, in the *grace* of faith (the light of faith), become a constitutive principle of the hearing of revelation. But grace as God's self-communication is not only a constitutive principle of the *capacity* for its acceptance (in what theology calls the supernatural *habitus* of faith, hope and love), but also of the *free act* of *acceptance*. It is so by what theology calls unmerited *efficacious* grace for the actual performance of the act. For this self-communication of God as the cause of its own acceptance is free even in regard to the production of its actual concrete free acceptance. Precisely because this act of acceptance is free and underivative in the concrete, such a self-communication can be accepted as a divinely personal one. Of course it may be said that the free effectuation of acceptance by God, the efficacious grace as such, is given in circumstances (whether these are explained on a Banezian or a Molinist basis) which can be distinguished from the supernatural self-communication as such. But even then it must not be overlooked that God's self-communication by the very fact that it is personal, free and unique in every instance requires these freely posited circumstances, which themselves are unmerited, as its own concrete conditions. The gratuitousness of efficacious grace as such is therefore required by the very nature of God's self-communication and only by it is the self-communication in each instance a unique event of love freely bestowed.

(ii) This free self-communication of God in Christ and his Spirit has to be accepted by the spiritual creature in a dialogue-partnership which itself is free. This presupposes that man is permanently constituted in a certain way (which of course was freely posited by God the Creator). Now this precedes God's self-communication, i.e., it is creatively pre-posited by the latter as the condition of its possibility. For this self-communication has to be received by man (as a partner already historically posited) as a free historical favour which cannot be reckoned with on the basis of the presupposed condition. In other words, it is not a transcendental condition of the self-realization of man, although man is essentially and obligatorily open to this self-disclosure of God (by the *potentia obedientialis* and supernatural existential) and if he refuses it his whole being is in ruin. On the other hand, that intrinsic constitution of man is such that it persists (if only in the form of absurdity and reprobation) if he shuts himself off from God's self-communication. This recipient of God's self-communication, which the latter presupposes as a condition of its own unmerited and solely self-initiated coming, is called in Catholic terminology the "nature" of man. The strictly *theological* concept of "nature" therefore does not mean a state of reality, intelligible in itself and experienced by us separately (apart from a grace inaccessible to experience) on top of which, according to revelation, an additional higher reality would be superimposed. Nature is rather that reality which the divine self-communication creatively posits for itself as its possible partner in such a way that in relation to it that communication does and can remain what it is: a free and loving favour. Nature in contradistinction to the supernatural is, therefore, understood as a necessary element in a higher whole, which is experienced in grace and explicitly declared in revelation. The difference between nature and grace must be understood on the basis of the radical unity of God's free self-communication as love. Nor does this theological concept of nature imply that it is identical with the domain of what can be experienced. That is ultimately a nominalist misconception. The case is rather that it is possible to experience what is not "nature" (cf., for example, Gal 3:1–5) and it is not self-evident *a priori* that everything in "nature" must *in fact* be experienced by man.

(iii) In this sense, the grace of God's self-communication is supernatural, in other words it is not owed to man (or to *any* creature) even prior to his unworthiness as a sinner. It is not posited with man's inalienable essence (his "nature"). Consequently in itself even in the absence of sin it could be refused to man by God (yet if offered it could not be refused by man without guilt). It is unmerited because it is a participation in the reality which in itself is solely that of God himself. Moreover, it can only be received if its very reception is made possible by God. And this again is not due to man. As well as the concept which we have just outlined of what is supernatural in itself and absolutely, and which transcends the essence, powers and intrinsic claim of every creature by the nature of the gift itself and not merely by the mode of its communication, theology also has a concept of what is "preternatural". This denotes a reality which indeed transcends the exigence of a given nature (e.g., of man in contradistinction to the angel) but which lies in some fashion within the domain (scope, aspiration) of a given nature. It cannot, however, be claimed as an appurtenance of the nature, either in itself or in the mode of its attainment (e.g., freedom from concupiscence; miraculous cure of an illness, etc.).

3. *Grace as forgiving*. All this does not mean that grace as forgiveness has been ignored or has become secondary. Man in the concrete always for his part finds himself in a doubly inescapable situation, as creature and as sinner. In concrete experience these two factors mutually condition and throw light on each other. The fallibility of the finite creature is of course of itself not purely and simply sin, but in sin that fallibility comes inexorably to light. And sinfulness inescapably compels man to understand that he is an absolutely finite creature for whom God's divinizing favour always and in every case is grace. To the extent therefore that divinizing grace is bestowed on the sinner and as the proffered self-communication of the *holy* God implies God's readiness to forgive and the acceptance of this (through grace) that grace is once again unmerited, by being conferred on one who is positively unworthy of it. Consequently, it is not surprising that the whole doctrine of justifying grace at the Council of Trent, though concerned with supernatural grace, is not conceived on the pattern of the "elevation" of a nature but of pardoning the impious

(*D* 790f., 793–802). The real need for redemption extends just as far and as radically as does man's capacity for elevation into the life of God.

This pardoning grace and, consequently, elevating grace, when given to man in original sin, is purely the grace of Christ (*D* 55, 790, 793f., 811f., etc.). Moreover, it is quite arguable that the elevating grace of man's original state was the grace of Christ. For in a Christocentric view of all created reality it is quite possible to assume that the creation and fulfilment of the world through God's gracious self-communication were willed by God from the start as factors of a divine self-communication to the non-divine, reaching its culmination, its full essence and historical irreversibility in the God-man. The incarnation and grace-given divinization of the world can then be regarded as mutually and necessarily interdependent elements of this one radical self-communication. Both factors are *free* because the one whole self-communication in its entirety is free, yet the one factor does not have to be thought of as separable from the other. By this origin from Christ, grace even as divinizing has an eminently historical and dialogal character. It is God's favour which, despite the fact that in essence it concerns all men always at all times everywhere and is indispensable to them (cf. *D* 160b, 1295, 1356, 1414, 1518, etc.) is dependent on the "event" of Jesus Christ. Consequently it possesses an incarnational, sacramental and ecclesiological character and unites man in grace with the life and death of Christ.

4. *Uncreated and created grace.* On the basic principle chosen it is readily intelligible that "grace" (of justification) as such and as strictly supernatural is first and foremost God himself communicating himself with his own nature: uncreated grace. On that basis any conception of grace which would reify it or treat it as an object and place it at man's autonomous disposal is excluded from the outset. The teaching of the Council of Trent about grace "inhering" in the soul (*D* 800, 821) was not intended to dispute this and was not put forward in connection with the problem of the distinction between created and uncreated grace (the latter is mentioned: *D* 13, 799, 898, 1013, 1015); it was simply intended to state the truth that justification consists, through genuine rebirth, in the constitution of a new creature, of a temple really inhabited by the Spirit of God himself, of a human being who is anointed and sealed with the Spirit and born of God; and that the justified person is not merely "regarded" forensically "as if" he were just but truly *is* so (*D* 799f., 821). Terms such as "inhering", "accidental", etc., in this connection can be understood entirely independently of the question of the distinction between created and uncreated grace. It is of course true that the concept of uncreated grace means that man himself is genuinely and inwardly transformed by this self-communication and that therefore in this sense there is a "created", accidental grace (i.e., not posited by the very fact of positing man's nature, but received by him). There is no agreement in Catholic theology on how exactly the relation between created and uncreated grace is to be determined. There is no unanimity whether created grace is to be regarded as effected by God (in the ordinary sense of efficient cause) as the presupposition and consequence of uncreated grace conferred by quasi-formal causality. (On this view it would resemble a material disposition for the "form" which, in communicating itself, actively produces this disposition as its own condition so that the two realities condition one another in reciprocal causality.) Nor is there agreement whether created grace is to be regarded as a factor necessarily accompanying uncreated grace (*actuation créée par l'acte incréé:* de la Taille). It is still disputed whether uncreated grace is to be regarded as more or less merely the consequence of created grace. This has mostly been the view since Trent but in a way that is surely inadequate and contrary to the trend of the later thought of Aquinas (cf. Dockx etc.). The special "indwelling" is then regarded as posited by created grace as such. With due regard for *D* 2290, it is at all events quite possible to regard uncreated grace as primary and as the grace which is the essential basis of the whole of man's grace-given endowment and as what alone renders intelligible the authentic and strictly supernatural character of grace.

5. *Actual and habitual grace.* a) *Official teaching of the Church.* On the *"habitual" grace of justification,* see above 1–4. In the sense which will be more precisely delimited below

in section b) the existence of *actual grace* has been defined, because against Pelagianism and Semipelagianism the absolute necessity of grace for absolutely every salutary act is a defined truth (*D* 103 ff., 176 ff., 811 ff.). Contrary to Semipelagian doctrine, these salutary acts include all (positive) preparation for faith and justification, hence grace anticipates man in his saving activity without any merit on his part (*D* 797) ("prevenient grace"; on co-operation with this grace see below, 6). In view of God's universal salvific will and of the sinfulness of man, it follows that there is also an assisting grace which is offered but does not produce its effect and which is therefore merely "sufficient", the existence of which has been defined against Jansenism (*D* 797, 814, 1093, 1295 f., 1521, 1791). The essence of grace cannot therefore be located in the irresistible omnipotence of God (*D* 1359–75). According to the (almost) universal teaching (both of Thomism and of Molinism, with regard to grace and freedom), and despite human freedom in acceptance and resistance, the distinction between merely sufficient and efficacious actual grace is prior to man's acceptance or resistance and has its ground in the sphere of God's election (otherwise the fact of final perseverance would not be a special gift of God: *D* 806, 826). It is illumination and inspiration (*D* 135 ff., 180, 797, 1521, 1791). It is regarded not only as unmerited but also as supernatural in the same sense as the grace of justification (cf. *D* 1789 ff.). This is also suggested by its absolute necessity for any saving act. It is not merely "moral" necessity which is in question, i.e., to make the saving act easier. Consequently it does not consist merely in the outward circumstances shaped by God's providence which favour man's religious action, but concretely and as a whole it is interior grace in the same sense as sanctifying grace.

b) *In speculative theology.* On the basis of the fundamental anti-Pelagian doctrine of Western theology regarding the necessity of grace for the salutary action of man (in the form which derives from Augustine: grace as inspiration of justifying love), grace in the first place is assistance for action (perpetually bestowed or constantly offered by the salvific will of God) and in this sense actual grace. (The state of grace of baptized children who are free from the stain of original sin but

who have not yet reached the use of reason is not examined in this connection.) We are not concerned here to describe why and how in the Middle Ages doctrine developed in such a way that the recognition of grace as supernatural concerned the "habitual" grace of justification, so that a salutary act and an act based on habitual grace were viewed as identical. At all events this fact shows that the concept of the supernaturally elevating assistance for every salutary act is not to be identified from the start with the concept of actual grace as this is almost universally understood today and deduced from the case of the grace-given act of preparation for justification. That view presupposes (without any real proof) that such acts cannot be performed on the basis of the antecedently offered grace of justification (a "habitual" grace in other words but dynamically actualized). It is also a fact that down to the present day no agreement has been reached whether a supernatural elevating actual grace over and above habitual grace is necessary in a justified person for every saving action, or whether habitual grace in itself is sufficient. If with the Thomists as opposed to Molina we assume the doctrine which, though disputed, is perfectly reasonable and indeed preferable, that the grace given for the act itself elevates the faculties of man (so that the salutary act as such is not only received but performed), it is possible to say that the Church's binding doctrine only imposes a distinction between actual supernatural elevating grace and habitual grace to the extent that it is certain by dogmatic definition that there are saving acts of not yet justified persons by which they prepare for justification with a prevenient grace which is absolutely necessary for them. There is no official pronouncement of the Church and no agreed teaching whether this necessary grace is the same as, or different from, God's self-communication which by giving itself also makes possible and effects its own acceptance. There is no decision, therefore, whether in adults habitual grace is the same as or other than that same communication of God when freely accepted. The sense of the distinction as far as it is a binding one is simply that grace is habitual inasmuch as God's supernatural self-communication is permanently offered to man (after baptism) and (in the adult) is freely accepted in the various degrees in which it is possible to accept it.

The same grace is called actual inasmuch as it is the basis of this act of acceptance in which it actualizes itself. The individual action in the concrete is essentially progressive and susceptible of indefinite renewal. (This conception also corresponds to the Thomist view of growth in grace.)

It follows from all this that the customary division of the treatise on grace since the Council of Trent into a section on actual grace and one on habitual grace is a very superficial one which does not do justice to the unity and nature of the one grace which divinizes the essence, powers and activity of man. All "actual" graces refer to the one dynamism for human action of the one divinizing grace as offered (actual grace for justification) or as already accepted (actual grace for merit on the part of the justified person). They are only distinguished from one another by the different degrees of actual vital acceptance of this one grace by man (grace for mere faith, for faith in hope, for love which integrates faith into itself).

6. *Grace as liberating grace of the free man.* Despite original sin, and even with concupiscence, man is free (*D* 792 f., 798, 814 ff.); therefore he freely consents to prevenient grace or freely rejects it (*D* 134, 140, 160 a, 196, 793 f., 1093, 1095, 1521, 1791, 2305). Consequently we must speak of mutual "co-operation" *(cooperari)* (*D* 182, 200, 797, 814). However, that does not in any way mean a "synergism" dividing up the saving operation. For not only the capacity for salutary action (the infused *habitus* or the prevenient sufficient grace) but also the free consent itself is God's grace (as was taken for granted in the controversy on grace between Molinism and Thomism, which is why the Church did not have to pronounce in favour of either of the two parties) (*D* 176 f., 182, etc.). It is therefore grace itself which sets free our (formal) freedom in capacity and in act for saving action, and heals it in itself. Consequently the situation of this freedom to say Yes or No to God is not that of autonomous emancipated choice (*D* 200, 321 f., 325). When man says No it is his own work; when he freely says Yes, he must attribute this to God as God's gift.

7. *Medicinal and supernaturally elevating grace.* The two doctrines — that of the difference between nature and supernaturally elevating grace, i.e., which endows with the gift of God himself, and that of concupiscence (as a spur to sin even against the natural law) which can only be overcome by a special help of God (the absence of which does not mean that the unjustified human being sins afresh in every action) — slowly led to a distinction being drawn between the necessity of grace for the divinized salutary act and the necessity of God's help for the observance of the law of nature. This is the distinction between elevating and medicinal grace. Though this distinction is not clear even in the Council of Orange (A.D. 529) and is not really brought out at Trent, the doctrine of the medicinal function of divine grace was nevertheless already present all the time (*D* 103, 132, 135, 186 f., 190, 806, 832, etc.), because of course this aspect of divine assistance is directly opposed to Pelagianism. The same is true of the doctrine that the substance of the natural law cannot in the long run be observed without this help (and in fact certainly is not). It had also to be maintained against the Reformers, Baius and Jansenius (see also the Augustinian school) that not only do persons who are not yet justified perform salutary acts with the help of grace, but also that the (presupposed) lack of it does not necessarily make every one of their actions a sin (*D* 817 f., 1025, 1035, 1037, 1040, 1297 f., 1301, 1395, 1409, 1523, etc.).

As a consequence the absolute necessity of salutary grace for a salutary act and the purely relative help for moral action in accordance with the natural law (the *actus honestus*) are not simply and solely two aspects of one and the same divine action in man, and medicinal help and supernatural grace must therefore be distinguished. From this it follows that the medicinal help can also be regarded as external and that it is still an open question in Catholic theology whether precisely as such (and even as purely sufficient) it is in every case gratuitous or not, and whether in every case it is to be considered to be a grace of Christ. The relation of these two kinds of assisting graces is not fully elucidated, however, by this necessary distinction.

Although the *possibility* of individual purely human acts in the domain or religious knowledge (*D* 1785 f., 2320, 2317) and of action in accordance with the natural moral law cannot be disputed, the question whether *in fact* there are moral acts which are merely good and reputable in themselves, but without any positive significance for salvation, or whether all such acts if they actually exist are also, through an elevating grace, salutary acts, is still freely discussed, for the second view (in the sense of Ripalda or Vazquez) has never been censured by the Church. The answer to this question largely depends on the open question as to what faith (without which there is no salutary act and no justification: *D* 1173, 801, 789, 798) is required as condition and element of the salutary act. If a "virtual" faith (in the sense for example of Straub) is sufficient, then justification by a baptism of desire and consequently salutary acts are possible in every man of goodwill even before contact with public revelation. If a psychological effect is also attributed to elevating grace, or at all events if it brings with it, as the Thomist doctrine maintains, a new cognitive perspective (a special *obiectum formale*, even if this cannot be grasped explicitly by reflection), and if this new supernatural perspective in which natural moral and religious objects would be grasped, can be regarded as a ("transcendental") kind of authentic divine revelation and therefore (if affirmed non-reflexively) as faith, then the problem can be solved even more simply. Every radically moral act would then occur in a supernatural perspective because of the elevating grace offered because of God's universal will to save. Consequently it also would constitute faith (in a "transcendental" way). For both these reasons, therefore, it would be a salutary act, and so every moral act *(actus honestus)* would *in fact* also be a salutary act. If this is the case, however (and it corresponds very closely to the optimistic attitude of Vatican II in regard to salvation [cf. *Lumen Gentium,* art. 16; *Gaudium et Spes,* art. 22], because it teaches the possibility of salvation and faith even for those whom the message of the gospel has not reached), then "medicinal" grace can in all cases be regarded as the dynamism of elevating grace and as its concrete accompanying (external) circumstances. Then, in the actual course of a totally Christocentric human history, medicinal grace would be an element in a coming of grace, which, through God's loving will to self-communication to the creature, aims at realizing all that is human and Christian in man.

8. *Further characteristics of grace:* a) It can be lost: see *Sin* I, *Justification, Penance* II.

b) It can grow: see *Works, Holiness.* On its relation to consciousness, see *Religious Experience, Mysticism* I, *Grace and Freedom, Faith* I, II.

9. *Grace and God's salvific will:* see *Salvation* I, *Predestination, Providence.*

BIBLIOGRAPHY. L. Bauer, "Gnade bei den Griechischen Vätern", *Theologische Quartalschrift* 98 (1916), pp. 467–91; 99 (1918), pp. 225–52; 100 (1919), pp. 426–46; 101 (1920), pp. 28–64, 155–86; J. van der Meersch, *DTC,* cols. 1554–687; H. Lange, *De Gratia. Tractatus Dogmaticus* (1929); M. Merlin, *S. Augustin et les dogmes du péché originel et la grâce* (1931); J. Terrien, *La grâce et la gloire* (1931); P. Dumont, "Le caractère divin de la grâce d'après la théologie scolastique", *RSR* 13 (1933), pp. 517–52; 14 (1934), pp. 62–95; P. Descoqs, *Le mystère de notre élévation surnaturelle* (1938); J. Gross, *La divinisation du chrétien d'après les Pères grecs* (1938); W. R. O'Connor, "A New Concept of Grace and the Supernatural", *Ecclesiastical Review* 98 (1938), pp. 401–13; H. de Lubac, *Surnaturel. Études historiques* (1946); J. Auer, "Um den Begriff der Gnade", *ZKT* 70 (1948), pp. 341–68; K. Barth, *Die Botschaft von der freien Gnade Gottes. These 6 der Barmer Erklärung,* Kirche für die Welt 14 (1948); O. Hardmann, *Christian Doctrine of Grace* (1948); G. de Broglie, "De gratuitate ordinis supernaturalis", *Gregorianum* 29 (1948), pp. 435–63; S. I. Dockx, *Fils de Dieu par grâce* (1948); H. Rondet, *Gratia Christi. Essai d'histoire du dogme et de théologie dogmatique* (1948); J. Trütsch, *Sanctae Trinitatis inhabitatio apud theologos recentiores* (1949); F. Walland, *La Grazia divinizzante* (1949); H. P. Lyons, "The Grace of Sonship", *ETL* 27 (1951), pp. 438–66; J. Simon, "Transcendance et immanence dans la doctrine de la grâce", *Revue de l'Université d'Ottawa* 21 (1951), pp. 344–69; J. Alfaro, *Lo natural y lo sobrenatural* (1952); M. J. Donnelly, "Sanctifying Grace and Our Union with the Holy Trinity", *TS* 13 (1952), pp. 33–58; W. A. van Roo, *Grace and Original Justice according to St. Thomas* (1955); J. Alfaro, "Transcendencia et immanencia de lo sobrenaturel", *Gregorianum* 38 (1957), pp. 5–50; P. Fransen, "Pour une psychologie de la grâce divine", *Lumen Vitae* 12 (1957), pp. 209–40; P. S. Watson, *The Concept of Grace. Essays on the way of divine love in human life* (1959); C. Journet, *Entretiens sur la grâce* (1961); K. Rahner, *Theological Investigations,* I (1961); J. Chéné, *La théologie de Saint Augustin. Grâce et prédestination* (1962); B. Stoeckle, *Gratia supponit naturam* (in German) (1962); M. J. Farrelly, *Predestination, Grace and Free Will* (1964); H. Küng, *Justification. The Doctrine of Karl Barth and a Catholic Reflection* (1964); P. J. Hefner, ed., *The Scope of Grace. Essays on Nature and Grace in Honor of Joseph Sittler* (1964); G. Hibbert, "Created and Uncreated Charity ... in St. Thomas", *Recherches de Théologie ancienne et médiévale* 35 (1964), pp. 63–84; H. Rondet, *Essais sur la théologie de la grâce* (1965); H. de Lubac, *Le mystère du surnaturel* (1965); B. Marthaler, *Original*

Justice and Sanctifying Grace in the Writings of St. Bonaventure (1965); H. A. Meynell, *Grace versus Nature. Studies in Karl Barth's Church Dogmatics* (1965); M. Schmaus, *Katholische Dogmatik,* III/2 (6th ed., 1965); K. Rahner, *Theological Investigations,* IV (1966).

Karl Rahner

III. Structure of De Gratia

1. *Definition and divisions.* a) The theology of grace *(De gratia)* is that part of a theological anthropology which deals with man as redeemed and justified. Rightly understood, therefore, this treatise should not speak in the abstract about grace but about man endowed with grace. For where man's reality is not envisaged in all its dimensions, the concept of grace in formal abstraction remains either an "experience" of the nature of man or a moral help to his moral life itself envisaged only in a very abstract way. The Church's proclamation is not adequately served by this, nor is full justice done to biblical theology which speaks of grace much more concretely. This part of an anthropology, dealing precisely with redeemed and sanctified man, has its natural place after Christology and ecclesiology, because these two treatises describe the cause, conditions and situation of man's justification. It is a secondary matter whether man's state as redeemed (as an "existential" analogous to the situation created by original sin, and antecedent to justification) is to be dealt with in soteriology itself or in a treatise on grace. This treatise must above all constitute a doctrine of the divinizing and forgiving endowment of man with grace (in his being and action) in all his dimensions, in all the spheres of his life. It therefore includes as an integral part the doctrine of the theological virtues and as a whole represents the dogmatic foundation which is essential to a radically dogmatic moral theology (cf. the description of a moral theology for the present day in Vatican II, *Optatam Totius,* art. 16).

Grace is ultimately the self-communication of the absolute God to his creature, and this self-communication itself has a history, which reaches in Jesus Christ its eschatological, irreversible culmination towards which it tended from the start and throughout, and which determined and formed the basis of its whole course from the beginning. Consequently the theology of man redeemed and justified (sanctified) by grace should include also a doctrine of man who was thus justified before Christ's time (but *through* Christ) or who (to some extent only apparently) stands outside the domain of the historical Christian message of salvation.

b) The essential themes of the theology of grace are as follows. (i) God's actual trinitarian self-communication itself to man in its fundamental character. As the fundamental act of God in relation to the nondivine, this includes (but as distinct from itself) both nature and grace. Nature is posited as its own condition for its own purpose. Grace includes the supralapsarian grace of God in the original state, which itself was already Christocentric. It also includes the grace of the infralapsarian order, after (original) sin, which was only "permitted" by grace on account of the latter's own absolutely triumphant power.

(ii) From this fundamental conception we have to work out the idea of supernatural justifying grace, both as uncreated and as the created grace deriving from it. And this must not be done only in a formal, abstract way restricted to the subjective interior life of the private individual (forgiveness of sins, indwelling of God, adoptive sonship, holiness). The Christological and infralapsarian character of this grace must be brought out, Christological in its dynamism towards sharing in the mysteries and death of Christ, towards the imitation of Christ, infralapsarian as being grace which is always threatened yet increasingly victorious again and again in overcoming concupiscence. This grace of justification has also to be seen in the appropriate way in each case, as divinization and redemption (liberation) of *all* dimensions of human reality. In other words, the individual *and* collective (ecclesial), anthropological *and* cosmic character (grace as transfiguration of the world) has to be brought out. Grace has to be considered in accordance with the transcendental dimensions of man as truth, as love and as beauty.

(iii) To this must be added the doctrine of the actual working out of this supernatural grace in the dialogue relation between God and man. This is free on both sides and it is free on God's part once again in this respect also: efficacious grace. Consequently this section must include: 1. The doctrine of actual grace, what formally constitutes it, its relation to justifying grace. 2. The formal aspects of the life of the justified in Christ (gratuity of grace even in the actual working out of justifying grace as such; hidden character of grace; experience of grace; freedom under grace and liberation of man's freedom by grace; grace as liberation from the Law) and its material dimensions (the doctrine of the theological and moral virtues and their acts). 3. The beginning of the divine life of grace (process of justification), its growth (merit), and the perils which always beset it (the justified person's proneness to sin; loss of grace). 4. The ecclesiological aspect and mission in the world of the life of grace (charisms). 5. The perfection of the life of grace (mysticism; confirmation in grace; holiness; martyrdom).

2. *Brief history of the theology of grace.* a) The Apostolic Fathers and the theologians of the first two centuries repeat the doctrine of Scripture, soberly stressing its moral demands but also starting to use the Hellenistic terminology of "divinization". The first theological reflections are made on the possibility of losing and recovering the grace of baptism (*The Shepherd of Hermas,* Tertullian).

b) The first great controversy on grace had to be waged in the 2nd and 3rd centuries against Gnosticism, i.e., against its doctrine of divinization, which made salvation non-universal, non-historical and a matter of one's "essential" constitution. It eliminated man's free acceptance of the free grace of God in favour of a cosmic history of God himself (Irenaeus).

c) The great age of the Greek fathers (from Origen onwards) developed a doctrine of grace on the basis of the Trinitarian questions of the period. Because the Spirit is truly God, man is truly divinized, and because man (without becoming God) is truly divinized, the Spirit must truly be God. As the Spirit is definitively inserted into the world by the incarnation of the divine Logos, the Greek doctrine of grace is optimistic about salvation. It also had to be on its guard against a kind of "actualism" in the doctrine of grace, which identified grace with an enthusiastic, mystical experience of grace (Messalianism). But it was familiar with a Logos mysticism which gradually introduced man in ecstasy into the incomprehensibility of God.

d) The Western doctrine of grace was less interested in intellectual divinization and its

cosmic aspects and more moralistic in tendency. It was also orientated towards the history of salvation and of the individual by the struggle against Pelagianism. Grace is the unmeritable strength of love for God which by free predestination delivers some men in original sin from the *massa damnata* of mankind and from their own egoism, liberates their freedom enslaved to sin and so makes them capable of the faith which operates in love (Augustine). In his theoretical works of controversy, Augustine no longer recognizes an infralapsarian *universal* salvific will of God. On the other hand he is the great teacher of the Church on original sin, the gratuitousness of grace and of predestination to beatitude, and on the psychology of grace.

e) The later patristic period (while preserving the genuine substance of the doctrine of grace of Augustine and of the Council of Orange: *D* 178–200a) and the early Middle Ages overcame, in opposition to predestinarianism, the thesis of a merely limited salvific will of God which would positively exclude many from salvation prior to their guilt (*D* 160a; 300; 316–25). The great age of Scholasticism gave precise formulation by means of a new philosophical (Aristotelian) terminology (habitus, disposition, accidents) to the nature of justifying grace, to the process of justification and to the theological virtues. The concept of the strictly supernatural character of salvific grace was slowly elaborated. It was not merely gratuitousness in regard to the sinner.

f) As against the theology of the Reformation, of Baianism and Jansenism, it was necessary to defend (especially at the Council of Trent, sessions V and VI) the freedom of man under grace, the truly inward new creation of man by habitual grace, its strictly supernatural character (in the post-Tridentine period against Baius) and the universality of God's will to grace (against Calvin and Jansenius). The controversy "De Auxiliis", concerning the more precise theories of how to reconcile human freedom with the divinely efficacious power of grace (Molina, Bañez) was left undecided in 1607 (*D* 1090, 1097) and has remained so until this day. Another equally open question is the problem which has been discussed since Petau (d. 1652), under the renewed influence of the Greek Fathers, whether by sanctifying grace a special relation not simply by appropriation is set up to each of the three divine persons. At the present day theology is concerning itself with the use of personalist concepts in the doctrine of grace, with the unity of nature and grace, without prejudice to their distinction, and with a better understanding of the biblical teaching on grace and of the theology of the Reformers.

See also *Grace* I, II.

BIBLIOGRAPHY. See also bibliography on *Grace* I, II; H. Rondet, *Gratia Christi. Essai d'histoire du dogme et de théologie dogmatique* (1948); G. Philips, "De ratione instituendi tractatum de gratia nostrae sanctificationis", *ETL* 29 (1953), pp. 355–73; K. Rahner, *Theological Investigations,* I (1961); H. Rito, *Recentioris theologiae quaedam tendentiae ad conceptum ontologico-personalem gratiae* (1964); O. Semmelroth, "Der Verlust des Personalen in der Theologie und die Bedeutung seiner Wiedergewinnung", *Gott in Welt, Festschrift K. Rahner,* I (1964), pp. 315–32; M. Flick and Z. Alszeghy, *Il Vangelo della Grazia* (1964), bibliography on the history of the doctrine, pp. 13–15; M. Schmaus, *Katholische Dogmatik,* III/2 (6th ed., 1964); H. Rondet, *Essais sur la théologie de la grâce* (1964); H. de Lubac, *Le Mystère du surnaturel* (1965); id., *Augustinisme et théologie moderne* (1965).

Karl Rahner

GRACE AND FREEDOM

1. *The problem.* a) The problem of the relation between grace and freedom, as a specifically theological question within Catholic theology, is how to maintain that man is really free in his salutary acts and could therefore refuse the grace offered for such an act, and that at the same time he necessarily requires interior divine grace for this salutary action. This grace does not become effective simply and solely through man's actual consent to it, but the consent itself is given by God's grace freely bestowed. God could also refuse precisely such an "efficacious" grace, without man thereby being excused if he sinned, because in any case he is capable (through "sufficient" grace) of performing the salutary act.

b) Beyond its attestation in Scripture, the problem of man's freedom and God's sovereign power and grace has its vital importance in the concrete: man cannot abdicate his own responsibility even in the matter of salvation, yet when he does act in a way ordered to salvation, he must give the honour

to God and acknowledge that it is God in his grace who has given him the power to act and the very act itself.

c) Theology then gives the problem its full theoretical extension and expresses it formally as the question of the relation between God's action (in his concursus) and man's free acts (including then both naturally good and morally bad ones).

2. *The correct starting-point for a solution.* a) The relation between God and the world is necessarily mysterious because God is *the* mystery, mystery as such. Any discussion of the topic can only proceed dialectically, in that tension of twofold utterance which the very nature of analogical language involves.

b) The relation between God and creature is characterized, precisely in contrast to any causal dependence otherwise met with within the world, by the fact that self-possession and dependence increase in direct, not in inverse proportion. It is God's causality itself which posits genuine difference from God and constitutes the creation of what is independent and has its own being.

This relation of a transcendental, non-predicamental kind culminates, without discontinuity, in the relation between God and the free subject together with his free act. The transcendental origin of the free act from God is precisely what posits it as free, and transfers it to the creature's own responsibility for itself. This ultimate creation in the authentic sense of the term, in which the idea of creation is at last fully realized, is the mystery of the "co-existence" of God and the free creature, and it is not susceptible of further analysis.

3. *The classical attempts at a solution.* All agree in attempting once more to mediate the mystery of this relation by indicating some third factor (of an ideal or real kind) by which, since it is distinct from God and from the free act, some intermediary may be found between the sovereignty of God's grace and independent freedom.

a) *Bañezian Thomism.* Bañez (d. 1604) claimed to be following Aquinas, but with what justice is disputed, for some consider that his teaching presents Scotist features. The kernel of his doctrine is the necessity and nature of *praemotio physica* for *any* action of a creature, not only for a positively salutary act. According to this view, a creature requires, in order to pass from potency to act, an absolutely indispensable "premotion", which consists of a transitory created entity produced by God *alone,* which is distinct from God (and his causality in respect of the act of the creature), and from the faculty and act of the creature, but which infallibly determines this act in its nature and actual existence. When it is a question of a free act, good or bad, the *praemotio physica* infallibly and antecedently moves to this action and its freedom.

God decides in predestination on a certain definite premotion, and so according to his own absolutely sovereign choice gives the creature the good or bad deed as the creature's own free act. Where this premotion by its own very nature moves to a positive salutary act, it is called efficacious actual grace, as opposed to sufficient grace, which is really distinct from it and confers the full power to act, but not the act itself.

Criticism. The proposition that God's transcendental causality of itself is also the cause of the free act formally as such in all its (positive) aspects, and that this causality, because divine, is logically prior to that of the creature as its ground, is certainly unassailable and necessary. But when with the *praemotio physica,* a finite entity, distinct from God and his transcendent activity, though caused by God, is introduced, and this entity, distinct from the free act of the creature, infallibly determines it and yet is supposed to cause it in its freedom, a contradiction is surely presented. A created reality which antecedently determines the existence of an act, abolishes freedom of choice.

b) *Molinism.* According to Molinism, God possesses sovereign freedom in regard to human freedom. Without detriment to it, he can direct it as he pleases, because in his *scientia media* he knows "conditionally future" free actions from their objective ideal reality. God knows what every free agent in every situation that God can bring about, would freely do or will do, if God were to or actually does, by his own free choice, produce this or that situation, internal or external. If therefore God wills to elicit a certain free action of a creature, he only needs to bring about the situation in which he knows by his *scientia media* that the creature in question will freely posit the act in question. Logically prior to the actual

free act, therefore, God knows and directs by his *scientia media* the creature's actual freedom without coercing it, because this direction itself is founded on God's knowledge of the *conditionally* future free decision of the human being *himself,* and the quality of this is not itself determined by God. If God on the basis of his *scientia media* selects and brings about a situation in which someone acts in a way ordered to salvation, this situation is in the Molinist sense an "efficacious grace", even if it is not intrinsically different from another, merely "sufficient" grace, with which the person concerned could have acted in a salutary way, but in fact does not, as God already knows, prior to the actual decision, as a conditional future.

Criticism. This rather over-ingenious solution of the problem does not answer the question of where the conditionally future free action derives its reality from (even if this is purely of the ideal order), if it is not to have it from God, and primarily from God. Moreover, it makes God's knowledge dependent on something not divine, and without postulating once again a ground in God himself for this non-divine element, not merely in its character as possible, but as a conditionally future free act.

If the very possibility of real freedom before God is grounded in its direct relation to God, rather than being restricted or threatened thereby, then neither a "conceptual" nor a "physical" intermediary can be inserted between it and God.

c) *Other attempts at solution.* These either attempt to explain the infallibility of divine grace from God's side, though without destroying human freedom, by declaring grace infallible, not as *praemotio physica,* that is, by reason of its ontological character, but as a psychological impulse, when it is conferred in sufficient strength to overcome concupiscence (Augustinianism of the 17th and 18th centuries). Or they are a syncretism of Thomism and Molinism, explaining easier initial salutary acts (e.g., to begin to pray) on Molinist principles, but more difficult ones on Thomist principles. Augustinianism offers a concrete description of the history of the human heart as it in fact occurs. But by conceiving efficacious grace as of such a kind that its psychological character in itself permits God infallibly to know how freedom will react to it, it presupposes a grace which no longer leaves a man free. The syncretist systems (Tournely, Alphonsus Liguori) of the 18th century combine the problems raised by the other systems, without preserving their advantages.

4. *Special problems.* The problem of the relation between human freedom and a grace which from God's side is certainly efficacious and which without detriment to the freedom of the creature, permits this freedom to be within God's disposition, is linked in the various theories of grace with the question of predestination. The efficacious grace selected by God on the basis of *scientia media* can be chosen *because* God absolutely wills the salvation of the human being in question (predestination antecedent to foreseen merits in the Molinist congruism of Suarez) or independently of this consideration (simple Molinism with an absolute predestination to beatitude as such solely on the basis of foreseen merits). Bañezian Thomism always views its own system on the supposition of a predestination to glory, antecedent (logically) to prevision of merits, because the latter of course are constituted precisely by the divine choice of the *praemotio physica* of grace.

Criticism. The question of predestination to blessedness before or after the prevision of merits would appear to be wrongly stated. That is made plain, if by nothing else, by the difficulties caused by predestination to damnation which, if viewed as positive and antecedent to demerits, is rejected by the Church as heretical Calvinism (*D* 816, 827). The absolutely transcendent God wills in his primordial, absolutely one, absolute act, a manifold world, in which the various items have quite definite relations of mutual interdependence, and of which the objective order is willed by God. But that does not mean that this finite order of connection within the manifold of the world has to be projected back into God too, so as to set up an order of several distinct divine decrees.

5. *Conclusion.* a) The endeavours of the various theories of grace to analyse even further the relation between God's universal causality and created freedom, and to distinguish a number of factors which to some degree permit the "concord" (Molina's term) of these two realities to be grasped, do not lead to any satisfactory results, as is shown by the very fact that since the 18th century theological controversy on the subject has stagnated.

b) It is probably correct to say that in this matter an attempt has been made to go beyond a point at which a halt has to be made, not out of mental laziness or theological scepticism, but because the point can clearly be seen to mark a limitation of principle. The relation between God and creature is a primordial ontological datum not susceptible of further resolution. In the fundamental transcendental experience of man's orientation towards God as the incomprehensible mystery, both man's independence and his derivation from God are simultaneously given. This experience is the most fundamental datum of the mind and even if it becomes the object of explicit reflection only later and imperfectly, it is logically prior, as the condition of the very possibility of existence as a person with intellectual knowledge and freedom. It culminates in the experience of the independence yet derivative character of freedom, and this manifests its specific nature. Consequently the relation God—freedom must be taken as primordial; there is nothing "prior" to it by which it can be rendered intelligible, any more than we, having come to know God "from" the world, can then understand the world anew, with God as starting-point.

Two facts established with certainty may not be contested because we cannot infer them one from another or both from a third, or because we are not in a position to exhibit a third which gives the how and why of their co-existence. Total origin from God in every respect, and independent freedom, are facts of that kind.

c) That is also the case as regards morally bad actions. They are ineluctably ours, and yet in everything about them which requires origination, they come from God. The morally good and the morally bad action, good and evil, are not, however, in themselves, morally or even ontologically perfectly equal possibilities of freedom. Evil, in the source of its freedom and in its objective embodiments, has less of being and less of freedom. To that extent it can and must be said that in its deficiency as such it requires no origination by God. This observation does not "solve" the problem of the relation between God and wicked freedom, but does show the creature's capacity to retain "something" wholly its own, the responsibility for which cannot be shifted to God, yet which does not require (like a good deed) to be returned to him thankfully as his grace.

d) In order really to "understand" the problem grace—freedom, to let it have its proper weight and to accept it, it is necessary to return to the frame of mind of a person at prayer. He receives himself, is, and gives himself back to God, by accepting the acceptance as an element in the gift itself. If one assumes that attitude of prayer (and by so doing in fact accepts the "solution" of the problem), there is no begging of the question, nor flight from it. One is only accepting what one undeniably is, both real and yet derivative, a creature which produced in freedom and is produced as grace as it acts.

See also *Mystery, Augustinian School of Theology, Predestination, Calvinism, Evil, Sin* I.

BIBLIOGRAPHY. F. Wörter, *Die christliche Lehre über das Verhältnis von Gnade und Freiheit von den apostolischen Vätern bis auf Augustinus,* 2 parts (1856–60); N. Del Prado, *De Gratia et libero arbitrio,* 3 vols. (1907); J. Stufler, *D. Thomae Aquinatis doctrina de Deo operante,* I (1923); A. d'Alès, *Providence et libre arbitre* (1927); F. Stegmüller, *Geschichte des Molinismus* (1935); P. Trugby, *Cognitio divina de obiecto indeterminato* (1937); B. Romeyer, "Libre arbitre et concours selon Molina", *Gregorianum* 23 (1942), pp. 169–201; H. Rondet, *Gratia Christi* (1949); T. U. Mullaney, *Suarez on Human Freedom* (1950); C. Siewerth, *Thomas von Aquin, Die menschliche Willensfreiheit* (1954); H. Rondet, "La liberté et la grâce dans la théologie augustinienne", *St. Augustin parmi nous* (1954); R. Guardini, *Freedom, Grace and Destiny* (1961); J. B. Metz, "Freiheit als philosophisch-theologisches Grenzproblem", *Gott in Welt,* I (1964), pp. 287–314; H. Schlier, "ἐλεύθερος", *TWNT,* II (1964), pp. 487–502; K. Rahner, "Theologie der Freiheit", *Schriften zur Theologie,* VI (1965), pp. 215–37; id., "Gerecht und Sünder zugleich", *ibid.,* pp. 262–76.

Karl Rahner